The American Revolution

The St. Martin's Series in U.S. History

The American Revolution
Nationhood Achieved
1763–1788

Harry M. Ward

University of Richmond

The St. Martin's Series in U.S. History

Editor: Louise Waller
Managing editor: Patricia Mansfield-Phelan
Project editor: Diana M. Puglisi
Production supervisor: Alan Fischer
Art director: Sheree Goodman
Cover art: Detail from John Trumbull, *The Declaration of Independence,* copyright
  Yale University Art Gallery

For information, write:
St. Martin's Press, Inc.
175 Fifth Avenue
New York, NY 10010

ISBN: 0-312-07162-0 (paperback)
    0-312-12259-4 (cloth)

Preface

The era of the American Revolution was a defining moment in history. It bore witness to the transformation of colonists into citizens of a new nation and the setting of goals for a free people by which to guide posterity.

Original materials for writing the history of the Revolution are abundant, and during the past half-century historians have expanded the prospects for study of the Revolutionary War era. Although much remains to be accomplished, monographs, biographies, and reappraisals of the broad contours of the Revolution have added greatly to our knowledge of the establishment of Independence and the birth of the Republic, and new perspectives have been initiated.

The American Revolution: Nationhood Achieved, 1763–1788 draws on the multifaceted contributions of recent historiography, as well as older sources and primary sources, in presenting a measured overview of the Revolutionary experience. The book treats the unfolding course of the American Revolution and its impact on American life and institutions from the commencement of a protest movement to the formation of a unique system of constitutional government.

The American Revolution is comprehensive—it embraces not just the war or ideology or political development but also the people behind the scenes whose lives were affected by the war. Given a fresh view of the experience during the period, the reader discovers an understanding of the events and decisions that evoke the meaning of the American character and nationhood.

Topical Considerations

While treating all major aspects of the Revolutionary era, *The American Revolution* seeks both to inform and to stimulate further inquiry. The book calls attention to certain topics minimized or overlooked by traditional historians of the Revolutionary era and covers some of these in depth. Some readers may expect greater coverage on two counts: the ideology of the Revolutionary movement and republicanism, and diplomacy. These subjects are treated in their essentials to allow room for supplementary reading. For ideology, excellent studies by Bernard Bailyn, Caroline Robbins, Gordon Wood, and others are available; for diplomacy, studies by Samuel F. Bemis, Jonathan Dull, and Richard B. Morris have been published.

Part 1 focuses on the development of the Revolutionary movement in the context of issues and controversy. The discussion of the Declaration of Independence considers how the document came to be written and the content and ideas behind it.

Part 2 narrates the key campaigns and battles of the Revolution according to various theaters of war, placing some emphasis on operations that have not been given their full due by other writers. The partisan war in the South (Tories versus Rebels) is discussed in general terms, but a breakdown of the action in the multiple localities is left to reading in other sources. In addition, Part 2 explores ways in which the War for American Independence expanded into a global conflict.

Part 3 discusses how Americans were affected by the war, getting behind the scenes to look at such events as the trading of secrets and the hardships of the many thousands who endured captivity. The Revolutionary War, like all wars, had its home front, involving the war effort and citizen morale. Many Americans were noncombatants—in association with military service or avoidance of it. There were persons from all walks of life who expressed loyalty to Britain, most of whom experienced severe ordeals.

Part 4 examines the making of state and national government, and shows how republicanism pervaded the social and cultural spheres as well as the political. The formulation of a new national constitution and its adoption sealed Americans irretrievably to the cause for which they had fought.

The book follows a logical progression. At the beginning of the Revolutionary period Americans protested against the acts and policies of the British government, which they deemed oppressive of the rights of Britons everywhere. Radicals and reconciliationists struggled to recast bonds in the relationship between the colonies and the mother country. With compromise failing, reluctant rebels fought to win independence. The "Spirit of '76" eroded, as did British determination. The war, nevertheless, gave distinction to Americans fighting for national liberty, sanctified in the effusion of blood.

Once the war was over, American citizens began to shape a government and society that agreed with the ideals of liberty and equality which had been proclaimed to justify their rebellion. The Revolutionaries-becoming-founders were mindful of forging Republican identity and a nation among nations.

Acknowledgments

I wish to thank the following individuals who reviewed *The American Revolution* for St. Martin's Press: David Ammerman, Institute of Early American History and Culture; Edward M. Cook, University of Chicago; Daniel Dupre, University of North Carolina at Charlotte; Constance B. Schulz, University of South Carolina; Rebecca Shoemaker, Indiana State University; and Sheila Skemp, University of Mississippi; their suggestions greatly aided in the improvement of this work.

I appreciate also those who critiqued segments of the book relating to the areas of their speciality: John Ferling, West Georgia College (the war); Sylvia R. Frey, Tulane University (social history and the "underside" of the Revolution); John L. Gordon, Jr., University of Richmond (Hanoverian England); and Melvin I. Urofsky, Virginia Commonwealth University (U.S. Constitution).

The staffs of the Virginia State Library, Reference and Archives divisions, and the Boatwright Library of the University of Richmond gave unstinting assistance.

Nancy E. Vick and Katherine S. Davison secured materials through interlibrary loans. I am grateful to the editors of St. Martin's Press, particularly Louise H. Waller, for guidance from the inception of this work to its completion, and to Diana M. Puglisi, who directed the editorial and production stages.

HARRY M. WARD
University of Richmond

Contents

PART 2
The Revolutionary War, 1776–1783

PART   3
The Underside of the Revolution

Maps

PART 1

The Gathering Storm

CHAPTER 1

The American Colonies
in 1763

The year 1763 marked a turning point in the history of America. With the conclusion of the French and Indian War, British North America now stretched uninterruptedly from Hudson Bay to the Caribbean and into the deep interior of a continent. The British government faced the challenge of developing a coherent imperial program for an enlarged empire. It had to reckon not only with the political maturity and rising economic self-sufficiency of the well-established colonies on the Atlantic seaboard but also with a distinctive American society and character. Failing to do so in any substantial measure, Britain was to learn that these colonies were capable of determining their own separate destiny.

"The American, This New Man"

American colonists were becoming increasingly aware of being something other than Britons. The mixing of diverse peoples in the New World helped forge a new identity. It was a Frenchman who eloquently discerned the traits of the emergent American. Michel-Guillaume Jean de Crèvecoeur (1735–1813), who had an American wife and settled on a farm in Orange County, New York, in the mid-1760s, penned *Letters from an American Farmer* (1782) in which he sought to define "the American, this new man." To Crèvecoeur, an American has "that strange mixture of blood which you will find in no other country. . . . Here individuals of all nations are melted into a new race of men, whose labours and posterity will one day cause great changes in the world." An American is also one "who leaves behind him all his ancient prejudices and manners, receives new ones from the new mode of life he has embraced, the new government he obeys, and the new rank he holds" (pp. 54–55).

One change in American life that was becoming increasingly perceptible was a quickening urbanization. While the vast majority of colonial Americans lived on farms, the population in cities grew by 36 percent in the two decades before 1760. The major urban areas still were small in 1760—Philadelphia had 23,750 people;

New York, 18,000; Boston, 15,631; Charleston, 8,000; and Newport, 7,500. Significantly, however, new villages were springing up to serve commercial needs, and some towns were becoming small cities. Overall, colonial population continued to double every 25 years, reaching 1.6 million by 1763. While colonial population became denser in some areas, it also experienced an outward pull: bold pioneers were ready to go beyond the Appalachian barrier. By midcentury, as Robert V. Wells (1982) notes, "both English and American observers were aware of rapid growth in the size and strength of the American population. For the former this produced anxiety, for the latter, a sense of confidence in the future" (p. 84).

The Colonial Melting Pot

The mingling of peoples in America indeed fits Crèvecoeur's metaphor of a melting pot. From 1700 to 1775 about 300,000 white immigrants came to America, most from places other than England. By the Revolution, one-half of the white colonists were of national origins different from England, and one-third were foreign born. In addition, in the eighteenth century some 350,000 Africans were imported into the colonies as slaves.

Most whites of the "new immigration" were either German or Scotch-Irish. The Germans, mainly peasants from the Rhineland, fled oppressive governments and economic blight; often they sought greater freedom of religion. They settled in central Pennsylvania (making up one-half of the colony's population) and also drifted southward into the Great Valley of Maryland and Virginia and into the Carolina piedmont. Occasionally, they were accompanied by Swiss immigrants. The Scotch-Irish, who had settled in the six northern counties of Ireland in the seventeenth century, came over to America en masse because of political and religious discrimination, oppressive landlordism, prohibitions on trade levied by the English government, and economic adversity. Like the Germans, they settled in Pennsylvania and moved into the backcountry of the southern colonies. The Shenandoah Valley of Virginia had a patchwork of Scotch-Irish and German farmers. Although some Scot Highlanders arrived in the wake of the abortive rebellions of 1715 and 1745, a large number immigrated in the decade before the Revolution. Smaller immigrant groups included the Dutch, Swedes, and French Huguenots of the "old immigration" and Jews, some 2,000 of whom had arrived by 1775 and settled in every colony. Newcomers readily received naturalization in the colonies where they resided. It became an irritant to the colonists when Parliament, in 1740, required for citizenship seven years' residence and taking the sacrament in the Anglican Church—a stipulation that was often overlooked, however. In 1773 Parliament forbade local naturalization altogether.

Usually, immigrants quickly blended into an anglicized culture and society, although Germans, like the Dutch earlier, tended to resist complete amalgamation. Yet immigrant groups made contributions to American life, especially language and agricultural techniques. The new immigration also strengthened religious pluralism, a factor that in itself created a climate for religious liberty and worked against the expansion of state–church establishments. Although immigration enriched American society, it also helped foster sectional feelings. On the eve of the Revolution, tidewater versus backcountry contention over political and economic matters was prominent everywhere in the colonies.

Even the prevailing British culture was not completely homogeneous, owing to different migrations to America. David Hackett Fischer (1989) argues that the pluralism among the British was healthy and derived from four separate British migrations: the Puritans to New England (1629–40); the small contingent of royalists to Virginia (1642–75); immigrants from the Northern Midlands and Wales to the Delaware Valley (1675–1725); and the Scotch-Irish to the Appalachian backcountry (1718–75). These groups, Fischer states, had "four different conceptions of order, power and freedom which became the cornerstones of a voluntary society in British America. . . . The interplay of four 'freedom ways' has created an expansive pluralism which is more libertarian than any unitary culture alone could be" (pp. 6–7).

Africans, most of whom came to America as slaves, lived in all the colonies, but were more numerous in the South. They made up less than 5 percent of the total population in New England and Pennsylvania and 10 percent in New Jersey, but numbered 40 percent in Virginia, Maryland, and Georgia, 25 percent in North Carolina, and 67 percent in South Carolina. Soon, miscegenation between blacks and whites occurred. Gary B. Nash (1974) notes that 8 percent of blacks in Maryland (1755) were mulattoes; 16.5 percent in Rhode Island (1783); and 20 percent in Chester County, Pennsylvania (1780). Africans, who were imported into the American colonies, themselves represented ethnic diversity. Although after 1700 most of them came from West and Central Africa, they still hailed from different geographical areas and societies. In the late eighteenth century, most slaves in the Upper South were American born and those in the Lower South African born. Life in America eventually obliterated most tribal distinctions.

The European-Indian contact added yet another dimension to American life, even though the number of Native Americans east of the Appalachians quickly dwindled after they began to succumb to the white man's diseases in large numbers and after they were driven westward by the new settlers. The two cultures failed to assimilate, despite some transculturalization, including native responses to the fur trade and missionary work and adaptation by whites of Indian words, clothing, and agricultural methods. Some miscegenation occurred, mostly involving those tribes who lived in close proximity to settlers in New York, the Carolinas, Georgia, and, of course, along the far frontier.

British Western posts served as an ethnic catchall, encompassing Indians, French fur trappers, and English, Scottish, Irish, and colonial merchant traders along with soldiers of the Royal American (60th) Regiment—which was itself a virtual Foreign Legion, consisting primarily of German and Swiss Protestants from Europe, Pennsylvania-Germans, and the "refuse of the army in Ireland" (Pargellis 1933, p. 112). There were also racially mixed people, and even black and Indian slaves, as was the case at Fort Michilimackinac (at the straits between Lakes Huron and Michigan). The Indian slaves were usually Pawnees (hence the name *pani* for such persons) captured by northern tribes and sold to the whites.

Some whites along the frontier, either by choice or by captivity, became members of Indian tribes. Crèvecoeur commented: "There must be in their [the Indians'] social bond something singularly captivating, and far superior to any thing to be boasted of among us; for thousands of Europeans are Indians, and we have no examples of even one of those Aborigines having from choice become Europeans!" (p. 306).

Colonial Society and Culture

Colonial society differed from Great Britain's in many ways other than just ethnic composition. In America, unlike Britain, there was widespread ownership of property, lack of a nobility, religious diversity, no ecclesiastical hierarchy, and ample opportunity for upward mobility in society. Still, America had an evolving class structure. In every colony, merchants or gentry dominated political and social life. By the time of the Revolution, the gap in wealth holding had widened to the point that an estimated 10 percent of the colonial population owned 51 percent of the taxable wealth. Historians agree that colonial society on the eve of the Revolution was experiencing a great amount of tension. Jack P. Greene (1973) points out that "among the realities of mid-eighteenth-century colonial social development" were "the destabilizing effects of rapid change" and "the frustrations created by a closing society" (p. 10).

By the mid-eighteenth century, the patriarchal family was undergoing change, partly because family units were less isolated and partly because fathers had less land to leave their sons. Many children were marrying without parental consent. Public development, such as the creation of almshouses and free schools, absorbed some family responsibility. Often the workplace moved out of the home, and, as a result, married women assumed a more defined sphere of responsibility—home, child care, and garden.

One characteristic of Crèvecoeur's "American" was a growing sense of loyalty to country. To the average colonist, "country" meant colony, but all the same an awareness of a broader attachment was becoming evident. Thus, Eliza Pinckney, proprietress of a large South Carolina plantation, when appearing at the British royal court in 1750, insisted that she be introduced as an American. John Dickinson, in England in 1754, wrote his mother:

> I shall return to America with rapture. There is something surprizing in it, but nothing is more true than that no place is comparable to our native country. It is some strange affection nature has implanted in us, for her wise ends. America is, to be sure, a wilderness and yet that wilderness to me is more pleasing than this charming garden (Colbourn 1969, pp. 274–275).

By the eve of the Revolution Americans could boast their own cultural and intellectual achievements. Fifty-three colonists were admitted as fellows of the Royal Society for Improving Natural Knowledge (founded in London, 1662). Even in the colonies there was an intercolonial fraternity of scientists. Learned organizations were founded, most notably America's first scientific society, the American Philosophical Society (1743). Colonial Americans gained international notice for their work in natural history (botany and zoology) and in natural philosophy (the physical sciences). In the late colonial period, many Americans went abroad to study medicine and returned to practice in the colonies. The College of Philadelphia (the present-day University of Pennsylvania) and King's College (now Columbia University) established medical departments in the 1760s. The prodigious output in published writings gave evidence of a growing awareness of the uniqueness of American life and environment. The belles lettres of the eighteenth century is vast. The writing of history moved from the depiction of chronological events and America as a lush garden to scholarly evaluation, as found in Thomas Hutchinson's three-volume history of Massachusetts (published in 1764, 1767, and 1828).

From 1763 to 1774 the colonists published 4,467 works, from broadsides to books, including 43 newspapers. As Richard L. Merritt has shown (1966), mention of American place names and symbols in the newspapers of five American cities increased from 13.2 percent for 1735–44 to 34.3 percent for 1765–75. Some 200 different almanacs were published before 1800, the best known being Nathaniel Ames's *Astronomical Diary and Almanack* (1725–64), which sold nearly 60,000 copies annually, and Benjamin Franklin's *Poor Richard's Almanack* (1753–55 under Franklin, and continuing until 1796), 10,000 copies.

Many Americans found education readily available. Although only New England had public school systems, elsewhere various kinds of private academies and schools emerged. Increasingly, southern planters began to send their sons to American colleges rather than to England for study. Overall, by the time of the Revolution, literacy for white male adults was about 75 percent (85 percent in New England), in contrast to about 60 percent in England. In America nearly all wealthy men and women were literate, while the literacy rate for farmers was about one-half and for poor persons of all occupations, one-third.

Religion helped form a national psychology. The early Puritans' tenaciously held idea of Providential destiny unfolding in a New Israel was transformed into a sense of Manifest Destiny—a secularization of the religious mission. The Great Awakening of the 1730s and 1740s made religion seem more vital and relative to the lives of colonial Americans. As John Higham notes (1974), the Great Awakening was "the moment in American history when ideology undertook the task of forging a new solidarity among individuals who had lost through migration and competition any corporate identity" (p. 12). The emotional and pietistic appeal of revivalist religion helped restrain any propensity for disorder or democratic upheaval.

Religion and patriotism began to merge during the colonial wars. Thus, Americans tended to view the struggle with France as a war between God's chosen people and the Antichrist (France). Reverend Samuel Davies, for example, preached to Virginia troops in August 1755 as follows.

> You are engaged in a cause of the utmost importance . . . to secure the inestimable blessings of liberty . . . from the chains of French slavery . . . to guard your religion . . . against ignorance, superstition, idolatry, tyranny over conscience, massa-

cre, fire and sword . . . to secure the liberties conveyed to you by your brave forefathers, and bought with their blood, that you may transmit them uncurtailed to your posterity.

After the Peace of 1763, the religious-patriotic zeal would be vented in defense of American liberties versus the corruption of England.

It was evident that Americans were beginning to think in continental terms. Commerce, frontier expansion, service in the armed forces beyond one's colony, and subscription to distant publications broadened the people's geographical interest. Religious groups, especially Quakers and Jews, as well as fraternal organizations, such as the Masonic order and ethnic societies, maintained ties among their brethren in different colonies. New Light preachers, artists, musicians, actors, and itinerant merchants were among those who traveled in a wide circuit. Businessmen and planters had intercolonial contact through their partners and agents. The postal service (first established in 1690 between Boston and New York), which came under control of the crown in 1711, eventually served all the colonies from New Hampshire to Georgia.

Constitutional Perspectives

Although the colonists gave little thought to principles of government before 1763, they nevertheless accepted certain ideas, such as those enunciated by John Locke and other English political writers: that government was derived from the people, that there was a contractual relationship between the people and their rulers, that power had to be limited, and that revolt against tyranny was justified. In the seventeenth century, while England was having its Civil War and Glorious Revolution, the colonists were also experiencing rebellions. The major uprisings were Nathaniel Bacon's in Virginia (1676), in which Governor William Berkeley was overthrown, and the revolts of 1689–90, which deposed not only the Dominion of New England and the existing governments in Massachusetts and New York, but also the proprietary rule in Maryland.

Two New England clergymen in particular expressed colonial views on the relationship between the people and their government. The Reverend John Wise, in his pamphlet, *Vindication of the Government of New-England Churches* (1717, reprinted 1772), declared that there should be three covenants: agreement upon majority rule; agreement upon rule of law; and an agreement by "those on whom Sovereignty is conferred" to guard "the Common Peace, and Welfare" and "the Subjects on the other hand, to yield them faithful Obedience." The people could withdraw their powers "when a Government so Settled shall throw itself from its Foundations" or "shall subvert or confound the Constitution." To Wise, "the end of all good Government is to Cultivate Humanity, and Promote the happiness of all, and the good of every Man in all his Rights, his Life, Liberty, Estate, Honour, &c. without injury or abuse done to any." The second clergyman, Jonathan Mayhew, minister of the West Church in Boston, upon the one hundredth anniversary of the execution of Charles I delivered A *Discourse Concerning Unlimited Submission and Non-Resistance to the Higher Powers* (1750). In this pamphlet he stressed the right of resistance to arbitrary authority: "no government is to be submitted to, at the *expence* of that which is the *sole end* of all government, the common good and safety of society." Views similar to Wise and Mayhew's increasingly found expression in New England election sermons and in oral disputations at college commencement exercises.

The American colonists developed ideas of a fixed (written) constitution unlike that of England, which was a combination of the Magna Carta, statute and local law, common law, and court decisions. Each colony had a basic constitution in the form of a charter. In addition, the proprietors of the Carolinas and East and West Jersey (New Jersey) had issued "concessions and agreements," and William Penn had granted his colony "frames of government." From time to time, royal instructions complemented these documents.

Although the colonists prided themselves on having all the rights of Englishmen, they occasionally tempered fundamental law with greater libertarianism than in Great Britain. Freedom of press and speech expanded in the colonies. One case in point was the 1735 verdict in the trial of John Peter Zenger for maligning the governor of New York. The jury's vote for acquittal recognized truth as a defense against a charge of seditious libel. (This principle was not acknowledged in English law until 1843.) Though of limited value in the colonial period (for example, criticism of a legislature remained unprotected), the principle in the Zenger decision provided an important step toward greater latitude for the freedom of expression.

The colonists never accepted the view that they were subject to the pervasive legislative power of Parliament. Acts of Parliament refrained from touching on the internal affairs of the colonies, except in rare instances when the stability of trade and finance relating to the empire as a whole was at issue. Parliament never seriously questioned the idea of the colonies being founded and governed through royal authority. When, for example, in 1733 the Massachusetts House and Council petitioned twice to have the governor's additional instructions from the crown withdrawn, the House of Commons replied that the petitions were "frivolous and groundless, an high insult upon his Majesty's government, and tending to shake off the dependency of the said colony upon the kingdom."

A greater sense of separation of powers prevailed in the colonies than in England. The British cabinet, as it was then developing (with ministers—heads of departments—selected from among members of Parliament), performed many executive functions. In the colonies, the governor, as representative of the king, had sole executive authority. Actually, the crown held greater sway in the colonies than in England. Royal governors had powers that the crown no longer exercised in the realm: they could veto legislation; summon, prorogue, and dissolve assemblies; dismiss judges; and create certain kinds of courts. Appointed at the king's pleasure, the royal governor was responsible to the crown only and invested with wide authority. He exercised absolute veto; commanded land and naval forces; appointed and removed officials; issued land grants; was legal head of the established church in the colony; pardoned criminals; issued letters of marque and reprisal; and enforced navigation and trade laws. He could be removed only by the crown, and he was answerable to the King's Bench (but not to any colonial courts) for suits of damages. In disputes between the governor and the legislature over appointments, the crown and not Parliament resolved the controversy. Connecticut and Rhode Island were governed principally by legislative authority, with the governors elected by and responsible to the legislatures. In Maryland and Pennsylvania, the governors owed their appointments to the proprietors, but they also had responsibilities similar to those of the royal governors.

Colonial councils served as an advisory board to the governor, an upper house of assembly, and, with the governor, the highest court of a colony. In the royal colonies, the crown appointed councillors from nominations by the governor (except in Massachusetts, where they were chosen by the lower house); in the nonroyal colonies of Rhode Island and Connecticut they were elected by the freemen; and in the proprietaries (Pennsylvania and Maryland) they were nominated by the governor and appointed by the proprietor. While selected from among the elite, councillors often had served in the lower house, and they usually had interests similar to those of the legislators. The lack of a "House of Lords" in colonial governments made the legislative and executive spheres more distinct. As Ian R. Christie and Benjamin Labaree have written (1976), the colonists

> agreed in theory that the best defense against corrupting tyranny was the mixed constitution—the three-legged stool of monarchy, aristocracy, and commons. But in fact the absence of a true aristocracy in America meant that the stool had only two legs, the royal prerogative expressed through the governors and the commons represented by the lower houses of assembly. Thus the all-important balance could not be achieved, and the assemblies therefore saw themselves standing alone as defenders of the people's "liberty" against the avaricious encroachment of executive "tyranny." (p. 18)

The colonial legislatures won the power of the purse—responsibility for initiating money bills and controlling expenditures. Thus, North Carolina refused to grant funds for sending troops to aid Virginia in an expedition against the French in western Pennsylvania in 1754 until the governor assented to a paper money issue. Similarly, during the French and Indian War, the Virginia House of Burgesses granted military appropriations only upon the stipulation that it supervise the expenditures. Because in most colonies a legislature had at least some control over the salaries of governors and other officials, the home government attempted to find some means to establish a permanent fund for the payment of such stipends, over which an assembly would have no control. This quest proved elusive, however, even with the British reform program of the 1760s and 1770s.

After 1696 the British sovereign and the Privy Council had joint authority, conferred by Parliament, to review colonial laws and decide whether they were to remain in effect. This practice, known as the royal disallowance, was not insisted upon for the corporate colonies of Connecticut and Rhode Island. In all, until the Revolution, 5.5 percent of colonial laws were disallowed—469 out of 8,563.

The royal disallowance proved a major annoyance for the colonies in their relationship with the British sovereign. On occasion the colonists were able to circumvent the process. Some legislatures, for example, evaded review by passing laws for a short duration. In Virginia the "Parson's Cause" gained fame because the colony abided by a disallowance decision but compromised its effect—thus obliquely challenging royal authority. After the price of tobacco rose as a result of the scarcity caused by a drought, the Virginia legislature had enacted the Two-Penny Act, which converted the pay of clergy from 17,280 pounds of tobacco per year to a fixed annual wage of 16s. 8d. per hundred pounds of tobacco (2d. a pound)—the same amount of tobacco but at less than the prevailing price. Though passed and then passed again on a short-term basis, in the hopes of avoiding royal review, the law was nevertheless disallowed. In the trial held at Hanover Court House in December 1763 to decide on the Reverend James Maury's claims for compensation for lost income to the amount of £288, the court, with the young Patrick Henry arguing brilliantly on behalf of the colony, accepted the jury verdict for an award of only 1d. for the plaintiff.

Representative government had a greater democratic base in the colonies than in England. It is true that in America the suffrage franchise entailed some form of property holding, residency, and age requirements, as in England, and women, servants, and slaves could not vote. In most colonies, however, in addition to real estate, personal property, payment of taxes, house tenancy, and leaseholding entitled adult white males to vote. In Albany and New York City, craftsmen and other tradesmen acquired the franchise by paying a small fee. Thus, while an estimated 15 percent of adult males could vote in eighteenth-century England, in the colonies the number was at least 50 percent, and in some areas as high as 75 to 90 percent.

Although the colonists were drawing closer together through intercolonial ties and an awareness of their American identity, little of lasting importance to colonial union was accomplished. Only twice before the Revolutionary period did the colonies join in a union. First, the New England Confederation (the United Colonies of New England), which lasted from 1643 to 1689, was formed by the Puritan colonies seeking to act in concert in matters of defense, Indian affairs, comity, economic development, and policies relating to religion. It proved of some value—not only was a treaty negotiated with New Netherland but also military efforts were coordinated during the Indian war of 1675–76 (King Philip's War). The second "Union" effort, the Dominion of New England, which put the northern colonies under a single royal government in 1686, lasted only three years, being undone by the colonists' own Glorious Revolution. Plans of imperial consolidation again emerged in the 1720s, but by this time the British ministry was reluctant to join the colonies together. Plans of union were intermittently proposed, with William Penn's scheme of 1698 and the Albany Plan of 1754 being the best known, but both the colonial legislatures and the British government were afraid of any redistribution of power. Nonetheless, delegates from several or more colonies came together from time to time throughout the colonial period to attend war and Indian conferences. In 1755, for example, governors from five colonies conferred with British army and navy commanders at Alexandria, Virginia, to plan offensive operations against the

French. Although none of these forms of cooperation endured on an institutional basis, they gave the colonists the benefit of experience and made them aware of options for future intercolonial collaboration.

On a broader scale, colonists kept paid agents in England to lobby with British officialdom. These men usually represented one or more colonial legislatures. The agents kept information flowing both ways and served the important function of sending home warnings of pending measures by the crown or Parliament.

Until the imperial crises began after 1763, the colonists never raised a constitutional challenge to Great Britain. They viewed their rights and political practices as fitting in with the principles of the British constitution, though adaptable to their own specific situations. As Lawrence H. Leder has written (1968), when "the Imperial crisis deepened," it "became obvious that there was no common and local ground on which the colonists could defend themselves against increasing British authority. If they were to find adequate safeguards for colonial rights, they could not rely upon local constitutional theory but would have to appeal to ideas broader in scope" (p. 117).

The writs of assistance case of 1761 in Massachusetts set a constitutional direction for the future. The writs (as provided by parliamentary law) authorized customshouse officials during daylight hours to compel the assistance of constables and other provincial officers in general searches for goods that had been imported without payment of duties. Initially, Boston merchants did not oppose the use of writs, but when efforts were made in 1760 to step up the practice, they became concerned.

Court authority for issuance of the writs had to be reestablished upon the death of a sovereign. With news of the death of George II in late 1760, 63 merchants petitioned the Massachusetts Supreme Court of Judicature to negate use of the writs. During the court hearing, James Otis, Jr., the chief counsel for the merchants, declared: "It is the business of this court to demolish this monster of oppression, & tear into shreds this remnant of Star Chamber Tyranny." Every man was a "natural sovereign," entitled to protection of "life, liberty, and property"— "inherent, inalienable, and indefeasible by any laws, pacts, contracts, covenants, or stipulations, which man could devise." Otis also stated that "an act against the constitution is void" (Gipson, 1967, pp. 124–126). Thus, Otis maintained, all Englishmen had certain fundamental rights that neither Parliament nor anyone else could invade. Otis was appealing to natural law as superior to parliamentary enactments. Over 50 years later, John Adams commented in reference to Otis's oratory: "Then and there the child Independence was born."

The Economic Outlook

For over a century leading up to the Revolution the colonial economy continuously expanded in all sectors. The diverse output of goods indicated a trend toward greater self-sufficiency. The colonists had few complaints about their participation in the English mercantilist system, for on balance, British mercantilist policies and regulation worked for the benefit rather than the detriment of the colonial economy. The mercantilist system sought a favorable balance of trade for the mother country, in value of goods and specie (coined money) exchange. It also aimed at creating an economic equilibrium within the empire, so that the mother country and the colonies would have complementary economies. The mercantilist system primarily stressed encouragement of English manufactures and the colonial production of raw materials.

The main drawback of the English mercantile system, from the colonial point of view, was the drain of specie from the colonies to England and the growing indebtedness of American merchants and planters to English and Scottish consignment firms. The colonies were forbidden to establish their own coinage. Colonial paper money emissions in the eighteenth century caused controversy over exchange rates, with colonial currency devalued in relation to specie.

The English regulation of navigation and trade caused little hardship and actually enhanced the colonial economy. The Navigation Acts of the seventeenth century prohibited foreign ships from carrying goods to the colonies as well as engaging in the coastal trade. The act of 1660 specifically forbade foreigners from acting as merchants or factors in the colonies and enumerated commodities that could be sent only to England. The list was expanded from time to time. The Staple Act of 1663 prohibited direct export of European goods to the colonies; instead, such trade had to be conducted through England. The Navigation Acts did not prohibit re-export of American enumerated commodities to foreign ports. Enumerated commodities consisted of 63 percent of the total value of colonial exports in 1760. American trade involving nonprohibited items had direct access to southern Europe, Africa, and South America, except where excluded by restrictions of foreign nations. The Navigation laws were a great boon to American shipbuilding and development of a merchant fleet. One-third of British merchant ships were built in the colonies.

Parliament enacted only a few laws restricting colonial production for the export trade; the purpose of these laws was to prevent competition with British goods. None of these laws had great impact on the colonial economy, for various reasons. The Woolen Act of 1699, for example, prohibiting export of wool or woolen manufactures, did not have much effect since sheep and wool did not exceed local demand. The Hat Act of 1732, concerned mainly with cutting off intercolonial trade in hats, affected only a minor industry. The Molasses Act of 1733 placed a 6d. duty on molasses as well as prohibitive levies on sugar, rum, and spirits imported from the West Indies. This law was evaded almost at will. The Iron Act of 1750, forbidding the further erection of mills for making high-grade iron and finished products, did not have much impact since the colonial iron industry had already expanded to its limits.

Americans produced a wide variety of commodities that supplied local markets and entered into the export trade. Even though American manufacturing was generally small scale (households, shops, and farms) and was hampered by primitive mechanization, industrial expansiveness was remarkable. Extractive industries in particular flourished, having the advantages of plentiful natural resources, minimal operational production requirements, proximity to sea lanes, and the encouragement of both the British and colonial governments. English bounties were given to encourage specific colonial production, such as naval stores (chiefly rosin, tar, turpentine, and pitch) and indigo. As a result, forest products (timber and naval stores), furs, iron, fishing, shipbuilding, and milling evolved into major industries. Household manufacturing moved into workshops maintained by skilled craftsmen.

Colonists found a wide market for southern staples, such as tobacco, rice, and indigo, and the leading exports in the northern colonies were pork, beef, livestock, grain, flour, and rum. Colonial ships carried their own goods in a shuttle trade with Great Britain or, frequently, in triangular commerce involving America–the West Indies–England and southern Europe–England–the colonies.

By the mid-eighteenth century, various factors contributed to the colonies' prosperity and increasing standard of living: expanded intercolonial trade and markets within the colonies; growing demand for grain in southern Europe; home and town industry; liberality of credit from Great Britain; increased population; expansion in the production of textiles and shoes; English capital for American enterprise; acquisition of land in the Appalachian region; and market value of goods that the colonists produced, climbing more than the rise in cost of wages.

Americans looked forward to further economic expansion and a rising standard of living, unencumbered by any additional mercantilist restrictions. Benjamin Franklin served notice on Great Britain in his OBSERVATIONS *concerning the Increase of Mankind, Peopling of Countries, &c* (1755), which he wrote in response to the passage of the Iron Act:

> The Danger . . . of these Colonies interfering with their Mother Country in Trades that depend on Labour, Manufactures, &c. is too remote to require the Attention of Great-Britain.
>
> But in Proportion to the Increase of the Colonies, a vast Demand is growing for British Manufactures, a glorious Market wholly in the Power of Britain, in which Foreigners cannot interfere, which will increase in a short Time even beyond her Power of supplying, tho' her whole Trade should be to her Colonies: Therefore Britain should not too much restrain Manufactures in her Colonies. A wise and good Mother will not do it. To distress, is to weaken, and weakening the Children, weakens the whole Family (Labaree 1959–90, 4:229).

The recession following the end of the French and Indian War left the colonists in no mood for any new imperial economic regulations and revenue measures. The withdrawal of British military forces in 1760 brought severe hardship to northern port cities. The lost contracts in supplying the armed forces hit the mercantile houses hard and especially the small retailers. Idle ships forced unemployment for seamen, maritime artisans, and tradesmen. Aggravating all this distress were the high prices and taxes occasioned by the war. Impoverished migrants poured into the cities. With the British economy also in a recession, American merchants and planters suddenly found themselves in a credit crunch. In the Chesapeake area, many planters faced bankruptcy. The tobacco price of 18s. hundredweight in 1763 fell to 12s. the next year. Bills of exchange were not honored in England. Yet planters bought more and more goods from England on credit, further increasing their indebtedness.

Impact of War and Peace

The colonies' military participation during the French and Indian War provided valuable lessons for the later creation of the Continental army during the Revolution. For one thing, it gave the provincials confidence in arms, even though they almost always fought alongside British regulars. In addition, two aspects of the colonial military experience had long-term effects. First, the war gave training to men who later became the senior officers of the Revolutionary army. Men like George Washington learned the art and organization of warfare principally from their association in the field with British seasoned veterans. Indeed, a professional American soldiery had its origins in the French and Indian War.

The second aspect was the mutual contempt between American and British soldiers. Beyond those who served in the field as militia, some 5,000 provincials enlisted as British redcoats for three years or the duration of the war. The desertion rate of American royal regiments greatly surpassed that of the British regular units. The reason for their discontent is easily found. American officers who joined British regiments were denied rank above captain. Moreover, British commanders denounced the fitness of American troops at every opportunity. General James Wolfe wrote in 1758: "Americans are in general the dirtiest, the most contemptible, cowardly dregs that you can conceive. . . . There is no depending upon them in action. They fall down dead in their own dirt and desert by battalions." General John Forbes was of the same mind regarding Virginia and Pennsylvania militia. Except for a "few of their principle [sic] Officers," they "are an extream bad Collection of broken Innkeepers, Horse Jockeys, & Indian traders," and "the Men under them, are a direct copy of their Officers, nor can it well be otherwise, as they are a gathering from the scum of the worst of people." Americans, in turn, considered British officers haughty and incompetent and the redcoat soldiery riffraff, and they had contempt for British fighting capabilities. Wrote Lieutenant Colonel Adam Stephen of the Virginia militia, after Braddock's defeat in July 1755: "You might as well send a Cow in pursuit of a Hare as an English Soldier loaded in their Way."

At the end of the war, some 10,000 British regulars were left in North America (mainly outside the 13 American colonies), a few of whom garrisoned posts in the western country. The colonists objected to a substantial peacetime military establishment, especially one to which they had not consented. It seems that Britain's chief motivation for leaving troops in America was that the king did not know what else to do with the British veteran soldiers who could not easily be fitted into civilian life. It was one thing, however, to station troops in America and another to put much of the burden for their cost on the colonies. During the war, the British government promptly reimbursed about two-fifths of the military outlay of the colonies. After the war, to relieve the oppressed English taxpayers, it was maintained, it was not unreasonable to expect Americans to pay for their own security. This was the Englishmen's point of view, but from the colonists' perspective the need for such protection in the first place was most questionable.

The Indian situation was continuing to prove dangerous. Pontiac's Rebellion of 1763 swept through the whole northern Ohio country, forcing all British forts west of Fort Pitt to surrender, except Detroit. The battle of Bushy Run of August 1763, in which the British colonel, Henry Bouquet, defeated the Indians, and the lifting of the siege of Detroit ended the Indian war. In the South there was always the possibility of hostilities. At the moment there was peace, which had followed the end of the Cherokee War of 1759–61.

The Proclamation of 1763 (a royal decree) made crown colonies of three territories that had been acquired from the war: Canada and East and West Florida. A line running along the crest of the Alleghenies was drawn to separate colonial settlements and Indian territory. All land claims west of the boundary were to be nullified. Westward population advance and land granting to settlers or speculators were left entirely to the disposition of the king. In the next year, the Plan of 1764 was imposed, placing the fur trade directly under royal control. Now only licensed traders could obtain furs; commissaries were to be appointed to supervise the exchange of furs between whites and Indians at designated sites. Northern and southern Indian departments, each under a royally appointed superintendent, took over the conduct of Indian relations from the individual colonies.

Land companies, pioneer settlers, fur traders, and colonial governments vehemently opposed the new policies. The proclamation went against the claims of many colonies to western lands, which were supported by provisions of the early colonial charters. Actually, the British government did not intend to maintain a permanent boundary, which, in fact, was adjusted several times before the Revolution to accommodate some of the pressures of westward expansion. Even most of the features of the Plan of 1764 were abandoned by 1768. Nevertheless, the colonists believed that the British program for the West ignored their legitimate interests.

In 1763 Americans had no thought of independence, but in England the idea was not so easily dismissed. The question had come up in government circles whenever proposals were made for creating some kind of union among the colonies and especially during the "Canada–Guadeloupe" debates of 1759–61, when England had to decide whether to accept Canada or the West Indian sugar island, Guadeloupe, from France in the peace settlement. With the acquisition of Canada from France and the Floridas from Spain, the colonies no longer needed British protection, and it was quite possible that they might now turn against England. Although Benjamin Franklin believed that the British government had nothing to fear on this account, in his *The Interest of Great Britain Considered, with Regard to the Colonies, and the Acquisition of Canada and Guadeloupe* (1760), he warned: "When I say such a union [of the colonies against England] is impossible, I mean without the most grievous tyranny and oppression. . . . The waves do not rise, but when the winds blow."

The peace settlement of 1763 bode ill for future American-British relations. Josiah Tucker, dean of Gloucester Cathedral and prolific essayist, observed in *The True Interest of Great-Britain Set Forth in Regard to the Colonies* (1774): "For an undoubted Fact it is, that from the Moment in which *Canada* came into Possession of the *English* an End was put to the Sovereignty of the Mother-Country over her Colonies. They had then nothing to fear from a foreign Enemy." It was "in the nature of the colonies to set up for themselves as soon as ever they find that they are able to subsist, without being beholden to the Mother-Country." Tucker, having the hindsight of a decade that had passed since 1763, also commented: "For if a Father is not able to govern his Son at the Ages of 14 or 16 Years, how can it be supposed that he will be better able when the Youth is become a Man of full Age and Stature, in the Vigour of Health and Strength, and the Parent perhaps more feeble and decrepid than he was before?"

CHAPTER 2

The View
from England

 The American Revolution occurred during a transition period in English economic, political, and social life. A steadily rising population in Great Britain (increasing 7 to 9 percent each decade and reaching 7.5 million in 1760) put demands on economic productivity. From 1714 to 1770 the leading sectors of the economy—agriculture, commerce, and industry—had expanded 40 percent. Although more than half of Britain's inhabitants were connected with agriculture and most manufacturing was still performed in the home, the Industrial Revolution was beginning to take effect—principally in the production of textiles, iron, and steel.

England's second enclosure movement (the first having been part of the Tudor period) was underway. Parliament forced rural workers to forego their claims for a share of commons or open field lands in return for tiny farms. Unable to pay their debts and the assessed cost of fencing and roads, many small farmers forfeited their lands and entered the workforce as hired hands and tenants of great landlords or found their way among the destitute poor of the cities. Yet the Englishmen, other than the very poor, benefited from the increased expansion and diversification of the economy. Real wages improved, though accompanied by exploitation and bad working conditions of industrial labor. As John B. Owen (1974) writes: "Most Englishmen by 1760 had more reason for confidence than they had had at the turn of the century" (p. 151). Class distinctions were becoming a little blurred, with greater social mobility and means for capitalist enterprise. Yet society remained stratified. Rank, by descending order and not necessarily by wealth, consisted of nobility, gentry (nonnobles, especially large landowners, entitled to a coat of arms), a large middle class of persons with nonmanual occupations (including professionals, merchants, shopkeepers, and prosperous craftsmen), freeholders (small landowners), tenant farmers, and laborers for hire.

The nobles and their relations filled most of the high offices, whether in the ministerial departments, church, navy, or army. Although the nobles themselves could sit only in the House of Lords (as peers), many of their family members were in the House of Commons. Generally, possession of real estate was a requirement for voting. In the counties, the suffrage franchise was based on the 40s. freehold

George III (1738–1820): The king who gloried "in the name of Briton" and was denigrated in the Declaration of Independence as "unfit to be the ruler of a free people." Mezzoprint by E. Fisher, from a painting by Benjamin West, published in 1778.   *National Archives*

(ownership of an estate annually yielding that amount of income). A more liberal allowance, however, was made for many of the boroughs, where one could vote either by being an "inhabitant householder," owning a hearth to boil a pot (potwalloper), or paying local taxes (the scot-and-lot borough franchise). Although members of the upper aristocratic families could find service in national-level positions, the lesser gentry and the middle sort, as in America, filled most of the local offices.

George III

George III (1738–1820) ascended the throne in 1760 at the age of 22 upon the death of his grandfather, George II. The young king's father, Frederick, prince of Wales, had headed an opposition party to his own father, George II, and had helped to topple the Robert Walpole ministry in 1742. Frederick died in 1751. Growing up amid the family squabbles, George III early had a disdain for parties or factions in government. John Stuart, the third earl of Bute, as tutor and confidant, had instilled in George the idea that a king was king of his people and not of Whigs and Tories.

England rarely had a sovereign more diligent, conscientious, dedicated, and of high personal morality than the third Hanoverian, yet he was obstinate and unimaginative. George III nevertheless became a masterful politician, playing the same game as the political leaders in the Commons, and staying closely attuned to public opinion. Fully accepting the settlement of the Glorious Revolution, he had no intention of usurping power from the legislature. Beginning early in his reign, however, George III suffered periodically from a manic-depressive disorder, brought on by what we now know to have been porphyria, a metabolic imbalance. (Today it is cured by barbiturates.)

During George III's rule, it was expected that the monarch should help make government policy, through influence on the ministry and Parliament, but be careful not to abridge the prerogatives of Parliament. George III did not harbor despotic ambitions. The story that as a youth he was told by his mother, Princess Augusta, "George, be a King!" has been shown to be apocryphal. Biographer John Brooke writes (1972) that British historian Lewis Namier "used to say that if the story were true it probably had reference to the King's table manners"—that the Princess most likely said, "George! sit up straight! do you want to look like your uncle Cumberland? George, be a King!" (p. 390).

George III was likely quite familiar with the popular work, *The Idea of a Patriot King* (1749), written by Henry St. John, viscount Bolingbroke, for the benefit of George's father, Prince Frederick. Though advocating a limited monarchy, Bolingbroke contended that the king should get rid of party government and choose his own ministers; he should "put himself at the head of his people in order to govern or, more properly, to subdue all parties." The king himself should be a sort of prime minister. To be a king for the people, George III sought to put an end to political parties. He insisted on his right to make appointments, especially pertaining to the royal household, the church, and the armed forces. He used patronage skillfully, and he applied royal funds to buy votes. George III followed parliamentary debates closely and rewarded those who sided with his point of view. An office, a pension, or a peerage might be available to the "King's Friends." George III customarily met with government ministers individually in a room called "the closet." As Edmund Burke complained: "The power of the Crown, almost dead and rotten as Prerogative, has grown up anew, with much more strength, and far less odium, under the name of Influence" (Langford 1981, 2:258).

Historically, English sovereigns had recourse to advice from the Privy Council. This body (131 members at the end of the eighteenth century) consisted of all adult males of the royal family, certain peers, prelates, and high-level officeholders, all of whom were normally appointed to the council for life. The Privy Council had become unwieldy and, since the time of the later Stuarts, had greatly declined in importance. A "cabinet council," selected from members of the Privy Council, since the reign of William III, began to assume the advisory functions of the Privy Council. It was also significant that members of the cabinet council were expected to be officeholders. The cabinet council acquired an enhancement of ministerial responsibility—the direction of policy and administration—during the reign of George I, who had limited skills in the English language and was indifferent to the intricacies of English government. But the old Privy Council still had certain functions. On matters pertaining to the American colonies it sat as a Committee of Council for Plantation Affairs (a committee of the whole). For routine business, only a few members attended, for example, in October 1763, only three attended: the two secretaries of state and the president of the Board of Trade. Most of the work of the Privy Council was pro forma, devoted to endorsing recommendations of the cabinet council, the Board of Trade, and heads of departments. Yet the king-in-council (king and Privy Council) served as a link to the colonies. In the colonies, as well as in Great Britain, all royal orders, letters, and grants had to pass through the hands of the Lord Privy Seal; it was from this source that colonial governors received their instructions. The Privy Council could hear appeals from colonial courts, since the colonists, as British subjects, had the right to appeal to the king. The role of the Privy Council as a supreme court for the colonies was also enhanced by its issuance of decisions on the validity of colonial legislation.

Parliament, Cabinet, Departments

In Hanoverian England during the 1760s–70s, membership in Parliament remained rather constant: the House of Lords was made up of around 220 members (in 1766 encompassing 26 bishops, 16 elected representatives of the Scottish peerage, and 180 hereditary English and Welsh nobles), and the House of Commons, 558 members, representing 315 constituencies, of which only 50 or 60 were contested. From England there were 489 members of the Commons; Wales, 24; and Scotland, 45. By the Septennial Act of 1716 (which replaced the Triennial Act of 1694), the maximum life of a Parliament was seven years.

No single American-born person sat in the 1761 Parliament, but from 1763 to 1783 there were five, all of whom had lived in the northern colonies: the merchants John Huske, Barlow Trecothick, and Henry Cruger; Staats Long Morris, brother of Gouverneur Morris and an army officer who had married the widow of the duke of Gordon; and Paul Wentworth, colonial agent and future loyalist. In addition, other members of the House of Commons were well versed in American affairs: West Indians, British merchants trading with the colonies, army and naval officers who had served in America during the Seven Years' War, and several members employed as agents for the colonies. One of the MPs, Anthony Bacon, was an agent for North Carolina and had been a storekeeper in Maryland.

Members of Parliament (MPs) rarely had to take a stand on issues affecting the whole realm or empire except in times of emergencies, such as war and peace. Petitioners from localities succeeded in having bills brought forward regarding transportation improvements, enclosures, commerce, and industry. Any heated contest most often arose out of local competing economic interests. As Edmund Burke noted in a 1780 speech, the House of Commons was becoming "a confused and scuffling bustle of local agency" (Pares, 1953, p. 2). Parliament thus gave little attention to colonial affairs. Also limiting legislative activity was Parliament's reluctance to meet longer than half a year, and even then there was high absenteeism. Customarily, country gentlemen attended only during the first four months of a year, with one-half the members of the Commons usually showing up at a given time. It was indeed a rare occasion for as many as 400 to be present.

In Parliament few members were independent. One-half of the MPs owed their seats to patrons, and 28 percent held an office or honor under the government.

Over half of the Commons owned large estates; 21 percent were younger sons of wealthy landholders; and 9 percent came from the business sector. Seats were bought and sold. "Rotten boroughs" (boroughs that had very few voters and yet elected members of Parliament) were becoming more prevalent during the latter half of the eighteenth century. Thirty percent of the MPs came from nomination boroughs; that is, they were obligated to a patron or a corporate group. Parliament avoided electoral redistricting. The industrial cities of Manchester, with a population of 130,000, and Birmingham and Leeds, each with 30,000 inhabitants, had no representation at all. Middlesex County, within the Greater London area, had 1 million residents but only eight MPs, whereas New Romney, with eight voters, returned two representatives, and the borough of Old Sarum, the "accursed hill" near Salisbury, with no inhabitants whatsoever, held one seat in the Commons. (Whoever owned the property, as did the Pitt family for a while, decided who was to be the MP.)

By the time George III ascended the throne, an inner cabinet (within the cabinet council, which was now sometimes dubbed the nominal cabinet) had appeared. The inner cabinet, of no fixed number, usually consisted of five to seven members, of whom there were always the first lord of the Treasury, chancellor of the Exchequer, the two secretaries of state, and president of the Privy Council. The inner cabinet, or what might be called the ministry, with its members coming from either house of Parliament, had responsibility for initiating and directing a legislative program. Although George III did not oppose the rise of a cabinet under parliamentary auspices, he insisted on making ministerial appointments. During his long reign, on several occasions he selected a prime minister (a designation that had first appeared in reference to Robert Walpole's leadership, 1721–42, as first lord of the Treasury and chancellor of the Exchequer) without deference to the Commons. Certain features of the modern cabinet became distinguishable by the end of the eighteenth century: unity within the cabinet; membership from the party that controlled the House of Commons; a prime minister; and the policy of collective resignations (or at least a change in office held) when a ministry had lost confidence in the Commons. Not until the late nineteenth century did the tenure of British ministries depend solely on the outcome of general elections.

Two government departments had primary responsibility for shaping imperial-colonial relations: the Board of Trade and the secretary of state for the Southern Department. The Board of Trade had 16 members, 8 of whom regularly attended meetings and were salaried at £1,000 a year. It advised on colonial appointments, drew up governors' instructions, and reviewed colonial legislation as to whether laws should be allowed; its recommendations went to the king-in-council and, if requested, to the House of Commons as well. In 1768 a third secretary of state was appointed, expressly for American affairs. In effect, he took over such duties from the secretary of state for the Southern Department. Edmund Burke commented that, since two secretaries were doing nothing, it was necessary to give them some help. Only three men served as secretary of state for America until the office was abolished in 1782: the earl of Hillsborough, 1768–72; the earl of

Dartmouth, 1772–75; and George Sackville Germain (Viscount Sackville in 1782), 1775–82. The secretary of state for America had the services of two undersecretaries and five clerks.

Still, imperial administration affecting the colonies lacked central control. Confusion and duplication characterized the bureaucracy. Besides the secretary of state for America and the Board of Trade, other agencies had some role in imperial administration: the Privy Council; the Treasury; the surveyor and auditor-general of the colonies; customs commissioners (a separate Board of Customs for America was established in 1767); the War Office (secretary at war); the Admiralty (with its 15 branches); Admiralty Courts; the surveyor of the King's Woods; the postmaster general; and the bishop of London. Most imperial policy was shaped by subministers. Many department decisions required endorsement by Parliament. Thus, drawing up and promulgating policies entailed a lengthy process. Some five to ten weeks elapsed in the making of a decision, and four or more weeks would pass before it would be known across the Atlantic in America.

Politics and Ministries

British politics of the 1760s and 1770s reflected a diminished rivalry between major political parties, though, of course, factional competition remained. Historically, a two-party system had grown out of "court" and "country" affiliations, and simply the "outs" versus the "ins." During the last years of Charles II's reign (1660–85), the "court party" became known as the Tories, and the "country party" the Whigs. Tories supported the royal prerogative and the continued hegemony of the Church of England, whereas the Whigs championed parliamentary supremacy, religious toleration, individual rights, and commercial development. The debates over the Exclusion Bill (designed to deny the Catholic James, duke of York, his rights as heir to the throne) during 1679–81 further accentuated party strife. At the time, the Tories favored the duke of York, while the Whigs backed Charles II's illegitimate son, the duke of Monmouth, for the succession. After the Glorious Revolution, William III, seeking reconciliation, brought both Tories and Whigs into his government. George I, owing his crown to the Whigs, relied mainly on that group in forming his cabinets. Contributing to the decline of the Tory party was the alleged attachment of many of its members to Jacobitism (the movement to restore the direct Stuart line for the royal succession). In 1761 only 113 members of Parliament were accounted Tories, and by 1780 there were practically none. In the 1760s, as Lewis Namier has written (1966), the Tories were mostly country gentlemen, who "worshipped the Throne and loathed the Court, believed in authority and disliked Government" (p. 183). Namier argues that now there were no real parties, only the politics of patronage and influence, with an oligarchy of wealthy families as the beneficiaries. By the 1770s the dominant force in Parliament were the King's Friends, most of whom came from the Whig ranks. Thus, a reversal of roles had been effected. As Frank O'Gorman (1975) writes, the Whigs:

[had] ceased to attack royal authority and proceeded to exploit it. The Tories, once the upholders of passive obedience to an established church and a divine right monarchy, accepted the Glorious Revolution, a constitutional monarchy and religious toleration. The party which had defended the Stuarts now became the advocate of Place Bills [excluding MPs from holding offices, pensions, or contracts from the crown], frequent elections and the purity and independence of the Commons. (p. 16)

As party distinctions blurred, factions, nevertheless, reappeared. Leadership of the remnant Old Whigs that had so long been headed by the duke of Newcastle now went to Charles Watson-Wentworth, second marquis of Rockingham (1730–82). Many of Rockingham's followers were also "young Whigs," such as Edmund Burke and eventually Charles James Fox, who entered Parliament in 1768 at age 19. Indeed, as Frank O'Gorman has shown, most new MPs of the period were very young; from 1734 to 1832 one-fourth were under the age of 25, and another one-fourth had not reached the age of 33. In October 1765 the duke of Newcastle complained to George Keppel, earl of Albemarle, that the young men coming into the Old Whig group "do not know the world; and what Ministers must do, and ought to do, to be able to serve the publick, and support themselves" (O'Gorman 1975, p. 127). The Grenvilles—Earl Temple and his younger brother, George Grenville—built up a following. The "Pittites" (followers of William Pitt) sought to be above politics and party, while also enjoying broad support from the middle class. As nominal Whigs, nonpartisan and attacking "patronage as corruption and party as faction," the Pittites, as George H. Guttridge (1966) notes, were instrumental "in clearing the way to a new toryism." By the mid 1770s "New Whigs" began to emerge; they were reform-minded and oriented more toward popular support than toward patronage.

From 1762 to 1770 five short-lived ministries, lacking party strength to govern alone, brought instability to the government. The earl of Bute, the king's friend, came to power after the collapse of the Pitt–Newcastle ministry in 1762. Though a Tory himself, Bute formed a cabinet made up mostly of Whigs, who had not held office under two previous ministries. Bute was resented for being an outsider (a Scotsman), for his close relationship with the king, and for securing the unpopular Treaty of Paris (1763), which ended the Seven Years' War (French and Indian War).

Bute's handpicked successor, George Grenville, took over as prime minister in April 1763. Grenville was respected for his conservatism, thrift, and administrative ability, and he staunchly advocated parliamentary supremacy over the colonies. Though enjoying wide support, Grenville was soon at odds with George III, principally because of disputes over patronage with Bute and Grenville's opposition to the inclusion of the Princess Augusta, George III's mother, in a regency should the king die or become incapacitated. George III was presumed to be near death several times during January–March 1765, suffering from a "violent cold" and high fever; the prince of Wales at the time was only 3 years old.

The ministry of the marquis of Rockingham, installed in July 1765, lasted hardly more than a year. Actually, the king's uncle, the duke of Cumberland, who held no office, guided the ministry from July until his death in October 1765—

thus, it is referred to as "the Duke's Administration, with Lord Rockingham at the Treasury." To some degree, the Rockingham ministry represented a return of the Old Whigs, with such appointments as Rockingham as first lord of the Treasury; Henry Conway, the administration's leader in the House of Commons and secretary of state for the Southern Department; William Dowdeswell, chancellor of the Exchequer; and the aging duke of Newcastle, Lord Privy Seal. Some of the King's Friends were included, such as the earl of Egmont, first lord of the Admiralty, and Viscount Barrington as secretary at war. Pitt remained aloof from the ministry. As Charles Townshend said of the Rockingham administration, it was "a Lutestring ministry, fit only for the summer." To gain any party cohesion was out of the question. The Rockingham ministry, though insisting on the principle of parliamentary sovereignty over the colonies, did not seek to implement it.

Replacing the Rockingham ministry in 1766 was a cabinet headed by William Pitt and the duke of Grafton, a nonparty alignment that excluded the Old Whigs. Pitt wanted to establish unity in Parliament and to end controversy with the American colonies, which were "too great an object to be grasped but in the arms of affection" (Ayling 1976, p. 344). Pitt, however, forfeited much of his prestige as the "Great Commoner" and as parliamentary leader when he accepted a peerage as earl of Chatham. Henry Conway, now secretary of state for the Northern Department, and Charles Townshend, the chancellor of the Exchequer, assumed responsibility for parliamentary leadership. Townshend's death in September 1767 and Pitt's resignation in October the next year, due to ill health, left the ministry in confusion.

With the pressing need for stability in government, George III called on one of the most loyal of the King's Friends, Frederick Lord North, to be prime minister. North, whose title was simply an honorary one (he was not made an earl until much later), had kept a low profile, although he had served in Parliament since 1754, was lord of the Treasury during 1759–65, and since 1767 had been chancellor of the Exchequer. Because he had not been outspoken on political principles and, for that matter, had not aligned himself with any political group, North began his ministry in January 1770 with broad approval. Of course, as Horace Walpole observed at the time, there was little to fear from any opposition ranks: "the several factions hated each other more than they did their common enemies. . . . Discord and interest . . . tore in pieces the opposition" (Brewer 1976, p. 65). But the Coercive Acts crisis of 1774 (see Chapter 4) polarized British politics, giving common ground on which critics of the North ministry could unite, led by such prominent politicians as Chatham, Burke, Earl of Shelburne, Fox, and Baron Camden.

From Whiggism to Radical Reform

Americans were acquainted with the "Real Whig" (Commonwealthmen) ideology in British political life, dating from the era of the Glorious Revolution. The Whig philosophy, with ties to the Puritan Revolution and its apologists, was expounded by such essayists as John Locke, Algernon Sidney, and Benjamin Hoadly. The Real Whigs ideology stressed government by consent of the people, resistance against arbitrary rule, separation of powers in government, and the inviolability of the individual's fundamental rights. To Locke, government, originating from a state of nature, was a contract between the people and those who ruled. Many Real Whigs, however, avoided Locke's contractual theory and rested their case on the historical argument that the British constitution had originated in Anglo-Saxon times based on the principles of limited and balanced government. Neither Locke nor other Whig writers advocated complete popular sovereignty; they maintained that all men were not politically equal or competent for participation in public affairs. But government should reflect the will of the people—those who had a property stake in society.

By the mid-eighteenth century, Whiggism overall had undergone a change. As George H. Guttridge (1966) writes:

> To its old face of contractual government, limited executive authority, and a balanced constitution it had added the aspect of parliamentary administration, the dispensation of influence, the exercise by deputy of royal functions, and the leadership of the church. . . . the rights which Locke had so strenuously maintained against the crown were turned into the perquisites of the aristocracy. . . . The reluctant revolutionaries of 1689 became the complacent conservatives of 1750, and to them whiggism stood less for the principles which had produced the Glorious Revolution than for the society which it had inaugurated. The process may be said to have reached its logical climax during the American Revolution. (pp. 10–11)

Most representative of the conservative Whiggism was Edmund Burke, MP (1766–94) and Rockingham's private secretary. Burke achieved fame as a prolific writer on English politics and for his oratory, which was often so lengthy that he was known as "the dinner bell of the House of Commons." He outlined his political philosophy in *Thoughts on the Causes of the Present Discontents* (1770). Burke's Whiggism went no further than limiting the power of the crown. The only way to prevent the influence of the King's Friends and use of "double cabinets," he said, was to establish party government. Burke believed that Great Britain should have a one-party aristocratic leadership. "When bad men combine," he said, "the good must associate." The country could not be well governed "until those who are connected by unanimity of sentiment hold to reins of power."

A reform movement for a more democratic constitution than that envisioned by Burke began to take shape in British politics, though its momentum belongs to a later time. The American crisis assisted British reformers in setting an agenda: no taxation without representation, a more extensive suffrage, and election districts proportionate to population. Americans, as John Brewer (1976) writes, "acted as an ideological midwife, bringing into the political world a qualitatively different sort of reform." English radicals could point to a parallel oppression in Great Britain and the colonies. Thus, the "American debate" provided the "opportunity and the arguments with which to present a case" for "greater participation in the political process" (p. 215).

British Radicalism and the Americans

Americans identified with the long ordeal of John Wilkes, MP and coeditor of the journal *North Briton* (so titled because of the revulsion toward Lord Bute, a Scotsman). Issue number 45 (April 23, 1763) of the *North Briton* set off a storm with its criticism of a speech by George III from the throne. The king's ministers were "the tools of despotism and corruption." Furthermore, "every friend of his country must lament that a prince" gives "the sanction of his sacred name to the most odious measures . . . from a throne ever renowned for truth, honour, and unsullied virtue." Wilkes was arrested a week later on a general warrant and imprisoned. The colonists could identify with such a transgression against liberty for they themselves had been aroused by the use of writs of assistance (general warrants, see Chapter 1).

Judge Charles Pratt (later Baron Camden), chief justice of the Court of Common Pleas, ordered Wilkes's release, but Wilkes was subsequently convicted of libel anyway and fled to France. Returning to England in 1768, he was promptly arrested as an outlaw, fined £1,000, and sentenced to 22 months in prison. Wilkes became the hero of the London crowds and coffeehouse radicals. There were cries of "Wilkes and Liberty!" and "No Wilkes, no King!" On May 10, 1768, 20,000 to 40,000 persons rioted near the King's Bench prison in St. George's Fields, London, where Wilkes was confined. The mob demanded Wilkes's release. Army units fired into the crowd, killing 6 and wounding 20 in the so-called Massacre of St. George's Fields. While in prison Wilkes was elected to Parliament three times from Middlesex, and on each occasion he was expelled for libel. On the fourth try, the Commons illegally installed a rival, Henry Luttrell. In 1774 Wilkes regained his seat in Parliament. Subsequently, he also served as lord mayor and as lord chamberlain of London. Although his conservative stance during the Gordon Riots of 1780 (a Protestant mob in London protesting removal of civil restrictions from Catholics) cost him much of his popularity, he had made his mark. Political reformers rallied around Wilkes for more than a decade, demanding freedom of the press and a more democratic and open Parliament. American newspapers kept alive the interest in Wilkes's predicament. Wilkes was toasted throughout the colonies as a defender of liberty. Subscriptions for his relief were taken in Boston and Charleston; a group of Virginians sent him a load of tobacco as a "small acknowledgment for his sufferings in the cause of liberty."

The British political reform movement on the eve of the American Revolution lacked cohesion and central leadership, and drew almost exclusively on an urban following. In London, taverns and some of the more than 550 coffeehouses were spawning grounds for radicalism. Various debating societies stirred popular discontent with the government. The most famous of these Societies was the Robin Hood Club (founded in 1613), which by the time of the Revolution had become primarily an organization of tradesmen for the purpose of discussing politics. In response to Wilkes's imprisonment, a group of friends led by John Horne (later called John Horne Tooke) established the Society for the Supporters of the Bill of Rights in February 1769. Its program called for more frequent elections of Parliament; fewer placemen (political appointees to government jobs) in the House of Commons;

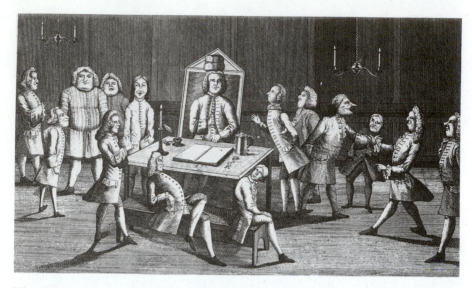

The Robin Hood, a debating society founded by London tradesmen in 1613, was strongly pro-American on the eve of the Revolution. *Reproduced by Courtesy of the Trustees of the British Museum*

equal representation; freedom of the press; elimination of cabinet government; freedom of thought and religion; manhood suffrage; and a pledge from candidates to work for reform. John Adams and Dr. Joseph Warren, both of Massachusetts, were elected members in September 1773. Stephen Sayre, an American merchant and banker in England, wrote to Adams, expressing his congratulations: "It affords me great pleasure to find so very respectable a gentleman of America disposed to unite with the Friends of Liberty in England for our mutual safety and defence" (Alden 1983, pp. 36–37). The Constitutional Society of 1775 grew out of dissension within the Society for the Supporters of the Bill of Rights. The new organization even took up a subscription on behalf of the widows and children of those Americans slain at Lexington and Concord. Similarly standing for reform, the Society for Constitutional Information was established by Major John Cartwright in 1780. Less active were groups of "Honest Whigs," as Caroline Robbins (1959) calls them, who met informally on a regular basis at the London Tavern and then at St. Paul's Coffeehouse.

British and American radicals corresponded with each other, exchanging ideas and pamphlets, and both agreed that it was the British government's purposeful design to curtail liberty. Americans in England associated with the radicals. Among those who participated in the meetings of the Honest Whigs were Benjamin Franklin, who resided in London for 16 of the 18 years before the Revolution, and Benjamin Rush, who was in postgraduate medical training at St. Thomas's Hospital in London during 1769–70.

Arthur Lee, a Virginian who studied both medicine and law in Great Britain, enmeshed himself in radical politics in London, serving both as a leader and as liaison for information between English and American radicals. He obtained mention of protest against the Townshend duties (see Chapter 3) in the famous Middlesex petition to Parliament, signed by 1,565 London citizens on behalf of John Wilkes. According to his biographer, Louis W. Potts (1981), from 1769 to 1776 Lee published (under 10 pen names but usually "Junius Americanus") 9 pamphlets, 170 essays, 17 petitions, and 50 letters to the press. Lee's output had the financial backing of a London merchant, Dennys DeBerdt. His first letters published in London newspapers in 1769 excoriated Francis Bernard, governor of Massachusetts, and Lord Hillsborough. Lee's major contribution was *The Political Detection: or, the Treachery and Tyranny of Administration, Both at Home and Abroad* (1770). America, said Lee, was a "nursery of British Liberty," where "the British constitution may arise anew, like a Phoenix from her parental ashes, to glory, strength, and happiness." The chief grievance of the Americans was having property taken away by Parliament, "wherein they are not represented; contrary to the most ancient and most important principles of constitutional liberty."

Radical Reformers on American Affairs

English radical essayists also linked the plight of British citizens on both sides of the Atlantic. Although some of the radical writings, especially during the war, were thought to border on treason, none of the authors was prosecuted by the government. Works by English critics of the existing political system quickly appeared in American editions. None was more influential on American political thinking than James Burgh's *Political Disquisitions: or, An Enquiry into Public Errors, Defects, and Abuses* (1774) in three volumes. Although only 67 of its 1,420 pages treated American grievances, American leaders relished its political philosophy. All five members of the committee in Congress commissioned to write the Declaration of Independence had copies. Burgh declared that "power in the people is like light in the sun, native, original, inherent, and unlimited by any thing human"; only the people or their representatives could alter the constitution. Every man had "inalienable property," which included "life, a personal liberty, a character, a right to his earnings, a right to religious profession and worship according to his conscience."

Other English radical writers also defended American freedom. Foremost among them were Dr. Josiah Tucker, dean of Gloucester, Major John Cartwright, Dr. Richard Price, a dissenting clergyman, and Mrs. Catherine Macaulay, who gained fame for her eight-volume history of England. Tucker (1774, see Chapter 1) contended that the Americans were applying the true principles of the British constitution, and he argued that independence would benefit both Britain and America. In *American Independence, the Interest and Glory of Great Britain* (1774) Cartwright stated that the Americans, having immigrated to the New World on their own, were subjects of the king and not Parliament. "When we shall have given birth, and the birthrights of freemen, to as many independent states as can find habitations on the vast American continent," declared Cartwright, then "Britain still will be great and free; the respected mother, the model, the glory of them all!" (Smith 1972, p. 154).

Price argued that Americans were defending liberty and the purity of the British constitution. Two of his pamphlets, *Observations on the Nature of Civil Liberty, the Principles of Government, and the Justice and Policy of the War in America* (1776) and *Additional Observations on the Nature of Civil Liberty* (1777), had great impact in America. In the second pamphlet, Price states that from the American Revolution "the Britons themselves will be the greatest gainers, if wise enough to improve properly the check that has been given to the despotism of their ministers, and to catch the flame of virtuous liberty which has saved their American brethren" (Knorr, 1968, p. 198). Macaulay's *Address to the People of England, Ireland, and Scotland on the Present Important Crisis of Affairs* (1775) was an inflammatory attack on both king and Parliament. She warned that if a "civil War" ensued with America, Englishmen would face ruin in their commerce, and that they would "be left to the bare possession" of their "foggy islands" and "under the sway of a domestic despot," or subjected to "some powerful European state" (Smith 1972).

Before 1765 the British public did not pay much attention to American affairs, although it was receptive to information about Indians and war. The Stamp Act (see Chapter 3) crisis changed all this. During the decade before the Revolutionary War, British newspapers filled their columns with materials from America—news and articles lifted in their entirety or in abstract from colonial periodicals, letters from Americans and their English sympathizers, and colonial and British state papers. Circulation of British newspapers greatly increased. Public opinion seems to have not been averse to the American cause. As late as October 1775, Temple Luttrell, having returned from a tour of England, reported "that the sense of the mass of the people is in favor of the Americans" (Bradley, p. 6). The parliamentary election of 1774, however, did not give hints of any growing pro-American sentiment. One hundred and sixty new members entered Parliament, but, as Edmund Burke observed, those who supported coercive measures toward the colonies "have been raised to near three hundred" (Sutherland and Guttridge, 3:135).

As the American war came, British radicalism stumbled on hard times. Petitions from both sides of the Atlantic were ignored by the king, Commons, and House of Lords. Merchants, who had successfully petitioned in the 1760s to remove or reduce taxation and trade restrictions on the colonies, now themselves were divided. Many felt that upholding parliamentary supremacy over the colonies had long-run benefits in the protection of British trade interests. The Revolutionary War, at least for a while, drew attention away from reform. There was now a wide gap between American and British radicalism—both as to objectives and means. The American radicals had gone too far: revolution.

CHAPTER 3

Revolt against Parliamentary Authority

 For a decade, beginning in 1763, the British government wrestled with the reform of imperial-colonial relations. The old colonial system, with its lax enforcement of the trade laws, was supplanted by clearer and more definite policies, supported by an enhanced enforcement machinery. Parliament insisted that the Americans recognize its supremacy just as did Englishmen in the realm. The Americans, however, questioned any parliamentary authority that encroached on their rights of self-representation in matters affecting their own property and personal liberty. Patriot leaders, with support of the masses, seized on one event after another to form a resistance movement, which, though slackening at times, did not retreat. By 1773 the movement was poised for confrontation with the whole of British imperial rule.

The Grenville Program, 1763–1764

On April 13, 1763, George Grenville, first lord of the Treasury and chancellor of the Exchequer, succeeded the earl of Bute as British prime minister. Grenville soon proved his ability at strong leadership. As Charles Yorke, in a speech to the House of Commons, said of Grenville, he was "a very worthy and able man . . . whose turn lay towards the revenue, and to that public economy which was so much wanted." The British ministry and Englishmen alike were concerned with the great expansion of the national debt, from £72,289,673 in 1755 to £129,586,789 in 1764. To help pay for the war effort, Parliament enacted new and additional taxes, and as a result merchants and landowners now found their tax liability substantially enlarged. Levies on cider and beer incited riotous behavior among the common people. Maintaining 10,000 troops in North America at an annual expense of £350,000 proved a major financial hardship for the British government. The British taxpayer thought it only sensible that the colonies contribute at least partially toward the cost of the American defense establishment. The colonists, of course, as noted earlier, had not asked for any kind of standing army in America.

There had been only a few precedents for parliamentary taxation of the colonies. The charter of Pennsylvania (1681) stated that the king could not tax Pennsylvanians unless "with the consent of the Proprietary, or chiefe governor, or assembly, or by act of Parliament in *England.*" The British post office in the colonies collected about £3,000 a year, which, however, represented fees rendered more for service than for taxation. The precedents of Parliament raising revenue, as minor as they were, included a 1672 law that imposed duties on certain goods transported from colony to colony and a 1729 law that required seamen to contribute 6*d.* per annum to help support Greenwich Hospital in England.

Grenville secured the passage of the Sugar Act (American Duties Act) on April 5, 1764. Debates in the Commons made it clear that the law was passed to raise revenue for maintaining troops, and not merely for regulating trade. The preamble of the act expressly stated that "it is just and necessary, that a revenue be raised, in your Majesty's said dominions in *America,* for defraying the expences of defending, protecting, and securing the same." Beginning on September 29, 1764, duties on a wide range of goods coming from foreign ports would be collected, including indigo, coffee, certain wines, and cloths (from Persia, China, and the East Indies). The law expanded the list of enumerated commodities (articles that had to be shipped exclusively to Great Britain, Ireland, or other English colonies). The levy on foreign sugar rose from 5*s.* to £1.7 per hundredweight. In contrast, the duty on foreign molasses went from 6*d.* to 3*d.* on each gallon.

The reduction in the molasses duty was a response to reality. The 6*d.* per gallon, established by the Molasses Act of 1733, had yielded only £21,652 over 30 years. The colonists smuggled in foreign molasses with almost complete impunity. With the change of purpose from prohibition to revenue raising and with improved means of collection, the molasses duty was expected to bring in about £45,000 annually. New Englanders felt they were being singled out to bear a disproportionate share of the new taxation. Molasses was in great demand in the region as a sweetener for baked beans, bread, pudding, and cornmeal, and for pickling fish. New England rum was a staple in the Indian, southern colonial, and African trade. In return for molasses from the foreign West Indies, New Englanders sent lumber, flour, cheese, and farm products. The Sugar Act came at a time of economic depression, with money and credit scarce.

A key ingredient of the Grenville program was the tightened enforcement of the trade and navigation laws. An order-in-council of October 4, 1763, required customs officials in America and the West Indies to reside at their stations and empowered them to call on civil and military officers for assistance. Among the many new regulations of the Sugar Act and its companion legislation, customs officials making a seizure on the basis of probable cause could not be liable for suits or damages against them. Any customs official convicted of accepting a bribe was subject to a £500 fine and disqualification from serving in any government post. In addition, an admiralty court for all America was established at Halifax, Nova Scotia. The new court could now draw cases away from the 11 district admiralty courts in the colonies, which were under the control of the royal governors. The colonists resented not only admiralty justice being dispensed from afar, but also the lack of juries in such tribunals and the closing of civil courts as a means of redressing admiralty court decisions.

The British ministry had not anticipated any general resistance to the Sugar Act because it lowered duties on molasses and affected primarily just one region of the colonies. What it had not anticipated was that the revenue-raising intent of the act would alert the colonists to the threat of taxation without representation. Americans soon learned that Parliament would further tax the colonies. Grenville's circular letter of August 1764 to all colonial governors requesting lists of kinds of public documents gave notice that a more pervasive form of revenue was to be raised in the colonies—a stamp tax. Before the passage of the Stamp Act, most colonial legislatures passed resolutions protesting the British taxation and sent petitions to England. The petition of the New York Assembly to the House of Commons on October 18, 1764, declared that, while the General Assembly had "no desire to derogate from the Power of the Parliament of *Great-Britain* . . . they cannot avoid deprecating the Loss of such Rights as they have hitherto enjoyed, Rights established in the first Dawn of our Constitution."

Several Americans penned rebuttals to the British claim to levy taxes on the colonies. *The Rights of the British Colonies Asserted and Proved* (1764) by James Otis, a Massachusetts lawyer and patriot leader, went through quick, successive editions in America and England, and was endorsed by the Massachusetts legislature and British radicals. Otis said that American rights were founded on the laws of God and nature, the common law, and the acts of Parliament. The people have natural rights, he asserted, that cannot be infringed on by government. No tax could be levied except by the people themselves or their representatives. Parliament had the power but not the right to tax the colonies. Although Otis was one of the few Americans who supported admission of colonists into Parliament, he thought such a course would not give Americans adequate representation in that body. Aiming mostly at the forthcoming Stamp Act, Stephen Hopkins, governor of Rhode Island, in *The Rights of the Colonies Examined* (1764), noted a constitutional distinction between the colonies and Great Britain. "In an imperial state," he said, such as the British empire, "no single part, though greater than another part, is . . . entitled to make laws for or to tax such lesser part; but all laws and all taxations which bind the whole must be made by the whole." Richard Bland's *The Colonel Dismounted: or the Rector Vindicated* (1764), concerned with the Parson's Cause controversy over royal disallowance of the Two-Penny Act in Virginia (see Chapter 1), anticipated the main argument that the colonists would use against the Stamp Act. "For our EXTERNAL government," Bland said, "we are and must be subject to the authority of the British Parliament, but in no others; for if the Parliament should impose laws upon us merely relative to our INTERNAL government, it deprives us . . . of the most valuable part of our birthright as Englishmen, of being governed by laws made with our own consent."

The Grenville program became an economic as well as a political issue. Northern merchants felt the impact on commerce produced by the new restrictions and enforcement measures, and farmers, with the constriction of the West Indian market, saw a decrease in prices for their commodities. Southern planters were affected by the Currency Act of 1764, which extended the provisions of the New England Currency Act of 1751 to the nine other colonies. No future paper money could be used for private debts. Legal tender (money that had to be accepted in payment of debts) already in circulation had to be retired as scheduled. Paper money could be issued for limited periods but only for payment of taxes. The act had been aimed primarily at Virginia, which had issued a large amount of paper money during the French and Indian War. By 1764 the colony had £230,000 in circulation, and the exchange rate was £160 paper money for £100 sterling. British merchants were insisting on hard money for payment of debts. Although Virginia planters were heavily indebted to British creditors, the Currency Act did not become a major grievance.

The Stamp Act Crisis

Encouraged by the colonies' relatively mild opposition to the Sugar Act, Parliament gave comfortable majorities to the passage of the Stamp Act, which became law on March 22, 1765. Stamp duties would provide additional revenue (£60,000) that would be used to support the American military establishment. The Grenville ministry considered the tax just, affecting everyone in America equally, and believed it would not be a heavy burden. Englishmen had paid a stamp tax since 1670, so why should not Americans do the same? A stamp tax in America did not mean an additional tax in Great Britain. Yet, before passage, strong opposition had mounted against it in Parliament, led by William Pitt and Edmund Burke in the Commons and Lord Camden in the House of Lords. Colonel Isaac Barré, who had served in the last war in America, stunned the Commons on February 12, 1765, in his reply to a speech by Charles Townshend. As reported by Jared Ingersoll to Thomas Fitch, governor of Connecticut, Barré declared:

> They planted by your Care? No! your Oppressions planted em [them] in America. . . . They nourished by your indulgence? They grew by your neglect of Em:— as soon as you began to care about Em, that Care was Exercised in sending persons to rule over Em . . . sent to Spy out their Lyberty . . . men whose behaviour on many Occasions has caused the Blood of those Sons of Liberty to recoil within them. . . . They protected by your Arms? they have nobly taken up Arms in your defence. . . . And believe me, remember I this Day told you so, that same Spirit of freedom which actuated that people at first, will accompany them still.

The Stamp Act placed duties on paper, vellum, and parchment to be used for public purposes, ranging from ½d. (for a newspaper sheet) to £10 (for an attorney's license). All legal and business documents, certificates for clearance of ships, court proceedings, pamphlets, newspapers, playing cards, and dice had to be stamped. The stamps were in the form of impressions in relief (like a modern notary seal). The annual burden per colonist would be only about 1s., equal to one-third of a day's labor. The program would be administered by an American Stamp Office in London; in the colonies there would be one stamp distributor for each of nine districts.

The passage of the Stamp Act reflected the British government's erroneous assessment of the American situation. In the first instance, the law bore directly on the most influential colonial citizens—newspaper owners and printers, lawyers, tavern-keepers, planters, and merchants. Moreover, it was passed too soon after the Sugar Act and at a time of economic stagnation and currency stringency. The colonists were already developing a consensus in opposition to taxation without representation. The stamp duties had to be paid in sterling, and violators could be prosecuted in the admiralty courts. But Britain's worst mistake was to levy a tax that affected almost everyone, directly or indirectly, at the same time and across sectional boundaries. Thus, the duke of Grafton aptly observed in a speech to the House of Lords in 1766: If "America is not sufficiently taxed, there are other means by which they may be taxed—don't tax them universally. By that means you join them when you should keep them asunder."

The American Response

The first reaction to the Stamp Act in America was registered in the Virginia House of Burgesses in its resolutions of May 30–31, 1765, introduced by Patrick Henry. Since the legislative session was closing, all but 39 of the 119 burgesses had gone home, leaving mostly the younger, more ambitious members present. During one heated debate, in the words of a French traveler who was standing in the lobby, Henry "stood up and said he had read that in former times Tarquin and Julius had their Brutus, Charles had his Cromwell, and he Did not Doubt but some good american would stand up, in favour of his Country." Speaker John Robinson interrupted Henry and accused him of speaking treason, saying he "was sorey to see that not one of the members of the house was loyal Enough to stop him, before he had gone so far." Henry then replied, asking pardon if he had "said any thing wrong," but "what he had said must be atributed to the Interest of his Countrys Dying liberty which he had at heart. . . . some other Members stood up and backed him, on which that afaire was droped."

Five of seven resolutions were adopted. The first four asserted the rights of Americans as transplanted Englishmen, secured by the royal charters. "Taxation of the People" was "the distinguishing Characteristick of *British* Freedom, without which the ancient Constitution cannot exist." The fifth resolution, which was rescinded on May 31, declared that "every Attempt to vest" the power of taxation "in any other Person or Persons whatsoever other than the General Assembly . . . has a manifest Tendency to destroy British as well as American Freedom."

Henry's sixth and seventh resolutions did not pass. The sixth said that Virginians were "not bound to yield Obedience to any Law or Ordinance" other than that of the General Assembly. The seventh stated that anyone claiming otherwise "shall be Deemed An Enemy to this His Majestys Colony." Newspapers outside of Virginia printed six or all the resolutions as if they had been sanctioned by the Virginia legislature. The colonies, except Georgia, North Carolina, Delaware, and New Hampshire, passed resolutions denouncing parliamentary taxation of the colonies as a violation of American rights.

Violence as a means of protest against the Stamp Act, or what Massachusetts Governor Francis Bernard called an "Ochlocracy, or government by a mob," began in Boston on August 14, 1765. The Loyal Nine, a group of artisans and small merchants, persuaded Ebenezer Mackintosh, a popular shoemaker, to lead a crowd to force Andrew Oliver, the stamp distributor, to resign. Oliver was burned in effigy and his home wrecked, whereupon he surrendered his post. On August 26 Mackintosh's rabble force sacked the home of Lieutenant Governor Thomas Hutchinson, causing £25,000 in damage. By the fall, the participants in this riotous behavior were called the Sons of Liberty. Demonstrators against the Stamp Act elsewhere were soon called by the same name. The Sons of Liberty, or the "Liberty Boys," had a threefold objective: to arouse the public, to force stamp distributors to resign, and to prevent the use of stamps. Although the Sons of Liberty belonged to the lower middle class, they were directed by the more prosperous lawyers and merchants. Two such patriot leaders in Boston formed a stark contrast—John Hancock, probably the richest man in America, and Samuel Adams, a failure at everything he had done previously and at the edge of poverty.

The New York Sons of Liberty tried to forge an intercolonial organization. Although this attempt did not succeed, the Sons of Liberty in different towns and colonies established committees of correspondence. The Sons of Liberty, especially in New York, gave evidence of developing into a class-conscious laboring movement. Had they joined forces with rebellious tenants on the great Hudson River estates, a great social upheaval might have occurred. Hence, as the stamp crisis subsided, merchants and upper class citizens in general refrained from further encouraging the growth of the Sons of Liberty movement. The Sons of Liberty, except at Charleston, South Carolina, were not an important force in the South, largely because the South had few urban areas and did not have a laboring class consciousness.

As a result of intimidation and mob action, stamp distributors resigned throughout the colonies, mostly before the Stamp Act went into effect on November 1, 1765. Ships were not permitted to land stamps. Ports, however, were opened in defiance of the Stamp Act, and clearances issued. While many people, especially debtors, favored keeping the courts closed because of refusal to use stamped paper, the justice systems, after some shutdowns, functioned without obeying the Stamp Act. If the British government had decided on coercion during the Stamp Act crisis, armed conflict might have erupted. The leaders of the New York Sons of Liberty called for organizing military defense, and it was estimated that 10,000 men in Connecticut and 40,000 in Massachusetts and New Hampshire were ready to bear arms.

When the Stamp Act crisis passed, the Sons of Liberty all but disappeared, many of them joining quasipolitical groups, such as the Mechanics party in New York. The intimidatory roles of the Sons of Liberty would at a later time be assumed by local committees of inspection and safety. Although the Sons of Liberty again appeared to some extent during the Townshend Act protest of the late 1760s, by 1773, the name "Sons of Liberty" meant simply any patriot.

An intercolonial Stamp Act Congress, initiated by the Massachusetts legislature, met in New York City on October 7–25, 1765, with 28 delegates from nine colonies. New Hampshire declined to participate, and the governors of Virginia, North Carolina, and Georgia refused to convene their legislatures for the purpose of electing delegates. Timothy Ruggles, a Massachusetts conservative, presided over the Congress. Petitions were sent to the king, the House of Commons, and the House of Lords. The Congress adopted a "Declaration of Rights and Grievances," which contained 14 resolutions. Although acknowledging "all due subordination to that august body, the parliament of Great Britain" in matters pertaining to the superintendency of the whole empire, the Declaration stated that Parliament could not "grant to his Majesty the property of the colonists." Only their own legislatures could levy taxes on the colonists. The Declaration complained of the lack of trial by jury in the admiralty courts and the "restrictions imposed by several late acts of parliament," which had adversely affected trade.

The nonimportation agreements among colonial merchants proved an effective protest against the Stamp Act. New York City led the way on October 28, 1765, when 200 merchants pledged not to purchase European goods until the Stamp Act was repealed. The movement spread throughout the colonies. British exports to America declined from £2,249,710 in 1764 to £1,944,108 the next year. As a result, merchants in Great Britain applied pressure on Parliament, through a flood of petitions from the port towns, for repeal of the Stamp Act. The Commons was receptive, voting for repeal by a margin of 275 to 167, with the Lords following suit, 105 to 71.

On the same day the Repeal Act went into effect, March 18, 1766, so did the Declaratory Act, an event little noticed by the colonists at the time. The Declaratory Act did not mention taxation but asserted that Parliament had "full power and authority to make laws and statutes of sufficient force and validity to bind the colonies and people of *America,* subjects of the crown of *Great Britain,* in all cases whatsoever." Furthermore, Parliament requested colonial legislatures to vote compensation for losses of persons victimized by the Stamp Act disturbances; this was met with only partial compliance. One American served notice on the British government regarding the Declaratory Act. George Mason, in a letter published in the London *Public Ledger* in September 1766, said that the colonies did not deny the supreme authority of Parliament, but "such another experiment as the Stamp Act would produce a great revolt in America."

Effects of the Crisis

The Stamp Act crisis clarified the American and British positions on the constitutional relationship between the mother country and the colonies, and gave rise to American consensus on the subject. The controversy paved the way for a "Whig–Tory" alignment in American politics, and awakened the interest of the people at large in political affairs. John Adams wrote in his diary for December 18, 1765: "The People, even to the lowest Ranks, have become more attentive to their Liberties, more inquisitive about them, and more determined to defend them, than they were ever before known or had occasion to be." Americans shared Governor Bernard's view of the crisis. In a letter of November 23, 1765, Bernard wrote: "The Question will not be whether there should be a Stamp Act or not; but whether America shall or shall not be Subject to the Legislature of Great Britain."

Daniel Dulany, a Maryland councillor, expounded the American constitutional view of the time in *The Considerations on the Propriety of imposing Taxes in the British Colonies, for the Purpose of raising a Revenue, by Act of Parliament* (1765). The pamphlet quickly went through five editions and was reprinted in England. Dulany argued that Americans could not be virtually or actually represented in Parliament; there was no mutuality of interest between American and British electors, or even nonelectors. Although Parliament was sovereign, he said, it was bound by the limits of propriety not to tax the colonists, who were not represented in Parliament. A division of legislative authority existed between Parliament and the colonial assemblies. Parliament could regulate trade, including raising revenue through import and export duties, but could not tax the colonies internally.

A more forthright viewpoint was expressed by Richard Bland of Virginia, who in *An Inquiry into the Rights of the British Colonies* (1766) claimed that the colonists had no obligation to accept any laws of Parliament. Americans in the New World had recovered "their natural Freedom and Independence." Virtual representation, the "putrid part" of the British constitution, was no more valid for England than for the colonies, he said. Recent parliamentary acts, which affected American commerce more severely than British, "constituted an unnatural Difference between Men under the same Allegiance, born equally free, and entitled to the same civil Rights." Any parliamentary act "that imposes *internal* taxes upon the colonies, is an act of *power*, and not of *right*."

The Townshend Acts

Charles Townshend, the brilliant chancellor of the Exchequer in the Pitt–Grafton ministry, took charge of the parliamentary program for America until his death in September 1767 at age 42. Townshend steered three laws through Parliament: the American Board of Customs Act, which established the agency in Boston in charge of all American customs officials; the Revenue Act; and the New York Suspending [of the legislature] Act.

Always a realist, Townshend decided to take the Americans at their word and therefore confined parliamentary taxation externally to duties on certain goods imported into the colonies—paper, painter's colors, glass, red and white lead, and tea. A 3d. duty per pound was levied on tea, the fourth largest British export to America. The Townshend Revenue Act was expected to raise £40,000 annually. The funds collected would be put into the British Treasury to pay the salaries of colonial officials, particularly governors and judges, thereby making them financially independent of the colonial legislatures. Actually, funds from the Townshend Revenue Act would not have created a completely independent civil list in America. Seven governors did rely on assemblies directly for their salaries (Massachusetts, New Hampshire, New York, New Jersey, Connecticut, Rhode Island, and South Carolina). Officials in North Carolina and Georgia, however, were already being paid with funds from the British Treasury. The legislatures in Connecticut and Rhode Island appointed all colony-level officials, and, in Pennsylvania, Delaware, and Maryland, the proprietors had the same responsibility. Thus, salaries paid by the crown in those colonies would not create much greater attachment to the British government. Permanent funds from a tobacco export tax, mandated by the legislatures, supported governors and other high public servants in Virginia and Maryland.

The colonists viewed the Townshend Revenue Act not only as a backhanded attempt to assert Parliament's right to tax Americans but also as further evidence of the British government's conspiracy to extend its authority over colonial affairs. Protests now mounted against any form of parliamentary taxation. Nonimportation began in Boston during October–November 1768 and spread elsewhere, although it did not have the full support of merchant communities and southern planters. The Massachusetts Circular Letter, written by Samuel Adams, was sent out by the legislature to all the colonies, most of which endorsed it. The document denounced the Townshend duties and all parliamentary taxation of the colonies, external and internal. The earl of Hillsborough, secretary of state for America, ordered the Massachusetts House of Representatives to rescind the letter upon penalty of dissolution. The legislators refused by a vote of 92–17, and the governor put an end to the assembly session. The names of those who voted for repeal of the Circular Letter were published in the newspapers, as a result of which 7 of the 17 lost their seats in the next election. Every colony other than New Hampshire condemned Hillsborough's action. The House of Burgesses in Virginia was also dissolved for supporting the Circular Letter; the members then met extralegally on May 17, 1769, at the Raleigh Tavern in Williamsburg, and formally adopted an "association" for nonimportation.

The Townshend Revenue Act proved a disappointment for the British ministry. The boycott in the colonies did have some effect. Up to January 1769, the Townshend duties brought in no more than £3,500. The new North ministry allowed for partial repeal. An act of April 12, 1770, removed all the Townshend duties except for tea, thus still adhering to the principle of the right of parliamentary taxation as stated in the Declaratory Act. The repeal provisions were satisfactory enough to the colonists that the protest movement collapsed.

John Dickinson, a Pennsylvania lawyer and legislator, clarified the American view in *Letters from a Farmer in Pennsylvania*, appearing serially in 12 issues of the *Pennsylvania Chronicle*, December 2, 1767–February 15, 1768, and republished both in other newspapers and as a pamphlet. Dickinson admitted that Parliament could levy duties, but only for the purpose of trade regulation and not for revenue. If members of Parliament "have a right *to* levy a tax of *one penny* upon us, they have a right to levy a *million* upon us. For where does their right stop?" Dickinson presented an indictment of parliamentary legislation that had affected the colonies, especially in the 1760s. "Let these *truths* be indelibly impressed on our minds," wrote Dickinson, *"that we cannot be* HAPPY, *without being* FREE—that we cannot be free, *without being secure in our property*—that *we* cannot be secure in our property, *if, without our consent, others may, as by right, take it away."*

A "Dreadful Tragedy"

The presence of British troops and naval units in America set the stage for civilian-military conflict. In 1765 the British army numbered 10,000 on the North American continent and 2,500 in the West Indies. Most soldiers were stationed in Newfoundland, Nova Scotia, and on the western frontier. In the 13 colonies, there were only 170 troops in all, garrisoned at New York, Albany, and Charleston. In the spring of 1766 a regiment (500 men, 350 fit for duty) joined the soldiers in New York City, and another regiment went to New Jersey; Philadelphia received part of a regiment.

American patriots considered the Quartering Act of 1765 as a measure providing for indirect taxation and strengthening Britain's military arm against the colonists. General Thomas Gage, the commander in chief in America, had requested such a law, mindful that during the French and Indian War the colonies had been negligent in making available quarters for British troops. The Quartering Act required local magistrates to order the billeting of British troops in colonial barracks, inns, taverns, and livery stables, and, if further need existed, governors and their councils were to provide quarters in "uninhabited houses, outhouses, barns, or other buildings" as well as food, beverages, bedding, and cooking utensils upon demand. The New York Assembly voted funds for securing lodging places but balked at allotting money for food and drink. Thus, Parliament passed the New York Suspending Act (one of the Townshend acts) to prevent the assembly from conducting any business until it fully complied with the statute. This compliance finally came in December 1769. Alexander McDougall, who became known as "the Wilkes of America," published a broadside, "To the Betrayed Inhabitants of the City and Colony of New York," which denounced the compliance of the New York legislature. His imprisonment for several months for contempt, without a trial, by the assembly was regarded as a suppression of freedom of the press.

Civilian-military violence flared up in New York City. On August 10, 1766, British soldiers cut down a symbolic liberty pole. The next day a mass meeting of several thousand persons provoked an encounter with the troops, who fired on the crowd, leaving a few wounded. The scene was repeated more than three years later when British soldiers cut down a liberty pole and put the sawed pieces in front of a tavern. On January 19, 1770, a mob armed with clubs and knives fought with soldiers with bayonets as weapons; during this so-called battle of Golden Hill, no one was killed, but several were wounded.

A naval squadron, commanded by Commodore Samuel Hood from headquarters at Halifax, operated in American waters, giving assistance to the customs service. Moreover, to bolster customs enforcement, Parliament in 1768 established four regional admiralty courts—the already existing court at Halifax and the addition of one each at Boston, Philadelphia, and Charleston. Naval officers renewed impressment, a practice that had caused a bloody riot in Boston during King George's War. On May 17, 1768, the H.M.S. *Romney* arrived at Boston from Halifax and proceeded to impress 18 men for the royal navy. On one occasion, a Boston mob rescued Thomas Furlong from an impressment crew. In response to the fury of the Boston populace, Hood abandoned impressment in 1769. But while excitement was still high over the practice, one incident provoked a large-scale riot. In June 1768 customs officials prepared to seize John Hancock's sloop, the *Liberty*, for nonpayment of duties on wine from Madeira. A mob assaulted and gravely injured Collector Joseph Harrison, his son, a customs clerk, and Comptroller Benjamin Hallowell; the victims, with the assistance of royal marines, took refuge on the *Romney*, as did all but one of the members of the Board of Customs. A grand jury refused to indict any of the rioters because no one would give testimony. Hancock's vessel, which was boarded by a crew from the *Romney* and towed out into the harbor, was ordered confiscated by an admiralty court. Because of the turmoil in Boston, Governor Bernard called for two British regiments to be sent to the city.

With the Massachusetts legislature dissolved because of its failure to rescind the Circular Letter, 70 delegates from 66 towns, most of whom were rural moderates, met as the Massachusetts Convention at Faneuil Hall on September 22. Not much of anything happened. Bernard ordered the convention to disband, which it did on September 29, just as the British 14th and 29th regiments from Halifax entered Boston. In early November two more regiments, the 64th and 65th, from Ireland, also arrived. There was no doubt that the troops were intended to back up the royal government in the colony. The 64th and 65th regiments departed for Halifax in summer 1769, while the others remained in Boston.

Radicals such as Samuel Adams discovered the excellent propaganda opportunity that could be had in exploiting civilian-military tensions. *The Journal of the Times* (the actual author unknown) recorded "events" for the period September 28, 1768–August 1, 1769, and almost daily reported instances of brutality and debauchery among British troops in Boston. Lieutenant Governor Thomas Hutchinson claimed that nine-tenths of the atrocity stories were false. First appearing in New York in October 1768, the *Journal* was carried in Boston and other colonial newspapers and even in the London *Gentleman's Magazine*.

The siege mentality combined with the high resentment in Boston against the soldiers made violence and loss of life inevitable, which was just what the radicals wanted. Violence had been a tradition in Boston. Each year Pope's Day (November 5), commemorating the English gunpowder plot of 1605 and William III's landing in England in 1688, was the cause of gang warfare, as North Enders and South Enders fought to take over each other's straw pope. In 1764 a 5-year-old boy was trampled to death. During the Stamp Act crisis, the two groups united as the Sons of Liberty to carry on their violence.

One incident in February 1770 raised the level of rage in Boston. When Ebenezer Richardson, a customs employee, tried to destroy an effigy in front of a

Samuel Adams (1722–1803), depicted here by John Single-ton Copley, contributed im-mensely to keeping the Revolu-tionary movement alive in the late 1760s and early 1770s through his politicking and effective use of propaganda. Thomas Hutchinson, governor of Massachusetts, said of him in 1771: "I doubt whether there is a greater incendiary in the King's dominion." *Depos-ited by the City of Boston. Courtesy of the Museum of Fine Arts, Boston*

friend's house and then began chopping down a liberty pole, a mob, made up mostly of the young, assaulted Richardson, who retreated to his house. There, with loaded musket, he fired into the crowd, killing 12-year-old Christopher Snider. Richard-son, who barely escaped a lynching, wound up in jail and was twice tried for murder, convicted, but pardoned by the king. On February 26, the day that Snider was buried, John Adams confided to his diary: "My Eyes never beheld such a funeral. . . . This Shewes, there are many more Lives to spend if wanted in the Service of their Country. It Shews, too that the Faction is not yet expiring—that the Ardor of the People is not to be quelled by the Slaughter of one Child and the Wounding of another."

Brawls were not uncommon between Boston's youth and the "lobsterbacks" (British soldiers). On March 2, three army privates entered Gray's ropewalk just around the corner from the barracks and asked for part-time work. One of the workers replied that he did have a job for him: he could clean up his outhouse. A fight with ropewalkers ensued. The soldiers, getting the worst of it, left but soon returned with some of their comrades, and again they were clobbered. On March 5 British officers broke up a similar fight in the streets. In the evening, Private Hugh White, on sentry duty on King Street a block from the customshouse, argued with a local apprentice and struck him with his musket. Threatened by a gang of youths, White retreated to the steps of the customshouse and pointed his musket at the group. Bells pealed from the Old Brick Church and then from other churches as well, which to the townspeople meant there was a fire. To John Adams the crowd that gathered was a "motley rabble of saucy boys, negroes and mulattoes, Irish teagues and outlandish jack tars." The mob soon was armed with stones, planks from a torn-down butcher shop, and bats used in the game of tipcat. Captain Thomas Preston and eight soldiers came to White's rescue. What happened next is the subject of conflicting accounts, but most likely, a soldier who had been knocked down fired accidentally or intentionally into the crowd, with others of the detachment then doing the same. Five persons died, three outright and two mortally wounded: Crispus Attucks (a mulatto laborer), James Caldwell (a young sailor), Patrick Carr (an immigrant Irishman), Samuel Gray (a ropemaker), and Samuel Maverick (a 17-year-old apprentice ivory carver). At a mass meeting at Faneuil Hall the next day, Samuel Adams demanded that the troops leave the city. For their own protection, the British garrison was withdrawn to Castle William, a fort in the harbor.

The trials of Preston and the soldiers were delayed until the fall. John Adams and Josiah Quincy, counsel for the defense, determined on fair proceedings, ensured that no Bostonian or Son of Liberty served on the jury. Thirty-eight witnesses testified for the defense. Preston was acquitted, as were six soldiers; the remaining two were convicted of manslaughter and were permitted to plead benefit of clergy, receiving, therefore, only the penalty of being branded on the thumb. Through the influence of Paul Revere's engraving, published in the *Boston Gazette*, the event of March 5 became known as the Boston Massacre. Now there were martyrs for the cause of American liberty. Massacre Day, marking the anniversary of what a Boston committee of inquiry called the "dreadful tragedy," became a patriotic holiday in Boston, attended by antigovernment demonstrations, fiery oratory, and various commemorative activity.

Irritants and Another Crisis, 1770–1773

Just enough provocation and controversy occurred in the interval between the Boston Massacre in 1770 and the tea episode of late 1773 to sustain a resistance movement. A rumor persisted that the Church of England, at long last, was ready to appoint a resident bishop in America, arousing fears of curtailment of religious liberty. Another irritant was Governor Bernard's ordering the Massachusetts legislature to Cambridge in 1769. Bernard acted under royal instructions. With Bernard departing for England on August 1, 1769, Lieutenant Governor Thomas Hutchinson kept the assembly at Cambridge until June 1772. Samuel Adams and other patriot leaders made much of the removal issue. Along with the presence of the troops in American cities, there were now two examples of the royal prerogative being employed against the wishes of the people—evidence that the king had joined with Parliament in a conspiracy against American rights.

In 1772 Thomas Hutchinson, now the governor of Massachusetts, announced that he and the five judges of the colony's Superior Court would be paid their salaries from the customs duties. At about the same time, Hutchinson's loyalty to the colony was called into question over letters he had written in 1768–69 to Thomas Whately, former member of Parliament and now deceased. The correspondence fell into the hands of Benjamin Franklin while in England. The speaker of the Massachusetts

House, Thomas Cushing, received copies of the letters, which were made public. Hutchinson had said that there must be "an abridgment of what are called English liberties" in the colonies. The Massachusetts legislature voted almost unanimously that the letters exhibited "the tendency and design" to "overthrow the constitution of this government and to introduce arbitrary power." Hutchinson wanted to have the Massachusetts charter amended. The letters were published in most colonial newspapers and, in pamphlet form, went through 10 printings in America and England within a year.

On June 9, 1772, the *Gaspée*, a customs schooner, ran aground in Narragansett Bay, Rhode Island, and a riotous boarding party put the captain and crew ashore and burned the ship. A royal commission consisting of chief justices of New York, New Jersey, and Massachusetts, the governor of Rhode Island, and an admiralty court judge investigated the incident and was instructed to send any persons accused to England for trial. Although the commission could order up military assistance, since it lacked cooperation from the local populace it concluded that there was insufficient evidence for prosecution. The British government's handling of the *Gaspée* affair, in which it bypassed the local authorities, was made to order for patriot propaganda.

With the prompting of Samuel Adams, the Boston town meeting created a committee of correspondence. The committee drew up two documents proclaiming American rights, which were published together as a pamphlet. By the middle of 1773, 50 Massachusetts towns had their own committees of correspondence, and at least 119 of 260 towns and districts endorsed the "Boston pamphlet." Benjamin Franklin, from England, wrote his son on September 1, 1773, that "the Resolutions of the New England townships" had "the Effect they seem intended for, viz. to show that the Discontents were really general, and their Sentiments concerning their Rights unanimous, and not the Fiction of a few Demagogues."

In March 1773 the Virginia Assembly appointed a standing committee to correspond with other legislatures, and by fall other colonies followed suit. By February 1774 all colonies, except Pennsylvania, had established committees of correspondence.

The tea tax reminded Americans that Parliament still claimed the right to raise revenue in the colonies, but the removal of all the other Townshend duties had somewhat muted colonial protests. The issue of "no taxation without representation" again became volatile following Parliament's response to the plight of the East India Company. By the end of 1772 this British firm was verging on bankruptcy. Eighteen million pounds of tea in British warehouses went unsold. The tax of 3*d.* on tea imported into America had encouraged smuggling, for the colonists preferred the cheaper Dutch tea. Along with an economic depression in Great Britain, the price of tea had greatly declined. Although the East India Company had a monopoly on the sale of tea in Great Britain and the colonies, it had a heavy tax burden: 25 percent upon importation; 25 percent "inland duty"; and 1*s.* per pound for domestic consumption. The Bank of London refused to make loans to the company. By the Dividend Act of 1767, the company had to pay the government annually £400,000 whenever dividends reached 6 percent. Such was the case in

"You'd have thought that the inhabitants of the infernal regions had broke loose," wrote one witness when tea belonging to the East India Company was thrown overboard in Boston Harbor on Dec. 16, 1773. There is no contemporary depiction of the event. Prentiss Whitney woodcut, 1830s–40s, Boston.
Courtesy of the American Antiquarian Society

1772, when the company requested a loan from the government, a reduction of the inland taxes, and a rebate of all duties on tea shipped to Ireland and America.

To obtain the desired assistance, the East India Company consented to the Regulating Act of 1773, which brought reform to the company's organization and gave the government a share in the administration of affairs in India. Concessions were made to the company in the Tea Act of May 10, 1773. Although the 3d. duty was retained, the £400,000 dividend levy was eliminated, and the company's tea shipped to America would have all duties in England canceled. East India tea now purchased in the colonies would sell at half the former price. During the summer of 1773, the East India Company designated American firms in the principal ports to receive 600,000 pounds of tea.

From the American viewpoint, not only was the Tea Act a restatement of the right to tax the colonies, but also there was fear that other British monopolist measures would follow. Tea smugglers could expect low profits with the cut in price of legally imported tea. Tea consignees in New York City and Philadelphia, facing severe intimidation, resigned. In Boston, however, the consignees did not give in, and Governor Hutchinson, who had a grudge to settle with local patriots dating back to the Stamp Act crisis, was determined that the tea be disembarked. According to customs regulations, once the tea ships entered the harbor, the cargoes had to clear customs. If the consignees declined to pay the duties, the tea would be seized and warehoused—eventually to find its way to the consumer. Another option was that the tea ships could return to England, but only if the governor granted a pass, something Hutchinson refused to do. The first of three tea ships, the *Dartmouth*, arrived on November 28; on December 2 the *Eleanor* joined it at Griffin's wharf, followed by the *Beaver* on December 15. The tea shipments had to clear customs or be sent back to England within 20 days. Thus, if neither condition were met, on December 17 the tea could be seized for nonpayment of duties.

Early on the evening of December 16, a crowd that had been stirred up by patriot oratory at the Old South Church descended on the wharf. Among them were small bands of men disguised as Mohawk Indians, who had daubed their faces with printer's ink or paint; a few had also draped themselves with blankets. The "Mohawks" boarded the three ships and threw overboard 340 chests of tea. Afterward, no one would swear to having recognized any of the perpetrators.

The Boston Tea Party "was the boldest stroke which had yet been struck in America," wrote the embattled Massachusetts governor in his history of the colony a few years later. The destruction of property sent to the colonies under the auspices of king and Parliament was an act of revolutionary defiance. Two weeks after the event, John Hancock informed his London agents: "No one circumstance could possibly have taken place more effectively to unite the Colonies than this manouvre of the Tea."

The tea episode was a culmination of a series of mob activity over a decade. As in earlier instances, the crowd response had a definite objective, enlisting broad support from the community. "Just as in a rite of passage," writes Peter Shaw (1981), before the patriots "could advance to a more autonomous stage of existence," they "had to undergo a process that released regressive tendencies" (p. 231). In the next stage, too, American patriots would institutionalize rebellion.

CHAPTER 4

From Resistance to Revolution

 News of the Boston Tea Party reached London on January 19, 1774. The king and the ministry, mindful of the retreat during the Stamp Act crisis of 1765–66, resolved not to back away from the present challenge in America. Parliament was either the supreme authority in the empire, as it was in the realm, or it was not. As Bernard Donoughue (1964) has written, the significance of the Boston Tea Party "is that it made the constitutional problem of England's American Colonies a stark issue of sovereignty" (p. 48). It was believed that only stern measures would convince the people of Massachusetts of their proper role as English subjects. General Thomas Gage, in England since June and soon to be sent over as governor of Massachusetts, advised the government that "in consequence of the present disorders in America, effectual Steps" should "be taken to secure the Dependence of the Colonies on the Mother Country." On February 4, 1774, George III informed Lord North of an interview with Gage: "he says they will be Lyons, whilst we are Lambs but if we take the resolute part they will undoubtedly prove very meek."

Initially, it was proposed that punitive action should consist of legal proceedings against the key radicals in Boston. The attorney general, Edward Thurlow, and the solicitor general, Alexander Wedderburn, were instructed to issue treason warrants for the arrest of the leaders thought to be responsible for the tea riot. Both law officers, however, balked at this process on the grounds that depositions taken from witnesses to the conduct of the radical leaders in Boston did not substantiate charges of treason.

On February 1, 1774, the earl of Buckinghamshire moved in the House of Lords that the question of the Boston rioting be laid before Parliament. Three days later, the ministry proposed that measures should be enacted to punish the Boston citizenry as a whole for condoning the rioting and destroying the tea. Opposition forces in Parliament—led by Edmund Burke, Isaac Barré, Charles James Fox, Rose Fuller, and William Dowdeswell—though favoring accommodation over coercion, generally did not set themselves against collective retribution. Rose Fuller's motion in the House of Commons, however, to make one grand concession by repealing the Tea Act failed by a vote of 182 to 89. Thus, Parliament entered on a punitive course toward Massachusetts.

The Intolerable Acts

Parliament now enacted five laws that the colonists deemed "intolerable." Three of these, the "Coercive Acts," targeted Massachusetts because of the tea crisis. On March 31, 1774, the king signed into law the first of the Coercive Acts, the Boston Port Act. The Boston port was interdicted from receiving or exporting goods, with the exception of military stores "for his Majesty's use." Fuel and food could be "brought coastwise from any part of the continent of America for the necessary use and sustenance" of the citizens of Boston, but only after clearing customs at Marblehead and if a customs officer and an armed guard accompanied such shipments. Boston would not be reopened as a port until payment was made for the lost tea.

To Edmund Burke, in Parliament, the punishment of culprits involved in the Boston Tea Party made sense, but he warned that it was a capital error to put sanctions against the innocent as well as the guilty.

Against Lord Dartmouth's advice not to go beyond the Boston Port Act, Parliament passed two more Coercive bills, the Act for Better Regulating the Government of the Province of Massachusetts Bay and the Act for the Impartial Administration of Justice, each signed by the king on May 20. These laws were reformative as well as punitive in intent. Under the Government Act, beginning on August 1, 1774, the Massachusetts council would serve by crown appointment rather than, as previously, be elected by the House of Representatives. The governor would appoint and could remove all judges and law officers without consent of council. Except for the annual election, town meetings could not be held without royal approval. The Administration of Justice Act permitted magistrates and military officers indicted for a capital offense to be tried in England or another colony. The colonists regarded this law as tampering with their constitutional liberties. Adam Stephen, a western Virginia planter, writing to Richard Henry Lee in August 1774 as Lee was about to make his way to the Continental Congress, indicated the feeling in Virginia over the Administration of Justice Act. "Can we be said to enjoy liberty," Stephen asked, "if the villain who ravishes our wives, deflours our daughters, or murders our sons, can evade punishment, by being tried in Britain, where no evidence can pursue him?"

The colonists also took offense at the "Act for the better providing suitable Quarters for Officers and Soldiers . . . in North America" of June 2, 1774. Though essentially a reenactment of the Quartering Act of 1765, the new statute emphasized the authority of a governor to order stationing of troops in quarters other than barracks. Whenever British troops were without quarters for 24 hours, a governor could, solely on his own authority, order the use of uninhabited houses, outbuildings, barns, and the like. With Thomas Gage both the commander in chief and the governor of Massachusetts, the colonists viewed the law as further evidence of combining civil and military authority and also as circumventing the powers of elected officials.

The fifth law, the Quebec Act of June 22, 1774, aroused colonists both North and South. The law had been in the making for many years. It revoked the Proclamation of 1763 as to Canada, but it enlarged the territory of Quebec, which was now to be bounded to the south by Pennsylvania and the Ohio and Mississippi rivers, thus creating a further barrier to colonial westward expansion. Colonial land speculators, including the Ohio Company, claimed western lands. The Quebec Act nullified Virginia's purported jurisdiction to territory north and west of the Ohio River, and could possibly lead to restrictions on bounty land grants promised by both the British and Virginia governments to veterans of the French and Indian War. The colonists insisted that the Camden–Yorke decision of 1757 that had upheld the acquisition of lands in India simply from a grant or purchase from the natives fully applied in America. The Quebec Act also revived the old antagonism toward French Catholics in Canada, who were given free exercise of religion and tax support for their churches. Representative government was denied in the Quebec province, with the governor and an appointed council having full legislative authority.

The Intolerable Acts transformed the argument between the colonies and Great Britain from a dispute over the right to taxation into a challenge to any parliamentary authority. Colonists understood that the Coercive Acts affecting one region could later be applied everywhere. Moreover, while the Coercive Acts were directed at Massachusetts, the Quebec Act was viewed as an affront to Virginia in particular. Thus, the British legislative program cut across geographical sections and created opposition by colonists who were affected generally and specifically.

Colonial Responses

Nearly six months after the Boston Tea Party, General Gage returned to Boston, on May 10, 1774, carrying a copy of the Boston Port Act. The protest movement had been put on hold until the future direction of the British government's actions could be discerned. Yet the colonies had made their opposition to the Tea Act quite clear. In Philadelphia and New York City, ships with cargoes of tea were forced to return to England. Customs collectors in Charleston, South Carolina, seized and warehoused tea for nonpayment of duties in December 1774. In the same month New Jersey had its own tea party. The *Greyhound*, with tea from Rotterdam bound for Philadelphia, to avoid the hostile temperament in that city sailed out of Delaware Bay into the Cohansey River, docking at the small village of Greenwich. Temporarily stored, on the night of December 22, the tea was taken by "persons unknown" and burned. Civil and criminal proceedings brought by the owners, John Duffield and Stacey Hepburn, were thwarted by local juries.

On May 13, 1774, the Boston town meeting asked the colonies to boycott British goods until repeal of the Boston Port Act. On June 5, the Boston Committee of Correspondence adopted a Solemn League and Covenant, which called for an end of importation and consumption of English goods after October 1. Rural areas in Massachusetts enthusiastically gave their support. The Boston Committee of Correspondence also issued an appeal to all the colonies to give economic assistance to the distressed citizens of Boston. The response was overwhelming. Supplies and cash poured in from far and wide. Three west New Jersey counties— Gloucester, Salem, and Hunterdon—alone sent a total of £1,124. Support in-

"A Society of Patriotic Ladies at Edenton in North Carolina" is seen here signing a petition to boycott English goods. A slave holds the inkwell, a child is lost under the table, and a dog shows its contempt for the proceedings. This British cartoon was probably drawn by Philip Dawes, London, March 1775. *Library of Congress*

cluded a wagonload of supplies from Henrico County, Virginia, and a sloopload of provisions from the Cape Fear region of North Carolina.

The Massachusetts Government Act met stiff resistance. The mandamus councillors, as the new appointees to the council were called, were intimidated from holding their commissions. Many of the 24 of 36 persons who accepted conciliar positions resigned. In the summer of 1774, Abijah Willard, one of the new councillors, traveled to Union, Connecticut, to collect debts. There he was abducted by a mob and threatened with confinement in Newgate prison (an abandoned cooper mine at Simsbury, Connecticut), whereupon he relinquished his office. One councillor, Israel Williams, and his son, were seized in February 1775 and "smoked"— locked all night in a smokehouse.

Organized Resistance Measures

Organizations to fight the British coercive measures spread at both the local and colony level. Town and county conventions or committees of safety sprang up in New England and elsewhere. During June–July 1774 at least half of the counties in Virginia held mass meetings and established committees whose resolutions were published in the *Virginia Gazette*. The influential Fairfax County Resolves, of July 18, 1774, declared that the colonists had all the rights of Englishmen and the sole right of taxation, that imports from England should be prohibited as of September 1, 1774, and that nonexportation would begin November 1, 1775, if the Coercive Acts were not repealed.

Royal governors prorogued assemblies that seemed ready to denounce the Coercive Acts and to support an economic boycott. Virginia led the way in forming extralegal bodies to function in place of the legislatures. On May 24, the House of Burgesses passed a resolution condemning the Coercive Acts and proclaiming a fast day for June 1. Two days later the council concurred, whereupon Governor Lord Dunmore dissolved the assembly. On May 27, 89 of the 103 burgesses met at Raleigh Tavern in Williamsburg and elected Peyton Randolph to preside. The group then adopted a nonimportation agreement, pledged nonconsumption of tea and other East India Company products, denounced the Boston Port Act and parliamentary taxation of the colonies, and directed a committee of correspondence to advise other colonies to join in a general congress. The idea of such a gathering had already been broached by patriot committees in Boston and New York City a week earlier. On May 30, 25 of the Virginia burgesses again met on their own to call for a provincial convention on August 1 in order to adopt economic sanctions and elect delegates to an intercolonial congress. For the same purposes, in New Hampshire members of the Assembly met on July 6 at a tavern in Portsmouth, with the resulting provincial convention of delegates from the towns convening on July 21.

Elsewhere, summonses came from local committees for colonywide conventions. During the spring and summer of 1774, seven colonies held extralegal provincial conventions. Most delegates were also members of the legislatures. Only in Pennsylvania, however, did a provincial convention and the legislature hold sessions simultaneously. The colony conventions declared American rights, denounced the Coercive Acts, and selected delegates for a general congress of the colonies. Georgia's convention at Savannah, however, was so divided that nothing was accomplished, not even selecting delegates for the proposed congress. Politics had radicalized enough people in the nonroyal colonies of Rhode Island and Connecticut that the legitimate legislatures took over leadership of the revolutionary movement in these colonies.

Merchants in Boston, Philadelphia, and New York City sought to prevent radical elements from dominating the protest movement. Rather than economic sanctions to be established locally, they favored an intercolonial congress to determine the course of action. Most of all they feared civil disorder. Especially in New York City, the conservative merchants held their own against the radicals. The struggle for leadership in that city also reflected the long-standing political division of the colony. The De Lancey merchant group was reluctant to support Boston. On May 16 they created a committee of 51 persons who sought to delay an economic boycott. Radicals Alexander McDougall and Isaac Sears of the Livingston faction created a committee of mechanics which challenged the claims of the Committee of 51 to speak for the city. On June 6 the radicals held a mass meeting calling for a trade boycott, a provincial congress, and a free hand for delegates to a general congress. The radicals, however, never secured majority support of the populace. Thus, at a mass meeting on July 19, the delegates selected to the impending congress mostly represented the merchants' point of view. New York did not hold a colony convention. It was not until May 1775 that a provincial legislature met, with radicals in control because by then the war had begun.

The first Virginia Convention, representing 60 of the 61 counties, met at Williamsburg on August 1–7, 1774, and set the economic sanctions that would be adopted by the ensuing Continental Congress. While there was agreement on nonimportation, conservatives such as Edmund Pendleton, Peyton Randolph, and Carter Braxton opposed nonexportation and nonpayment of debts. Finally, a compromise was reached. The convention resolved to form an "Association" pledging complete nonimportation after November 1 (including slaves) and if grievances were not redressed by August 10, 1775, nonexportation (including tobacco). Merchants were expected to sign the association, and those who refused were to be boycotted. The convention did not recommend stoppage of debt collections by the courts, but understood that the courts would not accept cases because an act regulating fees had lapsed on April 1. Of primary concern, of course, were the debts owed British creditors. County committees were charged with enforcing the association and preventing merchants from raising prices. As delegates to the Continental Congress, the convention elected Peyton Randolph, George Washington, Richard Bland, Benjamin Harrison, and Edmund Pendleton.

Threats of Armed Conflict

Even as delegates made their way to attend the Continental Congress, scheduled to begin in Philadelphia on September 5, events conspired to fuel the patriot cause with military ardor. On September 1, Gage and 250 regulars seized 125 barrels of powder stored near Cambridge. Militia poured in from the countryside. Joseph Warren and other members of the Boston Committee of Correspondence used their influence to prevent any violence. Soon a rumor was started that Admiral Samuel Graves and a British fleet had shelled Boston. The delegates of the Continental Congress heard of the "Powder Alarm" and the supposed bombardment of Boston on September 6. Not until two days later did they learn that the naval attack was false. As John Adams wrote his wife, Abigail, two weeks later:

> When the horrid News was brought here of the Bombardment of Boston, which made us compleatly miserable for two days, we saw Proofs both of the Sympathy and the Resolution, of the Continent.
>
> War! War! War! was the cry, and it was pronounced in a Tone which would have done Honour to the oratory of a Briton or a Roman. If it had proved true, you would have heard the Thunder of an American Congress.

With armed conflict threatening to erupt, Gage, on September 2, began fortifications on Boston Neck and within the city at Beacon Hill, Copp's Hill, Barton's Point, and Fort Hill. He asked for more troops from England. To Lord William Barrington, the English secretary at war, he wrote on September 25 that "the New England Provinces, except part of New Hampshire, are I may say in Arms, and the Question is not now whether you shall quell Disturbances in Boston, but whether those Provinces shall be conquered."

In the South there were no British troops, but a martial spirit was becoming evident, particularly in Virginia. In September 1774 Governor Lord Dunmore set out on an expedition to punish the Ohio Indians for depredations on the colony's far frontier. Patriots insisted that this foray amounted to a ploy by the governor to dampen the military zeal in Virginia. The colony had many seasoned veterans of the last war who were only too eager to seek glory again in military service. The expedition was successful. Colonel Andrew Lewis met the Shawnees and their allies at the battle of Point Pleasant (where the Kanawha joins the Ohio River) on October 10, 1774, and the Indians retreated back across the Ohio. Dunmore then negotiated the Treaty of Camp Charlotte, which led to a cessation of hostilities. While detained at Fort Gower at the junction of the Ohio and the Hocking rivers, the Virginia soldiers received news of the Powder Alarm and the subsequent actions of the Continental Congress. On November 5, the officers drew up the Fort Gower Resolutions, which were published in the *Virginia Gazette*. This document expressed allegiance to the king, but also pledged that

> as the love of liberty, and attachment to the real interests and just rights of America outweigh every other consideration . . . we will exert every power within us for the defense of American liberty, and for the support of her just rights and privileges; not in any precipitate, riotous or tumultuous manner, but when regularly called forth by the unanimous voice of our countrymen.

The resolutions, expressing the pride and confidence of the officers, were also intended to assure Congress there was no need to fear any danger from an American soldiery.

Increasingly, in the fall of 1774, the view on both sides of the Atlantic was that the crisis could not end except by a military solution. The colonies had in place the mechanisms of revolutionary organization on the local and colony level. A congress of the colonies would coordinate and control the revolutionary movement.

The First Continental Congress

One-half of the 56 delegates from 12 colonies attending the Continental Congress in Philadelphia on September 5, 1774, were lawyers, and 11 were merchants. None of the members represented their legislatures. John Adams wrote his wife that "it has taken us much time to get acquainted with the tempers, views, characters, and designs of persons, and to let them into the circumstances of our province." It soon became evident, however, that there were two main groups: the "reconciliationists" (or conservatives) and the radicals. Among the reconciliationists, led by such men as Joseph Galloway of Pennsylvania and James Duane and John Jay of New York, there was hope that, through petitioning and, if necessary, an economic boycott, England would be brought to terms. Radicals, such as John and Samuel Adams, Patrick Henry, Richard Henry Lee, and Christopher Gadsden, anticipated a break with the mother country. After gathering at the City Tavern early on September 5, Joseph Galloway, speaker of the Pennsylvania Assembly, offered the use of the State

House. But a majority of delegates preferred to accept an offer of the Carpenters Guild to meet in their hall, a decision that "was highly agreeable to the mechanics and citizens in general." Peyton Randolph, speaker of the Virginia House of Burgesses, was unanimously elected "president" of the Congress.

The first order of business was to settle the question of how to weigh votes in the Congress—"by Colonies, or by the poll, or by Interests [property, trade, etc.]." Patrick Henry argued for proportionate representation according to a colony's population. "The distinctions between Virginians, Pennsylvanians, New Yorkers and New Englanders, are no more," he said. "I am not a Virginian, but an American." Because small colonies might be denied influence and because it was difficult to assess the importance of each colony relative to another, the Congress agreed on one vote for each colony delegation.

Congress created two committees at the start: one to examine acts of Parliament relating to American trade and manufactures (with one delegate from each colony) and a "Grand Committee" (with two persons from each delegation) to report on rights. Radicals were disappointed in Congress's decision not to sanction an independent government for Massachusetts or military action. Congress also voted down Richard Henry Lee's motion calling upon the British army to evacuate Boston. The radicals gained a victory of sorts in the adoption, on September 17, of the Suffolk Resolves, which passed unanimously.

The Suffolk Resolves had been approved by a county convention in Milton, Massachusetts, on September 9 and were rushed to Congress by Paul Revere. Conservatives had little choice but to support the Resolves, for not to do so might suggest that they sided with Great Britain. They were consoled in that the Resolves sought commitment "to act merely upon the defensive." Among the 19 Resolves, although allegiance was pledged to George III, recommendations were made for nonimportation, withholding of local taxes from the provincial treasury, disregard of judges who held commissions under the Massachusetts Government Act, military training, and collection of arms.

On September 28, Joseph Galloway moved for adoption of his Plan of Union and an accompanying resolution stating that the colonies did not desire independence. James Duane seconded the motion. Most radicals did not outright reject the idea of union. Richard Henry Lee only advised that colonial assemblies should be consulted. Patrick Henry, however, was opposed. A union connected to Parliament, though it would "liberate our constituents from a corrupt House of Commons," would "throw them into the arms of an American Legislature, that may be bribed by that nation which avows . . . that bribery is a part of her system of government." Galloway's Plan of Union provided for a Grand Council, with members chosen by the colonial assemblies for three-year terms. A president-general, named by the king, would be the presiding officer. The Grand Council would be "an inferior and distinct branch" of Parliament. It could legislate on all affairs involving the relationship of the colonies to Great Britain and with each other. Any measure passed by the Grand Council required the assent of the president-general and Parliament, except in wartime for acts providing "aid to the crown." Congress, by a vote of six to five, tabled the plan, and it never again came up for discussion.

The Declaration of Rights and Resolves, adopted on October 14, proclaimed that Americans had rights "by the immutable laws of nature, the principles of the English constitution, and the several charters or compacts." The colonists were "entitled to life, liberty, & property, and . . . never ceded to any sovereign power whatever, a right to dispose of either without their consent." Their ancestors, upon emigrating from Great Britain, had brought with them "all the rights, liberties, and immunities of free and natural-born subjects, within the realm of England." Parliament could regulate trade for the good of the "whole empire," but could not raise revenue of any kind from the colonists without their consent. The document listed offensive acts of Parliament since 1763 that should be repealed. Thus, Congress now took another step in leadership of the revolutionary movement—providing unity in stating the foundations of American liberty and common grievances and goals.

Meanwhile, the delegates also gave attention to an intercolonial boycott of British goods. Several disagreements emerged. First, conservatives wanted economic sanctions limited to nonimportation; second, Virginians sought a delay of a year before nonexportation went into effect; and third, South Carolinians wanted to continue exporting rice. Congress finally voted for nonimportation to begin on December 1, 1774, nonconsumption on March 1, 1775, and nonexportation on September 10, 1775. It was also ordered that all manufactures "be sold at reasonable prices, so that no undue advantage be taken of a future scarcity of goods." The economic sanctions were designed to force the repeal of the resented parliamentary measures since 1763. Congress also resolved that

> We will, in our several stations, encourage frugality, economy, and industry, and promote agriculture, arts and the manufactures of this country, especially that of wool; and will discountenance and discourage every species of extravagance and dissipation, especially all horce-racing, and all kinds of gaming, cock-fighting, exhibitions of shews, plays, and other expensive diversions and entertainments.

To promote the new program, Congress called on the colonists to join into an "Association." Citizens in each locality should elect a committee "to observe the conduct of all persons touching the association." Violators of the association were to have their names published in the newspapers.

In concluding its session, Congress sent out four petitions—to the king and to the people of the "British colonies," Great Britain, and Quebec. The petition to the king asked that "royal authority and interposition may be used for our relief." The English people were warned of a "plan for enslaving your fellow subjects in America" by "wicked Ministers and evil Counsellors." Adjourning on October 26, Congress fixed its next meeting for May 10, 1775.

The Rift Widens

The first Continental Congress had acceded to Parliament's authority to regulate external trade of the colonies. This decision had been a tenuous one. It belonged to several prominent patriot leaders to articulate the position that the time had arrived to sever all ties with Parliament and declare allegiance only to the king. Thomas Jefferson prepared A *Summary View of the Rights of British Americans* for the instruction of the first Virginia Convention in August 1774. Jefferson had planned to attend as a delegate but fell ill, and had Patrick Henry and Peyton Randolph present the tract, which the convention had printed. The *Summary View* repudiated any "obligation" to Parliament and recited the "series of oppressions" of that body toward the colonies since 1763. As "expatriated" Englishmen who voluntarily came to America, the colonists had all the rights of subjects in the realm. "They were not sent out to be slaves, but the equals of those that remained behind." The king, as "the only mediatory power between the several states of the British empire," should recommend to Parliament "the total revocation" of all the offensive legislation, and, if necessary, veto acts of Parliament. The crown should also recall troops from America. "It is neither our wish nor our interest to Separate," said Jefferson. But if the king did not take charge and provide complete redress of grievances, then, Jefferson hinted, the colonists might disavow the sovereignty of the crown.

On August 17, 1774, James Wilson, a Pennsylvania lawyer and congressman, published a treatise that he had written in 1768: *Considerations on the Nature and Extent of the Legislative Authority of the British Parliament.* The king, and not Parliament, he said, could regulate the trade of the colonies. Parliament had no control over the colonies because "all men are, by nature, equal and free; no one had a right to authority over another without his consent." Wilson asserted that "allegiance to the king and obedience to the parliament are founded on very different principles. The former is founded on protection; the latter, on representation." The king "is intrusted the direction and management of the great machine of government. He therefore is fittest to adjust the different wheels." English and American prosperity "will be better preserved by the operation of the legal prerogatives of the crown, than by the exertion of an unlimited authority by parliament."

John Adams, under the pseudonym *Novanglus,* published 12 essays (between January 23, 1774 and April 17, 1775) in the *Boston Gazette* intended to refute the arguments in *Massachusettensis,* written by a Tory lawyer, Daniel Leonard. Adams referred to the history of parliamentary abuses, even long before 1763. He went further than Jefferson and Wilson. "I say, America is not any part of the British realm or dominions," said Adams. "Fealty to a body politic is only a frame in the mind, an idea. The British constitution is more like a republic than an empire."

Most localities had committees to enforce the association. The new organizations in the colonies afforded a broad participatory democracy. As David Ammerman (1974) estimates, by spring 1775, 7,000 colonists were serving either on the local committees or in the extralegal colony assemblies or conventions. One hundred and sixty town committees in Massachusetts accounted for 1,600 of that total.

The powers of the committees of safety (as most were called) to stifle public opposition to the policies of Congress and to create a community consensus strengthened the colonial resistance movement. As enforcers of the association, the committees of safety functioned as quasi-courts. They also set prices, inspected warehouses, investigated suspected Tories, and served as moral watchdogs of the community. Persons found not abiding by the association or other demands of a committee had their names published as an "enemy to America" or faced even physical intimidation.

Meanwhile, the American resistance stiffened Britain's punitive program for the colonies. The news of the association, arriving in England in December, spurred efforts to treat the colonial protest as rebellion. The British ministry now decided on reinforcement of the army and navy in North America and economic sanctions against the colonies.

Certain members of Parliament made a futile attempt to direct the government toward making real concessions to the American patriotic cause. On January 20, 1775, the earl of Chatham (William Pitt) asked for a resolution to request the crown to remove troops from America: the motion failed three to one. On February 1, Chatham introduced a bill for A Provisional Act for Settling the Troubles in America. It proposed the nonlevying of taxes on the colonies by Parliament, "except by common consent in their provincial assemblies"; repeal of the Intolerable Acts; colonial recognition of the crown's right to send troops to America for purposes other than coercion; and legalization of the Continental Congress on condition that the colonies make a "free grant" to the king to alleviate the national debt. The bill was rejected in the House of Lords, 61–32. On February 9, North's motion to declare Massachusetts in rebellion passed both houses. The English author, Horace Walpole, declared this was "a vote for civil war."

On February 27, the House of Commons, after a prolonged debate, adopted Lord North's Plan of Reconciliation. This resolution was designed mainly as a face-saving measure for the ministry. Under the plan, Parliament would enact taxes for the regulation of external trade only on condition that the colonial assemblies voted revenue for "the common defence" and for support of the British civil government and judiciary in America. The opposition group in Parliament charged that North's plan was for the purpose of "divide et delende"—splitting the opposition, so that further coercive measures could be pursued. By the same token, they maintained, the plan aimed at creating division in the colonies (especially to win over New York).

The new ministerial toughness, however, became evident in the enactment on March 30 of the New England Restraining Act. Beginning July 1, the trade of the four New England colonies was restricted to Great Britain and the British West Indies and after July 20 prohibited from the North Atlantic fisheries. On April 13, 1775, the act was extended to include New Jersey, Pennsylvania, Virginia, and South Carolina.

Military forces were strengthened at Boston. By April 1775, General Gage had 3,500 troops in the city, backed by the British North American Squadron of 29 ships with 196 guns (including four men-of-war—the *Boyne*, *Somerset*, *Preston*, and *Asia*).

Gage's immediate responsibility, as ordered by Lord Dartmouth, was to keep powder, arms, and artillery out of rebel hands. On December 13, 1774, a rumor spread that a British military force would soon be on its way to Fort William and

Mary at Portsmouth harbor to provide assistance to the six-man garrison there or take away the munitions. Paul Revere rode 60 miles to sound the alarm. The next day 400 men charged the fort and captured and then confined Captain John Cochran, the fort's commander, and five soldiers; the mob also hauled down the king's colors. On December 15 a patriot group returned to the fort and carried off 16 cannon, 60 muskets, and other military stores.

On February 26, 1775, Gage sent Lieutenant Colonel Alexander Leslie with 240 regulars to Salem to seize cannon, which were thought to have been delivered from Holland but were actually only old ship guns. The militia blocked entry into the town by raising the drawbridge. Reverend Thomas Bernard of Salem arranged a standoff. The drawbridge was lowered, and Leslie's men advanced 30 rods (165 feet) beyond the bridge and then withdrew. Meanwhile, local citizens removed the cannon from the town.

Tensions between the soldiery and citizens in Boston continued. There were isolated instances of redcoats harassing the townspeople, even pulling up the fence around John Hancock's yard. On March 8, British soldiers tarred and feathered Thomas Ditson for attempting to persuade a British soldier to desert. The annual commemoration of the Boston Massacre fired up the Boston populace. In his oration of Monday, March 6, delivered to a packed audience at the Old South Church, Dr. Joseph Warren stressed the need for commitment. "On you depend the fortunes of America," he told the assembly. As John Hancock exhorted to his audience to make a stand against tyranny, some British officers present "cried out, fie! fie! which being mistaken for the cry of fire" everyone sought to get out "as fast as they could by the doors and windows" (Force, 4th series, 2:18).

The New England colonies established independent companies and embodied militia regiments in order to counter any aggression that General Gage might intend. Colonies outside of New England did the same. The Maryland Convention at Annapolis, on December 14, 1774, resolved that "a well regulated militia, composed of the gentlemen, freeholders, and other freemen, is the natural and only stable security of a free government, and that such militia will releave our mother country from any expense in our protection and defence, will obviate the pretence of a necessity for taxing us on that account, and render it unnecessary to keep any standing army (ever dangerous to Liberty) in this province."

The second Virginia Convention, meeting at St. John's Chapel in Richmond on March 20–27, 1775, after much debate voted to put part of the militia in readiness. The convention, usurping the authority of the General Assembly, which the governor refused to reconvene, passed an ordinance reinstating the Militia Act of 1738 which had expired. The delegates also called for raising volunteer companies of 68 men in each county and a troop of horse from the tidewater area. The vote carried at 65–60. Those who opposed this action argued that establishing volunteer companies would provoke war, while all the colonies were not prepared and foreign aid was not promised. Patrick Henry's speech of March 23, apocryphally recounted by his later biographer, William Wirt, undoubtedly did win support for the ordinance. Surely Henry did exclaim, "We must fight!" as Wirt reported. The only known contemporary account of Henry's speech, by James Parker, a Scottish factor states:

You never heard anything more infamously insolent than P. Henry's speech: He called the K--- a Tyrant, a fool, a puppet and a tool to the ministry. Said there was no Englishmen, no Scots, no Britons, but a set of wretches sunk in luxury; they had lost their native courage and [were] unable to look the brave Americans in the face.

In Concord, Massachusetts, the Provincial Congress summoned an army of 30,000—one-half of which was to be raised in Massachusetts, and the rest in New Hampshire, Connecticut, and Rhode Island. The Provincial Congress also drew up Rules and Regulations for the Establishment of the Army, and ordered that if the British ventured out of Boston with artillery and baggage the colonists were "to oppose their March to the last extremity."

"The Way Is Open and Clear"

The British commander in Boston was already considering an expedition to Concord to seize military stores and hopefully apprehend ringleaders, when, on April 14, 1775, he received instructions from Lord Dartmouth, dated January 27, to take forceful action before the rebellion reached "a riper state." On April 18, General Gage ordered 21 companies (11 of grenadiers and 10 of light infantry—more than 700 men in all), under the command of Lieutenant Colonel Francis Smith, assisted by Major John Pitcairn of the Royal Marines, to be at the waterfront by 10 P.M. From there the detachment was ferried in flatboats across the Charles River. At midnight the British expeditionary force, assembled at Lechmere Point in East Cambridge, began their march to Concord. By a prearranged plan ("one if by land, and two if by sea"), sexton Robert Newman hung two lanterns in the steeple of Christ Church (Old North Church) to indicate the route of the British. Dr. Joseph Warren sent Paul Revere across the river and William Dawes, a young cordwainer, by way of Boston Neck to warn the rebel leaders at Concord. Both Revere and Dawes made it to Lexington, where they were joined by Samuel Prescott, a Concord physician, who had been visiting a lady friend. Headed toward Concord, all three were captured. But Prescott escaped in time to sound the alarm; Revere and Dawes were later released.

Just before dawn, the British detachment arrived at the meetinghouse in Lexington and discovered about 80 armed men on the green behind the church, led by Captain John Parker. Pitcairn called on the militia to throw down their arms and disperse, while one company of regulars, though not being ordered to, charged after the rebels. Arms fire ensued, lasting ten minutes. As the militia withdrew, they counted their casualties—eight killed and nine wounded; the British had one man wounded and no fatalities. British and American eyewitnesses had contrasting versions as to who fired "the first shot."

The British entered Concord at 8 A.M. While most troops searched for munitions, one company was stationed at the South Bridge over the Concord River, and three companies, under Captain Walter Laurie, guarded the North Bridge, a mile from the village green. The redcoats in Concord found two 24-pound cannon, 100 barrels of flour, 500 musket balls, which had been thrown into a pond, and gun carriages. A bonfire made of the gun carriages gave the militia the impression that the British were torching the town. Militiamen came down from the hills and engaged Captain Laurie's men in a sharp musketry. The fight lasted about three minutes; the British had three men killed and eight wounded, and the Americans, two dead and three injured. The militia broke ranks and ascended the hill. Smith, collecting all his men at the center of Concord, started on the return march at 12 noon. Unmolested for a mile, suddenly at Meriam's Corner the redcoats met an incessant fire from militia. At Lexington the British troops were joined by a relief column of 1,400 men under General Lord Hugh Percy. Two six pounders helped to scatter the militia. At 3:15 P.M. the retreat was resumed. On the whole distance back to Cambridge, some 4,000 militia fired on the beleaguered regulars from the cover of stone walls, trees, barns, and woods. Colonel William Heath, a militia officer, commented that the British minimized their losses by staying on the road, taking advantage of the stone fences, which "covered their flanks almost to the height of their shoulders." Counting losses, the British had 73 men killed, 174 wounded, and 26 missing; and the Americans, 50 killed and 34 wounded. Over the next several days some 10,000 to 12,000 militiamen gathered on the outskirts of Boston and Charlestown. As Lieutenant John Barker wrote on May 1: "The Rebels have erected the Standard at Cambridge; they call themselves the King's Troops and us the Parliaments Pretty Burlesque!"

Civil war thus erupted on April 19, 1775. Reverend Ezra Stiles commented: "It is happy that the Troops have given the first blow—the way is open & clear now for the Americans." In Virginia, Edmund Randolph noted that "the intelligence of the bloodshed at Lexington changed the figure of Great Britain from an unrelenting parent into that of a merciless enemy."

The fighting in Massachusetts galvanized further commitment and military preparation throughout the colonies. New Yorkers, who had not been very support-ive of the resolutions of Congress and of the revolutionary movement in general, now embraced the common cause. On April 29, 1,000 New York City citizens, "shocked by the bloody scene now acting in the Massachusetts Bay," signed them-selves into an association that pledged "to carry into execution whatever measures may be recommended by the Continental Congress, or resolved upon by our provin-cial convention [an extralegal session of the legislature which would meet on May 22], for the purpose of preserving our constitution and opposing the execution of several arbitrary and oppressive acts of the British Parliament." The association committees controlled the city; the customshouse was closed; ships were prevented from delivering provisions to the British army in Boston; and the arsenal was seized. Throughout the colonies, local militia and volunteer companies stepped up their drills. New England towns sent troops toward Boston. Even the discredited Pennsyl-vania legislature voted to raise 4,300 men for the defense of the colony.

Virginia almost had its "first shot" of the Revolution. The governor, John Murray, earl of Dunmore, aware that patriots would soon try to appropriate the powder in Williamsburg, determined to make the first move. During the night of

April 20–21 a squad of 15 marines, commanded by Lieutenant Henry Collins, from the British schooner, *Magdalen*, anchored in the James River, carted off 15 half-barrels of powder from the Williamsburg magazine. The shocked townspeople demanded the return of the powder. Dunmore was terrified. "All the People assembled," he reported, and "during their Consultation, continual Threats were brought to my House, that it was their Resolution to seize upon, or massacre me & every Person found giving me Assistance if I refuse to deliver the Powder immediately into their custody." Nevertheless, Dunmore had the powder taken to the British man-of-war *Fowey* in Chesapeake Bay. Militia rallied throughout central Virginia and prepared to march against the governor. Dunmore threatened to unleash slaves and burn Williamsburg. News of Lexington and Concord heightened the crisis. Patrick Henry collected 150 militia at Newcastle (in Hanover County, near Richmond) and headed toward the capital, adding militia on the way. At Doncastle's Ordinary, 15 miles from Williamsburg, Carter Braxton, one of the colony's conservative leaders, met with Henry and gave him a bill of exchange for £330 issued from the colony's treasury as payment for the powder. Henry and his troops then returned home. For the present bloodshed had been avoided. Dunmore remained aboard ship and began to form his own army. The *Virginia Gazette* said of the situation: "It is now full Time for us all to be on our guard, and to prepare ourselves against every Contingency. The Sword is now drawn, and God knows when it will be sheathed."

New England militia soon took offensive action, bringing further proof that a state of war existed between the colonies and Great Britain. On May 10, Ethan Allen's Green Mountain Boys and Benedict Arnold's band of Massachusetts and Connecticut militia seized Fort Ticonderoga on the western shore of Lake Champlain and its 50-man garrison, along with 78 cannon and 30,000 flints. Two days later, Crown Point, 10 miles to the northward, fell to a detachment led by Seth Warner; the nine enlisted men at the fort were made prisoners. On May 16, Arnold captured the British garrison at St. Johns, on the Richelieu River, an outlet of Lake Champlain.

When the second Continental Congress met on May 10, most of the same delegates were back. New members included John Hancock, Benjamin Franklin, James Wilson, and Thomas Jefferson, who temporarily replaced Peyton Randolph. With the news of Lexington and Concord fresh on their minds, there was unanimous agreement that the colonists must fight, but the conservatives, led by John Dickinson, held to the position of the first Continental Congress that only defensive measures be taken. The Lees and Adamses called for offensive warfare. On May 18, Congress learned of the capture of Fort Ticonderoga and Crown Point. There was also intelligence that General William Howe would soon be in America commanding a much enlarged British army. Thus, Congress, on May 26, resolved that the colonies "be immediately put into a state of defence" and, making yet one more effort at reconciliation, directed that a petition be sent to the king.

Congress agreed to a proposal from the Massachusetts Provincial Congress that it accept responsibility for the militia army about Boston. It had no choice but to take charge of the conduct of the war; not doing so, Congress would forfeit leadership of the Revolution. On June 14, it was voted that 10 rifle companies (six from

This miniature of George Washington, at age 45 or 46, by Charles Willson Peale, may have been made at the time of the Valley Forge encampment, 1777–78. *Courtesy of the Mount Vernon Ladies' Association*

Pennsylvania, two from Maryland, and two from Virginia) should join the forces around Boston; the enlistees would be in an "American continental army" and would be paid by Congress. Discussion turned toward appointment of a commander in chief. John Adams, much to the consternation of John Hancock, who had expected to be named to the position, recommended giving the commission to George Washington, which would meet the approval of "all America." The next day Thomas Johnson of Maryland formally nominated Washington. With no one else put forward, Congress unanimously elected Washington "to command all the continental forces, raised, or to be raised, for the defence of American liberty." Over the next week Congress named four major generals (Artemas Ward, Charles Lee, Philip Schuyler, and Israel Putnam), eight brigadier generals, and the several general officers for staff departments. Congressmen, seeing a danger in giving Congress complete powers of military appointment, compromised, agreeing that the individual colonies would name officers below field grade.

Taking charge of the army, as Jerrilyn G. Marston (1987) points out, "symbolized congressional acceptance of the old royal responsibility for protecting the continent" (p. 132). Much more than that, as the course of the conflict between the colonies and the mother country deepened, it meant that a logical consequence would be the repudiation of any crown authority over the colonies—and hence independence.

CHAPTER 5

Irrevocable Separation

 Americans braced for a bloody civil war. New England troops had skirmished with the redcoats at Lexington and Concord and were in control of Lake Champlain. The intercolonial Congress at Philadelphia established a Continental army, and the colonies, through their extralegal conventions and committees of safety, made preparations for war. The British army at Boston was now an occupying force, besieged by 15,000 armed patriots who formed an arc around the west of Boston, from Medford in the north to Roxbury in the south. On May 26, 1775, three British generals—William Howe, Henry Clinton, and John Burgoyne—landed at Boston, bringing with them troops that now gave General Gage an army strength of 6,500 men.

Acting on instructions from Lord Dartmouth, Gage, on June 12, issued a proclamation declaring Massachusetts in a state of rebellion and establishing martial law. Gage promised amnesty "to all who shall lay down their Arms, and return to the duties of peaceable Subjects," except for John Hancock and Samuel Adams. The verbose document, actually written by Burgoyne, whose literary pretensions would be better put to use as a playwright after the war, more amused than intimidated the Americans.

Neither the British nor the American governments made serious attempts at reconciliation. The war spread to northern and southern fronts. Doing battle with the king's soldiers, Americans, by early 1776, were ready to denounce any allegiance to the crown of Great Britain.

"Taking the Bull by the Horns"

New England militia settled in for a siege of Boston. If the patriots should gain the hills at Charlestown to the north or those at Dorchester to the south, they could exercise firepower on the British in the city and in the harbor. To the British point of view, some action was required to demonstrate military capability.

In June 1775 Gage planned to occupy Dorchester Heights. As a countermove, on June 15 the American commander, Artemas Ward, and his council of war determined to seize the hills above Charlestown, across the Charles River from

Boston. Such action would strengthen the siege of Boston and protect American lines from a British thrust.

On the night of June 16, Colonel William Prescott and 1,200 Massachusetts militia began to erect breastworks on Breed's Hill, on the lower part of the peninsula, just above Charlestown. Some work was also begun on Bunker Hill, to the north, near Charlestown Neck. At dawn the next day, British ship and shore batteries opened up on the American positions. At 2 P.M., 2,400 British troops landed at Moulton's Point. Smoke from burning buildings gave cover as the infantrymen, each with 40- to 50-pound packs containing three-day rations and 60 rounds of ammunition, moved across the open areas to outflank the American positions and thereby to seal off the neck connecting with the mainland. To cover the left flank, a Connecticut detachment under Captain Thomas Knowlton and Colonel James Reed's New Hampshire regiment assembled to the left and rear of Breed's Hill along a wooden rail and stone fence, which stretched 200 yards from the hill to the Mystic River.

Unable to penetrate beyond the fence because of the withering fire of the defenders behind it and from Breed's Hill, the British attempted a frontal assault on the hill. Failing, the redcoats threw off their packs and tried again, only to have their ranks again decimated. With bayonets drawn, they launched a final assault, from three sides of the hill, forcing the Americans, who were out of powder, to give way. Prescott took charge of the situation, though Brigadier General Israel Putnam was present, and ordered a retreat. One of the last to leave the redoubt was Dr. Joseph Warren, who, despite his rank as major general in the militia, was serving as a volunteer. Still trying to rally the men, Warren was shot in the head. The British buried him, along with his "seditious principles" on the spot where he had fallen. Later, after the British left Boston, the body of the Revolution's first martyred hero was exhumed, identified by two false teeth that had been made by Paul Revere.

After the retreat, the Americans fortified Winter Hill, west of the neck and two miles from Bunker Hill. General Howe, who had led the British expedition, with success being "too dearly bought," refused pursuit. British naval support would have greatly aided a British advance, but Admiral Samuel Graves, who had been negligent in making soundings up the Charles and Mystic rivers, was fearful of shoals and mud flats. At the battle, the British suffered 1,054 casualties, including 92 of 250 officers—226 killed and 828 wounded; the Americans had 140 dead, 271 wounded, and 30 captured.

The battle of Bunker Hill impressed Americans that the best strategy was to hold strong posts and invite the British to attack. This thinking would lead to the Americans' decisions to seize Quebec and New York City. The battle made Howe more cautious in future campaigns, and it showed that Americans could both stand and fight against British regulars and quickly and skillfully improvise fortifications. General Gage lamented that "these people shew a spirit and conduct against us, they never shewed against the French." He called for more troops. Writing to Lord Barrington, Gage summed up his predicament: "We are here, to use a common expression, taking the bull by the horns, attacking the enemy in their strong parts, I wish this cursed place was burned, the only use is its harbour . . . in all other respects its the worst place to act offensively from, or defencively."

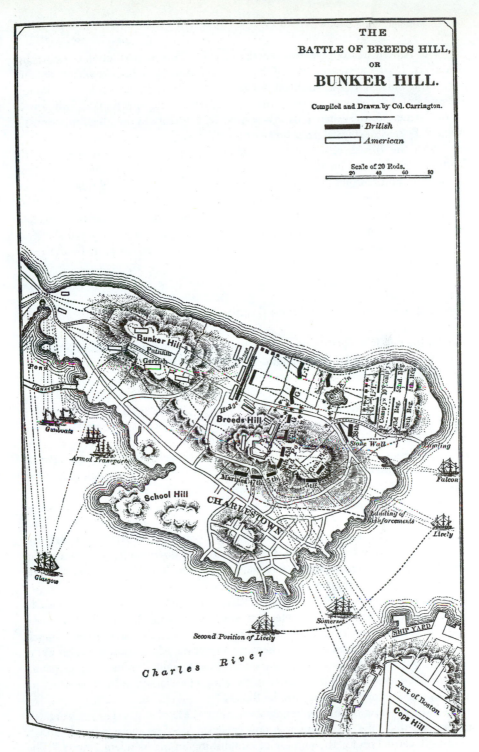

Battle of Breeds Hill, or Bunker Hill *Source: Henry B. Carrington, Battle Maps and Charts of the American Revolution (New York: A. S. Barnes & Co., 1881), p. 9.*

The American troops' steadfastness at Bunker Hill inspired confidence in the war effort. It also convinced people that the main reliance should be on a people in arms, the militia, rather than on a Continental army. Such a view weakened recruitment for the new intercolonial military force. While Bunker Hill was a tactical defeat for the Americans, it was a strategic victory in the long run, contributing to Britain's eventual decision to evacuate Boston.

With the British reluctant to do further battle, the American army around Boston gained some breathing space which they used to improve its fighting capabilities and resources. George Washington arrived at the Cambridge camp on July 3, and the next day, in general orders, he announced that the "Troops of the UNITED PROVINCES of North America" were now under the authority of Congress. While the commander in chief shaped a more proficient and professional soldiery, he made plans for an attack on Boston, which was delayed, in part, by the need for armaments.

End to Reconciliation

To rally the public's support and to bolster morale in Washington's army, on July 6, 1775, Congress agreed to a document, which it published the next day: *A Declaration by the Representatives of the United Colonies of North America, now met in General Congress at Philadelphia, Setting forth the Causes and Necessity of their taking up Arms*, written by Thomas Jefferson and revised by John Dickinson. The similarities between the *Declaration* and the later Declaration of Independence are striking; both, for example, listed the grievances since 1763. An important difference is that the 1775 document indicts mainly Parliament and only secondarily the king. Parliament, "stimulated by an inordinate passion for a power . . . unjustifiable," had brought on the war.

Congress also made one more effort to petition the king to end the violence in America and to restore the colonies' rightful relationship to Great Britain. This "Olive Branch Petition" of July 8, 1775, was entrusted to Richard Penn, the proprietor of Pennsylvania, to be delivered to Lord Dartmouth. The radicals in Congress had preferred to forego any such effort. On July 31, Congress formally rejected Lord North's proposal for reconciliation.

The king's proclamation of August 23, 1775, declared all the colonies in rebellion and called on loyal subjects to quell it. George III also had in mind supporters of the American cause in England, the rebellion having been "much promoted and encouraged by the traiterous correspondence, counsels, and comfort of divers wicked and desperate persons within this realm." When Congressman Samuel Ward of Rhode Island learned of the king's proclamation in November, he rejoiced that "we are all declared to be Rebels."

At the opening of the parliamentary session of October 26, 1775, George III announced that "the rebellious war now levied is become more general, and is manifestly carried on for the purpose of establishing an independent empire." The king said he was committing more land and naval forces to suppress the rebellion and was expecting offers of foreign assistance. "When the unhappy and deluded multitude, against whom this force will be directed, shall become sensible of their error, I shall be ready to receive the misled with tenderness and mercy." The king's speech touched off a bitter debate in both the Commons and the Lords, with the Opposition unsuccessfully trying to deny the usual expression of gratitude for the king's presentation and to prevent the use of foreign mercenaries. One casualty was Lord Dartmouth who resigned as secretary of state for America, and was replaced by a strong advocate of military coercion, Lord George Sackville Germain.

On November 1, Congress learned of the king's proclamation of August 23 and also that no notice would be taken of the Olive Branch Petition. It also heard rumors that the king was planning to hire foreign troops to be sent to America. Thus, more actions were taken to shore up the American cause. Congress established a Committee of Secret Correspondence to carry on diplomacy with foreign nations and created a Continental navy. Many members called for the establishment of state governments and a confederation, which would be the first steps toward independence.

The war was further defined as a contest between belligerents when the British Prohibitory Act of December 22, 1775, forbade all trade with the colonies while the rebellion continued; ships so engaged would be seized. Congress received news of this act in late February 1776. Thus, reconciliation had become a dead letter. General William Howe and Admiral Richard Howe brought British military forces to New York in the summer of 1776 with instructions to negotiate a peace. Nothing was accomplished, however. No new terms were offered, and by then the Americans had declared independence.

Preemptive War—Canada

A successful and perhaps speedy conclusion of the war, from both the American and British points of view, depended greatly on initial strikes before the enemy could mount effective opposition. Such a strategy could secure the loyalty of large segments of the population. The Americans would make a preemptive move into Canada and the British would do the same into the south. If the British could invade at will from Canada, then they would be in position to exact allegiance from the Indians and frontier settlements, control the Hudson, Lake Champlain, and Richelieu waterways, and drive a wedge between New York and New England. Sir Guy Carleton, governor of Quebec province, was already planning to launch an invasion. In anticipation of the arrival of a large number of reinforcements in August 1775 he regarrisoned St. Johns and began repairs on that fort as well as nearby Fort Chambly.

On June 27, 1775, Congress established the Northern army, giving the command to Major General Philip Schuyler, a seasoned veteran of the last war and a wealthy member of the Dutch New York aristocracy. Washington provided some troops from his army. A two-pronged offensive against Canada was planned: Colonel Benedict Arnold was to move up through Maine and the Canadian wilderness to

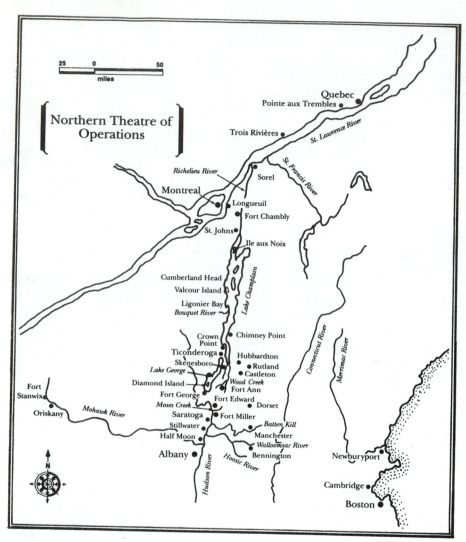

25   0   50
miles

Northern Theatre of
Operations

Quebec
Pointe aux Trembles •
• Quebec
St. Lawrence River
Trois Rivières •

Richelieu River
Montreal
Sorel
St. Francis River
• Longueuil
Fort Chambly
St. Johns •
Ile aux Noix

Cumberland Head
Valcour Island •
Ligonier Bay
Bouquet River
Lake Champlain

Crown
Point
• Chimney Point
Ticonderoga •
Hubbardton
Skenesboro •
• Rutland
Lake George
• Castleton
Diamond Island
Wood Creek
Fort Ann
Fort George •
Fort Edward
Moses Creek
• Dorset
Fort Stanwix •
Saratoga •
• Fort Miller
Oriskany •
Mohawk River
Stillwater •
Batten Kill
Half Moon •
Manchester
Walloomsac River
Albany •
Bennington
Newburyport •
Hudson River
Hoosic River
Connecticut River
Merrimac River

Cambridge •
Boston •
N

Northern Theatre of Operations *Source: Max M. Mintz,* The Generals of Saratoga *(New Haven, Conn.: Yale University Press, 1990), p. 95.*

Quebec, and the main Northern army was to proceed up Lake Champlain and on to Montreal, and then join with Arnold's detachment before Quebec. When Schuyler became ill, the field command was given to Brigadier General Richard Montgomery, a former British army officer who had settled on a small farm in New York in 1772.

Montgomery set out with 1,200 troops from Crown Point on August 30. Meanwhile, Ethan Allen and 100 or so militia and Canadians headed for Montreal, but upon reaching the outskirts of that city were captured by the British. Montgomery took St. Johns (a siege lasting from September 8 to November 12) and Chambly without a fight, and then entered Montreal on November 13, accepting the surrender of the 150-man garrison, though Sir Guy Carleton managed to escape to Quebec. Arnold, after a harrowing and remarkable journey, appeared at the outskirts of Quebec on the same day. He now had only 675 of the original detachment of 1,050 men. Montgomery linked up with Arnold on December 3. Since most American enlistments expired at the end of the year, an attack on Quebec had to be made quickly.

The battle plan at Quebec was twofold: Arnold was to assault the lower town from the west and Montgomery to attack from the opposite direction from the Plains of Abraham. As soon as the fight began on December 31, Montgomery was killed. Carleton, commanding a force of 1,800 regulars, Canadian militia, and sailors from the British ships in the St. Lawrence, easily repelled the invaders. Arnold was wounded in the leg. Colonel Daniel Morgan, in charge of the rifle companies with Montgomery, surrendered along with over 400 American troops. Carleton did not pursue the remnant American force, which lingered nearby, suffering from lack of supplies and the smallpox.

On April 1, 1776, Brigadier General David Wooster, a 64-year-old war veteran, arrived to take command of the American army that, having been reinforced, now numbered about 2,000. Major General John Thomas, who assumed command on May 1, raised the siege and brought the American army back to Sorel at the mouth of the Richelieu River. Thomas died of smallpox on June 2. Brigadier General John Sullivan arrived a few days later with a New York brigade. Meanwhile, Carleton received a reinforcement of 10,000 British and Hessian troops under Major General John Burgoyne. Sullivan gave Brigadier General William Thompson 2,000 men to cross back over the St. Lawrence and attack the British post at Three Rivers, probably not knowing that it was defended by some 6,000 British troops. The assault failed, and Thompson was taken prisoner. The American army retreated all the way back to Crown Point.

Schuyler was made the scapegoat for the Canadian fiasco, even though he had not taken an active role in the campaign. Horatio Gates, formerly adjutant general of the Continental army and before that a British officer, was given command of the Northern army on June 17, 1776.

Carleton remained in the field with his large army, planning to do what Burgoyne would attempt later—to move down Lake Champlain, capture Albany, and then descend the Hudson to link up with the British army in New York City. The British invasion, however, was put on hold, owing largely to the Americans' stubborn resistance at the battle of Valcour Island on October 11–13, 1776, a naval engagement offshore from Crown Point. Benedict Arnold commanded the small American fleet. Although Arnold lost 5 of his 16 ships and the British vessels suffered little damage, Carleton elected to halt the British advance. Arnold burned Crown Point, and the American troops held on to Ticonderoga. The American invasion of Canada had been a total failure. A major disappointment was that it did not win over the French Canadians, who considered the war an affair among Englishmen.

Preemptive War—the South

While the war in New England and upper New York became a contest of armies, in the South military conflict was slow to erupt. At the start of the war, the British ministry ignored the southern theater. However, intelligence coming into England from the royal governors indicated that coordinated operations of loyalists and minimal British forces could quickly put an end to the rebellion in the South. Governors Lord Dunmore of Virginia, Josiah Martin of North Carolina, Lord William Campbell of South Carolina, and Sir James Wright of Georgia beseeched the North ministry to send military expeditions to their colonies to act in conjunction with loyalist troops.

Backcountry settlers in North Carolina and South Carolina seemed ready to embrace the royal standard. Fresh in the minds of western North Carolinians were the Regulator movement and its crushing defeat at the battle of Alamance (near Hillsboro) in 1771 by troops led by the then royal governor, William Tryon. The Regulators, a vigilante group, had mostly protested use of the legal system to collect debts and the failure of colonial government to suppress outlaw bands. The backcountry residents resented only the eastern ruling elite—not the crown. Of course, a major factor in their loyalty to the king was an offer from the British government to confer free land and exemptions from quitrents to those who took up arms against the rebels. Lord North informed the king on October 15, 1775, that 2,000 troops sent to South Carolina, as recommended by Governor Campbell, would be "sufficient to set matters right" in that colony, and Georgia "will return to her duty as soon as South Carolina is brought to a submission." North observed that two motivators in particular could work toward securing royal government in the southern colonies: the fear that war might incite slave insurrection and "the exceeding want of European commodities."

By the end of 1775, the British government decided on a limited southern strategy, one that was intended to rally the loyalists and take the initiative away from the patriots. Meanwhile, southern royal governors, as best they could, sought to raise the royal standard locally. On the patriot side, the extralegal governments embodied troops both for home defense and for service in the Continental army.

In Virginia, Governor Dunmore collected a motley band of Scottish loyalists, watermen, and "Ethiopians" (runaway slaves), along with part of the 14th royal regiment, sailors, and marines—500 in all. He had the assistance of several British warships. Probably no one action did more to ruin Dunmore's cause than his proclamation on November 7 in which he not only called for Virginians to side with the king and established martial law, but also emancipated slaves and indentured servants belonging to the rebels. To Virginia planters, Dunmore's "Emancipation Proclamation" was a brazen call for slave insurrection. A week later, Dunmore's army routed Virginia militia at Kemp's Landing, 12 miles southeast of Norfolk. The Virginia Convention put several regiments, destined for Continental service, into the lower tidewater area to oppose Dunmore. Brigadier General Andrew Lewis first commanded these troops and was superseded for the period of

Recruits for the British Army in America. **The view of the British public was not unlike the American perception (post-1776) that the common soldiery consisted substantially of the dregs of humanity. Engraving by Henry William Bunbury.**   *Print Collection: Miriam & Ira D. Wallach Division of Arts, Prints and Photographs, The New York Public Library, Astor, Lenox and Tilden Foundations*

March to May 1776 by Major General Charles Lee, whom Washington sent southward to organize defenses. Lee was apprehensive that a British expedition would sail into the Chesapeake or show up at Charleston, South Carolina. "I am in a damned whimsical situation," he wrote Robert Morris; "I know not where to turn, where to fix myself. I am like a dog in a dancing school."

In December 1775 Virginia troops under Colonel William Woodford prepared to assault breastworks that Dunmore had set up at Great Bridge, on the South Branch of the Elizabeth River, near Norfolk. At dawn on December 9, Dunmore decided to attack; 120 regulars rushed onto the causeway and bridge, only to be cut down from arms fire at their front and flanks. Dunmore's troops had 17 killed and about 50 wounded. Woodford reported to the Virginia Convention: "This was a second Bunker Hill affair, in miniature, with the difference that we kept our part and had only 1 man wounded in the hand." The Virginia troops, now reinforced by Robert Howe's North Carolinians, entered Norfolk, while Dunmore's force remained shipbound. On January 1, 1776, Dunmore's little fleet bombarded the city; British sailors landed and set fires that consumed two-thirds of the city. Dunmore's seaborne force eventually anchored off Gwynn's Island in the Chesapeake near the mouth of the Rappahannock River. Bombardment from American shore batteries, on July 9, compelled the fleet to depart. Smallpox raged throughout the British ranks. When the patriots crossed over to Gwynn's Island, they found many dead or dying Negroes abandoned by Dunmore; one child was discovered "sucking at the breast of its dead mother." After raiding along the banks of the Potomac River for several weeks, Dunmore and the British naval commander agreed that a further "invasion" of Virginia was pointless. In early August Dunmore and one-half of the fleet sailed for New York, and the other half headed for St. Augustine and Bermuda.

Like Lord Dunmore in Virginia, Governor Sir James Wright of Georgia had hoped to preserve the royal authority but found the patriot forces too strong to oppose. When four British men-of-war appeared at the mouth of the Savannah River, the Georgia council of safety had Wright arrested and confined to the limits of Savannah, but Wright violated his parole and boarded the H.M.S. *Scarborough*. In February 1776 other British war vessels, with 200 troops, came into the river for the purpose of collecting supplies for the British army in Boston. As the British seized provisions from merchant vessels near Savannah, Georgia and South Carolina militia assembled for battle. The British squadron dropped down the river and out to sea; Wright sailed with it, and he did not return until 1779, after the British had captured Savannah.

Loyalists in the Carolinas, expecting a visit by a British expeditionary force, were encouraged to take up the royal standard. In November–December 1775 several thousand loyalists of the South Carolina upper backcountry assembled under arms but were confronted at the Reedy River by a militia force led by Colonel Richard Richardson. In this "snow campaign," the loyalist troops were routed, thus effectively ending their mobilization in the South Carolina "upcountry."

In North Carolina, Highland Scots of Cumberland County in the southeastern part of the colony and former Regulators of western Rowan County posed a formidable threat, but they acted too precipitately. Without waiting for the actual arrival of an expected British expeditionary force, Governor Josiah Martin, on June 10, 1776, issued a proclamation calling loyalists to arms. General Gage had sent Lieutenant Colonel Donald McDonald and Captain Alexander McLeod down from Boston to recruit in North Carolina. By mid-February 1776, 1,600 men, mostly Scots, assembled near Cross Creek (Fayetteville) and began their march for Wilmington along the Cape Fear River. Meanwhile, Colonel James Moore, with 1,000 troops (Continentals and militia), gave pursuit. Another rebel force of equal size, led by Alexander Lillington and Richard Caswell, dug in at Moores Creek, awaiting the approach of the enemy. The patriots removed the planks from the bridge and greased the sleepers with soft soap and tallow. On February 27, shouting "King George and broadswords!" the Scots ran onto the bridge; many toppled off into the water or were shot. The scene was much like Dunmore's defeat at Great Bridge. Moore's troops had arrived in time to assist in the battle. The victory was a crushing blow to the loyalists, and it made pointless any temporary appearance of a British expeditionary force in the Cape Fear region.

The first British offensive of the war was underway in February 1776 when General Henry Clinton set sail from Boston with 1,500 troops. At Cape Fear he expected to join an armada of 10 warships commanded by Commodore Sir Peter Parker; the fleet, setting out from Ireland, carried 2,500 troops under the charge of Major General Charles Cornwallis. The expedition was ill conceived, however: it would be in southern waters for a short duration before returning north for a New York offensive in summer 1776, and it was not large enough to accomplish any significant invasion or to rally the loyalists of the several southern colonies. Clinton arrived at Cape Fear on March 12, 1776, and Parker did not come until April 18. The North Carolina and South Carolina loyalists had been defeated and dispersed.

The expedition entered Charleston harbor on June 4. Clinton wanted a mainland attack, but Parker refused naval support. The immediate objective was to capture the rebel fort on Sullivan's Island. Contrary to the desire of General Charles Lee, who was now in Charleston superintending the city's defenses, Colonel William Moultrie and his force of 6,500 Continentals and militia were determined to make a stand.

By June 16 most of the British troops had debarked at Long Island, which was separated from Sullivan's Island by a water breach. At 11 A.M. on June 28, Parker's ships began bombardment of Fort Sullivan. British troops were to wade the breach over to Sullivan's Island. The water level at low tide was expected to be only 18 inches, but actually it was seven feet and so could not be forded. Three of Parker's frigates ran aground, and several others collided. Although more than 7,000 cannonballs battered Fort Sullivan, they did little damage, being absorbed in the spongy palmetto log walls. The crowning indignity for the British came when American cannonshot grazed Commodore Parker aboard the *Bristol* and "ruined his Britches . . . quite torn off, his backside laid bare, his thigh and knee wounded." The British suffered 64 killed, 13 wounded; the Americans, 17 and 20. After the battle, the failed British expeditionary force stayed for a while in the harbor and then sailed for New York. It would be two years before the British launched another southern strategy and offensive.

British Evacuation of Boston

Until the end of 1775, the British concentrated on breaking the rebellion in New England, more by strangulation than by conquest. They planned to do so by occupying Boston, closing off ports along the New England coastline, and, eventually, moving an army down from Canada to section off New England from New York. The rationale was that by reducing patriot capabilities in New England, which was regarded as the seedbed of the Revolution, colonists elsewhere might lose their will to fight. During 1775 to early 1776, however, Howe, who succeeded Gage as commander in chief, had too few troops to defeat Washington's army, which was still encamped just beyond Boston, and the patriot cause had gained substantial military backing throughout the colonies. Although British naval units bombarded and burned most of Falmouth (Portland), Maine, and shelled Bristol, Rhode Island, in October 1775 in retaliation for American privateers' preying on British ships, such actions were counterproductive, for the destruction of property further aroused the American public against Great Britain.

Washington had the difficult task of converting militia into a Continental army—reducing in number and realigning military units, settling squabbles over rank, persuading Yankee soldiers to serve under officers other than those whom they elected, exacting discipline, drumming up reenlistments, and working with Congress for reforms in organization and support services. Although Congress, on November 4, 1775, had voted for an army of 20,372 troops, divided into regiments of 728 each, in early January 1776 Washington had only 8,212 Continentals, of whom only 5,582 were fit for duty. It was not so much the number of soldiers that caused Washington to hesitate in opening warfare on the British in Boston, but the insufficiency of weaponry and powder, and especially the need for heavy artillery.

Yet Washington's predicament was not without a solution. While riding in the Cambridge camp one day in summer 1775, Washington met Henry Knox, a fat young man of 25 and a former Boston bookseller, who, with his wife, the daughter of the royal secretary of Massachusetts, had made his way through the British lines. Knox was fairly well versed in artillery and military engineering based on his reading of the books he had stocked in his shop for British officers. Washington took an instant liking to the jovial Knox, beginning a friendship that lasted throughout the war and many years afterward. Knox became attached to the army as a civilian consultant. Soon, however, in November, he was appointed colonel and commandant of the almost nonexistent artillery corps.

Knox proposed that captured artillery at Fort Ticonderoga be brought to Washington's camp and be used in the siege of Boston. This herculean task involved negotiating frozen rivers and the steep hills of the Berkshires in western Massachusetts. Washington approved and gave the assignment to Knox. Arriving at Ticonderoga on December 5, 1775, Knox selected the most serviceable equipment: 43 cannon (ranging from 4- to 24-pounders), 2 howitzers, and 14 mortars and coehorns; he also took with him 7,000 rounds of shot for the cannon, 2,000 muskets, and 31 tons of musket shot. On the first leg of the trip, the military freight went down by boat on Lake George. Then, employing local teamsters and using 124 pairs of horses, the cavalcade followed down along the west bank of the Hudson, crossing the frozen Mohawk River at its junction with the Hudson and then going on to Albany. To cross the Hudson, Knox cut holes in the ice, so that the extra water freezing would thicken the surface. On January 10, Knox started over the Berkshires with sleds pulled by 80 yoke of oxen; then came transit over the icebound Connecticut River at Springfield.

By the end of January, Knox had covered 300 miles and was able to present Washington the "noble train of artillery." The American commander in chief had also just received another military prize: from the captured British brigantine, the *Nancy*, a cargo that contained 2,000 firearms, flints, several tons of musket shot, and a 2,700 pound brass mortar. With his army now numbering 17,482 men, half of whom were militia, and the added weaponry and munitions, Washington was ready to attack Boston. The plan called first for seizure of Dorchester Heights (two high hills overlooking the city and the harbor) and then for an amphibious assault on the western part of Boston from the Charles River. On March 4, Brigadier General John Thomas, with 1,200 workers and 360 ox teams, began entrenchments on the heights. Several hundred trees were cut down to form an abatis, two redoubts were erected, and barrels were filled with dirt and stones to be rolled down the slopes in the event of a British attack.

Washington now began a light, intermittent bombardment of the harbor, while conserving powder. Fearing another Bunker Hill, Howe avoided an assault on the American position on Dorchester Heights. His only other alternative was to pull out of Boston. On March 17 the British army evacuated the city and boarded

Henry Knox (1750–1806) accomplished the feat shown in *Hauling Guns by Ox Teams from Fort Ticonderoga for the Siege of Boston, 1775,* **enabling Washington to emplace artillery on Dorchester Heights overlooking Boston, a factor that contributed to the British evacuation of the city in March 1776.**   *National Archives*

transports, which took them to Halifax, Nova Scotia. General Artemas Ward, whom Washington had displaced as commander in chief of the troops about Boston, led a procession into the city the same day that the British left. At the end of June, Howe's army of 24,000 regulars and 8,000 Hessians, assisted by a fleet of 130 men-of-war and transports, entered New York harbor. Washington, having guessed correctly the enemy's destination, had by this time stationed his army on Manhattan Island and western Long Island.

"'Tis Time to Part"

Events confirmed the separation between the colonies and Great Britain. The war would be prolonged and would end in victory for one side or the other; there would be no compromise. The king and the British Parliament remained adamant about a military solution. To Americans, not only was the king involved in the conspiracy against liberty, but he was also to blame for allowing the war to continue. He had tried unsuccessfully to purchase mercenary troops from Russia to fight against the Americans, and finally he had succeeded in obtaining 18,000 (and in the course of the war, 30,000) hirelings from the German states of Brunswick, Anhalt-Zerbst,

Thomas Paine (1737–1809), for a while himself a common soldier, rallied his countrymen to independence in *Common Sense* (1776) and to a fighting spirit in *The American Crisis,* a series of 16 essays (Dec. 1776–June 1782). Painted by John Wesley Jarvis.   *Gift of Marian B. Maurice © 1992, National Gallery of Art, Washington, D.C.*

Anspach-Bayreuth, Hesse-Cassel, Hesse-Hanau, and Waldeck for the same purpose. The Americans felt that the time had come to sever all ties with the British government. As yet, no American political writer had denounced allegiance to the king. That task would fall to an unlikely agent: an impoverished Englishman and former exciseman who had settled in Philadelphia in 1774—Thomas Paine. Paine found employment as a writer for the new *Pennsylvania Magazine.* Having attracted notice for his radical journalism, he was asked by Benjamin Rush and other patriots in Philadelphia to write a pamphlet that would present the case against the king. The result, the most influential political work in American history, was Paine's *Common Sense* (published on January 9, 1776, 47 pages, and selling for 2s.) which went through 120,000 copies in three months.

To Paine, the king was "a hardened, sullen-tempered Pharaoh" and a "Royal Brute" who had forfeited his right to rule the colonies. No distinction could be made between king and Parliament, he said, for they had joined forces. The whole British government was corrupt, and no real separation of powers existed. The present British royal line had been founded by "a French bastard landing with an armed banditti, and establishing himself king of England against the consent of the natives." The time for reconciliation had passed: "Every thing that is right or natural pleads for separation. The blood of the slain, the weeping voice of nature cries, 'TIS TIME TO PART." Paine devoted a good part of his essay to how Americans could establish a free and republican government, emphasizing a unicameral legislature, with its representatives elected annually.

Common Sense met enthusiastic praise everywhere. It "may justly be compared to a land-flood that sweeps all before it," said one writer in the *Connecticut Gazette* of March 22, 1776. "We were blind," but "the scales have fallen from our eyes"; the "doctrine of Independence . . . is now become our delightful theme, and commands our purest affections." Paine's writing convinced Americans to disown the monarchy and to replace it with a republic. Congress had before it the task of accomplishing both.

CHAPTER 6

Independence

During 1775 Americans had moved steadily toward independence, without realizing the necessity to declare it officially. The radicals had to bide their time. Conservatives and moderates wanted to be sure that independence had the full support of the people at large. They also favored an orderly progression toward independence—securing legal state governments, establishing a confederation, and opening negotiations with foreign governments that gave the prospect for alliances. Too-precipitate action might unleash democratic upheaval within the colonies.

There is some validity in Progressive historian Carl Becker's classic portrayal of New York politics at the start of the Revolution (1909). Becker stated that at this time two issues were "about equally prominent." One "was whether essential colonial rights should be maintained"; the other "was by whom and by what methods they should be maintained. The first was the question of home rule; the second was the question . . . of who should rule at home" (p. 22). Indeed, the New York provincial congress, in a letter to its congressional delegation on June 26, 1775, expressed doubts about the ability of revolutionaries to govern themselves:

> Contests for liberty, fostered in their infancy by the virtuous and wise, become sources of power to wicked and designing men; from whence it follows, that such controversies as we are now engaged in frequently end in the demolition of those rights and privileges which they were instituted to defend. We pray you, therefore, to use every effort for the compromising of this unnatural quarrel between the parent and child.

Thomas Paine's *Common Sense,* with its emphasis on unicameral legislatures, raised fears that the state governments that would be created would be excessively democratic.

Declaring independence had other risks as well. In areas of mixed ethnic culture and in those that were yet untouched by the war, citizens were lukewarm toward independence. This was especially the case in the middle colonies. To declare independence might be too drastic a step and draw persons to the British side. There was also apprehension that civil war might erupt among colonies with long-standing disputes. Indeed, Yankee and Pennsylvania settlers had fought the Pennamite Wars (1769–75) over land possession in the Wyoming district of Pennsylvania, and Virginia asserted jurisdiction to territory in far western Pennsylvania. Independence would create a national domain in the west. There was fear, too, that certain influential Congressmen who were members of the speculative land companies might seek the annulment of claims to western territory held by individual colonies. The British evacuation of Boston and news of the Howe brothers serving as a peace commission lessened a sense of urgency for declaring independence.

While many cautioned against independence, it became increasingly difficult to avoid a decision. The credibility and legitimacy of Congress as well as support for the war effort required a more definite commitment. By spring 1776 all royal governors had been ousted, and British authority in the colonies had been replaced by makeshift patriot governments. The Congress itself exercised sovereign powers—making war, issuing paper money (thus creating a national debt), and preparing to negotiate treaties. The king had disowned the colonies and now treated them as enemy nations.

With the breach between the colonies and the mother country now irreparable, it became clear that governments in America needed legitimization. As Elisha Douglass (1955) writes: "By 1776 the tolerant Whig attitude toward lawlessness underwent a transformation." Exercising government responsibilities "gave them a new appreciation of the necessity for order, authority, and subordination. The rascals had been turned out; therefore good patriots should settle down and show a proper respect for authority" (p. 18).

"Is Not America Already Independent?"

Samuel Adams sensed that a complete separation from Great Britain, which he had so long anticipated, was about to become reality. "Is not America already independent?" he wrote Samuel Cooper on April 3, 1776. "Why then not declare it. . . . Can Nations at War be said to be dependent either upon the other? I ask then again, why not declare for Independence?"

Those in Congress who would delay independence were now becoming a decided minority. Desperately, conservative James Wilson of Pennsylvania sought to have a vote on the issue before there could be much discussion on it, hoping that the delegates would find that they were still not ready to declare independence. Using the occasion of the arrival of the text of the king's speech of October 26, 1775, at Congress in early January 1776, Wilson made a motion (as reported by delegate Richard Smith of New Jersey) "& was strongly supported that the Congress may expressly declare to their Constituents and the World their present Intentions respecting an Independency, observing that the Kings Speech directly charged Us with that Design." On January 24, Congress appointed a committee, all of whom were conservatives (John Dickinson, Robert Alexander, James Duane, William Hooper, and James Wilson), "to prepare an address to the inhabitants of the United Colonies." Congressional committees usually had members of different views. With the composition of this panel as it was, the majority in Congress seemed to be saying that its recommendations would be taken lightly. The committee's report ("very long, badly written, and full against Independency," according to Richard Smith) was permanently tabled.

In order for a declaration of independence to promote unity rather than division among the people, obviously there was need for a unanimous vote of the congressional delegations. Approval rested very much with the quasilegislative bodies in the colonies, which elected the members of Congress. Wrote the ever-observant Smith in his diary of February 29, 1776: "Much was said about declaring our Independency on G Britain when it appeared that 5 or 6 Colonies have instructed their Delegates not to agree to an Independency till they, the Principals, are consulted." The mood in Congress, however, definitely turned toward independence. John Adams, in a letter to James Warren of April 16, 1776, observed: "There are such moderate Men here, but their Principles are daily going out of Fashion. The Child Independence is now struggling for Birth. I trust that in a short time it will be brought forth, and in Spite of Pharaoh all America shall hail the dignified Stranger."

Although no colony had instructed its delegates to vote for independence before spring 1776, in more than half of the colonies they were free to do so. As late as January 12, 1776, the Maryland convention ordered its delegates to Congress not to vote for independence or for any foreign alliance or "union or confederation of these Colonies, which may necessarily lead to a separation from the mother country" without its prior approval.

Many of the resolutions and other actions of committees of safety at the county or township level strongly suggested a de facto existence of independence. The Mecklenburg County committee of safety, meeting in Charlotte, North Carolina, on May 20, 1775, allegedly declared for independence, and on May 31 announced that all authority of the crown in the colony was suspended. A full text of neither resolution has survived, and not until the early 1800s did these resolutions receive much notice. John Adams saw a copy of the May 20, 1776, resolution in a Salem, Massachusetts, newspaper in 1819 and wrote Thomas Jefferson, saying that "if I had possessed it, I would have made the Hall of Congress Echo and re-echo, with it fifteen Months before your Declaration of Independence." Jefferson, however, replied that he thought the document "spurious" and wondered how it had so long escaped the attention of North Carolina historians.

Nevertheless, North Carolina was the first colony expressly to authorize its congressional delegates to vote for independence. On April 12, 1776, the fourth Provincial Congress unanimously "empowered" its members of Congress "to concur with the delegates of the other Colonies in declaring Independency." Virginia, in a resolution of the fifth Virginia convention, followed suit, being the first colony actually to instruct its congressional delegation to propose that independence be adopted: "it is necessary that every kind of authority under the said crown should be totally suppressed." Virginians assumed that now independence was a foregone conclusion; the Grand Union flag of Washington's army was hoisted over the Capitol at Williamsburg, and on June 28 the convention adopted a state constitution.

"The Ideas of Independence Spread far and wide among the Colonies," Samuel Adams gladly noted in a letter of April 30, 1776. The middle colonies at last were coming over to independence; in New Jersey, after all, one-half of the people had "N. Engd. Blood running in their veins." Even "our little Sister Georgia" has "warmly engagd in the Cause." Moderates in Congress, however, succeeded in their call for establishing regular state governments before turning to a discussion of independence. Radical John Adams had given such advice in his *Thoughts on Government,* written in March 1776 in the form of letters to several delegates who had returned home. Adams suggested particularly that new state constitutions provide for a bicameral legislature and frequent elections.

On May 10, Congress resolved that the "assemblies and conventions" of the colonies should create state governments, and it appointed a committee of John Adams, Edward Rutledge, and Richard Henry Lee to prepare a "preamble" to the resolution. On May 15, the preamble was adopted, six to four, with three colonies abstaining. The preamble asked that all vestiges of crown rule be repudiated: "it appears absolutely irreconcilable to reason and good Conscience" to take an oath to the king, and it was necessary "that the exercise of every kind of authority under the said crown should be totally suppressed."

One factor may have hurried independence: the fear that European powers might attempt a partition of the colonies. Russia, Prussia, and Austria, after all, had partitioned Poland in 1772. Great Britain, out of desperation, could offer to restore Canada to France and the Floridas and other territory to Spain in return for their intervention. James H. Hutson (1972) makes a strong case that the patriots' concern that they may have to go to war with countries other than Great Britain affected the timing of independence. If the colonies were independent, they would have the status of a nation among nations; efforts at partitioning would be less likely, and, instead, the crowned heads of Europe might give assistance to the United States, without the appearance of abetting revolution.

Rumors floated in early 1776 that France had sent 30,000 troops to the West Indies; actually, the number was 3,000. Benjamin Franklin assured General Charles Lee in February that "the Troops sent to the W. Indies have no inimical Views to us or our Cause" and that France was planning to go to war with Great Britain, even "without a previous Declaration." Others disagreed. John Adams, in April, said that he feared that Great Britain and France "will part the Continent between them," and Patrick Henry wrote a month later: "The half of our Continent offered to France may induce her to aid our destruction, which she certainly has the power to accomplish." Hutson observes that by the end of June "the tensions and apprehensions about a partition treaty became pervasive, cropping out in brief, fugitive newspaper pieces" (p. 893).

Another concern influenced the timing of a declaration of independence. On March 1, 1776, the congressional "Association" for boycotting British goods expired, and, if Congress took no action, American ports would be opened to British imports. Congress could continue a boycott or, with immensely more advantage, declare independence, thus nullifying all British trade laws affecting the colonies and giving the American government the capacity to enter freely in trade agreements with foreign powers. Two enactments of Congress helped to further the break of the colonies from the British trade empire. On March 23 Congress, responding primarily to the British Prohibitory Act, resolved that "the inhabitants of these colonies be permitted to fit out armed vessels [privateers] to cruize on the enemies of these United Colonies." On April 6, Congress declared that all goods, except empty casks and staves, could be exported to any place in the world other than Great Britain or her "dominions." Imports were to be allowed, except for East India tea and staves, from anywhere other than the British empire.

Decision for Independence

On May 27, the Virginia and North Carolina delegates presented their instructions to Congress. The question of independence, however, did not reach the floor until June 7, when Richard Henry Lee made a motion that was seconded:

> Resolved, That these United Colonies are, and of right ought to be, free and independent States, that they are absolved from all allegiance to the British Crown, and that all political connection between them and the State of Great Britain is, and ought to be, totally dissolved.
>
> That it is expedient forthwith to take the most effectual measures for forming foreign Alliances.
>
> That a plan of confederation be prepared and transmitted to the respective Colonies for their consideration and approbation.

The first resolution was debated two days (June 8 and 10), and it was decided to postpone a vote until July 1. As Thomas Jefferson wrote: "It appearing in the course of these debates that the colonies of N. York, New Jersey, Pennsylvania, Delaware, Maryland & South Carolina were not matured for falling from the parent stem, but that they were fast advancing to that state."

So "that no time be lost," on June 11 Congress appointed a committee to prepare a declaration of independence, consisting of Jefferson, Franklin, John Adams, Roger Sherman, and Robert R. Livingston. The next day a committee of 13, headed by John Dickinson, was named to draw up articles of confederation. Franklin did not attend the several meetings of the declaration committe, having just returned from an exhausting journey to Montreal as one of Congress's commissioners to win over the French Canadians. Moreover, his gout was acting up again. The committee members agreed on the general topics for a declaration. Jefferson, entrusted with the writing of the declaration, as he himself said, did not have to seek out new ideas or arguments. For philosophical statement, Jefferson drew from memory the principles set forth by John Locke and other Enlightenment writers and from George Mason's Virginia "Declaration of Rights." The case against the king he readily derived from two documents he had written—the 1774 Summary View and the 1776 draft of a Virginia Constitution—along with the

Benjamin Franklin (1706-90),
envoy extraordinary, interna-
tionally recognized scientist,
and member of Congress,
served on the committee to
draft the Declaration of Independence and concluded his
public career as a delegate to
the Constitutional Convention
of 1787. This 1785 portrait is
by Charles Willson Peale.
*The Historical Society of Pennsylva-
nia, Philadelphia*

declarations and petitions of Congress and recently published newspaper articles listing grievances.

Jefferson presented the draft of the Declaration of Independence to Congress on Friday, June 28, having shown it to Adams and Franklin, who made only a few minor changes. On Monday, July 1, Congress again took up the Lee resolution. Since the debates of June 8 and 10 had been rather exhaustive, there was little interest in further discussion. Announcement that the Maryland convention had rescinded its prohibition of its delegates to vote for independence caused a stir; only the New York delegation was now forbidden to vote for independence. John Dickinson spoke at length, again asking for a delay. The notes for his speech have been preserved. Dickinson said that there was still a chance to end the bloodletting, but if independence were adopted, "the War will be carried on with more Severity," with "Letting Loose the Indians on our Frontiers" and the burning of towns. Dickinson, as did other conservatives, favored union before independence; "not only Treaties with foreign powers but among Ourselves should precede this Declaration. We should know on what Grounds We are to stand with Regard to one another." Congress should wait for further news from England, he cautioned, which might pave the way for reconciliation. Independence offered no immediate advantage, either in the matter of foreign assistance or of additional matériel for the army.

In midafternoon, three of the six newly elected delegates from New Jersey (Richard Stockton, John Witherspoon, and Francis Hopkinson) strolled into the congressional chamber, and, since they had not been present for the June debates, they "expressed a great desire to hear the arguments" regarding independence. As John Adams recorded in his *Autobiography:*

> All was Silence: No one would speak: all Eyes were turned upon me. Mr. Edward Rutledge came to me and said laughing, Nobody will speak but you, upon this Subject. You have all the Topicks so ready, that you must satisfy the Gentlemen from New Jersey. I answered him laughing, that it had so much the Air of exhibiting like an Actor or Gladiator for the Entertainment of the Audience, that I was ashamed to repeat what I had said twenty times before. . . . The New Jersey Gentlemen however still insisting on hearing at least a Recapitulation of the Arguments and no other Gentleman being willing to speak, I summed up the Reasons, Objections and Answers, in as concise a manner as I could, till at length the Jersey Gentlemen said they were fully satisfied and ready for the Question, which was then put and determined in the Affirmative.

Adams won praise for his extemporaneous discourse, which he regretted was not recorded. To Stockton, John Adams was "the Atlas of American Independence," and Jefferson commented that Adams was "our colossus on the floor . . . not graceful nor eloquent, nor remarkably fluent, but he came out occasionally with a power of thought and expression, that moved us from our seats."

Edward Rutledge asked that the official vote on independence be postponed for a day. Meanwhile, Congress took an informal poll of the delegations: Pennsylvania and South Carolina opposed independence; Delaware was divided; and New York abstained. Nine states gave a clear majority in favor of independence. On July 2 a vote was delayed in hopes that Caesar Rodney of Delaware would arrive in time to put his delegation in the affirmative. Late afternoon, after riding 80 miles through heavy rains, Rodney made his appearance. The evening before, Rutledge, in conference with other delegates, declared that he would switch his vote, thus putting South Carolina in the majority column. Robert Morris and John Dickinson decided to absent themselves from the Pennsylvania delegation, and James Wilson changed his vote from no to yes; Pennsylvania could now vote four to three for independence. With New York abstaining, the 12 colony delegations gave Congress a unanimous vote for independence.

Congress discussed and edited the Declaration of Independence on July 3 and during most of the next morning. It deleted about one-fourth of the text, including the paragraph denouncing the king for fostering the slave trade, thus abiding by the wishes of the South Carolina and Georgia delegates who wanted to keep the slave trade open. In all, Jefferson, Adams, Franklin, and Congress made 86 changes; 480 words were dropped, leaving 1,337 in the document. Congress made a major incision into the Jefferson draft by rewriting and reducing much of the last two paragraphs of the original document and inserting Lee's resolution. Certainly, the document was improved by deleting Jefferson's condemnation of the British people, which read in part:

> they are permitting their chief magistrate to send over not only soldiers of our common blood, but Scotch & foreign mercenaries to invade & deluge us in blood. These facts have given the last stab to agonizing affection, and manly spirit bids us

The Declaration of Independence by John Trumbull shows, standing at center, left to right, John Adams, Roger Sherman, Robert R. Livingston, Thomas Jefferson, and Benjamin Franklin.   *Yale University Art Gallery*

to renounce for ever these unfeeling brethren. We must endeavor to forget our former love for them. . . . we might have been a free & a great people together; but a communication of grandeur & of freedom it seems is below their dignity.

Historians dispute Jefferson's later assertion that some members of Congress signed the Declaration on July 4. Most likely John Hancock, as president of Congress, did affix his signature, and perhaps also Charles Thomson, as secretary. With the New York delegates now having presented authorization to vote for independence, Congress, on July 19, resolved that "the unanimous declaration of the thirteen United States of America . . . when engrossed [put into final copy], be signed by every member of Congress." On August 2 the engrossed Declaration was signed by current members of Congress, although it was not until November 4 that all had done so. About one-fourth of the signers had not been present in Congress on July 4, and some of these had not been delegates at the time. Meanwhile, the committee to prepare articles of confederation brought in a draft on July 12. However, it would not be in a final form to be submitted to the states until November 1777.

A Charter of National Liberty

Congress justified independence in the court of all humankind. The "charter of national liberty," as Julian P. Boyd (1945) calls the Declaration of Independence, owes its force as a legal document predicated on inherent rights. It states criteria in fundamental law for revolution, evidence, and pronouncement of judgment. Americans were the wronged party and had acted in self-defense. To obtain justice, they are forced to assume the status of an independent nation. As Garry Wills (1978) writes: "The Declaration announced the failure of reform by petition"; Congress, therefore "had to restate the grievances for which redress had been sought through constitutional channels" (p. 65). Not for any "light and transient causes," but because of "a long train of abuses and usurpations" by the ruling government, Americans were driven to revolution and independence.

The idea of a new national identity pervades the Declaration of Independence. Liberty is placed in the context of a people and not of individuals. The Declaration does not address the conflict of power within the colonies, but rather that of Americans collectively versus the king as head of the British nation and empire.

"The Spirit of '76"

The Declaration embraced the "Spirit of '76"—the appeal to heroism and sacrifice in the fight for a nation's freedom. The document was read before the troops and before public gatherings at courthouses throughout the colonies, enhancing morale in the defense of one's country. Benjamin Rush, a few days after his election to Congress on July 20, wrote General Charles Lee: "The declaration of independence has produced a new era in this part of America. The Militia of Pennsylvania seem to be actuated with a spirit more than Roman." The "Spirit of '76," of a nation upholding its independence and honor through force of arms, inspired not only the revolutionaries of 1776 but also generations of Americans, not the least being the sons of the Revolutionaries who sought to emulate their fathers in the second War of American Independence (the War of 1812). American independence and freedom were to be defended and proclaimed before the world.

The Revolution was conservative in the sense that it sought to restore as well as assert liberty that should have been guaranteed and protected by the mother country. By breaking with Great Britain, Americans sought to redefine their own identity and to achieve this end through unity and common purpose. Thomas C. Barrow (1968) has written that the war was fought for "colonial liberation." Once the independence movement "becomes an open contest of strength, other divisions tend to become obscured. . . . the advocates of independence submerge momentarily whatever differences they may have and present a common front. It is a time of common effort, of mutual support within the forces interested in achieving self-determination" (pp. 458–59).

To gain independence and preserve national liberty requires that a pledge be made "to each other our Lives, our Fortunes, and our sacred Honor." The Declaration of Independence, as does the "Spirit of '76," seems to say that American liberty is given meaning through sacrifice made in the defense against external foes. "By *revolution*," Charles Royster (1984) writes, the Americans meant primarily the act of establishing republican political principles embodied in their new governmental institutions, the citizens' virtuous sacrifice of self-interest to maintain these principles, and the vision of a happy national future that such a citizenry could attain. Revolution established its primacy through the voluntary allegiance of Americans who understood the threat of permanent enslavement by Britain if they failed to resist. Voluntarism—free choice—was supposed to create a republican nation. . . . Yet even while invoking this ideal, Revolutionary rhetoric also resorted to another American claim to solidarity: the communal experience of violence. By contrasting the doctrine of voluntarism with the appeal to bloodshed, we can see the ways in which Americans, though aspiring to create a unique republic, nevertheless portrayed themselves in one of the oldest guises—a people at war. (pp. 27–28)

Thomas Jefferson's Document

Jefferson did not intend that his document would include an enumeration of rights; he was simply making the case that the usurpations and abuses of power by the king were justification for independence. Hence, he refers only to the "self-evident" truths of men being created equal and entitled to rights, among which were "Life, Liberty, and the pursuit of Happiness." It is government, with powers "derived" from the people, that protects rights. The people collectively, not as individuals, hold government responsible for the trusteeship of their rights, and, if government becomes "destructive of these ends, it is the Right of the People to alter or to abolish it, and to institute new Government." To resort to revolution is itself a right. Jefferson seems to be saying that majority will is the determining factor. Of course, man is entitled to the basic dignity of the human condition, but there is no recourse to the protection of rights except through the expression of the majority will or, in extreme necessity, revolution by the people, presumably representing a large number of the population.

Bernard Wishy (1958) notes a similarity between Jefferson's Declaration of Independence and the political theories of John Locke in reference to popular sovereignty and revolution. "Locke leaves us with a denial of the right of individual rebellion against the majority but not of revolution by *a people* against unjust rulers." The Declaration of Independence "says nothing about limits on a people itself. . . . Aside from the single mention of the rights of men in the famous second paragraph, all the references to the colonists are with collective nouns or plural pronouns. The evidence of the text establishes only the people as the source of political power and political change" (pp. 419–20).

Two significant critiques of the Declaration of Independence were immediately published in England: Thomas Hutchinson's *Strictures upon the Declaration of Congress at Philadelphia in a Letter to a Noble Lord* and John Lind's *An Answer to the Declaration of the American Congress*. Both pamphlets were concerned mainly with questioning the justifiability and accuracy of the complaints registered against the crown. Hutchinson's work reads like an apologia for British policy and laws during the period when he was a Massachusetts government official. He considers it absurd that Americans complained about their petitions being ignored in England, while "under the present free government in America, no man may, by writing or speaking, contradict any part of this Declaration, without being deemed an enemy to his country, and exposed to the rage and fury of the populace." Both Hutchinson and Lind question the premises set forth in the preamble of the Declaration. Hutchinson asserts that the colonies, "*politically* considered, never were a *distinct* people from the kingdom." Lind points to the contradiction between "self-evident" rights "to *enjoy* life, to *enjoy* liberty, and to *pursue* happiness" and the assumption that to secure these rights "Governments should be instituted." The Americans did not realize

> that nothing which can be called Government ever was, or ever could be, in any instance, exercised, but at the expence of one or other of those rights.—That, consequently, in as many instances as Government is ever exercised, some one or other of these rights, pretended to be unalienable, is actually alienated.

All that Jefferson is really saying, however, is that society exists to protect a people in the enjoyment of their rights and that men do not give up all of their sovereignty. Thus, persons may join with others to throw off tyranny.

Jefferson had hoped that the Declaration of Independence would carry the message of the universality of freedom and equality. The existence of slavery in America gave such an appeal a hollow ring; one-third of the signers were slaveholders. To members of Congress the right to property was a most cherished right, and, of course, slaves were property. Jefferson had wanted to put blame for American slavery on the British crown and was shocked when Congress deleted the long paragraph condemning the king for promoting the slave trade.

To Jefferson there was a distinction between those who were born within society and those who were not. In his definition of slavery, Africans held in bondage were "out of the protection of the laws" and, therefore, were not part of the social compact. Jefferson himself believed that slavery was wrong, but he did not quite know how to abolish it. He supported gradual emancipation, accompanied by the removal of the freed slaves from the white man's society. In 1770 he had argued in a court case that the child of a mulatto mother should be freed: "Under the law of nature all men are born free." In his second draft of a constitution for Virginia (1776), he put in a clause, which was rejected: "No person hereafter coming into this country shall be held in slavery under any pretext whatever." Although Jefferson did regard Africans as having certain inferior mental and physical qualities as compared to the white man, he thought such a view needed to be proved by scientific investigation.

Born equal, regardless of race, did not mean an equality of talent, mental and physical capabilities, or even opportunity. Jefferson, as did John Adams and others, believed in a "natural aristocracy." Interestingly, Congress struck from Jefferson's rough draft of the Declaration the word "independent" from the phrase "all men are created equal & independent."

The two British critics of the Declaration emphasized the obvious contradictions concerning equality. Hutchinson said that he would like to ask southern congressmen how they would justify "the depriving of more than one hundred thousand Africans of their rights to liberty and the pursuit of happiness, and in some degree to their lives, if these rights are so unalienable." John Lind took issue with the charge that the king "has excited domestic insurrections amongst us"—an allusion to Lord Dunmore's promise of freedom to slaves who would fight for the British:

> But how did his Majesty's Governors excite domestic insurrections? Did they set father against son, or son against father, or brother against brother? No—they offered *freedom* to the *slaves* of these assertors of liberty. Were it not true, that the charge was fully justified by the necessity, to which the rebellious proceedings of the Complainants had reduced the Governor, yet with what face can *they* urge this as a proof of tyranny? Is it for *them* to say, that it is tyranny to bid a slave be free? to bid him take courage, to rise and assist in reducing his tyrants to a due obedience to *law?* to hold out as a motive to him, that the load which crushed his limbs shall be lightened; that the whip which harrowed up his back shall be broken, that he shall be raised to the rank of a freeman and a citizen? It is their boast that they have taken up arms in support of these their own *self-evident truths*—that all men are created *equal*"—that all men are endowed with the *unalienable* rights of life, *liberty,* and the *pursuit of happiness.*" Is it for *them* to complain *of the offer of freedom* held out to these wretched beings? of the offer of reinstating them in that *equality* which, in this very paper, is declared to be the *gift of God to all;* in those *unalienable* rights, with which, in this very paper, God is declared to have *endowed all* mankind?

The rights mentioned in the Declaration, those of life, liberty, and the pursuit of happiness, are inclusive of particular rights possessed by human beings. Jefferson may have omitted the right to property because it was part of each of the general rights named. He may also have felt that the right to property derived more from the state than from nature. Moreover, reference to the right to property would conflict with the colonies' policy in sequestering royal land grants.

Although Jefferson would not deny that each person in society should be protected in fulfilling his or her physiological needs for food, shelter, and clothing, he had in mind, as did his contemporaries, that pursuit of happiness meant freedom to participate and share in public affairs. Society had no obligation to obtain happiness, but only to allow its pursuit. To the pursuit of happiness Jefferson would add another ingredient—development of intellect. For this end it was incumbent on government to encourage the diffusion of knowledge. In his *Notes on the State of Virginia* (written in 1781), Jefferson advised that the young be taught "how to work out their own greatest happiness, by shewing them that it does not depend on the condition of life in which chance has placed them, but is always the result of a good conscience, good health, occupation, and freedom in all just pursuits." The Declaration suggests no distinction between private welfare and public happiness. Later, the founding fathers would consider guarantees of personal rights, distinguished from public freedom, as in the Bill of Rights.

Jefferson's list of "a long train of abuses and usurpations" (to which he had appended in the rough draft, "begun at a distinguished period"—1763) is centered on the king. He makes only two direct references to Parliament: "He has combined with others to subject us to a jurisdiction foreign to our constitution . . . giving his Assent to their Acts of pretended Legislation"; and in the next to last paragraph, in conjunction with the only mention of the British people, "our British brethren"—"We have warned them . . . of attempts by their legislature to extend an unwarrantable jurisdiction over us."

The Declaration's bill of indictment against the king has four categories: articles 1 through 12—executive actions interfering with colonial governments and liberties; 13 through 22—assent to wrongful legislative acts; 23 through 27—recent actions (1775–76) of making war on the colonies; and number 28—refusal to hear the colonial petitions. Many of the charges are exaggerated and distorted as to actual fact. More properly, much of the indictment should have been brought against Parliament. But, of course, it was the king who was on trial, and he was guilty by his collusion with Parliament as well as by his own deeds.

The conclusion of the Declaration states that the right to revolution is being exercised. It is nationhood that is being proclaimed by the Congress "in the Name and by Authority of the good People of these Colonies." The colonies are now "FREE AND INDEPENDENT STATES," and as such have sovereign powers. The decision has been in the performance of solemn and sacred duty. There is confidence in the fulfillment of American destiny.

PART 2

The Revolutionary War, 1776–1783

CHAPTER 7

The Washington–Howe Campaigns

 Americans had reason to be confident in their resort to arms. Militia and Continentals had been successful in the North and South against royal troops, and even Bunker Hill had been a victory of sorts. In addition, the British had to evacuate Boston and withdrew from Charleston harbor. Although patriot forces had failed in Canada, so had Carleton's counterinvasion down Lake Champlain. Both the British and Americans looked to the remainder of 1776 and 1777 to strike blows that would end the war.

Advantage and Strategy

While the British had a large navy and a professional soldiery, the Americans had nearly every other advantage. Throughout the war the British government never committed enough troops for a full conquest. Recruitment was so difficult in England that in 1775 the total number of British soldiers, at home and abroad, amounted to only 48,000. By 1781, however, the army's strength had increased to 110,000 men (56,000 of whom were in the West Indies). The largest troop strength (British, loyalist, and German) in North America during the war was for the year 1780—38,000. Although Washington's army seldom matched the numbers of the enemy as to present and fit for duty, there was a large reservoir of manpower on which to draw. The Continental army never exceeded 17,000 effectives at all its locations, yet more than twice that number were usually enlisted. Militia turned out in large numbers in areas where the fighting took place, and militia units also assisted the Continental army. Both Heitman's *Historical Register* and the Department of Defense estimate that, of American men of fighting age, about 250,000 actually bore arms for the rebel cause, about 100,000 of whom were Continentals.

Initially, the British government believed that the colonies could be conquered with the support of that large segment of the population disaffected with the Revolution. This was not an unrealistic view, but any such success would depend on effecting the large-scale occupation of territory or at least on holding key posts over a broad area. Although the patriot war effort seemed to be backed by a relatively united populace, in actuality a majority of Americans, if not against the Revolution, were not necessarily for it. Many went with the tide—with whichever force could demonstrate it was winning and able to control territory. The British however, elected to fight a limited war, thus, their effectual occupation of large areas was all but impossible.

The Americans had an advantage in possessing a more effective command system. There were no competing high-level departments of government, even though Congress had its boards and committees. Washington had to answer to Congress, but he was given independence in conducting military operations. As commander in chief, he directed the main army; the Northern army and later the Southern army would also be independent, though they, too, were accountable to Congress. Both the American and British armies had to face the complexities of logistics and contracting for war matériel, but the American armies adhered to a clearer line of responsibility than did the British military forces.

The British system for military administration was multifaceted. From 1770 to 1778 the British army in Great Britain had no head other than the king, who was captain-general of all military forces. Normally, the king delegated his military authority to a prominent general. From 1778 to 1782 Lord Jeffery Amherst served as the officiating commander in chief, under the title of general on the staff. This office was primarily one for consultation on all military matters. The British war administration lacked coordination and often worked at cross purposes. There was always rivalry between the army and the navy. The British cabinet had overall reponsibility for determining military policy. Below the cabinet, four executive departments—Treasury, Board of Ordnance, Admiralty, and Army—each had their own bailiwick. The secretary at war rarely was involved in military policy decisions, his duties being chiefly administrative and financial. Actually, the man who had the greatest power in managing the war was Lord Germain, secretary of state for America. Germain enjoyed the support of the king. It was indeed a twist of fate that Britain's military leader had been convicted by court martial for disobedience at the battle of Minden (1759) and sentenced never to serve again in any army capacity. Seven of the 16 men on the court martial had voted for a sentence of death for Germain.

The British did not have an edge over the Americans in the quality of its officer corps either. It was unfortunate for the British cause early in the war that Sir William Howe and his brother, Lord Richard Howe, had been made peace commissioners as well as placed in the American military command. Their dual roles prevented them from pursuing either peace or war with full vigor. Although many British officers of high merit served in America and there was allowance for earned promotions, officer commissions were simply bought and sold in the British army. Most American general and field grade officers had fought in the last war and at one time or another had experience in recruiting their own men.

Various factors worked against British military success. Logistically, British armies had to depend substantially on supply from abroad, and they had limited opportunity for foraging. Americans had the advantage of interior lines—the ability to employ forces against an enemy faster than the enemy could make a countermove and lack of a barrier at their rear. Having interior lines also meant that they could maintain lateral communications and freedom for a wide range of movement. The Americans could afford to fight a defensive war, wearing down the enemy. In defending their own country, they had the capability of spontaneous mobilization and the availability of a wide range of economic resources.

The British decision for war entailed high risk. As John Wilkes warned, the Americans "will dispute every inch of territory with you, every narrow pass, every strong defile, every Thermopylae, every Bunker's Hill." With the difficulties of achieving victory, why did the king and majority of Parliament insist on prosecuting the war? As Richard M. Ketchum (1971) sees it, an overriding consideration, to borrow a later phrase, was the domino theory. Thus, the king could say in 1779 that, if America were to be independent, the West Indies would become "dependent" on America. "Ireland would soon follow, and this island reduced to itself, would be a poor island indeed."

The strategy of Howe's army, 1776–77, consisted of a conventional war of posts that aimed at conquest of territory instead of destroying Washington's army. The larger strategy included revival of the invasion from Canada and occupation of New York City, Philadelphia, east New Jersey, and Newport, Rhode Island. The British navy could be used for coastal raiding. Thus, New England and the middle colonies would be placed in a vise, with further options for expanding invasion into these areas. The British strategy, however, was shortsighted. It did not perceive the need for a political as well as a military strategy, notably, the establishing of rival governments. Moreover, it failed to coordinate military operations between Howe's army and the invading force from Canada. British naval units aided the land forces and thus neglected enforcing the blockade; American privateers managed to take a heavy toll of British shipping.

Realizing that success would not result from a war of posts, Howe, in 1777, decided it was necessary to provoke a direct confrontation with Washington's army. Thus, on January 20, he wrote Germain that there was no "prospect of terminating the war but by a general action." Yet, he soon lost his resolve, and during May–December Howe alternated between decisive battle and maneuver.

Washington was himself in search of a strategy. During 1775–76 he followed a strategic defensive that emphasized fortifications and inviting the British to attack as they did at Bunker Hill. After the battle of Long Island, the American commander in chief avoided pitched engagements, except at Brandywine. During most of the war, with British forces concentrated in the North in New York City, Washington preferred a war of attrition, attacking the enemy at their posts and interrupting their means of supply.

Retreat from New York

New York, along with New York City and the Hudson River, wrote John Adams to Washington in January 1776, formed "a Kind of Key to the whole Continent, as it is a Passage to Canada to the Great Lakes and to all the Indians Nations." A large harbor bay made New York City of utmost importance as a base for naval and army operations. Congress determined to hold the city, and Washington, with the assistance of General Charles Lee and others, shored up defensive positions along the banks of the Hudson, Harlem, and East rivers. Washington made the most extensive preparations on northwest Long Island, overlooking the one-mile channel of the East River between Brooklyn and New York City (on Manhattan Island). Washington stationed about half his army—5,800 troops, two-thirds of whom were militia—on a three- to four-mile stretch of the Heights of Guian. General Israel Putnam, who had no real knowledge of the terrain, at the last minute replaced General Nathanael Greene as the commander of the American force on Long Island.

For more than a month, Howe had been readying the British army that he had brought from Halifax to Staten Island to attack New York City. On August 22, the British conducted an amphibious landing on the beach of Gravesend Bay, at the southwest end of Long Island, eight miles from Washington's lines. On August 27 Howe deployed three divisions: General James Grant and 5,000 men up the Gowanus Road along the coast; General von Heister and 6,000 Hessians toward the American center through Flatbush Pass (present-day Prospect Park); and Generals Clinton, Percy, and Cornwallis, with 10,000 troops, on a turning movement on the American left in the Flatlands through Jamaica Pass, which was guarded by only a five-man patrol. Putnam sent troops forward under Generals John Sullivan and Lord Stirling (William Alexander, an American who had claimed a Scottish earldom). The enveloping actions of all three British divisions set the Americans to flight. At the battle of Long Island, the Americans lost over 1,400 men—312 killed and the rest wounded or captured—and both Stirling and Sullivan were made prisoners of war. The British had about 63 dead, 314 injured wounded and missing.

Instead of pressing a final assault on the American lines, Howe rested his army. With heavy rain over the next two days, Howe's troops, with bayonets drawn, undoubtedly could have overrun the American works. The Americans, however, had higher ground, and Howe was afraid of another Bunker Hill. On the night of August 29–30, under cover of a dense fog, Washington performed a near miracle. Having gathered all the small craft as he could, the American commander had the troops from Long Island ferried across to Manhattan Island, largely through the dexterity of John Glover's and Israel Hutchinson's regiments of New England fishermen. Howe learned of the evacuation, but did nothing until it was too late. He had missed the opportunity to capture half of the American army. Writes Sir John Fortescue, historian of the British army (1911):

Indeed, so obvious was the opportunity that Howe's neglect of it was ascribed less to incapacity than to desire to promote certain negotiations for peace, which had been recently opened by Lord Howe, under special powers, with Congress. Lord Howe's overtures were of course rejected. The capture of Washington's army might have made them welcome: not so its escape. No mistake is more common

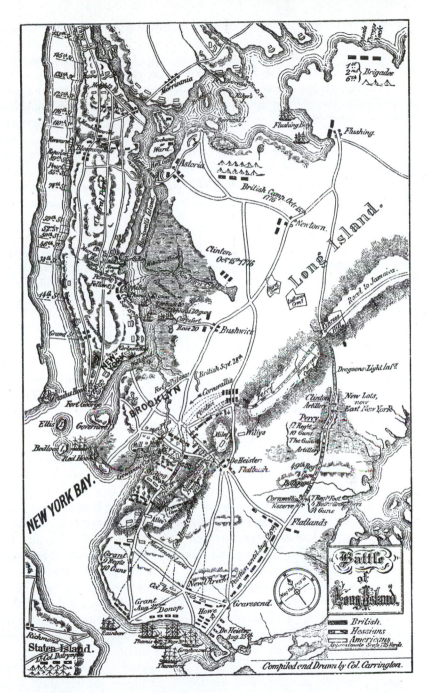

Battle of Long Island   *Source: Henry B. Carrington, Battle Maps and Charts of the American Revolution (New York: A. S. Barnes & Co., 1881), p. 17.*

nor more fatal in British statesmen than the attempt to wage war on the principles of peace. (p. 188)

Howe now decided to push the American army off Manhattan Island. This decision went against the advice of General Clinton, who recommended a major landing at Kingsbridge at the northern tip of the 13-mile island, which would have prevented an American escape over the Harlem River. If the British ships could cut a channel through the American-laid obstructions in the Hudson River and also patrol the East River, Washington's army could well have been sealed off on Manhattan. On September 15 the British debarked in force at Kip's Bay (34th Street). The American troops in the area, mostly militia, quickly fled just as Washington arrived on the scene. General George Weedon described the predicament, in a letter of September 20:

> The General was so exasperated that he struck Several Officers in their flight, three times dashed his hatt on the Ground, and at last exclaimed, "Good God, have I got such Troops as These!" It was with difficulty his friends could get him to quit the field, so great was his emotions. He however got off safe, and all the troops as you may think.

The American army stretched across the plateau of Harlem Heights in three lines: at present-day 147th Street, 153d Street, and 182d Street—between the rocky cliffs of Fort Washington on the Hudson and the Harlem River. On September 16, Washington sent a reconnoitering party under Captain Thomas Knowlton into the Hollow Way south of the American lines. Major Andrew Leitch and the Virginia 3rd regiment were sent to defend a pass, in assistance to Knowlton's Connecticut troops. The Americans engaged a British detachment in a buckwheat field (present-day 116th Street), and the enemy, as Weedon said, "got Cursedly thrashed," though both Leitch and Knowlton were mortally wounded. The battle of Harlem Heights was hardly more than a skirmish, but it vindicated the courage of troops who had a day before fled from the British.

Howe hesitated to resume an offensive, awaiting reinforcements and being reluctant to assault Washington's well-entrenched position on Harlem Heights. Just past midnight on September 21, a fire began at a wharf and, propelled by strong winds, swept through one-fourth of New York City, destroying 439 houses. Actually, Congress had prevented Washington from burning the city, on the grounds that American troops would be returning to it. The destruction greatly deprived the British of needed quarters for soldiers and refugee Tories. Suspicion for setting the conflagration fell on "some Rebels, who lurked about the Town," as Ambrose Serle, Howe's secretary, noted. Persons "were caught with Matches, and Fire-balls about them." One such culprit "was knocked down by a Grenadier & thrown into the Flames for his Reward: Another, who was found cutting off the Handles of the Water-Buckets . . . was first hung up by the Neck till he was dead and afterwards by the Heels upon a Sign-Post by the Sailors." Yet a conspiracy for starting the fire was never proved.

On October 12, British transports carried Howe's army to Throg's Neck, an isthmus in the East River, above the American lines. Finding the area too marshy and soon facing 1,800 opposing troops, the British army moved three miles northward to Pell's Point, where it fought with a small American force. The encounter served as a delaying action, allowing Washington's army to escape being trapped on Manhattan Island. Howe waited at New Rochelle until reinforced by 8,000 Hessian troops. Washington's army followed Howe laterally and took position on the hills above White Plains. Again Howe avoided a frontal attack, and on October 28 he sent the main British force across the Bronx River to attack the American right on Chatterton's Hill. General Alexander McDougall and Continentals and militia fought furiously before leaving the hill. Washington immediately withdrew to the next series of hills at North Castle. The battle of White Plains again had been a limited victory for the British commander. It seemed that the war was becoming one of maneuver.

Learning that Howe was returning to Manhattan, Washington divided his army, leaving Charles Lee with 5,000 men at North Castle and William Heath and 4,000 troops at Peekskill to guard the entrance into the Highlands. Washington took 5,000 men across the Hudson into New Jersey. Still unwilling to give up entirely a Bunker Hill strategy, Washington retained Fort Washington in upper Manhattan (present-day 184th Street), perched on a cliff 230 feet above the Hudson River. The post was now behind British lines. It had deficiencies—no water except from the Hudson, no palisades, and practically no outworks. Howe doubled back from White Plains to attack the fort. British vessels had already breeched the chevaux-de-frise (heavy-timbered boxes with iron spikes, sunk in the river to rip open the hulls of ships) and opened fire on the fort. On November 16, Colonel Robert Magaw surrendered Fort Washington to the British, along with its 2,800-man garrison.

With uncharacteristic alacrity, Howe sent Cornwallis over the Hudson to seize Fort Lee (opposite from Fort Washington) and to attack Washington's army. Fort Lee, with its 2,000 troops evacuated, was captured on November 20. Cornwallis gave up the chase when Washington's troops crossed the Delaware on December 7–8. Cornwallis's army now went into winter cantonment in New Jersey: the Hessians at Bordentown and Trenton, and the British at Princeton, New Brunswick, Maidenhead, Kingston, and Amboy. The line of armed camps in New Jersey could protect foraging parties. On November 30 Howe issued a proclamation that all rebels who put down their arms and swore allegiance to the king would be pardoned; British troops in New Jersey could offer protection to those who chose the British side. Howe also sent a military force to occupy Newport, Rhode Island. He had accomplished his strategic objectives for 1776. Yet Washington's army was intact, and opportunities to annihilate it had been missed.

"These are the times that try men's souls," wrote Thomas Paine in his first *Crisis* paper during the American retreat through New Jersey. Most enlistments in the Continental army expired at the end of the year, and a morale booster was needed in order to induce soldiers to stay in service. Washington had underestimated the enemy during the New York campaign, and Howe now demonstrated that he could make the same mistake. Each of the British garrisons in New Jersey presented an excellent opportunity for Washington to perform a coup de main. The American commander received new troops: 2,000 men who had been commanded by Lee, who himself had been captured by a British patrol at Basking Ridge, New Jersey; 500 troops brought in by General Gates; and 1,000 Philadelphia militia led by Colonel John Cadwalader.

Trenton and Princeton

Surprise was a key element in attacking any of the British garrisons, so as not to allow enemy troops from the various posts to group en masse. Obviously, the three Hessian regiments stationed across the Delaware River at Trenton made a fine target. Washington planned the assault for dawn on December 26. The Hessians would be celebrating the German two-day Christmas. Although the Hessian commander, Colonel Johann Rall, kept many of his troops on alert during the holidays, he let his guard down somewhat because of one incident. General Adam Stephen, without consulting Washington, on December 25 sent a small detachment commanded by Captain George Wallis over the river to test the enemy's outer pickets and to exact revenge from the Hessians for having killed one of Stephen's men in a boat. The American detachment fought briefly with Hessian guards and escaped. Rall, who had been warned that Washington was about to attempt some kind of action, concluded that the affair of December 25 had been the subject of his intelligence. The next day, Washington, descending with his troops on Trenton, was shocked to find Stephen's men wandering aimlessly, and he feared that they had given away any chance of a surprise. Actually, their contact with the enemy the day before had a contrary effect.

At dusk of Christmas Day, Washington, with 2,400 troops of Greene's and Sullivan's divisions, began the passage over the river in Durham boats (commercial vessels, 40 by 60 feet, 2 feet deep, with pointed keels). The river at the point of departure at McKonkey's Ferry had only thin cakes of ice, but a snow–sleet storm setting in at about 11 P.M. impeded the transit, and the troops were not entirely over until 4 A.M. The plan had called for two other crossings further down the river: General James Ewing, with 1,000 men, to move directly over to Trenton and to block a southward retreat by the Hessians at Assunpink Creek; and Colonel John Cadwalader and 2,000 troops, mostly militia, to go six miles below Trenton and attack the Hessian garrison at Bordentown as a diversion. Since the ice was thicker downriver from where Washington crossed, Ewing did not make it to the New Jersey side and Cadwalader arrived too late to be of service.

Debarking nine miles above Trenton, Washington split his troops into two prongs: Sullivan on the right taking the River Road and Greene on the left marching down Scotch Road. As the force approached Trenton, Stephen, Matthias de Fermoy, and Stirling circled around the town southward to Assunpink Creek in order to block an escape route. American artillery placed at the heads of the streets, a crossfire from Sullivan's and Greene's troops, and confusion in the orders given by

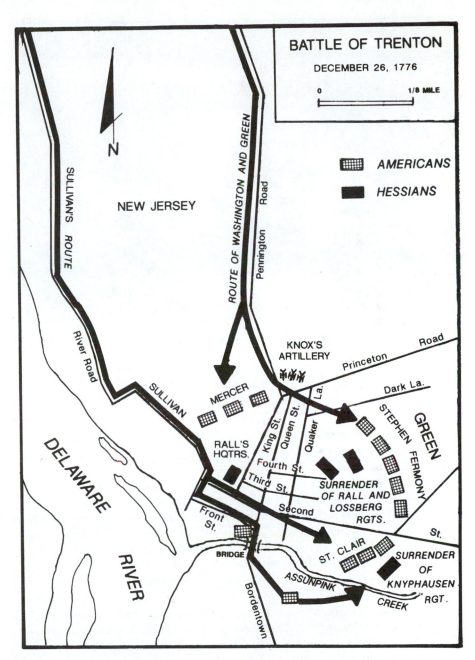

Battle of Trenton   *Drawing by Paul D. Kersey, Jr.*

John Trumbull's painting *The Capture of the Hessians at Trenton* reveals the actual likenesses of the key participants. Among the group, starting to the immediate right of Washington (seated on horse), are Generals John Sullivan, Nathanael Greene, and Henry Knox.   *Yale University Art Gallery*

Colonel Rall contributed to the quick American victory. Rall was mortally wounded. Casualties were remarkably minimal; the Hessians lost 23 killed and 83 wounded, and the Americans four dead and eight injured. Although 653 Hessians escaped, the Americans took 918 prisoners.

Trenton was a clear victory for Washington's army and gave renewed hope for the American cause, earning Washington respect at home and abroad. Though never a skilled tactician, he was good at improvisation. Henry Knox, whose artillerists played an important role at Trenton, wrote his wife: "Providence seemed to have smiled upon every part of the enterprise. Great advantages may be gained from it if we take the proper steps." Congressman Richard Henry Lee wrote General Stephen that "the *genius of America* seems now to be awakening from profound sleep."

Still, the army faced a crisis. Most of the Continentals would go home in January, leaving Washington with less than 2,000 regulars. Congressional bounties and the renewed confidence in the American army, however, eventually spurred enlistments, so that by late May 1777 Washington could count on over 8,000 Continental troops.

Having returned to Pennsylvania on December 27, Washington crossed the Delaware for the second time several days later. He had hopes of striking at another British garrison in New Jersey before going into winter quarters at Morristown.

Howe, shocked from the disaster at Trenton, ordered Cornwallis to collect the British-German troops in New Jersey and advance on Washington's army. At the second battle of Trenton, January 2, a small American force under Colonels Charles Scott and Edward Hand, posted halfway between Trenton and Princeton, conducted a running battle with British light infantry and Hessian jägers. The Americans steadily retreated through the woods between Princeton Road and Assunpink Creek. The fight continued on through Trenton, with the detachment finally finding refuge within Washington's lines.

Cornwallis planned to attack Washington the next day. A British officer warned: "My Lord, if you trust those people tonight, you will see nothing of them in the morning." Risking defeat if he stayed put or losing face if he retreated to Pennsylvania, Washington decided on maneuver. During the night of January 2, leaving campfires burning and 400 men behind as decoys, Washington took his army around Trenton and headed for Princeton. Belatedly discovering the American ruse, Cornwallis gave chase. As Washington's army came near Princeton, General Hugh Mercer's advanced party collided in an orchard with Lieutenant Colonel Charles Mawhood's regiments, who were on their way to join Cornwallis. Against a British bayonet charge, Mercer's troops fled, and Mercer himself was mortally wounded. Mawhood escaped through the woods, though 200 of his men were captured. Washington had hoped to stay ahead of Cornwallis and attack New Brunswick, but his men were too exhausted, and thus he led the Americans to high ground at Morristown for winter encampment. The British withdrew from New Jersey, except for posts at Amboy and New Brunswick. Significantly, the New Jersey campaign of the fall and early winter of 1776–77 showed how difficult it was for the British to hold territory.

A Season of Attrition

Morristown was ideally suited for the American winter cantonment. The small village, perched on a high plateau, was surrounded by hills and mountains. Here Washington could rebuild the army while keeping watch on British movements. The army was close enough to be on the flank of any British offensive up the Hudson or by land against Philadelphia. Washington kept light infantry in the field below the encampment to attack any roving British detachments, especially to prevent provisions and forage from coming into British hands. The British took a repeated pounding. Between January 6 and May 26, 1777, troops led by Charles Scott, William Maxwell, and others, together with independent militia, fought no less than 44 skirmishes, some of which were battle-scale. Casualties were high, and each side accused the other of wanton brutality. So successful was the American harassment that British garrisons suffered extreme hardship; insufficient diet resulted in scurvy and other illnesses. And without hay, horses could not be fed.

Washington learned the value of light infantry (so called because they traveled with the minimum of equipment and arms and could serve as both cavalrymen and infantrymen). Light infantry had been a missing component in the New York campaign of 1776. At Morristown, Washington designated one company from each regiment, on a revolving basis, as light infantry. The activity on the Jersey plains served to boost morale and made American soldiers more proficient in the art of war. General Adam Stephen, who had general charge of the operations, said that his "Division" was an "excellent school for a young soldier. We only fight eight or ten times a week—in short I have got my men in such spirits—that they only ask when the enemy come out and where they are—without enquiring into their numbers and so fall on." Charles Scott, promoted to brigadier general in April, had good advice for his men at the battle of Drake's Farm (near Metuchen, New Jersey), February 1: "Take care now and fire low bring down your pieces fire at their legs, one man Wounded in the leg is better than a dead one for it takes two more to carry him off and there is three gone leg them dam 'em I say leg them." Wrote British Lieutenant Colonel William Harcourt of the fighting in New Jersey, the Americans, though they "seem to be ignorant of the precision and order, and even of the principles, by which large bodies are moved," have "some of the requisites for making good Troops, such as extreme cunning, great industry in moving ground and felling of wood, activity and a spirit of enterprise upon any advantage . . . they are now become a formidable enemy."

Washington was tempted to do as the British commander had done—to establish outposts in New Jersey. Washington did station General Benjamin Lincoln and 500 men at Bound Brook, seven miles up the Raritan River from the substantial British garrison at New Brunswick. On April 12 Cornwallis made a surprise attack on the town, hoping to revenge the Trenton defeat, but after a sharp action Lincoln escaped with most of his troops. The British conducted raids into the countryside beyond the area covered by the American Continentals, and Tory militia were increasingly becoming a problem. General Stephen, as General Charles Lee had done before, tried to impress on Washington the necessity of securing as much of the state as possible. Stephen advocated an assault on the 1,200 Tory militia stationed in Bergen County. It was more important to keep the Continentals together, Washington replied: "To protect every Town, and every individual on this wide extended Continent is a pleasure that never can be realized. . . . it becomes me to place the Continental Troops in such a manner to answer a more valuable purpose than to give the Shadow (for it is no more) of security, to particular Neighbourhoods."

For summer campaigning, Washington considered his army of sufficient strength to offer battle on his own terms. On May 29 the American force shifted to Middlebrook, 20 miles to the south of Morristown. Here in the foothills of the Watchung Mountains, only eight miles from New Brunswick, Washington waited for Howe's next move. The British commander wanted to lure Washington out into the plains for a pitched battle. Assembling 18,000 men at Amboy, Howe, on June 12, set out in two columns and formed an eight-mile line. Although there was fighting between British and American forward units, Washington did not take the bait. All of a sudden, on June 19 Howe marched back to New Brunswick, and on June 29 the army embarked for Staten Island.

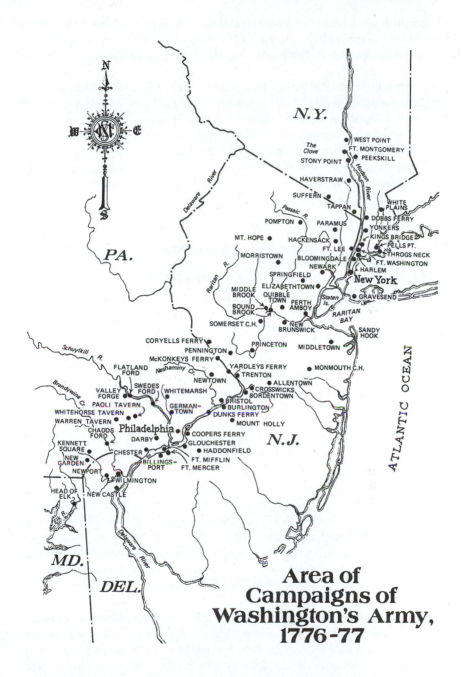

Area of Campaigns of Washington's Army, 1776-77

Area of Campaigns of Washington's Army, 1776–1777   *Drawing by Paul Nickerson, Richmond (Virginia) City Planning Commission.*

The British army boarded transports, and identifying the destination became a guessing game: the upper Hudson to assist a British invasion from Canada or Philadelphia by sea. Anticipating the first possibility, Washington moved his army to Smith's Clove, a pass in the Palisades near West Point. Howe did not appear, and Washington's footsore soldiers trekked back to New Jersey. With the British fleet being sighted off the Delaware capes on July 29, Washington took post at Germantown, just outside of Philadelphia. Again there was no enemy, and the American army started for the Hudson, though soon learning that the British were off the Maryland coast and then at the Virginia capes. Washington encamped at Neshaminy Creek, 20 miles north of Philadelphia. At last news came that, on August 25, the British had debarked on the Maryland shore at the head of Chesapeake Bay. Certainly, Philadelphia was Howe's objective. The British army had been aboard ship for 45 days.

Campaign for Philadelphia

Washington advanced his troops to Chads Ford on Brandywine Creek to block a British march on Philadelphia. Sullivan's division guarded the fords immediately to the north. Militia were stationed downstream, although a British crossing there was not likely because of the steep banks. Congress had fled Philadelphia, going to Lancaster and then to York.

On September 3 Howe marched out of Head of Elk (Elkton), Maryland. William Maxwell's Continental light infantry fought with Hessian troops at Iron Hill (Cooch's Bridge) on Christiana Creek. A week later the enemy stopped at Kennett Square, Pennsylvania, six miles directly west of Chads Ford. The two armies were about equal in size—the American, 11,000 and the British, 12,500. On September 11 the British army marched in two columns: Baron Wilhelm von Knyphausen with 5,000 men to Chads Ford, and Cornwallis and Howe and the rest of the army six miles up the Brandywine, outflanking Washington's right and crossing the creek. Washington had faulty reconnaissance and was caught entirely by surprise at the wide British turning movement. He hastened Greene's and Sullivan's divisions to meet the British attack on the right. Heavy fighting ensued in the vicinity of Birmingham Meeting House Hill. The Americans fought stubbornly but were forced to retreat. As it was now nightfall, Cornwallis halted his army and was joined by Knyphausen's men who had finally broken through at Chads Ford. American losses were 200 killed, 500 wounded and 400 captured; the British had 90 fatalities and 448 wounded.

Howe had shown the same tactical ability and swift movement that he had at the battle of Long Island. Again it was a wide envelopment that carried the day. Although Howe won a clear victory at Brandywine, he also missed another opportunity to destroy Washington's army. Johann von Ewald, a Hessian officer, commented that "had General Howe set out two hours earlier, or marched faster, Washington's army would have been caught between two fires, and could have been cut off from the Schuylkill and completely destroyed." On the other hand, Ewald also noted that the British stayed on the battlefield overnight and failed to send

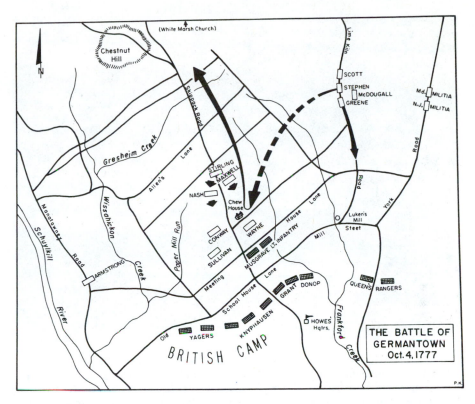

Battle of Germantown   *Drawing by Paul D. Kersey, Jr.*

troops in pursuit or to set up outposts; "if Washington had been such a great man as they proclaimed him to be . . . and had returned during the night, he would have been able to recover everything lost, double and triple."

Washington did elect to come back and fight again. He arranged his army at the crest of hills facing the Chester Valley, and Howe accepted the challenge. But a torrential rain drenched weapons, making a quagmire underfoot, and so Washington withdrew. Thus, what would have been a major battle of the Revolution became known as the "battle of the Clouds."

On September 19 the American army encamped at Skippack Creek, 20 miles above Germantown. A detachment under Anthony Wayne had been left on the other side of the Schuylkill River as a rear guard. At nighttime on September 21 General "No Flint" Charles Grey and three regiments charged into Wayne's camp near Paoli Tavern, using bayonets only. Two hundred Americans were killed, 100 wounded, and 71 captured. The British had a total of only 28 casualties. Samuel Hay, a major in the Continental army, recorded: "The annals of the age cannot produce such a scene of butchery."

Howe took his army to Germantown, five miles from Philadelphia. Keeping 8,000 troops, he sent Cornwallis and four regiments into Philadelphia and the rest

Germantown Battle, Chew's House. Precious time was lost in attempting to dislodge six companies of the British 40th regiment who had taken refuge in the Benjamin Chew house. American artillery could not penetrate the two-foot-thick stone walls. Engraving by Rawdon, Wright, and Harch from a drawing by Koeltner. *National Archives*

of the army to escort supplies from the Head of Elk. Washington, whose army numbered 8,000 Continentals and 3,000 militia, saw an opportunity to conduct a surprise attack on Howe's troops at Germantown, using a pincer movement against the enemy, who had the Schuylkill River at their rear. Stephen's, Greene's, and McDougall's divisions would take the Lime Kiln Road to engage the enemy's right; Sullivan's and Wayne's divisions and Conway's brigade would proceed down Skippack Road to the center of Germantown; and militia would form an envelopment on both the right and left. Two factors were essential to success: synchronization of the different columns arriving at Germantown and surprise. At 7 P.M., October 3, Washington's army began the 15-mile march to Germantown, expecting to begin the attack at dawn. Unforeseen factors thwarted the operation. A guard led the American left down the the wrong road. Conway's brigade engaged the enemy before other units had come up, thus alerting the whole British camp. Dense fog and smoke from buckwheat fields set afire by the British severely limited visibility. General Stephen complained that his and Greene's divisions "formed the battle at a great distance from the British and marched far through marshes, woods, and strong fences, [so that they were] mixed before we came up with the enemy."

Sullivan's, Wayne's, and Conway's troops gained the center of the town, and there was "the utmost reason to think they would have obtained a complete and glorious victory." Howe, however, was able to have his soldiers battle ready. A British regiment made a stand at the Chew house. Valuable time was lost in trying to eliminate this pocket of resistance behind the American lines. Knox's artillery had no effect against the thick walls. Stephen's troops broke away from Greene's column in the direction of the firing at the Chew house. Wayne's and Stephen's men fired on each other, thinking each was the enemy. Part of Greene's division, advancing further into the town, did not have the expected support from Stephen and Wayne. Sullivan, at the edge of Germantown, had trouble getting across fences and walls. Militia of the far flanks offered no assistance. Greene had to retreat, and the American withdrawal now became a rout. With the fog lifting, Howe gave pursuit for several miles.

The battle of Germantown on October 4 should have been an American triumph. Washington, in his general orders, said that he had "the mortification to assure the Troops they fled from Victory"; he warned that in the future the soldiers should not mistake "a particular Retreat" (one of maneuver) for a "general" retreat.

Despite the heavy American losses (152 killed, 500 wounded, and 438 captured while the British sustained about 550 casualties), Washington regarded the attack on the British encampment as one that showed the courage and capability of American troops. But the situation demanded scapegoats, and many officers were court-martialed for negligence or cowardice. General William Maxwell was tried and acquitted. But the 56-year-old General Adam Stephen, who had been a thorn in Washington's side as far back as the French and Indian War, was not so fortunate. Convicted of "unofficerlike behavior" in not rallying his troops during the retreat from Germantown and being "frequently intoxicated since in the service," Stephen was dismissed from the army.

On October 19 Howe's army entered Philadelphia, and Washington established camp at White Marsh. All that the American commander could do was to "hover" about the city, as he wrote Samuel Huntington on October 27, "to distress and retard their operations as much as possible." Eleven of 15 members of a council of war voted against an attack on Philadelphia.

To occupy Philadelphia, it was necessary for the British to have control of the Delaware River—for access of warships and bringing in supplies. The Americans held Fort Mifflin on the Pennsylvania side and, opposite it in New Jersey, Fort Mercer. Chevaux-de-frise had been placed in the river. A heroic defense at Fort Mifflin, led by Colonel Christopher Greene, stayed off a Hessian attack on October 22. Wrote Ambrose Serle, Howe's secretary, the Americans "certainly defended it with a Spirit, they have shown no where else to an equal Degree during the War." The British cleared a channel through the river obstruction and turned both ship and shore batteries on Fort Mifflin. On November 15 the American defenders set fire to the fort and evacuated it. Fort Mercer was abandoned on November 21.

Uneasy with the Americans near Philadelphia, Howe tried to force a battle. At midnight on December 4, he set his army in motion toward Washington's camp at White Marsh. The British took position on Chestnut Hill, a ridge three miles from the American camp. As before, Washington refused to fight on open ground. From December 5 to 7, clashes occurred between forward units of both armies. Predictably, Howe planned a wide flanking movement around Washington's right; to attack frontally meant facing strong breastworks and many heavy artillery pieces. Rather than go through the dense woods and the rough terrain to envelop Washington's army, Howe returned to Philadelphia.

Both sides figured that a clear victory in the Philadelphia campaign would end the war. With an American defeat of the British army in Pennsylvania, coming at the same time as the capture of the entire invading force from Canada at Saratoga, a termination of the war would have been most probable. The British ministry had a continuous burden, as it was, to justify the prolongation of the conflict.

The result of the campaign left both sides much as they were before. Mishaps and miscalculations had denied either army a complete victory. Both Washington and Howe had been cautious—fighting as few major engagements as possible and so not risking defeat. Nevertheless, the American soldiers acquired confidence in their fighting ability. But before they would go into battle again they had to endure the long winter at Valley Forge.

CHAPTER 8

From Victory to Stalemate in the North

Close upon the heels of Washington's unsuccessful Pennsylvania campaign came the great victory of the Northern army at Saratoga. Two major engagements occurred in the summer of 1778. Then the war in the north became one of encounters of excursionary parties and patrols along both sides of the lower Hudson River and in the southern Highlands above New York City. On a few occasions British naval units raided New England ports.

British strategy in 1778 shifted for the remainder of the war to dispersal of operations while keeping the New York City sector at a status quo. The war moved to the south and to the west, and expanded into a global conflict involving France, Spain, and Holland. American strategy, from 1780 to the end of the war, took into consideration the employment of allied military strength. In command of the main army, Washington tenaciously adhered to a defensive posture, avoiding major battles.

With the American troops greatly enfeebled from the hardships of the Morristown encampment of 1779–80 and not yet receiving the assistance of French land forces, General Sir Henry Clinton missed opportunities to strike at Washington's army. But, of course, Washington was always elusive. A British success in the North to complement the victories of the southern campaigns of 1778–80 might have persuaded the British government to make a greater commitment to winning the war.

Washington intended to attack the British in Manhattan whenever he managed to obtain sufficient manpower and resources to do so. This objective became all the more tempting after British troops were dispatched from New York City for duty in the South. If Washington did not have the full strength to drive the British from Manhattan Island, however, at least he controlled the immediate area to the west and the north.

During the military stalemate, the British government made one more effort to reach a peaceful settlement. A peace commission headed by the earl of Carlisle, empowered to concede to all American demands except independence, visited the United States from June to November 1778. It was doomed from the start, however, with Congress insisting on independence and the withdrawal of British troops as conditions for negotiations.

Burgoyne's Defeat

In June 1777, General John Burgoyne assembled his invading army at St. Johns on the Richelieu River, just above Lake Champlain. He had an army of 7,213 men (3,714 British and 3,016 German infantry and 473 artillerymen), assisted by 250 Canadians and Tories and 400 Indians. The objective was to move down Lakes Champlain and George and the Hudson River to Albany, and then link up with the British army from New York City. A British diversionary force, led by Lieutenant Colonel Barry St. Leger, began its march eastward from Lake Ontario, expecting to secure the Mohawk Valley as it progressed and to join Burgoyne's army at Albany. Success would be a strategic victory, taking New York out of the war and isolating New England. The British invasion, however, was premised on miscalculations: the British failed to realize the difficulty of the land route along Lake George; they overestimated Indian support; and they anticipated little opposition by Continental and militia forces. It was also assumed that Howe's army would come up the Hudson.

Burgoyne warned the people of New York and New England that if citizens aided the rebel army or withheld provisions and forage, he would "give stretch to the Indian forces under my direction" and there would be "devastation, and famine, and every concomitant horror that a reluctant but indispensable prosecution of Military duty must occasion." To Burgoyne's credit, he did warn his Indian auxiliaries against indiscriminate killing. But the proclamation had an effect quite the opposite of what the British general had intended and a tragic incident resulted in powerful propaganda for the Americans. Jane McCrea, daughter of a Presbyterian minister who was bethrothed to a loyalist, David Jones, was murdered and scalped by several Indians. Burgoyne demanded that his Indian allies surrender the culprits. The Indians refused, and largely owing to the dispute, they left the British army. Burgoyne, however, was perceived as not trying hard enough to have the murderers apprehended, thus alienating those who had been sympathetic to the British cause. Burgoyne was therefore denied assistance from two sources that he had counted on—Indians and loyalists.

An invasion such as Burgoyne's had been anticipated by the Americans ever since their own failed campaign against Canada in 1775–76. Major General Philip Schuyler, commander of the Northern army, placed Major General Arthur St. Clair in charge of 3,400 men to check the British advance. St. Clair abandoned Crown Point and did the same with Fort Ticonderoga on July 5, when the British moved cannon onto Mount Defiance (Sugar Loaf Hill), 1,500 yards to the southwest, across the outlet between Lakes George and Champlain. St. Clair's troops retreated to safety, but a rear detachment of 600 men fought a British force under Generals Simon Fraser and Baron Friedrich von Riedesel at Hubbardton (Vermont) on July 7, resulting in heavy casualties on both sides and capture of half the rebel force. Cutting their way through trees felled by the Americans, Burgoyne's army took almost a month to traverse the 23 miles to Fort Edward on the Hudson, which St. Clair's troops had evacuated.

On August 3, St. Leger's expedition, consisting of 750 regulars and Canadians and 1,000 Indians, began a siege of Fort Stanwix (Rome) on the upper Mohawk, defended by Colonel Peter Gansevoort and New York Continentals. Indians and loyalists ambushed a militia force, made up mostly of German patriots under General Nicholas Herkimer, at nearby Oriskany on August 6. Herkimer was mortally wounded, and the militia retreated to Fort Schuyler (Utica). Benedict Arnold and 950 Continentals from the Northern army relieved Fort Stanwix. With his Indians refusing to fight, St. Leger headed back to Canada. Leaving 700 troops at Fort Stanwix, Arnold returned to the American army on the Hudson.

Simultaneously, Burgoyne received another setback. With provisions running low, the British general sent Lieutenant Colonel Friedrich Baum and 900 troops to raid stores at Bennington. Making contact with American militia on August 14, Baum set up breastworks on a hill. Brigadier General John Stark assaulted the enemy position from the flanks and rear on August 16. In the bloody affair Baum was killed. Stark then turned on a British relief column of 640 men led by Lieutenant Colonel Heinrich Breymann. In both engagements, known as the battle of Bennington, 207 British forces were killed and 700 captured; of the 2,000 Americans involved, 30 were killed and 40 wounded. Burgoyne had lost one-seventh of his army.

On September 14, Burgoyne's troops crossed to the west side of the Hudson River at Saratoga and marched southward on the river road. The British general had now completely outdistanced his supply line from Montreal. Major General Horatio Gates, who had replaced Schuyler as commander of the Northern army, drew up his force of 7,000 (2,700 Continentals, the rest being militia) on Bemis's Heights (site of Johann Bemis's Tavern) near Stillwater. Here, four miles from the British army, Gates awaited a British attack. Burgoyne found himself in a perilous situation, facing a well-entrenched enemy, running short of supplies and ammunition, and having almost no routes available for escape. The Americans controlled all passes and fords on the east side of the Hudson. Burgoyne expected an army from New York City to come to his aid. But Clinton, who waited for reinforcements from England, went only so far, on October 6, as to capture Forts Clinton and Montgomery on the lower Hudson.

The battle of Saratoga (or more correctly, the two engagements at Stillwater— Freeman's Farm and Bemis's Heights) determined Burgoyne's fate. At the first battle of Stillwater (Freeman's Farm, September 19), the British advanced in three columns. Daniel Morgan's riflemen and Henry Dearborn's infantry temporarily broke through on the British right, with sharpshooters taking a deadly toll of British officers and men, and Benedict Arnold's troops furiously attacked the British center. Gates, insisting on securing his fortified positions, refused to send reinforcements to Arnold. At dusk the two fatigued armies ceased fighting. Although the British occupied the battlefield, it was as much an American victory; the Americans suffered one-half the number of the British casualties of 600. Afterward,

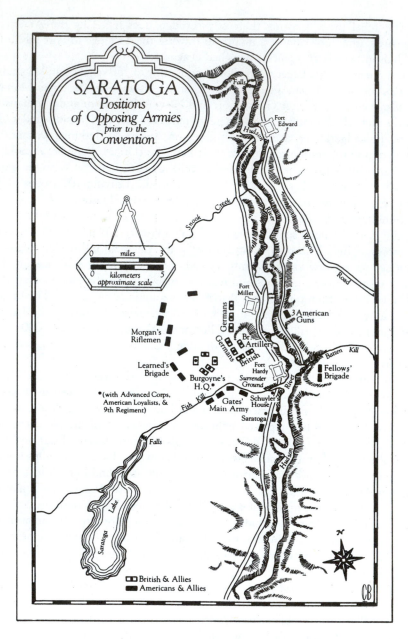

Saratoga: Positions of Opposing Armies   *Source: Gerald Howson, Burgoyne of Sara-toga (New York: Times Books, 1979), p. xvi.*

Arnold quarreled with Gates over tactics and over Gates's failure to recognize his heroism, after which Gates relieved him of his command.

At the second battle of Stillwater (Bemis's Heights, October 7), Burgoyne again attacked in three columns. Generals Ebenezer Learned and Enoch Poor held the American center and right; Morgan's and Dearborn's troops "poured down like a torrent" on the British far right, forcing an enemy retreat in that sector. Benedict Arnold, against orders, rode out into the fray, taking charge of some Continentals and Lieutenant Colonel John Brooks's Massachusetts militia. Unsuccessful on the left, Arnold's troops swung completely to the other side of the battle and captured Breymann's redoubt. Indeed, it seemed that Arnold was everywhere, constantly exposing himself to enemy fire. A musket ball fractured Arnold's thighbone, in the same leg that was wounded at Quebec. Although he had arrived in battle after it was well underway, Arnold certainly deserves to share honors with Morgan for the American victory. The British withdrew to Saratoga.

Negotiations for the surrender of the British army began on October 13, culminating four days later in an agreement to the terms of the "convention" at Saratoga. According to the terms of the surrender, Burgoyne's whole army could return to Europe on condition that it was not employed again in America. But when the Saratoga Convention received no ratification from either Congress or the British crown, Burgoyne's army remained in America as prisoners of war. The British abandoned Fort Ticonderoga on November 8, 1777.

Valley Forge and the Conway Cabal

The encampment at Valley Forge from December 1777 to June 1778 afforded Washington's army a strong defensive position. Located 20 miles from Philadelphia, the site formed a triangle, bordered by the Schuylkill River on the north, Valley Creek on the west, and a ridge sloping eastward. The men built log huts, housing 12 persons each, and the officers found quarters in private homes. Unfortunately, Valley Forge was not located in a rich farming area, and many Tories lived in the neighborhood. What is more, supplies had to be brought in from a distance over deeply rutted roads. Light infantry and militia patrols occasionally encountered small British detachments. "One of the Gallentest things that has happened this war," wrote General George Weedon, occurred on January 20, 1777, when Captain Henry Lee and eight men held off a British force of 200 at Spread Eagle Tavern, five miles from Valley Forge.

Ineptness in the commissary and quartermaster departments and depreciation of the Continental currency contributed to a shortage of food and clothing. Many soldiers had only a blanket for their outer covering and one pair of well-worn shoes. Meat and flour were scarce, as was the usual daily ration of one gill of whisky or rum. But a mild winter, plenty of firewood, and little prevalence of disease compensated for the deficiencies. Congressional reforms—creating the staff departments of commissary of issues and purchases and allowing commissions to be taken by persons involved in transactions—eventually helped to speed the flow of goods to the army.

A high rate of desertion (as many as 10 a day), resignations of hundreds of officers, and the lag in recruitment and reenlistment diminished the ranks. Morale, however, improved with the coming of spring and with news of the French alliance. Surgeon Ebenezer Crosby, writing to Norton Quincy in April 1778, reported that the army "tho' small, is tolerable healthy, better clothed and on a much more respectable footing than ever before."

The soldiers at Valley Forge did not know what to think of the "illustrious stranger" who arrived on February 23, 1778, bearing a letter of introduction from the president of Congress. Friedrich Wilhelm Ludolf Gerhard Augustin, Baron von Steuben, speaking only German and French, warmly assumed the role of the army's drillmaster. The American emissaries in France, Benjamin Franklin and Silas Deane, had passed Steuben off as a former lieutenant general in Prussian service, though he had never held a rank higher than captain. In May 1778 Congress appointed Steuben major general and inspector general of the army. Partly out of bemusement and partly because of Steuben's evident ability, the soldiers responded to Steuben's training exercises as prescribed in a handbook that he had written, translated into English by one of Steuben's French assistants, Pierre Duponceau. Steuben established a model company of 47 men. He simplified drills, reducing the motions in the manual of arms and the number of steps per minute in marching. For battle maneuvers, Steuben taught the troops to march not in Indian file as they had been accustomed to, but in columns of fours. The use of compact formations showed to advantage on May 20 at Barren Hill, located halfway between Valley Forge and Philadelphia. Here Lafayette, with 2,200 men, interrupted a British foraging expedition. The British command responded by rushing a force of 7,000 troops to the scene. Finding a road that was unknown to the enemy, Lafayette and his soldiers managed to escape, not the least aided by the close order of the troops.

Despite all the progress in the American military, dissension over rank threatened to disrupt the officer corps. Congress's giving preferment to foreign officers created especial resentment. Such was the case of Phillippe Tronson de Coudray, who was promoted to major general. To prevent the resignation of several of Washington's generals, the Frenchman was shifted from the line to the staff. The controversy became moot, when de Coudray accidentally drowned in the Schuylkill River on September 15, 1777. Another problem of morale occurred when Congress restructured the army in early 1778 without giving much attention to claims of seniority. The jealousies among general and field grade officers proved a constant irritation to Washington. While in Congress, John Adams had written his wife about the situation in May 1777: "I am wearied to Death with the Wrangles between military officers, high and low. They Quarrell like Cats and Dogs. They worry one another like Mastiffs. Scrambling for Rank and Pay like Apes for Nutts."

The elevation of Thomas Conway to major general and inspector general (Steuben's predecessor) on December 13, 1777, brought the controversy over Congress's preferment of foreign officers to a head. Conway, an Irish-born Frenchman had served competently as commander of the third Pennsylvania brigade during the

Fredrich Wilhelm Augustin von Steuben (1730–94), here painted by Ralph Earl, as Inspector General of the Continental army, introduced practices that improved discipline, fighting ability, and morale of the soldiers.   *National Archives*

battles of Brandywine and Germantown. Nine American brigadier generals with greater seniority petitioned Congress against Conway's promotion. Conway had already earned ill will for expressing his displeasure over the conduct of American officers and soldiers. He also became the center of an alleged conspiracy to remove Washington as commander in chief.

In the fall of 1777 Congress appointed a new Board of War, consisting of men of military experience who were not members of Congress. General Horatio Gates, the hero of Saratoga and former adjutant general, was named president of the panel. The possibility was raised that the board and certain congressmen who were known to be critical of the military leadership might favor censure or removal of Washington as commander in chief. Historians have discounted any real conspiracy, but Washington himself acted as if he thought there was one.

The American commander in chief had good reason to be concerned. His army had suffered two major defeats—at Brandywine and Germantown. Washington's military leadership seemed weak because of his total reliance on his council of war, which consisted of general officers, to make operational decisions when following his own judgment might have been for the best. Washington appeared as too cautious a general. John Adams complained that he "was sick of fabian systems in all quarters." Some congressmen, such as James Lovell of Massachusetts, expressed fear that Washington was becoming too venerated. Certainly, on many people's minds, a rotation in the high command might be a healthy change. Gates might well be the better general. Although critics of Washington were known both in Congress and the officer corps, it was Conway's misfortune to become the scapegoat for an alleged conspiracy. If there was one it existed mainly among Board of War members and disgruntled Congressmen.

An alert to a supposed "Conway Cabal" appeared in a letter from General Stirling to Washington on November 3, 1777, which enclosed a message from Colonel James Wilkinson, Gates's adjutant, to Major William McWilliams, Stirling's aide-de-camp, which read: "In a letter from Genl. Conway to Genl. Gates he says: 'Heaven has been determined to save your Country; or a weak General and bad Councellors would have ruined it.' " Washington wrote Conway a curt letter, which included the quotation. Conway admitted that he had been critical of his commander in chief, but declared that he had not written the offending passage. Transferred by Congress to an unimportant command at Albany, Conway resigned his commission on April 28, 1778. Benjamin Rush, surgeon general of the army's middle department and former congressman, was almost alone in coming to Conway's defense.

Defending his honor, Conway fought a duel with Brigadier General John Cadwalader and was shot in the jaw. Thinking he was near death, Conway wrote Washington: "You are in my eyes the great and good man." Conway recovered and returned to Europe, becoming a general in the French army. As a result of the alleged cabal, Congress showed greater circumspection in its relations with Washington. It now regarded Washington all the more as the indispensable military leader and showed greater respect for Washington's opinions.

Monmouth

General William Howe sailed for England on May 24, 1778. His successor as the commander of the British army in America, General Sir Henry Clinton, had never approved the long occupation of Philadelphia. Thus, on June 18, the British army evacuated the city and, with its huge baggage train, headed slowly eastward across New Jersey. Washington now had the opportunity either to harass the enemy's march or provoke an outright battle. With a detachment under Benedict Arnold sent into Philadelphia, the American army left Valley Forge. Washington initially decided on a limited engagement with the enemy's rear and left flank, employing 1,500 men under General Charles Scott. Ultimately, the plan was altered to commit a large force against the British. Lafayette took charge of an attack force of 4,200. Charles Lee, who had been released by the British as a prisoner of war only a month before, now insisted, by right of his military seniority, on commanding the forward troops, and Washington acquiesced.

On June 26, the British army encamped in woods opposite Monmouth Court House. Washington ordered Lee to deploy at advantage, but otherwise gave no specific instructions. At dawn on June 28, Lee sent the brigades of Scott, Maxwell, Varnum, and troops under Colonels Richard Butler and Henry Jackson to attack the rear and left flank of the British army, which had resumed its march. Clinton assaulted the American center, hoping to drive Lee's troops into ravines. Lee sent orders to Scott to hold the position on the left, but the instructions were not delivered inasmusch as Scott was well into a retreat. Troops at the center were forced back, and seeing this, Maxwell's and Wayne's troops on the left also retreated. Lee planned to make a stand on a ridge fronted by a morass. Washington, bringing up the main army, was shocked to see what he considered a full withdrawal from battle. He met Lee, and the two men argued. Washington took over the field command himself, lining up troops at the position Lee had selected. Savage fighting ensued. By late afternoon, the battle became chiefly an artillery duel, with Knox's guns having the advantage of high ground. The near 100 degree temperature, lack of water, and heavy packs brought both armies to exhaustion. The battle ceased at dusk. Clinton withdrew a short distance and rested his troops before resuming the march. The darkness of the night, the rugged ground, and dense woods discouraged pursuit. The British army reached Sandy Hook on June 30 and ferried to New York City, Staten Island, and Long Island. Washington missed an opportunity to attack the enemy during their debarkation.

Washington led his army across the Hudson to White Plains and awaited Clinton's next move. The battle of Monmouth had resulted in 106 American dead (37 of whom died of sunstroke), 161 wounded, and 95 missing, and the British, 65, 155, and 64, respectively. On the march from Philadelphia, Clinton lost 580 men by desertion.

Lee insisted on a court-martial to vindicate his conduct. This was customary practice in the military: an officer's honor must be upheld above all else. Washington only too gladly complied and had Lee arrested. At the court-martial, held from July 4 to August 12, with General Stirling as president, Lee was found guilty on all three charges: "disobedience of orders, in not attacking the enemy"; "misbehavior before the enemy . . . by making an unnecessary, disorderly and shameful retreat"; and "disrespect to the Commander-in-Chief" as expressed in two letters to Washington (June 28 and July 1). His sentence was suspension from command for one year.

Much of the damaging testimony at Lee's trial came from men who might themselves have been held culpable for their decisions in the face of the enemy—Generals Scott, Maxwell, and Wayne. More inexcusably, young officers, ambitious and hoping to court favor with Washington, were also prosecution witnesses. As expected, Lee's own aides defended him. Unquestionably, Washington's own initial indecisiveness was as much to blame for not gaining a victory as Lee's had been. Lee's biographer concludes that Lee at most was guilty of disrespect to his commander in chief. Lee had substantial support in Congress, which had to confirm the verdict. By taking his side of the quarrel with Washington to the public and to Congress itself, however, Lee worsened his case. Even then, when Congress made its decision on December 5, with many members absent, the votes of six state delegations were against Lee, two for, and three divided. Congress had little choice; to have overturned the sentence would have shown a lack of confidence in Washington. As Benjamin Rush wrote John Adams on October 27: "The Congress I believe disapprove of the sentence, but are so much afraid of the workmanship of their own hands, that they are afraid to reverse it." Lee resigned. Had Lee accepted a mild reprimand from Washington instead of a court-martial, he would have retained his position as second in command of the Continental army.

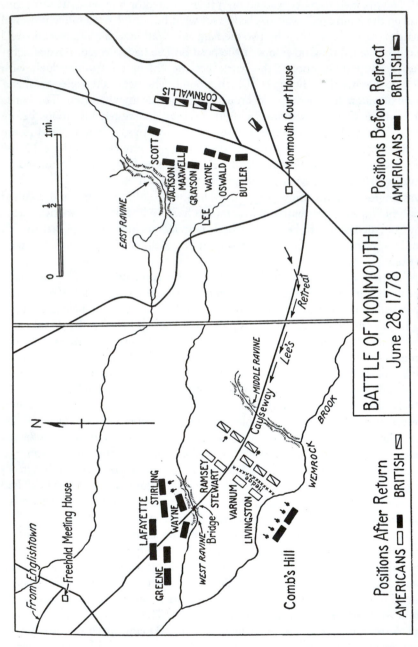

Battle of Monmouth *Reprinted with permission of Macmillan Publishing Company from The War of the Revolution by Christopher Ward. Copyright 1952 and renewed © 1980 by Macmillan Publishing Company.*

Containment

The war greatly expanded in 1778 and 1779, leaving New York–New Jersey only one of many sectors. With the entry into the war of France in 1778 and Spain in 1779, the British government decided on a global strategy. Unable to bring the war to Europe because of the lack of allies and insufficient naval power for an effective blockade owing to the commitment of fleets elsewhere, the British emphasized securing the flanks of empire. Instead of reinforcing the main army at New York, British troops went to Canada and Nova Scotia. Military campaigns on the North American continent had as objectives control of the Mississippi and Ohio valleys and the South (first the Floridas and Georgia and then the Carolinas). Naval campaigns would be conducted in the Caribbean Sea and the Indian Ocean.

American strategic planning now considered the possibilities of an allied war effort. Washington hoped that an American-French army, aided by French naval units, would drive the British out of Manhattan Island, but this goal always eluded him for lack of manpower or other factors.

The first military benefit of the French alliance was the availability of the French navy for operations in American waters. In July 1778 Admiral Charles Hector Théodat Count d'Estaing arrived off Sandy Hook with 12 ships of the line and four frigates, carrying 4,000 soldiers, to take part in a combined naval-land expedition planned against British-held Newport, Rhode Island. General Sullivan and nearly 10,000 troops (6,000 of whom were militia commanded by John Hancock) lay siege to the Rhode Island port. D'Estaing reached Rhode Island on July 29 and on August 10–12 maneuvered against a fleet sent from New York under Admiral Lord Howe. A violent storm came up, however, scattering and damaging vessels of both fleets; the only fighting that took place was between single ships. Howe returned to New York.

On August 15, Sullivan pushed toward the British lines above Newport. D'Estaing reappeared on August 20 but refused to debark any troops; the next day he sailed for Boston. Disgusted over the French withdrawal, 5,000 of the militia went home. The British commander, General Robert Pigot, reinforced by troops under Clinton, now had 7,000 men. The British constructed strong fortifications. On August 29 both sides attacked, resulting in an American retreat. Without naval assistance and lacking sufficient manpower, further effort to oust the British at Newport was abandoned. Needing manpower for the southern campaigns, the British pulled out of Newport in October 1779.

Breaking up camp at White Plains, Washington dispersed his army from Peekskill, on the Hudson, to the Connecticut border. Except for winter cantonments of the main part of Washington's army at Middlebrook in 1778–79 and Morristown in 1779–80, the American forces remained in the southern Highlands of New York. After October 1778 the most distant British outpost above New York City was Kingsbridge, at the northern tip of Manhattan and on the Post Road, the main artery that connected New York City and Boston.

The rest of the war in the North was punctuated by foraying parties of both armies above Manhattan and in eastern New Jersey and by British naval raids along the southern and extreme northern New England coastline. For hit and run tactics, the Americans relied on light infantry. In July 1778 Congress ordered that 16 companies for that service be drawn from the three divisions in Washington's army and be organized into four regiments of four companies each; those selected were 20 to 30 years old. Use was also made of dragoons; these, too, were mounted infantrymen, but unlike the light infantry, they were self-contained groups and did not come from the regular army itself. General Charles Scott commanded the Corps of Light Infantry during the summer and fall of 1778. Anthony Wayne then took charge of this special force in Washington's army until it was disbanded in December 1779.

Westchester County, which included the towns of White Plains and Yonkers, became the site of numerous small military encounters during 1778–82. Scott commented that there was occasionally "scattering fur," and Johann Ewald, a Hessian officer, observed that "enemy patrols" frequently ran into his "sneak parties." One unusual engagement, on August 31, 1778, was the battle of Indian Bridge on the Saw Mill River at present-day Woodlawn Heights, just inside the boundary of New York City today. Lieutenant Colonel John Graves Simcoe's Queen's Rangers and Lieutenant Colonel Banastre Tarleton's dragoons ambushed a detachment of Americans and 60 Wappinger Indians. The Indians were herded into a field and slaughtered—the first instance of "Tarleton's quarter" (showing no clemency toward the defeated).

The little war around New York City exhibited yet more brutality. In September 1778 a general foraging party of 5,000 troops under Cornwallis landed in New Jersey and moved northward along the Hackensack River Valley while Knyphausen and 3,000 men also went up the east side of the Hudson for large-scale foraging. An additional objective of the Cornwallis expedition was to envelop the Hackensack Valley, thereby rounding up any patriot troops and giving encouragement to Tories of the region. Some speculated that the British were starting a military campaign, but Washington soon determined this was not the case. Yet, as Clinton wrote Lord Germain on October 8, 1778, if Washington were "tempted to quit his mountains [southern New York Highlands] to interrupt our foraging in the Jerseys, I had a good chance of having a fair stroke at him." As Clinton later said in his memoirs, Washington would "have met me in an angle between the mountains and the river, on terms replete with risk on his part, and little or none on mine." Washington only sent light infantry and dragoons to harass the British foraging.

On September 27 British detachments moved toward the New Jersey–New York border. Lieutenant Colonel George Baylor and the Third Continental Dragoons took position on a hill overlooking the river, bedding down for the night in Cornelius Haring's farmhouse, barns, and other outbuildings. Early on the morning of September 27, General Charles "No Flint" Grey, being apprised of Baylor's location by Tory spies, suddenly rushed on the sleeping men, bayoneting them, while shouting "no quarters to rebels!" Weapons were plummeted into haystacks, from which blood drifted down through the rafters. Of Baylor's 120 troops, 30 were killed, 50 captured, and 40 escaped. Some of the Americans were killed after surrendering. The British buried the slain in tanning vats; reinterment years later revealed multiple wounds on the bodies, confirming the atrocity.

During the summer of 1779 Clinton twice attempted to draw Washington into a major battle. On June 1 British troops captured two Highland forts on the Hudson, Stony Point and Verplanck's Point. Washington took his army from the winter's encampment at Middlebrook (New Jersey) to Smith's Clove and prepared to resist a British advance to West Point. Clinton, however, dropped back down the Hudson. In the second attempt, in July, General William Tryon, with 2,600 troops transported in 48 vessels, raided the Connecticut coast and destroyed many of the buildings in New Haven, Fairfield, and Norwalk. Washington did not come to Connecticut's defense, as Clinton had anticipated.

Further up the New England coast at the entrance of Penobscot Bay, Maine, the British established a naval base, which was besieged by 2,000 New England militia and seamen, supported by three Continental navy ships and a Massachusetts fleet, beginning on July 25. Upon the arrival of a British naval force under Sir George Collier, the Americans retreated up the Penobscot River leaving their ships behind—a total British victory. The British retained the post until the end of the war.

As a countermove to the British invasion of Connecticut, Washington sent Anthony Wayne's corps of light infantry to attack Stony Point and a detachment under Colonel Rufus Putnam to seize Verplanck's Point, on the east bank of the Hudson across from Stony Point. Although Putnam failed because Clinton had reinforced Verplanck's Point, Wayne met spectacular success. At dusk on July 16, 1779, Wayne's force of 1,200, under orders not to fire but to rely solely on bayonets, stealthily crept through a deep morass and a double row of abatis and stormed into the Stony Point fort. Wayne's men killed 63 and wounded 71 of the enemy, and captured the remaining 442 troops of the garrison; the American loss was 15 dead and 85 wounded. To Wayne this coup was revenge for the massacre of his soldiers at Paoli (on September 21, 1777; see Chapter 7); to Clinton, Stony Point was another Trenton.

Washington, however, had no plan to hold Stony Point, and it was immediately evacuated, with its works dismantled. For a northern war that had become a stalemate, the Stony Point victory greatly boosted the morale of Washington's army. It also deterred Clinton from further offensive action in the Highlands along the Hudson. Wayne's feat was soon duplicated on a smaller scale, during the night of August 18–19, when Major Henry Lee, with 400 men, silently approaching through the marshland, successfully assaulted the British post at Paulus Hook, killing 50 of the enemy and capturing 158. The post (in present-day Jersey City), however, was too near the British in New York City to be retained by the Americans.

In summer 1780 Lieutenant General Knyphausen, acting as British commander in chief in New York until Clinton's return from the Charleston expedition (see Chapter 9), sought to accomplish what Clinton had been unable to do the previous year—to lure Washington's army into a major battle. Knyphausen had learned of rumors that the Continentals were near mutiny, and he expected that loyalists would rally to support a British expedition in New Jersey. On June 7 Knyphausen, with 5,000 men, set out from Elizabethtown, New Jersey, toward Morristown, where Washington still had the main part of his army from the winter cantonment. But because of strong resistance by the New Jersey Continental brigade and militia, Knyphausen fell back to Connecticut Farms, a small village near Springfield. After some fighting, Knyphausen returned to Elizabethtown. Washington left Morristown and, encamped at Short Hills, had Greene take charge of Continentals and militia at Springfield. On June 23, Knyphausen's army attacked the American forces at Springfield. But the Hessian-British commander hesitated to continue fighting when Greene withdrew his troops to heights above the town. Burning most of the 50 buildings in the village, Knyphausen returned to Elizabethtown and crossed on pontoons over to Staten Island. Sarcastically, a British captain, Archibald Robertson, commented: "A very pretty expedition; six thousand men having penetrated 12 miles into the country—burnt a village and returned." This was the last British military effort in New Jersey.

A French squadron, commanded by Charles Louis d'Arsac, Chevalier de Ternay, arrived at Newport harbor on July 10, 1780, and a few days later Lieutenant General Jean Baptiste Donatien de Vigneur, Comte de Rochambeau, debarked with 5,000 troops. The French ships had kept three days ahead of a fleet from England, under Admiral Samuel Graves, headed for New York. Admiral Marriot Arbuthnot, at New York, made no effort to intercept the French squadron. Clinton later commented that "there is little doubt that our not being able to crush this reinforcement immediately in its arrival gave additional animation to the spirit of rebellion, whose almost expiring embers began to blaze up fresh on its appearance." The French army remained inactive, not moving near Washington's Westchester County encampments until June 1781. The British kept the ships of Ternay (who died on December 15, 1780) blockaded at Newport. Without French naval power, Washington hesitated to mount an attack on New York City.

Other than continuing patriot–loyalist militia clashes and small raids, the last battle involving American troops and any part of the British army from New York City occurred when Benedict Arnold, now a British general after having switched sides (see Chapter 15), sought to draw off a part of Washington's army heading southward for the Yorktown campaign (see Chapter 10). Arnold raided and burned most of New London and captured Forts Griswold and Trumbull in the vicinity. Most of the American casualties were suffered after the surrender of the garrisons, thus again giving credence to the American charge of British brutality.

At the Close of the War: The Newburgh Addresses

Washington's army made its final cantonment of the war at New Windsor in the Hudson River Highlands, 60 miles from New York City. The commander in chief established his headquarters at nearby Newburgh, where many of the officers also resided.

With pay far in arrears, soldiers and officers alike were in a near-mutinous mood. Officers also complained that Congress had not implemented its resolve of

1780 that would allow them to retire at half-pay pensions. The discontent created a dangerous situation. In December 1782, a group of officers at Newburgh representing each of the state Continental lines at the "Cantonments, Hudson River" sent a petition to Congress, with the warning: "Our distresses are now brought to a point. We have borne all that men can bear." Pay should be sent to the army as soon as possible, they argued, as "The uneasiness of the soldiers is great and dangerous; any further experiments on their patience may have fatal effects." The officers said that instead of a pension they would accept a lump sum equal to "full pay for a certain number of years."

Nationalists in Congress—men such as Alexander Hamilton, James Madison, Gouverneur Morris, and Robert Morris—saw the growing discontent in the army as an opportunity to pressure the state delegations to confer on Congress new powers to raise revenue and to fund the national debt. Efforts at securing an amendment giving Congress authority to collect import duties had failed. Arthur Lee, in Congress, wrote Samuel Adams on January 29, 1783: "Every Engine is at work here to obtain taxes. . . . The terror of a mutinying Army is played off with considerable efficacy."

Congress rejected the December 1782 petition. Colonel Walter Stewart brought the news to Newburgh and also made it known that Congress planned to dissolve the army. Young officers were especially resentful. On March 10–11, 1783, two anonymous papers circulated among the officer corps, both purportedly written by Major John Armstrong, Jr., an aide-de-camp to General Gates, who had returned to the army and was Washington's second in command, replacing Lee. One of the "addresses" gave notice for a meeting of field officers, and the other emotionally played on grievances and suggested that the officers could take action to solve their problems with Congress. If the officers did not want to "grow old in poverty, wretchedness and contempt" and had "spirit enough to oppose tyranny under whatever garb it may assume; whether it be the plain coat of republicanism, or the splendid robe of royalty," then they should "awake" and redress themselves.

Washington immediately sent copies of the addresses to Congress and called a meeting of the generals, field officers, one officer from each company, and a "proper representation from the staff of the army" for the purpose of adopting measures "as most rational and best calculated to attain the just and important object in view." Washington spoke at the gathering, appealing to loyalty, patriotism, and honor. At one point he adjusted his glasses, saying, "Gentlemen, you must pardon me. I have grown gray in your service and now find myself growing blind." After he left, Gates, as presiding officer, steered the meeting to adopt resolutions professing attachment to American liberties and to Congress. Thus the so-called Newburgh Conspiracy ended. But questions have remained: to what extent, if any, were officers determined to take action? Was there really a conspiracy? Historian Richard H. Kohn insists that Gates was at the center of a plot by officers to resort to forcible action in seeking redress from Congress. By assuming leadership of the discontented officers, Gates sought to restore his own military reputation. "Gates and his young zealots evidently lost all sense of reality and began planning a full-fledged coup d'etat," writes Kohn (1970, p. 200). They "openly advocated mutiny" (1972, p. 152). The

Horatio Gates (1728–1806), the "hero of Saratoga," as commander of the Southern army, found General Charles Lee's warning to be prophetic: "Take care lest your Northern laurels turn to Southern willows." Portrait by Charles Willson Peale.   *Independence National Historical Park Collection*

would-be conspirators had become disillusioned with Washington's leadership, at least in the way he argued their case before Congress. Other historians disagree with Kohn, claiming that no direct evidence supports any kind of conspiracy designed to change or overthrow the government. In any event, by summer 1783 the army disintegrated, with officers and soldiers accepting furloughs that in all practicality became dismissions from military service.

CHAPTER 9

The War Turns Southward

From the start of the Revolutionary War, Congress and the southern patriot governments took measures to secure Georgia and to wrest East Florida from the British. On March 1, 1776, Congress named Charles Lee commander of military forces in the South and at the same time appointed four of six new brigadier generals—Robert Howe (North Carolina), Andrew Lewis (Virginia), James Moore (North Carolina), and John Armstrong (Pennsylvania)—to command Continental troops in the Southern department. After the British withdrawal from Charleston harbor in the summer of 1776, the Georgia–East Florida sector received the primary attention of American forces in the South. Georgia was hardly more than a frontier settlement, consisting of 18,000 whites and 15,000 blacks, in an area along the Savannah River and stretching down the coast to the Altamaha River. Only 4,000 white males (divided between loyalists and patriots) were eligible for military service. South Carolina loyalist refugees, who had fled to East Florida, in conjunction with British regulars and Indians, raided into Georgia. In August 1776 Lee left Robert Howe and Colonel William Moultrie in charge of 1,500 Virginia and North Carolina Continentals in Georgia. Subsequently, an American invasion of Florida floundered, and the British countered with a successful campaign into Georgia.

In 1778 the British ministry decided on a revised American strategy that had the prospect of success and that might arouse greater public support in England for the war effort. William Knox, undersecretary to Lord Germain, had lived in Georgia for five years, and had persistently argued that the American war had been waged at the wrong place. Reports from refugees from the southern colonies and former governors and lieutenant governors of North Carolina, South Carolina, and Georgia emphasized the advantages of bringing the war to the South. A southern strategy could be carried on with limited means and it was thought that loyalists and neutrals, who were considered a majority of the population, would rally to the royal standard. A southern conquest would deprive the rebels of the ability to export goods, which provided their principal means of paying for military supplies. Confiscated rebel estates could be used to cover part of the cost of military operations as well as to afford relief for loyalist refugees. With British control of southern ports, food and lumber to supply the army could be brought in from the West Indies.

Step by step, a British offensive in the South could bring pacification from Georgia to Virginia. Campaigns could be carried on in the wintertime; British forces in the North had lost much of what territory they had gained during that season. Also favoring a British southern strategy were calculations that rebels would find it difficult to raise troops because of the sparseness of population, the fear of slave uprising, and the enmity of the poorer classes toward the patriot aristocracy.

On March 8, 1778, Lord Germain sent a "Most Secret" letter to the newly appointed British commander in chief in North America, Sir Henry Clinton, instructing him to limit warfare in the North to coastal raids and a blockade and to begin offensive operations in the South. Using substantially loyalist forces, Clinton was to restore royal government in Georgia and the Carolinas. It was a risky venture at best, and so the British government refused to commit a sufficient number of regular troops. Patriot militia and Continentals had the ability to harass and strike back at British forces, which discouraged loyalists and neutrals from taking up arms. The British policy of offering pardon to those who subscribed to an oath of allegiance to the crown and also paroling captured patriot militia angered loyalists who were opposed to conciliation. In the end, territorial occupation failed, and the British had to return to conventional operations—a war restricted to maneuver of armies and battle.

East Florida–Georgia, 1777–1779

In early 1777 Tory rangers from Florida raided in Georgia. On February 18, 1777, Fort McIntosh, near the Satilla River, surrendered to the British. An American excursion into Florida aborted, owing largely to rivalry between regular and militia commanders. General Lachlan McIntosh of the Continental army and Governor Button Gwinnett of Georgia argued over command, and in a duel between the two men in May, Gwinnett was killed. On another attempted invasion, Colonel Samuel Elbert and 400 Georgia Continentals descended the St. Johns River, while Colonel John Baker and 200 mounted Georgia militia went overland. Before joining Elbert, Baker was attacked by British rangers, regulars, and Indians at Thomas Creek on May 17, 1777, resulting in all of the invading force returning to Georgia.

A year later, Robert Howe, now placed in command of the Southern department by Congress, led Continentals into Florida, supported by Georgia and South Carolina militia and naval units under Commodore Oliver Bowen. On June 29 Howe found his immediate objective, Fort Tonyn, on the south side of St. Marys River, burned and abandoned by the British. Governor John Houstoun of Georgia refused to release militia to Howe, thus thwarting a further invasion. Georgia militia, under Brigadier General James Screven, were routed on June 30, 1778, at Alligator Bridge (over a branch of the St. Marys) by Major James Mark Prevost's British regulars and Thomas Brown's Tory rangers.

With Admiral d'Estaing's fleet leaving North American waters for the Caribbean, General Clinton at last felt he had enough leeway to send an expeditionary force to the South—3,041 troops, commanded by Lieutenant Colonel Archibald Campbell, and a fleet under Admiral Hyde Parker. General Augustine Prevost, in charge of 2,000 regulars and loyalist militia in Florida, was ordered to cooperate in an invasion of Georgia and South Carolina. Campbell and his army of Scotch Highlanders, Hessians, and New York loyalists debarked at the mouth of the Savannah River in late December 1778 and headed for the Georgia capital. General Robert Howe, with 750 Continentals and 150 militia, attempted to block the British advance about one-half mile southeast of Savannah. An old slave, Quamino Dolly, informed the British of a path through a swamp around the American right. Campbell made a diversionary attack at Howe's front and sent a detachment of Highlanders under Captain Sir James Baird through the swamp trail. Undetected, Baird surprised Howe's troops from the rear. It was a complete disaster for the Americans. Campbell moved upriver and captured Augusta on January 29, 1779.

While Campbell cleared American forces from the Savannah River, General Augustine Prevost was doing the same along the coast. Prevost, with 900 troops, on January 10 captured Fort Morris at Sunbury, 30 miles south of Savannah. The British now expected to receive ample aid from loyalists. Campbell issued a proclamation offering full pardon to Georgians who affirmed British allegiance and promising to punish those who did not do so. Loyalist militia, however, soon met a rebuff. Andrew Pickens and patriot militia pursued Tories under Colonel James Boyd. Catching up with them at Kettle Creek, Georgia, on February 14, Pickens won a crushing victory. After Kettle Creek, loyalists from the interior of the South never again went into the field on their own except when in an adjunct status with the British army.

General Benjamin Lincoln, who had been assembling an army at Purrysburg, South Carolina, sent Brigadier General John Ashe and 1,600 North Carolina and Georgia Continentals to attack Augusta. On February 13, Campbell evacuated the town. At Briar Creek, Georgia, on March 3, Major J. M. Prevost, with 900 men, made a circuit around Ashe's camp, attacking the Americans from the rear. It was a catastrophe for the Continentals, who sustained a loss of 150 killed and 227 captured; all but 450 of the survivors went home instead of rejoining Lincoln's army. The British 71st regiment had charged the rebels, yelling "Remember poor Macalister!" This was a reference to a British sergeant who had been hacked to pieces by patriot marauders. The British victory at Briar Creek offset Pickens's success at Kettle Creek and forced General Lincoln temporarily to delay his planned offensive in Georgia.

When Lincoln's army crossed into Georgia on April 20, General Prevost, hoping to draw American troops away from the state, marched toward Charleston. General William Moultrie, with part of Lincoln's army that had been detached in South Carolina, went into that city. Prevost started a siege, but upon learning that Lincoln was moving toward Charleston, he withdrew toward Savannah, leaving a 900-man garrison at Stono Ferry as a rear guard under Lieutenant Colonel Charles Mawhood. Lincoln, with 1,200 men, at midnight of June 19 attacked this British post but had to break away when British reinforcements arrived from Johns Island. Lincoln occupied Charleston where, with militia additions, he assembled a force of 6,500 men.

Meanwhile, as a hint of future British strategy, an expeditionary force of 2,000 under Commodore Sir George Collier and Brigadier General Edward Mathew on

Benjamin Lincoln (1733-1810) had the mortification of being forced to surrender a whole American army to the British at Charleston, May 12, 1780. Portrait by Henry Sargent. *Massachusetts Historical Society*

May 6 sailed into the Chesapeake. The purpose of the invasion of lower tidewater Virginia was to destroy trading resources, tobacco, and magazines that had been accumulated for the French fleet and to interrupt the flow of American supplies heading southward. The British force removed stores from Portsmouth, burned American vessels, and destroyed provisions at Suffolk, including 9,000 barrels of salted pork and 8,000 barrels of pitch, tar, and turpentine. The Virginia government called on the services of Continental Brigadier General Charles Scott, who was in the state recruiting for the Southern army. Scott put several regiments of regulars and militia into the field, but before any military action took place the Collier–Mathew force departed on May 24 for New York.

From Charleston, General Benjamin Lincoln made plans to clear the British out of Georgia. But fearing the effects of a torrid climate and the "sickly" season, both Lincoln's and Prevost's armies remained inactive during the summer of 1779. For the fall, Admiral d'Estaing, in the West Indies, let it be known that he would participate in combined operations against Savannah. In early September the French fleet of 33 warships and transports carrying 6,000 soldiers entered the Savannah River. The British sank vessels in the river to block passage near the town. D'Estaing debarked 3,500 troops eight miles from Savannah and spent several weeks in making preparations for battle. Lincoln, with 1,500 troops (half of whom were militia), joined the French on September 16. The heavy artillery brought from the French ships began a bombardment of Savannah on October 4. Prevost had a force of 2,360 regulars as well as the services of about 1,400 sailors, volunteers, and armed blacks brought in from neighboring plantations. He had used the delay in the advance of the allied forces to improve fortifications. Several strong redoubts guarded each end of the town. Lincoln wanted to engage in regular siege operations, but d'Estaing became impatient. D'Estaing had already overstayed his proposed time and was fearful of a possible British naval attack. Furthermore, many French soldiers and sailors were sick from having been so long at sea, and provisions were in short supply. Thus, it was decided to storm the British fortifications. The attack on October 9 went awry from the start. A South Carolina militiaman deserted to the enemy and revealed that the main assault would be against the Spring Hill redoubt. Prevost, therefore, sent more men to this post. An American detachment approaching under cover of a swamp came into open view instead of following a depression in the terrain, and was raked by heavy fire. Troops were trapped in the abatis and ditch around the redoubt. Count Casimir Pulaski, at the head of his 200-horse Legion, tried to breach the obstructions between Spring Hill and another redoubt, and was mortally wounded. Some British soldiers left their positions and engaged allied troops in fierce hand-to-hand fighting.

The storming of the Savannah fortifications, one of the most hotly contested battles of the Revolution, like Bunker Hill entailed horrendous casualties for the attacking force: for the French, 183 killed and 454 wounded; for the Americans, 244 and 583, respectively; and for the British an estimated 40 killed and 63 wounded. The allies had casualties of one-third of their forces who were engaged in the action.

D'Estaing and his fleet sailed away on October 19, and Lincoln's remnant army returned to Charleston. The failure at Savannah gave heart to loyalists to assist in future British operations in South Carolina. For the Americans, French assistance had twice proved disappointing. The British hold in Georgia was all the more secure. As General Clinton wrote after the war, "the universal dejection occasioned in the rebel country" by the "miscarriage of the French and their combined efforts before Savannah" served as an invitation to capture Charleston.

Charleston

The winter of 1779–80 favored a British invasion of South Carolina. With Washington's army in cantonment, Clinton could spare part of his 25,000-man force in New York City. He had a strong base at Savannah, and the French fleet had left American waters. On December 26, 1779, Clinton and Admiral Marriot Arbuthnot set out from New York with 8,500 troops and 5,000 seamen aboard 14 warships and 90 transports—their destination Charleston. Because of great damage caused by a succession of storms on the way, the fleet anchored at Tybee Island at the mouth of the Savannah River for repairs. Not until February 11, 1780, did the expeditionary force debark at Johns Island, 30 miles south of Charleston. Avoiding the harbor forts, the British then occupied James Island, directly across from Charleston Neck. With the arrival of 1,500 men from the Savannah garrison and a 2,500-troop reinforcement from New York under Lord Rawdon, Clinton had a land force of 12,500 for the siege operations. Besides 500

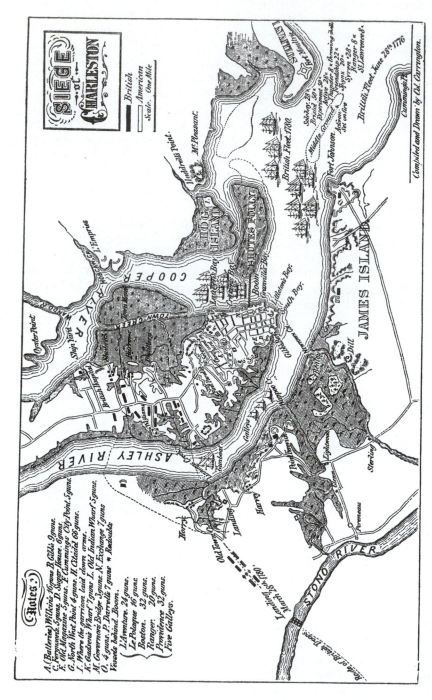

Siege of Charleston *Source: Henry B. Carrington. Battle Maps and Charts of the American Revolution (New York: A. S. Barnes & Co., 1881), p. 61.*

132

troops commanded by General Isaac Huger stationed at Monck's Corner to keep open an escape route across the Cooper River, Lincoln had an army in Charleston of 2,600 Continentals and 2,500 militia and armed citizens. Included were 750 Continentals marched southward from Virginia by General William Woodford.

On March 29, British troops crossed the Ashley River to the Charleston peninsula, 14 miles above Charleston. On April 10 the first parallel (trenches parallel to the entrenchments of the besieged) was completed within 600 to 800 yards of the American lines at the edge of the city; seven days later the trenches were brought 300 yards closer.

Lincoln believed Charleston to be defensible, especially if he were "supported by the people of the country." He did not seriously consider escape. There would have been considerable risk in pulling out of the city anyway. The British in pursuit along any of the navigable rivers could cut off the Americans in their retreat, and South Carolina militia refused to leave the city. On April 8 Clinton summoned Lincoln to surrender, to which came Lincoln's reply that he would defend the city to the "last extremity." The British stepped up artillery fire and on April 13 began bombardment of the city. If Lincoln had any intention of evacuating the city, it was now too late. On April 14 the last escape exit was closed off when Tarleton's Legion and Patrick Ferguson's loyalist militia routed Isaac Huger's troops at Monck's Corner; for good measure, Cornwallis occupied nearby Haddrell's Point on April 26. The British opened a third parallel within 100 yards of the American lines, thus being in a position to take their works by storm. On May 8, Clinton sent Lincoln his "last summons" for surrender, which was declined. The next day, wrote one British officer, "the Rebels began with huzzaing and a violent Cannonade from every Gun they could fire seemingly at Random as if in a drunken Frensy, and without doing us any harm. We fired very little but from our Mortars." Lieutenant Governor Christopher Gadsden, who had insisted on the defense of the city, now applied to Lincoln to surrender, supported by two petitions bearing signatures of 407 citizens. Lincoln complied, and just past noon, May 12, more than 5,000 American Continentals and militia lay down their arms. Among the captives were six American generals— William Woodford, Charles Scott, William Moultrie, Lachlan McIntosh, James Hogun (militia), and Louis Le Bègue de Presle Duportail (Continental army chief of engineers). Continental officers were confined to Haddrell's Point, five miles east of Charleston across the river, and enlisted men were placed aboard prison ships in the harbor. Militia were allowed parole. The siege took the lives of 89 Americans, with 138 wounded; the British lost 76 and 189, respectively. This was the worst American defeat of the war; for the British, it was revenge for Saratoga. The way was now open for the British army to move into the interior of the Carolinas with force.

Clinton left Cornwallis a free hand in conducting southern operations. Two days before embarking for New York on June 5, Clinton issued a proclamation requiring all inhabitants in South Carolina to renew their allegiance to the king. Many did so, but Carolinians, who had been willing to remain neutral, were now forced to take sides.

Charleston had surrendered before another Virginia detachment of Continentals could reach the beleaguered city. Colonel Abraham Buford's 350-man regiment

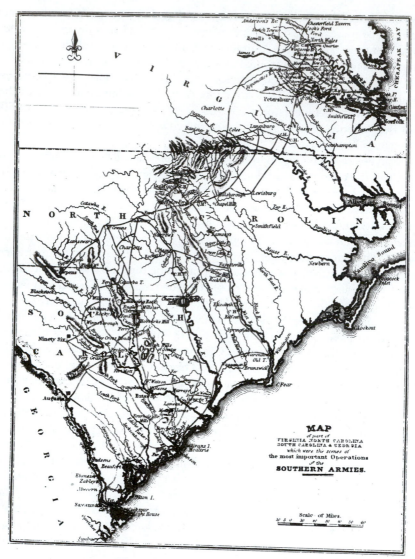

Operations of the Southern Armies   *Virginia State Library and Archives.*

and a small party of Lieutenant Colonel William Washington's cavalry had advanced to the Santee River, 40 miles above Charleston. After the fall of Charleston, Brigadier General Isaac Huger ordered Buford's troops to withdraw to Hillsboro, North Carolina. Cornwallis took to the field in pursuit of the Virginians, but unable to catch up sent Tarleton and 300 of his dragoons on ahead. Covering 105 miles in 54 hours, Tarleton, on May 29, overtook Buford at the Waxhaws, near the North Carolina border. Buford made the mistake of huddling his men on open ground and ordering them not to fire until the enemy was within 30 feet. With bugles sounding, Tarleton's cavalry swept down on the Americans with drawn bayonets. Despite Buford hoisting a white flag, the butchery continued; not even the wounded were spared. The Americans had 113 killed, 150 badly wounded, and 53 captured. Dr. Robert Brownsfield, an eyewitness, wrote:

> Not a man was spared . . . for fifteen minutes after every man was prostrate, they went over the ground, plunging their bayonets into everyone that exhibited any signs of life, and in some instances, where several had fallen one over the other, these monsters were seen to throw off on the point of the bayonet the uppermost, to come at those beneath.

The atrocity called for vengeance, and "Tarleton's quarter!" became a rallying cry of American troops in the South.

On June 8, 1780, Thomas Brown and his King's Rangers reoccupied Augusta. Cornwallis established a line of posts in the South Carolina interor; the British also held Georgetown, Charleston, Beaufort, and Savannah on the coast. At the end of June 1780, Cornwallis reported that rebel resistance in South Carolina and Georgia had ended. In order to control the two southernmost states, the British commander felt it was necessary also to bring the war to North Carolina.

The anticipated British offensive into the interior of the Carolinas stirred a savage warfare between loyalist and patriot militia during June–August 1780. The British were dealt a severe blow when Colonel Francis Locke, on June 20, crushed a loyalist force under Colonel John Moore at Ramsour's Mill, North Carolina. Other rebel victories over loyalists, who expected to join in the British operations, occurred at Williamson's Plantation (July 12), Flat Rock (July 20), and Thicketty Fort (July 30) in upper South Carolina. Thomas Sumter and patriot militia fought to a bloody draw in engagements with loyalist troops at Rocky Mount (August 1) and Hanging Rock (August 6) in South Carolina.

Camden

Camden, the northernmost of the British chain of forts, was the key to the territorial war in upper South Carolina and an invasion of North Carolina. A thriving commercial community of largely Scotch-Irish Presbyterians and Irish Quakers, it was an important entrepôt for provisions and livestock. Here Cornwallis expected to establish his forward base of operations.

General Horatio Gates, appointed by Congress as Benjamin Lincoln's replacement to head the Southern army, arrived at Coxe's Mill, North Carolina, on July 25, 1780, to take charge of Continentals and militia. Washington had sent Delaware and Maryland regulars, commanded by Baron Johann De Kalb. Virginia and North Carolina militia would make up two-thirds of Gates's army. Cornwallis, heeding a warning from Lord Rawdon, who commanded at Camden, that a large American army was approaching, set out from Charleston, arriving at Camden on August 13. At Camden, Cornwallis had 2,239 men, 1,900 of whom were fit for duty.

Gates marched for Camden, hoping to catch Rawdon by surprise. He was unaware that Cornwallis was coming to Rawdon's aid. The American force endured great hardship; food was scarce, and the soldiers subsisted mainly on green corn and unripe peaches; occasionally they killed stray cows, making soup thickened with hair powder.

On August 11 Gates found Rawdon blocking a bridge at Lynches Creek, 15 miles above Camden. Gates missed an opportunity by not conducting a flank attack on the enemy. Rawdon returned to Camden, and Gates took post at Rugeley's Mill, where he was reinforced by more Virginia and North Carolina militia, bringing his army to 4,100.

The American commander decided to move closer to Camden. At 10 P.M. on August 15, in utter darkness (it was a new moon), the army began its march, just as Cornwallis came out on the same road toward Gates. Many of Gates's troops were in no condition to fight, suffering from diarrhea brought on by having eaten half-cooked meat and molasses mixed with cornmeal mush. Cornwallis expected to surprise the Americans at their camp at Rugeley's, and Gates anticipated doing the same against Rawdon at Camden. The frontal troops of both armies moved silently toward each other through the hot, humid night. Suddenly they collided about eight miles from Camden. The generals waited until dawn for full-scale action.

At the battle of Camden, August 16, Gates placed De Kalb's Continentals on the right, North Carolina militia under General Richard Caswell in the center, and Virginia militia under General Edward Stevens on the left. Swamps were on both flanks. At dawn the British charged the American lines. The militia immediately gave way. As Colonel Otho Williams of the Maryland Continentals observed:

> General Stevens . . . put his men in mind of their bayonets; but the impetuosity with which they [the enemy] advanced, *firing* and huzzaing, threw the whole body of the militia into such a panic that they generally threw down their *loaded* arms and fled in the utmost consternation. The unworthy example of the Virginians was almost instantly followed by the North Carolinians. . . . A great majority of the militia . . . fled without firing a shot.

The Delaware and Maryland Continentals stood firm but were soon left alone on the battlefield and surrounded by the enemy. De Kalb received a dozen wounds and died three days later. Gates had tried to rally the militia several times, only to find that they had "taken the Woods in all directions." It was not long before Gates himself mounted the fastest race horse in the army (son of Colonel George Baylor's Fearnought) and rode away posthaste, with Tarleton in close pursuit, not stopping until he reached Charlotte, 60 miles distant. The Americans lost 250 killed and 800 wounded (who were captured) in the battle, and the British 68 dead, 245 injured, and 11 missing. The American army was annihilated; only 700 of the soldiers showed up later at Gates's headquarters in Hillsboro.

As an enhancement of the victory at Camden, Tarleton's dragoons surprised Thomas Sumter and his militia at Fishing Creek, near the junction with the Catawba River, on August 18. Catching the Americans literally napping, Tarleton

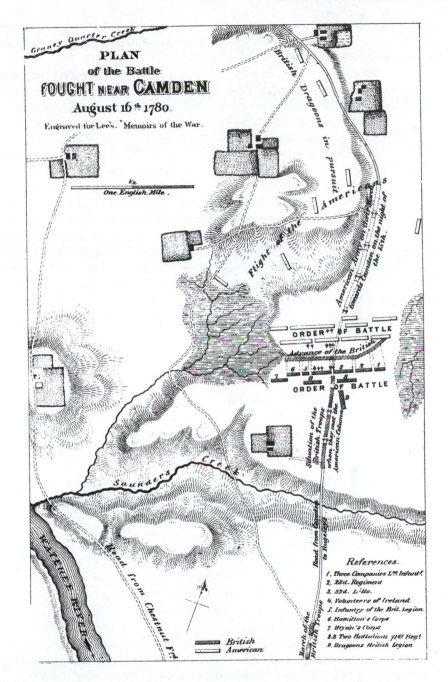

Plan of the Battle Fought Near Camden   *Source: Henry Lee, Memoirs of the War in the Southern Department of the United States (New York: University Publishing Co., 1869), p. 282.*

cut them off from their weapons. Again it was "Tarleton's quarter." One hundred fifty of the militia were slaughtered, and 300 captured; Sumter managed to escape. The British had only 16 killed and six wounded.

Despite their spectacular triumphs, the British knew that they were not winning the war. Patriot militia turned out in greater numbers. Only four days after the battle of Camden, Francis Marion and his militia force ambushed a detachment of British regulars and loyalists at Nelson's Ferry near Camden, recovering 150 Maryland Continentals who had been captured at Camden.

Meanwhile, rebel partisans renewed warfare in Georgia. Colonel Elijah Clarke led 500 militia on an assault on Augusta on September 14. Capturing the town's forts, Clarke could not, however, carry the White House (McKay's Trading Post), a half mile west of the town, where Thomas Brown and his band of loyalist militia and Cherokee Indians had sought refuge. With their water supply cut off, Brown and his men had to subsist on drinking their own urine and eating raw pumpkins. A Tory force under Colonel John Harris Cruger from Ninety-Six arrived on September 18 to relieve the siege. Clarke had to retreat so quickly that he left behind the wounded. Brown, himself wounded twice in the leg, took his revenge by having 13 of the captives hanged from a gibbet in the stairwell of the White House and turning over others to the Indians to be tortured to death.

King's Mountain

On September 8, Cornwallis began his invasion of North Carolina, reaching Charlotte on September 25. Gates's army at Hillsboro was in no condition to offer resistance, but rebel militia harassed British foraging parties and demonstrated the vulnerability of the British supply line. Cornwallis ordered Major Patrick Ferguson from Ninety-Six into North Carolina to raise loyalist militia in the backcountry. A daring officer, Ferguson had the distinction of having invented a breech-loading rifle that could fire six shots a minute. (The British army would not adopt this weapon for another 90 years.) Ferguson was to conduct operations parallel to the movement of Cornwallis's army.

Recruiting loyalist militia in western Carolina, Ferguson made the mistake of sending an American parolee, Samuel Phillips, to the far frontier to announce that Ferguson "would march his army over the mountains, hang their leaders and lay their country waste with fire and sword, if they did not desist from their opposition to the British arms." On October 1, Ferguson proclaimed:

> Gentlemen:—Unless you wish to be eat up by an inundation of barbarians, who have begun by murdering an unarmed son before the aged father, and afterwards lopped off his arms, and who by their shocking cruelties and irregularities, give the best proof of their cowardice and want of discipline; I say, if you wish to be pinioned, robbed, and murdered, and see your wives and daughters, in four days, abused by the dregs of mankind—in short, if you wish or deserve to live, and bear the name of men, grasp your arms in a moment and run to camp.

At the battle of King's Mountain, Oct. 7, 1780, the "Overmountain Men" from the frontiers of the Carolinas annihilated a Tory force led by Major Patrick Ferguson, in what proved to be a decisive blow to British expectations in winning the southern backcountry. From a painting by Alonzo Chappel. *Library of Congress*

Ferguson's pronouncements had a countereffect, enraging the overmountain men. Colonels Isaac Shelby and John Sevier joined their Watauga men to those of William Campbell's Virginia recruits and some South Carolinians, and went into the field seeking Ferguson. The loyalist force took refuge on King's Mountain. Here Ferguson and 1,000 troops thought they could repel an assault from the rebels of equal number. The level summit of 500 by 60 to 180 yards was surrounded by steep, wooded slopes, rising 60 feet from the countryside. Ferguson sent word to Cornwallis at Charlotte, 35 miles away, to bring up reinforcements. On October 7, the patriot force, climbing up through the forested and boulder-scattered slopes, found Ferguson's troops an easy mark on the relatively treeless ridge. Ferguson, charging at the Americans several times, fell with seven rifle bullets through his body. The Americans took 698 prisoners, leaving 163 wounded to die among those who had already been killed; many of the prisoners were shot, and a week later nine were hanged. The American loss at King's Mountain was 28 dead and 62 wounded.

King's Mountain proved a definite turning point in the war in the South. Cornwallis gave up any further attempt to subdue backcountry North Carolina and withdrew to Winnsboro, South Carolina. The victory emboldened patriot militia in the Carolinas and precluded the possibility of the British creating an effective loyalist "home guard."

Nathanael Greene (1742–86), here painted by Charles Willson Peale, wore down the enemy in the southern campaigns of 1780–82 and won a military reputation second only to Washington's. *Independence National Historical Park Collection*

The victory contributed to a more determined American war effort in the South. Nathanael Greene, upon Washington's recommendation to Congress, replaced Gates as commander of the Southern army; Greene assumed charge of his new troops at Charlotte on December 2. Congress persuaded Daniel Morgan to return to the army by giving him the well-deserved promotion to brigadier general that he had so long sought. Greene put Morgan in charge of a light infantry corps— 400 Maryland and Delaware Continentals, two companies of Virginia riflemen, and 100 dragoons of Lieutenant Colonel William Washington. Ordered southward from Washington's army, Lieutenant Colonel Henry Lee and his Legion, a cavalry regiment, joined Greene's army.

Cowpens

If not the tactician (moving troops to advantage on the battlefield), Greene proved himself a superb strategist (capable of the maneuvering that wins campaigns). Before leaving Charlotte for Cheraw, South Carolina, on December 16, 1780, Greene made the unorthodox decision to divide his army in the face of the enemy. He would thereby force Cornwallis to move against one of the wings of the American army, while the other could strike at the string of British posts in South Carolina. Also, a divided army could better secure food. Greene directed Morgan and his light infantry to join militia in operations between the Broad and Pacolet rivers. Morgan was to "spirit up" the people, "annoy" the enemy, collect provisions, and move against the

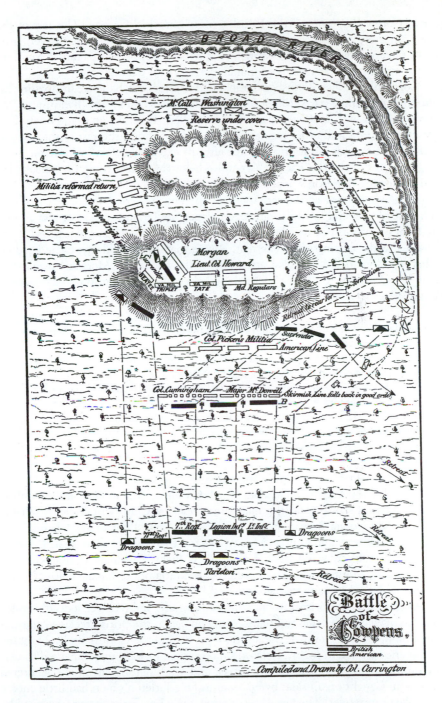

Battle of Cowpens   *Source: Henry B. Carrington,* Battle Maps and Charts of the
American Revolution *(New York: A. S. Barnes & Co., 1881), p. 71.*

rear of Cornwallis's army if the British general attacked Greene. The rest of the American army formed a "camp of repose" at Cheraw on the Pedee River, from where Greene could assault British forts, in conjunction with Francis Marion's militia, and disrupt Cornwallis's communications with Charleston.

Cornwallis, still at Winnsboro, responded to Greene's challenge by dividing his own army into three parts: Major General Alexander Leslie, who had just arrived from New York with 2,500 troops, to hold Camden; Tarleton, up from Ninety-Six, with his dragoons and other regulars, to fight Morgan; and the rest of the army to intercept the remnant of Morgan's force after its expected defeat by Tarleton.

Tarleton crossed the Pacolet, six miles below Morgan's camp on January 16, 1781. Knowing Tarleton's approach, Morgan selected ground for battle—at the Cowpens, where once cattle were rounded up. The area consisted of a wide plain, intersected by several low hills, an "open wood," as Tarleton called it, and ground free from underbrush or marshes. Six miles to the south, the swollen Broad River curved, thereby cutting off any retreat. Aware that Tarleton always came head on in battle, Morgan did not give attention to the far flanks. Morgan's own statement years later (or so Greene's early biographer, William Johnson, 1822, claims) explains the battlefield selection:

> I would not have had a swamp in the view of my militia on any consideration; they would have made for it, and nothing could have detained them from it. And as to covering my wings, I knew my adversary, and was perfectly sure I should have nothing but downright fighting. As to retreat, it was the very thing I wished to cut off all hope of. I would have thanked Tarleton had he surrounded me with his cavalry. It would have been better than placing my own men in the rear to shoot down those who broke from the ranks. When men are forced to fight, they will sell their lives dearly. . . . Had I crossed the river, one half of the militia would immediately have abandoned me. (1:376)

Morgan arranged his troops in three lines: in the front, 150 Georgia and North Carolina riflemen; then 300 Georgia, North Carolina, and South Carolina militia under Andrew Pickens; and the main line, held by Continentals, with reliable Virginia and Georgia militia on the left. Cavalry stayed out of sight behind the second hill. Morgan told militia to fire twice, and then they could retreat. (Morgan knew they would anyway.) Behind all were William Washington's dragoons and Georgia mounted infantry. Pickens ordered his militia not to fire until 40–50 yards and then "Mark the epaulette men [officers]."

As expected, the British troops charged frontally, and received a deadly volley from the riflemen and other militia. Coming on again, the British received another telling blow, and, as planned, the militia went behind the Continentals. Thinking the Americans were in flight, Tarleton's men rushed forward in complete disorder. The militia returned to fight on the flanks, and Washington's cavalry now entered the action. Caught on all sides by heavy arms fire, Tarleton's men had little choice but to die or surrender. The few who got away, including Tarleton, were pursued by Washington and 140 horsemen. Militia resisted the temptation to inflict "Tarleton's quarter" on the captives. The American victory was complete. The British lost 100 killed, 229 wounded, and another 500 prisoners of war—nine-tenths of Tarleton's force. Cornwallis thus had been denied most of his light infantry—the choicest part of his army. American casualties were 12 dead and 60 wounded.

The battle of Cowpens on January 17, 1781, had valuable lessons. It demonstrated tactics whereby regular-militia armies could effectively perform in open battle and the superiority of the rifle over the musket. It impressed on Cornwallis the difficulty of conquest of the Carolinas. For the rest of the Southern campaign, Greene modeled his own tactics on those of Morgan at Cowpens.

CHAPTER 10

Collapse of the British Southern Invasion

Britain's southern military operations in 1781 extended to two fronts: the Carolinas, to be secured by Cornwallis, and an army based in Virginia for the purpose of interrupting supplies and draining off manpower for the American Southern army. In a short time, however, a spirited British offensive failed, resulting in a strategy of defensive actions to hold key posts and seaports.

Although recoiling from Tarleton's unexpected and disastrous defeat at Cowpens, the British commander in the South thought he could still beat the American Southern army. Cornwallis did not at first appreciate the problems of distancing himself from naval and logistical support. He believed that quick and decisive victories would arouse loyalists to arms. But conquest of the American Southern army did not occur, and loyalists did not rally in strength. With the army on the move or garrisoned at isolated locations, the British held no territory in the South.

The Carolinas, January–May 1781

Just after the battle of Cowpens, though he was only 25 miles from Morgan's troops, Cornwallis, with his army understrength, feared to go further afield and risk defeat. On January 18, however, the situation changed with the arrival of the remnant of Tarleton's force and reinforcements under General Leslie, bringing Cornwallis's army up to 2,500 seasoned troops. Morgan had 2,000 men. Cornwallis hoped that by swift marches he could cut Morgan off before Morgan rejoined Greene, and then get between Greene and Virginia and destroy Greene's army.

Greene rode 125 miles to confer with Morgan at Sherill's Mills on the east bank of the Catawba. For the time being, it was decided to keep Morgan's force detached. Back at Salisbury with his small army, Greene, having learned that Cornwallis had burned most of his baggage, tents, and wagons so that all the British army could serve as light infantry, decided to play the same game—engaging in quick marches to lead Cornwallis on a chase. Greene retreated northward, and Morgan, to the west, did the same.

144

Cornwallis, who always liked flanking movements, marched westward of the Broad River, intending to catch Morgan. But Morgan kept a two days' march ahead of Cornwallis. Denied his prey, the British commander headed toward Greene's troops, now on their way to Guilford Courthouse. There Morgan's force and Henry Lee's Legion linked up with Greene. Could Greene now, upon finding favorable ground, challenge Cornwallis in battle? At the time Greene's troops numbered 2,036, but only 1,426 of these were Continentals. A council of war voted against making a stand. Greene, therefore, decided to retreat across the Dan River into Virginia. He sent militia General Andrew Pickens to obtain recruits, intercept British foragers, and cut off enemy intelligence. A mixed force of 700 Continentals and militia operated as a light corps to cover the retreat of the main army and to remain close to Cornwallis's troops. Colonel Otho Williams of the Maryland Continentals, commanded this detachment in place of Morgan, who was ill and had returned home.

If Cornwallis could overtake and crush Greene, he could then move into Virginia, free the prisoners of war now interned near Charlottesville, and attack Richmond. Both Greene and Williams won the race to the Dan River and crossed over to Virginia. Cornwallis came up to the swollen stream, but, denied boats, he marched southwest and encamped at Alamance Creek. With Cornwallis at a safe distance, Greene now returned to North Carolina and again made his way toward Guilford Courthouse. Reinforced with North Carolina and Virginia militia, the American army now totaled 4,400 (1,490 of whom were Continentals). Cornwallis had only 1,900 effectives.

Able to afford battle, Greene drew up his troops 1¼ mile from the courthouse at the crest of a long, rising hill. The forested area was split by a road, zigzagging rail fences, and many ravines. The American troop arrangement was similar to that of Morgan's at Cowpens, except that Greene did not allow for a reserve and the lines, at 300 yards apart, were too distant to support each other. Virginia militia gathered at the edge of the woods, backed by a second line of North Carolina militia; Continentals formed the third line. Virginia riflemen and William Washington's cavalry covered the right flank, and on the left were Lee's Legion and William Campbell's overmountain men.

Cornwallis rose to the challenge. At New Garden, 12 miles southwest of Guilford Courthouse, the British southern commander, with a scarcity of supplies, had only two choices: fight or retreat. However, he still wanted a victory that would rally the North Carolina Tories. At daybreak of March 15, 1781, the British army marched up the Salisbury Road toward Guilford Courthouse, and at noon the two armies clashed. The American militia fired several volleys as ordered and then retreated. Although the third line held, the British broke through the 5th regiment of Maryland Continentals. The right and left flanks of the Americans withstood bayonet charges. Cornwallis further massed against the American third line, using his artillery effectively, though some of the grapeshot hit British as well as American soldiers. At 3:30 P.M. Greene ordered a general retreat, halting three miles distant at Troublesome Creek. Although Cornwallis had gained the field, this victory had been at great cost. One-fourth of the British army were casualties—93 killed and 439 wounded (39 of whom died); Greene had 78 dead and 183 wounded.

Although acquiring a lifetime reputation as one of Great Britain's greatest generals, General Charles Cornwallis (1738–1805) brought the British southern campaign to failure, culminating in the entrapment and capitulation of his army at Yorktown. Engraving by Benjamin Smith (London), from a painting by John Singleton Copley, published 1798.
Virginia State Library and Archives

With his army greatly weakened, Cornwallis could hardly afford to remain on the offensive in the interior of North Carolina. He stayed two days at Guilford Courthouse and then marched 200 miles to his supply port, Wilmington, arriving there on April 7. Had Cornwallis dropped down to Camden and joined Lord Francis Rawdon's troops there, he would have again had a strong enough force to do battle with Greene. Instead, Cornwallis preferred an invasion of Virginia, and on April 25 he started for Virginia to link up with the British troops already in the field there.

Taking advantage of the distance between the American and British armies, Greene concentrated on driving the enemy from their posts in South Carolina and Georgia. Eight thousand British troops manned garrisons at Ninety-Six, Fort Granby, Fort Motte, Fort Watson, Nelson's Ferry, Georgetown, Orangeburg, Charleston, Augusta, and Savannah. Greene's army had dwindled. The six-week enlistments of the North Carolina and Virginia militia had expired, and Greene had only 1,400 men: 1st and 5th Maryland and 1st and 2d Virginia Continental regiments; Henry Lee's Legion; Robert Kirkwood's Delaware light infantry; and William Washington's dragoons. Yet, with the assistance of militia under Thomas Sumter and Francis Marion, the British posts could be subdued one at a time. Greene detached Lee's Legion and Captain Edward Oldham's 5th Maryland regiment to join Marion's militia to clear out the enemy in the South Carolina low country. On April 14, Lee and Marion attacked Fort Watson, on the Santee River, 60 miles northwest of Charleston; here Lieutenant James McKay commanded 80 regulars and 40 Tories. Not having siege guns, the American assault bogged down. The defenders refurnished their water supply by digging a well and tunneling from it to a nearby lake. Upon the suggestion of militia Colonel Hezekiah Maham, the

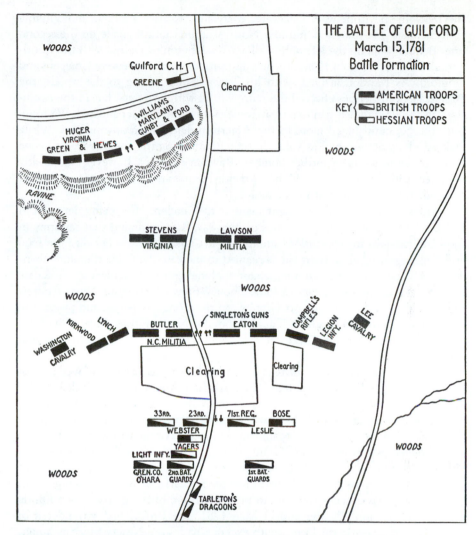

THE BATTLE OF GUILFORD
March 15, 1781
Battle Formation

KEY:
━━ AMERICAN TROOPS
▭ BRITISH TROOPS
▭ HESSIAN TROOPS

WOODS

Guilford C. H.
GREENE

Clearing

WOODS

WILLIAMS
MARYLAND
GUNBY & FORD

HUGER
VIRGINIA
GREEN & HEWES

RAVINE

STEVENS
VIRGINIA

LAWSON
MILITIA

WOODS

WOODS

KIRKWOOD   LYNCH
WASHINGTON
CAVALRY

BUTLER
N.C. MILITIA

SINGLETON'S GUNS
EATON

CAMPBELL'S
RIFLES
LEGION
INFT.

LEE
CAVALRY

Clearing

Clearing

33RD.   23RD.   71ST. REG.   BOSE
WEBSTER   LESLIE

YAGERS

WOODS

LIGHT INFY.

GREN. CO.   2ND. BAT.
O'HARA   GUARDS

1ST. BAT.
GUARDS

WOODS

TARLETON'S
DRAGOONS

The Battle of Guilford   *Reprinted with the permission of Macmillan Publishing Company
from* The War of the Revolution *by Christopher Ward. Copyright 1952 and renewed © 1980
by Macmillan Publishing Company.*

Americans constructed a tower out of logs (Maham tower), whereby they delivered
rifle fire downward into the stockade. On April 23 Fort Watson surrendered, the
first of the South Carolina British posts to do so.

Greene marched toward Camden, where Rawdon had 900 troops—the 63d
regiment and Tories. While camped on Hobkirk's Hill, a sandy ridge covered by
pines, a mile east of Camden, on April 21 Greene learned that 500 British troops
under Colonel John W.T. Watson were on their way to reinforce Rawdon. In order
to intercept this body he arranged his army, backed by Hobkirk's Hill. On April 25
Rawdon came out of the village to do battle. The American lines were dissected by

the road. In the front were Delaware, Maryland, North Carolina, and Virginia Continentals. Two hundred and fifty North Carolina militia made up the second line. Behind them on the left were William Washington's cavalry. With the Continentals holding the front line, Greene's disposition was the reverse of Cowpens and Guilford. As Rawdon arrived, with his Tory riflemen taking to the woods, the American Continentals charged the narrow front with bayonets, but in the confusion that resulted they began to retreat; some of the militia then panicked. Washington probably contributed more to the American defeat than anyone else. While making a long detour, he lost valuable time in attacking the enemy's rear. Greene chose to withdraw from further combat. Rawdon's victory, however, was dearly obtained, with 38 killed and 230 men wounded or missing; the Americans counted 18 dead, 108 wounded, and 136 missing.

Although Watson's detachment made it to Camden, after being detained in fighting off Lee's and Marion's troops on the way, Rawdon found that his army in the Carolinas was in a precarious situation. At Camden he was cut off from food and forage, and rebel partisan bands seemed to increase daily. He therefore abandoned Camden and ordered Lieutenant Colonel John H. Cruger to evacuate Ninety-Six and join Lieutenant Colonel Thomas Brown in Augusta; Major Andrew Maxwell also was to give up Fort Granby, on the Congaree River, and proceed to Orangeburg, 50 miles south of Camden on the North Edisto River. Rawdon's dispatches to both officers were intercepted, however, and as a result, neither post was evacuated.

Thomas Sumter's militia, instead of joining Greene as ordered, moved against Fort Granby (present-day Columbia, S.C.), where Maxwell commanded a 400-man garrison. Sumter, discovering the post too strong, marched on to Orangeburg, which surrendered on May 11. Meanwhile, on the next day, Lee and Marion forced the capitulation of Fort Motte, located at the junction of the Congaree and Santee rivers, taking 80 prisoners; Fort Granby fell to Lee on May 15, without loss on either side. Rawdon ordered the British post at Nelson's Ferry on the Santee abandoned upon news of the fall of Fort Motte. Similarly, on May 23, Georgetown, on the coast, was evacuated by sea to prevent seizure of the garrison by a militia force under Marion. By the end of May 1781, the British had surrendered or evacuated every post in the Deep South except Charleston, Ninety-Six, Savannah, and Augusta.

While American regulars and militia subdued the British Carolina posts, much of the war in the South shifted to Virginia. The state had been relatively untouched by military operations since Dunmore had been expelled in 1776. Only the brief incursions into the lower tidewater area by the Collier–Mathew expedition in May 1779 and by the troops under General Alexander Leslie in October 1780 on their way to join Cornwallis's army had brought home to Virginians the reality of warfare. General Clinton, the British commander in chief in America, was now willing to keep a force in Virginia at the mouth of the Chesapeake in order to disrupt that state's war effort as well as to be available to join Cornwallis should he bring his army to Virginia. But he preferred to limit the main southern British army to the task of securing the Carolinas and Georgia. Cornwallis ignored

Clinton's instructions for this purpose and instead insisted on remaining on a broad-ranging offensive. He even went over the head of his commander in chief by gaining approval for the conquest of Virginia from Lords Dartmouth and Germain, the principal British ministers conducting the war strategy. Cornwallis himself had noted that "small expeditions do not frighten" Virginians. A full invasion of Virginia would disrupt the state's economy and the major logistical support for the American Southern army.

The British Invasions of Virginia

On December 20, 1780, Benedict Arnold, now a brigadier general in the British service (see Chapter 16), set out from New York City with a 1,600-man force for Virginia. Arriving at Hampton Roads ten days later, he immediately ascended the James River. Arnold's goal was Richmond, the state's new capital, in an area that was the hub for processing men and supplies for Greene's Southern army.

Arnold's Success in Virginia

Taking only 800 of his men with him, the turncoat general reached Jamestown, where 20 sloops were captured. Arnold then ferried further upriver. At Hood's Point, 14 miles below the mouth of the Appomattox, the Queen's Rangers, under Lieutenant Colonel John Graves Simcoe, surprised a group of Prince George County militia and made them captives. On the morning of January 4, Arnold and his troops debarked at Westover plantation (25 miles east of Richmond), where he greeted the proprietress, Mary Willing Byrd, his widowed cousin-in-law. Arnold was aware that he would be no match for the fully assembled militia of central Virginia. Indeed, if captured he would face the highest gibbet in the land. Yet the expedition was a well-calculated risk. Militia had to be collected, and General Steuben, in Virginia to raise Continental troops as well as to command state militia in the field, had not yet obtained any sizable force.

At Westover, Simcoe and Lieutenant Colonel Thomas Dundas, with whom Clinton had ordered Arnold to consult on all decisions, advised that a one-day march to Richmond could be undertaken "with perfect security" and that a large amount of munitions and other supplies could be quickly destroyed. Arnold agreed on a hit-and-run attack on Richmond. Governor Jefferson and other state officials, startled suddenly to find a British army in their midst, fled the capital. Arnold's march to Richmond began on the afternoon of January 4 down the Darbytown Road. Some militia, ordered by Steuben "to give the Enemy a few fires," came out to offer resistance. Their commander, Major Alexander Dick, formerly a captain of marines in the Virginia and Continental navies, however, thought it was the better part of discretion to withdraw to the hills of Richmond. Dick, together with 200 to 300 militia, took position on Richmond (Church) Hill, just east of the town. At noon on January 5, as Arnold's troops marched into Richmond by a road at the waterfront, a Hessian detachment quickly moved up Richmond Hill, whereupon

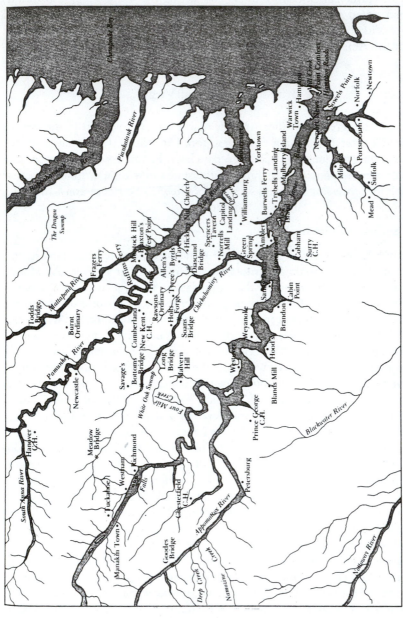

Southern Virginia: James and York River Area *Reprinted from Lafayette in the Age of the American Revolution: Selected Letters and Papers, 1776–1790—Volume IV: April, 1781–December 23, 1781, edited by Stanley J. Idzerda, Robert Rhodes Crout, Linda J. Pike, and Mary Ann Quinn. Copyright © 1981 by Cornell University. Used by permission of the publisher, Cornell University Press.*

the militia fled, after delivering a few shots at the enemy, killing one of the German soldiers.

While Arnold occupied the Virginia capital, half of the invaders, led by Simcoe, went six miles further up the river and destroyed the foundry at Westham, returning in the evening. Arnold left the tobacco untouched, probably because he expected to return for it later. Nevertheless, the depredations in Richmond were extreme. Most of the town was consumed by fire. The frame building that served as the capitol, an old warehouse belonging to a Scottish mercantile firm, was spared. It is not known if Arnold himself ordered the burning of Richmond. Ironically, Arnold donated 20 guineas to James Buchanan, a Richmond merchant, for aid to the poor; an infuriated Jefferson ordered the sum to be returned.

At 1 P.M. on January 6, exactly 24 hours after he entered Virginia's capital, Arnold headed back to Westover—not too soon, as Jefferson summoned 4,600 militia from 21 counties to be placed under Steuben's command. Militia General Thomas Nelson also raised several hundred militia, stationing them on the James below Charles City County Courthouse (near Westover). Arnold's force encamped at Westover on January 7–10. On the night of January 8, he sent a 40-man cavalry patrol under Simcoe to gather intelligence. Learning that there were militia at the courthouse, Simcoe suddenly alarmed these militia when a British bugler sounded a charge, giving the impression of a large number of British troops. Simcoe's men rushed into the courthouse, and there was some exchange of fire. So much confusion resulted that the Americans "fled on all sides," some not stopping until they reached General Nelson's camp on the Chickahominy River, and then many of Nelson's men were so agitated they themselves hastily departed for Williamsburg. At the "battle" of Charles City Courthouse, several Americans were killed.

When an "easterly wind" finally came on January 10, Arnold left Westover and floated down the river. The raid of the traitor-general had been most effective— destruction of munitions, burning of the capital, driving away the state's government officials, and taking away many slaves, 40 of whom were one-third of the slaves of Benjamin Harrison's Berkeley plantation, adjacent to Westover. Upon his return to the Chesapeake, Arnold established a base of operations at Portsmouth.

Phillips's Command

Since it appeared that the enemy had come to stay in Virginia, Washington sent Lafayette southward with 1,200 New Jersey and New England troops. On March 14, Lafayette and the Continentals arrived at Yorktown, where they joined 1,000 Virginia militia under General John P.G. Muhlenberg at Suffolk to keep an eye on the British at Portsmouth. Lafayette planned to attack Arnold, with the aid of a French fleet. But this opportunity did not present itself. Convinced that Muhlenberg could check any further operations by Arnold, Lafayette left for Maryland after a two-week stay. Just as he did so, General William Phillips, recently exchanged as a prisoner of war with the Convention army (Saratoga captives) in Virginia, arrived at Portsmouth with 23 transports carrying 4,500 men. Phillips assumed the command of the British armed forces in Virginia.

The Marquis de Lafayette (1757–1834), joined the American army in July 1777 as a major general at age 19, and from Nov. 1778 to the end of the war commanded a division. Painting by Charles Willson Peale, 1777. *Virginia Historical Society*

Washington, learning of the new military buildup, instructed Lafayette to return to Virginia as commander of all troops in that state, in effect superseding Steuben in this capacity. The young Frenchman stayed nearly a month in Baltimore gathering clothing and supplies for his army. On April 14, he wrote the French minister in the United States: "I'm on my way and the Susquehanna has been my Rubicon; I am going to run after General Phillips but I do not hope to catch him"; he would either command in Virginia or "form my junction with General Greene."

On April 18, Phillips, with Arnold second in command, led British troops up the James toward Richmond. The expeditionary force consisted of the light infantry, part of the 76th and 80th regiments, the Queen's Rangers, Hessian jägers ("huntsmen," light infantry), and Tarleton's Legion. Phillips had several options: raid quickly and return to Portsmouth, join Cornwallis in the Carolinas, or stay in central Virginia to await a junction with Cornwallis's army. On the way up the James, Lieutenant Colonel Robert Abercromby and a detachment were sent up the tributary Chickahominy River, destroying the state shipyard, several ships, naval stores, and warehouses. Jefferson and other Virginia officials were again caught off guard and could not quickly get a large militia force into the field. Steuben, still in charge of military forces in Virginia, did, however, what he could to thwart the British advance.

Phillips's army crossed the James at City Point (now Hopewell, five miles northeast of Petersburg). Steuben, who had joined with Muhlenberg's troops from the lower tidewater area, hurried to Petersburg. On April 25 the American force went out to intercept the advancing enemy. Each American soldier was amply supplied with rum, one hogshead per regiment, which Steuben had impressed from the town merchants. " 'Now Boys drink and fill your canteens,' was the word that came," wrote one Virginia militiaman, " 'but don't drink too much as we are going to fight to-day.' " At 10 A.M. the British army marched for Petersburg. Steuben's troops, as instructed, met the oncoming enemy, pausing to fire several times while retreating. Steuben held out for awhile on a hill near Blandford Church, but the British light artillery was too much, and the Americans were forced to cross over the Appomattox River, tearing up the bridge after them. Unlike the men confronted by the earlier invasion by Arnold, Virginia militiamen at the battle of Petersburg (or Blandford Church) had fought bravely.

Steuben retreated up the James, with Phillips's army in pursuit. On April 27 Arnold and a detachment of the Rangers moved to Osborne's on the James, 13 miles below Richmond, where he discovered 20 ships of the Virginia navy. Arnold sent a flag to the naval commander, James Maxwell, demanding surrender and half of the cargoes. Maxwell said he would fight to the end. Arnold then brought up his small artillery. The American cannon on shipboard could not be raised high enough above the water to be effective against Arnold's troops on the river's banks. Maxwell had no choice but to scuttle the large warships—setting afire the *Renown* and the *Jefferson;* the *Tempest,* however, intact, drifted to the British side of the river. Altogether Arnold's men took over ten ships that were not sunk, thus winning a total victory over the Virginia navy.

Phillips in the meantime had marched to Chesterfield County Courthouse, where he burned a "range of barracks for two thousand men," the jail, and the interior of the courthouse, in addition to seizing supplies. Phillips then headed eastward, linking up with Arnold at the James River on April 28. The next day the combined force marched for Richmond. Steuben, who had been collecting militia, did not try to halt the British advance.

At the town of Manchester, across the river from the Virginia capital, the British burned 1,200 hogsheads of tobacco and some buildings and "plundered the inhabitants of their furniture, killed a large number of cattle, hogs, etc." But soon Phillips had a rude surprise. Lafayette had arrived at Richmond on April 29. At dawn the next day, as the British general prepared for a river crossing, he saw silhouetted against the skyline on the hills an American army of nearly 3,300 troops—Lafayette's Continentals, 2,000 militia, and 60 dragoons. Steuben's men and General Thomas Nelson's militia had joined Lafayette. Because Phillips could not use artillery to advantage, he refrained from taking his army into Richmond. It is said that Phillips swore an oath against Lafayette, whose father had been killed by Phillips's artillery at the battle of Minden during the Seven Years' War.

The British immediately went down the river to Petersburg. On May 7, Phillips received a letter from Cornwallis announcing that his army would soon link up with the British troops in Virginia. Lafayette took station on the banks of the Appomattox across from Petersburg. Phillips died on May 14, from disease, probably yellow fever, and was buried in an unmarked grave. Cornwallis reached Petersburg on May 20 and "formed a junction with the corps under Arnold," who had succeeded Phillips. Arnold requested and received permission to return to New York, carrying with him his rightful share of one-eighth of the spoils of the Virginia campaigns.

The Road to Yorktown

In Virginia, Cornwallis's combined army, with the arrival of 2,000 more troops at Portsmouth, totaled 7,000 men. Lafayette had 3,200 troops, half of whom were militia "not used to war." For the present he dared not challenge Cornwallis to battle. Whenever an expected detachment of Continentals under Wayne should arrive, however, Lafayette felt that he could strike the British "one Blow," and "Being Beat, I may at least Be Beat with some decency."

Cornwallis now had a free hand in Virginia, although he understood that Clinton would probably order him to participate in an invasion of Pennsylvania or would direct him to keep a garrison on the Chesapeake and send most of his army to New York. Nevertheless, Cornwallis thought his options limited. For the time being, Cornwallis would "proceed to dislodge La Fayette from Richmond, and with my light troops destroy any magazines or stores in the neighbourhood which may have been collected either for his use or for General Green's army." He would then remain at "the neck of Williamsburgh," engaging in no action until hearing further from Clinton.

On May 24, Cornwallis crossed the James and encamped at the Byrd plantation at Westover. There General Leslie with the 17th and 43d regiments and two German battalions came up; Cornwallis kept the 43d regiment and sent the rest of the new troops back to Portsmouth. The British general now had 5,500 to 6,000 troops in the field—one of the largest field concentrations of British troops during the war; another 1,200 to 1,500 men were stationed at Portsmouth. With Lafayette marching northward, Cornwallis decided to give chase. At Raccoon Ford, 30 miles west of Fredericksburg, Lafayette awaited Wayne's arrival.

At Hanover Junction on the North Anna River, Cornwallis, concluding that nothing more was to be gained by pursuing Lafayette any further, moved his army westward, sending Tarleton's dragoons to destroy stores at Old Albemarle County Courthouse and Simcoe to attack Steuben's Continental recruits (destined for Greene) at Point of Fork, located where the Rivanna and Fluvanna flow into the James. Both missions were accomplished spectacularly. Tarleton succeeded in routing Jefferson from Monticello and capturing seven members of the Virginia Assembly in Charlottesville. Simcoe, with 300 infantry and 100 dragoons, spread out his men to look like they numbered more than they did, so scaring Steuben and his 540 men, who thought they were facing the whole British army, that they retreated 50 miles in two days. Simcoe and Tarleton rejoined Cornwallis at Elk Hill (island), 40 miles west of Richmond.

At last, on June 10, Wayne arrived at Lafayette's encampment at Raccoon Ford with 900 troops—three regiments of Pennsylvania Continentals and 100 artillerymen. Lafayette now lagged along parallel to Cornwallis's retrogressive march, cautiously following the British commander to Richmond. Cornwallis held Richmond, June 16–20, during which time he set fire to "a number of houses" and destroyed 2,000 hogsheads of tobacco. He then descended the James, with Lafayette in pursuit.

The British army entered Williamsburg on June 25, while Lafayette halted 10 miles distant at Bird's Ordinary. Lafayette sent Colonel Richard Butler to Spencer's

Ordinary, at the forks between Williamsburg and Jamestown, at the same time that Cornwallis dispatched Simcoe to destroy boats on the Chickahominy and reconnoiter the area. On his return, Simcoe ran across Butler, and the battle of Spencer's Ordinary (June 26) was fought, with about 30 casualties on each side.

Lafayette's troop strength swelled to 4,565 men: 2,325 were regular infantry, cavalry, and artillerymen; and 2,240 were militia infantry and cavalry. Wayne, who was "anxious to perform wonders," and his troops kept watch on the enemy. In a field at Green Spring plantation, the British left cannon and a few soldiers to decoy the Americans, while most of the main army was concealed in the woods. Wayne ordered an attack, thinking he had run across the British rear guard. British troops poured from their forest cover, and a heated engagement ensued. Wayne, who always thought that the best defense was an offense, attacked but then had to back off. Lafayette came up with the rest of the American army, and the British withdrew. At the battle of Green Spring (July 6), the Americans suffered between 150 and 300 casualties, and the British about 70. The next day Cornwallis crossed to the south side of the James and headed for Portsmouth.

The British general sent Tarleton to destroy stores westward and to intercept any detached units of Lafayette's army. Cornwallis also wanted to divert Lafayette from attacking the British army. Tarleton and his dragoons rode to Petersburg and then through Amelia, Bedford, and Lunenburg counties. For 15 days (July 9–24) Tarleton cut a swath through the backcountry, covering 400 miles.

At Portsmouth, Cornwallis received orders from Clinton to establish a base at Old Point Comfort or Yorktown. Cornwallis therefore sailed up the York River and on August 14 established posts both at Yorktown and on the opposite bank of the half-mile-wide river, at Gloucester. Complained Cornwallis, "the position is bad, and of course we want more troops."

Lafayette had no plans for engaging the enemy. Writing to Washington, he said: "The war in this country is becoming a war of depredation," and "there is no longer a suggestion of large maneuvers." He asked to return to Washington's command and leave Steuben in charge of the troops in Virginia. Instructed by Washington, however, to prevent Cornwallis from escaping toward North Carolina, Lafayette established camp at the head of the York River on August 16. Wayne, who went to the Richmond area, did not join Lafayette until the beginning of the siege in late September.

The British invasion of Virginia had now come to a standstill. The operations of the armies of Arnold, Phillips, and Cornwallis had only accomplished selective interference with the war effort in that state, while causing a substantial elevation of commitment among the people to drive out the British. A two-front war in the South was working to the Americans' advantage.

Siege of Yorktown and Gloucester

While Cornwallis pondered the next shift in British military strategy, some events occurred that made his predicament at Yorktown determinative of the outcome of

Washington and His Generals at Yorktown. **Lafayette is at Washington's right and General Comte de Rochambeau to his immediate left. Others are not identified, though one, the artist noted in a letter, is Lieutenant Colonel Tench Tilghman (1744–86), aide-de-camp to Washington. Tilghman brought the news of Cornwallis's surrender to Congress. Print from Charles Willson Peale's painting.**   *Colonial Williamsburg Foundation*

the whole war. For a year, except for reconnaissance and the probing of New York City's outer defenses, military operations in the North had ceased. The Comte de Rochambeau's 5,500 French troops, stationed in Rhode Island, had been idle since their coming to America in the summer of 1780. In May 1781 Washington learned that Admiral comte de Grasse with a French fleet was headed for the West Indies. At a conference between Washington and Rochambeau on May 21–22 at Wethersfield, Connecticut, it was decided that Rochambeau's army would march to the Hudson, that an attack on New York City was a priority, and that both generals would appeal to de Grasse to come northward to assist in a siege of New York City. It was hoped that such action would pressure Clinton to draw off some troops in the South, thus easing Greene's and Lafayette's situations. Rochambeau and the French army joined Washington at Dobbs Ferry on July 6, 1781.

Arrival of French Support

Washington changed his plans when, on August 14, he received news that de Grasse, with a large fleet and French troops, was sailing for the Chesapeake and could remain in Virginia waters until October 15. Here was an unique opportunity, through quick action, to bring to bear on Cornwallis at Yorktown the combined

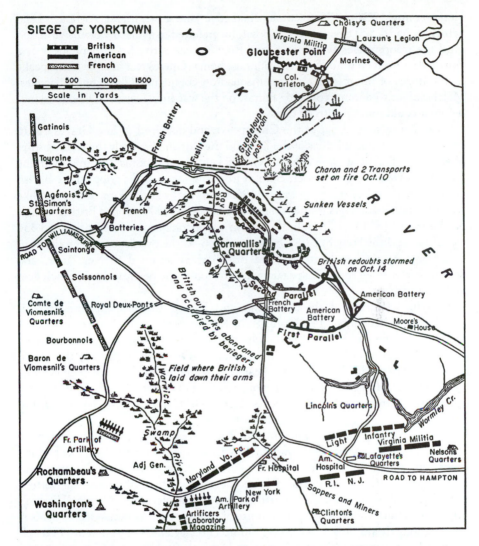

Siege of Yorktown   *Reprinted with the permission of Macmillan Publishing Company from*
The War of the Revolution by Christopher Ward. Copyright 1952 and renewed © 1980 by
Macmillan Publishing Company.

forces of Washington, Rochambeau, de Grasse, Lafayette, and the Virginia militia.
Leaving one-half of his army in the New York Highlands under General William
Heath, Washington with 2,500 men and Rochambeau's army headed southward
through New Jersey, making a feint as if to ready an attack against Staten Island,
thus deceiving Clinton of the real objective.

As Washington and Rochambeau made their way to Virginia, de Grasse's fleet of
34 warships, along with transports carrying 3,200 land forces, arrived in Chesapeake
Bay and anchored in Lynnhaven Inlet. Three regiments under General Claude

Henri, comte de Saint-Simon, were debarked at Jamestown Island. Although Lafayette now had 5,500 troops at his disposal, he preferred to avoid any offensive action until the troops under Washington and Rochambeau arrived. On September 5, a British fleet from New York under Admiral Thomas Graves reached the Chesapeake in the hopes of intercepting a French squadron commanded by Admiral Jacques-Melchoir Saint-Laurent, comte de Barras, on the way from Newport, Rhode Island, before it could join up with de Grasse.

De Grasse slipped out of the Chesapeake and managed to lure Graves out to sea. The French had 24 ships of the line and the British, 19. Only the leading ships of each fleet fought at close combat. Graves kept the rest of his fleet in a rigid line formation. Heavy fire of French cannon from the lower decks crippled six British vessels. As Thomas J. Fleming writes (1963), Graves "was thinking and acting like an admiral on maneuvers, rather than as the savior of 7,500 trapped British soldiers on the shore" (p. 134). Overall, the action was inconclusive. The British had 336 casualties, and the French, 220. On September 6–7, the two fleets sailed southward to an area near Cape Hatteras. The British then returned to New York, and de Grasse reentered the Chesapeake, where he found the newly arrived French fleet under de Barras.

To the cheering of the American and French troops camped near Williamsburg, on September 14, Washington, Rochambeau, and a band of horsemen rode through the ranks. Washington, observed Major St. George Tucker, embraced Lafayette "with an ardour not easily described." The army units from the North were ferried from Head of Elk and appeared at Williamsburg during September 14–17. The allied forces now totaled more than 19,000 men: 8,845 Continentals; 7,800 French troops; and 3,000 militia. Cornwallis had an army–navy strength of 9,725 men.

On September 18 Washington and Rochambeau conferred with de Grasse aboard the *Ville de Paris* at Hampton Roads, and it was agreed that combined operations should fit into a 40-day timetable. On September 28 the army was arranged for battle. The American force consisted of three divisions (Lafayette's, Lincoln's, and Steuben's), Knox's artillery, several cavalry units, George Weedon's brigade of militia, and two separate units of militia, each commanded by Robert Lawson and Edward Stevens. Weedon's militia brigade and a detachment of French troops (duc de Lauzan's 600-man Legion and 800 marines) were sent across the river to oppose a 1,000-man garrison at Gloucester Point, commanded by Lieutenant Colonels Thomas Dundas and Banastre Tarleton. On October 3, a large foraging party led by Tarleton and Lauzan's Legion and Colonel John Mercer's second militia regiment clashed, with the British retreating and the allies then tightening their lines about Gloucester.

On September 30, the enemy abandoned all advanced posts about Yorktown. Already there were signs of the British hardship: starving horses driven from Yorktown and bands of sick and starving blacks, many with smallpox, dying in the woods.

During October 6–11, the allies established a parallel (a 2,000-yard trench with several redoubts) extending from the Hampton road to the river. Three days later the heavy bombardment of Yorktown commenced. A second parallel, 400 yards closer to enemy lines, though not reaching to the river because of two enemy redoubts on the right, was completed on October 14. That night the simultaneous storming of redoubt 9 by French troops led by Guillaume comte de Deux-Ponts and redoubt 10 by an American detachment under Alexander Hamilton succeeded. New trenches linked the captured redoubts to the second parallel, only 250 yards from the British lines.

Toward Surrender

Time was running out for the British army at Yorktown and Gloucester. Cornwallis had forgone the opportunity to attack Lafayette before the arrival of the allied forces. Earlier he could have retreated to the Carolinas, or at least he could have broken out of the York peninsula and therefore have had an advantage of maneuverability. Cornwallis expected that Clinton would again send another fleet to the Chesapeake and either reinforce him or transport his army away. Although there was not much Clinton could do, with the southern British army effectively under siege by an immensely superior army-naval force, preparations were being made in New York for Cornwallis's relief. Unfortunately, the constant bickering between the admirals and generals, over such questions as where British reinforcements should land, consumed valuable time. Moreover, attention in New York was given to entertaining the 16-year-old William, duke of Clarence and future king, who had just arrived. Not until October 19 did an English fleet leave from New York for Virginia; maneuvering off the Capes, October 28–30, it returned home.

In desperation, Cornwallis knew that all he could do now was surrender or attempt an escape at great risk. Anticipating a British move to retreat across Gloucester Neck, Washington had ordered General Weedon's militia to fell trees, tear up roads and bridges, and drive off livestock in the area.

On the night of October 16, while a British party attacked one of the American redoubts and the allied batteries fired an "incessant cannonade," Cornwallis started sending his troops across the river. One thousand men made it to the opposite shore, when suddenly a "violent storm" came up, preventing the rest from crossing. The squall sank or dispersed the small boats that Cornwallis had assembled; two boatloads of British troops were driven downstream and were captured. Seemingly as if by an act of Providence, the escape scheme had gone awry.

At 9 P.M. on October 17, a British drummer boy appeared on a parapet and began a steady roll, and a British officer raised a white handkerchief. The American batteries became silent. At several conferences at the Moore house in Yorktown, British and American commissioners negotiated the capitulation of Cornwallis's army. The British held out for a while for immediate parole of the army, which Washington refused. The American commander in chief, however, allowed the British sloop, *Bonetta*, to take 250 Tories and American deserters, without inspection, to New York.

On October 19 at 3 P.M., the British army marched up the road from Yorktown. In a field Benjamin Lincoln, second in command of the American army, received the surrender from Brigadier General Charles O'Hara. British bands played martial airs, which included, as tradition has it, an old Jacobite serenade to the Scottish rebel leader, Bonnie Prince Charlie, "When the King Enjoys His Own Again"—a tune which had also been adapted to the nursery rhyme "The World Turned Upside Down."

An hour later the Gloucester garrison paraded out and stacked arms before French troops and Mercer's Virginia militia regiment. Because of the Virginians' intense hatred for Tarleton and his infamous "Tarleton's quarter," other Virginia militia were not permitted to participate in the ceremony.

In all, the British surrendered 7,241 troops and 800 naval prisoners. American casualties during the siege numbered about 125, of whom possibly 70 were fatalities; the French loss was 60 killed and 193 wounded. British dead has been estimated at 156, with 326 injured and 70 missing. On October 21, prisoners of war, escorted by militia General Robert Lawson, began their march for Williamsburg and then to Winchester. With Pennsylvania, Maryland, and Delaware Continentals led by St. Clair and Wayne sent to reinforce Greene, Washington's army returned to the Hudson. Staying until spring, the French army made its way to Newport, Rhode Island.

Ending the War in the South

The collapse of the British military presence in South Carolina and Georgia proceeded rapidly. Greene's immediate objective after the capture of Fort Granby in late May 1781 was to seize the two remaining interior posts in South Carolina and Georgia—Ninety-Six and Augusta. As Greene moved to Ninety-Six, he detached Lee to join Pickens's militia for an attack on Augusta.

In Augusta, Lieutenant Colonel Thomas Brown commanded 250 Tory militia and 300 Creek Indians at Fort Cornwallis and 80 British troops at Fort Grierson, a half mile distant. Browne's men sallied out in bayonet charges on several occasions but were forced back to their forts. A Maham tower (see p. 000) erected by the Americans again made the difference, resulting in the silencing of the British artillery. Browne surrendered both garrisons on June 6. Lee now hastened to rejoin Greene at Ninety-Six.

Greene's army reached Ninety-Six on May 22. At the stockaded village Lieutenant Colonel John H. Cruger commanded 600 troops, mostly Tories. Greene's 1,000 Continentals and some militia were reinforced on June 8 by Lee's corps and Pickens's militia. The American siege operations were extensive (including the establishment of three parallels)—as were the British exterior defenses, which included ditches and abatises. Greene, learning that Rawdon was approaching with 2,000 men, hurriedly attempted to storm the British works before these troops could arrive. The Americans concentrated their attack at the Star Redoubt and Fort Holmes, at opposite ends within the stockade. The British sallied out and exacted a heavy toll among the Americans entangled in the outer works. The

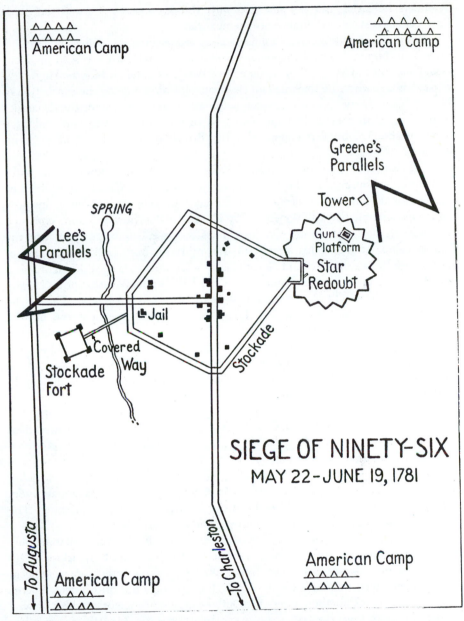

SPRING

Lee's
Parallels

Greene's
Parallels

Tower ◇

Gun
Platform

Star
Redoubt

⌂ Jail

Covered
Way

Stockade
Fort

Stockade

American Camp

American Camp

American Camp

American Camp

SIEGE OF NINETY-SIX
MAY 22 - JUNE 19, 1781

To Augusta

To Charleston

Siege of Ninety-Six   *Reprinted with the permission of Macmillan Publishing Company from* The War of the Revolution *by Christopher Ward. Copyright 1952 and renewed © 1980 by Macmillan Publishing Company.*

defenders held on, and on June 20, with Rawdon nearby, Greene retreated. Rawdon's troops entered Ninety-Six the next day.

Rawdon pursued Greene 25 miles and at Orangeburg was joined by Cruger's force from Ninety-Six and Lieutenant Colonel Alexander Stewart's 3d regiment from Charleston. Greene, now outnumbered two to one, headed for the High Hills of the Santee, where he remained for six weeks. Rawdon ordered the evacuation of Ninety-Six and returned to Charleston with part of his force, leaving the remainder of his army with Stewart at Orangeburg. With the ailing Rawdon now taking a leave of absence, Stewart commanded the British troops in the field in South Carolina.

On August 22, Greene resumed the offensive, following Stewart as he withdrew to Eutaw Springs, on the Santee River 40 miles above Charleston. Joined by Pickens's and Marion's militia and Jethro Sumner's three North Carolina Continental troops, Greene had 2,400 men (1,256 Continentals). Stewart's army consisted of 2,000 regulars and Tories. On September 8, Greene took position near the British camp, arranging his army with the militia in front backed by a line of Continentals. Lee's Legion and North Carolina Continentals held the right flank, and Maryland and Delaware Continentals the left. William Washington's cavalry and Robert Kirkwood's Continental light infantry formed the reserve. During the action which began at 9 A.M., the whole American front line gave way, but the Continentals withstood the enemy charge. The American reserve now also engaged the enemy, who were thrown into confusion. Both sides, however, claimed victory. The British retreated to Charleston. The battle of Eutaw Springs was one of the most costly in the war for both sides. The Americans had 139 (including 17 officers) killed and 375 wounded; the British sustained a loss of two-fifths of their army—866 casualties, of whom 85 were killed and 430 missing.

Greene, buoyed by the news of the victory at Yorktown, moved to various encampments about a 30-mile radius of Charleston. The British evacuated Wilmington, North Carolina, on November 8 and Dorchester, on the Ashley River 15 miles northwest of Charleston, on December 1, 1781. Greene sent Generals St. Clair and Wayne with Continental troops to Georgia. This force put Savannah under siege in January 1782 but did not have the strength to compel surrender. The British garrison, however, marched out for Charleston on July 11.

With peace a certainty by mid-1782, neither side in the South planned any widescale military operations. There was but a "little warfare, always irksome," in quest of supplies, wrote Henry Lee: thus, "incursions into our territory were occasionally attempted; sometimes with success, but generally the British detachments were forced to regain their lines, without the accomplishment of their views." What may have been the last action in the South was the skirmish at Combahee Ferry, 40 miles southwest of Charleston, on August 27, 1782: an attack led by General Mordecai Gist on a British force of 300 regulars and 200 Tories while on a foraging mission. During the nighttime encounter, the British held their own and escaped down the river. The evacuation of Charleston on December 14, 1782, presided over by Cornwallis's successor in the Carolinas, Major General Alexander Leslie, marked the end of the war in the South.

CHAPTER 11

Securing the Frontier

 American westward settlement by 1775 had just begun to penetrate into the trans-Allegheny region. The frontier line, starting at German Flats in the Mohawk Valley (70 miles from Albany), extended southwest along the eastern edge of the Appalachian plateau through Pennsylvania, Maryland, and Virginia, and then veered eastward in the Piedmont section of the Carolinas to Savannah, Georgia. Only the new settlements in the Kentucky bluegrass country reached beyond the mountains. The schemes of the great land companies for bringing pioneers into the western territories had all but fizzled.

The trans-Appalachian West, from the mountains to the Mississippi, did not figure to be a zone contested by the British and American armies. Manpower and resources were needed for the war in the East. In time, however, to protect pioneer settlers and to keep open communications for trade, war in the West became a reality.

The Native American Factor

The Indian population south of the Great Lakes and east of the Mississippi was sparse. In the frontier regions 40,000 to 50,000 natives lived north of the Ohio River (including about 10,000 Iroquois in upper New York), and about 75,000 resided south of the Ohio. Principal Indian groupings in the "Ohio country" were the Shawnees, Delawares, Chippewas, Wyandots, Potawatomis, Miamis, Ottawas, Menominees, Sauks, and Foxes. The Six Nations of the Iroquois consisted of the Mohawks and Tuscaroras just west of the Hudson River and also, moving westward, the Oneidas, Onondagas, Cayugas, and Senecas. Most southern Indians belonged to the "Five Civilized Tribes": Cherokees (in the mountain areas of North and South Carolina, Tennessee, and Georgia); Creeks (primarily in South Carolina, Georgia, and Alabama); Seminoles (Florida); Choctaws (Mississippi and Alabama); and Chickasaws (Mississippi).

By the start of the Revolution, frontier Indian relations had stabilized. The Iroquois mixed freely with settlers. By the Treaty of Fort Stanwix of 1768, they had relinquished all claims to lands west and south of the Ohio River. Pressured to take sides, the Iroquois, with the exception of the Oneidas and Tuscaroras, supported the British cause.

Indians in the South divided their allegiance. Reservation Indians, such as the Catawbas, who had almost been wiped out by a smallpox epidemic in 1759 in South Carolina, had little choice other than to contribute to the American war effort. Cherokees along the Virginia–Carolina frontier had been defeated by British regulars and militia during the Indian War of 1759–61. Yet settlers, in violation of treaties and the Proclamation of 1763, moved into the Cherokee country, making it a matter of time before hostilities would recur. The Creeks did not face much of a problem with the expansion of American settlements. They were unmolested in their far-flung trade emporium. Their long-standing feud with the Choctaws distracted from contention with the whites. American Indian diplomacy during the war succeeded in neutralizing the lower Creeks, a policy that was aided by Spain's entry into the war as an American ally, resulting in Spanish invasion of the British-held Floridas. Upper Creeks were mostly pro-British, and bands of this group occasionally assisted British military operations in the South.

The Indians of the Ohio country remembered the chastisement of Pontiac's War of 1763 and the battle of Point Pleasant in 1774. At the beginning of the Revolution they preferred a status quo, going their own way and profiting from the British trade. These tribes north and west of the Ohio River, however, recognized that British policy, according to the Proclamation of 1763, was one of containment of white westward expansion. The British continued their practice of doling out presents to the tribes, to a much greater extent than the American government could afford. It was not unexpected, therefore, that at one time or another the Algonquin tribes of the Ohio and Illinois country would side with the British, even if it meant going on the warpath together with their former enemies, the Iroquois.

Western Native Americans could not identify with the cause of Independence. The "American view of a righteous struggle against tyranny was not expanded to include American Indians," writes Dorothy V. Jones (1982). "It did not address itself to the problem of economic dependence that underlay Indian political sovereignty." Furthermore, "the American vision had the fatal flaw of making white Americans the leaders in the universal well-being that was to come when the vision was fulfilled" (pp. 120–21). The widespread Indian resistance may be seen as an extension of the pan-Indian revivalistic movement that had brought on Pontiac's War in the early 1760s. Militants had kept alive a distrust and hatred of whites encroaching on their lands. On the eve of the Revolution, delegations from northern and southern tribes several times exchanged visits. War made for Indian solidarity. As Gregory E. Dowd writes (1992): "Breeches within many Indian communities temporarily closed, religious nativism became submerged beneath a broader movement against Anglo-America, and the largest, most unified Native American effort the continent would ever see erupted with the American Revolution" (p. 46).

Militarily, the British had a scant presence in the area bounded east to west by the Alleghenies and the Mississippi and north to south by the Great Lakes and the Ohio River. Redcoats served only at fort-trade centers at Michilimackinac, Detroit, and Niagara. Thus, the British preferred a defensive strategy in the West.

Congress and the British government initially sought to avoid warfare in the West, including the employment of Indian auxiliaries. The war would be won or lost in the East, it was thought. Notwithstanding the military plans, Indians soon became involved.

Ethan Allen called on Indian support for the Canada invasion of 1775. Some Stockbridge Indians (Christian Indians, mainly remnant Mohegans) left their reservation in far-western Massachusetts to assist American troops. Thus, British policy changed accordingly. Guy Johnson, who had succeeded his uncle, Sir William Johnson, as imperial superintendent of the Iroquois and the northwestern Indians, received orders from Lord Dartmouth to encourage the Indians "to take up the hatchet" in summer 1775. On March 8, 1776, Congress followed suit in sanctioning military use of Indians in situations that it might approve. Under congressional auspices, General Philip Schuyler of the Northern army had the support of the Oneidas and Tuscaroras. On March 6, 1778, Congress instructed the Board of War to enlist southern Indians in Continental service. Except for a few Choctaws and reservation Indians, this policy had no success. The American government's greater priority was to ensure Indian neutrality. To superintend Indian relations, Congress, on July 12, 1775, established commissions (made up of three to five persons), each of which would administer three Indian departments: northern—tribes in New York and the Fort Pitt area; middle—the Ohio country; and southern—the southwestern sector. The British, having over twenty years' experience with the southern and northern Indian superintendencies, had an advantage in conducting Indian relations. They also had agents and British officers who resided among or near Indian tribes.

Regardless of both the British and the Americans' defensive strategies, it was realized that the West had to be won. Both sides ordered troops on a limited scale into the West. Savagery was provoked as much by the frontiersmen as by the Indians. The Americans' military action and destruction were bold reminders of the intent to encroach on Indian lands. Indeed, conquest itself was a means to that objective.

Indian War in the Southwest

Encouraged by British agents and visiting delegations from northern tribes, the Cherokees once again saw an opportunity to even the score with settlers along the southwestern frontier. Despite treaties and the Proclamation of 1763, frontier encroachment had continued into their hunting grounds, especially along the Watauga and Nolichucky rivers. Even the Watauga settlers had formed their own government in 1772. Dragging Canoe, son of the famous Little Carpenter (Attakullakulla), and the Overhill (westernmost) Cherokees repudiated the Treaty of Sycamore Shoals (actually a private purchase agreement in 1775 made by a faction of the Indians and the Transylvania Company). The treaty ceded that part of Kentucky and Tennessee bounded on the north by the Kentucky River and on the south by the Cumberland River. The British supplied arms to the Cherokees.

Hostilities began in the Georgia backcountry and in late June 1776 quickly spread to the Virginia–North Carolina frontier. Overhill Cherokees led by the Great

Warrior raided settlements on the Watauga and Nolichucky, invested Fort Caswell (Fort Watauga), and also put Fort Chiswell (near present-day Wytheville, Virginia) under a two-week siege. Militia quickly rallied. Evan Shelby defeated a band of Cherokees at the battle of Long Island (in the Holston River) on July 20, 1776.

In Georgia, Colonel Samuel Jack and 200 men drove away the Indian raiders and burned Cherokee towns between the Tugaloo and Chattahoochee rivers. South Carolina offered a £75 bounty on Cherokee scalps. Colonel Andrew Williamson led 1,000 South Carolina militia into the area of the Lower Towns (upper South Carolina Piedmont), destroying many of the Indian villages. Williamson's troops then joined with General Griffith Rutherford's 2,400 North Carolina militia in an expedition against the valley towns of the Middle Cherokees (60 miles west of the Lower Towns), laying waste to crops and 36 Indian villages.

To attack the Overhill Cherokees, the Virginia government sent out militia under Colonel William Christian. Christian's army of 1,800 men, "well equipped and in high Spirits," reached the French Broad River, destroying Indian towns on the way. There was ample evidence of Indian atrocities. At the house of Chief Dragging Canoe, the Virginians, according to John Redd, a soldier in the campaign, "found 7 scalps hanging up nicely painted and put in hoops and just in front of the town a stake to which Draggon [Dragging] Canoe had a short time before bound a small boy [Samuel Moore] and burnt him entirely up, and while the boy was burning the Indians held their dance."

The American campaigns into the Cherokee country brought the Indians to terms. The Cherokee War officially ended in May 1777 with the Indian leaders and commissioners from South Carolina and Georgia signing the Treaty of DeWitt's Corner, whereby the Cherokees surrendered almost all their territory in South Carolina. By a second treaty with Virginia and North Carolina commissioners at the Long Island on the Holston, the Cherokees ceded their lands east of the Blue Ridge Mountains. Dragging Canoe, however, refused peace and led a group, including several hundred warriors, to Chickamauga Creek (near Chattanooga) in the Tennessee River Valley.

The conclusion of the Cherokee War left the southwestern frontier in relative peace. There would yet be some trouble with the Chickamaugas (as the Cherokees under Dragging Canoe were called), Middle Cherokees, and the far-western Chickasaws. In 1778 a Creek war threatened briefly. Overall, however, the Creek Nation, split between neutral and pro-British factions, preferred peace with the Americans, though on occasion bands of warriors aided British forces. For example, 250 Creek warriors assisted the British in the capture of Augusta in September 1780. The defeat of the Cherokees had an important deterrent effect on the Creeks.

From their new location, the Chickamaugas made sorties against the Tennessee frontier settlements. Furthermore, as Governor Patrick Henry pointed out to Governor Richard Caswell of North Carolina, in January 1779 these Indians thwarted communication with "our posts on the Mississippi and Ohio" and prevented trade with New Orleans. British agents encouraged the Chickamaugas to persist in hostilities, thus maintaining a sort of "second western front." Two militia forays in 1779 did considerable damage to towns and crops of the Chickamaugas but increased the Indians' thirst for revenge.

In 1780, under British prompting, some of the Overhill Cherokees, resenting further land encroachments by the whites, also began raiding. Colonel Arthur Campbell and Lieutenant Colonel John Sevier, with 700 Virginia and North Carolina militia (many of them fresh from the battle of King's Mountain), defeated a combined force of Cherokees and Chickamaugas at the battle of Boyd's Creek on December 16, 1780. The following spring Sevier again campaigned against the Middle Cherokees and their Tory allies, and the next year led a force against the Chickamaugas, destroying their towns from the Hiwassee to the Coosa (in northern Alabama) rivers. The Chickamaugas then moved into the mountains, from where they harassed the Cumberland settlers of middle Tennessee. On April 1, 1781, Dragging Canoe and his followers lay siege to Bluff Fort (at present-day Nashville). At the battle of the Bluff near the fort, the pioneers won the field largely because they turned their many dogs loose on the attackers. Beginning in 1781, the Chickasaws from the Mississippi country also assaulted the Cumberland settlements.

Although the Chickamaugas and Chickasaws made trouble for the settlers in central Tennessee and beyond for another decade, peace existed along the southwestern frontier. Indians and militiamen had fought essentially a border war. Neither Congress, except for negotiations of its Indian commissioners, nor the American regular military forces had any role in quelling the Indian uprisings.

The Fort Pitt Sector, 1775–1779

Congress at first neglected the Ohio country, primarily because it was claimed by Virginia. The state and not the national government had responsibility for securing the region to the American cause. Pennsylvania also asserted jurisdiction over the immediate vicinity of Fort Pitt. Virginia, however, insisted on being in charge of this post. Fort Pitt, which was now part of a thriving village, was the key to domination of the upper Ohio Valley.

At the outbreak of the war in 1775, Captain John Connolly commanded Virginia militia at Fort Pitt. Soon exposed as a loyalist, he was forced to leave. Connolly then schemed to raise a frontier regiment, to be equipped at Detroit, which he hoped to lead in the capture of Fort Pitt and Alexandria, Virginia, and then to join up with Governor Lord Dunmore's loyalist force in Virginia. The plot never materialized, and Connolly wound up in the prisons of Philadelphia and Baltimore.

Virginia militia remained stationed at Fort Pitt as well as at the posts established by Dunmore in 1774: Fort Henry (Wheeling) and Fort Randolph (at Point Pleasant at the junction of the Kanawha and Ohio rivers). Captain Robert Campbell and then Captain John Neville succeeded to Connolly's command at Pittsburgh. In 1777 Virginia accepted Congress's offer to take over Fort Pitt and garrison it with Continental troops. Brigadier General Edward Hand assumed the command at Fort Pitt and the related posts.

While the Shawnees, Delawares, and Mingos (Ohio Senecas) of the eastern Ohio country were willing to abide by the recent peace treaties, certain bands of these tribes went on the warpath in 1777. These Indians terrorized Kentucky settlements, and, joined by Wyandots, assaulted Fort Henry (September 1–2). Nearby, they ambushed a patrol led by Captain William Foreman. (Twenty-six of the 34-man party were killed.) Any hopes of Shawnee neutrality was ended by one dastardly deed. Cornstalk, the Shawnee chief, went to Fort Randolph in December 1777 under a flag of truce to try and bring about peace. Militiamen, seeking revenge for the Indians' killing of one of their companions, burst into the fort and murdered Cornstalk and his son, Elinipsico. As Randolph C. Downes writes (1940): "with the death of these Indians the friendship of the Shawnee nation for the Americans perished forever" (p. 206).

Although there were insufficient troops on the upper Ohio to carry out a major campaign against the Indians and their British allies, General Hand did attempt an expedition in February 1778 versus Sandusky, a British commercial and military post. This ineffectual "squaw campaign," as the frontiersmen derisively called it, was forced to turn back because of high waters. Meanwhile, the situation around the upper Ohio became even more perilous. In May 1778, 400 Shawnee, Wyandot, and Mingo warriors held a week's siege of Fort Randolph and then moved into the Greenbrier River region, where they assaulted Fort Donnally.

With the northwestern frontier aflame with Indian warfare, which the British could exploit, Congress further committed itself to securing the Ohio country. Brigadier General Lachlan McIntosh was summoned from Valley Forge to command the western department, replacing Hand, who had asked to be recalled. Congress voted $900,000 for a 3,000-man expedition against Detroit. Two more Continental regiments—the 8th Pennsylvania under Colonel Daniel Brodhead and the 13th Virginia under Colonel John Gibson—were added to McIntosh's troops at Fort Pitt. In November 1778, General McIntosh established Fort McIntosh on the Ohio River at the mouth of Beaver Creek (30 miles northwest of Pittsburgh) and Fort Laurens, 70 miles further to the west (near present-day Bolivar, Ohio), as bases for a campaign against the Indians and the British at Detroit. An American offensive out of Fort Pitt, however, did not proceed very far. McIntosh, with 1,500 troops, scoured some of the Indian territory, but since the enlistments of many of his soldiers had expired during the winter of 1778–79, he had to abandon any full-scale campaign. During January and February 1779 Indians assaulted Fort Laurens. Holding on to this post, deep in the Indian country, became daily more precarious; food was in short supply, and disease at the garrison was rampant. Congress therefore decided there would be no forward stations that could not be adequately supported. Fort Laurens was abandoned on June 16, 1779. The Ohio country frontier again was left to take care of itself. Immediate attention would be given to the Iroquois problem in an area that was vital to provisioning the Continental army and to winning the allegiance of frontier settlers.

The Ohio Indians, intimidated by George Rogers Clark's western campaigns and the capture of the governor of Detroit (see "Kentucky and the Illinois Country, 1777–1779," pp. 173–176), were relatively quiet during 1779. The main Indian problem of the Fort Pitt sector soon shifted to the north with the Senecas of western New York. Colonel Daniel Brodhead, who had replaced McIntosh as commandant at Fort Pitt, led a 600-man force up the Allegheny River toward the Seneca country. The expedition was intended to be in conjunction with the more eastern Sullivan–Clinton Indian campaign. On the 400-mile round trip to the New York border, Brodhead's troops fought a small skirmish, took a few scalps, and destroyed Indian villages and fields, without losing a single soldier. If the results were meager, the expedition did relieve pressure on the western Pennsylvania settlements.

The Iroquois

The alliance of the Mohawks, Onondagas, Cayugas, and Senecas of the Six Nations with the British reflected in part the assiduousness of Sir William Johnson, the northern Indian superintendent, who had persuaded the Iroquois to participate in British military operations during the last two colonial wars. Upon Johnson's death in 1774, his work among the Iroquois was carried on by his son, Sir John Johnson, his son-in-law, Daniel Claus, and his nephew, Guy Johnson, the new Indian superinten- dent. But the main key to the alliance was the Mohawk chief, Joseph Brant (or Thayendanegea). Brant had attended an English school in Lebanon, Connecticut, and was an Anglican convert. His sister was the common-law wife of Sir William Johnson. The loyalist leader, John Butler, who resided in the Mohawk Valley as deputy Indian superintendent, also exerted a major influence among the Iroquois.

The British–Indian Invasion

The New York frontier had not spread very far westward at the start of the Revolu- tion, and the Iroquois were on relatively friendly terms with the pioneer settlers, both Whig and Tory. But the war interrupted this coexistence. The Iroquois assisted the British during the American invasion of Canada during 1775–76 and the Burgoyne campaign of 1777. The British strategy from Fort Niagara was to create irregular warfare along the New York-northeastern Pennsylvania frontier, with the employment of forces consisting of American Tories, Indians, and Canadian regu- lars and militia.

The grain- and timber-rich Mohawk and upper Susquehanna valleys, under the control of the rebels, offered inviting objectives for a British–Indian invasion. On July 3, 1778, Colonel John Butler, with a 1,100-man force from Niagara—400 Tories, a regular company, a militia regiment, and 500 Indians (mostly Senecas)— descended on the Wyoming Valley. The region, 30 miles long and three miles wide along the north branch of the Susquehanna River, contained a populous, if scat- tered, community. Colonel Zebulon Butler, a Continental officer on furlough, commanded 60 Continental soldiers and 300 militia, most of whom were concen- trated at Forty Fort, the principal of eight posts in the area. With refugees crowding into Forty Fort, the American commander decided to go out and fight a pitched battle with the invaders. Colonel John Butler spread his Indians in the surrounding

This painting by William Berczy is the most lifelike portrait of Joseph Brant (1742–1807), the great Mohawk war chief, who with his British allies, terrorized the New York–Pennsylvania frontier during the Revolutionary War.
National Gallery of Canada, Ottawa

woods, and the Americans were caught in a deadly crossfire. The defenders fled back toward the fort, only to be shot down or captured. According to John Butler's report, the Americans had 24 officers and 268 privates killed; the losses on the other side were one Indian killed, and two Tory rangers and eight Indians wounded. Only about 60 American soldiers escaped. John Butler did what he could to restrain the Indians, preventing them from plundering and also destroying the stores of liquor. All the captured Americans, including the noncombatants, were paroled on promise that they would not bear arms. Nevertheless, Butler gained the opprobrium of being a butcher; actually, the killing of surrendered soldiers occurred after he had departed. The Senecas stayed behind and slaughtered 70 soldiers. When these Indians later reached Niagara, they had 227 scalps. The famous legend that the Senecas' Queen Esther (the half-breed Esther or Catherine Montour) had personally tomahawked 15 American prisoners, who were shackled in a circle on a large rock, rests on no real proof.

The Wyoming Valley "massacre" did not involve the killing of noncombatants. Yet terrorized settlers of the whole northeastern Pennsylvania flooded the roads leading eastward. Refugees also came out from the settlements on the Delaware River. British–Indian raids continued after the Wyoming bloodbath. In September 1778 Captain William Caldwell, filling in for the ailing Butler, led Tory rangers and Indians on an attack on the settlements at German Flats on the Mohawk River, there destroying all the buildings. Butler was soon back in the field and raided communities on the Lackamaxen branch of the Delaware River.

On November 11, 1778, Captain Walter Butler (son of John Butler) together with 200 of his father's rangers and 500 Indians (Joseph Brant's Mohawks and Chief Cadaraquas's Senecas), moved against the Cherry Valley community, which consisted of 40 houses and 300 inhabitants, along the Mohawk River (40 miles west of Albany). Colonel Ichabod Alden commanded about 250 soldiers (including the 2d Massachusetts Continental regiment) at Fort Alden. He had ordered local settlers out of the fort and permitted officers to live in private houses. The invading force attacked the houses where the officers were billeted and then converged on the fort. Alden was killed as he raced from one of the houses. With the Indians going off in different directions seeking plunder, Butler decided not to take the fort. Twelve American soldiers were killed and 12 captured; in addition, some 30 noncombatants perished. Joseph Brant helped to save the members of one family, whom he knew, by having them put on his war paint. The Cherry Valley fight was hardly an event of wanton slaughter, but it was viewed as such by the frontiersmen, who now further embodied themselves in arms. An important effect was Congress's determination that the best defense on the frontier was an offense.

The Sullivan–Clinton Expedition

Acting on petitions from settlers of the New York-northeastern Pennsylvania frontier, Congress, on February 25, 1779, directed Washington to provide for "the chastisement of the savages." Washington offered the command of the Indian expedition to General Gates, who refused on grounds of age. Major General John Sullivan, who had a reputation for daring but otherwise was of questionable competence, was then selected. According to the plan of operations, Sullivan, with a division of Continental troops (William Maxwell's New Jersey brigade, Enoch Poor's New Hampshire brigade, and Edward Hand's Pennsylvania and Maryland troops), would set out from Easton, Pennsylvania, and march by way of Wyoming up the Susquehanna and at Tioga (near the New York border) form a junction with Brigadier General James Clinton's New York brigade. Clinton was to proceed up the Mohawk to Canajoharie and then make his way down Lake Ostego and the Susquehanna to Tioga. The army numbered 4,445: Maxwell, 1,137; Poor, 1,101; Hand, 732; and Clinton, 1,475. The combined force was to scour the territory of the Mohawks and eastern Senecas. It was also arranged, as already mentioned, for Colonel Daniel Brodhead to march northward out of Fort Pitt into the western Seneca country. Because of logistical problems, Sullivan's division did not reach Tioga until August 11. Even then Joseph Brant and Indians were raiding as far east as Minisink, New York, on the Delaware River.

On August 13, the main part of Sullivan's troops marched 12 miles up the Chemung River to the site of an Indian encampment. At the battle of Chemung, Hand led a charge against the Indians, who fled. The American loss was 7 dead and 13 wounded. After destroying a village, the troops returned to Tioga, where they linked up with Clinton's brigade on August 22.

Near Chuknut (Newtown), on August 29, the Sullivan–Clinton force engaged Joseph Brant's Indians and Walter Butler's Tory rangers. The Indians had been waiting a long time in ambush, and short of food, each warrior had been allocated a daily diet of seven ears of corn. The Indians had erected "some works on the other side of a morass," observed Lieutenant William Barton; upon a cannonade "they gave a most hideous yell and quit their works." After this "severe scattering engagement," the Americans went "in hot pursuit." The loss was 4 dead and 38 wounded, and for the Indians, at least 14 killed, 11 of whom were scalped by the Americans.

The Sullivan–Clinton army continued its trek up the east side of Seneca Lake and then westward as far as the Seneca town, Gathtsegwarohare, on the Genesee River, destroying villages and crops on the way. Major Jeremiah Fogg described the venture as "hunting wild turkeys, with light horse." The "nests are destroyed," he said, "but the birds are still on the wing." American forward parties killed Indians; Timothy Murphy, a scout, collected 33 scalps. One misadventure occurred on September 13 when the Indians ambushed a detachment under Lieutenant Thomas Boyd. This officer and Michael Parker were taken prisoner; both men were horrendously tortured—they were whipped; stabbed; their nails, tongues, and eyes were plucked out; their ears were cut off; their intestines were removed; and finally they were beheaded. The Sullivan–Clinton army started for home on September 14. Forty villages had been destroyed, with the loss of only about three dozen men.

Continuing Indian Hostilities

The Sullivan–Clinton expedition did not put an end to Iroquois warfare as had been expected. The Indians returned to their devastated villages and were bent on retaliation. They figured in the British strategy of 1780 for a general Indian invasion of the whole northwest frontier. Brant and Sir John Johnson attacked settlements along the Schoharie River. Johnson, with British regulars, Tories, and Indians caused havoc in the Susquehanna Valley, laying siege of Middle Fort in October 1780 before moving back up the Mohawk Valley. General Robert Van Rensselaer with 800 New York militia went in pursuit, catching up with the enemy on October 19. Johnson was hastily setting up breastworks when the Americans attacked just after sunset. This battle of Klock's Field (or Fox Mills) was indecisive, and the British and Indians headed back to Oswego without being pursued.

The Iroquois remained engaged in the war during 1781. Brant and his Mohawks ranged as far west as the mouth of the Big Miami on the Ohio, where on August 24 he fought troops under Colonel Archibald Lochry, who were on their way to join George Rogers Clark. None of the Americans escaped—6 officers and 30 privates were killed, and 12 officers and 52 privates were made prisoners. On July 10, Colonel Marinus Willett, with New York Continentals and militia, defeated several hundred Tories and Indians led by John Docksteder, near Canajoharie, on the Mohawk River.

In late 1781 Major John Ross and Walter Butler, with a force of 1,200 (Indians and British troops from Canada), raided settlements in the Mohawk Valley to within a short distance of Schenectady. Willett caught up with the enemy, which resulted in the battle of Johnstown (October 25). This proved the last major engagement of the war on the New York frontier. Ross retreated up the north side of the Mohawk. Some

Oneidas, in service of the Americans, overtook Walter Butler on October 30 and promptly killed him, shouting "Sherry Valley! Remember Sherry Valley!" In declining to chase after the enemy, Willett wryly commented, in a letter to Governor George Clinton of November 22, 1781: "In this situation to the compassion of a starving wilderness, we left them in a fair way of receiving a punishment better suited to their merit than a musket ball, a tomahawk or captivity." With news of the American victory at Yorktown and subsequent intimation of peace, in a few months Indian hostilities on the New York frontier ceased altogether.

Kentucky and the Illinois Country, 1777–1779

Beginning in 1775, a steady stream of pioneers entered the lush bluegrass region of central Kentucky by way of the Cumberland Gap and the Ohio River. By 1776 Kentucky had a half dozen settlements or "stations," with the principal sites being Harrodsburg on the Dix River and, to the eastward, Boonesborough on the Kentucky River. Judge Richard Henderson's Transylvania Company failed to establish a government, and in 1777 Kentucky became a county of Virginia. Indians of the Ohio country not only viewed the Kentucky settlements as an intrusion on their hunting grounds but also feared that the newcomers would stake out homesteads across the Ohio and threaten their own communities.

The "Year of the Three Sevens" was a bloody one in Kentucky. As Dale Van Every states (1977), the Indian offensive "was a spontaneous and unorganized expression of chronic Indian aversion to white settlers" (p. 108). Black Fish's Shawnees and other Ohio Indians raided at will in Kentucky. Harrodsburg and Boonesborough endured successive assaults during the spring and early summer. Heroic deeds were recorded, such as Simon Kenton's saving Daniel Boone's life during the Indian attack on Boonesborough on April 24, 1777. Both men were caught outside the fort, and Boone had a broken ankle and could not move. As two Indians readied to tomahawk and scalp Boone, Kenton shot one and clubbed the other, and then raced back inside the fort with Boone on his back. The Indian invasion of 1777 left only three stations in Kentucky—Boonesborough, Harrodsburg, and Logan's Fort (at St. Asaph's, 20 miles southeast of Harrodsburg).

In February 1778 Shawnees captured Daniel Boone, a captain in the Kentucky–Virginia militia, while saltmaking at Blue Licks, on the Middle Fork of the Licking River. Instead of meeting an expected terrible fate, Boone was adopted as a son by Black Fish himself and renamed Sheltowee (Big Turtle). After several months as a trusted "Shawnee," Boone learned of a planned attack on Boonesborough and managed to escape to give the Kentuckians timely warning. Black Fish and 400 Indians and French Canadians under Dagniauis de Quindre lay siege of Boonesborough for ten days, September 7–16, 1778. The Indians' efforts to set fire to the fort and to tunnel under the walls failed, and the invaders withdrew. The arrival in August of 100 Virginia and 50 North Carolina riflemen at the fort had enabled the defenders to survive the attack.

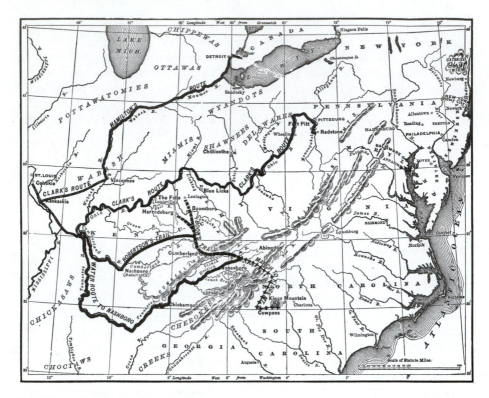

The West during the Revolution   *Source: Theodore Roosevelt,* The Winning of the West, *vol. 1 (1908). Courtesy of the Putnam Publishing Group.*

The Indian warfare aroused Kentuckians and the state of Virginia to take the offensive. George Rogers Clark traveled to Williamsburg with a plan for carrying the war in the West to the British and for conquering the Northwest for Virginia. Governor Patrick Henry and the Virginia council commissioned Clark lieutenant colonel and gave him the authority to recruit seven companies of militia (350 men). In addition to an order to defend Kentucky, Clark also had secret instructions to take possession of French-speaking villages in the Illinois country, and if possible, mount an assault against the British post at Detroit.

Meanwhile the British determined to press the war in the West. Lieutenant Colonel Henry Hamilton, commandant at Detroit, had at his disposal 500 regulars and Tory rangers. The British war office authorized Hamilton to employ Indians to create diversions and alarms but not to harm peaceful settlers. Hamilton, however, encouraged Indian war parties and gave the Indians presents for their services. Because Indians returned to Detroit with scalps, Hamilton soon had the reputation as the "Hair-buyer," which strictly speaking was not the case.

Clark collected whatever recruits he could at Redstone on the Monongahela— about 150 volunteers chiefly from the Shenandoah Valley and Holston River settle-

George Rogers Clark (1752–1818), the "conqueror" of the Old Northwest, 1778–79, shown here at middle age in the uniform of a Revolutionary War officer. Painted by Kentuckian Matthew Harris Jouett (1787–1827), the first major western artist. The Filson Club, Louisville, Kentucky

ments. General Edward Hand, commander at Fort Pitt, provided boats and supplies. Proceeding down the Ohio, picking up about 50 more men, at Corn Island (across from present Louisville), Clark read his secret instructions to his troops, which caused some of the men to desert. Upon reaching the mouth of the Tennessee River, Clark learned of the Franco-American alliance. On June 26, the expedition set out on a 125-mile march for Kaskaskia. At dusk on July 4 Clark and his men entered this French settlement, located near the place where the Kaskaskia River emptied into the Mississippi. The community was taken by total surprise. When Clark announced the news of the alliance with France, Chevalier Phillippe de Rocheblave, commandant of the local Fort Gage, surrendered without resistance. Captain Joseph Bowman secured Prairie du Rocher, 17 miles to the northwest, and Cahokia, further up the Mississippi across from Spanish St. Louis. Captain Leonard Helm was dispatched with 25 men to take possession of Fort Sackville at Vincennes on the Wabash River 100 miles above the Ohio, a mission accomplished without incident. In December, however, Hamilton launched a counteroffensive from Detroit and forced Helm to surrender Fort Sackville.

To recapture the Vincennes post, in February 1779 Clark set out from Kaskaskia overland with 170 men, fording the cold, rain-swollen streams along the way. Arriving at Vincennes after dusk, on February 22, Clark spread his men on the hills, giving the impression that he had a much larger force. Brisk arms fire continued throughout the night. Hamilton had only 79 men at the fort, half of whom were Frenchmen who refused to fight. His Indian allies fled from the village, and the townspeople gave Clark powder that they had hidden from the British commander. The next morning Clark paraded four Indians and one Frenchman disguised as an Indian, whom he had captured, in front of the fort and had them tomahawked. Commented Hamilton: "This horrid scene was transacted in the open Street. . . . The Blood of the victims was still visible for days afterwards, a testimony of the courage and Humanity of Colonel Clarke." Hamilton surrendered on February 24. He and 26 other prisoners were brought through Kentucky to Williamsburg. For a month Hamilton was fettered with irons in the town's common jail. He did not gain parole (release upon promise not to fight) until October 1780, whereupon he went to New York City, where he was exchanged. After visiting England, Hamilton returned in 1782 as lieutenant governor of Quebec.

Clark built Fort Nelson at the Falls of the Ohio (Louisville), where he made his headquarters for the next three years. In the spring of 1780 he began construction of Fort Jefferson on the Mississippi just below the mouth of the Ohio River. Clark still had unfinished business in the Northwest—to attack the British at Detroit—but this proved to be an elusive quest. Even though Congress voted a sum of $932,743 in 1779 toward raising 3,000 volunteers (2,500 to be from Virginia and Kentucky) for a march on Detroit, not enough militiamen were willing to participate in such an expedition.

War in the West, 1780–1782

The British western offensive of 1780 aimed at breaking George Rogers Clark's hold on the Illinois country and Kentucky. The upper Mississippi River would be secured as far south as Fort Jefferson, and raids would be made in Kentucky, with the ultimate goal of taking Fort Nelson. Captain Emanuel Hesse from Michilimackinac led a force of 950 that included Indians of the western Great Lakes region (even Santee Sioux) through Wisconsin and down the Mississippi. Colonel Arent De Peyster, who had replaced Hamilton as lieutenant governor of Detroit, sent Colonel Henry Bird with 150 whites and 1,000 Indians into the Ohio country and Kentucky.

The war on the Mississippi now had an international cast. In 1779 the Spanish had taken Baton Rouge and Natchez. The British campaign of 1780 in part was an effort to interrupt Spanish control of the Mississippi. Hesse's expedition arrived on May 26 at St. Louis, the Spanish administrative capital of upper Louisiana. Captain Fernando de Leyba, with a garrison of 350, withstood the attack. Because the Indians were discontented and feared the arrival of an army under Clark, Hesse made a rapid retreat. Clark organized a force of American, French, and Spanish volunteers, commanded by Colonel John Montgomery, which pursued Hesse as far as the Rock River and burned Indian towns in Illinois.

Bird's expedition left Detroit with 150 soldiers and 100 Lake Indians and on the way picked up about 700 Ohio Indians. The invading force carried artillery with them, a first for British troops in the West. Major Alexander McKee, former Indian agent at Fort Pitt, had charge of the Indians. On June 9 the army reached the banks of the Ohio. Because the Indians were interested mostly in plunder and did not want to face Clark's troops, instead of striking at Fort Nelson, Bird's force attacked stations along the Licking River. Ruddle's Station was compelled to surrender, and Bird burned the fort. The Indians slaughtered 200 of the 300 inhabitants—men, women, and children. Mrs. John Ruddle's infant was tossed into the fires, and when she leaped to save the baby she was tomahawked and also thrown into the flames. A few escaped, and 50 prisoners were brought to Detroit. Martin's Station, five miles away, capitulated on June 28 without firing a shot. This time Bird was able to prevent a massacre. Realizing, however, that he was losing control of the Indians, Bird refused to attack Bryan's Station and Lexington, 20 and 25 miles southeast, and headed back to Detroit.

Retaliation

Shocked by the bloodletting, Kentuckians were eager to seek vengeance against the Indians. George Rogers Clark, assisted by John Bowman and Benjamin Logan, with 970 men, crossed the Ohio on August 1, 1780, on a punitive expedition against the Shawnees. The Kentucky militiamen destroyed Chillicothe on the Little Miami and then marched on its sister town, Piqua, 12 miles away on the Mad River, a tributary of the Great Miami (present-day Springfield, Ohio). In August 1970 at the battle of Piqua, the largest military encounter of the American Revolution west of the Alleghenies, Clark faced 1,500 Indians under Blackhoof. Fighting fiercely outside the town, the Indians retreated to within their stockade. While Clark's six-pound brass cannon splintered the log walls of the fort, the Indians escaped out the back way. Clark counted 14 dead and 13 wounded among his men; the Americans took 73 scalps, and then looted and burned the town and fields. Lacking provisions to go any farther, the army recrossed the Ohio and disbanded at Covington.

In 1781 the Virginia garrisons at Kaskaskia, Cahokia, Vincennes, and Fort Jefferson were withdrawn. It was difficult to obtain supplies in the Illinois country because the French and Spanish settlers along the Mississippi did not accept Virginia paper money. Furthermore, available manpower was needed to protect Kentucky from Indian depredations.

The Indian situation in the Ohio country became more threatening with the Delawares abandoning neutrality, except for a band of the tribe who had been converted to Christianity by Moravian missionaries. Early in 1781, Colonel Daniel Brodhead led 300 regulars and militia from Wheeling toward the Delaware towns on the Tuscarawas and Muskingum rivers. At Coshocton, the main village of the Delawares, Brodhead found only 15 warriors, all of whom were killed. The women and children were left unmolested. Because the creeks and rivers were at flood level, the Brodhead expedition returned to Wheeling. A result of the campaign was that the Delawares moved westward to the Sandusky River, forcing their peaceful Moravian-converted kinsmen to accompany them.

The last year of the war in the West was one of almost unalleviated bloodshed and tragedy. Bands of Indians, principally Wyandot and Shawnee, raided in Kentucky; Delawares struck along the Pennsylvania frontier.

Colonel David Williamson and 300 Washington County (Pennsylvania) militia set out to punish the Delawares. At the outskirts of the Indian village of

Gnaddenhutten, on the east bank of the Muskingum, on the morning of March 8, 1782, they found Moravian Delawares, most of whom were working their fields. Clothing belonging to Mrs. Robert Wallace, who had been tortured and killed by Indians, was discovered in the area. Williamson had the Moravian Delawares brought to two buildings in the village, with the men assembled in one and the women in the other. Williamson asked his militiamen what to do with the captives; all but 18 voted to kill them. Sitting on the floors with their ankles shackled, singing hymns, the Christian Indians were tomahawked one by one. Ninety were slaughtered—29 men, 27 women, and 34 children. The militia burned the buildings with the bodies. Two Indian boys managed to escape.

Counter-Retaliation

The Gnaddenhutten atrocity stirred the Delawares to revenge. They joined up with other Ohio Indians in raiding Kentucky settlements. Another militia expedition of 400 mounted volunteers, commanded by Colonel William Crawford, a former Continental officer and a friend of George Washington, entered the Delaware country. On June 4, 1782, Crawford fought Delawares and Shawnees on the upper Sandusky. The next day, upon the arrival of a British reinforcement and more Shawnees, the militia troops were routed. Crawford and a small party lost their way and were captured by the Delawares. Even though Williamson had been responsible for the Gnaddenhutten massacre, a special torture was reserved for Crawford, inflicted by 35 braves and 70 women and children—an ordeal of various kinds of slow burning and mutilation, lasting two hours.

The Indians persisted in raiding Kentucky. On August 10, 1782, a band of warriors struck at Hoy's Station, a few miles south of Boonesborough. Captain John Holder pursued the Indians and was ambushed, with seven of his men killed. Five hundred Wyandots, Shawnees, Lake Indians, and a few Canadian rangers lay siege of Bryan's Station, August 15–17, and then moved westward across the Licking River to Blue Licks. Kentucky militia quickly rallied, and John Todd, Daniel Boone, and other officers with 182 men went after the Indians, without waiting to be reinforced by Benjamin Logan's troops. At Blue Licks, on August 19, the Indians counterattacked, sending the Kentuckians into flight. Among the 77 militia dead were Todd, Colonel Stephen Trigg, and Boone's son, Israel. To avenge Blue Licks, George Rogers Clark, with 1,050 mounted Kentucky volunteers, in what would be the last campaign of the Revolution, marched into the Ohio country. Though failing to engage the enemy, the expedition destroyed New Chillocothe (or New Piqua) for the second time, along with five other Indian villages.

The end of the war brought a few years' peace to the Northwest. The British now sought alliance with the Indians for nonmilitary purposes, chiefly to enhance the fur trading system. Eventually, small bands of Indian marauders plagued the Ohio River traffic and the northern Kentucky settlements, resulting after 1789 in renewed Indian warfare.

CHAPTER 12

The International Conflict

 Once the Americans decided for war and independence, it became imperative that they obtain recognition and material support from abroad. The United States could invite trade from neutral countries. Active foreign intervention, especially in naval and troop commitments, could contribute immeasurably to American victory.

France, with a score to settle with Great Britain for the loss of its North American empire, waited for an opportunity for revenge. Étienne-François, duc de Choiseul as minister of foreign affairs (1758–70) and also of war and the navy (1761–70) set France on a course of military preparedness. Charles Gravier, comte de Vergennes, foreign minister beginning in 1774, favored war with Great Britain. He feared that a British-American reconciliation would make the French West Indies vulnerable to attack. Vergennes's objective was not so much designed to produce territorial conquest but to improve the French position in world trade.

Acting on a report from a French observer in America that the colonies would soon declare independence, Louis XVI, on May 2, 1776, directed that 1 million livres' worth of munitions be sent to the colonies through the fictitious commercial firm of Hortalez and Company, headed by Pierre Augustin Caron de Beaumarchais, a playwright and courtier. By September 1777 Beaumarchais had spent 5 million livres for supplies sent to America. Silas Deane, agent for the Congressional Secret Committee of Correspondence, arrived in Paris in July 1776 and helped to prod the French for further assistance. The matter of the French contribution soon led to a bitter controversy both within and outside of Congress. The radical faction in Congress supported the contention of Arthur Lee, who had joined Deane in Paris as an agent, that the aid was a gift, whereas Deane, who was accused of being in a profit-making arrangement with Beaumarchais, insisted that the supplies were in the form of purchase. Congress refused to pay. Hortalez and Company was dissolved in 1783; not until 1835 did Congress bestow on Beaumarchais's heirs a partial settlement of 800,000 francs. Other aid included turning over ships to the Americans and allowing American merchantmen and privateers to use French ports.

Allies and Neutrals

In proposing his resolution for independence on June 7, 1776, Richard Henry Lee stated that "it is expedient forthwith to make the most effectual measures for forming Alliances." Four days later, Congress named a committee—John Adams, Benjamin Franklin, John Dickinson, Benjamin Harrison, and Robert Morris—to draw up a plan for treaties. The "Plan of 1776," approved on September 17, set forth a model for treaties of commerce and amity. Its goals were to end Britain's monopoly of American commerce, to avoid restrictive tariffs, and to allow neutrals to use the ports of belligerents, with only contraband of war prohibited. The principle behind the plan was "free ships make free goods." The plan defined contraband as excluding food and naval stores.

The French Alliance

The Americans thus entered into a "new diplomacy"—the idea of a world order versus power politics, to be attained chiefly by removing economic barriers. Congress let it be known that it sought only commercial relations with France and not a military relationship, for any entangling political-military alliance might make the United States too dependent on France. Congress proceeded to appoint plenipotentiaries to foreign courts—Arthur Lee, Benjamin Franklin, and Silas Deane. The three commissioners arrived in Paris by late 1776 and promptly discovered that they did not get along with each other.

Despite the personality conflicts, the three envoys made progress in negotiations, although they learned that France and Spain would provide full assistance only through formal alliances. Lee, Franklin, and Deane, therefore, went beyond their instructions and began working for military alliances. On February 2, 1777, Congress approved the change in objective.

With the Saratoga victory in 1777, France was assured that the United States would be a formidable ally against Great Britain. On February 6, 1778, the American envoys signed two treaties with France—one, in accord with the "new diplomacy," a Treaty of Amity and Commerce; and the second, a Treaty of Conditional and Defensive Alliance, which would bring France into the war. On May 4, 1778, Congress voted unanimously to ratify both treaties. The treaties recognized American independence and gave the United States favored nation status in commerce. France reserved the right to acquire British islands in the West Indies; each side agreed not to conclude a separate peace with Great Britain. The military alliance would go into effect only in the event of war between France and Great Britain. In mid-March 1778 when the treaties were announced by France, the two countries broke off diplomatic relations, and a state of war began during the summer with naval fighting in the Channel and the appearance of Admiral d'Estaing's warships off the coast of Rhode Island.

The Spanish Alliance

Spain withheld open recognition of the United States, although Arthur Lee's visit to that country in early 1777 had yielded secret aid and a friendlier disposition to

The Western European Theater   *Reprinted with the permission of Macmillan Publishing Company from* The War of American Independence: Military Attitudes, Policies, and Practice, 1763–1789 *by Don Higginbotham. Copyright 1971 by Macmillan Publishing Company.*

the American cause. Spain hesitated to enter the war (despite the defensive alliance of the third Family Compact of 1761 between the Bourbon rulers of France and Spain) for fear of American expansion beyond the Alleghenies and incitement of Spain's American colonies to rebellion. For the price of neutrality, the Spanish government proposed a peace congress in Madrid to mediate the Anglo-colonial dispute on the basis of recognition of American independence and leaving territory as it was actually possessed—*uti posseditis*. Thus, Great Britain would retain New York and other areas. Spain, however, insisted on the recovery of Gibraltar and Minorca. Great Britain refused to accept the proposals. As a result, on April 12, 1779, Spain joined France in the war with the signing of the Convention of Aranjuez. Both countries pledged to help achieve each other's objectives: for France, an expanded role along the African coast and in India, acquisition of Dominica in the Caribbean, and British compliance with the Anglo-French commercial treaty of 1713 (free trade in the East Indies); and for Spain, recovery of Gilbraltar, Minorca, and East and West Florida and expulsion of the British from Central America. Both countries agreed to stay in the war until American independence was secured.

Diplomatic Efforts in Other Nations

Diplomatic success with France and Spain encouraged a helter-skelter application for recognition and aid at the courts of Central and Eastern Europe, an endeavor that historians have labeled "militia diplomacy." Benjamin Franklin favored more of a "watchful waiting" policy. Writing to Arthur Lee on March 11, 1777, Franklin said that "a virgin state should preserve the virgin character, and not go about suitoring for alliances, but wait with decent dignity for the application of others." John Adams expressed a different view in his letter to Robert R. Livingston on February 11, 1782: "Your veterans in diplomatics and in affairs of state consider us as a kind of militia, and hold us perhaps, as is natural, in some degree of contempt; but wise men know that militia sometimes gain victories over regular troops even by departing from the rules."

Arthur Lee took it upon himself to leave Paris for Berlin in May 1777; he achieved nothing. Baron von der Schulenburg informed him that Frederick II (the Great) considered that Prussia "had too great a friendship for the King of Great Britain to enter into any connections with his rebellious subjects." Equally frustrated, Ralph Izard, appointed by Congress as envoy to Tuscany, learned in Paris that he would not be received, and declined to go to Florence.

In May 1777, Congress selected William Lee as commissioner to visit Prussia and Austria, but neither country permitted him to enter its capital. At the time Prussia and Austria were fighting each other in the War of the Bavarian Succession. Without mutual trade with the United States, the two countries were unwilling to recognize American independence or to conclude treaties of friendship and commerce. Eventually, Lee on his own initiative went to Holland and in September 1778 signed a draft of a secret treaty of amity and commerce with Jean de Neufville, a merchant and representative of the Dutch foreign secretary; neither of the two was authorized to enter into negotiations.

Henry Laurens, a former president of Congress, was appointed minister to Holland in 1780. Unfortunately, Laurens was captured at sea by the British, with a copy of the draft "treaty" in his possession. Laurens wound up in the Tower of London, and the British used the pretext of the treaty to declare war on Holland on December 21, 1780. John Adams, now Congress's peace commissioner, negotiated a loan from the Dutch of 5 million guilders at 5 percent for ten years, and in 1782 secured a treaty of amity and commerce between the United States and Holland.

Francis Dana of Massachusetts, in Europe as John Adams's secretary, had an assignment to enlist Russia in a treaty of amity and commerce. From 1781 to 1783, unable to speak either Russian or French, he vainly applied to be received at the court in St. Petersburg. Although the United States could not offer Catherine II anything to persuade her to enter into a treaty, the monarch did endorse principles of the American "new diplomacy" regarding neutral rights.

Neutral Maritime Rights

Protection of the maritime rights of neutrals during wartime had been a troublesome issue in international relations for centuries. By the eighteenth century, the nation-states agreed generally to the principle of *consolato del mare*—that is, neutral property (except contraband of war) was protected on enemy ships, but enemy property on neutral ships could be captured. This principle was modified in time so that neutral vessels were free to carry all goods other than contraband of war into the ports of belligerents. Large nation-states, however, frequently set their own rules, even to the extent of confiscating neutral vessels trading with the enemy. Great Britain was willing to respect the rights of neutral shipping with the enemy as long as there was no effective blockade, but persistently held to the position that all naval supplies (such as ship timber, sailcloth, cordage, pitch, tar, and turpentine) were prohibited from trade with the enemy.

To give international sanction to neutral maritime rights and to seek adherence to a narrow definition of contraband of war, on March 10, 1780, Russia's Catherine II proclaimed the Declaration of Armed Neutrality and invited other countries to join in a League of Armed Neutrality for mutual protection of neutral rights. Catherine proceeded to arm the Russian merchant fleet. The declaration had as much to do with the balance of power as with trade. Catherine's foreign minister, Count Nikita Ivanovich Panin, hoped to construct a "Northern system," which would enhance Russian influence in Europe. Sweden and Denmark joined the league in 1780; Prussia, Portugal, and Austria in 1781; and the Kingdom of Naples in 1783. Spain and France accepted its principles, as did the United States. Holland was not permitted membership in the league because it was feared that such action might provoke retaliation by Great Britain.

The League of Armed Neutrality generally adhered to the criterion of "free ships make free goods." Specifically, neutrals could freely trade at ports and along the coasts of nations at war; neutrals could carry goods belonging to belligerents except contraband of war; neutral shipping was to be excluded from an effectively blockaded port; and naval matériel was defined as noncontraband of war.

On October 5, 1780, the American Congress passed a resolution approving Catherine II's declaration. Although the League of Armed Neutrality accomplished little, it planted firmly in international law a definition of rights of maritime trade by neutrals during wartime. More importantly, the League of Armed Neutrality bolstered the United States' international position while isolating Great Britain.

The American Navy and Privateers

Because of the pressing need to support the army with manpower and supplies and the great advantage of British seapower, Congress did not make naval affairs a priority. It did create a small navy, first administered by a congressional committee, then from 1779 to 1781 by a Board of Admiralty, and finally by a marine agency in the office of the Superintendent of Finances, Robert Morris.

By February 1776 a Continental navy had gone to sea, commanded by Commodore Ezek Hopkins, and in March it captured a fort at New Providence (Nassau, in the Bahamas) along with a large quantity of cannon and military stores. During the war Continental naval ships for the most part operated singly and in American and West Indian waters. After Congress dismissed Hopkins in June 1778, there was no unified command. In all, Congress commissioned only 22 men-of-war (21 frigates and one ship of the line) for the navy; by 1781 just two were left. Yet the miniscule navy had some success, capturing 196 ships and collecting $6 million in prize money. Most states had little navies, often manned by militia, that sought chiefly to protect inland waters.

Congress and the states commissioned about 2,000 privateers during the war. Privateers were privately owned vessels, which carried letters of marque and reprisal from Congress or state governments, allowing seizure and possession of enemy merchant ships. Service on privateers held great attraction because both officers and men shared in all the proceeds from their prizes. Privateers, usually commissioned for a single voyage, operated mainly off American coasts and in the West Indies, where they could use French, Spanish, and Dutch ports. Some American privateers, often coming from French ports, sailed in European waters. During the war Continental and state-commissioned privateers captured 3,087 vessels (as indicated in the records of Lloyd's of London), with 879 ransomed or retaken. New ships used for privateering increasingly became larger, averaging 20 guns and a crew of 150 to 200.

Privateering both harmed and benefited the American war effort. The public did not receive any revenue from the captures, and some of the 11,000 seamen who served on privateers might otherwise have enlisted in the American land forces. Profits from privateering, however, gave rise to new fortunes, which spurred American maritime expansion.

Life on the high seas, in the navy or on privateers, entailed great risk to life and limb. There were many heroes, mostly unsung. Two commanders of naval vessels who stand out as legendary heroes for their valor are Gustavus Conyngham and John Paul Jones. During 1777–79 Conyngham terrorized British commerce in the

English Channel and in the Baltic and North seas, to the extent that London maritime insurance rates rose 28 percent. On one daring excursion he circumnavigated the British Isles, taking prizes along the way. Captured twice, Conyngham was lodged each time in Mill Prison (at Plymouth, England); following his second confinement, he was exchanged after about a year. He successively commanded such vessels as the *Charming Peggy*, the *Surprise*, and the *Revenge*. Conyngham captured 27 British ships and sank or burned 33 others.

John Paul Jones entered the Continental navy in December 1775, commissioned a lieutenant. Previously, he served on British rum–slave ships in the Caribbean. On the run for having killed a sailor, he changed his name from John Paul, adding his new surname Jones, probably to conceal his identity from the British. Jones found a patron in wealthy North Carolina congressman Joseph Hewes. Congress made Jones a captain in 1776 and ordered him to raid off the British Isles. Among Jones's many deeds was an attack on Whitehaven, a seaport along the Scottish coast, in April 1778. In August 1779 he commanded a refitted French merchantman, the *Bonhomme Richard*, and four small French ships. On September 23, 1779, Jones's little squadron came upon a 41-ship British merchant fleet, convoyed by two men-of-war, the *Serapis* and the *Countess of Scarborough*, at Flamborough Head off the Yorkshire coast. In the famous sea fight, Jones lashed his vessel to the larger *Serapis*; both vessels caught fire. Asked by the *Serapis*'s com-

Although John Paul Jones (1747–92) and other American naval commanders had many exploits to their credit, the duel between Jones's *Bonhomme Richard*, and the British *Serapis*, off the York coast, near Flamborough Head, Sept. 23, 1779, caught popular fascination. After Jones's capture of the *Serapis*, the *Bonhomme Richard* sank. Engraving from painting by Richard Paton.
National Archives

mander if he wanted quarter, Jones exclaimed: "I have not yet begun to fight!" American naval sharpshooters picked off sailors, and the *Serapis* surrendered, with Jones then taking it over after his own ship went down. The French frigate, *Pallas*, had kept the *Countess of Scarborough* from coming to the aid of the *Serapis*. The two-ship battle, one of the most bitter of its kind in naval history, resulted in Jones losing 150 killed and wounded out of his crew of 322. An estimated 100 British sailors were killed.

Allied–British Naval War—Europe

Armed conflict between England and France began on July 27, 1778, at the battle of Ushant (a Channel island off the coast of France). The fleets were nearly equal: 30 ships of the line under Admiral Augustus Keppel were pitted against the Brest fleet of 32 warships, commanded by Admiral Louis Guillouet, comte d'Orvilliers. The indecisive engagement came at a high price: the British lost 133 killed and 373 wounded, and the French 161 killed and 513 wounded. The British gave chase afterward but were outmaneuvered. One outcome was that it convinced the French of the need for Spanish naval assistance.

In accord with the Convention of Aranjuez, as soon as Spain entered the war, preparation began for a combined French and Spanish fleet to clear the English Channel and establish a beachhead in the southern British Isles. The story of the "second Armada" calls to mind the Spanish Armada of 1588, though it did not seek to conquer England and did not have the disastrous consequences of the earlier armada. The French and Spanish fleets joined at La Coruña, Spain, just above Cape Finisterre—66 ships of the line (100 in all), commanded by d'Orvilliers. At the French Channel ports, an invasion force of 40,000 troops was collected. The original objective was to seize Portsmouth and the Isle of Wight, which would be held until it was exchanged for Gibraltar. To avoid a long siege, the plans were changed to make landings at Falmouth and Plymouth on the south coast of Cornwall and to hold position throughout the winter.

The "invasion" threat caused great alarm in England. Most ships of the navy had sailed to other parts of the world and only Admiral Sir Charles Hardy's fleet of 39 ships of the line was available to challenge the Allied expedition. Fortifications were built at Plymouth, and hulks of ships were sunk across the mouths of the harbors. A royal proclamation of July 9 called for removal of all horses and livestock from the coast in the event of an Allied landing. Prisoners released from jail joined in the military defense.

The two fleets sighted each other off the southern tip of England on August 31. Hardy moved further up the Channel toward narrow waters, hoping for enemy pursuit. In early September he was reinforced by six more ships of the line, making his total 45. D'Orvilliers had second thoughts about continuing operations; he lacked confidence even in defeating Hardy. D'Orvilliers was short of about 7,000 seamen, and the army was still at Brest. Smallpox, scurvy, and typhus spread aboard the Allied vessels, and water and provisions were in insufficient supply. Hardy's fleet included seven double-decker ships with copper bottoms; these vessels could stay at sea for long periods and could in the future cause havoc to an anchored Allied fleet and transport vessels. The two fleets scarcely did more than parade in the Channel; the British fired no shots, and their loss consisted of one warship that inadvertently ran into the enemy. The "invasion" threat ended with d'Orvilliers taking his fleet to Brest on September 14.

French-Spanish naval strategy called for a siege of Gibraltar and Minorca and offensives in the Caribbean and the Indian Ocean. An Allied siege of Gibraltar began in July 1779 and lasted until the end of the war. The British garrison of 7,000, commanded by Lieutenant General George Augustus Eliott, determinedly held on despite acute shortages of supplies and the difficulties of facing relentless bombardment from a vastly superior force (at times numbering 40,000 men). Only three times did large-scale relief reach Gibraltar. Admiral Sir George Brydges Rodney and a fleet of 22 ships of the line and eight frigates, convoying 66 storeships and transports and 300 merchantmen, set out from Plymouth in December 1779. On the way down the coast of Spain, Rodney captured a small Spanish squadron and its convoy bringing supplies to the besiegers of Gibraltar. On January 16, 1780, the Rodney fleet engaged a Spanish naval force of 11 ships of the line and two frigates off Cape St. Vincent, at the southwest tip of Portugal. At this "Moonlight Battle," the British won a complete victory, with only four of the Spanish vessels escaping. Rodney then relieved both Minorca and Gibraltar, and on February 13 headed across the Atlantic for the Leeward Islands. The Spaniards had their revenge in August 1780, about 250 miles west of Cape St. Vincent, when an Allied fleet from Cadiz seized a large British convoy (55 of 63 ships) carrying troops and supplies to the British West Indies. A second British relief fleet, under Vice Admiral George Darby, made it to Gibraltar in April 1781.

The Allies launched full-scale assaults against Minorca and Gibraltar. Minorca fell in February 1782, but Gibraltar held on. A combined Allied fleet, assembled at Algeciras on the Spanish coast, unsuccessfully conducted a grand attack by sea during September 11–18, 1782. A new weapon used by the British—red-hot iron shot—set many enemy vessels afire. In the attack, some 2,000 French and Spanish seamen perished. The third and final relief of Gibraltar came in October of the same year, when a large fleet, ultimately destined for America and India, arrived, commanded by Admiral Richard Lord Howe. The British landing went unchallenged because a hurricane had disrupted the Allied fleet a few days before. On October 20, however, Allied men-of-war caught up with the British off Cape Spartel (Tangier, Africa); during a fight of several hours casualties were heavy, but neither side lost or had any vessels crippled.

As the war broadened, the British planned to capture the Dutch-held Cape of Good Hope, which would enhance the East India Company's operations. Commodore George Johnstone headed a naval expedition to that area, and in April 1781 he anchored at Porto Praya (La Praya Bay) at the island of Santiago in the Cape Verde Islands to take on supplies and water. A French fleet, commanded by Admiral Pierre de Suffren de Saint Tropez, France's greatest seafarer of that era, sailed into the harbor, not knowing beforehand the British were there. A short battle ensued, with Suffren putting out to sea and Johnstone in pursuit. But the British admiral gave up the chase. Suffren proceeded on to the Cape of Good Hope, where he left cannon and two battalions of troops to assist the Dutch defenders. When Johnstone arrived, he found the Cape garrison too strong to attack; sending part of his fleet to India, he returned to England. In 1782 the British captured Dutch forts on the Gold Coast of Africa. Elsewhere, in the North Sea, a number of minor actions occurred between Dutch and British squadrons.

On balance, the naval war in European waters was indecisive, but it importantly distracted from use of British sea power in North America and the West Indies.

War in the Caribbean

The Allied–British war in the Caribbean started in September 1778 when François-Claude-Amour, marquis de Bouillé, governor of Martinique, landed 2,000 men and captured Dominica. The British quickly retaliated, with Rear-Admiral Samuel Barrington wresting St. Lucia from the French in December 1778. Admiral d'Estaing, arriving from Boston with his fleet shortly after the capitulation, failed to recover the island. D'Estaing took St. Vincent in June 1779 and on July 6, in a bloody sea battle versus Vice-Admiral John Byron, captured Grenada. Byron had attacked before his ships were in proper formation, and his fleet was heavily damaged; the British lost 183 killed and 346 wounded, and the French 166 killed and 763 wounded.

Nearly a year passed before the next major naval battle. The fleets of Admiral Rodney and Rear Admiral, comte Luc Urbain de Guichen, fought off Martinique on April 17, 1780. Neither side gained advantage, with the French suffering the greater number of casualties and the British the heavier ship damage. The two admirals fought again at the battle of St. Lucia Channel on May 15, 1780.

In January 1781 Rodney received instructions to seize Dutch possessions in the West Indies. With the Dutch in the Caribbean not learning of war between England and Holland, Rodney quickly captured St. Eustatius, as he said, "as sudden as a clap of thunder." St. Eustatius, the "Golden Rock," though only six miles long and three miles wide, was the great trade center of the Caribbean and had been a mainstay of the Americans for supplies. The British also seized Dutch St. Martin and Saba.

As the war was about to end, British fortunes in the West Indies collapsed, a factor that gave American diplomats an advantage in the peace negotiations. The French captured St. Eustatius in November 1781, along with £250,000 pay destined for British troops in North America. Subsequently, St. Vincent, Dominica, St. Kitts, and other islands also fell. By February 1782 the British held only Jamaica, Barbados, St. Lucia, and Antigua. But then the war in the Caribbean suddenly reversed itself, with the British victory at the Saintes Passage on April 12, 1782, the last battle between the large fleets in the West Indies. On April 8, 1782, Admiral de Grasse set sail from Martinique with 35 ships of the line escorting 150 merchantmen to Haiti, in

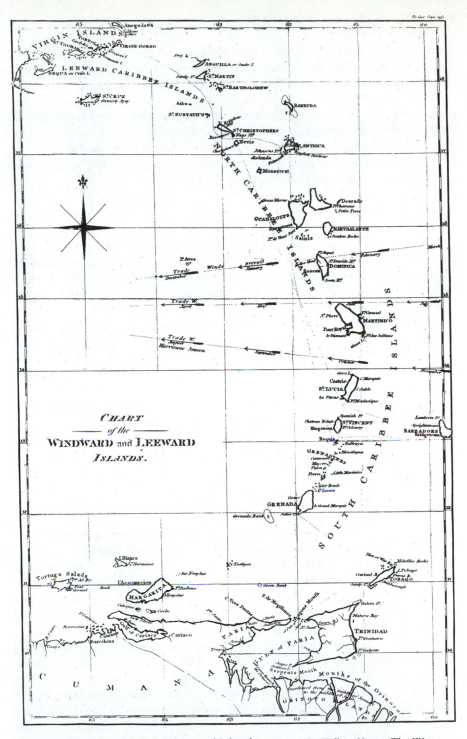

Chart of the Windward and Leeward Islands *Source: Sir William Young, The West-India Common-Place Book (London, 1807), opp. p. 195. Virginia State Library and Archives*

anticipation of launching a Spanish-French attack on Jamaica. As de Grasse's fleet entered the channel between Dominica and Guadeloupe, in which were the Saintes Islands, he came across Rodney's fleet. Rodney sent Admiral Hood and eight ships on ahead as a decoy. De Grasse took the bait and sent half of his fleet in pursuit. Just then the rest of Rodney's war vessels closed in and dissected the French naval force into three groups, which never reformed. The British captured the *Ville de Paris,* along with de Grasse himself, and four other vessels, which had all the artillery intended for an invasion of Jamaica. Rodney did not continue pursuit. Hence, the British victory was not as lustrous as it could have been and did little to affect the final round of peace negotiations.

While the battle of the Saintes aborted the invasion of Jamaica, Spain achieved other objectives in the Caribbean and along its coasts. General Juan Manuel de Cagigal, the governor of Cuba, and a fleet of 59 vessels, including the *South Carolina,* a South Carolina state vessel commanded by Captain Alexander Gillon, captured New Providence in the Bahamas from the British on May 7, 1782. "Nueva Providencia" and the Spanish Bahamas, however, lasted only 11 months, surrendering to British attackers on April 19, 1783.

In 1779 Bernardo de Gálvez, governor of Louisiana, and a motley force of regulars, militia, Indians, and local American and German settlers captured British posts along the lower Mississippi River—Manchac, Baton Rouge, and Natchez. On March 12, 1780, the British surrendered Mobile after a month and a half Spanish siege. Gálvez failed to take Pensacola, the strong British base in West Florida, in 1780, but the next year, with 7,000 soldiers and sailors, he conducted a successful siege of the garrison, aided by an explosion of its powder magazine. Brigadier General John Campbell and 900 defenders surrendered on May 10, 1781; thereafter the Spaniards proceeded to take control of all of West Florida.

The East Indies

In India the British ruled with a strong hand over the territories of Bengal and Madras and dispersed East India Company stations under Warren Hastings as governor-general (1774–84). The French had all but been driven out of India during the last war. The main base for French operations in the East Indies was Île de France (Mauritius), with 6,500 colonists, in the western Indian Ocean. The Anglo-French confrontation in the East Indies during the Revolution occurred primarily off the Coromandel Coast of southeast India and off eastern Ceylon.

As soon as news of war between France and England arrived in India during July 1778, British forces seized Chandernagor, a French post in Bengal. An army under General Sir Hector Munro and the East India squadron, commanded by Commodore Sir Edward Vernon, attacked the French-held Pondicherry to the south on the Coromandel Coast; the British troops numbered 10,500 (1,500 being Europeans). The French fleet in the area withdrew. After a bloody siege, the garrison of 3,000 (900 Europeans) surrendered on October 17, 1778. The British lost 224 killed and 693 wounded, and the French, 200 killed and 480 wounded. By spring 1779 all French possessions in India had fallen to the British, and the French stayed away from India for the next two years.

A more serious threat to British hegemony in India were the wars with the Indian state of Mysore and with the Marathas of west-central India. Hyder Ali, sultan of Mysore, invaded the Carnatic in September 1780 and annihilated a British force of 4,000 under Colonel William Baillie. The struggle turned to Britain's favor when General Sir Eyre Coote defeated Hyder Ali at the battle of Porto Novo in July 1781. Rival Maratha chiefs now began fighting among themselves.

The British expanded their conquest by the capture of Trincomali, a Dutch post in eastern Ceylon, in January 1782. At last, a French naval force returned to the Indian Ocean, commanded by Admiral Suffren. The French admiral, aided by the Mysorean adventurer, Tippu Sahib, captured Cuddalore in April 1782. The British East India navy was reinforced, with Rear Admiral Sir Edward Hughes in command. Hughes and Suffren fought five major naval battles: Sadras (India), February 17, 1782; Providien (Ceylon), April 12, 1782; Negapatam (a Dutch port in India), which the British captured, July 6, 1782; Trincomali, now captured by the French, August 31, 1782; and Cuddalore (failure of a British army and naval siege), June 20, 1783.

The French naval war in the Indian Ocean had a measure of success. Although the naval engagements were indecisive, the British fleet suffered heavy damage. Suffren managed to keep the sea lanes in the Indian Ocean open, and he was able to give encouragement to the Indian rebellions against the British. Suffren had also secured the important base of Trincomali. The Anglo-Dutch Treaty of 1783 returned Trincomali to the Dutch, compensating the British with a much lesser port, Negapatam, and free navigation of the Molucca Islands (East Indonesia).

Toward Peace

In August 1779 Congress drew up basic terms for a peace: recognition of independence; withdrawal of British forces; a definition of boundaries that included the Mississippi River; and restoration of fishing rights off Canadian waters. John Adams became sole peace commissioner. Any progress was delayed largely because the British government would not acknowledge American sovereignty as a precondition for peace.

On June 15, 1781, Congress appointed a peace commission made up of John Adams, Benjamin Franklin, Henry Laurens, John Jay, and Thomas Jefferson. The commissioners had discretionary authority but were instructed to insist on independence and include the French in the negotiations. Henry Laurens, a prisoner of war in London, did not join the other commissioners in Paris until late 1782. Jefferson declined to serve.

After Yorktown, Great Britain was willing to make peace. Further prosecution of the war seemed bleak, not only because of the defeat of its armies, but also because the navy was weak and undermanned, the French and Spaniards were winning in the Caribbean, and a French fleet threatened India. In February 1782,

Parliament resolved that the war be terminated, and the North ministry resigned on March 20, 1782. A member of the opposition in Parliament, the marquis of Rockingham, became prime minister. His secretary of state for home affairs, William Lord Shelburne, arranged for negotiations to begin, and Richard Oswald, an 80-year-old Scottish merchant, was sent to Paris to talk with Franklin. At the time Adams was in Holland negotiating the Dutch treaty, and Jay had not yet arrived from Spain where he had been the American minister. Charles James Fox, the British secretary for foreign affairs, sent Thomas Grenville to discuss peace directly with the French foreign minister, Vergennes. Rockingham died in July 1782, and Shelburne succeeded him as prime minister. Fox resigned from the ministry, and Shelburne took sole responsibility for peace negotiations through Oswald, who was joined by Henry Strachey in October 1782.

There was not much progress at first. The British insisted that the United States renounce claims to the trans-Appalachian territory and part of Maine as well as rights to the northern fisheries. Franklin suggested that the United States acquire Canada. By fall 1782 Adams and Jay had returned to Paris, and, with significant compromises made between the American and British negotiators, Jay drafted a provisional treaty. The British government now acknowledged that it was dealing with the "13 U.S." The American commissioners kept France out of the proceedings because they surmised that France intended to hold out to ensure that Spain received Gibraltar and that the Americans would be denied the western territory and navigation of the Mississippi River. On November 30, the British and American negotiators signed the provisional treaty, which was essentially the same as the later final treaty. Two clauses, formerly objectionable to the Americans, were now inserted; they pertained to collection of prewar debts and restoration of loyalist rights and property.

Vergennes, though shocked to learn of the separate treaty between the United States and Great Britain, knew that France and Spain had no choice but to conclude their own treaties. On January 20, 1783, then, the United States, France, and Spain signed "preliminary" treaties with Great Britain. To France, Great Britain ceded Tobago in the West Indies and Senegal and Goree Island in West Africa, along with fishing rights off Newfoundland; Great Britain recovered all the rest of its Caribbean islands. While Great Britain kept Gibraltar, Spain received the two Floridas and Minorca.

Great Britain proclaimed an end of hostilities on February 4, 1783, and the American Congress, receiving the text of the treaty on March 13, did the same on April 11, 1783. Congress approved the preliminary treaty on April 15. The peace treaties were all signed by their respective parties at Versailles on September 3, 1783. Congress ratified the Treaty of Paris on January 14, 1784, and ratifications were exchanged on May 12, 1784.

The final treaty between the United States and Great Britain acknowledged the independence of the United States and set boundaries at the St. Lawrence River, 45th parallel to the Great Lakes, the middle of the Great Lakes and from Lake Superior up the Rainy River to the Lake of the Woods, the Mississippi River, and the 31st parallel and the St. Marys River bordering the Floridas. The Americans could fish off the Grand Banks and in the Gulf of the St. Lawrence, and they could dry and cure fish on the unsettled shores of Labrador, Magdalen Island, and Nova Scotia. It was also agreed that debts owed creditors in each country be paid. Congress recommended that the states restore loyalist rights and property, that the British evacuate all military forces from the United States ("without . . . carrying away any negroes or other property of the American inhabitants"), that all prisoners of war be exchanged, and that both countries have the right of free navigation of the Mississippi. Of course, the treaty disappointed both sides in a few respects— namely, regarding the actual collection of debts and the restoration of loyalist property. Moreover, nothing was said about the thousands of slaves who went off with the British during the war. Nevertheless, the Treaty of Paris of 1783 may be regarded as a "birth certificate" for the United States, a recognition of the status of a nation among nations by the former mother country.

PART 3

The Underside
of the Revolution

CHAPTER 13

The Home Front

 Those Americans who lived within reach of moving or occupying armies and in major port towns experienced more hardships of the war than other civilians. Armies in the field appropriated provisions, wagons, forage, and livestock. Although both American and British military commanders severely punished soldiers for plunder, still robberies by military personnel and marauders occurred. The "Neutral Ground" (the area between the American and British armies) above New York City, eastern New Jersey, and the Carolinas, in particular, witnessed theft and destruction of property. Legal impressment entailed a burden, as bills for indemnification given by agents for seized items, though priced slightly above current value, rapidly depreciated, and farmers could only expect future redemption.

The war caused some temporary or permanent displacement of population. Citizens removed themselves from areas of warfare or from British occupation. At Newport, Rhode Island, and vicinity between 2,000 and 3,000 persons fled from the British forces. Throughout the states Tories departed on their own or were forced to leave. But Americans who supported the rebel cause and lived away from military forces went about their affairs much as usual. Economically, however, nearly everyone felt some effects of the war, negatively or positively. Fortunes were made from war profiteering and speculation, and the wartime economy led to expanded employment and productivity. Many of the lower and middle economic classes, however, especially in the towns and cities, faced shortages in essential goods and were caught in a price–wage squeeze. Citizens expressed dissatisfaction over the inability of governments to exact uniform and effective economic regulation.

Frustrations

Trade disruption, army requisitions, and the reluctance of farmers to sell for depreciated currency caused food and fuel shortages among civilians. Where tea was unavailable, substitutes were made from checkerberries or from sage and other resinous plants (balm tea). Salt was produced from lye in walnut ashes. Maple syrup took the place of sugar. A thick molasses (with a "tartist" flavor) came from the grinding of cornstalks and boiling the juice; such a concoction was distilled into rum.

There were other scarcities as well. Lieutenant Colonel Ebenezer Huntington wrote his brother from Norwich, Connecticut, on May 3, 1779, that "this whole part of the Country are Starving for want of bread, they have been drove to the necessity of Grinding Flaxseed & oats together for bread." A Boston town committee in March 1778 recommended that "on no Occasion whatsoever" should citizens "have more than *Two Dishes* of Meat on the same Day on their Table," and they should "avoid the Use of *Poultry* & every other Superfluity as much as possible." It was also advised that Bostonians should "make two dinners per week on fish, if to be had."

In the beginning, American patriots expected the war to be short, especially after the victories of Trenton and Burgoyne's surrender. Washington, who repeatedly positioned his army to avoid general battles, sought a pitched engagement during the Philadelphia campaign in the fall of 1777, hoping that a defeat of Howe's army would conclude hostilities. In his general orders of September 5 (just before the battle of Brandywine), the American commander in chief told his troops that for the British "their all is at stake—they will put the Contest on the event of a single battle—If they are overthrown, they are utterly undone—The War is at an end." The battle of Germantown produced the same expectation. Wrote General George Weedon four days after this engagement: "The Grand cause was in my opinion in one Quarter of an hour of being finally settled that day, to the eternal honor of America."

Of course, the war continued, spurred on by the British victories in the South. All the same, it was obvious that the British could not secure a wide swath in the territory of the new nation. Many Americans became war weary, and they felt that they had already given their full measure toward winning Independence. All that was needed was for the British army to go away. In disillusionment over the war effort and enduring economic hardship, even patriots had thoughts of reaccommodation with the British empire; many contemplated a return to the halcyon days when British rule was not oppressive. Thus, it is not surprising that residents of Prince George County (in the upper tidewater region of Virginia) put their names to a petition in summer 1781 calling for the legislature to make peace. At that time, Cornwallis was invading Virginia. Lafayette had an officer seize the petition, and it was "torn to pieces." Fragments of the document, however, were collected and preserved, and were kept by generations of the Ruffin family before surfacing at the Virginia State Library. Because of plundering and militia call-ups, as the document states, many Virginians had been "reduced to indigence so justly apprehensive, that their wives & helpless Children run the risk of shortly wanting even a morsel of Bread." If "the Sword be not quickly sheathed and Peace restored," this "land of warfare will . . . sink under the more dreadful effects of griping Penury and famine." Thus, "to stop the further effusion of Human Blood," the Virginia government should accept any truce terms and work for an "accommodation" with Great Britain, to renew "ties of friendship and interest, with the Parent Country."

"Patronesses of American Liberty"

American women contributed to the war effort in many ways. George Washington mentioned in February 1781 that from the commencement of the war women "have been the patronesses of American liberty." On the home front women also experienced additional work tasks, economic hardship because of the absence of their husbands, and even violence.

From time to time, instances of sexual assault by soldiers occurred, as revealed by affidavits collected by a congressional committee on British and Hessian atrocities. One example is that reported by a New Jersey resident in late December 1776 from information received from a Continental officer. In this case, British light infantrymen, who pretended to be "Searching for Rebels" near Princeton, asked a young woman to show them "Secret Places" in a barn. She complied, knowing that no American soldiers were hiding there. When inside the barn, one enemy soldier "Laid hold on her Strangled her to Prevent her crying out while the other Villain Ravisht her, and when he had done, he Strangled her Again While the Other Brute Repeated the horrid crime Upon her again."

Farmers and villagers in and around army encampments could expect direct contact with officers and soldiers. Officers were usually quartered in residences, paying their own way and with little objection from the householders. Nevertheless, citizens were always apprehensive of the soldiers nearby, for they were aware of the soldiers' potential for rowdyism, assault, or damage to property. A major complaint was the taking up of fence rails and trees; such was the case when Washington's troops, settling in at Valley Forge, sought wood for fuel and the building of huts. Lydia M. Post, a Long Island housewife, whose husband served in the Continental army, commented typically on the depredations in her neighborhood.

> They [Hessian soldiers] take the fence rails to burn, so that the fields are all left open, and the cattle stray away and are often lost; burn fires all night on the ground, and to replenish them, go into the woods, and cut down all the young saplings, thereby destroying the growth of ages. But worst than all, robbers come over from the main shore in boats, and keep us in constant alarm! They belong to no party, and spare none; freebooters, cowardly midnight assassins, incendiaries, indiscriminate, bold, and daring. (1970, 1859, p. 75)

Mrs. Post, however, did not seem to mind Hessian officers staying in her home, since they assured protection.

Phebe Bliss of Concord, Massachusetts, was one of many who rented out space in her home for military use; she took in British prisoners of war. Having young officers in and around one's home enlivened the social scene. Thus, Sally Wister, a 16-year-old Quaker girl who lived at her father's farm 15 miles from Philadelphia, noted in her diary of October 19, 1777: "I feel in good spirits, though surrounded by an Army, the house full of officers, the yard alive with soldiers,—very peaceable sort of men tho'. They eat like other folks, talk like them, and behave themselves with elegance; so I will not be afraid of them." Not everyone, however, agreed that military service enhanced good qualities in men. A pension deponent recalled that at the end of the war in Fauquier County, Virginia, the father and family of a prospective bride objected to the marriage with a soldier because "he was thought a dissipated man. All thought his habits as contracted in the army were such as to unfit him for marriage."

Aid to Military Dependents

Widows and orphans of soldiers often found themselves destitute. About one-fifth of the Continental soldiers were married, and their wives and children were also in desperate straits. Some form of allotment was available from state and local governments, and recruiting officers often promised the same to enlistees. Washington condemned such aid, however, as a drain on the army's meager financial resources. Writing to General William Maxwell on May 10, 1779, he said that "all that the common soldiery of any country can expect is food and cloathing. . . . The idea of maintaining the families at home, at public expence, is peculiar to us; and is incompatible with the finances of any government."

Various efforts—all too insubstantial—were made to relieve the distress of soldiers' wives and families. The Pennsylvania Assembly established pensions for the families of those militiamen killed or wounded in the war and required that local relief officials provide food and other essential items to families of poor militiamen in the field, not to exceed 20s. per week.

State and local governments, in general, gave limited direct aid to soldiers' families, but seldom quite enough. Charitable donations came from private sources, such as churches and individual persons. With currency depreciation rampant, one form of assistance permitted soldiers' families to purchase goods at a previous price, and another granted food assessed to a soldier's future pay—with the shortfall made up from public revenue. Such policies were slightly implemented and received little popular support. Thus, the Connecticut Courant of September 8, 1777, queried: "How is it that the poor soldier's wives in many of our towns go from door to door, begging a supply of the necessaries of life at the stipulated prices, and are turned away, notwithstanding the solemn agreements of the towns to supply such?"

Virginia repealed a law requiring counties to provide relief to military families because the cost was too great, but did permit assistance to the neediest cases to the amount of one barrel of corn and 50 pounds of pork for each person annually. Counties on their own decided on varied kinds of relief. Thus, on April 18, 1778, the Botetourt County court ordered that a cow and £15 worth of grain be given to Mary Alsop, whose husband was "engaged in the Continental service," and to their two children. Also on the county level, soldiers' wives who were thought capable of making wise purchases received cash grants. The Virginia legislature continued provision for the support of widows of fallen soldiers. Typically, the Hanover County court, on January 7, 1782, stipulated that Mary Anne Jolly

> widow of James Jolly a soldier who died in the service of the United States be allowed four barrels of Corn and 200 weight of Pork, for the year 1781 and the

same for the present year: being the allowance for herself and 3 children under the act of Assembly "For Recruiting the State's Quota for the Continental Army" and that the Commissioners of the specific tax for this County do furnish the same.

Women's Volunteer Societies

Anticipating war aid societies and the Red Cross in future wars, American women during the Revolution formed volunteer groups for the purpose of providing for the soldiers' material needs. One such organization had great success and inspired the formation of similar groups in several states—the Ladies Association of Philadelphia, founded in the summer of 1780 by Esther DeBerdt Reed, wife of Joseph Reed, the president of Pennsylvania. Women, divided into 11 teams, solicited door to door in the city and suburbs for money to purchase linen to make shirts for soldiers. A broadside, *The Sentiments of an American Woman,* published on June 10, 1780, and reputedly written by Mrs. Reed, called upon women to move beyond their previous "barren wishes for the success of so glorious a Revolution" and "aspire to render themselves more really useful." Women should emulate the deeds of great ancient heroines and Joan of Arc. "Our ambition is kindled by the fame of those heroines of antiquity," so the document declared, "who have rendered their sex illustrious, and have proved to the universe, that, if the weakness of our Constitution, if opinion and manners did not forbid us to march to glory by the same path as the Men, we should at least equal and sometimes surpass them in our love for the public good." Any good citizen will "applaud our efforts for the relief of the armies which defend our lives, our possessions, our liberty," and soldiers themselves will say, "this is the offering of the Ladies." The appeal of the Ladies Association was an early published declaration of women's equality in America.

Mrs. Reed died of dysentery on September 18, 1780, shortly before her thirty-fourth birthday, and Sarah Franklin Bache (Mrs. Richard Bache and daughter of Benjamin Franklin) succeeded to the leadership of Philadelphia's Ladies Association. The Ladies collected $300,766, equal to $7,500 specie, from 1,645 women, ranging from 7s. 6d. from a black servant to a donation by General Lafayette, on behalf of his wife, for $175 in specie. Mrs. Reed and others had wanted to give two dollars in good money to each soldier—a proposal, however, that Washington quashed because he feared the scheme would only heighten the soldiers' awareness of being paid in depreciated paper money. Instead, the women purchased linen and made shirts—2,200 in all during 1780–81. The marquis de Chastellux, a French traveler in America, commented on the Philadelphia women's war effort in his journal of December 1, 1780:

> This work consisted neither of embroidered tambour waistcoats, nor network edging, nor of gold and silver brocade—but of shirts for the soldiers of Pennsylvania. The ladies had bought the linen from their own private purses, and had gladly cut out and stitched the shirts themselves. On each shirt was the name of the married or unmarried lady who made it.

Women elsewhere made similar contributions. In Northboro, Massachusetts, 44 women spun 2,600 miles length of yarn to be used in making uniforms. While in Baltimore with a detachment from Washington's army in the spring of 1781, before marching for Virginia, General Lafayette persuaded the ladies of that city to make summer clothes for his troops.

Dr. Benjamin Rush grasped the significance of the effects of "total war" on women's lives. In a letter to John Adams on July 13, 1780, he said:

> The women of America have at last become principals in the glorious American controversy. Their opinions alone and their transcendant influence in society and families must lead us on to success and victory. My dear wife, who you know in the beginning of the war had all the timidity of her sex as to the issue of the war and the fate of her husband, was one of the ladies employed to solicit benefactions for the army. She distinguished herself by her zeal and address in this business, and is now so thoroughly enlisted in the cause of her country that she reproaches me with lukewarmness.

Rush also advised that now, with the increased involvement of American women in the war effort, Great Britain would do well to sue for peace. After all, he commented, " 'The Romans govern the world,' said Cato, 'but the women govern the Romans.' "

Generally, women's role in the production of textiles increased during the war years. The American Manufactory of Philadelphia employed about 400 women in this line of work and individual households also made clothing for the army. By mid-1776, 4,000 women in Philadelphia were spinning cloth in their own homes. Families also made more of their own clothes than before the war.

Women collected scrap metal for the war effort in the form of pewter plates, pots, and lead from window casings for the making of bullets. Mrs. Nathan Sargent of Massachusetts even removed pewter inscriptions from family gravesites. Although women made bullets at home, they made little stride in employment in the munitions industry. A few, however, may have worked in the Westham arms foundry near Richmond, Virginia, as George Muter, the state commissioner of war, observed in a letter to William Obryan on November 28, 1780: "The manager at the Foundry informs me, that of the hands sent up last, a Considerable number were women. Women not answering for the business there, any further than they are necessary for Cooking & Washing, I hope you can be able to dispose of them otherwise."

Women managed farms and stores while their husbands served on military duty. For the families of small farmers, this meant work in the field as well. Elizabeth Adkins, in a pension deposition, recalled that when her husband was drafted into military service during the summer of 1775, "He was gone all summer" and she "had to plough and hoe his corn to raise bread for the children." Men in service writing home to their wives often referred to "our farm" instead of "my farm." Despite broadened activities, expanded employment opportunities for women outside the household remained limited.

Wartime Finance

To meet the expenses of the war, Congress and the states resorted to paper currency, loan office certificates (bonds), and additional taxes. Depreciation of the currency caused difficulties in economic transactions, as well as inflation of prices and wages, and it tended to defraud those who received public compensation. Poor citizens in particular were hard pressed to find means to pay taxes.

The issuance of paper money offered some advantages. Unlike specie, it did not leave the country, and thereby it stimulated accumulation of wealth at home. Whatever depreciation occurred was distributed among all groups. On the other hand, the more paper money depreciated, the more debtors insisted on forcing it on creditors. The success of a paper money issue depended on a slow rate of depreciation. Indeed, this was the case at first, but then repeated emissions of paper money and a growing refusal to accept it in payment of debt led to almost complete devaluation.

Beginning in 1775, Congress issued $6 million in paper money, and thereafter each year, except in 1777, it greatly expanded the amount of currency in circulation. Congress pledged the public credit of the 13 states, each of which was responsible for withdrawing an assigned quota of the total amount issued. In all, Congress issued $200 million in paper money. (This was the limit set by Congress on September 3, 1779.) Congress hoped, in vain, that loans from foreign alliances would arrive soon enough to support the currency. Rapid depreciation set in by 1779; at the end of the year, the Continental money was worth $42.1 to one dollar in specie. Counterfeiting (to which the British greatly contributed) further hastened devaluation of the paper money. In March 1780 Congress ordered new bills issued at 40:1 and the old currency destroyed; for every forty dollars in old currency destroyed, the states would receive two dollars in the new Continental currency. But the program met with little success. Old currency remained in circulation; by July 1780 it was valued at 64.5:1, and in December of that year, at 100:1.

Last-ditch efforts were attempted locally to stabilize the currency. For example, in Philadelphia in November 1780, a committee of merchants headed by Frederick Muhlenberg, speaker of the Pennsylvania Assembly, agreed on a ratio of 75:1. The committee drew up a document to that effect which was to be subscribed to by householders and merchants; those who refused to sign were "to be held up to the Populace as enemies to their Country." Such actions, however, came to no avail.

In addition to paper money, Congress sought to finance the war by floating interest-bearing bonds (loan office certificates) in large denominations ($300–1,000), redeemable by the states. A Continental Loan Office was created on October 3, 1776, and each state appointed a commissioner of the Loan Office. The certificates were offered at 4 percent interest, which was increased to 6 percent in February 1777. The certificates were not very attractive inasmuch as interest in the private sector was 8 to 18 percent. The Loan Office certificates also depreciated. By the time the Loan Office closed in 1781, the people had purchased about $62 million in certificates, which in specie value amounted to $7,648,000.

The states issued paper money to the total amount of $209,524,776, with

Virginia and the Carolinas relying most heavily on this form of public finance. New England and Virginia issued 6s. bills; New York and South Carolina, 8s.; and elsewhere, 7½s. The bills lacked adequate security, however. Only Delaware and Georgia backed their currency with real estate—Delaware with mortgages, and Georgia with confiscated loyalist estates. The other states based their paper currency on the promise to pay (anticipation of tax revenue).

Additional state taxes had to be levied in order to reduce the amount of Continental currency and certificates and to supply and pay the armed forces, according to congressional requisitions. States expanded the usual tax base, such as revenue from port duties, property and per capita taxes, and fees, and sought new funds from excise and income taxes. Wartime tax measures led to some reform, as in Virginia, where eventually an equal land tax (regardless of quality of land) was replaced by an ad valorem land tax. Maryland abolished its poll tax, which had put an undue burden on the poor, and substituted a graduated property tax.

Virginia had as wide a variety of wartime taxes as any state: taxes on real estate, cash capital, mortgages, salaried income, interest received, various livestock, hogsheads of tobacco exported, manufactures, and luxury items such as carriages and billiard tables. A per capita levy was in the form of a poll tax and 5s. on every tithable person above age 21. One-half of most taxes could be collected in tobacco or hemp. Especially burdensome to the poor was the "specifics" tax, first levied in May 1780. "Due for every man, free or slave, and every female slave above age 16" were one bushel of wheat or two of corn or barley; or 10 pecks of oats and 15 pounds of hemp; or 28 pounds of tobacco. Spoilage, transportation problems, difficulty in finding persons who would serve as tax agents, and general resistance from the public thwarted the collection of this special wartime tax.

As the war continued, tax resistance began to mount in the states. At Gloucester, Rhode Island, in 1783 a mob released prisoners jailed for nonpayment of taxes. Daniel Morgan wrote Thomas Jefferson on March 23, 1781, on the situation in Frederick County, Virginia, shortly after he had returned home from his victory at Cowpens:

> When I arrived at home, I found the people in a ferment about the Taxes; and some went so far as to say they would not pay them. . . . This circumstance convinces me that a small force ought to be kept up in each county as well to enforce the Laws as to defend the States, for had great Britton it in her power to send ever so many men in the field against us, I should still be in hopes to repel them, but when ever I see the Laws trampled on with Impunity I shall begin to despair.

How unrealistic Virginia lawmakers were in levying the "specifics" and other tax measures is seen in the rather pitiable petitions of backcountry farmers. One from Montgomery County of May 28, 1782, pleaded that "Families residing on the Mountains & remote Parts of the Frontier Counties . . . cannot possibly make Payments in Hemp." Another from Botetourt County of June 3, 1782, asked that payment of taxes be in something that could be afforded—deerskins, shoes, linen, woolen cloth, butter, cheese, or bacon.

Wage–Price Controls

Real or contrived scarcities of domestic and imported goods available to consumers and currency depreciation fed inflation. Army agents often overpurchased supplies. The prices of imported goods were high because of the risk of capture from Europe and the West Indies, though offset somewhat by privateering. In addition, farmers withheld commodities from the market for higher prices and hard money. When there were wage–price regulations, employers tended to keep wages but not prices within the legal limits.

At the start of the war, prices and wages held stable, but by 1778 they had spiraled upward. From July 1778 to November 1779, as Steven Rosswurm (1987) notes, in Philadelphia and vicinity wholesale prices for flour, beef, sugarloaf, and molasses (63 percent of the foodstuffs bought weekly by laborers) had increased 1,100 percent. George Washington observed in April 1779 that "a wagon load of money will scarcely purchase a wagon load of provisions." To prevent scarcity, Congress and the states ordered temporary export embargoes. On several occasions, Massachusetts enacted a "Land Embargo," forbidding transportation to other states of rum, molasses, cocoa, linen, wood, and various food supplies.

Congressional and Local Measures

Artificial shortages imposed by monopolists drove up prices: engrossers purchased all of an available commodity, and forestallers acquired goods before they reached the market. Washington thought there was no greater crime than this practice. Writing to Joseph Reed on December 12, 1778, he said he would like to bring "those murderers of our cause (the monopolizers, forestallers, and engrossers) to condign punishment. . . . I would to God that one of the most atrocious of each State was hung in Gibbets upon a gallows five times as high as the one prepared by Haman [for Mordecai, in the biblical book of Esther]." No punishment "is too great for the Man who can build his greatness upon his Country's ruin."

Congress recommended that states seize and forfeit the grain and flour of engrossers. State and local governments passed antimonopoly measures, but they were difficult to enforce. On February 8, 1779, Massachusetts enacted a law against "monopoly and forestalling," which provided that no person other than bakers could purchase grain or flour more than what was needed to feed his family until the next harvest; another law in June required selectmen to seize hoarded goods, with payment in "the common currency of this state." Actually, intimidation and threats of harm had greater effect on monopolizers than legal sanctions. Elizabeth Drinker, on May 26, 1779, wrote that in Philadelphia "the Bell-man went about the City at near ten this night—desireing the people to arm themselves with guns or Clubs, and make a sarch for such as had sent any Flour, Gun Powder &c out of town, with great threats to the Torys."

Congress encouraged price controls at the local level. In creating the "Association" in October 1774, Congress advised "that all manufactures of this country be sold at reasonable prices," and "vendors" should sell at "accustomed" rates. During

1775–76 Congress suggested maximum prices for tea, coffee, salt, sugar, and other imported goods and a markup of purchases for the army at 5 percent.

It was difficult to achieve a united front for price controls. In urban areas, whereas small shopkeepers wanted a ceiling of prices only on food and firewood, artisans and laborers favored general price controls. Wholesale importers and prosperous merchants desired higher prices not only because of profitability but also because as creditors they would receive higher interest payments.

Although measures were passed to prevent overcharging, such as paying a fine up to equal the price of goods, complicated legal proceedings made for little enforcement. Public-spirited citizens, however, banded together from time to time to try to keep prices in check. Mass meetings and extralegal committees brought pressure to bear on merchants to hold prices down. However, threats of direct action and being branded in the press as "enemies of the country" proved only a slight deterrent.

The Wage Picture

On the labor front, the demand for skilled and unskilled workers rose. Industrial production expanded to support the war effort, and jobs were vacated by persons on military duty. Some extra employment needs were met by the increased use of blacks, children, apprentices, and foreign artisans. Even prisoners of war were hired out; in Pennsylvania during the summer of 1777 Hessian captives earned ls. per day. Occasionally war-related industries employed American troops, but Washington opposed this practice as a distraction from duty. Southern states drafted slave laborers for public service. South Carolina paid owners 10s. per day, but Georgia, only 3s. In Virginia slaves worked in the lead mines of the western counties—some of them as punishment for aiding the British; others belonged to loyalists. Exemptions from military service were freely given to laborers in occupations affecting the supply and transportation of troops.

Because of labor shortages, workers were in a position to insist on fringe benefits (such as board and room), better jobs, more steady employment, and payment in specie or goods. Still, wages did not keep pace with money depreciation and inflation. Overall, workers, unlike others in the economy, such as merchants and farmers, profited little from the war.

Relations between industrial employers and employees deteriorated. At Fredericksburg, Virginia, in 1781, workers at the state arms factory almost walked out because of wages paid in paper money. General Adam Stephen, who had a gunnery near his home at Martinsburg, Virginia, heard constant complaints from his plant manager, especially about work slowdown, grumbling, employees taking leave without notice, and problems in retaining skilled workers. Once when the manager, Anthony Noble, returned from having made a delivery of weapons, he "found the Hands all Idle, standing out for more wages, and not a single Gun made."

Coordinate Regulation

Congress, state legislatures, and intrastate and interstate conventions at one time or another adopted measures to fix wages and prices, but with almost no success. A convention of 13 delegates from New Hampshire, Massachusetts, Rhode Island, and Connecticut met at Providence, Rhode Island, during December 25–31, 1776, and drafted a wage–price code on almost everything except real estate. It recommended rates for farm labor at 3s. 4d. per day and for mechanics and tradesmen computed according to "usages and custom." Congress, responding to the Providence convention, recommended that the states pass regulations for wages, prices, and profits at the 1774 (pre-nonimportation) level. Only New England adopted regulations; New York, Pennsylvania, and the southern states did not.

Massachusetts led the way in attempting to fix a definitive standard for wage–price regulation. In its antimonopoly act of 1777, the legislature specified rates for wages and for domestic commodities in Boston, with the expectation that the towns would follow suit. Imported goods could sell at wholesale 175 percent above the cost at the place of origin; retail sales were allowed only a 20 percent markup. Other New England states also took some action. Little compliance resulted; many towns did not elect committees to oversee enforcement. A Springfield, Massachusetts, conference of New England and New York delegates, meeting July 30–August 5, 1777, recommended the abandonment of price regulations, and by fall of that year the New England states had ended their price-fixing programs.

Realizing that economic regulations could be effective only if all the states adopted them, Congress on November 22, 1777, called for three regional conferences: delegates of Georgia and South Carolina to meet at Charleston; North Carolina, Virginia, and Maryland to meet at Fredericksburg, Virginia; and the eight northern states at New Haven, Connecticut. The conferees were to establish prices for commodities, labor, and charges of innkeepers. The New Haven conference was the only one to convene, with delegates attending from all the northern states except Delaware. A report of January 13, 1778, recommended a wage–price scale; it suggested mainly that the price of labor, manufactures, and domestic products be 75 percent above the rates of 1774 and that innkeepers could charge 50 percent above current liquor prices. Only several New England states made any effort to implement these guidelines.

Because of the ill success in implementing price regulations and because many states refused to participate in such a program, Congress, on June 4, 1778, advised the repeal of all price-fixing acts. It declared: "Limitations upon the prices of Commodities are not only ineffectual for the Purposes proposed, but likewise productive of very evil Consequences to the great Detriment of the Public Service and grievous Oppression of Individuals."

Still, efforts to establish and coordinate price-fixing did not cease altogether. From time to time, conventions of towns within the states of Massachusetts, New Hampshire, Connecticut, Rhode Island, New York, Pennsylvania, and Delaware attempted to establish wage–price codes. A leading example is the Concord meeting of July 1779, with representatives from 140 Massachusetts towns, which set maximum prices; 75 towns ratified the agreement. On June 6, 1780, the Pennsylvania Assembly, responding to local demands, set the "Average Price of Common Labor" at 20s. per day; although courts of quarter sessions were charged with enforcing this rate, there is no evidence that they did.

A final interstate price-fixing effort was made in 1780. Upon a call by the Massachusetts Assembly, a Hartford convention of New England delegates, on October 28, 1779, adopted a resolution summoning a meeting in Philadelphia of representatives from all the northern states southward to Virginia. The Philadelphia convention met January 29–April 4, 1780, with delegates from all the invited states except New York and Virginia who refused to participate. It appointed a committee to prepare a list of prices and to report at a later meeting. With New York's and Virginia's refusal to attend, the convention did not meet again. But even the failure of the interstate conferences pointed to needs that would be addressed when a new national government was created under the Constitution.

Industry

The war put severe limits on trade and all but destroyed the New England fishing industry; at the same time, it acted as a stimulant to manufacturing. Shipbuilding recovered some of its losses through the construction of American privateers and warships. The war promoted American manufacturing of flour, munitions, iron and other metal products, leather, clothing, distilled liquors, salt, and lumber. The states offered subsidies, premiums, and loans to encourage production of war-related materials.

Domestic-household manufacturing prospered beyond what it had been before 1774. The marquis de Chastellux (November 17, 1780) described a typical household clothing industry during a visit to West Hartford, Connecticut:

> The inhabitants engage in some industry in addition to their prosperous agriculture; some cloths and other woollen stuffs are manufactured here, rather rough, but durable and suitable for clothing people who live in the country, that is in any town other than Boston, New York, or Philadelphia. I went into a house where they were preparing and dyeing the cloth. This cloth is woven by the country people, and is then sent to these little factories, where it is dressed, pressed, and dyed for two shillings "lawful money" per yard.

Craftsmen engaged in further subsidiary work; for example, blacksmiths made bayonets and repaired muskets, and carpenters built cannon carriages.

Each state had a munitions program, including the establishment of public-owned manufactories of weapons and gunpowder. The gunneries helped bring America into the age of the Industrial Revolution by employing the principles of plant integration, specialization, and continuous production. An arms manufactory complex included a number of forges, water-powered mills for grinding and polishing barrels and ramrods, lock and bayonet shops, and a fitting and assembly place. Congress established the Board of War and Ordnance in June 1776, and a year later installed Thomas Butler as the "Public Armourer," to supervise the network of arms and gunpowder production.

Economic Mob Action

Hoarding of necessary goods, price-gouging, and refusal to accept paper currency in purchases were all practices that would set off mob action. One of the earliest mob disturbances was the salt riot in Virginia in summer 1776. Before the war, Virginians had depended on Great Britain and the West Indies for most of their salt supply. From spring to summer 1776 the price increased from 1s. to 15s. per bushel. Backcountry farmers descended on warehouses in Hanover and Henrico counties, just outside of Richmond, and carried away the salt supplies.

Women sometimes took matters into their own hands. Women from the North End in Boston became infuriated with a bachelor merchant, Thomas Boylston, who had a hogshead of coffee that he refused to sell at a fair price. A crowd of not "your Maggys but respectable Clean drest women" marched on Boylston's store. Abigail Adams wrote her husband on July 31, 1777:

> A number of females, some say a hundred or more, assembled with a cart and trucks, marched down to the warehouse and demanded the keys, which he refused to deliver. Upon which, one of them seized him by the neck and tossed him into a cart and discharged him; then opened the warehouse, hoisted out the coffee themselves, put it into a truck and drove off.

About the same time a mob of women in Beverly, Massachusetts, seized two hogsheads of sugar from a merchant and forced him to sell at the legal price. A Boston newspaper of October 9, 1777, reported a similar instance in East Hartford, Connecticut: "a corps of female infantry . . . marching westward about one mile, in martial array and excellent order . . . attacked and carried without opposition from powder, law or conscience, Mr. Perkin's store, in which was lodged a quantity of sugar designed for the army of which they plundered and bore away in triumph 218 lb."

In Boston during spring 1777 a mysterious figure who went under the name of Joyce, Jr. (undoubtedly borrowing from the name of the person who arrested Charles I and who was one of the two masked executioners of the king) published a warning:

> Whereas there are several Merchants, Shopkeepers and others in this Town, who have a large Quantity of Dry Goods, and West-India Produce, which they have secreted, and still refuse to sell, altho' the good People of this State, and the Army, are in immediate Want of such Articles; and others that do sell, are guilty of many wicked and evil Practices, in adulterating certain of their Goods, and others refusing Paper Currency. . . . I HAVE therefore thought fit to issue this my NOTIFICATION, strictly charging and commanding all Persons who are guilty of any or all the Vices and Enormities herein before enumerated, that they forthwith cease all such nefarious Practices, otherwise they may rely on Judgment without Mercy; as I am determined to punish with Rigour all such notorious Offenders.

Joyce, Jr. lived up to his threat. On April 19, 1777, as Abigail Adams reported, five merchants

Abigail Adams (1744–1818), shown here at age 22 in a painting by Benjamin Blyth, often commented on political subjects and the need for racial and social justice in her correspondence with her husband, John Adams, and friends. *Massachusetts Historical Society*

were carted out of Boston under the direction of Joice junior, who was mounted on horseback, with a red coat, a white wig, and a drawn sword, with drum and fife following. A concourse of people to the amount of five hundred followed. They proceeded as far as Roxbury, when he ordered the cart to be tipped up, then told them if they were ever caught in town again it should be at the expense of their lives. He then ordered his gang to return, which they did immediately without any disturbance.

Philadelphia abounded with turbulence during 1779. On January 12, 150 sailors, on strike for higher wages, marched to the docks and unrigged ships. Soldiers soon arrived and put an end to the demonstration; 15 of the strikers were arrested. During May 24–31, gangs roamed the streets, intimidating merchants, especially flour factors, and threw several dozen of them in jail, from where they were eventually released by the courts. Wrote Elizabeth Drinker, on May 25, "Men with clubbs &c have been to several Stores, obliging the people to lower their prises."

Mob action peaked in Philadelphia with the "Fort Wilson" riot of October 4. Some 150 to 200 city militiamen, protesting price increases, marched up Walnut Street toward the house of James Wilson, who had been involved in speculation and had defended merchants brought before price-control committees. Several dozen merchants, lawyers, and army officers, including Generals Thomas Mifflin and William Thompson and Captain Robert Campbell of the Continental army, joined Wilson at his home. "With the Drum after them, beating the Rogue's March," the militiamen paraded past Wilson's house, giving three cheers. Just as the rear had passed, Captain Campbell fired a pistol at the militiamen from the third floor. The militiamen faced about and fired into the house. During the ten-minute "battle," Campbell and five militiamen were killed, and 14 wounded. President Joseph Reed, accompanied by the Philadelphia First Troop Cavalry (the "silver stocking" militia) and some of Colonel George Baylor's Continental dragoons, rode to the scene and 15 militia demonstrators were arrested and fined. As a result of the mob action, the government distributed food to the poor. During the crisis some citizens fled the city, as Samuel Patterson wrote Caesar Rodney on October 16, "for fear of Vengeance." A year later, in June 1780, with the city again threatened with disturbances, President Reed declared martial law.

The economic riots occurred with virtual impunity for the participants. Rioters consisted of the "middling" as well as the "lower sort." The mobs had singular objectives and quickly dispersed. In most instances, as extralegal arms of the community, mobs acted to enforce laws, which governments had been unwilling or unable to do.

CHAPTER 14

The Common Soldier

 The enlisted men of the Revolution, ragtag and bobtail and hardly more than faces in a crowd, were subject to the disdain of officers and the general public alike. Washington, surveying the quality of his raw recruits, in a letter to Lund Washington of August 20, 1775, declared: "I dare say the men should fight very well (if properly officered) although they are an exceedingly dirty and nasty people." Yet common soldiers unflinchingly endured adversity and the hardships of service, a core of them staying with the army throughout the war. Thus, an appreciative Washington could state in his Farewell Orders of November 2, 1783, that "the unparalleled perseverance of the armies of the United States, through almost every possible suffering and discouragement, for the space of eight long years, was little short of a standing miracle."

Many men volunteered for soldiering in the Continental army out of a sense of patriotic obligation. Unfortunately, once they had performed a single tour of duty, they did not reenlist. Others, coming from the dregs of society, viewed service as a security of livelihood. Adventure and glory held attraction to enlistees, as did awards of bounties. The assiduity of recruiting officers reaped in volunteers. Some militia were drafted into regular service for short periods at a time. Recruits poured in during the *rage militaire* of 1775; thereafter, enthusiasm for enlistment rapidly dwindled as sullen veterans—either discharged, on furlough, or deserting—returned home.

If, as John Adams observed to his wife, the Continentals who paraded through Philadelphia on August 24, 1777, did not have "quite the air of soldiers," the American fighting men had one great advantage over the enemy. A visiting Frenchman, in the summer of 1777, noted this difference:

> the European soldier, his will, his personality, in fact his very instinct for self-preservation have been stifled and destroyed. In battle he is a mere machine, motionless, without personal feelings, controlled only by hidden springs. . . . Must we not admit that it is far better to command an army of free men fighting for their independence, whose inborn love of liberty is manifested even in their methods of waging war? Such men may be conquered but they will still preserve this spirit of freedom which they have imbibed with their mother's milk. (Echeverria and Murphy 1977, p. 205)

In combat, American Revolutionary War soldiers, as have their counterparts throughout the ages, experienced paralyzing fear, while others were indifferent to their own safety, fighting courageously and with hatred of the enemy. To most soldiers, writes John Ferling (1980), "a battle often seemed a melee of events to be endured, not understood" (p. 102). Accentuating the terror of combat in the eighteenth century was its close-at-hand method of fighting. Younger and single men performed in battle better than those who were older or married. In American wars overall, as Ferling notes, soldiers were sometimes reluctant to fire on an enemy: one-fourth did not fire at all, and three-fourths did not use their weapons effectively.

The soldiers generally reacted to battlefield gore in a matter-of-fact manner. Thus, Sergeant Elisha Bostwick of the 7th Connecticut regiment observed at the time of the battle of White Plains:

> as we were on the declivity of the hill a cannon ball cut down Lt. Youngs Platoon which was next to that of mine; the ball first took off Chilsons arm which was amputed & he recovered it then took Taylor across the Bowels, it then Struck Sergt. Garret of our Company on the hip and took off the point of the hip bone. Smith & Taylor were left on the Spot. Sergt. Garret was carried but died the Same day now to think, oh! what a Sight that was to See within a distance of Six rods those men with their legs & arms & guns & packs all in a heap.

As British and American army units drew up for battle, the soldier would have time for only a moment's reflection on his past life and on the danger of being killed, wounded, or captured. It was an ordeal of courage and stamina. Yet he had but little choice but to mesh with the flow of movement with his comrades—to engage in fighting, retreat, or flee in panic. A greater test of morale were the long marches and camp duty, beset with deprivation and suffering.

Recruitment

As the war lengthened, Congress discovered that men did not fight out of patriotism alone and that it was necessary to add a mercenary incentive. In 1776 Congress voted $20, 100 acres of land, and a $20 yearly clothing allowance as bounties for enlistment of privates. The land bounty for officers ranged from 150 acres for ensigns to 500 acres for colonels and generals. In 1779 Congress raised the money bounty for enlisted recruits to $200. At that time pay was 20s. a month. Enlistments were for the duration of the war, though a slightly smaller bounty was given for a three-year service. States also provided bounties for Continental enlistees and for their militia in the field, with amounts surpassing Congress's offer. Joseph Plumb Martin, who reached the rank of sergeant, commented on the land bounties: "Congress did indeed appropriate lands under the denomination of 'Soldier's land,' in Ohio state or some state, or a future state, but no care was taken that the soldiers should get them." Bounties for short-term enlistments of militia assigned to

Continenal service spurred recruiting. General John Paterson, writing to General William Heath on March 31, 1780, however, lamented that the troops at West Point were "nine months' abortions, sent here with bounties . . . naked, lifeless, and dead, who never saw action, are now counting days, hours, and minutes they have to tarry in service." Several months later, Paterson noted that bounties had "little purpose than to hire the populace to visit the army."

The nondisabled enlisted man had no expectation of a military pension. Other than establishing the Invalid Corps that remained in service during the war, Congress left to the states the relief of the military disabled. Not until 1818 did Congress pass a law to aid any war veteran impoverished and in "need of assistance from his country" for support—$20 per month for officers and $8 for privates and noncommissioned officers who had served to the end of the war, or for nine months. In 1828 all surviving enlisted and officer veterans who had joined for the war and served to the end were granted pensions of "full pay" as of March 3, 1826. The pension act of 1832 granted pay, not to exceed that of a captain's salary, for all who had served on active duty two years—Continentals, state troops, militia, and navy. A smaller pension for life was also given to those who had served six months. Remarkably, at this late date there were 24,260 claimants (by January 1833), with the average annual pension of $75.97. The last Revolutionary War pensioner, Daniel F. Bakeman, died on June 30, 1867.

In response to a congressional resolution, by spring 1778 11 states had instituted a draft from among militia for service in the Continental army. For those selected, typical was a draft notice in Chelsea, Massachusetts, of May 1778:

To Dea. John Sail, SIR:

This is to inform you are this evening drafted as one of the Continental men to go to General Washington's headquarters, and you must go or find an able bodied man in your Room, or pay a fine of twenty pounds in law. money in twenty-four hours.

Samuel Clark, Capt.

Not too unexpectedly, "Deacon Sail" paid the fine, thereby avoiding service.

Characteristics of Enlistees

Because recruits were so scarce, less than desirable persons were often allowed to enlist. It was believed that service would be good for the riffraff, while at the same time removing them as burdens to communities. Typical of the socially undesirable recruits were the "liquor listees" at taverns, inducted by overzealous recruiting officers. Congress prohibited this practice, and such persons could be discharged but seldom were they actually released. Service offered escape from family domination, debts, jail, servitude, and apprenticeship. In some instances convicts and loyalists were pardoned if they joined the army. Thus, John Sanders, a horse thief in New Jersey, sentenced in 1776 to two floggings, had his second whipping suspended when he entered the army. Tories sentenced to death in a Morristown, New Jersey, court, were given pardons upon joining the army. Although Congress prohibited the enlistment of prisoners of war, this restriction was not heeded.

Recruiting officers often overlooked the age of inductees. The basic physical requirements for service were a height of five feet and two inches and an age span of 16 to 50. Claude Blanchard, a French commissary, in the summer of 1781 commented on Washington's troops on the Hudson: "There were some fine looking men, also many who were small and thin, and some children twelve or thirteen years old. They have no uniforms and in general are badly clad."

The majority of soldiers who remained in service had known poverty. "The hard core of Continental soldiers," writes John Shy (1976), "the soldiers at Valley Forge, the men who shouldered the heaviest military burden were something *less* than average colonial Americans" (p. 173). Regarding Peterborough, New Hampshire, Shy found that of about two dozen men who had long service (of 170 who had enlisted, most of the town's adult males), seven resided outside the town, two were transients, two had deserted from the British army, two were black, six were legal paupers after the war, one was a landless day laborer, one had been jailed for debt, and one was mentally ill.

Continental troops, whether deservedly or not, had a bad reputation. A French officer, observing the American army, wrote that "the regular regiments were composed entirely of vagabonds and paupers; no enticement or trick could force solid citizens to enlist as regulars, inasmuch as they had to serve as militia anyway." Colonel Francis Johnston wrote General Anthony Wayne from Albany on November 17, 1776: "I have been assiduous in my Endeavours to enlist, but all such as are fit for service are already engaged, the Others are only *Food for Worms*— miserable sharp looking Caitiffs, hungry lean fac'd Villains."

Communities were glad to be relieved of misfits. In 1776 Captains Alexander Graydon and David Lennox, officers in the Pennsylvania line, went to the eastern shore of Maryland, hoping to recruit unemployed seamen. At a tavern they met a "gentleman of note," Dan Heath, who "helped us . . . to recruit, a fellow, he said, who would do to stop a bullet as well as a better man, and as he was a truly worthless dog, he held, that the neighbourhood would be much indebted to us for taking him away." Soldiers, mustered out of service, who could not find employment reenlisted. General Heath wrote the Massachusetts Council in March 1780 that there were many discharged soldiers in the state, with whom "no persuasions could induce them to enlist." But after having visited their friends, "they are now out of business, are destitute of money and clothing, the times difficult, and the demand for labourers not yet come. Some employment they must seek for a support." Hence, such persons had an "inclination to reingage in the army."

A study of the Virginia Continental line, using a sample of 658 privates and noncommissioned officers, shows that of 419 men whose ages were known, 90 percent were under age 25; the median age of new recruits was 20; 21 soldiers were ages 14–15; most had no education, often signing their names with an "X"; and 82 percent were born in Virginia. Of the 658, only 5 were of foreign birth. Most Virginia soldiers left the army after their initial enlistments expired. Mark E. Lender's (1980) examination of several hundred men of the New Jersey brigade indicates that 90 percent were poor and that half were landless or had too little land to farm; only 4 to 5 percent were foreigners. Most of the enlistees were laborers or workers who had some craft skills. One-half of the New Jersey troops had not resided where they enlisted.

A 1973 study of Maryland Continental soldiers by Edward C. Papenfuse and Gregory A. Stiverson reveals that a Baltimore company of 102 men comprised no farmers at all; there were 35 laborers, and the rest were listed as having tradesmen's skills. A Maryland roster of 1782 indicates that 40 percent of enlistees were foreign born (England, Ireland, Scotland, or the European continent accounting for most of these). As elsewhere, Maryland enlistees came from the poorest level of society. Even for the native-born soldier from Maryland, "poverty was endemic," and "in view of his marginal economic existence it is not difficult to understand the attraction of the enlistment bounty which was equivalent to approximately one-quarter of the total assessable property owned by the average recruit or his family" (p. 124).

Black Enlistees

About 5,000 blacks enlisted with the American army during the Revolution. After 1776 Congress authorized the service of free Negroes in the Continental army. All states, except South Carolina and Georgia, allowed free blacks to substitute for draftees and also subjected them to the draft. The New England states permitted slaves to join the army on their own, with their owners being compensated at public expense. Blacks fought in battles throughout the war, beginning with Lexington, Concord, and Bunker Hill. The adjutant general's report of August 24, 1777, listed 755 blacks in 14 brigades of the Continental army. A Hessian officer in October 1777 observed that no American regiment "is to be seen in which there are not Negroes in abundance and among them are able-bodied, strong, and brave fellows." Slave recruits had several advantages over whites: blacks tended to enlist for the duration of the war, and, as former slaves, they were not as likely to desert and return home.

While African Americans served mostly in racially mixed units, there were several all-black groups: a Massachusetts company styled the "Bucks of America," the second company of the 4th Connecticut regiment, and most significantly, the 1st Rhode Island regiment. In February 1778 the Rhode Island government was hard-pressed for recruits since the British controlled two-thirds of the state. Thus, the legislature provided for enlistment of two regiments (one actually raised). The act mentioned that in history there had been "frequent precedents of the wisest, the freest and bravest nations having liberated their slaves and enlisted them as soldiers in defence of their country." Any slave entering the service became "absolutely" free; their masters received compensation up to £120 for the enlisted slave. Although Rhode Island repealed this law after several months, slaves still joined the army. Colonel Christopher Greene (a white officer) commanded the black regiment, which initially consisted of about 140 men and later about 250. The regiment saw major service during the war, including the battle of Yorktown. After Greene was killed on May 14, 1781, at Points Bridge, Croton River, New York,

Lieutenant Colonel Jeremiah Olney had charge of the regiment until its disbandment on June 13, 1783. At that time, Olney praised his men as having shown "unexampled fortitude and patience through all the dangers and toils of a long and severe war."

Congress's plan in 1779 to enlist 3,000 slaves in the South, with compensation for masters, went awry with opposition from Georgia and South Carolina planters. Thousands of blacks fled to the British armies during the war, but only a few, such as those who served in Dunmore's "Ethiopian corps" in 1775–76 and as "Black Dragoons" in the Carolinas, were put under arms. Some Hessian units, however, welcomed blacks as regular soldiers.

Most blacks in the American armies and militia and British forces were engaged as service troops, such as drummers, fifers, trumpeteers, orderlies, guides, cooks, pilots on waterways, teamsters, artisans (blacksmiths, sawyers, carpenters, and the like), and pioneers (laborers). Some of these were inducted into military service, and some were not. Pioneers generally were forbidden to carry arms; instead, they performed menial work, such as erecting fortifications, repairing roads, felling trees, foraging, digging latrines, and cleaning streets.

The British made ample use of service troops, much in the same way as did the Americans. Several hundred blacks in Cornwallis's army acted as batmen (orderlies) and body servants. Each field officer could have two blacks as servants, and captains, subalterns, and sergeants in the staff departments, one each. Most of the black fugitives, however, served as pioneers, notwithstanding General Clinton's proclamation in June 1779, which promised that blacks deserting the rebels would have "full security within these Lines" to pursue "any Occupation which he shall think proper." General Phillips organized 250 black defectors into a company of pioneers, led by a white officer, for erecting fortifications around Portsmouth, Virginia, in 1781. At the same location, Cornwallis set 1,000 blacks "to cut wood and work on the trenches." Typical of the many blacks who responded to the British for service was John Twine, a free man from Petersburg, Virginia. Originally he was a wagoner for a Virginia regiment; in 1779 he defected and became a servant to a British officer. Wounded in a battle, he went to England after the war.

Clothing and Food

"Poor Fellows! they exhibit a picture truly distressing—More than Half Naked and above two thirds starved." Thus wrote Quartermaster General Nathanael Greene in January 1780 when the army at Morristown was acutely short of supplies. From the soldier's point of view such a situation was often the case. Not only delays in purchase and transportation, but also the inferior quality and mismatched sizes contributed to clothing shortages. Clothes were acquired in only three sizes. As Washington wrote the clothier general, James Mease, on July 18, 1777, with men forced to wear undersized garments, "the Clothes do not wear out fairly, but tear to pieces."

Insufficient clothing made for unsanitary conditions. On May 13, 1778, General Anthony Wayne appealed to Richard Peters, secretary to the Board of War, from Valley Forge: "give us linen that we may be Enabled to Rescue the poor Worthy fellows from Vermin which are now devouring them. . . . Some hundreds we thought prudent to Deposit some six foot under Ground—who have Died of a Disorder produced by a want of Clothing." Clothing sent by a state could be used only for its own troops, who had the cost of clothing deducted from their pay. On many a cold night an enlisted man shivered on the ground under a single blanket, which, as Private Joseph Plumb Martin complained, was frequently too short and made of "thin baize, thin enough to have straws through without discommoding the threads."

Soldiers suffered extremely because of want of shoes. At times they went about their duty assignments and endured long marches while practically barefoot. Sergeant John Smith, on the retreat from New York during November 1776, wrote that "our soldiers had no shoes to wair; was obliged to lace on their feet the hide of the cattle we had kill'd the day before." Joseph Plumb Martin reported a similar experience. He made himself a pair of moccasins from "a small piece of rawhide," which

kept my feet (while they lasted) from the frozen ground, although . . . the hard edges so galled my ankles, while on a march, that it was with much difficulty and pain that I could wear them afterwards; but the only alternative I had was to endure this inconvenience or to go barefoot, as hundreds of my companions had to, till they might be tracked by their blood upon the rough frozen ground.

Colonel William Shepard, in January 1778, noted that "at least 400 men in the Brigade which I belong to that have not a shoe nor a stocking to put on."

During the early part of the war, the closest soldiers came to uniforms were hunting shirts and leggings. Eventually, upon induction into the service, an enlistee could expect to receive a long jacket, waistcoat, belt, breeches, stockings, shoes, and a hat, and, as accoutrements, a knapsack, blanket, canteen, gun, cartridge pouch, bayonet, and bayonet belt. In November 1775, Congress decreed that all clothing be dyed brown. Not until 1779 did the army adopt blue coats as the standard uniform. Facings on the coats designated particular military units. But only New York and New Jersey troops constantly wore the blue and buff uniforms often thought to have been the usual attire of the whole Continental army. Soldiers wore either knitted wool caps or cocked hats, turned to the left to allow them freedom when doing the manual of arms.

Improper cooking and lack of a balanced diet was a major cause of illness. A soldier's fare fell short of the rations promised by Congress. Supposedly, a soldier each day was to have one pound of beef, three-fourths pound of pork, or one pound of fish; one pound of bread or flour; one pint of milk; a gill of rum, brandy, or whisky; and a quart of spruce beer or cider. Spruce beer, easily brewed, was a popular beverage that also had a health benefit as a deterrent to scurvy. To make spruce beer, one boiled needles of evergreen trees for three hours, then strained the liquid into casks, adding yeast and sugar or molasses and allowing for fermentation.

On a weekly basis, a soldier could also expect three pints of peas or beans or equivalent vegetables and one-half pint of rice or a pint of Indian meal. Even regular rations were often deficient. As Joseph Plumb Martin noted, a pound of beef "when it had gone through all its divisions and subdivisions, would not be much over three quarters of a pound, and that nearly or quite half bones!" Flour was frequently "eaten half-cooked." All too often, a repast consisted of "a little musty bread and a little beef."

The worst suffering for lack of food in Washington's army occurred at Morristown in December 1779 and early 1780, the most severe winter of the eighteenth century. During the first week in January the snow was four to six feet deep, thus preventing supplies from reaching the army. Days at a time, the men went without meat and bread. Joseph Plumb Martin declared that

> we were absolutely, literally starved. . . . I did not put a single morsel of victuals into my mouth for four days and as many nights, except a little black birch bark which I gnawed off a stick of wood. . . . I saw several of the men roast their old shoes and eat them, and I was afterwards informed by one of the officers' waiters, that some of the officers killed and ate a favorite little dog that belonged to one of them.

Soldiers plundered the countryside for food and for the most part escaped the stern punishments reserved for such behavior.

Camp Life and Discipline

For the long encampment, soldiers of Washington's army were sheltered in log cabins or makeshift shacks constructed of soil, interspersed with straw and brush. Roofs consisted of turf, dirt, oak shakes, and sometimes pieces of old tents. By regulation, huts were supposed to be 16 by 18 feet and at least 6 feet high. Each of some 2,000 huts that formed the "Log Town" at Valley Forge provided for 12 men, with three bunks in each corner. A chimney and fireplace was located at the center or back side. Living in the huts was decidedly unhealthy; even though there were two windows, ventilation was inadequate, and offal collected nearby. The men burned gunpowder and tar, which they thought had curative powers. Albigence Waldo, a surgeon with the Connecticut line, wrote that at Valley Forge his eyes "started out from their Orbits" because of the "great Cold & Smoke."

During most of their service, however, the men had to rely on tents, of which there were always shortages. The usual tent for enlisted troops measured 6½ feet square and 5 feet in height, accommodating six men; two strung together sheltered 18 men.

Daily Activities

The daily routine began at dawn when reveille was sounded by drums and fifes and the firing of a cannon. After breakfast, troops exercised in front of the company's huts or tents. There always seemed to be a parade, a review, or an inspection at either the regimental or brigade level. In between, soldiers were detailed to some kind of work. At sunset a cannon signaled retreat; tattoo, at 9 P.M. meant all lights out. Roll calls were held frequently at different times during the day in order to detect any desertion as quickly as possible.

Fatigue details involved such chores as cooking, cutting wood, cleaning snow from roads, rebuilding bridges, transporting supplies, erecting entrenchments, barracks, and magazines, hauling firewood, making cartridges, and serving as the "grass guard," watching over horses while feeding. "Camp Colour men" cleaned up and constructed latrines, and in general cleared an area of "nausances," such as "filth, bones &c . . . throwing the Same into the pits and Covering the filth therein" with fresh dirt every morning. Enlisted men served as sentinels within the camp and also, in groups, at outposts (covering the roads) and piquets (supporting the outpost guard). One responsibility of the camp guard was to keep men from leaving camp after retreat, an offense punishable by up to 100 lashes.

The army command refrained from promoting recreational activity and discouraged otherwise harmless pastimes on the grounds that they invited gambling. Occasionally, there were celebrations, such as one for St. Patrick's Day (when news was received that the Irish supported the American cause), during which the men were permitted to drink excessively. According to the congressional articles of war, soldiers were expected to attend religious services on Sunday. Swearing was prohibited, as were gambling at cards, billiards, and dice. If caught in any of these forbidden amusements, soldiers faced "exemplary punishment." While liquor was part of the daily ration, soldiers could not sell it, upon penalty of 21 lashes. Even though frowned upon by officers, physical contests, such as snowball fights and boxing, were held by the soldiers. Swimming was discouraged; usually, once a week officers would lead their men to a stream to bathe. It was feared that too much spiritedness not directly connected to military prowess might encourage riot or mutiny.

Rules of Conduct

Discipline in the Continental army aimed at more than just good order and the shaping of effective combat units. As John Ellis (1974) states, military discipline "was imposed from above by those of a certain social group who feared the consequences of allowing too much initiative to the ordinary soldiers. . . . it was used as a counter-revolutionary tool to suppress any radical tendencies among the rank-and-file" (p. 71). General Anthony Wayne, writing to Sharp Delany on December 15, 1776, commented that discipline meant "only to put a necessary Constraint on the principle of freedom to prevent it growing into licentiousness which it unavoidably would if not Curbed in an army." General William Heath observed that soldiers were "promiscuous crowds" before being disciplined.

Heavy drinking, which often resulted in a hangover ("barrell fever"), did not in itself bring severe penalties—at most, confinement in a guard house to sober up. Imbibing to excess, however, was a form of defiance, and it rendered soldiers temporarily unfit for duty. Worst of all, it was the root of serious offenses. Captain Joseph Bloomfield lamented that "it is strange when men have Money that are fond of Drink, what Pains they will take to stupify themselves"; drunkenness "is undoubt-edly the *primum Mobile* of all mischief & disorderly Conduct."

Unlike officers, enlisted men were subject to corporal punishment. Such correc-tion was intended to have a maximum deterrent effect among the troops. While punishment of the American enlisted man was never quite as brutal as that of the British and European enlistees, still it often entailed great suffering. Dr. James Thacher, an army surgeon, questioned the use of physical violence in discipline. Corporal punishment, he said, "will never reclaim the unprincipled villain, and it has a tendency to repress the spirit of ambition and enterprise in the young soldier."

Whipping was reserved for major infractions of military regulations and of-fenses that were deemed criminal, such as stealing and plundering. In many in-stances, whipping substituted for the maximum penalty, death. As Thacher notes, especially harsh corporal punishment was meted out for "aggravated cases and with old offenders." Sentenced to be flogged, "putting on a new shirt," the culprit was tied to the "Adjutant's Daughter" (whipping post), his back bared, in the presence of troops at parade. Drummers and fifers performed the flogging, using a whip "formed of several knotted cords, which sometimes cut through the skin at every stroke." The flesh became bloody and lacerated with welts.

The maximum lashes were 100, compared to 1,000 in the British army. (Wash-ington had unsuccessfully asked Congress to allow 500.) In rare instances, several hundred stripes were ordered to be given over several days. The usual limit was 39. One extreme case that took place among General Putnam's troops in the New York Highlands in September 1777 involved Samuel Sturdivant, sentenced to 300 stripes (100 on each of three days) for collecting a bounty for enlisting in one company and doing the same for another. Putnam approved the sentence but commuted the whipping to 34 lashes the first day and 33 each of the next two days.

Other corporal punishment included the pillory and the old European torture of riding the "wooden horse," a sharply ridged seat, with the victim straddled, his legs weighted down to apply full pressure to the base of the spine. A common punishment for hardened offenders was running the gauntlet, with 100 or so sol-diers formed into two lines six feet apart; each man struck a blow with a stick at the culprit, whose pace might be regulated by bayonets against his breast. At Morris-town in January 1780 a New York soldier, convicted of trying to desert, was sen-tenced to run the gauntlet "through the Brigade to which he Belongs and Be Confined in A Dungeon for the Space of one Month on Bread and water."

Death was the maximum penalty for mutiny, plundering, sedition, repeated desertion, abandoning a post, cowardice or misbehavior before the enemy, striking an officer, sleeping at or abandoning a post while on duty, and throwing away arms and ammunition. Two-thirds of a court-martial had to agree to a death sentence. Washington has been criticized for his readiness to use capital punishment, but he knew its limits. He believed that too extensive resort to executions would adversely affect morale and recruitment. Writing to Major Henry Lee, on July 9, 1779, Washington warned: "Examples however severe ought not to be attended with an appearance of inhumanity otherwise they give disgust and may excite resentment rather than terror."

While bad conduct was readily punished, Washington did little to recognize the meritorious conduct of the common soldier. Not until orders of August 7, 1782, did he establish a definite award system. A purple heart of cloth or silk, worn on the left side of the chest, could be presented for exceptional meritorious behavior, particularly relating to battle performance. For service of three years at good behavior, a soldier could wear a narrow angular white stripe on his left arm, and for six years, two stripes.

The Soldier's Last Resort—Mutiny

As if depletion in the ranks of soldiers through sickness, desertion, and discharges were not enough, Washington and other American commanders had to face the reality of the worst of their fears—mutiny. A soldier's revolt could spread and cause the army to disappear and could even dangerously threaten the existing government.

Although group desertions had plagued the American Revolutionary War armies since their inception, it is remarkable that no major mutiny occurred until 1780. During the first six months of that year there were three soldiers' revolts. On January 1, 100 Massachusetts troops at West Point, believing that their three-year enlistments had expired, started a march homeward. General William Heath, recounting the situation in his *Memoirs*, noted that "they were pursued and brought back: some of them were punished; the greater part of them pardoned. Some others at other posts, conducted in the same manner, and were treated as the first mentioned. Those whose time of service was expired were all discharged with honour."

On May 25, 1780, at Morristown, two Connecticut regiments paraded without officers, as surgeon James Thacher reported, "and in the spirit of mutiny resolved to march into the country to relieve themselves from present difficulties, and to furnish themselves with provisions at all hazards." The men had been on short rations (with no meat for 10 days) and unpaid for five months. They resented new recruits being given large bounties, and they were also probably demoralized over the scheduled execution of 11 men the next day. (Actually, all but one would be reprieved at the gallows.) Two other Connecticut regiments and a Pennsylvania detachment pursued the mutineers, who were persuaded to return to camp with impunity. A month later, 31 men of the 1st New York regiment at Fort Schuyler, for "want of pay and the necessary clothing, particularly shirts," left camp on their own, intending to go to a British post on the St. Lawrence. Lieutenant Abraham Hardenbergh led a party of Oneida Indians in pursuit, catching up with some of the escapees, killing 13 of them.

The Pennsylvania Affair

A full-scale revolt erupted among the Pennsylvania line stationed at Mount Kemble, near Morristown, on January 1, 1781. A primary factor in the uprising was a dispute over the definition of tours of duty. In late 1776, Congress had allowed for three-year enlistments or for the duration of the war. Unfortunately, some recruiting agents had put all enlistees on the rolls as serving for three years or for the duration. Soldiers insisted on the three-year limit, while the army claimed enlistment was for the war. The Pennsylvania troops were also angry over news that the state's recruiters were now paying $25 bounty in specie for six months' enlistments. The Pennsylvania soldiers already in service had received bounty money in depreciated currency and had not been paid for nearly a year. In celebration of the New Year, liquor flowed freely.

At about 9 P.M. soldiers left their huts and began shouting. The officers had almost quieted them when shots were fired throughout the camp. The soldiers again demonstrated, and officers came down on them, brandishing swords. In early morning, General Anthony Wayne sent a dispatch to Washington, informing him of "the general mutiny." Captain Adam Bettin had been killed, said Wayne, and two officers seriously wounded, among others who were attacked by "muskets, bayonets & stones."

> Nor have the rioters escaped with impunity—Many of their bodies lay under our horses' feet, and others will retain with existence the traces of our swords and espontoons. They finally moved from the ground about eleven o'clock last night, scouring the grand parade with round & grape shot from four field pieces, the troops advancing in solid column with fixed bayonets, producing a diffusive fire of musketry in front, flank & rear.

Wayne appeared with pistols drawn, but the soldiers threatened to kill him if he fired. The mutineers declared that they were marching on Philadelphia and would force Congress to give them satisfaction. Wayne was able to move the New Jersey brigade from the area to Chatham, where it would be positioned to contest any British advance. With Colonels Walter Stewart and Richard Butler, Wayne went on ahead of the mutineers as they marched southward.

The mutineers went as far as Trenton. There they established a "committee of sergeants" to negotiate with the authorities, naming as its president Sergeant John Williams, a deserter who had been sentenced to death but pardoned. Washington, with his own troops on the verge of mutiny, decided not to go to Philadelphia to meet the Pennsylvania soldiers. He directed Wayne to avoid any further force. Washington, however, did order about 1,000 troops from the West Point and Highlands command to march for Philadelphia under General Robert Howe. As it turned out, this contingent was not needed.

General Henry Clinton at New York saw an opportunity to take advantage of the American mutiny. To invade New Jersey, however, would be too risky, for such action might drive the mutineers back into the fold of the American army. Instead, he sent two agents, a British sergeant, John Mason, and a New Jersey resident, James Ogden, to the mutineers, offering them their back pay and the option either to enlist in the British army or remain neutral. Many mutineers were inclined to accept these terms, but it was decided that the soldier's cause would best be served by adhering to strict American loyalty. Clinton's two agents were arrested and hanged by the mutineers at Trenton on January 11. The leaders of the mutiny met with representatives of Congress and the Pennsylvania government at Trenton, whereupon all the revolters' demands were met: discharge of any soldier claiming to have completed a three-year enlistment, issuance of back pay and new clothing, and a promise of no punishment for the mutiny. By the end of January, 1,250 Pennsylvania troops were discharged, leaving only 1,150, most of whom were given two months' furlough. Many of the discharged men reenlisted. The success of the mutiny and the leniency of the authorities soon inspired a revolt of other Continental troops.

The New Jersey Mutiny

The New Jersey brigade had many of the same grievances as the Pennsylvanians. They had petitioned the New Jersey legislature for redress, only to be told that their application reflected "indecent and undeserved Reflections upon the Representatives of this State." During the night of January 20, 200 members of the brigade stationed at Pompton refused to take orders from Colonel Israel Shreve, an overweight officer and a man deemed incompetent even by Washington. The disaffected troops marched to Chatham, where the rest of the brigade was bivouacked. Colonel Elias Dayton, the brigade's commander, ordered the newcomers to disperse, and most of them did so. Dayton offered pardon and promised to support the soldiers' grievances. The would-be mutineers returned to Pompton, where they still voiced demands and refused to take orders from officers.

Washington now had a mutiny he could handle. Unlike the Pennsylvania affair, the New Jersey mutiny involved only a few soldiers. He ordered 600 troops from West Point, commanded by General Robert Howe, to suppress the mutiny. Howe was instructed "to compel the mutineers to unconditional submission" and to "execute a few of the most active and most incendiary leaders." At dawn on January 26, Howe's troops surrounded the rebels while they were sleeping in their Pompton camp. The mutineers were ordered to be on the paradeground within five minutes. Outmaneuvered and outnumbered, the New Jersey troops had no choice but to comply. Immediately, a drumhead court-martial sentenced three leaders to be shot by 12 comrades who had also participated in the mutiny. Three in the firing squad would shoot at the head, three at the chest, and the other six would complete the execution if needed. Two of those sentenced were quickly dispatched; Sergeant Major George Grant, another of the condemned, was pardoned. Thacher wrote of the scene that "this was a most painful task" for members of the firing squad, "being themselves guilty . . . when ordered to load some of them shed tears." The "wretched victims, overwhelmed by the terrors of death, had neither time nor power to implore the mercy and forgiveness of their God."

Other Mutinies

At York, Pennsylvania, on March 19, 1781, a dozen men in the Pennsylvania line were arrested for "exciting mutiny" in telling other soldiers not to join in the march for Virginia, which was scheduled to begin four days later. General Wayne immediately held a court-martial; six were sentenced to be shot, of whom four were actually executed. Wayne boasted: "Thus was this hideous monster crushed in its birth."

The Southern army was also on the verge of mutiny. General Nathanael Greene wrote Governor Benjamin Harrison of Virginia in April from his camp near Dorchester, South Carolina, that "all the public stores are delayed on the road. Our army literally naked, badly fed, and altogether without spirits. Certainly this is pushing an army to desperation. Mutiny appears in many forms." Indeed, at this very time Greene took action to quash an incipient mutiny. It seems that certain enlisted men conspired to seize Greene and other officers and to turn them over to the British if demands for clothing and pay were not met. A sergeant's wife turned informant. One leader was immediately shot, and Sergeant George Goznal (sometimes referred to as Gornell), who "was pitched upon—as one who used those mutinous expressions," was hanged two days later on April 23, 1782. Others who were under suspicion for plotting mutiny were sent to work at the munitions laboratory at Salisbury, North Carolina; 12 more thought to be implicated successfully deserted, making their way to the British lines at Charleston.

Two mutinies late in the war caused some consternation in Virginia. In 1782 Virginia Continentals at Cumberland Old Court House, under Colonel Thomas Posey, mutinied when ordered to join General Greene. The causes of the mutiny were simple: first, many of the troops who had been taken prisoners at Charleston had only recently been exchanged and, therefore, objected to being sent to South Carolina again; second, the men had not been paid, and the one month's pay the officers received was in depreciated paper money. A fracas ensued with a sergeant "run through the body" by an officer. The troop's commandant had the barracks set afire. The men were then marched about eight miles, after which it seems that tempers cooled.

Then in April 1783 the enlisted men of Colonel George Baylor's regiment of Continental dragoons, consisting mostly of Virginians, mutinied at their camp on the Congaree River in South Carolina. Thereupon the mutineers set off for Richmond to demand redress of their grievances from the Virginia government. After going about 100 miles, the mutineers paused and sent a petition to the Virginia governor. The petition was signed by 10 sergeants and corporals. The mutineers had no radical intent; only out of desperation and need for survival had they taken matters into their own hands. The main grievance was that they were almost starving. General Daniel Morgan was called out of retirement and was asked to meet with the mutineers and lead them to Winchester. This was done without incident. Morgan employed Captain Robert Morrow to provide supplies for the mutineers, which were paid for by the Virginia government. At Winchester, it is assumed the mutineers were soon allowed to go home. As elsewhere, the granting of indefinite furloughs, which were all too willingly and perhaps unwittingly accepted, proved to be the best means of averting further trouble with a discontented soldiery.

The last mutiny, in June 1783, was the most dangerous. The war was over, and the enlisted men were scheduled to be furloughed indefinitely. Many saw such a discharge as a ploy by the government to deny them their overdue pay. Eighty soldiers of the Pennsylvania line at Lancaster marched on Philadelphia, where they were joined by 300 men from the local barracks. On June 21 the combined troops, with "fixed bayonets and drums beating," went to the statehouse, where both Congress and the Pennsylvania Council were meeting. The soldiers declared that they would "let loose an enraged soldiery" on Congress if demands were not met immediately. Sentinels were posted at the doors of the room where Congress was in session. The soldiers, however, had second thoughts, and after three hours retired to the barracks. This was the only instance in American history in which an armed band invaded the premises of Congress. The Pennsylvania Council refused to call on the state militia. Congress then appealed to Washington for help, and the commander in chief again ordered General Howe and troops from the Highlands to the rescue. Howe, with a force of 1,500, arrived in Philadelphia after the crisis had passed. Congress fled to Princeton, and the mutinous soldiers desisted from any further action. Several leaders were court-martialed and sentenced to death, but were pardoned by Congress. The mutiny, as did all the others, underscored the need for stronger powers of Congress and gave impetus to a nationalist movement.

CHAPTER 15

The Noncombatants

For every Continental soldier actively engaged in service, whether in the field or in a staff capacity, there were one or several non-combatants—persons under military obligation who avoided duty, and civilians accompanying the army. As had been customary in the American colonies and in Europe, the presence of a limited number of civilians in camp or on a march was tolerated on the basis of necessity. While noncombatants complemented the regular soldiery, the number of effective fighting men was reduced by evasion of military service, physical disability, absenteeism, and desertion.

Allowance for Nonservice

The states liberally granted exemption from military duty to all individuals employed in tasks deemed essential for the war effort. As in colonial times, all white males between the ages of 16 and 50 were regarded as members of local militia and were expected to attend musters and drills and even to take to the field when called upon during wartime. The militia obligation during the Revolutionary War also entailed the possibility of draft for service in the Continental army. Not surprisingly, many people sought exemption from militia duty.

Exemptions permitted by the states included persons over or under age; those with physical impairment; indentured servants, excepting apprentices, unless consent for induction was given by their masters; religious pacifists; artisans performing military-related work; millers; clergy; employees of military staff departments, such as storekeepers, teamsters, and stock drivers; postmasters and postriders; and paroled soldiers who actually were still prisoners of war. Typically, the Virginia House of Delegates in 1780 resolved that "the workmen employed in the public shipyard, foundery, ropewalk, and other public works, be exempted from military duties of all kinds." Special exemptions were sometimes given, as when the Virginia Assembly declared that Samuel Trotter could avoid military duty "untill his Child which is under a Grevious Indisposition Recovers or is Removed from him." In October 1782 the legislature exempted the rector, professors, masters, and tutors of Liberty Hall Academy in Rockbridge County "and in all other seminaries and public schools and also students" under age 21. Nevertheless, much bickering took place between citizens and the government over who actually deserved exemptions.

The states followed suit on Congress's urging for a Continental army draft in 1777. Militia were divided into "classes" or "squads," and on a rotating basis lots were drawn; those with tickets that said "service" entered the Continental army or other active duty in the field. In the New England states each draft group was selected according to ratable property, thereby ensuring that all ranks of society would bear an equal responsibility. There were individual draft evaders and even collective resistance. In Virginia riots to prevent drafts at militia musters occurred during 1778–81 in the counties of Accomac, Augusta, Frederick, Hampshire, Lancaster, Loudoun, Northumberland, Richmond, Rockbridge, and Westmoreland. Ringleaders were arrested and forced to go bond for future good behavior. John Augustine Washington wrote Richard Henry Lee in June 1778 that a major factor for draft resistance in Virginia was that the poorer sort of people "believe it is a war produced by the wantoness of the Gentlemen."

The principal legitimate means of avoiding conscription was to hire a substitute. Sometimes when an individual himself could not find a substitute, this was done for him, and he was assessed a fine. In 1780 Pennsylvania allowed a person selected for induction to pay a fine equal to the daily rate of labor for the time absent from service and also a wealth tax of 15s. per "hundred pounds of property." Even those who could least afford it hired a substitute. Thus, Philip Bailey of Bedford County, Virginia, retained John Oglesby in his stead "as he was a poor man and having tobacco growing upon rented land" and "was fearful if he left it at this time he would lose his crop." An entire militia squad might collect money to pay for a substitute. Just such a group intimidated Joseph Plumb Martin of Connecticut into reenlisting; thus, "they were now freed from any further trouble, at least for the present, and I had become the scapegoat for them."

Conscription, as Charles Royster (1979/1981) observes,

> remained primarily a technique for determining who would hire a substitute rather than for alloting military service. The means of evading conscription reached new heights of refinement every year of the war. Men charged with providing a recruit sent a man to camp but failed to pay his full bounty. Then they connived at or even encouraged his desertion, thus both filling their draft quota and saving themselves the expense of a full bounty. The most popular method of evasion seems to have been signing up men who were physically unfit or otherwise exempt. The quota was filled, but the ringer was sent home when he reported to camp. (p. 267)

There were complaints that substitutes were found from among vagrants, British deserters, and prisoners of war. In Maryland, "imported convicts" were recruited who had not finished the required indenture of seven years. Washington decried this practice as bringing in men "not capable of doing the duties of Soldiers," harming recruitment, and encouraging men to desert and then enlist as a paid substitute.

In one case in Virginia in 1781, General Steuben refused to accept a substitute because of his extreme youthfulness and ordered that a man be sent in his stead. This policy seemed to work, as Steuben noted: "The new recruits are coming in daily and since the treatment the two men from Brunswick [County] met with, the people seem afraid to bring in the dwarfs and children they formerly counted upon." Governor Thomas Jefferson observed in March 1781 that "Baron Steuben has sent" to Richmond "a number of Levies raised . . . whom he declines retaining as unfit for Service." The Virginia House of Delegates quickly resolved that these rejects be used for state garrison duty and in arms manufacturing.

In the South the most vexing problem with the use of substitutes centered on the recruitment of servants and slaves. Masters called up by the draft tried to pass slaves as free in order for them to serve as substitutes. Virginia eventually required a certificate of freedom signed by a justice of the peace in order for a black to enter military service. In October 1783 the Virginia legislature ordered the emancipation of any slave who had been enlisted as a substitute. It was a foregone conclusion that white servants so serving would automatically be released from future servitude upon completing a tour of duty.

Conscientious Objectors

For those Americans opposed to all wars and who refused to acknowledge any military obligation there was some relief. Exemptions for conscientious objectors which were granted by the state governments pertained almost entirely to members of pacifist churches: Quakers and related small groups—Rogerines, Nicholites, and Shakers—and the German-speaking sects—Mennonites, Amish, Dunkers, Moravians, and Schwenkfelders. These groups went on record denouncing warfare. The Schwenkfelder declaration of May 1, 1777 said typically: "on account of scruples of conscience we can not take up arms and kill other men." The Virginia Yearly Meeting of the Society of Friends in May 1778 announced: "We cannot take up arms either offensively or defensively, or Join in promoting Measures which tend to the distruction of our fellow creatures."

While all states permitted nonservice for persons with scruples against war, most required fines to pay for substitutes. The Quaker groups, however, opposed any kind of concession abetting the war effort. Quaker meetings pronounced excommunication ("disownment") upon any member who "trained with militia," "acted in military service," "enlisted in military service," or hired a substitute. The Moravians and Schwenkfelders also forbade payment of money for substitutes, but this injunction was often breached, with no sanctions on members who did so; soldiers were not excommunicated. A North Carolina Moravian declaration of May 21, 1778, stated: "We Brethren do not bear arms, and we neither will do personal service in the army; but we will not refuse to bear our share of the burden of the land in these disturbed times if reasonable demands are made." The Moravians willingly gave financial and material aid, such as clothing and care for the wounded.

In some instances the authorities demanded that pacifist bodies attest to the good standing of persons seeking exemption from military service. Because slackers might seek refuge in their churches, Moravians refused to accept any new members as long as the war lasted.

In addition to burdens placed on them for not subscribing to loyalty oaths, religious pacifists faced penalties for evading military service. A few Quakers were briefly imprisoned in New England. For avoiding the militia and the draft, persons were expected to provide a substitute or pay a fine. The required payments varied: New Jersey, 10s. for each muster and review missed, raised to six times this amount in 1780; Massachusetts £10 or imprisonment of two months; New York, £10 and an extra £10 when called up; Pennsylvania, £2 10s., which was raised to £40 in 1778; Virginia and Maryland, £10; North Carolina, £25 in 1777 and the next year, threefold taxes; and South Carolina, up to £500 for not serving when militia entered the field. Those refusing service, payment of a substitute, or the fines faced attachment of property.

The only severe treatment of Quakers for nonmilitary service occurred in the southern states. For example, 14 Quakers from Frederick County, Virginia, in September 1777, were forcibly marched to Washington's army north of Philadelphia, several with muskets tied to them. The commander in chief ordered them to return home. Two Friends drafted for service as guards for the Convention army at Charlottesville experienced brutality. John Pemberton, a North Carolina Quaker, was given 40 stripes with a nine-cord whip, and William Davis of Virginia underwent 39 lashes. Neither man would carry a weapon or do any kind of service, including tending the sick. Davis told the commanding officer that "Our Saviour was Stiled the prince of pease and they that follow'd Must follow him in Pease." Both men were finally released.

"Followers of the Army"

Sutlers, hired staff personnel, and women, some of whom were with their children, made up the civilian contingent of the American armies in the field. While they provided material service and helped to boost morale, these noncombatants were nevertheless a constant source of friction.

Sutlers

Sutlers were licensed civilian storekeepers who sold liquor, provisions, and other supplies to the troops. With the Revolutionary army subsisting mainly on bread and meat, Washington also allowed local farmers to establish markets with the army.

Only licensed sutlers could sell liquor in camp and within a seven-mile radius. An exception was made for "houses of Entertainment to accommodate Travellers and Strangers, who must be necessarily in the Vicenity of the Camp." Congress prohibited officers to "scuttle or sell to the soldiers." Sutlers had to "Shut up their houses at Taptoo [tattoo]," when soldiers were expected to bed down. At Valley Forge in April 1778, Washington directed that there should be only one sutler for each brigade, "who shall have one Sutling Boothe within the limits of the Brigade."

A sutler could only sell, at fixed prices, to officers and soldiers of the brigade to which he was assigned. Any sutler who violated any of the army regulations could have his entire stock seized and be "render'd Incapable of ever serving as Sutler in the army again."

Hired Staff Personnel

Numerous civilian suppliers and their agents came into camp. Especially in times of severe shortages, persons were contracted, by direct authority of Congress, to bring the army supplies and clothing, outside the jurisdiction of the Quartermaster or Commissary departments. Staff departments hired their own employees, with or without congressional approval.

There was a constant demand for a large number of employees in the departments of the Quartermaster General, Clothier General, Commissary General of Purchases, Commissary General of Issues, and Commissary of Military Stores. Civilians, with soldiers sometimes filling in, worked in such occupations as clerks, magazine-storekeepers, coopers, laborers, teamsters, and artificers (such as blacksmiths, wheelwrights, tanners, harness makers, and arms repairmen). Artillery artificers, however, were usually army personnel. The Quartermaster Department, with 3,000 employees in 1780, had two important subsidiaries—the Forage and Wagonmaster departments. Wagoners, retained at about £10 per month and $1 per day for hire of each horse, "enlisted" with the army for a period of time, without rank. Nathanael Greene, as quartermaster general at Morristown in December 1779, directed the hiring of 100 wagoners for one year or longer for service with any part of the army at the going wage, along with a $100 bounty and a suit of clothes. Poor farmers were the most likely to sign up as wagoners.

Wagoners, driving their teams into the army camps, often exhibited a more haggard appearance than did the foot soldiers. They worked 13- to 14-hour days, endured all kinds of weather, and slept along the road and in barns and haystacks. Prone to gambling and excessive drinking, wagoners sometimes proved untrustworthy, embezzling supplies and using their vehicles to transport private goods. To lighten loads, it was not uncommon for them to throw cargo off to the side of the road or to drain brine from salt pork—thus spoiling the meat. To remedy these problems, Congress, in 1780, ordered that wagon department personnel be drawn from the army and not the civilian population.

The British armies engaged civilian personnel for logistical purposes, much as did their American counterparts. Among the 80 "follower" prisoners of war at Yorktown in 1781 were purveyors, commissaries, conductors, a wagon master, clerks, issuers, and artificers.

Women

Women accompanied the armies; this was a long-standing practice in European warfare. Though usually limited to about six per company, women "followers of the army" exceeded this number. It is estimated that about 20,000 women went with the American armies during the war, while the British officially had some 12,000 women with their troops in America. Commissary figures for the British army in or near New York City for August 22, 1781, showed that rations were supplied to 23,489 men, 3,615 women, and 4,127 children. Women with the army were expected to perform useful work, whether to assist their husbands, lovers, and relatives or in hire of military units, in such tasks as washing, mending clothes, nursing, cooking, and carrying ammunition. Black women, mostly slaves, served as nurses and cooks. Those officially on rosters were entitled to rations and privileges.

Not only did women perform work that freed men for fighting, but they also contributed to morale. As Washington explained to Robert Morris on January 29, 1783: "I was obliged to give Provisions to the extra Women in these Regiments, or lose by Desertion perhaps to the Enemy, some of the oldest and best Soldiers in the Service."

Women volunteers were recruited as nurses for army hospitals, most of which, however, were located at a distance from the army in the field. As early as February 21, 1776, Thomas Carver, quartermaster and steward of hospitals, advertised in a Watertown, Massachusetts, newspaper for nurses to serve at Cambridge and Roxbury; "the preference . . . will be given to Boston and Charleston women." At Valley Forge (May 13, 1778) Washington called on commanders of regiments to "assist Regimental Surgeons in procuring as many Women of the Army as can be prevailed on to serve as Nurses . . . who will be paid the usual Price." Most skilled nursing, however, was performed by male surgeon mates; the duties of women as nurses were similar to those of a modern orderly.

Life for women in the army meant drudgery and severe hardship. On the march they had to tote heavy iron pots, small children, and baggage. They slept, as did the soldiers, on open ground or in tents. Many were destitute, as were the men in their lives. On marches, women tagged along at the rear of the army. Washington's orders for September 13, 1777, stated: "No woman under any pretence whatever to go with the army, but to follow the baggage." The British army had a similar policy. When the British entered Philadelphia on September 26, 1777, "Baggage wagons, Hessian women, & horses, cows, goats & asses brought up the rear." Hannah Winthrop, a Cambridge matron, described a dismal scene of women with the Saratoga Convention prisoners upon their arrival at Cambridge in November 1777:

> I never had the least Idea that the Creation produced such a sordid set of creatures in human Figure—poor, dirty, emaciated men, great numbers of women, who seemd to be the beasts of burthen, having a bushel basket on their back, by which they were bent double—the contents seemd to be Pots and Kettles, various sorts of Furniture—children peeping thro' gridirons and other utensils, some very young Infants who were born on the road; the women bare feet, cloathd in dirty raggs, such effluvia filld the air while they were passing, had they not been smoking all the time, I should have been apprehensive of being contaminated by them.

During a military campaign, Washington especially found women with the army a hindrance to operations. "The multitude of women," he stated on August 4, 1777, "especially those who are pregnant, or have children, are a clog upon every movement." He occasionally issued orders to prevent new women camp followers from joining the army and to get rid of those whose services were not considered necessary. Several times he declared that women could not ride in the army wagons.

The Americans had less trouble than the British with camp follower-prostitutes. The American troops were away from cities most of the time, and soldiers were often stationed in the vicinity of their homes. Foreign troops had the real money to spend. Yet prostitutes did show up in American camps, and at times measures had to be taken. General Artemas Ward ordered in June 1775 that no "lewd women" would be permitted to come into camp; in February 1776 two such persons were drummed out. During the Philadelphia campaign, Washington's orders of August 24, 1777, instructed his division generals to "take every precaution" to prevent "the straggling of soldiers . . . and likewise to prevent an inundation of bad women from Philadelphia; and for both purposes, a guard is to be placed on the road between the camp and the City, with particular orders to stop and properly deal with both." At least one of Washington's generals himself became a little too friendly with alleged prostitutes. Thus, one of the charges of a court of inquiry into the conduct of Major General Adam Stephen (November 1777) was that he had been "seen in open view of all the soldiers very drunk taking snuff out of the Boxes of strumpets" when the army was on the march in New Jersey the previous summer.

British and Hessian commanders could do little to curtail the fraternization of their soldiers with prostitutes in the large cities. It seems that the officers took up with the best looking women, while most common soldiers had to be content with "artillery wives." The "bitchfoxly jades, jills, haggs, strums" garnered in trade at the New York City brothels at the "Holy Ground" around St. Paul's Church and at Canvas Town, between Great Dock and Canal streets. Many prostitutes also followed the British army, taking "fierce pleasure in annoying and insulting the prudent and decent women . . . adjacent to their line of march." Legend has it that 3,500 women from the brothels of London, Liverpool, and Southampton were sent over as the "intimate property" of the British army in America. A Captain Jackson was given a fee for making the arrangement. One vessel transporting the women was lost at sea; hence 50 black women were picked up in the West Indies. Denied permission to return to England with the army at the end of the war, these "Jackson Whites and Blacks" exited the city and settled across the river in the Ramapo Mountains of New Jersey.

Women as well as the men in the American army, faced courts-martial when charged with transgressions such as thievery, plundering, and stripping the dead. Order books noted punishments. In rare instances, a woman convicted received a lashing, but more frequently she was simply drummed out of the army. At such time, the drums usually beat the *Rogues March* (the same cadence used to drum men out of the army) or the *Pioneers March;* "idle women" were drummed out to the beat of the *Whores March.*

At Valley Forge, Washington was especially concerned with women who "pass and repass from Philadelphia to Camp under a pretence, of coming out to visit their friends in the Army and returning with necessaries to their families, but realy with an intent to entice the soldiers to Desert." General Orders for January 29, 1778, noted:

"Mary Johnson Charged with laying a plot to Desert to the Enemy found guilty and Sentenced to receive 100 Lashes and to be drum'd out of the Army by all the Drums and Fifes in the Division." A day earlier, Ann McIntosh and two soldiers were acquitted of "mutiny and desertion." Orders, on February 4, entreated all officers to try and prevent "interviews" with visiting women and to forbid soldiers "under the severest penalties from having any communication with such persons and ordering them when found in Camp to be immediately turned out of it."

One way unwanted women could enter a camp was to pass as men. At the encampment of the New Jersey brigade at Elizabethtown in November 1778, Lieutenant William Barton became suspicious of a newcomer and had a physician engage in some "searching," which resulted in "Pulling out the Teats of A Plump Young Girl." She said she wanted to visit a young soldier, whom her father had forbidden her to see. The next morning "she came to me and said she Dreamd I had discharg'd her, I then orderd the Drums to beat her Threw the Town with the whores march; they did so which was Curious seeing her dress'd in mens Clothes and the whores march Beating."

Still, the army needed good public relations. Getting young ladies of good character who visited a camp to leave could be handled with delicacy. Lieutenant James McMichael, on August 3, 1777, reported from the American army camp near Germantown:

> The largest collection of young ladies I almost ever beheld came to camp. They marched in three columns. The field officers paraded the rest of the officers and detached scouting parties to prevent being surrounded by them. For my part, being sent on scout, I at last sighted the ladies and gave them to know that they must repair to headquarters, upon which they accompanied me as prisoners. But on parading them at the Colonel's marquee, they were dismissed, after we had treated them with a double bowl of Sangaree.

Both armies had notable camp followers. Baroness Fredericka Charlotte Louise von Riedesel, taking her three daughters with her, accompanied her husband, the commander of the German troops, during the long trek and captivity of the Convention army. Sally S. Boothe calls her "the most patrician campfollower of the American Revolution." At Valley Forge, many wives of general officers appeared, including Martha Washington, Catherine "Kitty" Greene, Lucy Knox, Deborah Putnam, Molly Stark, and Lady "Kitty" Stirling. Martha Washington, who acted as the official "hostess" at headquarters, visited the army at Cambridge in fall 1775, at New York City in spring 1776, at Morristown in spring 1777, and at Newburgh, 1782–83. Mrs. Washington said that she timed her visits between the closing guns of one campaign and the beginning of another. At war's end, the commander in chief submitted a bill of £1,064 to Congress for the "lawful" expenses incurred during Martha's sojourns in camp and also in Philadelphia.

Women with the army could expect to be in a combat situation. To enlist as a soldier, of course, was out of the question, unless one adopted a disguise. Without entrance medical examinations, deception as to gender was not all that difficult to accomplish. The most famous woman soldier was Deborah Sampson, who was born at Plymouth, Massachusetts, in 1760. In April 1781 at Bellingham, Massachusetts, attired in male clothing, she enlisted as a Continental soldier under the name of Robert Shurtliffe. Marched with other recruits to West Point, she served in General Paterson's brigade. Like other soldiers she carried a musket, knapsack, bayonet, a cartridge box, and 30 cartridges. Even though wounded in a skirmish with Tories in Westchester County, New York, her true identity went undetected. Taken with a fever and supposedly dying in Philadelphia in 1783, just before the disbandment of the army, a surgeon discovered Deborah's actual sex. She was honorably discharged. In 1784 Deborah married Benjamin Gannett and resided at Sharon, Massachusetts, the rest of her life. On January 20, 1792, the Massachusetts legislature, in granting her a sum of £34, resolved that Deborah Sampson "exhibited an extraordinary instance of female heroism by discharging the duties of a faithful, gallant soldier, and at the same time preserved the virtue and chastity of her sex unsuspected and unblemished, and was discharged with a fair and honorable character." Deborah Gannett died on April 27, 1827. Congress afterward gave a military pension to her husband.

The exploits of two women followers of the army have become legend. Margaret (Molly) Corbin accompanied the army to Manhattan Island in 1776. Her husband, John Corbin, was a private in a Pennsylvania regiment whose duties included loading and sponging out cannon. John was a member of a gun crew stationed at Laurel Hill, overlooking the Harlem River. The British crossed the river and attacked. When John was wounded, Margaret assumed her husband's artillery duties. She was hit by grapeshot, as a result of which she lost the use of an arm. John died from his injuries, and Margaret became a prisoner of war. Upon release, she enrolled in the Invalid regiment at West Point. In 1779 Pennsylvania awarded her $30, and Congress granted her a lifetime disability of one-half month's pay of a private, a suit of clothes, and permission to draw rations from army stores. Margaret lived out her life near West Point.

Mary Ludwig Hays (1754–1832), or "Molly Pitcher," was the wife of a private in a Pennsylvania state regiment, John Casper Hays. John was also a gunner. At the battle of Monmouth he collapsed, either from the heat or a wound. Molly took over the sponging, loading, and firing of the cannon. As Joseph Plumb Martin recorded the event, she

> attended with her husband at the piece the whole time. While in the act of reaching a cartridge and having one of her feet as far before the other as she could step, a cannon shot from the enemy passed directly between her legs, without doing any other damage than carrying away all the lower part of her petticoat. Looking at it with apparent unconcern, she observed that it was lucky it did not pass a little higher, for in that case it might have carried away something else, and continued her occupation.

John died soon after the war; a second marriage, to George McCauley, did not last. Living in Carlisle, Pennsylvania, Mary Hays received a state pension of $40.

There were perhaps many other women, single and married, who pitched in to help during battle. One of these, Anna Maria Lane, resided in Virginia after the war. She enlisted in her husband's unit in the guise of a man, probably joining Washington's army in September 1777. Within a month, she was wounded in battle. Long after the war, she petitioned the state of Virginia for a pension. Governor William H. Cabell, endorsing her claim in his annual address of January 1808, referred to her as "very infirm, having been disabled by a severe wound, which she received WHILE FIGHTING AS A COMMON SOLDIER, in one of our Revolutionary battles, from which she never recovered, and perhaps never will recover." The legislature, in granting the pension, said that Mrs. Lane "in the revolutionary war, in the garb and with the courage of a soldier, performed extraordinary military services, and received a severe wound at the battle of Germantown." Anna Maria Lane died on June 13, 1810.

Unfit for Duty: The "Sick"

Manpower reports (or "returns") in the American armies always showed a high number of soldiers "sick" and sometimes designated "sick absent" and "sick present." Not only were the sick unfit for combat, but also they put a strain on military operations and provisioning.

Smallpox and dysentery all but destroyed the American army invading Canada during 1775–76; in May 1776 only 3,000 of 7,000 men were fit for duty (Blanco 1986, p. 157). Throughout the war, about one-fourth to one-third of the troops in Washington's army were physically incapacitated. A return for the army, on the Delaware, December 22, 1776, counted 3,180 of 11,423 men sick and unfit for duty (Lesser 1976, p. 43). When the army reached Valley Forge in December 1777, 32 percent of troops were considered absent and present sick (Blanco 1979, p. 168). Of 11,133 American soldiers, including militia, at Yorktown in 1781 1,000 were reported as absent sick and 700 as present sick (Freeman, *Washington*, 5:514).

A program for inoculating the whole army for smallpox in March 1776 and also for new recruits starting in April 1777 greatly reduced the mortality rate from this disease. Other than inoculation, however, the Americans had little in the way of preventive medical procedures. Until the French Alliance of 1778, drugs, obtained mostly from overseas, were acutely in short supply.

Many diseases and ailments debilitated the armed forces. Unsanitary conditions and deficient diet were major causes of the prevalence of ill health. Washington placed the blame primarily on the excessive use of "animal food, untempered by Vegitables, or Vinegar, or by any kind of Drink, but water and eating indifferent bread." Lack of personal hygiene, open latrines, rotting remains of cattle in camp, and spoiled meat brought on communicable diseases. Washington became increasingly insistent on sanitary codes and their implementation.

Respiratory and contagious illnesses were widespread. The most feared diseases, traced to contamination, were typhoid and typhus, which were often referred to as "putrid fever" or hospital or jail fever. A report on 396 patients at the general military hospital at Albany of August 20, 1777, indicates a wide variety of illnesses:

Dysentery	81	Dropsy	4
Intermittent fever	79	Jaundice	2
Diarrhea	61	Rupture	2
Rheumatism	22	Scorbutic	4
Cough	25	Pleurisy	3
Convalescent	17	Hemorrhoids	1
Debility	17	Hemoptysis	2
Luesvenerea	14	Nephritis	3
Fever	13	Asthma	1
Whooping cough	10	Paralysis	2
Head itch	9	Cholera	1
Measles	8	Hypochondria	1
Putrid fever	6	Scrofula	3
Bilious fever	4	Opthalmia	1

From lack of cleanliness and sleeping on the ground, soldiers acquired the "Itch"; mites would burrow into the skin, resulting in scabs and stripping off portions of skin. Hog's lard, pine tar, and sulfur were used as ointments for this malady. General Johann De Kalb wrote that upon arriving at Valley Forge his troops were "infected with the itch, a matter which attracts very little attention either at the hospitals or in camp. I have seen poor fellows covered over and over with scab." De Kalb ordered his "seven regiments to put up barracks large enough to hold all these unfortunates, so that they can be subjected to medical treatment away from the others."

To treat the sick and wounded, the army had a network of hospitals: field (camp and "flying" or "marching") hospitals and general hospitals (a safe distance from military operations). Many of the treatment centers were temporary: huts, barns, churches, or taverns—crowded and poorly ventilated places—would be used. A congressional committee report of August 1777 showed 3,745 men in army hospitals. Congress established the Hospital Department on July 27, 1775. Eminent doctors successively held the position of director general and chief physician of the army: Benjamin Church, 1775; John Morgan, 1775–January 1777; William Shippen, April 1777–January 1781; and John Cochran, January 1781–1783. In April 1777 the Hospital Department was reorganized into districts—middle, eastern, northern, and southern—each directly superintended by a deputy director general and deputy apothecary general. The chief hospital for officers, caring for 380 patients, was located at Moravian dormitories in Bethlehem, Pennsylvania. During the war, 1,400 doctors enlisted in the medical service.

Disciplining patients and getting those who had recovered back to their units posed problems. Dr. Benjamin Rush wrote General Greene on December 2, 1777, from Princeton that he had 500 sick and wounded charges, "many of whom have complaints so trifling that they do not prevent their committing daily a hundred irregularities of all kinds." He warned that "the sick cannot be governed without military authority." On March 21, 1777, from Morristown Washington complained to Dr. William Shippen that discharged soldiers, "instead of joining their Corps they belong to, go Stroling about the country at their own option, to the great detriment of the Service." As a result, measures were taken that patients upon release had to report to the nearest commanding officer in the field.

For those disabled by wounds or illness, Congress, on June 20, 1777, established the Corps of Invalids, consisting of eight companies, with appropriate officers and noncommissioned officers. Colonel Lewis Nicola supervised this organization. Some of the "Invalids" were assigned to duty at garrisons, hospitals, arsenals, and magazines. On December 9, 1782, Congress created a retirement board, allowing certain "Invalids" a pension instead of staying in the service. The corps was disbanded on June 18, 1783. As early as August 26, 1776, Congress provided pensions for disabled veterans and over several generations increased the amount of compensation slightly and the coverage as well, so that eventually active militia as well as Continental service qualified for the disability benefit. In 1816, 185 officers and 1,572 enlisted men of the Revolutionary War received disability pensions.

Deserters

A continual stream of officers and soldiers leaving the Continental army greatly reduced its fighting capacity. Furloughs were liberally granted to officers, frequently in the expectation that they would aid recruiting back home. Many officers lingered for indefinite stays; countless others, as was their privilege, resigned. Like enlisted personnel, many officers had not been trained in the rigors of war, and they had families who suffered financial hardship. Enlisted men could not resign and had to serve out their tours of duty. No distinction was made between being away without leave and desertion.

During 1777–78 some brigades had one-half of their troops on furlough. Many of these never returned. At Valley Forge, about 2,000 soldiers deserted. James H. Edmonson (1971) has made estimates of the rates of desertion from the Continental army. From an average strength of 20,241 troops in 1778, 3,612 deserted (reflected in weekly returns); according to 11 monthly returns in 1779, 1,762 of 19,809; for a nine-month period in 1780, 1,354 of 13,808; from the monthly returns of 1781, 609 of 6,290; in 1782, 692 of 8,699 (monthly returns); and for the first six months of 1783, 463 deserters. Fifty percent of all desertions occurred during the first six months of service and 65 percent during the first year. Sylvia Frey (1981) notes that British official reports indicate 3,701 desertions from the British army in North America and the West Indies during the war.

Any of innumerable reasons would prompt American soldiers to take unauthorized leave. Lieutenant General Knyphausen of the German troops in British service remarked in March 1780 that "there has been a great desertion" from Washington's army at Morristown; "tired of the war, and dissatisfied with the depreciated value of their money, a general discontent pervades the army." The factors leading to American desertion included disaffection; homesickness; the bounty system—leaving the army and reenlisting for the bounty offered; lack of regular pay; failure to receive promised bounties; fear of smallpox and other diseases; lack of clothing; hunger; the need to return home for planting or harvesting; destitute families; fear of being wounded, captured, or killed; unfitness of officers; a quest for other opportunity, such as privateering (in which participants could share in the spoils); and emergencies at home, such as sickness or an Indian threat. Ebenezer Huntington, a lieutenant colonel of a Connecticut regiment, summed up the distress that soldiers felt when they got news from home. In a letter of December 21, 1778, he observed:

> Not a Day Passes my head, but some Soldier with Tears in his Eyes, hands me a letter from his Wife Painting forth the Distresses of his family in such strains as these, "I am without bread, and Cannot get any, the Committee will not Supply me, my Children will Starve, or if they do not, they must freeze, we have no wood, neither Can we get any. *Pray Come Home.*"

Washington found that pardoning deserters to lure them back into the army did not always produce the best consequences. He issued general amnesties for limited periods: April 6 to May 15, 1777; October 24, 1777 to January 1, 1778; March 10 to July 1, 1779; and finally, in early 1782. Such pardons, he observed in a letter to the Board of War, on April 9, 1780, "tend to encourage future desertions than bring in any number of those who have already gone off."

As if American discontent was not sufficient to cause desertion, the British provided incentives to encourage Americans to desert. Howe awarded each American soldier coming into British lines £3, and, if carrying a weapon, £4. Many of those who accepted this opportunity were British- or Irish-born. The Americans, of course, used various propaganda tactics to promote desertions from the enemy, such as printing and distributing leaflets to German prisoners in their own language.

Many American desertions occurred when recruits failed to show up at a rendezvous for induction ("clearing a division"). This desertion was not viewed as severely as deserting when under arms.

At first, punishment for desertion was relatively mild, only 39 lashes; later, it was raised to 100. In September 1776, however, Congress made death the punishment for all types of desertion, though this penalty was not mandatory. States had leeway in exacting punishment. Thus, in Virginia, if a deserter surrendered within two months he was pardoned but had to remain in service two years; if he did not surrender within two months, he was given five years' duty with the state guard or navy, or a similar term working in the public mines.

Death penalties for desertion were given to 225 men during the Revolutionary War, according to Allen Bowman, of which 40 are known to have been carried out. Undoubtedly, many more executions took place since individual commanders meted out penalties on their own. Washington had qualms about military executions for desertion, but he was firm in his belief that, if employed very selectively, execution had exemplary effect. Washington did what he could to restrain his generals from capital punishment without his approval. He turned down Henry Lee's request to use decapitation; however, one of Lee's officers, Captain Philip

Reed, on his own, had a deserter shot and beheaded at Smith's Clove, New York, with the trophy placed on a gallows. One method regarding deserters under capital sentence that Washington sanctioned was to march a condemned group to the gallows and then to reprieve all but one (usually a multiple offender); thus, both severity of punishment and mercy could be demonstrated.

Execution was most likely for captured American deserters who had served in the British army. Such a turncoat might even be shot immediately upon surrender, as happened after the battle of Quaker Hill in Rhode Island on August 29, 1778. Captain Robert Kirkwood of the Delaware Continentals, serving in Greene's Southern army, noted that five American-turned-British soldiers, captured at the battle of Hobkirk's Hill, were hanged en masse on May 1, 1781, and on May 19, three more, who had been captured at Fort Granby, were executed.

Apprehending deserters was difficult, despite rewards offered by Congress, the commander in chief, and officers, who frequently advertised in local newspapers, and penalties for harboring military defectors. One sure way to escape being arrested for desertion was to find hideouts, such as in lower New Jersey, Vermont, the rugged western country of the Carolinas and Pennsylvania, or even in faraway Kentucky. Most deserters, however, successfully acquired refuge among family and friends, and even in their communities.

CHAPTER 16

Behind Enemy Lines

Intelligence gathering and care for prisoners became important ancillary tasks for the armies. The British insistence that the Revolutionary War was a civil war complicated matters both as to the definition and culpability of persons engaging in espionage and to the status and treatment of prisoners of war. The Americans, of course, contended that the Revolutionary War was a war between nations, and, therefore, traditional rules of warfare governed all aspects of the conflict.

Intelligence

Battles and wars have been won or lost by the quality of intelligence of an enemy's planned operations, disposition of manpower, logistics, and military strength. Even knowledge of such intangibles as fitness and morale was highly important during the Revolutionary War. The composition and size of military forces constantly changed, as did the options available to the armies. With Tories and Whigs prevalent in any given military zone, recruits for intelligence service for one side or the other could readily be found. At the start of the war, General Gage made good use of informers, as did his successors.

Washington, who kept close oversight of clandestine operations throughout the war, considered the establishment of intelligence networks a priority. Upon assuming command of the Continental army at Cambridge in July 1775, Washington, as one of his first acts, enlisted an agent "to go into the town of Boston to establish secret correspondence for the purpose of conveying intelligence of the Enemys movements and designs." General Orders for July 9 required that the commanding officer at Roxbury send Washington "a report every day in writing, sealed up . . . of all the material Occurrences of the preceding day; mentioning particularly, all Arrivals of Ships and Vessels in the bay; and what changes and alterations are made in the Stations of the Men of war, Transport's, and floating batteries &c."

Almost daily throughout the war, Washington perused intelligence reports from officers and agents in the field. Most letters to Washington from his generals and other officers contained some intelligence, with the knowledge that this was what the commander in chief expected. While the American army was stationed above New York City, before and after Yorktown, Washington had a chief of intelligence, first General Charles Scott (in the summer and fall of 1778), then also briefly, Colonel David Henley, and finally, on a permanent basis, Major Benjamin Tallmadge. Washington made funds available for field commanders to pay informers. He expected American secret agents to position themselves near British headquarters. Thus, Washington told Tallmadge in March 1779 that "all great movements, and the fountain of all intelligence must originate at, and proceed from the head Quarters of the enemy's army."

Both armies gleaned valuable information from refugees and deserters. News about the enemy was also supplied by the many persons allowed to cross enemy lines on business or to take care of personal affairs. General William Maxwell called these travelers "licensed spies"; some were actually double agents. It was a guessing game which side had the advantage in debriefing such persons, but the information that was given could be tested against information that came from other sources. General Henry Clinton, who was lenient toward spies, boasted of the double agents in the employ of the British. Tories on parole for good behavior often aided British espionage. One such person was Archibald Kennedy, who, restricted to his wife's farm in New Jersey, served as a go-between for secret correspondence sent to the British. There were also agent provocateurs; these were quite successful in New York state in leading loyalist bands into entrapment.

Both sides used counterintelligence in the form of duping one another with fraudulent letters and reports. Such a document might be "found" or permitted to be seized by the enemy. Thus, on one such occasion, in the winter of 1777, Washington was notified of the arrival of a merchant, who was thought to be a British spy, at the American encampment at Morristown. Washington instructed his brigadier generals to prepare muster returns showing triple the actual troop strength of 4,000 men he had under his command. The merchant-spy became friendly with one of the brigadier generals, who at one point absented himself from his headquarters while the British agent was present. Finding the faked report, the spy quickly left and brought the report to General Howe. As Elias Boudinot commented, the disinformation convinced Howe "that we were too strong to attack & saved us thro' the Winter" (Miller 1989, p. 21).

The British proceeded more slowly than the Americans in developing an espionage network. At first the British preferred to rely mainly on tactical reconnaissance—information discovered by British patrols—but with the occupation of Philadelphia and New York City, British intelligence activity expanded. Loyalist refugees had family connections in New Jersey and the Hudson Valley. Provincial loyalist commanders, particularly Brigadier General Cortlandt Skinner and Colonel Beverley Robinson, made good use of their kinship relations. John André, in New York City, created an intelligence network from his contacts in Philadelphia. Major Oliver De Lancey, who replaced André as Clinton's chief intelligence officer, established a forward intelligence headquarters in the Bronx (New York), from where he coordinated British patrols, interrogated refugees, and sent out spies.

Eventually, Washington placed his confidence in residence spies, respectable citizens who were discreet and so could keep above suspicion. Elaborate arrangements were made under total secrecy for regular contacts with secret agents by couriers, who themselves were businessmen and the like free to travel across military lines. American intelligence developed a sophisticated use of codes. The ciphers most used were (1) transposition of the alphabet by substituting one letter for another; (2) designation of words, using a certain dictionary, by an arabic page number, *a* or *b*, for the column, and a Roman numeral for the line; and (3) substitution of numbers for words, syllables, letters, and names of places or persons. In 1779 Washington instructed agents to use the "sympathetic stain," a formula for invisible writing invented by Sir James Jay, a physician brother of John Jay who had just returned from England. This process, which required one chemical for writing and another for developing, was considered superior to the invisible ink that had been used.

The British preferred codes to the use of any kind of invisible ink. They had one system that the Americans did not practice: placing a grill (such as the shape of an hourglass) over a letter page, with the open space thereby revealing the intelligence.

Both armies employed spies of two classes: (1) military or civilian personnel sent behind enemy lines and (2) subjects of the enemy, civilians or soldiers, who were secretly hired to provide intelligence to the opposite side (which activity constituted treason). According to the rules of war, a soldier in uniform in an enemy area was not considered a spy; if caught, he would be treated as a prisoner of war. A soldier in civilian disguise upon rejoining his army also had immunity from being considered a spy if later captured by the enemy.

Military Spies

At the beginning of the war, some persons of divided loyalties, even within the ranks of the American army, conducted espionage for the British. Revelation of first the espionage activities conducted by Benjamin Church, director general of army hospitals and chief military physician, and then the Hickey plot led Congress to adopt legislation imposing harsh punishment for spies and traitors.

Benjamin Church and the Hickey Plot

Church, a Boston physician, had been a member of the Massachusetts Provincial Congress and a high-ranking patriot leader. Unknown to the American authorities, he was one of General Thomas Gage's paid informers and supplied information on Lexington and Concord before the British raid of April 19, 1775. He also alerted the British to the American intention to fortify Bunker Hill. One of his dispatches to the British commander, reporting on American troop strength, munitions, and plan to attack Canada, fell into Washington's hands. Church was brought up before a council of war and then remanded to civilian authorities. Congress resolved that the turncoat physician should be jailed in Connecticut and be denied recourse to pen, ink, and paper; he was not to converse with anyone except in the presence of a county sheriff or magistrate. Church endured confinement until 1780, when, because of ill health, he was allowed to leave for the West Indies, upon pain of death if he returned. On the journey, both ship and passenger were lost at sea. Church's wife went to England and was awarded a £150 annual pension.

Equally shocking as Church's espionage was the Hickey "mutiny." Not long after Washington brought his army from Boston to New York City in the spring of 1776, a large ring of counterfeiters was uncovered, involving soldiers and civilians. The group passed bogus bills supplied by the Tory governor, William Tryon. One of those arrested, Thomas Hickey, a sergeant in Washington's personal guard, boasted to his jailmates that he would join the British when they came to New York, and he intimated that he planned an assassination plot against Washington. The civilian authorities turned Hickey over to Washington. Tried by court-martial for sedition, mutiny, and "treasonably corresponding with, enlisting among, and receiving pay from the enemies of the United American Colonies," he was condemned and hanged on June 28, 1776, before a throng of 20,000 spectators. Civilians, such as the mayor of New York City, David Matthews, had also been implicated in the Hickey plot. Upon prompting from Washington, Congress, on June 24, 1776, resolved that "all persons, members of, or owing allegiance to any of the United Colonies," who "shall levy war against any of the said colonies . . . or be adherent to the King of Great Britain, on others the enemies of the said colonies . . . giving to him or them aid and comfort, are guilty of treason." It was "recommended" that the colonial legislatures "pass laws for punishing such persons . . . as shall be proveably attainted of open deed, by people of their own condition, of any of the treasons before described."

Spying was also deemed a capital offense punishable by a military court, as Congress so resolved on August 21, 1776:

> That all persons not members of nor owing allegiance to, any of the United States of America, as described in a resolution of the Congress of the 24th of June last, who shall be found lurking as spies in or about the fortifications or encampments of the armies of the United States, or of any of them, shall suffer death, according to the law and usage of nations, by sentence of a court martial, or such other punishment as such court martial may direct.

Whereas both military and regular courts were reluctant to mete out the extreme penalty for espionage, severity was expected in cases involving military personnel posing as civilians while operating as spies behind the lines of an enemy. Soldiers understandably refrained from volunteering for such hazardous missions. With so many civilians acting as informers, deserters crossing lines, and the development of intelligence networks, the need to employ soldiers as spies became less necessary as the war progressed. The fate of Nathan Hale and John André proved a deterrent for the lone infiltration of enemy lines by a soldier in disguise.

Nathan Hale

Nathan Hale, a 21-year-old captain in Colonel Thomas Knowlton's regiment of New England rangers, agreed to gather information on Howe's army after the battle of Long Island. Hale, a 1773 graduate of Yale and easily recognizable from powder scars on his face, was not a very likely candidate as a spy in an area not far from his Connecticut home. He had no training as a secret agent, no cover had been planned for his mission, no contacts were arranged with American patriots, no money was provided, and no line of communication was established. In all probability, he would have to carry notes on his person. Having been a teacher for two years, Hale assumed "the character of a Dutch schoolmaster." Leaving the American camp at Harlem Heights, the young would-be spy went ashore at Huntington, Long Island, and then crossed British lines into New York City, having changed from his uniform to a civilian suit. The presence of a schoolmaster at the military front in itself aroused suspicion. Arrested on the night of September 21, Hale may have been recognized by a relative or an acquaintance, but it is generally assumed that, trying to return to American lines by a boat in the river, he mistook an American for a British crew. Without granting him a trial, General Howe had Hale hanged the next day.

John André and Benedict Arnold

Major John André (1750–81) was one of the most promising young officers in the British army. A prisoner of war on parole in Pennsylvania after his capture at St. Johns in 1775, André became deputy adjutant general of the British army in America and Clinton's intelligence chief. In his intelligence capacity he was involved with Major General Benedict Arnold of the Continental army.

Benedict Arnold, hero of the Canada and Saratoga campaigns, began secret negotiations with the British in June 1779 which would lead to his treason. While American commandant at Philadelphia, he confided in Joseph Stansbury, a Tory glass shop proprietor, that he was interested in changing sides; Stansbury, in turn, notified General Clinton to this effect. As the conspiracy unfolded, Arnold forwarded secrets of American military strength and installations, as well as information on congressional proceedings.

Arnold acted from mixed motives. He had disliked the entry into the American war by the French, and probably really did believe his treasonable actions would contribute to a quick termination of the war to the best interests of both the Americans and the British. But mercenary gain appears to have been the overriding consideration. Arnold was disgruntled because Congress had not reimbursed him for substantial out-of-pocket money that he had incurred during military service. He had an expensive courtship with Peggy (Margaret) Shippen, 20 years younger than he and the daughter of Edward Shippen, a prominent Philadelphia lawyer. During the British occupation of Philadelphia (1777–78) Peggy had freely socialized with British officers, including John André. After marriage to Arnold in April 1779, Peggy continued to exhibit expensive tastes. Besides the need for money, injured pride as an officer also shaped Arnold's decision to betray his country. Arnold was disgusted at his conviction by court martial, January 1779, for malfeasance while American commandant in Philadelphia, principally for using public wagons for his own profit. Washington reprimanded him, according to the only sentence of the court martial, but, in recognition of Arnold's superb war record during the northern campaigns, granted Arnold's request to be commandant at West Point. At that post, Arnold continued his correspondence with the enemy, offering to turn West Point and other Hudson River forts over to the British in exchange for £20,000 (reduced to £10,000 if the British were unable to occupy West Point), a general's commission in the British army, compensation for his property that would be confiscated, and a lifetime annuity of £500.

To confirm an agreement for Arnold's defection, André arranged to meet with the American commander. On the evening of September 21, 1780, using the name of John Anderson, André rowed ashore from the British armed sloop, the *Vulture*, which had moved up the Hudson River, and conferred with Arnold near Haverstraw, New York. Arnold consented to surrender the garrison and its 3,086 men. The meeting lasted until dawn, much later than had been anticipated. Meanwhile, unauthorized American artillery fire from the Hudson shore forced the *Vulture* to drop down the river, depriving André of his planned means of return. There was no choice now but for André to travel some 15 miles through the "Neutral Ground" to the British post at Kingsbridge. Arnold had his friend, Joshua Hett Smith, serve as a guide for part of the way. Unfortunately, Arnold gave André documents to carry with him relating to the manpower and defenses of West Point. He had also scribbled out a note for André:

Headquarters Robinson House Sept 22d 1780

Permit Mr. John Anderson to pass the guards to White Plains, or below, if he chooses, he being on Public Business of my direction

B. Arnold
M. Gen.

So as not to be taken a prisoner of war, André took off his scarlet uniform jacket and put on a civilian's brown coat and a "gentleman's hat." Spending the night of September 22–23 near Crompond, eight miles from the river, Smith and André parted company, and André went on alone. Traversing the "Neutral Ground" was perilous. Cowboys (pro-British) and the patriot Skinners pillaged at will and robbed the unwary, even sometimes disregarding victims' political affiliations. About three miles from his destination, André happened upon three men—John Paulding, Isaac Van Wart, and David Williams. André thought he was fully protected from discovery. If he was apprehended by patriots, he would show Arnold's pass; if he was detained by Cowboys or others attached to the British interest, he would identify himself as a British officer. Since one of the three intruders wore a Hessian coat, André mistook these "volunteer militiamen" for Cowboys, and when challenged, announced that he was a British officer. André was searched, and the West Point papers were found in his boots. André was brought before Lieutenant Colonel John Jameson of the second regiment of light dragoons at North Castle. Jameson dispatched a letter to Arnold that he had detained a John Anderson, on whom incriminating evidence had been found.

The prisoner was then placed in the custody of Major Benjamin Tallmadge, who at the time was Washington's chief intelligence officer.

Jameson's letter arrived at the Robinson House, Arnold's headquarters, on Monday, September 25, when the West Point commander was having breakfast with two of Washington's officers. The commander in chief himself was expected to arrive at any moment to conduct a scheduled inspection of West Point. Arnold, upon reading Jameson's message, knew that André had been captured and that his own complicity would soon be known. With a last word to his young wife (who after his departure went into hysterics), Arnold hurriedly galloped down to the river bank and commandeered a barge to take him to the *Vulture*. Not finding Arnold, Washington, accompanied by Generals Knox and Lafayette and Lieutenant Colonel Alexander Hamilton, expecting that Arnold had gone on to West Point, visited that post. Upon their return to the Robinson House, Washington and his companions were told of the capture of André and surmised correctly that Arnold had been the source of the purloined papers.

Meanwhile, Major Tallmadge interrogated his prisoner, whom he noticed had a gait that suggested that he had been "bred to arms." André confessed his true identity and involvement and put it all in writing in a letter to Washington. He was then brought under heavy guard to West Point and from there sent down the river to Tappan, where he was confined in a local residence. Washington sought to exchange André for Arnold, who was "hackneyed in villany," but Clinton refused, and after conviction by a military court, André was hanged on October 2, 1780.

Benedict Arnold displayed the same boldness and courage as a British general that he had when in the American army. His daring raid in Virginia was a high risk. Both Generals Muhlenberg and Lafayette in that state attempted to capture him, but were thwarted by tight British security. Lafayette had orders from Washington to hang Arnold on the spot. Even Governor Thomas Jefferson placed a reward of 5,000 guineas on Arnold's head. But the most enterprising effort to apprehend the archtraitor was that of Sergeant Major John Champe, a Virginia soldier in the Continental line. Champe, posing as an American deserter, "escaped" his unit, Major Henry Lee's Light Dragoons, and reported to British officers in New York City. Champe met Arnold on a New York street and agreed to sign up for Arnold's new legion. The American plot was to kidnap Arnold when he went into the garden at his residence as he was accustomed to do to relieve himself. An American boat was waiting in the Hudson to receive the gagged prisoner. As it was, Arnold changed his address the very day of the planned abduction. Champe had no choice but to go with Arnold's troops to Virginia, from where he escaped; finally making it back to Washington's army, he was discharged. Champe could have been hanged by the British for deserting Arnold's army, up to the point that he resumed his status in the American army.

Other Military Espionage Cases

Other American soldiers performed heroically in the espionage service. Sergeant Daniel Bissel of the 2d Connecticut regiment, had a similar experience to that of Champe. Bissel was sent into New York City for intelligence purposes. He, too, signed up in Arnold's legion but did not get away from British service until September 1782. Another, Captain David Gray, who had served in the American northern army, from 1777 to 1782, posed as a deserter and joined up with Colonel Beverley Robinson's intelligence chain among the Tories in New York, New Hampshire, and Vermont. Gray delivered letters between the British command in New York City and the Tories, while sending information about their contents to Washington's headquarters. Enoch Crosby (supposedly the model for James Fenimore Cooper's *The Spy*) was a Connecticut shoemaker who entered the American army. Returning from a visit home, he met a Tory stranger in Westchester County, New York. Crosby let it be known that he wanted to join the British army. Thereafter, on several occasions, Crosby was admitted into the confidence of Tory military leaders; with information supplied by Crosby, American troops were able to capture loyalist military companies.

The British also made use of military spies. William Demont, adjutant to Colonel Robert Magaw of the 5th Pennsylvania regiment, deserted to the enemy on November 2, 1776, carrying with him the plans of Fort Washington, a deed that greatly facilitated the capture of that post. Demont remained with the British army and then settled in England. During the northern invasion of 1777, Captain Thomas Scott of the British 53d regiment, in disguise, conveyed messages between Clinton and Burgoyne through areas occupied by American troops.

Civilian Espionage

Very few civilian spies were executed by the commanders of the main armies. The usual stability in position and close proximity of the armies to each other made observation easy. Persons of divided loyalties willing to give information to the enemy were everywhere, and to impose the death penalty freely would only alienate the local populace as well as bring retaliation from the other side. Washington, Howe, and Clinton especially realized that humaneness had its own propaganda effect. Washington, however, unhesitantly executed certain spies, particularly those who attempted to promote mutiny and desertion in the Continental army.

General officers, who did not report directly to Washington, were the more likely, on their own authority, to put spies to death. For example, at New Windsor, General George Clinton had Daniel Taylor executed for spying. Taylor, when apprehended, had swallowed a hollowed-out silver bullet, which had a message inside. The object was "recovered by a prescription of tartar emetic." Clinton remarked, "out of thine own mouth shalt thou be condemned." General Israel Putnam, at his winter quarters at Redding, Connecticut, in February 1779, allowed the execution of Edward Jones, who had passed on intelligence and provisions to the British army.

One of Washington's most resourceful spies was John Honeyman, a New Jersey butcher and weaver, who, in his beef buying and horsetrading, was able to move uninhibited within British lines. Honeyman collected essential information needed for planning the Trenton attack of December 26, 1776, and he also helped to persuade the Hessian commander, Johann Rall, that Washington would not soon recross the Delaware.

During 1779–80 Washington greatly depended on a spy known simply as "Z." (He was probably Lewis Johnston of New Brunswick, New Jersey.) Washington's generals frequently forwarded intelligence, citing the source as "Z," which meant the information conveyed was reliable. Whenever the secret service became too risky, "Z" would not be heard from. On March 15, 1779, an exasperated Washington wrote Brigadier General William Maxwell from the Middlebrook encampment: "We have heard nothing in a long Time from Z. Has he dropped the correspondence? or what is become of him. If we are to depend no further upon him, you should endeavour to open some other channel for intelligence."

Washington especially prized the use of resident spies—those persons of social and business reputation who resided behind enemy lines. One such operative par excellence was Haym Salomon, a Jewish immigrant merchant. Salomon had a good knowledge of German and became a commissary supplying Hessian troops under General von Heister. Salomon sent Washington valuable information and helped American prisoners to escape. Eventually, he fell under suspicion and was put in the Provost prison. He was suspected of being involved in a plot to burn the dock and British ships in New York's harbor. Salomon escaped, leaving behind his wife and children. In Philadelphia, he became an important broker and commission merchant, even to the extent of advancing large amounts of cash to the Continental army, for which he was never fully repaid.

"The Manhattan Project"

The most successful intelligence chain was Washington's "Manhattan project," which came into being in late 1778. The identities of the two key participants in this endeavor were so secret that they were not known until about 1930 (when they were discovered through the investigations of historian Morton Pennypacker). The two spies in the secret correspondence went by their code names: Culper, Jr. of Oyster Bay (Robert Townshend) and Culper, Sr. of Setauket (Abraham Woodhull). Pennypacker regarded Townshend as the "most active spy of the Revolution."

Townshend, a merchant, established residence in New York City. He and James Rivington were proprietors of the Coffee Room, which British officers liked to patronize. Townshend was the "society reporter" for Rivington's Tory newspaper, the *Royal Gazette*, in which British officers were always hoping to see their names printed. Thus, Townshend could readily obtain military information without arousing suspicion. Austin Roe, and, to a lesser extent, Jonas Hawkins, handled business arrangements on Long Island for Townshend and in the process conveyed intelligence. At Setauket, 55 miles from New York City, Roe turned messages over to Woodhull. Nearby, the wife of Judge Selah Strong used her clothesline to signal (by displaying a certain number of handkerchiefs) the location of Lieutenant Colonel Caleb Brewster's whaleboat, which brought the intelligence across Long Island Sound to the Connecticut shore. Then the messages were relayed "pony-express" style to Washington's headquarters.

Aiding Townshend in New York were Hercules Mulligan, an Irish tailor, and a woman, evidently Townshend's common law wife, known only as Agent 355. Washington insisted that the Culpers and their associates observe absolute secrecy; even he never learned their identity. The Culpers were adept in the use of the "sympathetic stain" (see p. 243). Also, a letter with a secret message was folded differently from others.

One coup of the Culpers was to learn that Clinton planned to attack the newly arrived French troops at Newport in July 1780 before they had a chance to organize their defenses. Ten British warships sailed for Newport along with 800 men on transports. Washington, learning of this development from the Culpers, caused misleading documents, which implied the American army was preparing to come down from the Highlands and attack New York City, to fall into British hands. As a result, Clinton canceled the expedition to Rhode Island.

After Benedict Arnold switched sides, he tried to expose the identities of American spies in New York City. The Culpers laid low for a while in great fear, but their precautions had been so complete that Arnold never did discover their roles as spies. Unfortunately, however, both Agent 355 and Hercules Mulligan were arrested, probably because Arnold knew something about their involvement before defecting to the British. Agent 355 was confined aboard the prison ship, *Jersey*, at the time that she was pregnant with Robert Townshend's child. After giving birth, she disappears from history—she was probably one of the prison's casualties. The Culpers continued their work as secret agents until the evacuation of New York City.

Because of James Rivington's close business association with Robert Townshend, it is believed that Rivington himself became an American secret agent—as he claimed after the war. If so, he did not change sides until 1779, when he opened his coffee shop with Townshend. Admittedly, as the king's printer and as, reputedly, a staunch Tory, Rivington had the ideal cover. Rivington is credited with conveying to Colonel Allen McLane the Royal Navy's secret code. Perhaps this is why the French fleet off the Virginia capes so readily outmaneuvered the British ships commanded by Admirals Graves and Hood. As an expert bookbinder, it would have been an easy matter for Rivington to glue a message inside a bookcover or to employ similar means.

Other Civilian Espionage Activity

Since the Revolutionary War was such a long war, many tales of individual exploits surfaced. These included, for example, the activities of Mrs. Ann Bates, who, married to a soldier in the British army and posing as a pedlar, visited encampments of units of Washington's army in the summer and fall of 1778. She was finally recognized by a British deserter and, heading back to New York City as quickly as possible, was seized by a party of General Charles Scott's light infantry. When brought before the general, she explained that she was a soldier's wife "in the Centre Division & had forgot something about five or six Miles below the Plains." Scott, unaware of her real mission, wrote out a pass for her. In another case, Mrs.

Lydia Darragh of Philadelphia is said to have eavesdropped on British officers living in her home and heard of a planned night attack on Washington's army at Chestnut Hill. She then, as legend has it, rode through the lines on the pretext of obtaining flour and gave Washington ample warning. And James Armistead Lafayette, a black slave in Virginia, was persuaded by General Lafayette to go to the British in Yorktown, posing as a refugee. The British army retained him as a spy. After the surrender, Cornwallis, much to his dismay, discovered that James was actually in the American service (for which role James was awarded his freedom by the state of Virginia).

British Prisoners of War Held by Americans

Most British prisoners were stationed in the interior of Pennsylvania and Virginia, where there was plenty of food and less chance of warfare, regular or partisan. Congress originally wanted to entrust each of the states with care for army prisoners. Such a policy, however, would have impeded prisoner exchanges, caused complications in maintenance, and deprived Washington and other Continental army commanders of contact with the prisoners for intelligence purposes.

Congress created a special commissariat that was to be responsible for all enemy prisoners. On June 6, 1777, Elias Boudinot accepted the office of commissary general of prisoners; his successors were Colonel John Beatty of the 6th Pennsylvania regiment, May 28, 1778 to March 31, 1780; and Abraham Skinner of Pennsylvania, September 15, 1780, to the end of the war.

Lancaster, Pennsylvania, where, for most of the war, about 2,000 enemy soldiers were confined, served as the major repository for captured British troops. The overflow went to York, Carlisle, Reading, Lebanon, and Hebron, Pennsylvania. Many captives hired out as farm servants and as workers in iron foundries, and both armies allowed officers to live at lodgings of their choosing within a permitted zone. In December 1775 Congress even ordered that prisoner officers could "sell their bills for their sustenance."

By the Saratoga Convention of October 17, 1777, Burgoyne's defeated army of 5,871 troops (British, 3,379; German, 2,492) were to be sent back to Europe on condition that they would not return to fight in North America. Congress, however, repudiated the terms of the agreement, by one pretense or another, for fear that the released captives in Europe would free more soldiers to be sent to America. At first, a hassle between Congress and General Howe over which port should serve as the debarkation point of the troops delayed implementation of the Convention. Then Congress cited other grounds for detaining the prisoners in America. Supposedly, the captured army did not surrender all its arms (turning in only 648 cartridge boxes). In addition, debts incurred in America had not been paid in cash as promised. The most ridiculous assertion of all was that there was no witness to the king's signature in the ratification of the Convention. Thus, the Convention army was destined to remain in America for the duration of the war. It was kept intact.

After the surrender, the Convention troops were marched 215 miles toward

Cambridge, Massachusetts, arriving there on November 7–8, 1777. In the following April, while the Hessians stayed at the barracks on Prospect Hill in Cambridge, the British soldiers were relocated 53 miles inland at Rutland, Massachusetts, under a militia guard commanded by General William Heath. Desertion, encouraged by the Americans, was rife. Between October 17, 1777 and April 1, 1778, 733 had escaped. The entire band of a German regiment fled and was soon performing for American soldiers in Boston.

Because of the scarcity of provisions, the Convention army was ordered to be settled on a 400-acre tract (the property of Colonel John Harvie) in Albemarle County, Virginia (five miles from Charlottesville). Five divisions (4,000 soldiers) began their journey on November 4, 1778, arriving at their destination in mid-January 1779. The 628-mile march was managed by Colonel Theodorick Bland. Each state that the captured army passed through provided guards. Again, many deserted; by November 1780 the force had been reduced to only 804 British and 1,503 German troops (2,307 in all).

In Virginia, the local populace initially resented having so many enemy prisoners in their midst, fearing food shortages. When Baroness Riedesel (wife of the commanding general of the German troops) arrived with her two children, she went to a house and asked for food, only to be told, "The corn we need for our slaves because they work for us, but you come here to kill us." But the newcomers were soon deemed a desirable element. The prisoners built a neat little village at the "Albemarle barracks"—336 log huts, 24 feet by 14 feet (each structure lodging 18 men)—and they tended their own livestock and gardens. (General Baron Riedesel donated 200 pounds of seed.) At this prison complex the men had their own "coffee room," equipped with billiard tables. The captive troops remained healthy: during the first three months there were only four deaths, two of them infants'.

The British general, William Phillips, whom Jefferson called "the proudest man of the proudest nation on earth," resided at Blenheim, the home of Colonel Edward Carter, and Baron and Baroness Riedesel and family rented Colle, near Monticello, owned by the absent Philip Mazzei, Jefferson's Italian friend. Jefferson entertained Phillips and Riedesel and other officers at Monticello, and other Virginians did the same. Then, as now, the international intellectual and social community transcended war. Officers were allowed to reside within a 100-mile radius, many of them choosing to stay in Staunton and also as far away as Richmond. The British officers marveled at the crudeness of Virginia society, slave life, and the indolence of the gentry. Lieutenant Thomas Anburey and Baroness Riedesel wrote remarkable accounts of their impressions.

As the war moved south, there was greater demand in Virginia for provisions for the Southern army. The possibility that Cornwallis's army might attempt to rescue the Convention troops increased. For these reasons, it was decided to move the prisoners out of Virginia. In September 1781 they went to Maryland, the British soldiers going to Frederick Town and the German troops to Fort Frederick. Officers again had freedom of the area. Eventually, the enlisted men were removed to the barracks at Lancaster, Pennsylvania, and the officers went to New Windsor, Connecticut. At the end of the war, the Convention army had all but disappeared; 1,500 elected to stay in America. Many of the Germans intermingled with their kinsmen along the Shenandoah Valley and in Pennsylvania.

British prisoners held by Americans fared very well because they were detained in open country, enjoying fresh air, a healthy diet, and productive work. Of course, the same thing could not be said of the many loyalist prisoners confined to crowded jails and makeshift prisons. The amenities afforded to British prisoners could not be matched in the treatment of captive American soldiers in America because the British effectively occupied very little territory and their armies were based in urban seaports.

American Prisoners of War in British Custody

With the refusal to recognize the belligerent status of the American cause and subsequent problems at exchange, the British held large numbers of American prisoners. Most captives taken in North America—those from the army and navy—entered the New York City prison system. Americans who surrendered during the Canadian invasion of 1775–76, however, wound up in various buildings and jails in Quebec and Halifax, Nova Scotia. By the end of 1776, the British had 4,430 prisoners of war detained in New York City, the majority from the capitulation of Fort Washington. Joshua Loring, appointed commissary general for prisoners in early 1777, supervised the prison system in New York City and was generally responsible for British prisoners of war in America. Actually, William Cunningham, the provost-marshal, had the day-to-day responsibility for the keep of the prisoners.

At least 13 buildings in New York City, including several churches and the closed King's (Columbia) College, were used by the British to hold American prisoners of war. Many prisoners were incarcerated over a long period of time at sugarhouses (sugar refineries), the most prominent being the Liberty Street Sugarhouse (five stories with its windows covered with boards), and the Provost and New Bridewell jails. Officers had the freedom of the city, provided they paid for their room and board and refrained from any subversive activity.

Provost-Marshal Cunningham had a reputation for brutality in the treatment of prisoners. He seemed to have had a thirst for revenge, going back to the time before the war when he was roughed up by the New York Sons of Liberty. Cunningham saw to it that the prisoners had short rations, little heat, and poor sanitary conditions. Typhus claimed many lives. As Richard H. Amerman (1960) states, Cunningham "boasted that he killed more rebels with his own hand than had been slain by all the king's forces in America" (p. 266). Just before his own execution in London on August 10, 1791, for forgery, Cunningham confessed that during his tenure as provost-marshal in New York City there had been over 260 "private executions" of "American prisoners and obnoxious persons." This is obviously an exaggeration, but as a result of disease and other causes, only 800 of the Fort Washington captives were alive at the time of their exchange in 1781.

The American military prisoners from the fall of Charleston in May 1780 consisted of 1,977 Continental soldiers, 246 Continental officers and 1,000 militia. The prison ships—*Torbay, Pack-Horse,* and *Peter*—received the Continental enlisted men; 800 died within eight months, and 500 accepted British service outside of North America. The Continental army officers (including six brigadier-generals) were assigned to the sandy and mosquito-infested Haddrell's Point (Mount Pleasant, South Carolina), eastward across Charleston harbor; the captives had freedom of movement for a six-mile radius. Militia were placed on parole in the city. Some prominent civilians were sent to St. Augustine.

Eventually, most prisoners of the British army in America faced confinement in the notorious prison ships at New York City. The first use of a vessel for this purpose was the *Whitby* in October 1776. Thirteen prison ships, mostly old transport vessels that had hauled cattle and other supplies, were anchored at the Wallabout, a shallow tidal basin across from New York City in Brooklyn, at Paulus Hook, or in the Hudson and East rivers. Three hospital ships—the *Stromboli, Scorpion,* and *Hunter*—received the moribund patients. The 7,000 prisoners (soldiers, seamen, and some civilians) aboard the floating jails experienced abominable living conditions. Prisoners spent days below deck and only visited topside briefly in shifts. The overcrowding and wretched sanitation caused the spread of disease, especially jail fever (typhus), smallpox, yellow fever, and dysentery. Infrequent bathing in saltwater, with no soap, left skin a parchment color. Wooden tubs, used as latrines, were emptied once a day over the side of a ship at the same place where water was drawn for drinking (sometimes in the latrine tubs). The sole cooking utensil, a copper boiler, had two sections: one for boiling peas, oatmeal, and pudding (flour and raisins) in freshwater, and the other for cooking salt pork or beef in saltwater. Boiling corroded the copper, and the meat often spoiled. Prisoners knocked biscuits against the deck to get rid of worms. The diet lacked fruit and vegetables.

The worst of the prison ships was the *Jersey,* launched in 1736 as a hospital ship and in 1780 converted into a jail. The *Jersey,* which had a reputation as "Hell" or "Hell Afloat," had a manifest of 800 to 1,100 prisoners. Ebenezer Fox, a 16-year-old cabin boy from a Massachusetts ship, gave this description: "The portholes were closed and secured. . . . Two tiers of holes were cut through her sides, about two feet square and about ten feet apart, strongly guarded by a grating of iron bars." Prisoners were scarcely clothed, and often were kept on starvation rations; troublemakers were beaten and put in iron shackles. Five to six prisoners succumbed daily. Every morning came the order: "Rebels, turn out your dead." Corpses were buried in shallow graves in the loose sands of the Wallabout, and in time many of the bodies became exposed. In all of the New York prison system—on land and shipboard—it is estimated that 8,000 to 11,500 died, more than all those killed in military action of the war.

More fortunate than their counterparts in the New York prison system were the captives from the wide-ranging naval vessels and privateers who wound up in England. Other seafaring prisoners were detained at places close to where they were captured: New York City, Charleston, Halifax, Barbados, and St. Lucia. In England, Mill Prison, a four-building complex at Plymouth, and Forton Prison, consisting of two large structures near Portsmouth and Gosport, became the principal repositories for captives taken in European waters. Forton Prison accommodated a total of 1,200 prisoners from June 1777 to November 1782—200 to 400 at a time. Mill Prison had no more than 625 prisoners, with the daily average about 300.

Although there was always the threat of solitary confinement in the "Black hole," Americans fared better in the English prisons than in New York. Mill and Forton never filled to capacity. Fresh air, exercise in the yards, quarantine, and the burning of infected clothing and bedding warded off disease; freshwater and soap were available for bathing. The British Commission of Sick and Hurt Seamen made the welfare of the prisoners a primary concern. The prisoners could attend classes and keep books to read. Not surprisingly, they remained high-spirited. The Fourth of July was a festive occasion. When prisoners learned at the end of the war that the British Admiralty ordered them to be sent to France, proclaiming "You all now have received His Majesty's most gracious pardon," there were shouts of "Damn His Majesty and his pardon too."

Parole, Retaliation, and Exchange

Parole

Both armies were liberal in their parole of officers until they could be exchanged. As early as November 17, 1775, Congress allowed officers captured in the invasion of Canada a "parole of honor"—freedom within a six-mile radius of their residence. This became the general policy for both armies. Enlisted personnel, however, were subject to close detention.

At times, the British required a parole status for adult male citizens (presumably as militia) in territory they supposedly controlled. Prisoners could achieve release from such parole by taking an oath of allegiance and promising not to take up arms against the British; violation of the arms promise could be considered a capital crime. General Clinton in South Carolina, after the fall of Charleston, issued a proclamation freeing officers of restraint of parole if they took an oath of allegiance. Colonel Isaac Hayne, one of the Charleston prisoners of war, wanting to return to his family, who had the smallpox, complied. Ordered to join the British army, he considered his parole nullified and instead joined up with American militia. Captured by the British at Horseshoe, South Carolina, he was taken to Charleston. Lieutenant Colonel Nisbet Balfour, commandant at Charleston, and Lieutenant Colonel Lord Rawdon were determined to make an example of Hayne. Condemned only by a court of inquiry, Hayne was hanged on August 4, 1781. The execution was counterproductive for the British; it infuriated South Carolinians, many more of whom now actively supported the American cause.

Law of Retaliation

Execution of those who violated their declared allegiance and then fought for the enemy, and even of those who were considered spies was rare simply because each side had recourse to retaliation. American and British commanders often resorted to the threat of retaliation. For example, early in the war, Lieutenant Colonel Ethan Allen, captured at Montreal and brought to England in irons, was threatened with execution. When the British general, Richard Prescott, was taken during the Canadian campaign by the Americans, Washington wrote General Howe, on December 18, 1775 that

> whatever fate he [Allen] undergoes—such exactly shall be the treatment & Fate of Brigadier [Richard] Prescot now in our hands.
>
> The Law of retaliation is not only justifiable in the Eyes of God & man, but absolutely a duty which in our present circumstances we owe to our Relations Friends & fellow Citizens.

On September 1, 1776, Prescott was exchanged for General John Sullivan, and Allen, who was finally paroled in New York City, was exchanged for Colonel Archibald Campbell, in May 1778.

Retaliation occurred widely in the Carolinas. After Scottish loyalists were defeated at Kettle Creek (February 14, 1779), five persons were hanged as traitors. The British executed some rebel captives at Camden, Ninety-Six, and Augusta. After the battle of King's Mountain (October 7, 1780), nine of Major Patrick Ferguson's loyalist militiamen were summarily hanged by the victorious American "over mountain men." In May 1781 Colonel Henry Lee hanged several British militiamen at Fort Motte.

After Yorktown, Washington faced his most difficult decision involving retaliation. Captain Richard Lippincott of the Associated Loyalists, whom General Clinton had empowered as a military organization, hanged Captain Joshua Huddy of the New Jersey militia in Monmouth County. Huddy had been accused of killing Philip White, captain of a loyalist band of militia. Clinton would not surrender Lippincott to Washington for trial. Washington, therefore, directed that an officer from among the Yorktown captives be selected by lot and hanged if the British persisted in not delivering up Lippincott. Captain Charles Asgill, a 19-year-old son of a wealthy baronet, had the unlucky draw. Asgill came close to execution. Fortunately, Asgill's mother contacted comte de Vergennes, the French foreign minister at Versailles, who interceded with Washington to spare Asgill. Washington finally appealed to Congress, which ordered "that the life of Captain Asgill should be given as a compliment to the King of France."

Prisoner Exchange

The Americans expected that under the prevailing rules of warfare there would be a quick return of prisoners. Normally, cartels for prisoner exchange (quid pro quo, with money payment added to cover any discrepancy) would be arranged. Congress, on December 2, 1775, declared for a policy of citizen for citizen, officer for officer, and soldier for soldier. But the British refused to allow cartels for prisoner exchange because this would constitute recognition that the war was between two nations and not a civil war. Congress was also at a disadvantage until October 1777 in that the British held many more prisoners than did the Americans.

Throughout the war, most prisoner exchanges were partial and accomplished under the auspices of individual commanders. The capture of Hessians at Trenton gave the Americans a bargaining position, and the surrender of Burgoyne's army made for a near equality in the number of prisoners held by each side. Thus, negotiations began for limited prisoner exchange. In March 1778 at Germantown, commissioners arranged for the exchange of some prisoners. Three prisoner-of-war conferences convened at Perth Amboy, New Jersey (in December 1778, April 1779, and March 1780) failed, largely because Clinton wanted a mixed exchange, whereas Washington insisted that the exchanges of officers and men be handled separately. The Perth Amboy meetings did establish a ratio for prisoner exchange that was used in the future. The formula had privates as the lowest common denominator. The exchange rates were as follows.

Lieutenant general	1,044
Major general	372
Brigadier general	200
Colonel	100
Lieutenant colonel	72
Major	28
Captain	16
1st lieutenant	8
2d lieutenant, ensign	4
Sergeant	2
Corporal, drummer, fifer, private, and volunteer	1
Adjutant, quartermaster of regiment and corps	6
Surgeon to regiment and corps	6
Mates to regiment and corps	4

Thus, after Yorktown, Cornwallis could be exchanged for 1,044 privates or by "composition" of officers and soldiers. In May 1782, however, Cornwallis was exchanged, one-on-one, for Henry Laurens, former president of Congress and emissary to Holland, who had been captured by the British on his way to Europe.

The first major breakthrough for a general exchange came from negotiations between General Nathanael Greene, commander of the Southern army, and Cornwallis. Commissioners appointed by the two armies (Captain Frederick Cornwallis for the British and Lieutenant Colonel Edward Carrington for the Americans) met on May 3, 1781, at the Claudius Pegree house (near present-day Cheraw). The resulting agreement, approved by Washington and Clinton, allowed all Continental army prisoners of war in the South to be paroled. Thus, in July 1781 nearly 900 officers and men in the first delivery were brought to Jamestown Island in Virginia and marched to Richmond for discharge.

With the fall of the North ministry, at last Parliament, on March 25, 1782, passed an act acknowledging American captives as prisoners of war. A cartel held in fall 1782, attended by Andrew Elliott and General James Campbell and Generals Henry Knox and William Heath, however, came to naught because the British refused to accept the American demand for reimbursement for provisioning the Yorktown captives.

The recognition of prisoner-of-war status now cleared the way to free American captives in England. Of course, John Paul Jones taking 200 prisoners from the British warship, *Drake*, and 504 from the *Serapis* made for parity. Benjamin Franklin also contributed to freeing the prisoners in England through his diplomatic skills. In August 1782, 833 Americans from Mill and Forton prisons arrived at Boston and Philadelphia.

In May 1783 Washington met with Sir Guy Carleton, who had replaced Clinton as commander in chief of British forces in America, for the purpose of arranging a general exchange. A complete exchange, however, had to await finalization by the Treaty of Paris ending the war.

CHAPTER 17

The Loyalists

 "Pray tell me, what is a Tory?" a New Yorker asked in February 1778, to which he received the reply: "A Tory is a thing whose head is in England and its body in America, and its neck ought to be stretched." Thomas Jefferson, writing in 1781, was a little more circumspect: "A Tory has been properly defined to be a traitor in thought, but not in deed." Although the term *Tory* did not have the currency in colonial America that it had in England, American patriots of the Revolutionary period used it to refer to a wide variety of persons, ranging from those disinterested in the American cause to those whose actions gave proof of their attachment to the British side. The word *loyalist* did not come into usage until toward the end of the war when the British gave the name to refugees seeking their protection. Historians have made Tory and loyalist interchangeable. While a distinction might be made as to Tory meaning one with a pro-British disposition of mind and allegiance and loyalist as a person overtly siding with the British, loyalist here will be used in the broad sense.

It is reasonable to assume that at the start of the war more than one-half of all Americans were willing to accommodate their differences with Great Britain in a peaceable manner. John Adams said that two-thirds of Americans (one-third loyalist, one-third neutral) were of such persuasion. Joseph Galloway, Whig leader turned loyalist, in an examination before Parliament in 1779, insisted that four-fifths of the colonists were loyal or well disposed to the crown, and had the British taken adequate measures the rebellion would have been quickly subdued.

Although most British sympathizers preferred neutrality, they went along with repression by patriots in order to keep out of harm's way. Those not content to be passive, but who by deed or open expression opposed the rebel cause, faced various kinds of recrimination. From the beginning, the loyalists were at a disadvantage, for the patriots had the momentum. Loyalists were simply bent on preserving the status quo in British America. They lacked any significant intercolonial unity and leadership. The British government seeking exclusively a military instead of a political solution, and delaying in the use of loyalists in a military capacity, saw much of a vital native resource disappear.

The Loyalist Perception

On the eve of the Revolution, many Americans cautioned against breaking with Great Britain and against war. Foremost among those sounding alarms were some substantial merchants and planters, crown placemen, Anglican clergy, and conservative lawyers. In addition, many of the common people—yeomen, artisans, and laborers—wondered what stakes were high enough as to risk bloodshed and destruction. Most opponents of the Revolutionary movement who articulated their views admitted the need for reform in imperial relations and even for limitations on parliamentary authority over the colonies. But they believed that there were no irreconcilable differences between England and America. They thought that war would disrupt the social fabric and create mobocracy, further division between colonies, and American legislative tyranny.

The loyalist apologists held to a more historical view than did the patriots. History, the loyalists maintained, had demonstrated that inequality and imperfection were the lot of humankind. Government should be guided by reason and be dispassionate in protecting the rights of individuals. It should also work for the greater good rather than abide by the wishes of a fickle and impermanent majority.

A common theme of the loyalist writers was that the colonists had enjoyed liberty with little governmental interference. In *Massachusettensis* (17 essays published in the *Massachusetts Gazette*, December 12, 1774, to April 3, 1775), Daniel Leonard, a wealthy lawyer, warned of the threat of sacrificing "real liberty to licentiousness." The British government had protected the colonists from "internal rapacity and violence" and from foreign interference. The American patriots aimed at despotism. Leonard said that he had seen "the small seed of sedition when it was implanted." It had grown into "a great tree; the vilest reptiles that crawl upon the earth are concealed at the root; the foulest birds of the air rest upon its branches." Peter Oliver, who had served as chief justice of the Massachusetts Superior Court, in an address to the colony's soldiers in 1776, advised them that if "Heaven, in righteous judgment should suffer you to conquer . . . the ambition and desperation of your leaders will then demand the fruit of all their toils." Oliver, like Peter Van Schaack, a New York lawyer, recalled how the English Civil War (1642–49) had brought forth the dictatorship of Oliver Cromwell.

Anglican clerics emphasized the need for law and order under proper authority. Jonathan Boucher, a parish rector in Maryland and tutor of George Washington's stepson, had the extreme view, that God had ordained the state and government, and therefore rebellion was against God Himself. Samuel Seabury, an Anglican clergyman in Westchester County, New York, published four pamphlets condemning the rebel cause. Like others, he deplored violence. If he were to be enslaved, he would rather "let it be by a king at least, and not by a parcel of upstart lawless committeemen. If I must be devoured, let me be devoured by the jaws of a lion, and not gnawed to death by rats and vermin."

Some writers believed that there was an inviolable compact between the colonies and the mother country. William Smith, Jr., a New York councillor and later chief justice of Quebec, pointed out that "neither of the contracting parties may dissolve this compact as long as their joint aim in the union, to wit, their mutual prosperity, can be attained by it." Smith, who felt that all grievances could be resolved in a negotiated settlement, hoped that an American parliament, elected by the assemblies, would be allowed, with full power for colonial taxation.

Personality characteristics may have predisposed some Americans to resist the Revolutionary movement. N.E.H. Hull and others, in a 1978 study, made a "personality inventory" of a small grouping of New York loyalists and revolutionaries, and found that the loyalists had a greater propensity for order, conformity, stereotyped thinking, traditionalism, submission to authority, and power relationships. Of course, persons on both sides shared some of the same qualities. But, this study does suggest a kind of loyalist mentality, at least among those in the upper echelon of society.

Divided Loyalties, 1774–1776

Americans were finally forced to take sides in 1774, when the colonies adopted economic sanctions against Great Britain. Local committees of safety and inspection sprang up everywhere and soon were keeping an eye on everyone's essential loyalty. The committees sought to detect disaffection even as expressed in conversation and correspondence. As the war began, they became the guardians of patriotism and exacted impositions on those deemed unfriendly to the American cause.

Persons were hailed before committees for "speaking Words inimical to the Cause of America" and were forced to sign recantations, which were usually published in the newspapers. Thus, for example, John Morris of Caroline County, Virginia, confessed "that I have made use of certain expressions foreign to the good of this Country. I do confess myself heartily sorry for It." The most recalcitrant received brief jail sentences and, in rare instances, were banished. The most frequent mode of suppression required persons to post bond for future politically correct behavior. Besides checking on loyalty, the committees held to account those engaged in deviant behavior, such as refusing to attend militia musters and showing contempt of a committee. In Virginia, writes Dale E. Benson (1970), "justice was often crippled by local planters less concerned about the rights of accused persons than the threat to society such persons represented" (p. 319).

On October 6, 1775, Congress urged the state and local makeshift governments "to arrest and secure every person in their respective colonies, whose going at large may in their opinion, endanger the safety of the colony or the liberties of America." One form of implementation of this policy was the banishment of "alien enemies." After Independence, most states, citing the Staple Statute of 27 Edward III, Chapter 17, expelled many natives of Great Britain who were partners or employees of British merchants. Banishment of foreign merchants had been a traditional wartime practice in England. British merchants in Virginia, unless they could show "themselves friendly to the Cause of America" or had wives and children in the state, were given 40 days' notice that they had to leave. If they refused, they were confined. Their property was held in trust, and after an official inquiry and waiting period, the property was taken over by the state and sold. In late 1776 and throughout 1777 a large number of British and Scottish merchants left America.

Neutrality was permitted until Independence. Thereafter, all states enacted laws compelling oaths of allegiance. The oaths were doubled-edged: renouncement of George III and a pledge of allegiance to a state. In South Carolina royal officials and others who did not subscribe to the oath had 60 days to remove themselves and their families; the state paid passage to Great Britain or the West Indies for those who could not afford it. Those who left the state to avoid the oath but later returned faced the death penalty. Enforcement of this penalty was unrealistic, but in all states nonjurors were subject to forfeiture of civil liberties. The oaths of allegiance drew a sharp line of distinction between patriots and loyalists, and also served to coerce persons to declare their support of the American cause.

Still, there was a high degree of disaffection and loyalism, owing to a variety of circumstances. Local conditions and the presence or close proximity of British armed forces were major factors. Loyalists had strength in numbers in maritime regions and in the backcountry. In the Carolinas, backcountry settlers harbored bitter resentment against the lowland patriot aristocracy, at whose hands the western uprising of 1771 had been brutally crushed. Generally, Scottish Highlanders in the South supported the crown; it is said that having been defeated in the British rebellions of 1715 and 1745, they did not want to be three-time losers. Those involved in the Indian trade on the frontier also inclined toward loyalism.

Except for the upper levels of society, no predominant patterns emerge to establish a loyalist profile according to occupations. Of course, royal placemen, wealthy merchants and landholders, lawyers, Anglican clergy, and physicians who were trained in Great Britain, if they were included among the governing elite, mostly joined the side of the crown. In these ranks were the great New York landholders, who had received their estates through royal grants. They were supported by many of their satisfied tenants. Some tenants became loyalists because they remembered their defeat in the antirent riots of the 1760s and the king's role in saving their leader from a death sentence. Some tenants, however, did join the patriots in expectation that they would acquire land from the breakup of the large loyalist estates. Of 104 members of the New York City Chamber of Commerce, 57 became loyalists and 21 preferred neutrality. Yet throughout the colonies, the majority of loyalists were of the common sort. It has been estimated, for example, that in Massachusetts the loyalist ranks consisted of one-third professionals, gentlemen, and merchants, one-third farmers, and one-third artisans and small shopkeepers.

The conscious (or cultural) minorities, who felt isolated and unprotected, tended to be either neutral or loyalist. Chief among these were those individuals who most retained a close ethnic identity, namely, Germans, Dutch, and Scots. Recent immigrants from England also tended to be loyalists. These groups felt detached from the mainstream of American life as well as from the political controversy. Black slaves were attracted to the British because they hoped for "freedom and a farm." To some extent Americans also divided according to religion, with Quakers, German pacifists, Methodists, and southern Presbyterians inclined to be neutral or loyalist.

Persecution

Loyalists had to contend with the infliction of extralegal and legal punishments. They were fortunate if they lived in areas that had a large number of British as well as American sympathizers, intermingled among kin and neighbors. Those loyalists who lived near a war zone or were a distinct minority were in greatest danger of persecution. In the partisan war in the Carolinas, torture and slaughter were rampant on both sides.

Tarring and Feathering

Vigilante actions sought to exact revenge as well as to compel outward conformity. For example, a person known to have drunk to the health of the king or the like would be forced to proclaim open support of the American cause. Tarring and feathering (with pine tar and goose feathers) was an effective means of intimidation, and often removed a layer of the skin and caused infection. Peter Oliver, who claimed the practice was a New England invention, had a recipe for it:

> First, strip a Person naked, then heat the Tar untill it is thin, & pour it upon the naked Flesh, or rub it over with a Tar Brush, *quantum sufficit*. After which, sprinkle decently upon the Tar, whilst it is yet warm, as many Feathers as will stick to it. Then hold a lighted Candle to the Feathers, & try to set it all on Fire; if it will burn so much the better. But as the Experiment is often made in cold Weather; it will not then succeed—take also an Halter, & put it round the Person's Neck, & then cart him the Rounds.

One use of this "invention" stands out, among many. In May 1777 when General Francis Nash and North Carolina Continentals passed through Richmond, Virginia, a spunky shoemaker appeared at the door of his shop and shouted, "Hurrah for King George!" The shoemaker followed the troops to outside the town, continuing to hurrah for the king. General Nash ordered the troublemaker to be taken to the nearby James River and dunked.

> The soldiers tied a rope around his middle, and seesawed him backwards and forwards until we had him nearly drowned, but every time he got his head above water he would cry for King George. The General having then ordered him to be tarred and feathered, a feather bed was taken from his own house, where were his wife and four likely daughters crying and beseeching their father to hold his tongue, but still he would not. We tore the bed open and knocked the top out of a

tar barrel, into which we plunged him headlong. He was then drawn out by the heels and rolled in the feathers until he was a sight but still would hurrah for King George. The General now ordered him to be drummed out of the West end of town, and told him expressly that if he plagued him any more in that way he would have him shot. So we saw no more of the shoemaker.

Legal Punishments

Legal penalties covered all degrees of loyalism, from behavior exhibiting nonsupport for the American cause to treason, entailing punishment ranging from reprimand to death. The states that had the harshest treatment of loyalists were New York and South Carolina; a little less severe states were Massachusetts, New Jersey, and Pennsylvania. After the war started, five kinds of legal punishment were used: confinement, exile, deprivation of civil rights, confiscation of property, and execution.

Persons of suspected or proven disloyalty were subject to house arrest, a travel ban, and imprisonment, even in the most dank of cells. The "Catacomb of Loyalty," an abandoned copper mine at Simsbury (now East Granby), Connecticut, is the best known of the dismal Tory jails. Admittance to Newgate Prison, as it was called, was by opening a barred trap door and climbing 70 feet down the shaft to the ground level of the caverns. In the darkness and dampness, disease flourished and clothes became moldy and rotted away. On May 18, 1781, as the wife of one of those confined was being lowered down for a visit, prisoners scurried up the ladder, overpowered their guards, and escaped, killing one of the guards.

In times of military emergency, many Tories, otherwise deemed harmless, had to go into the interior of a colony or to another colony. Thus, in the Carolinas and Virginia suspected persons were moved from coastal areas. In 1776 many New York Tories were shifted to Pennsylvania, New Hampshire, and Connecticut, and for seven months (in 1777–78) 20 Philadelphia Quakers were interned at Winchester, Virginia.

All states forbade those who refused to take the patriot oaths of allegiance from holding office, suing for debts, serving on juries, and buying or selling lands. In some states, avowed loyalists could not practice trade or their professions. Eight states provided for banishment of declared loyalists, and five disfranchised them. In most places they had to pay extra taxes. In Virginia, for example, in 1777 they had to pay double, and in 1778, treble taxes.

Respected native loyalists who kept their views to themselves and lived quietly otherwise went unmolested. A prime example is Thomas, sixth Lord Fairfax, the proprietor of 5 million acres in Virginia's Northern Neck. As his biographer, Stuart E. Brown, states (1965), Fairfax, "democratic in bearing," and "a Whig by birth and by heritage, was a non-conforming conformist if there ever was one" (p. 176). Infirm at 84 years of age in 1777 but not so much as not to bed down "a Negro wench," Fairfax paid his extra taxes but was allowed to continue collecting quit-rents from the portions of his lands that had been granted to settlers. The added tax liability was offset by the increased rent revenues produced by wartime prosperity. Fairfax, as did other men of great wealth, faced a difficult dilemma. Had he declared for the patriots, his estates (such as Leeds Castle, in England) may have been subject to British confiscation. At the close of the Revolution (Lord Fairfax having died in 1781), the state of Virginia lay claim to quit-rents due and to lands of the Proprietary not yet granted to settlers on grounds that Lord Fairfax's heirs in England were alien and absent loyalists. The state, in 1785, abolished quit-rents on the Fairfax lands, thereby converting quit-rents to taxes payable to the state. A compromise in 1796 provided that the state receive Fairfax lands that had not been granted to settlers by 1793, but relinquish claim on lands appropriated before that date.

Acting on recommendations by Congress, the states declared that levying war and aiding the enemy by citizens constituted treasonable offenses, punishable by death. Five states included conspiracy to levy war. Executions were not frequent, with sentences carried out by order of courts, courts-martial, or a legislature (bill of attainder). Wallace Brown, in *The King's Friends* (1965), gleaning information from the testimony of loyalist claimants, estimates that 65 executions for treason occurred, ranging from none in Georgia and New Hampshire and one in Delaware to 15 in New York and 20 in South Carolina. These figures are not all inclusive and are misleading. In the case of Virginia's four executions, for example, charges of treason were compounded with other offenses, such as murder or robbery. James Madison, writing to George Washington on June 20, 1782, commented on why executions for treason were infrequent, despite the widespread collaboration with the enemy: "In Civil War between people of one Empire there can, during the Contest, be no Treason at all, or each party assuming the other to be Traitors, shall be able, by the same or different Laws, some made during the very Contest, to effect more Carnage than by the Sword."

The states enacted laws for misprision of treason (crimes less than treason), such as persuading persons to abandon allegiance, discouraging enlistment in American forces, speaking or writing against the government or the war effort, attempting to give intelligence to the enemy, corresponding with British officials, giving arms and supplies to the enemy, enlisting in the king's service, and inciting disorders. These offenses were punishable by fines, deportation, imprisonment, or involuntary military service; New York and South Carolina, however, made them felonies carrying the death sentence.

Following Congress's advice of November 1777, all states had laws for confiscation of loyalist estates. Most confiscations affected exiles. Loyalists frequently avoided confiscation by selling their estates, usually at less than full value, or assigning their property to relatives or friends. The confiscation of loyalist property gave the states and citizens (as prospective purchasers) a financial interest in persecuting loyalists. Confiscated estates usually sold at less than one-fourth of value. Interestingly, the British government did not appropriate American real estate in Great Britain.

Insurgents—Outlaws

Loyalist uprisings were isolated, ill planned, and for the most part amounted to banditry. One of the most successful of the free-ranging loyalist groups was led by

James Moody, a Sussex County (New Jersey) farmer, who, in April 1777, with 74 neighbors refused an oath of allegiance and fled to the British lines. Moody, who received a commission in the British army as ensign and then lieutenant, operated with his band in New Jersey. The daring feats of this "Scarlet Pimpernel of New Jersey," as one writer calls him, included regular seizure of the Continental army's mails and abduction of American officers. He escaped from captivity several times. His most ambitious exploit was his attempt to steal important papers from the Congress, which was meeting in Philadelphia; the project was foiled only in its last stage. After the war, Moody settled in Nova Scotia. Another gang that terrorized patriots in the North was one led by Claudius Smith. Pillaging in the Highlands above New York City, Smith gave most of his loot to the British and the poor, and thus earned the sobriquet, "Robin Hood." Proclaimed an outlaw by Governor Clinton and with a high price on his head, Smith fled to Long Island, where he was caught by a Connecticut posse and hanged on January 22, 1779.

For three years, Josiah Phillips's marauders, finding refuge in the Dismal Swamp, terrorized Norfolk and Princess Anne counties in lower tidewater Virginia. Phillips, a landless laborer, received a commission from Governor Lord Dunmore to raise men for the British service. After Dunmore left Virginia, Phillips led a bandit gang of upward to 50 persons in plundering. Militia were reluctant to pursue the band, which had protection from a network of relatives and friends. The gang murdered a militia captain. Finally, the Virginia legislature voted a bill of attainder for treason, stating that Phillips had one month to surrender, and if he did not give himself up he would be put to death on sight. Captured after the time limit, Phillips and three others were convicted in court of treason, robbery, and murder, and hanged in December 1778. Virginia's leaders were proud that, after all, no one in the state was executed under a bill of attainder.

Similar to the Phillips's marauders was the Doane loyalist gang of Bucks County, Pennsylvania, that functioned from 1781 to 1783. The group, led by Joseph Doane and his five sons, specialized in stealing government tax collections. The leaders were in the pay of the British army. Eventually, three leaders were slain, several hanged, and the others made good their escape.

On Maryland's Eastern Shore in 1777 500 loyalists from Somerset, Worcester, and Dorset counties, joined together under the command of Hamilton Colello. Colonel William Smallwood, with the 7th and 22d Virginia Continental regiments, who were passing through the state, and Maryland militia made ready to fight, whereupon the loyalists dispersed. Captured insurgents who took the oath of allegiance were pardoned; those who did not were imprisoned.

In April 1778 Maryland loyalists from Queen Anne and Kent counties, together with some Delaware residents, staged an uprising. General Howe had sent handbills to the area, stating that a reconciliation was near at hand. A band of 300 to 400 loyalists, led by Cheney Clows of Delaware, built a fort on the Chester River and committed robberies and abductions in the area. The governor sent out a militia force, and after exchange of gunfire, the insurgents evacuated the fort and dispersed. Clows successfully fled to join the British army in Philadelphia. One other ringleader was sentenced to be hanged but was pardoned.

The board of Associated Loyalists of America in New York planned a loyalist uprising in Maryland in 1781, one that it was hoped would assist British troops in the invasion of the Chesapeake area. The plot quickly collapsed. John Caspar Frietsche and six others were sentenced to be hanged, drawn, and quartered for high treason. Four had their sentences commuted, but Frietsche and two others were hanged.

During 1779–81, the Virginia frontier threatened to erupt in loyalist rebellion. A motley group of nearly 100—including Germans, indentured servants, Continental army deserters, English and Welsh immigrants who had been promised by the British 450 acres free of quit-rents, and newly arrived landholders—took an oath to the king and planned to collect more followers and then destroy the state lead mines and join forces with the British in the Carolinas. Colonels William Preston and Charles Lynch, with western militia, managed to suppress the uprising before it gained momentum. Those insurgents who immediately took the American oath of allegiance escaped punishment; those who did not were whipped until they shouted "Liberty Forever" and also agreed to take the oath. In 1781 John Claypool and others in the far-western part of Virginia (now Hardy County, West Virginia) refused to pay taxes and planned to join Cornwallis's army. General Daniel Morgan and militia captured the ringleaders, some of whom were arraigned for treason but eventually released.

The civil war in the Carolinas, 1780–82, waged in the form of loyalist militia groups and those who served in units of the British army versus patriot militia and Continentals, rapidly degenerated into hit-and-run raids on farms and plantations by small armed bands. William Cunningham and some 60 loyalists, calling their band the "Bloody Scout," carried terror from the outskirts of Charleston to the backcountry. David Fanning conducted dozens of raids in both Carolinas. Other armed bands, mostly considered to be of loyalist sympathies but often merely freebooters, caused havoc in South Carolina and Georgia. Some of these raiders had been followers of Joseph Coffel. Thus, groups of bandits that preyed on backcountry settlers were generally called "scoffelites." David Ramsay, in his 1809 history of South Carolina, commented on this element:

> A great proportion of them was an ignorant unprincipled banditti; to whom idleness, licentiousness and deeds of violence were familiar. Horse-thieves and others whose crimes had exiled them from society, attached themselves to parties of the British. . . . The necessity which their indiscriminate plundering imposed on all good men of defending themselves, did infinitely more damage to the royal cause than was compensated by all the advantages resulting from their friendship. (I, 259)

Of course, patriot groups also committed depredations and atrocities.

Daniel McGirt (or McGirth), who had been a member of the British Tory rangers in the South, led an interracial gang that preyed on wealthy plantation owners, sometimes without bothering to discern the victim's political affiliation. Maroon outlaws, taking refuge in the swamps along the Savannah River, plundered settlements in South Carolina and Georgia. Some of the maroons were slaves who had gone over to the British but had refused to depart with them.

The Provincial Service

Although loyalist Americans rallied to take up arms in support of British military operations, as organized corps they did not figure significantly in British strategy until 1778. A policy until 1779 kept loyalist units in a separate establishment, whereby they were not entitled to retirement rights or to the same pay as British regular troops. Besides the cost factor, the delay in organizing the loyalists was also due to overconfidence, expectation of a short war, a belief that the loyalist population would fight on its own, the issue of rank between provincials and regulars (a problem during the last war), and contempt for Americans as incompetent and inexperienced soldiers. The British thought a large professional army concentrated on Washington's troops would be sufficient to win the war.

Nearly 50,000 loyalists fought for the British cause during the war. From 1775 to 1781, 50 distinct loyalist units were created, consisting of 312 companies. Of the loyalists in arms, 21,000 were engaged in the Provincial Service (which carried regular army status), 19,000 of whom were American; the other 2,000 were recruited from Nova Scotia, Florida, Canada, or from recent British immigrants. As with the American armies, loyalist soldiers came and went, the standard enlistment being two years. The Provincial Service had 9,659 men in December 1780.

Some loyalist regiments drew a substantial number of recruits from prisoners of war and immigrants. Captured Americans crowded into prison ships and the like, brutalized, diseased, and near starvation, regarded enlistment with the British a matter of survival. Of 405 American troops captured in Canada in December 1775, 111 joined the British army. A favorite tactic of British commanders in ports was to prevent newly arrived immigrants from leaving the vicinity and promising that enlistees would be entitled to the same allotments for their families as those given regular British soldiers.

The largest and most active of the loyalist military units were the Queen's Rangers (Lt. Col. John G. Simcoe); Volunteers of Ireland (Lord Rawdon); New York Volunteers (Lt. Col. George Turnbull); British Legion (Lt. Col. Banastre Tarleton); King's American Regiment (Col. Edmund Fanning); Florida Rangers (Lt. Col. Thomas Brown); Loyal American Regiment (Col. Beverley Robinson); De Lancey's Brigade (Brig. Gen. Oliver De Lancey); New Jersey Volunteers (Brig. Gen. Cortlandt Skinner); Loyal Highland Emigrants (Lt. Col. Allen Maclean); and King's Royal Regiment of New York (Col. John Johnson).

The Exiles

One in 40 Americans became a refugee. In 1783 the United States had a population of about 2,950,000; 80,000 or more Americans fled the country, mostly at war's end. Nearly one-half of the refugees went to England, Scotland, and the West Indies (chiefly Jamaica, Dominica, Antigua, Grenada, Bahamas, and Bermuda), whereas the remainder settled in Canada and the Maritime Provinces (Nova Scotia–New Brunswick and Cape Breton and Prince Edward Islands). Nova

Scotia–New Brunswick received 30,000 exiles, and Canada, 10,000. The refugees in Canada, by order of the government in Quebec in 1789, were designated United Empire Loyalists, and they and their descendants ever since have been entitled to affix U.E. (Unity of Empire) after their names.

Places of Exile

New England loyalists left the area upon the British evacuation of Boston in March 1776 and were soon joined by a scattering of loyalists from other states. By the end of 1776, 3,000 resided in Great Britain. Most of these loyalists had been connected with the British government in America. Fleet Street, London, became a receptacle for many prominent loyalists; some went into the countryside and Bristol, whereas southern Scottish-Americans returned to their homeland. Some of the refugees received government pensions. Thomas Hutchinson, former governor of Massachusetts, had one of the highest awards (£500), but he had to refuse appointment to a baronetcy because he lacked the funds to support this position. The exiles in Great Britain were an unhappy lot, painfully separated from the rest of their families, homesick, snubbed by English society, and learning of the loss of their estates in America.

The British government offered inducements to settle in Canada and Nova Scotia–New Brunswick. Newcomers in Canada received homesteads and did not have to pay quit-rents for 10 years. Those who wanted to be "real farmers" could acquire 200 acres beyond a nine-mile radius of a town. Loyalist military veterans were eligible for large land grants: field officers, 5,000 acres; captains, 3,000; lieutenants, 2,000; and enlisted men, 300. So many loyalists moved into the region north of the Great Lakes that in 1791 a new province (west of the Ottawa River) was set off from Quebec.

By 1784 out of Nova Scotia's total population of 42,747, 28,347 were loyalists; more than 20,000 of these had left New York City during April–September 1783. The new town of Shelburne (originally called Roseway Harbor and also New Jerusalem) accommodated many of the immigrants, and by 1785 the community boasted 1,400 buildings and 3,000 house lots. Shelburne, however, proved to be an ill-fated experiment. The soil was bad, the harbor froze in winter, and most of the newcomers had no experience in fishing and farming. Within several years people began leaving for Great Britain, the West Indies, and other Nova Scotia towns or returning to the United States. In 1798 storms swept away the wharfs, and two years later Shelburne was a deserted city. Another town, created for the loyalists from a dense forest, was St. John's, across the Bay of Fundy. So many loyalists went to this location that New Brunswick was established as a separate province in 1784.

Black loyalists in the immediate postwar period fared much worse than their white counterparts. Overall, 4,000 left New York City, 6,000 left Charleston (evacuated December 14, 1782), and 4,000, Savannah (evacuated July 11, 1782). Most black loyalists were runaway slaves. Those from the southern states mainly wound up in East Florida, the West Indies, or England. Three thousand blacks, enrolled in General Sir Guy Carleton's "Book of Negroes," left New York City on evacuation day, November 25, 1783, for Nova Scotia. The experience in Nova Scotia was a nightmare for them. Only one-fourth of the immigrants received lands (an average of 34 acres), and these were mostly uncultivable. Deprived of rights, their status was scarcely more than peonage. In Nova Scotia, the black loyalists resided principally in Shelburne, Halifax, and Birchtown—the largest of their communities. Halifax became a rough town; in 1785 alone, 20 criminals were hanged (three of them blacks) for minor offenses. One black was executed for stealing a bag of potatoes. In Shelburne blacks lived in segregated quarters; they were given no tools, capital, credit, or livestock, and to qualify for public rations they had to perform labor, which was not required of the whites. Race riots on July 26, 1784, drove all the blacks out of Shelburne to Birchtown. Many died from disease in Birchtown.

Relief for black loyalists came from the Sierra Leone Society, sponsored by British humanitarian leaders such as Thomas Peters, John Clarkson, and Granville Sharp. The society acquired land at Sierra Leone, on the west coast of Africa, for the purpose of resettling black loyalists from London and Nova Scotia. The evacuation from Nova Scotia began on January 15, 1792, when 15 ships bearing 2,000 black loyalists sailed for the "Province of Freedom," along St. George's Bay at the mouth of the Sierra Leone River. Here the capital, Freetown, was established. In 1808 Sierra Leone became a crown colony.

Compensation

In England, loyalist refugees lobbied for compensation for losses sustained in America. Parliament responded in July 1783 by establishing the Commission of Enquiry into the Losses and Services of the American Loyalists. The commission conducted a thorough investigation of claims, with members holding hearings in London, Canada, Nova Scotia, and New Brunswick. It received 3,225 claims and made awards to 2,291 loyalists for a total amount of £8,216,126. The commission refused to consider properties outside the United States, unpaid salaries, fees, and rents, lost business profits, and debts owed by Americans. Claimants had to submit proof, chiefly mention in a confiscation law, a bill of attainder, or other official proceedings, supported by depositions of witnesses. Applicants had to demonstrate absolute and continual British loyalty during the war. Many persons did not apply because of the difficulty in obtaining documents and the cost involved in developing a case. The compensation represented 37 percent per claim. Forty-seven blacks applied for pensions or compensation. Of these, only one received compensation for property; three were awarded small annual incomes; and 20 were given small amounts of money. Parliament afforded minimum compensation for the loss of proprietorships in America, chiefly to the Penn and Baltimore families.

In addition, the British government awarded one-half pay pensions to about 500 loyalist officers, annual pensions to 204 persons for loss of official or professional income, and payments to 588 widows, orphans, and others. Overall, the

The Province of Freedom: The "Free Black Settlement." **The view is looking northward across St. George's Bay of the Sierra Leone River, Africa. A British flag flies from a tree stripped of its branches. From the French edition of John Matthew's** *Voyage à la Rivière* **de Sierra Leone (1797); first published in 1791.** *By permission of the British Library*

cost for compensating and resettling American loyalists amounted to about 30 million pounds.

Some loyalists' hopes of returning to America and recovering losses were buoyed by the peace treaty of 1783 and resolutions of Congress. Article five of the treaty stated that Congress would "earnestly recommend" to the state legislatures that they "provide for the restitution of all estates, rights and properties" belonging "to real British subjects" or to those under British protection who had not borne arms against the United States. Other loyalists would have the liberty to visit unmolested any part of the United States for 12 months in order to seek restitution. In addition, persons who were owed debts should have "no lawful impediment" for their recovery. Article six precluded any further confiscation or persecution. On May 30, 1783, Congress resolved that the states abide by articles five and six and that no person should "suffer any future loss or damage, either in his person, liberty or property" and that those under confinement for loyalism, "at the time of the ratification of the treaty in America, shall be immediately set at liberty, and the prosecutions so commenced be discontinued."

The states ignored the treaty provisions and the congressional resolution of May 1783, and enacted laws preventing suits against those who had purchased confiscated loyalist lands. Eight of the 13 states banned the return of certain loyalists. Connecticut, for example, passed a law requiring the deportation of returning exiled loyalists, and should they manage to stay in the state they were subject to a whipping of 10 to 20 lashes once a month. Of course, if loyalists were not allowed to return, they could not become naturalized citizens and thereby have easy access to the courts. Some states justified their restrictive legislation on the basis that the British had not provided indemnity for slaves they had taken away and also had not evacuated the western posts. In a few years, however, tensions eased, and certain leaders, such as Alexander Hamilton, James Madison, Benjamin Rush, and Aedanus Burke in their respective states, led successful campaigns to repeal antiloyalist legislation. By 1787 most states had done so. However, the confiscations of the war years remained largely intact, and the federal government eventually assumed responsibility for resolving the debts question.

PART 4

The New Nation

C H A P T E R   18

Sovereign Republics

 The new states established governments based on the sovereignty of the people. Before the war, few American political writers defended complete democracy. The ideal was a mixture of democracy, aristocracy, and monarchy. It was believed that unchecked majority rule of the people would result in anarchy and mobocracy. With Independence, American leaders considered republicanism to be their objective in the creation of government. The term *republicanism* had hitherto been confined largely to usage in England to condemn Whig ideas. The publication of Thomas Paine's *Common Sense* in January 1776 gave the terms *republican* and *republicanism* wide currency in America.

Republicanism primarily meant the rejection of monarchy and the British constitution and embraced the notion that government should be based on a community of equals. Roger Sherman, writing to John Adams on July 20, 1789, referred to an English dictionary definition of republic as "a commonwealth without a king." Samuel Johnson's dictionary of 1775 mentioned that a republic was a "government in which the supreme power is lodged in the people." Americans tended to make the distinction that a republic was a government of the people, but not necessarily a pure democracy. At times the terms *democracy* and *republic* were used interchangeably. A writer in the *Providence Gazette* of August 9, 1777, observed: "By *a democracy* is meant that form of government where the highest power of making laws is lodged in the common people, or persons chosen out from them." By the mid-1780s, to most Americans the fundamental characteristic of a republic was government through representatives chosen by the people. It was assumed that as a whole the people were virtuous, and since they naturally sought liberty in *res publica* (public affairs), tyranny would be impossible. For safety, powers conferred by the people should be prescribed and limited. John Adams said in his *Thoughts on Government* (1776) that "the very definition of a republic is 'an empire of laws, and not of men.'"

At the heart of republican government was the people's right to select their own representatives for the making of laws. All persons should have equal recourse to government. The Americans repudiated any ideas of virtual representation, such as in England, and thus provided the means for direct and equal representation in their lower houses of assembly. This was not materially different from the colonial period, except that the new governments allowed for fairer distribution of represen-

275

tation, according to population and geography. Some states reapportioned their legislatures and recognized districts, primarily in western areas, that had either been underrepresented or not represented at all. In shaping their new governments, state leaders strove to achieve some conservative balance by retaining certain property requirements and instituting checks and balances. Still, the change from colony to state governments indicated liberalization, chiefly by giving the lower houses of the legislatures preponderant authority.

To equalize access to government, state capitals were located centrally. The Virginia removal law of 1779 stated that "the equal rights of all inhabitants required that such seat of government should be as nearly central [as possible]." By 1789 five states established new capitals: from Charleston to Columbia, South Carolina; from New Bern to Raleigh, North Carolina; from Newcastle to Dover, Delaware; from Williamsburg to Richmond, Virginia; and from Savannah to Louisville, Georgia.

State Constitution-Making

The former royal and proprietary colonies wrote constitutions. The two autonomous colonies of Connecticut and Rhode Island, which had only an external link with the crown, kept their charters of 1662 and 1663, respectively. Connecticut did not adopt a constitution until 1818, and Rhode Island, in 1842.

In writing the state constitutions, the framers developed a unique theory of government created by a constituency expressing itself—"out of doors," by the people in convention. Only Massachusetts, however, combined the use of a special constitutional convention and popular ratification. The other states, though having some involvement of the constituency at large, adopted their constitutions with some form of legislative approval.

On November 3, 1775, Congress advised New Hampshire to bring together "a full and free representation of the People" for the purpose of adopting a constitution, and a day later it issued a similar summons to South Carolina. The Congressional Resolutions of May 10 and 15, 1776, called on all the states "to adopt such Government as shall, in the Opinion of the Representatives of the People, best conduce to the Happiness and Safety of their Constituents in particular, and America in general." From 1776 to 1788, 14 states (including the territory of Vermont) adopted constitutions: one each for 11 of the 13 states and Vermont, and two each for South Carolina (1776 and 1778) and New Hampshire (1776 and 1784). Eight state constitutions went into effect in 1776, four of them before the Declaration of Independence. These constitutions, as most of the others to follow, were adopted by provincial bodies sitting as legislatures. New Hampshire enacted its constitution (the first state to do so) on January 5, 1776, as a regular legislative action. The South Carolina provincial congress, on March 26, 1776, also passed a law for a constitution, which was intended to be a temporary one for the duration of the war. On March 19, 1778, South Carolina, through amendments, became the first state to rewrite its constitution. The fifth

Virginia Convention, on June 29, 1776, ratified a constitution, and the New Jersey provincial congress did the same on July 2.

Delaware and Pennsylvania were the first to call special conventions to draft their constitutions. After accepting a constitution on September 21, 1776, the Delaware Convention declared itself a legislative body. In Pennsylvania, a convention of delegates from the county and Philadelphia committees of inspection, adopted a constitution on September 28, 1776. Neither the Delaware nor the Pennsylvania constitution was submitted to a referendum. Dual convention-legislative bodies enacted constitutions in Maryland (November 8, 1776), North Carolina (December 14, 1776), Georgia (February 5, 1777), and New York (April 20, 1777).

On June 15, 1777 the Massachusetts legislature, which had reaffirmed the charter of 1691 without the royal trappings, resolved itself into a convention. This body, on February 28, 1778, submitted a constitution to the towns for approval. Largely through the influence of a pamphlet, the *Essex Result,* written by lawyer Theopolis Parsons, the constitution failed by a vote of 9,972 to 2,083. Criticism emphasized the need for broader representation, lack of a bill of rights, and insufficient separation of powers. In rejecting the constitution, however, three towns (Lexington, Concord, and Beverly) called for a specially elected convention to meet at Cambridge in September 1779. A constitution, crafted mainly by John Adams, was approved on March 2, 1780, and sent to the towns, which ratified it by the requisite two-thirds majority.

The making of the Massachusetts constitution helped to establish the principle that the people should have a role both in drafting and in ratifying a constitution. It also served to distinguish clearly between fundamental and statutory law. In 1781 Thomas Jefferson was mindful of the unique American constitutional development. In his *Notes on Virginia,* he observed:

> The other states in the union have been of opinion, that to render a form of government unalterable by ordinary acts of assembly, the people must delegate persons with special powers. They have accordingly chosen special conventions to form and fix their governments. . . . If they be right, we shall only have the unnecessary trouble of meeting once in convention. If they be wrong, they expose us to the hazard of having no fundamental rights at all.

Five state constitutions provided means for amendment. In Georgia a constitutional convention would meet upon petitioning representative of one-half of the voters and one-half of the counties. Sixteen of the 24 members of the Pennsylvania Council of Censors could order the holding of a constitutional convention, which could vote amendments; the legislature could not change the constitution. In Maryland, two-thirds of the senators and representatives could propose amendments, which would go into effect by a similar vote after an election had intervened. South Carolina permitted amendment by a majority vote of both houses of the legislature. Massachusetts had a requirement for polling the towns in 1795, and if two-thirds of the voters at that time so favored, a convention would meet for the purpose of drafting amendments.

Bills of Rights

Six states—former colonies Virginia, Delaware, Pennsylvania, Maryland, North Carolina, and Massachusetts—and Vermont, which declared its independence from New York in January 1777, initially prefaced a "declaration of rights" (bill of rights) to their constitutions. Two states added a bill of rights at a later time, New Hampshire in 1784 and New York in 1787. The constitutions of New Jersey, South Carolina, New York (1777), and Georgia, though lacking bills of rights, noted certain common law protections within their constitutions. Since the constitutions set limits on powers of government, the declarations of rights were mainly in the form of prescriptive guidelines rather than mandatory injunctions, with the frequent use of the word *ought* rather than *shall;* the word *shall* was reserved for setting forth the duties and functions of government. The enumeration of rights was not meant to supersede the common law, which all the states recognized as being substantially in force within their respective jurisdictions.

The framers of the state constitutions recognized that the long colonial experience had expanded upon and modified English guarantees of rights. Thus, the Massachusetts constitution stipulated that colonial laws were in full force unless repealed by legislation, "such parts only excepted as are repugnant to the rights and liberties contained in this Constitution."

The states' declarations of rights significantly afforded positive protection of the rights of individuals and not just those of the majority. "The use of a bill of rights to curtail the power of the sovereign majority was a new step in the development of Western constitutionalism," writes Willi Paul Adams (1980).

> Since 1776, bills of rights had acquired a new function, one that was no less essential in the republican system than it had been under the monarchical. They now not only obliged those in public office to adhere to specific modes of procedure but also delimited certain areas of individual behavior over which the sovereign majority relinquished control. (p. 145)

"A DECLARATION of RIGHTS made by the representatives of the good people of *Virginia,* assembled in full and free Convention," written mostly by George Mason and adopted unanimously on June 13, 1776, after sharp debate, served as a model for other states. The preamble of this first declaration is suggestive of Jefferson's Declaration of Independence, in stating

> That all men are by nature equally free and independent, and have certain inherent rights, of which, when they enter into a state of society, they cannot, by any compact, deprive or divest their posterity; namely, the enjoyment of life and liberty, with the means of acquiring and possessing property, and pursuing and obtaining happiness and safety.

The Virginia "Declaration" contained 16 articles, seven pertaining to the relationship of a free people to the government and nine enumerating rights of citizens. Thus, citizens had guarantees against self-incrimination, arrest without knowing one's accuser, excessive bail or fines, cruel and unusual punishments, and general warrants of search and seizure. All persons were entitled to the right to vote, jury trials in both criminal and civil cases, freedom of the press, and the "free exercise of religion, according to the dictates of conscience." Due process in general was guaranteed: no person could be "deprived of his liberty except by the law of the land, or the judgment of his peers." Standing armies, "in time of peace, should be avoided, as dangerous to liberty; and that, in all cases, the military should be under strict subordination to, and governed by, the civil power." Interestingly, the Virginia "Declaration" omitted references to speech, assembly, petition, habeas corpus, grand jury process, counsel, double jeopardy, ex post facto laws, and bills of attainder.

John Adams remarked that Pennsylvania's declaration of rights was "taken almost verbatim" from the Virginia declaration; Pennsylvania, however, as did North Carolina, forbade the imprisonment of debtors. All state constitutions guaranteed the right to bear arms, civil over military power, and free elections. Six states provided for freedom of the press. All of the states' declarations proclaimed freedom of worship. Massachusetts' document had one of the stronger statements: "no subordination of any one sect or denomination to another shall ever be established by law." None of the declarations provided for absolute freedom of religion, although some progress was made in that direction during the 1780s through legislative enactment. Five states retained public support for churches.

Separation of Powers and Judicial Review

The British experience in mixed government proved instructive to the framers of the state constitutions. Of course, to the American patriot mind, a true checks and balances system in Great Britain had been perverted by the fused tyrannies of king and Parliament. Yet separation of powers was needed to prevent unbridled exercise of power. A republican view of government also meant that any particular social element should not be embodied exclusively in any branch of government.

The framers of the American state constitutions did not wish to diverge too much from the previous colonial political systems; they wished only to make them more democratic. They agreed with the view of the English jurist, Sir William Blackstone, that two houses of legislature and an executive (to Blackstone, the king) "jointly impel the machine of government in a direction different from what either, acting by itself, would have done; but at the same time in a direction partaking of each, and formed out of all; a direction which constitutes the true line of the liberty and happiness of the community."

Such checks and balances between the legislature and the executive might not be enough, however, to ensure an overriding interest of the public good. Thus, Americans began to grope for means to establish an independent judiciary, one that would be charged with holding the Constitution inviolable. Baron de Montesquieu's *The Spirit of Laws* (English translation, 1750) had a great influence on American political thinking. To Montesquieu there were "three sorts of power"—legislative, executive, and judicial; there could be "no liberty if the judiciary power be not separated from the legislative and executive." These views found expression in the state constitutions. The Virginia constitution, for example, stated that "the legislature, executive, and judiciary departments, shall be separate and distinct, so that neither exercise the powers properly belonging to the other; nor shall any person exercise the powers of more than one of them at the same time." According to the Massachusetts "Declaration of Rights" (part one of the 1780 constitution), "the legislative department shall never exercise the executive and judicial powers, or either of them: The judicial shall never exercise the legislative and executive powers or either of them: To the end it may be a government of laws and not of men."

Yet the framers of the state constitutions distrusted completely independent departments that would be unanswerable to each other. Thus, in most state constitutions, legislatures elected the executive councils and also appointed judicial and executive officers.

Although the state constitutions avoided the question of judicial review (courts passing on the constitutionality of laws), court judgments in the 1780s contributed to the shaping of this doctrine. In Pennsylvania and Vermont, however, the situation was different. In these states an elective Council of Censors could determine infractions to the state constitution and propose amendments. Allan Nevins (1924) comments that "these two remarkable institutions had the same influence in both States: they delayed the recognition of a distinction between the Constitution and statutes, and the development of a judicial enforcement of that distinction" (p. 169).

In *Holmes v. Walton* (1780), a New Jersey law providing for six-man juries in cases regarding confiscation of loyalist property was overturned because of conflict with the Constitution. The Virginia Court of Appeals, in *Caton v. Commonwealth* (1782), by a vote of six to two, upheld the constitutionality of the Treason Act, as to the legislative pardoning power. The Mayor's Court of New York City, in *Rutgers v. Waddington* (1784), contrary to state law, allowed, in an action for trespass, Elizabeth Rutgers to recover property that she had abandoned during the war and that had been used by the British army. The decision contended that the New York law contravened the Articles of Confederation of the national government and the peace treaty of 1783. In *Bayard v. Singleton* (1787), the North Carolina Supreme Court invalidated an act confirming titles of persons who had purchased confiscated loyalist lands.

Trevett v. Weeden (1786) sparked wide controversy. Creditors in and outside Rhode Island charged that an enforcement law of that state requiring acceptance of its paper money violated the obligation of contracts. The case arose when John Weeden, a butcher in Newport, Rhode Island, refused to accept paper money from John Trevett in payment for meat. The state supreme court decided not to pass judgment in the case, thus in effect refusing to abide by the enforcement law. The court in exercising judicial restraint was in agreement with James Varnum, Weeden's counsel, who had argued "that the legislature have the uncontrollable power of making laws not repugnant to the constitution; the judiciary have the sole power of judging of those laws, and are bound to execute them; but cannot admit any act of the legislature as law, which is against the constitution."

Suffrage and Officeholding

Qualifications for voting and officeholding, though liberalized, remained much the same under the state constitutions as under the colonial governments. Separation from Great Britain and the democratic bases of the new state governments necessitated some changes.

The voting franchise was still limited to free white adult males, with an age requirement usually of 21 years and residency from six to twelve months. Only one state had a religious test for voting: South Carolina required expression of a belief in God and in a future state of rewards and punishment.

Concerning a "stake in society," the new governments showed both a continuity with the past and a liberalizing trend. Although American political leaders wanted republican government founded on the consent of a broad electorate, many could agree with John Adams that the suffrage should be limited to men of property. Writing to James Sullivan, on May 26, 1776, Adams asked, "is it not true" that men "who are wholly destitute of property, are also too little acquainted with public affairs to form a right judgment and too dependent on other men to have a will of their own?" Would not giving propertyless men the vote, Adams further queried, "make a fine encouraging provision for corruption by your fundamental law? Such is the frailty of the human heart that very few men who have no property have any judgment of their own."

All of the original 13 states required property ownership or payment of taxes to vote. Vermont was the only state to have universal manhood suffrage. New Hampshire, Pennsylvania, and North Carolina granted the suffrage to all taxpayers. In other states, voting in the lower house required ownership of real estate that carried a stipulated assessment, the maximum being £40, or capable of returning an annual rent, such as 40s. In some states, a vote for members of the upper house of the legislature had a higher property condition (e.g., in New York, real estate valued at £100). The 1780s saw some change in electoral procedure. Several states adopted secret balloting as a substitute for viva voce voting and scheduled elections for November instead of May, enabling persons to vote after the cultivation of their crops.

Plural officeholding was eliminated. Five states and Vermont had no property qualification for membership in the lower house of the legislature; three states, including Vermont, had none for senators. Nine states had no property conditions for the executive. Maryland and New Jersey had the highest property requirement for assemblyman, £500. South Carolina, by its constitution of 1778, had the top requirement for property qualifications for members of the upper house and for governor—£2,000 and £10,000 property evaluation, respectively.

Clergymen were not eligible to serve in the legislature in some states, and in South Carolina, Delaware, and New York, they were barred from any office. A half dozen states made declarations of being either a Protestant or a Christian a requisite for public office. Even under the liberal Pennsylvania constitution of 1776, legislators had to avow belief "in one God" and "acknowledge the Scriptures of the Old and New Testament to be given by Divine inspiration."

Legislature and Executive

To achieve republican government, the American revolutionaries determined that the locus of power should lodge in the lower houses of assembly, the direct representatives of the people. Unicameralism had a strong advocacy in some states, and indeed it was adopted in Pennsylvania, Georgia, and Vermont. Thomas Paine's *Common Sense* stirred debate on whether or not to have a one-house legislature. He argued "that the more simple any thing is, the less liable it is to be disordered, and the easier repaired when disordered." An anonymous writer published in 1776 *The Interest of America,* which noted that "one branch of Legislature is much preferred to more than one, because a plurality causes perpetual contention and wasted time"; furthermore, "it might open a door for ill-disposed aspiring men to destroy the state." Critics feared that a single house would have a tendency to act recklessly. Ideally, an upper house would consist of men of wisdom to complement men of virtue in the lower house.

In all states, the lower houses were elected by the people, from the towns in New England or counties or parishes elsewhere. All but one state had annual elections for the lower house; South Carolina provided for two-year terms. The lower houses of legislature had authority to originate money bills, though the Maryland, South Carolina, and New Jersey senates also insisted on having this same right. Thomas Jefferson was among those who complained of insufficient checks on the power of the legislatures: in 1781 he wrote that "173 despots [the number of Virginia legislators] would surely be as oppressive as one. . . . An *elective despotism* was not the government we fought for."

As a balance to the larger property qualifications for senators, the states provided that the upper houses also reflect popular sovereignty. Thus, senators were elected by the people, except in Maryland, which used an electoral college. (Two persons from each county and one each from Annapolis and Baltimore met to select 15 senators from their ranks.) Senates had full legislative powers, except for limitations on initiating appropriations: in Virginia the senate could only accept or reject but not amend money bills. The senates tended to be representative of the middle levels of society rather than just wealthy landowners, lawyers, and merchants, which had been characteristic of the past colonial councils.

The states experimented with weak executives. Eleven states, including Vermont, set one-year terms for governors; South Carolina, two years and Delaware and New York, three years. Several states set limits on successive terms. In Virginia a governor could serve three single-year terms in four years—thus, in 1779 Patrick Henry had to step aside, with Thomas Jefferson succeeding him as governor. Executives were elected by the legislatures in eight states (by joint ballot of both houses in New Jersey, Delaware, Virginia, and North Carolina) and by direct popular vote in New Hampshire, Rhode Island, Connecticut, Massachusetts, New York, and Vermont. Pennsylvania had a plural executive in the form of the Supreme Executive Council, with one member from Philadelphia and each county, elected for staggered seven-year terms; it did not have veto power. New York's Council of Revision, consisting of the governor, chancellor, and supreme court judges, had the power of veto, though it could be overridden by two-thirds vote of both houses. Nine governors had no kind of veto power at all.

Six governors shared appointive powers with the legislature. Most states had councils of state (privy councils), elected by the legislature or the people, to advise and assist governors in their executive functions. New York had a unique body: a Council of Appointment, consisting of the governor and four senators (one selected annually by the assembly). This body had full power to appoint officials at all levels of the state government. Thus, New York presented enormous opportunity to build up a political machine through patronage, a fact not lost on George Clinton, who served as governor from 1776 to 1795. The relatively strong executive powers in the New York and Massachusetts constitutions served as models for the framers of the later federal Constitution.

Division and Disillusion

The Revolutionary War era brought into government more of the ordinary type of person rather than members of the elite. Contributing to this change were "two simultaneous and interlocking developments," writes Jackson Turner Main (1973b): "the declining prestige of the 'better sort' and a rising confidence of the 'middling sort' in their own ability" (p. 203). A large number of people found opportunity for public service in the enlarged legislatures and the armed forces. War prosperity provided the means for upward mobility, politically and socially as well as economically. Even those who did not expand their "stake in society" entered the legislative ranks as never before. The new legislatures contained persons from all walks of life above laborer. Increased representation from the backcountry gave a new leaven to representative government. In Georgia, the thousands of Carolinians and Virginians who moved into the interior part of the state led to a shift in political power geographically. In the legislatures of six states (South Carolina, Virginia, Maryland, New Jersey, New York, and New Hampshire), the proportion of wealthy members dropped from 46 percent to 22 percent, with Virginia experiencing the least change, 60 to 50 percent.

Many new leaders in New England rose from humble beginnings. Samuel Huntington of Connecticut, for example, son of a small farmer, had almost no schooling and at age 16 was apprenticed to a carpenter. He studied law on his own and was admitted to the bar. Huntington sat in the assembly and council and the Continental Congress (1775–84), serving as its president (1779–81), and was governor of Connecticut (1786–96).

Emerging Political Blocs

If the political changes led to less deference in government (ordinary people catering to the wishes of a wealthy elite), economic and sectional conditions were important in molding broad political alignments. Two opposing political blocs emerged in the legislatures, whom Jackson Turner Main calls the Cosmopolitans and Localists. Most Cosmopolitans lived along the coast or navigable rivers and in urban areas. They had a broad outlook and were well connected, with their ranks formed by prosperous merchants, lawyers, and other professionals. They wanted to maintain an orderly society and to promote economic progress. Localists lived mainly in the interior rural areas and had a narrow view of issues. Many were subsistence farmers and debtors. They sought leniency in payment of debts, less government, and a lowering of the tax burden.

The postwar recession, reaching its worst phase in 1786 and lasting until 1788, exacerbated political alignment. Localists secured noncompliance with the obligations of the peace treaty of 1783, issuance of paper money as legal tender, nonpayment on quotas of national expenses, limitation on actions for debts, and allowance for payment of debts in commodities or land instead of cash. In the mid-1780s seven states had paper money in circulation, and cheap money advocates had been barely defeated in four other states. Even when the rag money–debtor groups were not victorious, they instilled fear among the wealthier classes, who began to question the emphasis on democratic government. Localists were never able to control the legislature in Massachusetts. In the interior of that state, after 1780, citizens rioted regularly to prevent courts from conducting proceedings. In 1784–85 they ceased such action and simply protested by ignoring government, refusing to send representatives to the legislature, and withholding taxes. Similar resistance occurred in Vermont, New Hampshire, Maine (part of Massachusetts), New York, New Jersey, and Virginia.

Party organization was slow to form. Cliques and factions existed but mostly as alliances. The lack of patronage control and coordinating mechanisms hindered party development. Furthermore, "the absence of stable party or factional designations in elections," writes William N. Chambers (1963), "made it extremely difficult for voters to hold representatives responsible for their acts." Popular impact on government decisions was "thwarted by the looseness, semi-visibility, disorder, personal ties, and confusion of faction" (pp. 26–27).

Pennsylvania came the closest to approaching a party system. The Constitutionalists (Radicals) held sway against the Republicans (Anti-Constitution). The Constitutionalists, largely representing western Scotch-Irish and German communities, supported the democratic constitution of 1776 and opposed the special privileges of men associated with the Philadelphia merchant–financial establishment. In power, the Constitutionalists secured briefly the state's suspension of the charter of the Bank of North America. This institution had high interest rates and dividends and promoted imports, which drained specie from the economy. The Constitutionalists also reintroduced paper money and funded certificates to benefit speculators. The Republicans kept up their attack on the Constitution of 1776 and by 1790 gained power, whereby they scuttled the old constitution for one with a bicameral legislature. In New York, Governor Clinton was forging together a political constituency of farmers, artisans, and small entrepreneurs.

Interstate Disharmony

Jealousies and rivalries threatened interstate accord. In particular, states bickered over their share of war debts. Quarrels became most pronounced, however, concerning the levying of tariff duties. From 1782 to 1785, all states, except New Jersey, placed duties on imports (affecting both interstate as well as foreign commerce), for the purpose of revenue only. By 1786 the New England states, New York, and Pennsylvania had increased import duties to make them protective. The northern protectionists advocated fewer imports in order to protect new industries and halt the flow of specie to England. Much of the states' tariff regulation was imposed in retaliation against England for dumping goods and for its almost total exclusion of American ships from the West Indian carrying trade. The states also could not export cured meat, fish, and dairy products to the British West Indies. Besides import duties, eight states (New York, Pennsylvania, Delaware, New Hampshire, Massachusetts, Maryland, Virginia, and North Carolina) also had tonnage duties discriminating against Great Britain. But it was the added duties for the transshipment of goods once in America that caused great acrimony among the states. In 1787 New York went so far as to require entrance and clearance fees on vessels bound for Connecticut and New Jersey. Connecticut merchants retaliated by boycotting goods from New York, and the state of New Jersey placed a heavy tax on a New York lighthouse built at Sandy Hook on the New Jersey side of the harbor.

State boundary disputes, jurisdictional rivalry, and the questions of separatism in the West were all mostly resolved by the end of the decade through the states' own actions or through assistance by Congress. Sectional animosity continued unabated, however, in relation to commerce, navigation, and Congress's western policies. Eight northern states and five southern states grouped against each other in opposing interests. A heated sectional controversy arose over the location of the nation's capital during 1783–84, only to be resolved to the satisfaction of almost no one by making New York City, in 1785, the temporary seat of government. Each section had its own preferred location. Southerners desired a site on the Potomac. Such a location, as Jefferson wrote to George Rogers Clark in December 1783, would "cement us to our Western friends when they shall be formed into separate states."

By the mid-1780s many Americans had become disillusioned over their governments' failure to create harmony or to enhance public virtue. Taxes were burdensome, debtor laws defaulted creditors, interest-bearing government and military certificates were hoarded by the rich, and the legislatures acted irresponsibly in issuing paper money. Propertied interests especially felt victimized by their assemblies, whereas the poorer elements of society thought government was not fully responsive to their needs. As David Ramsay of South Carolina wrote Benjamin Rush in 1783, "This revolution has introduced so much anarchy that it will take half a century to eradicate the licentiousness of the people." George Mason, writing to William Cabell on May 6, 1783, expressed a similar opinion: "Frequent Interferance with private Property & Contracts, restrospective Laws destructive of all public Faith, as well as Confidence between Man & Man, and flagrant Violations of the Constitution must disgust the best & wisest Part of the Community, occasion a general Depravity of Manners, bring the Legislature into Contempt, and finally produce Anarchy & public Convulsion."

James Madison, in Congress during the winter and spring of 1787, wrote a memorandum, "Vices of the Political System of the U. States," in which he outlined the deficiencies in the state governments and their relations with the Confederation. As to the states themselves, he noted the "multiplicity of laws" among the states ("a nuisance of the most pestilent kind"), "mutability of the laws," which were daily being "repealed and superseded before any trial can have been made of their merits," and also the need for restraining the majority "from unjust violations of the rights of the minority, or of individuals." Unchecked sovereignty of the people threatened the viability of republican government itself.

Although few persons wanted to disengage the state governments from the republican principles on which they were founded, the experience of the states in attempting to solve all their problems as small and competing nations demonstrated the need to strengthen the central government. In that way, the states could be assisted in establishing their own credibility and in coordinating solutions relating to their mutual concerns.

CHAPTER 19

The Confederation

Graduating from Harvard at age 19, John Quincy Adams was assigned as his part in the commencement to deliver a ten-minute "English Oration, upon the importance and necessity of public faith to the well-being of the Community." Already having served as a secretary to diplomatic missions abroad, Adams expressed his dismay over what he considered America's failure in national government. "At this critical period, when the whole nation is groaning under the intolerable burden" of "accumulated evils," said Adams, "it is natural to enquire, what were the causes" which have led "to the deplorable situation," and "what measures might still be adopted, to realize those happy days of national wealth and honour, which the glorious conclusion of a just and successful war, seemed to promise." Others in the 1780s spoke of "a critical period," and historians have treated the Confederation period as a time of crisis and ineptitude in government.

Nevertheless, the Confederation has had its staunch defenders. Patrick Henry, at the Virginia ratifying convention in 1788, declared:

> The Confederation, this same despised government, merits, in my opinion, the highest encomium—it carried us through a long and dangerous war; it rendered us victorious in that bloody conflict with a powerful nation; it has secured us a territory greater than any European monarch possesses—and shall a government which has been thus strong and vigorous, be accused of imbecility, and abandoned for want of energy?

Historians in the twentieth century, such as Charles A. Beard, Merrill Jensen, E. James Ferguson, and Jackson Turner Main, have viewed the Confederation favorably. Richard B. Morris (1956) aptly sums up Jensen's assessment:

> Jensen sees the Articles as a constitutional expression of the philosophy of the Declaration of Independence, the Constitution as a betrayal of those principles. To Jensen the Articles were designed to prevent the central government from infringing upon the rights of the states, whereas the Constitution was designed to check both the states and the democracy that found expression within state bounds. (p. 243)

The Confederation brought the Revolutionary War to a successful conclusion, did what was expected of it, provided frugal government, developed lasting national policies, and avoided further warfare of any kind. Had its shortcomings been correctable by an adequate amending process, it might well have afforded a strong national government. It might also have had clearer lines of responsibility than did the succeeding government, which had a division of powers among its branches.

The First National Constitution

On June 12, 1776, Congress named a committee of thirteen to draft articles of confederation. John Dickinson, as chairman, assumed the task of writing the document. Dickinson was one of those who advocated union before independence. By taking steps toward independence and union in June 1776, Congress sought to placate both conservatives and radicals. In July, Congress rejected the initial draft. Eventually, after debates over a variety of suggested amendments, Congress, on November 15, 1777, accepted the Articles of Confederation in final form, and on June 26, 1777, ordered ratification by the state legislatures through their congressional delegates.

By July 9, 1778, eight states had accepted the Articles of Confederation. The other ratifications came in more slowly, with Maryland, on March 1, 1781, the last to approve. Maryland had delayed until Virginia consented to surrender to Congress its territorial claims north and west of the Ohio River.

The great defect of the Confederation as a national government was that it was established by the states and not by the people, hence functioning, except for federal territories, in relation to the states and not directly with the people. Although the Articles pledged "perpetual union," the Confederation typified a "league of friendship" wherein "each state retains its sovereignty, freedom and independence, and every Power, Jurisdiction and right, which is not by this confederation expressly delegated to the United States, in Congress assembled." The Confederation had no coercive power over states or individuals within the states.

For representation, the Articles of Confederation took a cue from the earlier Albany Plan of Union (1754). Each state voted as a unit in the unicameral national legislature; delegations consisted of not less than two or more than seven persons. Congressmen, elected annually, were limited to three terms in six years; the president of Congress (like a speaker of the House) was chosen from among the members to one annual term in three years. A vote of nine states ratified treaties and passed laws on matters relating to war, peace, and emitting and appropriating moneys. Except for amendment, which required the consent of all delegations, other business could be transacted by a simple majority, seven states.

Congress had the authority to decide on peace or war, carry on hostilities, engage in diplomacy, raise an army and navy (appointing the superior officers), borrow and issue money, determine the alloy and value of coin "struck by their own authority, or by that of the respective states," adjudge prize cases, settle interstate boundary disputes, manage Indian affairs, make requisitions on the states for money and men (in case of war), set standards for weights and measures, and establish and regulate post offices. The Articles recognized comity among the states: return of interstate fugitives; reciprocity as to the privileges and immunities of citizens; and "full faith and credit" for each state's "records, acts, and judicial proceedings." States were restrained from entering into treaties, alliances, or confederation on their own, conducting foreign affairs, or making war, unless invaded. As serious liabilities, Congress could not regulate commerce or enforce financial requisitions and treaties. The Articles prescribed that any remedy pertaining to the authority of the Confederation be in the form of a simple amendment. With unanimity required, however, that was all but impossible. During the debates over the Articles in Congress, the New York delegation had proposed a vote of eleven states to pass an amendment. Had this been incorporated into the Articles, there would have been less need in the future to write a new constitution.

Congressional Administration

The Confederation Congress created single-headed executive departments to coordinate its major business, although there were still the usual standing and special committees. Before 1781 administrative concentration had proceeded as far as the establishment of a Board of War, Board of Treasury (in addition to the treasurer, comptroller, auditor, and two Chambers of Accounts of three commissioners each), Board of Admiralty (naval and marine affairs), and a standing Committee for Foreign Affairs.

On January 10, 1781, Congress designated a Department of Foreign Affairs. Robert R. Livingston, chancellor for the state of New York, served as secretary for Foreign Affairs from August 1781 to June 1783, and John Jay served from 1784 to 1789. The principal duties consisted of recommending policy and acting as liaison between Congress and American and foreign diplomats.

The Department of Finance was created on February 7, 1781. Robert Morris served as the superintendent of Finance (February 20, 1781–November 1, 1784). He had responsibility "for Regulating the Treasury and Adjusting the Public Accounts." The office included the treasurer, comptroller, register, auditor, and clerks. Morris, as superintendent, presided over payment of the civil list and interest on loans. He also had charge of contracting for army supplies and their transportation. An arduous task was the liquidation and settlement of accounts at home and abroad. After Morris's resignation, amid sharp criticism of conflict of interest and excessive power, Congress dispensed with having one financier and appointed a three-man Board of Treasury (1784–89). The initial appointees refused to serve, but in January 1785 Arthur Lee, Samuel Osgood, and Walter Livingston accepted membership on the Board. Duties centered primarily on further settling war accounts.

Congress established a war department on February 7, 1781. After some politicking by would-be office-seekers, General Benjamin Lincoln received the appointment as secretary at War. Since the office was potentially irksome to General Washington, Lincoln was regarded as the ideal appointee. Not only did he have an amiable disposition, but also, since his release as a prisoner of war (after the Charleston debacle) his status in the army was generally little more than that of supernumerary. The secretary at War kept returns of army personnel, supplies, and equipment, made estimates for needed supplies and recruits, transmitted orders and resolutions of Congress to the army, signed commissions, and generally reported on military affairs to Congress. Lincoln held the post from October 30, 1781 to October 29, 1783. Until General Henry Knox took over the department on May 8, 1785, the sole clerk in the office, Joseph Carleton, assumed the duties of the secretary at War. Since 1775, the Congress had employed a postmaster general; Ebenezer Hazard held this position during 1782–89. Although the three new executive heads were merely agents of Congress, the establishment of these offices represented an important step toward the later single-headed departments within an independent executive branch.

Besides executive functions, Congress exercised limited judicial authority. The Confederation, of course, lacked any independent judiciary, except for the adjudication of maritime (admiralty) cases. Article IX of the Articles of Confederation empowered Congress to appoint "courts for the trial of piracies and felonies committed on the high seas" and also tribunals "for receiving and determining finally appeals in all cases of captures." In January 1780 Congress established a three-man "Court of Appeals in Cases of Capture," and in April 1781 it designated certain state judges to hear cases on maritime crimes. Before setting up the special judiciary, the marine committee, any one of several naval boards, and a special committee on appeals tried admiralty cases. Of 104 admiralty trials decided by congressional tribunals for the period of 1776–87, 49 were reversed by state courts.

According to the Articles of Confederation, Congress, upon the petitioning of parties involved, could resolve boundary disputes. Only one such case was decided. Five commissioners appointed by Congress, meeting in Trenton, New Jersey, December 1782, awarded political jurisdiction of the Wyoming district in the Susquehanna Valley to Pennsylvania rather than to Connecticut. A congressional decision, not going through adjudication, had impact on another boundary controversy. Congress made known its approval of Vermont becoming a state; New York, however, would not relinquish its claim to the territory until 1790.

The Articles of Confederation gave Congress authority to appoint a "Committee of the States" to "sit in the recess of congress." This body, consisting of one delegate from each state, could carry on regular legislative functions. As in the Congress, nine states made a quorum. From June 4 to August 13, 1784, this experiment was tried; most of the time, however, the Committee could not muster the requisite majority. Rather than providing continuity and leadership, it thus underscored a major shortcoming of the Confederation. Complained Charles Thomson, secretary of Congress, to Jacob Read, on September 17, 1784: "A government without a visible head must appear a strange phenomenon to European politicians and will I fear lead them to form no very favorable opinion of our stability, wisdom or Union."

Public Finance

Although the Confederation lacked sufficient revenue to retire the national debt, income from states and other domestic sources met operational expenses and some payment toward debt obligations. The cost of government administration was minimal: in 1785, $85,715; in 1786, $117,430; in 1787, $128,332; and in 1788, $94,610. The Confederation, however, fell behind in payment of interest on French loans and contracts. After 1784 the Confederation, seeking to avoid possible retaliation on shipping and to maintain good credit with at least one country, kept up interest payments on Dutch loans. Unfortunately, the borrowed foreign capital was used to pay interest on previous loans. In all, Dutch bankers supplied seven loans to the United States (1782 and 1784–89), amounting to about $4 million.

In 1783 Congress assumed for itself the debts of the Continental army. The national debt at the end of that year stood at $41,207,861, foreign debt accounting for $7,907,037 and domestic debt, the remaining $33,300,824; annual interest amounted to about $2.4 million. The domestic debt consisted of loan certificates (government bonds) issued by Congress, notes given for purchases by the army quartermasters and commissaries, and certificates for the back pay of soldiers and a one-sum pension of five years' full pay to officers. All the certificates issued were interest bearing. Lacking funds, Congress had to forgo payment of much of the interest and principal on the domestic debt.

Robert Morris, as superintendent of Finance, set four goals, which he made a condition for his staying in office: (1) settlement of the credits and debits between the states and Congress; (2) apportioning the expenses of the war among the states (payment through requisitions); (3) reserving for Congress the exclusive holding of the "preferred debt" of the principal and interest of the loan office certificates (invested in by merchants and other men of wealth); and (4) granting Congress an independent source of revenue (other than land sales). The last two objectives were not to be accomplished.

Morris, like Alexander Hamilton later, hoped not only to have a funded national debt, but also to wed public and private financial interests through a national bank. He succeeded in having his Bank of North America incorporated by Congress (December 31, 1781) and by the states of New York, Massachusetts, and Pennsylvania. The bank opened its doors on January 7, 1782. Morris expected a capitalization of the bank at $400,000, with $400 a share. The bank would service outstanding loan obligations of the government and afford it credit. The bank loaned the Confederation the amount of $1.2 million. The Bank of North America's role as a national bank, however, was short-lived. For a while the bank's notes were received in payment of taxes collected in most states for use of Congress in discharge of the states' indebtedness to the United States. But the bank notes soon fell below specie value, which hindered their acceptance. Morris's institution also did not receive as much capital as expected. The government severed connection with the bank at the time of Morris's departure from the finance department in 1784.

Liquidation of the domestic debt proceeded steadily. Morris sent commissioners into the states to settle claims on the quartermaster and commissary departments and for military pay. Paymaster General John Pierce declared a final settlement in the form of pay certificates issued to the troops. Settlements were also made on accounts of persons who had lent money or property during the war. Soldiers received notes of $200 to $300 for their claims, and officers were given certificates, the amount ranging from $1,500 for lieutenants to $10,000 for generals.

States were amiss in meeting requisitions. A report of a congressional committee in early 1786 showed that $15,670,000 had been levied in requisitions, of which only $2,457,897 had been paid—hardly enough to cover the interest on the foreign debt. Four requisitions, from August 1786 to August 1788, also elicited little response.

Beginning in 1784, states were allowed to pay part of their quotas in indents (certificates issued by the Confederation for interest on loan office certificates). Nine states accepted indents for state taxes. Congress permitted one-fourth of state requisitions to be paid in indents. This partial assumption of the "preferred" national debt weakened the central government. As E. James Ferguson writes (1961):

> More ominous than the fragmentation of debt servicing, however, was the fragmentation of the debt itself which accompanied the progressive disintegration of the indent system. By 1786 the states were advancing into Congress's last preserve: they had begun to assume public securities. As they did, the public debt disappeared into state debts. (p. 228)

To maintain the public credit, Congress desperately needed independent income. John Adams wrote Robert R. Livingston from Paris, July 18, 1783, that if the United States did not "show to the world a proof that they can command a common revenue . . . we shall be soon so far despised" that it would not be long before "we are involved in another war." The only major source of independent income for the national government was from the sale of western lands. But this revenue developed very slowly, yielding only $760,000 through 1788.

Nationalists in Congress labored to find revenue through import duties. All the states at one time or another approved conferring upon Congress such a power not merely as a revenue solution but also as a means of bringing order out of domestic and foreign trade relations. Unfortunately, not all states agreed at the same time and thus did not achieve the unanimity required for an amendment.

In February 1781 Congress requested that it be empowered to levy a 5 percent impost (import) duty on all foreign goods sent to America. By 1782 all states except Rhode Island had ratified the impost amendment. Rhode Island objected primarily because the impost would put a heavier burden on commercial states and federal collection would violate the state constitution. In 1783 Congress tried again, allowing states to appoint collectors, who, however, could be removed by the federal government, and placing a time limit of twenty-five years for an impost. All states but New York supported the impost. New York, already resentful that Congress had backed Vermont for statehood, insisted that the state have full control over collections and that paper money be accepted as payment. Congress refused New York's restrictions. The failure of an impost amendment gave an important argument to nationalists, who emphasized the government's impotency under the Articles of Confederation.

Foreign Relations

Although the economic recession lasted until the late 1780s, the prospects for expanded trade were bright. The United States had a most favored nation status for trade with the British Isles and unrestricted entrance at the ports of France, the Netherlands, Spain, and the northern European countries. Trade opportunities opened in the Pacific and in the Far East. The round-the-world voyage of Captain Robert Gray and the *Columbia* (1787–89) touched the Pacific Northwest and China, inaugurating an otter skin and tea trade. Americans discovered that fabulous profits could be made in the Far East. With the backing of Robert Morris and associates, the *Empress of China* made a voyage in 1784 from New York to Canton, with a cargo of furs, lead, and ginseng, returning on May 11, 1785, with tea, silk, and other commodities. Samuel Shaw, who was in charge of the commercial aspects of the voyage and later became consul at Canton, reported that the Chinese "styled us the *New People.*" By 1789 fifteen trading vessels from New England ports and New York and Philadelphia were plying the China trade.

Differences persisted with Great Britain. Americans were banned from the carrying trade with the British West Indies and from shipping certain commodities there. Newfoundland and Nova Scotia were closed to American fishermen, and whale oil, fish, and salted meats could not be exported to Great Britain. British citizens were forbidden to purchase any ship built or repaired in America, which greatly hurt American shipbuilding; production of all vessels in New England during 1789 totaled only eleven ships. In violation of the Treaty of 1783, Great Britain held on to western posts in American territory and also refused to make compensation for slaves exiting with the British forces during the war. By the same token, the United States had not made any progress in the payment of prewar debts owed to British creditors by American citizens or in the reversal of confiscation of loyalist property. John Adams, minister to Great Britain, 1785–88, found a cool reception from British officials, who told him that the Confederation government did not have authority to negotiate or enforce commercial treaties, and it was useless to treat with thirteen independent sovereignties.

Negotiations with Portugal and Denmark also failed, but the Confederation succeeded in obtaining commercial treaties with Holland (1782), Sweden (1783), and Prussia (1785). The Prussian treaty incorporated a provision that indicated a shift from the American "Plan of 1776," which advocated "free ships make free goods" to the principle that neutral goods should be free on any ship. France and the United States signed a consular treaty (relating to the status of consuls in the two countries) in 1788, which was ratified by the government under the Constitution the following year. With gifts worth $10,000, Thomas Barclay concluded a treaty with the sultan of Morocco (ratified in 1787–88), which nullified the payment of tribute by the United States. The government had less success, however, with the other Barbary states. Algiers, Tunis, and Tripoli demanded exorbitant sums for trade in the Mediterranean. Two American ships were seized by Algerian pirates in 1785, with the crew of twenty-one imprisoned and treated as slaves; the survivors were not released until 1795 when a treaty was finally signed.

Diplomacy with Spain not only ended in failure but also accentuated sectional division. Spain did not accept the provisions of the Treaty of Paris which granted Americans free navigation of the Mississippi and drew the Spanish-American boundary at the 31st parallel. Starting in 1784, Spanish officials in Louisiana kept American vessels out of the lower Mississippi and closed the mouth of the river to American goods. The Spanish government asserted claim to the Yazoo Strip, located between 31° and 32° 28′.

The Spanish envoy, Don Diego de Gardoqui, arrived in 1785 with instructions to negotiate a treaty but not to concede navigation of the Mississippi. John Jay, then secretary for Foreign Affairs, submitted a treaty to Congress that avoided the navigation rights and only provided for a favorable commercial treaty with Spain. Debates in Congress agitated sectional antagonism. Northeastern interests feared western political power and commercial competition. Along strict north-south lines, the treaty failed in Congress by a vote of seven to five, two votes short of the necessary nine. Westerners, such as James Robertson of the Cumberland settlements in Tennessee and James Wilkinson of Kentucky, now flirted with the idea of accepting allegiance to Spain, whereas others talked of separation from the United States and independence, which would serve Spanish interests by the creation of a buffer state.

The National Domain

Congress inherited the trans-Appalachian to the Mississippi territory (except Kentucky) that had been reserved by the British crown. Ironically, Congress would adopt a program of controlled and orderly expansion to which the colonists had objected under British rule. Seven of the thirteen states asserted rights to western territory, based primarily on the "sea-to-sea" clauses in the colonial charters. Beginning with the New York cession in 1780 (accepted by Congress in 1781), gradually other states surrendered western territory.

With the establishment of a national domain, Congress urgently needed a land policy. Congress still had to make good the promises of lands to soldiers and officers. The value of military certificates redeemed in land would increase. Public land sales would help to discharge the national debt, and occupation of western territory would bolster national defense.

On October 10, 1780, Congress resolved that ceded lands "shall be disposed of for the common benefit of the United States, and be settled and formed into distinct republican states, which shall become members of the federal union, and have the same rights of sovereignty, freedom and independence, as the other states." The vote of the Virginia Assembly on January 2, 1781, to cede the enormous tract north of the Ohio to the Great Lakes and west to the Mississippi paved the way for the creation of a national land policy. The Virginia cession included some conditions unacceptable to Congress, particularly that all land company purchases from Indians be voided and that Virginia be guaranteed possession of its remaining western territory (namely, Kentucky). In December 1783, however,

Virginia reenacted its cession law, all but removing the previous restrictions. Congress had to act soon; otherwise it might lose control over the northwest region. Thus, on March 1, 1784, Virginia territory north of the Ohio, except for a district of Virginia military bounty lands, was transferred to Congress.

In defining a system for land occupation, Congress chose the New England practice of prior government survey and establishment of townships (usually rectangular) rather than the southern land policy of allowing persons with land warrants to choose location and bear the responsibility and expense of surveys.

In 1784, Congress sought to enact laws for a western land system and for territorial government. A land ordinance was mired in debate, but on April 23 Congress adopted "a plan for a temporary government of the Western territory," which had been written by a committee headed by Thomas Jefferson. This Ordinance of 1784 projected ten states for the whole of the Northwest Territory, each having a minimum population of 20,000 "free inhabitants" and a "republican" government.

A land ordinance passed on May 20, 1785 adopted the New England system. Government survey would precede settlement. Townships (36 square miles) were to be divided into sections of 640 acres each; one section was to be reserved for the United States and another for schools. Sections would be offered for sale at $1 an acre. Public auctions were to be held by loan office commissioners in each state. Public surveys began in late 1785, under the direction of Captain Thomas Hutchins, the geographer of the United States, assisted by one surveyor from each state. First laid off were the Seven Ranges (one range being a tier of townships, south to north) in eastern Ohio for military lands.

The opening of the western lands did not spur any land rush. The first auction, September 21 to October 9, 1787, brought only $176,090. Several factors deterred pioneering in the Ohio country. Cheaper lands were available elsewhere: tracts in Maine and western New York sold for 50 cents an acre, and in the Lake Erie–New York–Pennsylvania triangle, 75 cents an acre. To eastern small farmers and laborers, 640 acres was too much and too expensive. Prospective settlers were also reluctant to go westward because they feared Indian hostility.

Inevitably, speculators entered the picture. General Rufus Putnam and other veteran army officers founded the Ohio Company in Boston on March 3, 1786. This organization counted on a stock subscription of 1,000 shares at $1,000 each, for a total of $1 million. The investment, however, could be in the form of loan office and military pay certificates. Persuaded by insistent lobbying, Congress granted the Ohio Company 1.5 million acres of land, to be paid in six equal installments. The extra 500,000 acres was gratis in order to allow for inferior land. Congress accepted the Continental certificates toward purchase, even though they had depreciated to 12 percent of face value. Considering the extra acreage and the depreciation, the Ohio Company obtained lands at only about 8 cents an acre. The company, however, could not meet the pay schedule, and in 1792 Congress terminated the agreement but allowed the company to keep 750,000 acres already received. The first town founded in the Northwest Territory, under the auspices of the Ohio Company, was Camp Martius (soon renamed Marietta), at the mouth of the Muskingum River.

Land Speculation, 1783–90   *Source: David C. Skaggs, ed.,* The Old Northwest in the American Revolution: An Anthology *(Madison: The State Historical Society of Wisconsin, 1977), between pp. 150 and 151. University of Wisconsin Cartographic Laboratory.*

Congress awarded two other large land grants similar to the terms of the Ohio company; to John Cleves Symmes, a New Jersey member of Congress, 1 million acres between the Great and Little Miami rivers and to the Scioto Company, headed by William Duer, secretary to the Board of Treasury, 5 million acres, between the Ohio Company grant and the Virginia Military District. Duer dispatched Joel Barlow, a lawyer and poet, to Europe to sell shares. Barlow, in turn, employed a smooth-talking Englishman, William Playfair, to peddle shares in France. Playfair sold 150,000 acres and then disappeared with the money. Meanwhile, 600 Frenchmen arrived in America, only to find that they had been defrauded. Congress, however, sympathized with the victims and gave them lands in and around the new town, Gallipolis, on the Ohio River. Despite their failures, the three land companies attracted settlers to the Ohio country. By the late 1780s, a steady stream of pioneers drifted down the river in flatboats, setting up homesteads north and south of the Ohio. In November 1788, at the future site of Cincinnati, the Symmes associates laid out Losantiville (*L* for the Licking River in Kentucky, *os* Latin for mouth, *anti* for opposite, and *ville* for town).

In one of the rare instances when it had a quorum, Congress, on July 13, 1787, enacted "An Ordinance for the government of the territory of the United States North west of the river Ohio." This law (called the Northwest Ordinance), which superseded the Ordinance of 1784, set three stages of political development. Until the adult male population reached 5,000, the territory would have a governor named by Congress, a secretary, and three judges (who also had local ordinance-making power); when population surpassed 5,000, the territory would also have an elected legislature, a council appointed by the governor, and an ex officio delegate in Congress. When any particular area within the territory had 60,000 "free inhabitants," the people thereof could frame a state constitution and acquire statehood upon approval of Congress. Only five states could be carved out of the Northwest Territory. The Northwest Ordinance also raised to the national level constitutional recognition of individual rights: freedom of religion, habeas corpus, jury trial, bail, security of contracts, due process, no cruel or unusual punishment, and abolition of slavery. The Northwest Ordinance of 1787 met some criticism for its conservatism, namely, the large size of the prospective states; the property qualification of 50 acres for the suffrage; and lack of self-government at the first stage.

The two territorial ordinances (1785 and 1787) were lasting achievements of the Confederation. Not only did they establish U.S. territorial policy as to land granting and government, but they also gave evidence of congressional intent to create republican governments in territories becoming states and to ensure that the United States would remain a federation and not an empire.

Indian Relations

The American advance westward intruded upon Indian lands. Most tribes, north and south, had sided with Great Britain during the war, and Indians in the Ohio country looked for support from the British in Canada. Indeed, British troops were still garrisoned in posts within the territorial limits of the United States—at Michilimackinac (at the intersection of Lakes Michigan and Huron), Detroit; Niagara; Point au Fer and Dutchman's Point on Lake Champlain; Sandusky and Presque Isle on Lake Erie, and Oswego and Oswegatchie in the western Mohawk Valley. Southern Indians came within the orbit of Spanish Florida and Louisiana.

Congress, by the Ordinance of 1786, established Indian departments north of the Ohio, headed by Richard Butler, and south of that river, first under Dr. James White and then Richard Winn. Georgia infringed on the federal prerogative by its own treaties with the Creeks at Augusta in 1783 and Galphinton three years later. Responsible Creek leaders, however, repudiated these treaties. Although Georgia land speculators encroached on Indian lands, the southern Indian frontier remained stable during the period of the Confederation.

Fort Harmar, built in late 1785, was located at the junction of the Muskingum and Ohio Rivers. "Camp Martius," nearby, became Marietta, the first U.S. settlement in the Northwest Territory.   *Illustration from John W. Monnette,* History of the Discovery and Settlement of the Valley of the Mississippi *(New York: Harper & Brothers, 1846)*

The northern Indian frontier was on the verge of erupting into an Indian war. To Congress, frontier defense along the Ohio was a compounded one: to secure voluntary Indian withdrawal (despite Congress's being on record that the northwest lands belonged to the Americans by right of conquest); to protect settlers from Indian hostility; and to keep squatters off government and Indian lands.

In the spring of 1785, Congress ordered that the American army should consist of a mere 700 troops and be sent to the northwest frontier. The soldiers were recruited from the states of Connecticut, New York, New Jersey, and Pennsylvania. By 1787 the little army had built Fort Harmar, on the west side of the mouth of the Muskingum River, Fort Knox (Vincennes), and Fort Finney, near the falls of the Ohio. Besides protecting federal surveyors, the "American Regiment" functioned mainly as a constabulatory police force. It had its hands full chasing squatters, burning their houses and barns, only to find that the interlopers soon returned. Secretary at War Henry Knox reported the gravity of the problem to Congress on April 19, 1787: "If the disposition, to seize the public lands be not curbed in the first instance . . . all future attempts to remove intruders may be abortive. Their numbers may be so great as to defy the power of the United States."

In March 1784 Congress elected five commissioners to negotiate with the northwest Indians. At the Treaty of Fort Stanwix, October 22, 1784, the Iroquois disclaimed any rights to land in the Ohio country. On July 21, 1785, the Wyandots, Delawares, Ottawas, and Chippewas agreed to run the Indian boundary along a diagonal line from the Cuyahoga River in northeast Ohio to Vincennes on the

Wabash. Several Shawnee chiefs endorsed this pact at the Treaty of Fort Finney negotiated on January 31, 1786. The Shawnees, however, quickly repudiated the treaty, and along with other Indians set upon a series of depredations in the Ohio Valley. As a result, Colonel Benjamin Logan and Kentucky militia destroyed Shawnee towns and crops along the Great Miami River. George Rogers Clark conducted a similar expedition toward the tribes on the Wabash River. Clark's troops, however, mutinied, and nothing was accomplished.

An Indian resistance movement began to materialize. Knox reported to Congress on July 18, 1787, that he had received "indisputable evidence that a general confederacy has been formed of nearly all the indians to the Northward of the Ohio within the limits of the United States." Joseph Brant, the great Mohawk chief of Revolutionary fame, allegedly headed the confederacy. The deterioration of the Indian situation in the northwest, coming at the time of insurgency in Massachusetts, pointed to the need for a strong central government.

Crisis and Transition

The Confederation seemed to be faltering not so much from a lack of power but from the want of energy. Seldom did more than seven state delegations attend Congress. Frustrations ran high. The Connecticut delegates wrote the governor of Connecticut on April 12, 1786: "Our affairs seem to indicate the approach of some great crisis. Our Trade in a very distracted situation, Britain watching for some opportune season to revenge her smarts, the fickle Indian nations ready to join those who best can supply their wants, the states unwilling or neglecting to adopt any one Measure . . . for Mutual benefit." Congress avoided action where it could. It rejected consideration on eight amendments prepared by a special committee on the revision of the Articles of Confederation in August 1786.

While Congress was becoming lethargic, a crisis of domestic insurrection arose. In September 1786 Governor John Sullivan of New Hampshire called out 2,000 militiamen to disperse several hundred farmers threatening the legislative assembly after it had reneged on a promise to issue paper money. On October 31, Vermont farmers attempted to close courts in Windsor and Rutland counties, and similar action occurred in York County, Pennsylvania, in November 1786 and January 1787. New York appeared to be on the verge of another tenant uprising. Virginia farmers in April 1787 burned down the King William County Courthouse, and in August stopped judicial proceedings in Greenbrier County. In Massachusetts, rioting turned into insurgency and threatened rebellion.

"Shays's Rebellion" in Massachusetts occurred because of the extreme poverty of farmers, burdened by debts and tax collections. Coastal merchants, denied credit in Europe and forced to pay specie for imports, demanded payment from their debtors. Thus, a chain of debt collections developed. The cost of being sued was enough in itself for a poor man to lose his property. The $200 average taxes for a year exceeded the average cash income of a family. A debtor could lose everything, his whole estate and even "the last potato in his cellar and the only cow in his barn." Many debtors were imprisoned. The farmers became angry when the Massachusetts Assembly failed to pass paper money and debtor stay laws.

The people of the interior counties of Berkshire, Hampshire, and Worcester, from August to December 1786, stopped the courts from functioning. Insurgent militia embodied in large numbers, with western and central Massachusetts divided into four regimental areas. Daniel Shays, once a captain in the Continental army and himself a dirt farmer, was one of the influential leaders, and his name became the rallying cry of the movement. The Massachusetts Assembly supported Governor James Bowdoin's request for tough measures to uphold the laws. The Riot Act prohibited twelve or more armed persons from congregating in public, under penalty of whipping, imprisonment, or forfeiture of all property. This law also granted the governor power to call out the militia to suppress insurrection.

In January 1787, Bowdoin summoned a volunteer militia force of 5,000, commanded by General Benjamin Lincoln. Coastal merchants and professionals contributed £6,000 for the maintenance of this army for three months. On January 21, Lincoln and 4,000 men entered the field.

An immediate objective of the insurgents was to seize the federal arsenal at Springfield, with its 450 tons of military stores. Defending the federal property was Major General William Shepard and 900 militia. On January 25 Shays, with 1,500 men, marched on the arsenal. He was to have been joined by Luke Day's insurgents, then at West Springfield. Day had sent a message to Shays to postpone the attack for one day, but the message was intercepted by Shepard. The Massachusetts militia general brought artillery fire upon the advancing Shayites, killing four of them and wounding twenty. The routed Shayites retreated toward Petersham. Early Sunday morning, February 4, marching through a blizzard, Lincoln's army caught up with the insurgents, who were sleeping in houses and barns. One hundred and fifty were captured, and the rest fled. The legislature voted pardons, conditioned upon denial of certain civil rights, to all the insurgent troops but Shays and Day, who had prices placed on their heads. Some of the Shayites conducted a few forays against merchants and military leaders in western Massachusetts and Massachusetts retailers across the border in New York. Despite the promise of pardons, a special Massachusetts court of oyer and terminer condemned to death thirteen insurgents for high treason, but these eventually merited clemency. The only persons executed were two young men who had been convicted of theft. Shays settled on the New York frontier, dying in 1825 at age 84.

Shays's Rebellion strained the credibility of the Confederation. "Is not their attack on the Arsenal a declaration of war against the United States?" asked Jeremy Belknap of Ebenezer Hazard on February 2, 1787. On October 20, 1786, however, Congress did take a step to increase its army by voting for the recruitment of 2,040 troops; the stated purpose was to meet the crisis in northwestern Indian affairs, even though everyone knew that the measure was aimed at the Massachusetts uprising. Only two companies of artillery were raised, about 100 men, and these were sent to Springfield. Congress repealed the army act on April 4, 1787. Massachusetts beseeched Congress to replace the state troops called up for the emergency with federal soldiers. But Congress refused, not only because of the difficulty that had already been encountered in attempting to increase the army but probably also because Massachusetts had the situation well in hand and further measures might spread the alarm.

Although Shays's Rebellion sent shock waves throughout America, some thought the threat to government overrated. Thomas Jefferson wrote James Madison from Paris, January 30, 1787: "Turbulence" in protest is "productive of good. It prevents the degeneracy of government. . . . I hold it that a little rebellion now and then is a good thing, & as necessary in the political world as storms in the physical."

Even before Shays's Rebellion had taken its full course, the momentum grew for holding a convention to rewrite the national constitution. In May 1785 commissioners from Virginia and Maryland met at Mount Vernon and worked out a reciprocity agreement for use of the Potomac River, including tariffs and fishing rights. Following a suggestion from the Mount Vernon conference, twelve delegates from five states (New York, New Jersey, Pennsylvania, Delaware, and Virginia), though nine states were invited, met at Annapolis on September 11–14, 1786, and adopted a report prepared by Alexander Hamilton. The report called for a general convention to meet in Philadelphia on the second Monday of May 1787 to "devise" such provisions "necessary to render the constitution of the Federal Government adequate to the exigencies of the Union." On February 21, 1787, Congress finally endorsed the Annapolis resolution, with the understanding that the forthcoming convention would merely submit amendments.

The Confederation, though deficient in powers, made some definite accomplishments, most notably pertaining to western lands. It provided a valuable experience and clarified issues. As James Madison wrote in *The Federalist*, number 40: "The truth is that the great principles of the Constitution proposed by the [Constitutional] convention [of 1787] may be considered less as absolutely new than as the expansion of principles which are found in the Articles of Confederation."

CHAPTER 20

Impulse for Social Change

 "The American war is over: but this is far from being the case with the American Revolution," wrote Benjamin Rush in 1787. "It remains yet to establish and perfect our new forms of government; and to prepare the principles, morals, and manners of our citizens for these forms of government, after they are established and brought to perfection." If American social reform of the last quarter of the eighteenth century seems modest and comports mainly with the Enlightenment of the age, the Revolution, in the immediate postwar period, inspired action for the betterment of humanity. More importantly, it set forth ideals to be achieved in the course of time.

The American Revolution, by avoiding the excesses of the French Revolution and other modern upheavals that profoundly disturbed the social and political fabric, allowed for continuity and consensus in a progressive development. As Richard B. Morris has written (1967):

> We broke with England to achieve political independence, freedom from external controls, emancipation . . . of the bourgeoisie from mercantile restraints, but in the process of achieving those goals we had aroused expectations, encouraged aspirations, and created a climate conducive to a measurable degree of social reform. (p. 84)

From the beginning of the twentieth century, historians have sought to recognize the social impact of the Revolution. None provoked more discussion and interest on the subject than did J. Franklin Jameson in his *The American Revolution Considered as a Social Movement* (1926). In this little book containing several lectures delivered at Princeton University, Jameson declared:

> The stream of revolution, once started, could not be confined within narrow banks, but spread abroad upon the land. Many economic desires, many social aspirations were set free by the political struggle, many aspects of colonial society profoundly altered by the forces set loose. The relations of social classes to each other, the institution of slavery, the system of land-holding, the course of business, the forms and spirit of the intellectual and religious life, all felt the transforming hand of revolution, all emerged from under it in shapes advanced many degrees nearer to those we know. (p. 9)

Although Jameson overrated progress toward reform during the Revolutionary era and although his generalizations were too sweeping, he brought attention to the Revolutionary impetus for change that unfolded throughout American history.

The Revolution spurred desire for humanitarian improvement in America. The Declaration of Independence emphasized rights of persons as human beings. In a republic, which the Americans sought to achieve, people were expected to serve the public good.

Status of Women

The trends of the late colonial period continued as to women's legal and economic status. Women who entered the workplace engaged in work ranging from managing businesses to serving in nurturant occupations; they were variously teachers in small private schools for girls, tutors, music and dancing instructors, governesses, nurses, and midwives. In Pennsylvania newspapers between 1762 and 1776, fifty women proprietors advertised their taverns. Single women had the same rights as men in business, as states expanded the legal rights known as feme sole trader. But married women who wished to engage in a commercial operation still had to have their husbands' approval or at least no objection from them.

Few changes that occurred during the Revolutionary era affected women's property status. Essentially, the English common law was in effect. The property of a married woman (feme covert) was under the control of the husband. After the birth of the first child, the husband gained control over real estate belonging to his wife as "tenant by the curtesy." Married women, however, could retain full property rights through prenuptial agreements and could hold husbands accountable through the equity procedure for the administration of their property. Single women had complete control over their property.

One change that did take place in the area of property rights related to inheritance. Primogeniture—leaving the estate to the eldest son—was abolished in all states where it had existed: in Georgia (1777), North Carolina (1784), Virginia (1785), Maryland and New York (1786), South Carolina (1791), and Rhode Island (1798). In addition, Pennsylvania and the other New England states did away with the biblical double portion for the eldest son. Primogeniture had been applicable only when a person died intestate, and since most people left wills, it had never been much in practice. In 1788 the Connecticut Supreme Court determined that a married woman could devise her real estate (even though it was under the care of her husband) as inheritance to anyone she chose.

On the negative side, as Linda K. Kerber notes (1980), "the erosion of dower rights was the most important legal development directly affecting the women of the early Republic" (p. 147). Hitherto, in most colonies (states), a widow had the full use during her life of one-third of her deceased husband's estate (the dower), regardless of will or intestacy. After the Revolution, states began to encroach on the widow's third by stipulating that, if there were more than two children of the marriage, the widow would receive a share of the estate equal to that of each of the children.

After the war, some women asserted greater initiative in making decisions affecting their lives. Their wartime experiences of having to cope alone while their husbands were away, their volunteer participation in the war effort, and, above all, their feeling that they had a primary role in shaping a virtuous citizenry contributed to the attitude that women were fully capable of exercising independent wills. Reliance on parental approval in the selection of a husband now diminished. New England funeral sermons of the period stressed a wife's character molded by "Conscience and religion" rather than by attributes of domesticity. Men and women who remained single did not fall under the stigma that they did in colonial times, and increasingly more persons preferred the unmarried state. Robert V. Wells (1972) notes that, among Quakers in Plainfield and Rahway, New Jersey, 9.8 percent of daughters born before 1786 never married by age 50, while, similarly after 1786, the ratio was 23.5 percent.

Women found divorce more widely available in some states. Nancy F. Cott (1976) notes that in Massachusetts, of 229 petitions (from 128 women and 101 men) to the governor and council (with several exceptions to the legislature) from 1692 to 1786, one-third came after 1774. The greater incidence of women seeking divorce during the Revolutionary era indicated women's growing self-assertiveness and awareness of citizenship and legal rights.

Before the Revolution, only New England permitted absolute divorce, through judicial proceedings; Pennsylvania followed suit in 1785. In 1787 New York allowed divorce through the Court of Chancery on grounds of adultery only. In the South, before the war, no kind of divorce was granted, although legal separation was often tantamount to divorce. The Revolution destroyed the Anglican church's control over marriage, and southern states began to permit private bills of divorce submitted to the legislature, which alone could nullify a marriage. Grounds for divorce, varying among the states, included adultery, desertion, bigamy, cruelty, impotence, and nonsupport. In 1786 Massachusetts permitted divorce if the husband had been convicted of a major felony. Under the new divorce laws, a woman as the innocent party could recover control over her own property. One Revolutionary change in Virginia was to legalize marriages performed by dissenting preachers.

The Revolution helped liberalize women's attitudes and behavior relating to public life. Only one state, however, afforded any form of suffrage to women. The New Jersey constitution gave unmarried women, with property worth £50, the right to vote; this provision was rescinded by an amendment in 1807. Although women were excluded from voting, it was recognized that they could speak out more freely and openly on issues. Of 2,000 petitions from individuals sent to Congress during 1776–87, 43 came from women (26 of whom were widows). Yet the idea of two separate spheres of men and women worked against women's participation in institutionalized public life. Although substantial gains in women's rights were not made until the future, forced discrimination came under increasing denunciation. Abigail Adams, writing to her absent husband on March 6, 1776, offered a gentle warning: "Remember the Ladies . . . Remember all Men would be tyrants if they could. If particular care and attention is not paid to the Ladies we are determined to foment a Rebellion, and will not hold ourselves bound by any laws in which we have no voice, or Representation." She was not so much concerned with the alteration of gender roles as with the need for legal provision of equal rights for women.

The Republican Family

The family was becoming less patriarchal and more companiate. Just as the colonies had repudiated royal paternalism, so, too, the family should be founded on mutual trust and respect, without a domineering head. Fathers regarded themselves more as benefactors than as controllers of the family. Attention was paid to the individuality of children. As James Henretta writes (1973): The "tendency for parents to find the fulfillment and justification of their own lives in the success of their children marked the appearance of a new and different type of family life, one characterized by solicitude and sentimentality toward children and by more intimate, personal, and equal relationship" (p. 30). For republican ideals to be achieved for the whole of society, it was necessary first to establish virtue in private life.

True marriage in a republican society should be symmetrical, as Jan Lewis points out (1987); that is, the partners should attain mutuality and reciprocity. This did not mean that marriage was totally egalitarian, but that men and women had separate roles, each of which together formed the whole. "Like republicanism, the doctrine of symmetrical marriage subordinated individual interest to the greater good of the whole. Accordingly, marriages based upon interest were to be loathed; true marriage was the model for disinterested benevolence" (p. 709). As in republican society in general, conflict should be avoided in the family. Wrote Nancy Shippen of Philadelphia, in May 1783: "Equality is the soul of friendship: marriage, to give delight, must join *two minds,* not devote a slave to the will of an imperious Lord."

Women's influence was a key to establishing a virtuous family. Even in love and courtship women should seduce men to virtue. A man, for his part, as the *Massachusetts Magazine* of March 1789 stated, should treat his wife "with delicacy as a woman, with tenderness as a friend." To fulfill the role of wife and mother and the custodian of virtue in the home, a woman needed education. Benjamin Rush, in *Thoughts upon Female Education* (1787), advised women to be prepared "to be an agreeable companion for a sensible man," able to educate her children and to assist in the family's business affairs. Thomas Jefferson, concerned with the education of his daughter, Martha, confided to the marquis de Barbé-Marbois on December 5, 1785: "The chance that in marriage she will draw a blockhead I calculate at about fourteen to one, and . . . the education of her family will probably rest on her own ideas and direction without assistance." Jefferson was right; his son-in-law, Thomas Mann Randolph, by whom Martha bore twelve children, had spells of insanity and was financially irresponsible.

The late eighteenth century witnessed many changes relating to childbearing and infant care. Especially in major urban areas, male physicians, as family doctors, expanded their practice to include midwifery. By 1807 five medical schools recognized obstetrics as a branch of medical science. The attendance of male physicians,

Mrs. Richard Tilghman (Mary Gibson) and sons, 1789. Mrs. Tilghman (1755–90) was the wife of Major Richard Tilghman (1740–1809). The family, one of the wealthiest in Maryland, lived on Gross Coate plantation in Talbot County on the eastern shore of Chesapeake Bay. William Gibson (1785–1844) was age four and John Lloyd (1788–1832) a year old at the time of this painting by Charles Willson Peale.   *Maryland Historical Society, Baltimore*

instead of female midwives as had commonly been the case earlier, transformed childbirth from an open affair, with the presence of a crowd of friends and family, to a restricted one. The trend reflected the growth of privatization in family life. Infant care increasingly became entrusted wholly to the mother rather than to servants. Opposition developed to wet-nursing as being profane and against natural law. More attention was being paid to the child's health. Child-rearing attitudes also changed, especially in Calvinist New England.

American parents emphasized individuation in child development, instead of repression and the inculcation of precepts. Philip Greven, in his classic study (1977), discerned themes of child rearing in the colonial period: evangelical (New England), moderate (middle colonies), and genteel (southern colonies). The evangelicals sought to break the child's will and to bring a denial of self and surrender to God; moderates emphasized self-control instead of self-repression; and genteels stressed self-assertion, with lax discipline. Now parents were generally inclined to view their children as unique persons with special needs. The greater leniency in child rearing in New England by the time of the Revolutionary era was owing in large measure to the loosening bonds of Puritanism and to growing prosperity. In New England, children's names showed greater variety as less reliance was placed on the Bible and parents and grandparents for names; middle names were also added. In the South, use of names of the parents' sisters and brothers (babies' aunts and uncles) continued to be common, emphasizing a sense of lateral kinship.

Child nurture was most important in the new nation. It was the mother's responsibility to shape the mind and will of a growing child; indeed, republican mothers were expected to raise responsible and patriotic citizens. Wives replaced husbands as having the primary role in overseeing the mental development of young children. The vast literature in magazines and elsewhere that began to appear on motherhood and child rearing scarcely mentioned husbands as fathers. Englishman William Buchan's *Advice to Mothers,* appearing in several American editions, offered a typical view on a mother's responsibility in child rearing:

> Every-thing great or good in future life, must be the effect of early impressions; and by whom are those impressions to be made but by mothers. . . . Their instructions and example will have a lasting influence, and of course, will go farther to form the morals, than all the eloquence of the pulpit, the efforts of school-masters, or the corrective power of the civil magistrate, who may, indeed, punish crimes, but cannot implant the seeds of virtue. (1809 ed., p. 107)

The youthfulness of the population contributed to an emphasis on family life. In 1770 the majority of the population (52.5 percent) was under 20 years old; one-third were below age 10. Thus, one-half of the population needed care or supervision. Although a large number of children per family was still the rule, especially among rural people, blacks, and immigrants, the family size of whites in urban areas began to decrease. White births averaged 7.4 per family in the late seventeenth century, 6.4 in the late eighteenth century, and 4.9 for the first half of the nineteenth century. The decline indicated that women were gaining more control over their bodies. Women tried various means of contraception, the most popular being the prolongation of the lactation period. Thus, Elizabeth Drinker, in 1799, told her daughter, Sarah Drinker Downing, who had just given birth, that "she was now in her 39th. year, and that this might possiably [*sic*] be the last trial of this sort, if she could suckle her baby for 2 years to come, as she had several times done heretofore." With fewer children, women could be better mothers. Yet, despite the liberalization and elevation of her place in the family, a married woman's role remained primarily in the context of domesticity.

Structure of a New Society

Upward Mobility

Social status, based on wealth and influence, did not vary much from the prewar to the postwar eras. But there were marked changes in attitudes, and few barriers to upward economic and social mobility existed. Lower- and middle-class Americans showed less deference toward their betters. Although many of the wealthy and important engaged in an ostentatious style of living that set them apart from others, no longer did custom or law prescribe that the lower classes should know their places as to dress, social options, or how persons were addressed. Ironically, as social distinctions became blurred, there was a widening economic gap between the well-to-do and the rest of society. The great planters of the Chesapeake area held their

**Billiards in Hanover-Town, Virginia. This drawing by Benjamin Henry La-
trobe, November 1797, suggests that this popular indoor sport was a social
equalizer. Note the contrast in the clothes of the participants.** *Maryland Historical Society, Baltimore*

own by branching out in the commercial cultivation of wheat in addition to
tobacco, and their counterparts in the Deep South found better ways to raise rice
(through irrigation and selected seeding) and, with the coming of the cotton gin in
the 1790s, expanded cotton production. Many plantation owners and small farmers
struck out for the "land of the western waters," replicating the society they had
known back east.

In the North, however, there was a measurable turnover among the wealthy.
Some old families lost their wealth because they were Tories; others failed to capital-
ize on new means for profits. A parvenu class could be found in the major cities, having suddenly made their fortunes in trade, privateering, and land speculation.
French, Dutch, and German merchants appeared in Philadelphia after the war. In
1785 that city had 514 merchants, 60 percent more than in 1774. Northerners and
foreigners moved into southern cities and became wealthy from retail and industrial
pursuits. Thomas Rutherfoord typified the new breed; a Scottish emigré who came to
Richmond in the 1780s, he soon built up a large flour-milling industry and also profited handsomely in land speculation. From Boston, James Bowdoin wrote Thomas
Pownall on November 20, 1783, saying that "when you come you will scarcely see
any other than new faces . . . the change which in that respect has happened within
the few years since the revolution is as remarkable as the revolution itself."

By 1800 it was evident that some Americans were amassing great wealth; William Bingham of Pennsylvania by then was America's first "millionaire," and John Jacob Astor was not far behind. By the 1820s in New York City, 4 percent of the population owned one-half of the noncorporate wealth. Yet Benjamin Franklin's comment in his *Information for Those Who Would Remove to America* (1782) was undoubtedly accurate as to the immediate postwar period: although there were few people in the United States "so miserable as the Poor of Europe," there were "very few that in Europe would be called rich."

The cities became congested with the "poorer sort," many of them rural migrants, foreign immigrants, and free blacks. In Philadelphia, for instance, the poor were cramped into small dwellings at the northern and southern perimeters of the city.

The American Worker

The American Revolution marked a transition period for American labor. Although the factory system was yet to evolve, labor was being placed on an industrial basis. The war favored quantity in production as well as quality. More work was being brought under one roof. The patriarchal relationship between master craftsmen and their journeymen and apprentices deteriorated into a disinterested business association. American workers became more class conscious. They had already learned the value of collective action from their Revolutionary War experience, beginning with the activities of the Sons of Liberty. The ideology of the Declaration of Independence would be the inspiration for a labor movement, as labor platforms in the future would testify. The first authentic labor strike in America occurred in 1786 when journeymen printers of Philadelphia conducted a successful "turn-out" that forced employers to pay a minimum six dollar weekly wage. In the 1790s strikes were held by carpenters, shoemakers, masons, and seamen. During that decade workers began to convert their mutual aid societies into trade unions.

At least lower-level American workers had less competition from indentured servants. For one thing, immigration traffic in contract labor had ceased during the war. Moreover, while, for a decade or so after the war, a sizable number of German redemptioners and Irish servants (approximating the numbers of the prewar years) arrived, chiefly in Pennsylvania and Maryland, the institution was moribund. The prewar dumping of transported felons, though never in great numbers, ceased but not entirely so until several states in the 1780s passed laws prohibiting this practice. Many indentured servants had gained freedom through their military service during the war. Several states passed laws making indentured contracts more closely enforceable, thus curtailing the laxity of masters in not abiding by their promises of training, freedom dues, and the like. Also affecting the indentured system was Great Britain's prohibition in 1788 of emigration of skilled servants. Interestingly, few voices spoke out against indentured servitude. Even George Washington, in 1784, ordered the purchase of white servants. Indentured servitude had never been the most reliable kind of labor, and escape from the obligations of servitude was easy, involving nothing more than fleeing westward. Thus, by 1817 the system had disappeared.

Americans were still a nation of farmers. Even among rural people there was a social gradation: the large landowners at the top, and then, in descending order, the yeoman farmers, tenant farmers, unmarried sons of farmers, squatters in settled areas and on the fringes of the frontier, and landless whites who drifted about as hired hands. Slaves, of course, remained at the lowest rung in society. In urban areas, the great merchants, industrialists, and landholders had the highest social distinction, followed by professionals and then shopkeepers, artisans, laborers, and the unemployed. Interestingly, in the postwar period the status of clergymen had slipped, owing to various factors, not the least being a greater secularization of society and an increase in the number of not-too-well-educated evangelical preachers.

The New Republican Society

One effect of the Revolution was that the people opposed nobility of any kind. The establishment of the Society of the Cincinnati in 1783 created a furor of protest. The organization, largely conceived by General Henry Knox, intended to create an order of Continental army officers and their direct descendants. George Washington served several years as the Society's first president general. Numerous writers attacked the Society as representing foreign influence and as a step toward the overthrow of American democracy. Judge Aedanus Burke of South Carolina, in a 1783 pamphlet, said: "the order is planted in a fiery, hot ambition, and thirst for power; and its branches will end in tyranny." John and Samuel Adams, Thomas Jefferson, John Jay, and Elbridge Gerry were among prominent leaders who condemned the Society. Even Benjamin Franklin commented that the eagle medallion worn by members around their necks resembled a turkey. Because of the hostility in America to an order of military "nobility," the national organization voted to remove the requirement for hereditary membership, but state branches failed to go along. The fraternity declined, and by 1832 Massachusetts was the only one of the original thirteen states to retain a chapter. Subsequently, in the late nineteenth century the Society was revived, allowing for membership by collateral descent. If the new republican society after the Revolutionary War still allowed for privilege, founded on land and money, the highest accord, that of gentleman, came not from wealth or birth but from merit.

The Revolution reinforced old honorary distinctions for those who had engaged in public office, with the use of such appellations as Judge, Colonel, and the like. Of course, titles sometimes represented little more than a manner of speech. Herman Bowman, an early Kentucky pioneer, recalled a humorous incident involving General Charles Scott, who moved from Virginia to Kentucky in the mid-1780s. Scott was sitting in a log tavern when "a tolerably well dressed Stranger" from New England came in and asked for a half pint of whiskey. The tavernkeeper told him that he did not sell whiskey in such small quantities.

"Stranger I will join you and pay half," said Scott. "Therefore landlord, give us a pint of your best." The whiskey was brought, and Scott, who drank first, addressed the newcomer: "Colonel, your good health."

"I am no Colonel," replied the stranger.

"Well then," said Scott, "Major, your good health."

"I am no Major," replied the New Englander.

"Then your good health, Captain."

"I am no Captain, Sir," said the stranger, "and what is more, never held a commission in my life."

Amused, Scott explained, "Well then by heavens, you are the first man in Kentucky that ever wore a cloth coat and was not a commissioned officer."

African Americans

If all persons were indeed endowed with natural and fundamental liberty, race of itself could not justify human bondage. The most convenient way to rationalize slavery in view of the Revolutionary ideology was to demean the character of African Americans. Proslavery advocates pointed to hostile stereotypes of blacks' mental and behavioral characteristics. Nature and environmental development, it was argued, made for separateness between blacks and whites. Blacks were best suited to certain occupations and climatic conditions. It was further asserted that blacks, if freed en masse, would exhibit vice and ignorance that would contaminate republican society. Even those southerners who condemned slavery justified it as a fact accomplished, and they had the biased opinion that black bondsmen had a natural propensity toward savagery, dishonesty, and sexual promiscuity.

John Taylor of Caroline County, Virginia, who wrote prolifically on southern rights and agriculture, exemplifies the early southern apologist for slavery. Although he considered slavery an evil, he thought, nothing could be done about it. Those blacks who had been freed found themselves as outcasts. "The situation of the free negro class is exactly calculated to force it into every species of vice," he said (1803). "Cut off from most of the rights of citizens, and from all the allowances of slaves," freed blacks are driven into "crime for subsistence; and destined to a life of idleness, anxiety and guilt." Free blacks, furthermore, are readily exploited by "the domination of some interest or combination." On the other hand, "slaves are docile, useful and happy, if they are well managed" (pp. 117 and 182–84). As a caste, enslaved African Americans, for their own good and the good of republican society, should be closely confined to their existing status. During the antebellum period, slavery apologists would go to even greater lengths to further the idea that African Americans were mentally and morally inferior.

After the war, pent-up demand led to increased prices for slaves. In Georgia, a "seasoned Negro" valued at £40 in 1776 brought £210 in 1782. New slaves arrived from Africa and the West Indies. Georgia's slave population doubled from 1775 to 1790. So many slaves were imported that states resorted to prohibitive duties and even temporarily closed off the slave trade. South Carolina shut off the trade in 1787, reopening it during 1800–1807 (during which time nearly 40,000 slaves entered the state). Under the federal Constitution, in 1808 all foreign slave trading by Americans was prohibited. From 1790 to 1807 more slaves were imported into North America than during any other similar period in colonial times.

Slavery spread westward. Two-thirds of Georgia's slaves in 1775 were located 20 miles from the coast; in 1790 half of the state's slaves resided in the backcountry. From 1790 to 1810, 75,000 Chesapeake slaves accompanied planters to Kentucky and Tennessee. The migration separated slave families, although occasionally planters took most of their slaves with them. The domestic slave trade became a thriving interregional enterprise.

Blacks hearkened to the message of independence, only to discover that liberty was not meant for them. Tensions among slave communities accentuated fears of collective slave resistance. The slave revolts in the West Indies during the 1790s were all too real and threatened to be contagious. At last, so it seemed, American slaves were ready to rebel. The Gabriel conspiracy of 1800 in central Virginia led to the execution of twenty-seven slaves, and two years later in Virginia, ten more were executed. In 1802 a slave conspiracy in eight counties of North Carolina cost the lives of a dozen blacks. Plantation brutality was still commonplace. Slaves could be put to death for a variety of crimes. In Virginia during 1783–1814, the state compensated owners of 438 slaves executed, 31 for killing a master or an overseer.

Slaves sought to establish community and kinship ties. Separated from relatives and friends when sold westward, they remarried and formed new families. In the upper Southwest, however, smaller numbers of slaves were held, making it difficult to form a sense of black community. The selling of so many slaves directly imported from Africa in the lower Southwest contributed to the preservation of African culture. In the late 1780s, three-fourths of slaves sold at Natchez were new arrivals from Africa. In contrast, slaves and free blacks in the North favored creating a creole culture, obliterating the African past. One trend during the Revolutionary period was the anglicizing of slave names. Discarded were Cato, Scipio, Caesar, Pompey, and the like as well as African forenames such as Cuffee, Cajoe, or Quash in favor of English forenames and surnames. Blacks took on names indicating skills, such as Carpenter or Cooper or just simply English names such as Brown or Smith. Freeman and Newman were not unusual names for freed slaves.

"The growth of the free Negro population was one of the most far reaching events of the revolutionary era," writes Ira Berlin (1976, p. 352). The war provided the opportunity for freedom. Some slaves were manumitted for military service, and others by the private actions of their masters or, in the North, by governmental abolitionist measures. A number of slaves who had gone over to the British stayed in America and struck out on their own. Masters increasingly hired out slaves to urban industries, with the bondsmen allowed to keep a small part of their earnings, which they used to purchase their freedom as well as that of relatives. The attention of the Chesapeake states to the cultivation of cereal crops, requiring less intensive labor than tobacco, made slaves available for hire. In the Upper South alone, the free black population expanded by 90 percent from 1790 to 1800. The growth of the number of freedmen in the South, however, stirred fears of greater potential for slave resistance. Thus, eventually the southern states either banned free black immigration or required posting high bonds upon entry, which if not paid led to enslavement. Other restrictive measures placed on free blacks in the South included payment of special taxes, exclusion from militia service, and prohibition to bear arms.

Freedmen in northern urban areas were largely limited to menial labor, although there were craftsmen. Blacks in the cities had the advantage of physical proximity, and thus it is not surprising that they began to form mutual aid societies. The African Union Society was founded in Newport, Rhode Island, in 1780 and the Free African Society in Philadelphia in 1787. Prince Hall, a free black and war veteran, was the founder of black Masonry in America. The African Lodge opened in Boston in 1787 under a charter from the British Grand Lodge; in the 1790s lodges were also formed in Providence and Philadelphia. "Blacks certainly played their part in making post-Revolutionary War America a nation of joiners," writes Benjamin Quarles (in Berlin and Hoffman, eds., 1983, p. 297). In the South, small independent black churches appeared that affiliated with white congregations, especially the Baptists, and were under the "watch-care" of white pastors. In the North, Richard Allen, a former slave who purchased his freedom, led the movement for independent black churches. In 1787 he and other African Americans withdrew from St. George's Methodist Church in Philadelphia, and in 1794 he founded Bethel Church, the first congregation of a new denomination—the African Methodist Episcopal Church. Absalom Jones, who had also purchased his freedom, established St. Thomas's African Episcopal Church in Philadelphia in 1794.

Antislavery

During the colonial period few voices were heard denouncing slavery. On the eve of the Revolution, however, Quaker leaders, such as Anthony Benezet and John Woolman, along with their English counterparts, drew the lines of battle. With the coming of the Revolution, the debate over slavery was joined in full force. For abolitionists to counter the argument of the alleged negative personal characteristics of blacks, it was necessary to demonstrate that all men were equal in natural endowment and that human bondage was the result of environmental factors—or simply the unfortunate circumstance of being enslaved.

Blacks could be educated. Anthony Benezet, who founded a school for black children in 1770, challenged his pupils to be "citizens of the world." Individual blacks achieved on their own. Lemuel Haynes (1753–1833), son of a black father and white mother, in 1780 became a licensed Congregational minister and held pastorates in Connecticut, Vermont, and New York. From 1788 to 1818 he preached 5,000 sermons. Haynes declared that liberty was a natural and inalienable right of all men, "a Jewell . . . handed Down to men from the cabinet of heaven"; God made distinctions among men "as to natural ability, but not as to natural right." Benjamin Banneker (1731–1806), born in Maryland of free Negro parents, by the 1770s had won a reputation as an astronomer. In 1789 he was a member of the survey team for designing the District of Columbia. Banneker did a variety of scientific work, published an almanac, and founded a peace movement. Phillis Wheatley (c. 1753–1784), a Boston slave until freed in 1778 and author of *Poems*

Phillis Wheatley (1754–84), brought from West Africa at age six and sold to John and Susannah Wheatley of Boston, became a poet, celebrated on both sides of the Atlantic. By an unidentified artist, after Scipio Moorhead's engraving; published in Phillis Wheatley's *Poems on Various Subjects, Religious and Moral* (London, 1773).   *National Portrait Gallery*

on Various Subjects, Religious and Moral (1773) and *Liberty and Peace: A Poem* (1784), was but one among other African Americans who gained recognition for achievement.

Antislavery environmentalism found expression in many writings. Benjamin Rush, for example, in his *Address . . . upon Slave-Keeping* (1773), stated:

> Slavery is so foreign to the human mind, that the moral faculties as well as those of the understanding are debased, and rendered torpid by it. All the vices which are charged upon the Negroes in the southern colonies and the West Indies, such as Idleness, Treachery, Theft, and the like, are the genuine offspring of slavery, and serve as an argument to prove that they were not intended, by Providence for it.

Even some proponents of slavery could agree that slavery had a debilitating effect on the character of the Negro. But with the reality of so many persons of color in bondage, discipline and control of such a potentially disruptive and dangerous lower class mattered the most.

Religious groups in the South offered slaves salvation but little else. In the North, Congregational preachers began to attack slavery. In 1776 Reverend Samuel Hopkins, a pastor in Newport, Rhode Island, published an appeal to Congress, *A Dialogue concerning the Slavery of the Africans.* To Hopkins, slavery was a "sin of a crimson dye"; there was "no reason to expect deliverance till we put away the evil of our doings." Quaker meetings began to adopt the policy of excommunicating slaveowners. Philadelphia Quakers had a guiding role in establishing America's first antislavery organization in 1775—the Society for the Relief of Free Negroes Unlawfully Held in Bondage, reinstituted in 1787 as the Pennsylvania Abolition Society.

Anglicans and Presbyterians, for the most part, remained above the controversy over the holding of slaves. The New York and Philadelphia Synod of the Presbyterians in 1786, though going on record favoring an eventual abolition of slavery, noted that immediate emancipation would be too "dangerous"; church members should only support the education of slaves and the opportunity for slaves to purchase their freedom. Evangelicals in the South at first headed toward antislavery, but, with so many converts from the slaveowning class, they hedged their views. The objective of evangelical ministers was to save individuals and not society as a whole. Still, the owning of slaves or the desire to do so was denounced as the sin of covetousness. The Methodist Conference of December 1784 in Baltimore, which marked the beginning of a separate Methodist Church in America, ordered all members to free their slaves within a year. Because of the hostility of Virginia Methodists and other southerners, this policy was revoked in 1785.

Most antislavery supporters accepted gradual emancipation. Slaves had first to be educated and prepared for freedom. Even some enlightened southern planters saw the inevitability of freeing the slaves. George Washington (with 216 slaves at the time) wrote Lafayette on May 10, 1786, congratulating the Frenchman for his emancipationist views. To set slaves "afloat at once," commented Washington, "would, I really believe, be productive of much inconvenience and mischief; but by degrees it certainly might, and assuredly ought to be, effected; and that too by Legislative authority."

Antislavery organizations made headway in the North but not in the Deep South until after 1800. The New York Society for Promoting Manumission of Slaves was established in 1785, with John Jay and Alexander Hamilton as members; Jay became the Society's president in 1787. In 1794 the American Convention of Abolition Societies began meeting annually, with delegates from nine chapters from the states of Rhode Island, Connecticut, New York, New Jersey, Pennsylvania, Delaware, Maryland, and Virginia. The Convention condemned slavery and the slave trade, and favored lifting restrictions on free blacks.

The antislavery movement had success in the North. The Vermont Constitution of 1777 banned slavery, as did the Northwest Ordinance of 1787. Massachusetts abolished slavery through judicial decision. In that state's lower courts Nathaniel Jennison successfully sued for recovery of his slave, Quock Walker, while Walker won a case for assault by Jennison. Out of these contradictory decisions came a judgment of the Massachusetts Supreme Judicial Court in favor of Walker. Chief Justice William Cushing charged the jury to free Walker: the Massachusetts Constitution

sets out with declaring that all men are born free and equal—and that every subject is entitled to liberty, and to have it guarded by the laws, as well as life and property—and in short is totally repugnant to the idea of being born slaves. This being the case, I think the idea of slavery is inconsistent with our own conduct and

Constitution; and there can be no such thing as perpetual servitude of a rational creature, unless his liberty is forfeited by some criminal conduct or given up by personal consent or contract.

Jennison was convicted of assault and fined £40. Walker thus gained his freedom. Although slaves were sold for a while longer in the state, the case helped eradicate slavery in Massachusetts. That state's census of 1790 reported no slaves.

Elsewhere in the North, provision was made for gradual emancipation. Although the development in New Hampshire is obscure, it seems that the courts interpreted the state constitution of 1783 as meaning that after that date no persons would be born into slavery. In 1792 New Hampshire had 150 slaves. Officially, slavery did not end in New Hampshire until a law was passed in 1857 declaring all blacks free and full citizens. Connecticut and Rhode Island bestowed gradual emancipation by statute. A Connecticut law of 1784 freed all slave children born after the law went into effect when they reached age 25. That same year Rhode Island allowed freedom for all black children born after March 1, 1784. Not until 1843 did Rhode Island have a constitutional provision prohibiting slavery.

New York and New Jersey moved more slowly. New York had a gradual emancipation law in 1799, and New Jersey in 1804; slavery was officially abolished in New York in 1827 and in New Jersey, in 1846. The Pennsylvania Abolition Act of 1780 liberated all black children born after the date the law took effect, when they reached age 28. Blacks in the state, however, did not acquire full legal rights until 1847. A Pennsylvania law of 1788 freed slaves of persons entering the state intending to settle there. Ironically, most of the provisions of the northern states for gradual emancipation did not immediately free a single slave. Those in servitude at the time the laws were passed remained in slavery for life.

Betterment of Humanity

A virtuous republic should look after all the people, even the undesirables, protect public health, and, in general, provide for social stability. A free people should be compassionate. As Benjamin Rush said, "peaceful and benevolent forms of government" are based on "mild and benevolent principles."

Americans prided themselves that their republican governments made for greater humanity than in England. At first, the Revolutionaries stigmatized luxury as the bane of society; then they shifted to the condemnation of idleness: the people should be industrious. Even Benjamin Franklin said that the best way to help the poor was "not making them easy in poverty, but leading or driving them out of it." It was believed that each human being had a moral faculty. Thus, even paupers, criminals, and the insane had capabilities for improvement. Although the more concerted attempts to rehabilitate outcasts belong to the next century, important strides in attitudes and reforms occurred in the Revolutionary era.

Customarily, an insane person had been treated as a demoniac, locked up in a jail cell or confined to a room or a shed by family members. The asylum movement in America began with the establishment of the "Public Hospital for Persons of Insane and Disordered Minds" (later named Eastern State Hospital) at Williamsburg, Virginia, in 1773. Benjamin Rush was instrumental in creating a second asylum facility—a new wing for the mentally ill at the Pennsylvania Hospital, which opened in 1796. Rush thought that disordered minds could be improved through changes in body or environmental conditions. He has earned the reputation as America's first psychiatrist for his diagnoses of a "species" of "mania" and "phobia" and his specific treatments for patients, although the excessive bleeding, purging, emetics, and blistering prescribed did not work wonders.

Efforts were also made to bring health care to the indigent. The Philadelphia Dispensary for the Poor, established in 1786 and supported by voluntary contributions, employed four physicians and an apothecary to inoculate persons and to assist the poor medically free of charge; the physicians made house calls in the poor neighborhoods. Charitable societies to aid impoverished widows and their children sprang up in the major cities. The Society for the Relief of Widows of Decayed Pilots, founded in 1788 in Philadelphia, had government subsidization in the form of one-fourth of ship tonnage duties collected.

Boston and Philadelphia each had a "humane society" for the purpose of lifesaving, modeled after the Royal Humane Society of London. The Philadelphia Humane Society (1780) had as its goal to rescue "those whose animation may be suspended by drowning, breathing air contaminated by burning charcoal, hanging, exposure to choke-damp of wells, drinking cold water while warm in summer, strokes of the sun, lightning, swallowing laudanum, etc." The Massachusetts Humane Society, founded in 1786, recommended as one of the "methods of treatment" for drowning victims the use of a "fumigator," which pumped tobacco smoke into the rectum. "If a fumigator should not be at hand, the common pipe will answer the purpose of applying this vapour to the bowels. So easy and important an operation should be repeatedly performed, as the good effects of tobacco smoke have been proved in many cases." The societies provided rescue stations and built huts on beaches to be used by shipwrecked sailors.

Postwar America may not have been an "Alcoholic Republic," to borrow the title of a book by W. J. Rorabaugh (1979), but people of all ages and professions imbibed plentifully of spirituous liquors (whisky, rum, gin, and brandy) and about anything else, such as beer, cider, and wine. Besides recognizing medical problems associated with alcohol consumption, Benjamin Rush helped create an awareness for temperance reform. In 1784 he published a pamphlet, *An Inquiry into the Effects of Ardent Spirits upon the Human Body*. Alcohol consumption, Rush pointed out, caused disorderly conduct, illnesses, disfigurement, such as "dropsy of the Belly" and "rum buds" on the skin. Although westerners in the 1780s learned how to make bourbon whisky from corn, consumption of distilled liquors did decline somewhat, owing to the federal excise tax on whisky in 1791 and decreased trade with the West Indies. Before 1810, however, the only groups to register disapproval of the use of spirituous liquors were the Methodists and the Quakers.

The desire for humaneness brought into question the use of cruel and unusual punishment. An antigallows movement developed, influenced by the writings of

Cesare Beccaria and other European reformers. Benjamin Rush, America's foremost leader in the cause of abolishing the death penalty, in an address to a learned society in March 1787, stated his wish "that the time is not very far distant when the gallows, the pillory, the stocks, the whipping post and the wheelbarrow will be connected with the history of the rack, and the stake, as marks of barbarity." Though not going as far as England with its capital penalties for 160 crimes, most American states had a wide range of felonies punishable by death. Virginia, for example, had made twenty-nine crimes capital offenses; Delaware, twenty; New York, sixteen; Connecticut, fifteen; and Pennsylvania, thirteen. Burglary and other crimes against property were punishable by death in most states. Indeed, the wave of executions for burglary in the 1780s created a revulsion against an extensive death penalty. In 1794, Pennsylvania set an example for other states in making murder the only capital offense. The revised Virginia code of 1796 retained only murder and treason. States also began to phase out corporal punishment, such as public floggings, but this was to be a slow process. (Delaware, for example, did not do so until the twentieth century.) The penitentiary idea of solitary cells, whereby prisoners would not corrupt each other, was put into effect at Philadelphia's Walnut Street Jail in the 1790s, in the new state prisons of New Jersey in 1797, and in Virginia and Kentucky in 1800.

Reform to alleviate the punishment of debtors progressed substantially during the 1780s, although much remained to be done. Persons were imprisoned for the smallest indebtedness, and they were assessed the cost of their jail keep as well. In the prison systems of Philadelphia and New York City, debtors outnumbered all other inmates. Changes began when the Pennsylvania and New York constitutions permitted the imprisonment of debtors only if there was a strong case of fraud. In 1784 New York provided for the release of debtors if they went through bankruptcy proceedings and 75 percent of the creditors gave their approval. In 1789 the state passed a law limiting imprisonment to thirty days if the debt was less than £10. Massachusetts, in 1788, allowed for the release of debtors if they could not pay debts or prison expenses.

Social welfare systems for helping the poor underwent little change after the war. In the cities, the almshouse (poorhouse) and workhouse (for persons guilty of minor infractions) were the mainstays for relief, along with some "outdoor" aid, such as firewood, food, or other essentials. Home relief, in the form of direct financial or material assistance, characterized welfare aid in towns and rural areas.

The influx of immigrants and war refugees, fires, and economic hard times put a strain on municipal relief. Programs became more centralized and specialized, and state governments extended their authority over local aid programs. The increase in transiency led to changes in settlement policy in New England. It had been the practice of New England towns to "warn-out" newcomers—that is, refuse relief if such persons could not claim legal residence. A Massachusetts law of 1794 ended the warning-out system; though still providing for removal of newcomers, localities had to give relief to them for up to three months.

In the South, a significant change occurred with the transfer of welfare responsibility from the Anglican parish to the county. An overseer elected by the freeholders in each county had charge of the poor, collecting funds through taxes and administering relief.

The humanitarian impulse of the Revolutionary era brought definite achievements, even if they were, in many instances, only small beginnings. Significantly, the reform movements recognized that to ameliorate suffering and injustice environmental conditions had first to be improved. Americans awakened to a broader sense of community and to specific problems facing a republican society.

CHAPTER 21

Republican Culture

 Independence challenged Americans to affirm their own cultural identity. The virtues most esteemed in creative endeavor were those of ancient republics—simplicity, frugality, a high moral sense, industry, patriotism, and public spirit. Culture and liberty, it was felt, should be intertwined. One dilemma Americans faced was to decide how far progressive individualism should go in view of the goals of collective harmonization. Though selectively adopting the best of the Old World ideals, Americans were not burdened by a lengthy past. In that respect, as the German romanticist author, Johann Wolfgang von Goethe, noted: "*Amerika, du hast es besser*" (America, you have it better). Americans had faith that in the future the quality of the arts and sciences on its shores would surpass that of Europe.

The classical iconography in America's public symbols testified to the nation's attachment to the ideals of ancient republics. The Great Seal, adopted by Congress in 1782, shows an eagle with one talon holding a sheaf of thirteen arrows and the other an olive branch. On the beak is attached an announcement of "E pluribus Unum"; on the back of the seal there is a truncated pyramid under the "Eye of God"; at the top is "Annuit Coeptus" ("he has favored our beginnings"), and below is "Novus Ordo Saclorum" ("a new order of the ages," expressing, in a sense, "a new covenant we give ourselves"); at the base of the pyramid is "MDCCLXXVI," indicating the year of renewal. An act of Congress in 1792 established that one side of a coin should have an eagle and the other, a figure of Liberty, clad in classical garments and wearing a Phrygian cap, the symbol of a liberated slave. Interestingly, in using the Roman symbol of an eagle, it was the American bald eagle that was adopted. When heads of personages were introduced on the currency, they were, and still are, either in profile or in three-quarters view, according to the practice in antiquity.

Religion

From the time of the first Great Awakening (1720s–40s), American religion became more and more adaptable to a sense of national identity and purpose. Americans had always had an idea of providential mission, ever since the founding of the colonies. Such millennial expectation, however, now translated into a secular context, one of manifest destiny for the nation. As Catherine L. Albanese writes (1976), "Jehovah had stopped making history, while the nation of patriots was obligingly making it for him" (p. 105).

Historians have debated whether a "civil religion," a term introduced by Jean-Jacques Rousseau in his *Social Contract* (1762), was being formed in America. Rousseau had in mind a public philosophy, independent of religion, to which citizens would subscribe for uplifting moral direction. Because Americans recognized a suprapolitical sovereignty and along with it natural law and liberty, as expressed in the Declaration of Independence, and expected church and state to complement each other in achieving a Christian republic, it may be said there was a "civil religion." But it was a nation under God. Thus, James Madison, in a "Memorial and Remonstrance" to the Virginia Assembly in 1785, stated:

> It is the duty of every man to render to the Creator such homage, and such only, as he believes to be acceptable to him. This duty is precedent . . . to the claims of Civil society. Before any man can be considered as a member of Civil Society, he must be considered as a subject of the Governor of the Universe; and if a member of Civil Society who enters into any subordinate Association must always do it with a reservation of his duty to the General Authority, much more must every man who becomes a member of any particular Civil Society do it with a saving of his allegiance to the Universal Sovereign.

Religion and the republican state reinforced each other. There was no need for conflict. If the fusion of purpose between church and state did not arise from a "civil religion," a motivating force was the growing awareness of national community, which found expression in the majority will. As Alexis de Tocqueville was to write in *Democracy in America,* concerning his travels in America in 1831:

> All the American clergy know and respect the intellectual supremacy exercised by the majority. . . . They readily adopt the general opinions of their country and their age. . . . Thus it is, that, by respecting all democratic tendencies not absolutely contrary to herself, and by making use of several of them for her own purposes, Religion sustains a successful struggle with that spirit of individual independence which is her most dangerous opponent. (abridged ed., 1964)

The Revolution left an ambiguity in the relationship between church and state. It certainly aided the breakdown of church establishments. Only in New England did state support of churches survive in the form of multiple assessment (with people in localities choosing which groups were to receive tax money). This practice was finally abolished in Connecticut in 1818 and Massachusetts in 1833. Jefferson's Statute of Religious Freedom, introduced in 1779 and passed in 1786, ended church tax support in Virginia, despite the strong opposition led by Patrick Henry in favor of multiple assessment. Yet government favored religion in many respects, as manifested in state laws versus blasphemy; local ordinances for Sabbath observance; clergymen named to public office; federal and state chaplains; the Northwest Ordinance provision of federal funds for religion; tax exemption of church property; and state and national days of fasting, thanksgiving, and prayer. In 1791 even Baptists and Congregationalists in New England asked Congress to set up a committee for licensing the Bible.

The Revolution brought reorganization to the churches, resulting in national-ization of denominations. The Anglican Church, which had so long existed with the king as the head of the church and under the jurisdiction of an English bishop, struggled to recreate itself independently in America. Finally, the General Conven-tion, meeting at Christ Church, Philadelphia, during July–August 1789, with three bishops already installed by state groups, established the Protestant Episcopal Church in the United States. Presbyterians, Lutherans, and Dutch and German Reform adherents held synods during the 1780s and 1790s to promote a greater American identity. Congregationalists, amid competition from other groups, strengthened their national ties. The Catholic Church in America, no longer under the jurisdiction of the vicar apostolic in London, received its own recogni-tion. In 1784 John Carroll was appointed prefect apostolic in charge of church affairs in the United States; in 1790 he became bishop at Baltimore and in 1808, archbishop. Besides Baltimore, in 1808 the church had dioceses at New York, Philadelphia, Boston, and Bardstown, Kentucky; and by 1826, also at Richmond, Charleston, Cincinnati, St. Louis, and New Orleans.

Baptist and Methodist groups grew phenomenally. Methodists, united by their "Christmas Conference" at Baltimore in 1784, spread rapidly to the South and the West, as did the Baptists, mainly "separate" converts from the Congregationalists. Although the old "regular" Baptists and the Separates attempted national coopera-tion by consenting in 1787 that their churches be called United Baptist Churches, they had no success in establishing a national organization. By the end of the century, the church superstructure consisted only of some forty local church associa-tions. Francis Asbury (1745–1816) became the great leader of the Methodists, and Isaac Backus (1724–1806) had an important role among Baptists, even publishing a three-volume history of the denomination (1777–96). Methodist membership rose from 10,500 in 1781 to 76,150 in 1791. Methodists reaped converts in the northern port cities from artisans, young women, and recently freed slaves. Circuit riding of Baptist and Methodist itinerant preachers brought religion to rural areas and the frontier, and by the 1790s a second Great Awakening spread from New England to the southern frontier. Many Americans were looking for a freer and more open religion, one that could give vent to emotion and enthusiasm. As Donald G. Mathews writes (1969), the Revolution "provided a political and social world view which was conducive to building a new religious community based on common participation in a holy life" (p. 35).

Education

By the time of the Revolution, substantial development had occurred toward gen-eral education in the colonies. Tuition-based elementary schools and academies were found everywhere, as were charity schools. Only New England, however, had a public school system, with an elementary school required for towns and, for the larger urban areas, also a Latin Grammar School. The Boston school system of the 1780s consisted of a South and a North Grammar School, a North and a South Writing School, and a "Writing School in Queen Street." Everywhere and at all levels the war had an adverse effect on education, with funds diverted for the war effort and teachers enlisting in military service.

After the war, education expanded greatly, especially in the proliferation of private-venture schools and neighborhood district schools. The academy movement was most noticeable in the South, either as "old field schools," presided over by an itinerant schoolmaster and meeting in a log cabin or barn, or as an "academy" in the urban areas. These secondary schools sought a broader curriculum than did the Latin grammar schools.

Most state constitutions mandated public education, although, outside New England, little was accomplished until later, and virtually nothing was accomplished in the South. Georgia, however, required each county to have a school at public expense in 1777 and in 1783 provided that 1,000 acres in each county be set aside to support academies. In 1784 New York created a general education board, the Regents, which granted charters and financial assistance to schools and colleges. The Land Ordinance of 1785 reserved one lot in each township in the western country for a school, and the Ordinance of 1787 stated that schools and education should "forever be encouraged."

The republican ideology called for a popularly educated democracy. Education would serve as a social instrument to inculcate knowledge, discipline, and, not the least, respect for the state that was considered necessary for a well-ordered society. An enlightened citizenry would thwart tyranny. One major change was to move away from a strictly classical education to a more practical one. Benjamin Rush thought that American education should enter the modern age. Writing to John Adams on July 21, 1789, he asked

> Who are guilty of the greatest absurdity—the Chinese who press the feet into deformity by small shoes, or the Europeans and Americans who press the brain into obliquity by Greek and Latin?
> Do not men use Latin and Greek as the scuttlefish emit their ink, on purpose to conceal themselves from an intercourse with the common people?
> Indeed, my friend, I owe nothing to the Latin and Greek classics but the turgid and affected style of my youthful compositions and a neglect of the English grammar.

Rush proposed a public education system in Pennsylvania which in the lower grades stressed "reading, writing and arithmetic," and in the upper levels included history, commerce, principles of money, science, "art of war," and "practical legislation." The *Thoughts upon the Mode of Education Proper in a Republic* (1786), to which was appended the public school plan, noted that "the business of education has acquired a new complexion by the independence of our country" and that the main purpose was to "convert men into republican machines."

Southern gentry opposed universal education, both because it would be wasteful of tax money and because educating all of the poor might prove dangerous to the social order. Thomas Jefferson, however, was willing to apply democracy to education to the extent of tapping genius from among the poor. He introduced a Bill for the More General Diffusion of Knowledge in the Virginia Assembly in 1778, only to have it finally rejected in 1786. Jefferson's plan would establish local school districts, each with a school where all children (the poor, tuition-free) attended for three years, learning reading, writing, and arithmetic as well as Greek, Roman, and American history. Female students could also attend. After the three years, one of ten children, whose parents were unable to pay, would be admitted to grammar schools to learn Latin, Greek, English grammar, geography, and higher arithmetic. After the first year, one-third of the tuition-free students would be discharged, and after the second, there would be left only one poor student, who would then be entitled to attend the College of William and Mary tuition-free.

Robert Coram (1761–96), a teacher and an editor at Wilmington, Delaware, proposed a national system of public education in his *Political Inquiries: To Which Is Added, a Plan for the General Establishment of Schools Throughout the United States* (1791). States would be divided into school districts, and a land tax would support education. Coram suggested instruction in the arts as well as the sciences. "A system of equal education" would prevent "barbarity, war and poverty" and "give every citizen a power of acquiring what his industry merits" and "an opportunity of acquiring knowledge and fitting himself for places of trust."

Women's education improved. While originally attending schools only during the summer when the boys were on vacation, New England girls were now being integrated into the regular sessions, and by 1810 they were fully accepted into the town schools. The academies began to have "female departments," and small private academies for girls appeared. The illiteracy rate of women declined, falling from twice that of men in the colonial period to a par with them by the mid-nineteenth century.

The Young Ladies Academy in Philadelphia, founded in 1787, became the prototype for similar institutions. About 100 students studied the same curricula as the boys did in their schools. Benjamin Rush presented an address at the school on July 28, 1787, which was soon published as *Thoughts upon Female Education*. Rush concluded by saying: "It will be in your power, LADIES, to correct the mistakes and practice of our sex . . . by demonstrating that the female temper can only be governed by reason and that the cultivation of reason in women is alike friendly to the order of nature and to private as well as public happiness."

Education promoted cultural identity. Benjamin Franklin in *A Scheme for a New Alphabet and Reformed Mode of Spelling* (1768) had urged the Americanization of the English language. Noah Webster, setting himself to this task, published *A Grammatical Institute of the English Language* (1783–85) in three parts: a spelling book (which sold 60 million copies by 1890) for standardizing spelling differently from the British; a grammar text; and an anthology (resembling the later McGuffey readers), which contained selections from European and American writers. Webster's *Dissertations on the English Language* (1789), first given as popular lectures, expounded on his theories of language and cultural nationalism. "As an independent nation," Webster said, "our honor requires us to have a system of our own, in language as well as government." Jedediah Morse's *Geography Made Easy* (1784) and *American Geography* (1787), used as textbooks in the schools, further defined a national identity. As Morse noted in a magazine piece in 1787: "We are independent of Great Britain and are no longer to look up to her for a description of our own country."

The colleges experienced hard times during the war. About one-fourth of the students had enlisted in the armed forces, and several institutions had their buildings, at least temporarily, used as army barracks. After the conflict, however, higher education expanded greatly. To ensure a quality leadership and avoid aristocratic rule, it was argued that a republican government should promote university-level education. Of nine colleges founded before 1776, only one was nonsectarian; of fourteen established during 1776–96, ten had public support. Georgia charted a state university in 1785 (opened 1801), followed by North Carolina (1789; opened in 1795). William and Mary and the College of Philadelphia (University of Pennsylvania) became state schools. New York attempted to erect a University of the State of New York, intending that King's College (Columbia) be the nucleus of the system, but the effort failed. In 1780 Virginia gave 8,000 acres belonging to Kentucky Tories to found a public school "to promote the diffusion of knowledge even amongst the most remote citizens whose situation, a barbarous neighborhood and savage intercourse, might otherwise render unfriendly to science." Transylvania Seminary thus was established in 1785 in Lincoln County; in a few years the school moved to Lexington and in 1798 became Transylvania University. Other institutions chartered as colleges before 1790 were Liberty Hall (later Washington and Lee) and Hampden-Sydney in Virginia in 1782, Washington College (1782) and St. John's College (1784) in Maryland, Dickinson College (1784) in Pennsylvania, and the College of Charleston (South Carolina) in 1785. Professional training became available in law at William and Mary and the College of Philadelphia; the Litchfield Law School in Connecticut, founded by Tapping Reeve and the first institution of its kind in America, opened in 1784. Moreover, Americans no longer had to travel to Great Britain and Europe to study medicine; the Harvard Medical School (1782) joined the College of Philadelphia and King's College, which had had medical departments since the mid-1760s, in offering professional medical training.

College curricula became more practical and secular; however, without an elective system, students had to take all courses offered. At William and Mary the two divinity professorships disappeared; the five professorships at the school now consisted of Law and Peace; Anatomy and Medicine; Natural Philosophy and Mathematics; Modern Languages; and Moral Philosophy, the Law of Nature and Nations, and the Fine Arts. At Harvard and other colleges as well, the medieval curricula gave way to modern concerns, although classics were still emphasized. Women were not allowed to attend college. Ezra Stiles, president of Yale, in 1783 examined 12-year-old Lucinda Foot, daughter of a pastor, and presented her with a certificate attesting that but for her sex she would be admitted to study at the college.

Some proponents of a federal education system advocated the founding of a national university. Benjamin Rush, in a letter entitled "To Friends of the Federal Government: A Plan for a Federal University," published in the *Federal Gazette* (Philadelphia), on October 29, 1788, had in mind a graduate school, taking in those who had finished college. Besides delving into the "principles and forms of government" and "everything that relates to peace, war, treaties, ambassadors and the like," students would pursue the arts, sciences, and history and also participate in "athletic and manly exercises." Rush's elitism was evident; he proposed that after thirty years no one could serve in government who had not obtained a degree from the national university. James Madison and Charles Pinckney, at the Constitutional Convention in 1787, sought authority for Congress to establish such an institution.

Literature

The wider horizons occasioned by the war and the expansion of education made for a larger reading public. More publications reached mass audiences. Whereas there had been 37 newspapers at the start of the war (78 in all appearing from 1704 to 1775), there were 90 by 1790, and 376 by 1810. From 1775 to 1795, twenty-seven magazines began publication, six more than the whole colonial period, though most lasted hardly more than several years. Kenneth Silverman (1987) notes that the presses increased production of belles lettres (literature to entertain): 7 items in 1763; 45 in 1773; and 105 in 1787. Almanacs, as popular as ever, began to include short pieces on history, especially Revolutionary War events. Samuel Stearns, who published a number of almanacs during 1770–94, issued the *United States Nautical Almanac* in 1783, the first of its kind in this country.

Americans wanted a literature of their own, one that drew on native themes and subjects. Most efforts, however, were derivative of British models and were too affected with neoclassicism. This was especially true of American poetry, which preferred the neoclassical style, with rhyming couplets, each stating a single thought.

Two poems, written just before the war for delivery at commencement exercises at Yale and Princeton, respectively—John Trumbull's "A Prospect of Our Future Glory," published in his *Essay on the Use and Advantages of the Fine Arts* (1770), and Philip Freneau and Hugh Henry Brackenridge's *A Poem on the Rising Glory of America* (1772)—set the stage for the theme of the Rising Glory of America. Indeed, many writers referred to the age-old idea of *Translatio studii*, that the arts and civilization moved westward. Thus was the glory of Greece, Rome, and England, and now to be America.

When not writing of the present and future progress of America, the poets produced mock heroic satire. Most prominent in this genre were the Connecticut Wits—John Trumbull, Timothy Dwight, David Humphreys, Joel Barlow, and Lemuel Hopkins, all of whom attended Yale. The group collaborated on the *Anarchiad* (published serially, 1786–87), which praised national union and condemned the boorish farmers of Shays's Rebellion. Best known of Trumbull's poems is *M'Fingal*

(1776 and as a complete work, 1782), which satirizes events and leaders of 1775 and tells the ordeal of a contentious Scottish Tory in New England. Timothy Dwight wrote America's first epic poem, *The Conquest of Canaan* (1785), which describes the American Revolution in a biblical context, with Joshua representing George Washington. David Humphreys rather pompously continued with the rising glory theme with *Poem on the Industry of the United States* and *The Glory of America* in 1783 and *Poem on the Happiness of America* (1786). Joel Barlow's *The Vision of Columbus* (1787 and revised as the *Columbiad*, 1807) was the most ambitious and serious poem of the Revolutionary era and early Republic. Columbus, while in prison, is visited by a "radiant seraph," who shows him the successive stages of American empire and finally the establishment of a league of all nations to promote "the political harmony of mankind."

Americans turned to the perfection of rhetoric. *Lectures in Rhetoric and Belles Lettres* (1782 and published in America, 1784) by Reverend Hugh Blair, an Englishman, became very influential in America, going through forty editions before 1840; it was adopted as a text at Yale (1785) and Harvard (1788). Blair maintained that, although essayists and orators should be acquainted with classical works, they should avoid "artificial and scholastic rhetoric" and "false ornament"; good sense is "the foundation of all good composition, and simplicity" is "essential to all true ornament."

Few persons before 1800 undertook the task of writing American history. Jeremy Belknap contributed a three-volume history of New Hampshire (1784, 1791, and 1792), noted for its impartial treatment, and David Ramsay, a Charleston physician, wrote *History of the Revolution in South Carolina* (two volumes, 1785) and *History of the American Revolution* (1789); his three-volume *History of the United States* was published posthumously (1816–17). A Federalist, Ramsay stressed the rise of a republican and national American character. From an Antifederalist viewpoint, Mercy Otis Warren wrote *History of the Rise, Progress, and Termination of the American Revolution* (completed in 1788 but not published until 1805), which emphasized the ongoing nature of the Revolution. English-born William Gordon traveled the states to produce *History of the Rise, Progress and Establishment of the Independence of the United States of America* (1789); the work became the most popular of the Revolutionary War histories, but was later shown to have been substantially plagiarized from the British *Annual Register*. The future historians of America now had a usable past with definite bounds, from beginnings to nationhood. As John Lendrum, author of *A Concise and Impartial History of the American Revolution* (two volumes, 1795) put it: "Perhaps no people on the globe can trace the history of their origins and progress with so much precision."

Reading novels, a very popular pastime in England, soon found an eager constituency among young American women. Republican moralists frowned on this kind of literature because it took women into a flight of fancy away from the sober realities of everyday life. It was also argued that novels caused readers to lose their republican simplicity, embrace foreign fashions, and waste time. Yet, by the early nineteenth century, novels had great popularity in America. Interestingly, the themes of most early American novels involved illicit sex and a doomed heroine.

Liberty Displaying the Arts and Sciences. **This 1792 painting by Samuel Jennings conveys the message that, in the American Republic of the future, African Americans could expect not only to be free but also to enjoy the pursuit of happiness.**   *The Library Company of Philadelphia*

Besides the seduction and abandonment of young women, these novels usually had a subplot detailing the financial ruin of a man, such as a father, who had been too trusting of a friend. Thus, a message warned against entering into a deficient contract, whether as to chastity or business. Probably the first American novel (now attributed to William Hill Brown, though previously to Sarah Wentworth Morton) was *The Power of Sympathy* (1789), based on a real-life tale in Boston of seduction, incest, and suicide.

Susannah Rowson's *Charlotte Temple* (1791, first American edition 1794) enjoyed phenomenal success in America, eventually going through nearly 200 editions by the twentieth century. Rowson was an Englishwoman who lived for a while in the United States. The novel tells of a young Englishwoman who comes to New York on the promise of marriage, but is abandoned and dies in childbirth.

American authors also soon discovered the art of blending American and European themes. Hugh Henry Brackenridge's *Modern Chivalry* (published in parts, 1792–97), chronicles the experiences of an American captain and his Irish servant on the frontier (a Don Quixote and Sancho Panza relationship). It remained for

Charles Brockden Brown (1771–1810) to establish the American Gothic romance, beginning with *Wieland* (1798), using totally American sources. Despite the lightness of fare, the early American novel paid homage to republican virtue. Writes Cathy N. Davidson (1986): "Virtually *every* American novel written before 1820 . . . at some point includes either a discourse on the necessity of improved education . . . or a description of then-current education . . . or, at the very least, a comment on the educational levels and reading habits of the hero and even more so the heroine" (p. 66).

Art and Architecture

The fine arts reflect a nation's character as well as its progress. Although some considered the arts a frivolity, others viewed them as a means of edification and inspiration. The marquis de Chastellux, a traveler in America in the early 1780s, offered advice to Americans in the essay "The Progress of the Arts and Sciences in America," which he sent to Reverend James Madison, president of the College of New Jersey, in January 1783. The fine arts "far from rendering nations vain and frivolous . . . tend to preserve them from the excesses of luxury and the caprices of fashion," and "can certainly not be considered either as dangerous or harmful. . . . as long as a taste for the Arts can be reconciled with rural and domestic life, it will always be advantageous to your country."

Conditions favored patronization of the arts during the early Republic. Fortunes were made, and the new middle class was attracted to an aristocratic style of living. Art could reveal the ideology of the nation and advance moral values.

Few Americans engaged in sculpture as a fine art, although there were the woodcarvers and artisans working in decoration. Yet neoclassic sculpture was prevalent, executed largely by foreign-born artists. Thus, the French sculptor Jean Antoine Houdon produced a statue of Washington for the rotunda of the Virginia capitol building. He visited Mount Vernon in 1785 to obtain Washington's life mask and proportions. The statue arrived in Richmond in 1788 but was not installed until 1796.

The number of native and foreign-born artists more than trebled in the major cities after the war. For example, from 1726 to 1776 New York City had only eight painters who advertised and for 1779–99, thirty-four. The most prominent artists of the early Republic—Trumbull, Peale, Copley, Stuart, and Earl—all studied with Benjamin West in England. West (1756–1843), a Pennsylvania Quaker, went to Europe in 1760, spent three years in Rome, and, stopping off at London on his way home, never returned to America. He was the royal portrait painter and a member of the Royal Academy for thirty years.

John Trumbull (1756–1843), son of a Connecticut governor, resided in America only nine years between 1780 and 1812, when he returned from England for good. Trumbull made a lifetime work of depicting the great events of America's national history. Most of the persons who appeared in his canvases were based on sketches Trumbull made of them in real life.

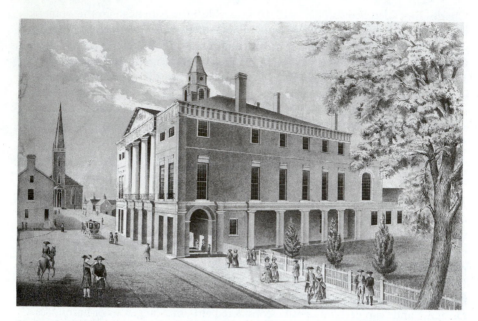

Federal Hall, Wall Street & Trinity Church, New York in 1789. Federal Hall served as the U.S. Capitol, 1785–90.   *Eno Collection, Miriam & Ira D. Wallach Division of Arts, Prints and Photographs, The New York Public Library, Astor, Lenox and Tilden Foundations*

Charles Willson Peale (1741–1827), after a period in England (1767–69), settled in Philadelphia. He painted leaders of the Revolution with brilliant realism, though of a formulaic quality. As Joseph J. Ellis comments (1979): "Part doll and part demigod, the typical Peale figure suggests a benign otherworldliness that wins our affection because of, rather than in spite of, its naivety" (p. 58).

John Singleton Copley (1738–1815), often regarded as the foremost American artist of the eighteenth century, had two careers: thirty-seven years in Boston and then forty years in London. His portraits—with sharp delineation of form, a chromatic colorization, and contrast in light—have almost a three-dimensional effect. In England, Copley painted grand historical scenes.

Gilbert Stuart (1755–1828) was a leading portrait painter in London before his return to the United States in 1793. He was a master of transparent color and meticulous realism; his subjects are depicted with almost photographic accuracy. Stuart experimented with dots of pigment, anticipating Impressionism. Washington sat for three portraits from which Stuart made many copies. Finally, Ralph Earl (1751–1801) brought a frank Yankee realism to his portraits, isolating or silhouetting his subjects.

Neoclassicism affected architecture on both sides of the Atlantic. Excavations at Herculaneum (1738) and Pompeii (1748–63), both of which were destroyed by the eruption of Mount Vesuvius in A.D. 79, with their priceless treasures and a flood

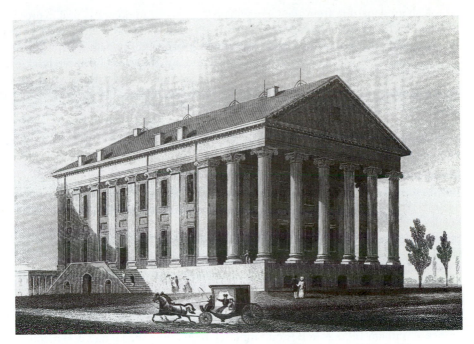

The Virginia capitol was designed by Thomas Jefferson from the Maison Carrée, a temple built by the Romans in Nîmes, France. The Virginia General Assembly first met in the capitol in 1788, and it is still in use today. A stucco exterior was added in 1798, and steps to the portico and two wings in 1906. *Virginia State Library and Archives*

of publications relating to antiquity, stimulated a revival of classical styles. In America, the Federal style, 1780–1820, incorporated Roman classicism along with the *style Louis Seize* (Louis XVI) and late Georgian. An example of mixed Georgian and classical styles was the renovation in the mid-1780s of City Hall in New York City for use as the Federal Hall, the seat of Congress. Pierre Charles L'Enfant (1754–1825), who presided over the project, added large columns and an entablature on the "state" balcony and modified rectangular columns fronting the ground-level corridors.

Thomas Jefferson, while minister to France, convinced the Virginia government to build as the state capitol a replication of the Maison Carrée, a Roman temple of the first century A.D. in Nîmes, which had been restored by Louis XVI. The Virginia "temple" was completed in 1789. Jefferson had written James Madison in August 1784 praising Maison Carrée as

> One of the most beautiful, if not the most beautiful and precious morsel of architecture left us by antiquity . . . it is very simple, but is noble beyond expression. . . . You see I am enthusiastic in the subject of the arts. But it is an enthusiasm of which I am not ashamed, as its object is to improve the taste of my countrymen, to increase their reputation, to reconcile to them the respect of the world, and procure them its praise.

A sharp departure from the Georgian style occurred in domestic architecture. The new architecture featured a large portico, a "Federal doorway," with a semicircular window over the door that had radiating sash bars and side windows, a gentle sloping or flat roof surrounded by a balustrade, and outside walls of painted brick or stucco. The interior design included a spiral staircase and rooms with rounded ends or with projecting bays.

Music and Theater

Music, as entertainment and refinement, brought families and communities closer together. The new academies stressed musical instruction. As Kenneth Silverman writes (1987): "What the age called the 'power of music' seemed to some pedagogues a means of producing the empathy necessary for republican life, inducing people to place the public good above their own" (p. 477). Singing schools flourished, and American composers published tunebooks.

Two native-born composers stand out. Francis Hopkinson (1737–91), America's first secular composer and a signer of the Declaration of Independence, had as his most ambitious work *The Temple of Minerva* (1781), a cantata "consisting of an overture, arias, ensembles, and choruses in praise of the American alliance with France." William Billings, a Boston tanner by trade, published a half dozen collections of his anthems, psalms, and fuguing tunes, in which he also discussed musical theory. One New England pastor said of Billings: "He was a singular man, of moderate size, short of one leg, with one eye, without any address, and with an uncommon negligence of person. Still he spoke and sang and thought as a man above the common abilities." Billings's *Chester* became the war hymn of the Revolution and one of the favorite marching songs. Its opening stanza:

> Let tyrants shake their iron rods
> And slav'ry clank her galling chains.
> We fear them not—we trust in God.
> New England's God forever reigns.

Concerts and the musical theater continued to be popular. European virtuosos came to America, the best known being pianist Alexander Reinagle (1756–1809), who arrived in 1786. George Washington attended Reinagle's concerts. A prolific and versatile composer, Reinagle's works ranged from pieces in the style of Carl Phillipp Emanuel Bach to songs for the theater. Light opera, in the form of ballad opera or comic opera (operetta), was popular in the first years of the Republic. Although full European operas were not staged, their arias were often performed in stage productions.

Theater experienced a vigorous revival. The American Company, under the direction of Lewis Hallam and John Henry, had gone back to England for the duration of war but returned to America in 1783. The company dominated the theater from New York to Annapolis. Dennis Ryan and the American Company of Commedians were popular in the southern circuit, from Baltimore to Charleston. A few other troupes were also formed. Colleges also began producing plays. In the cities, a battle royal raged as to whether or not to allow theater. Opponents argued that theater contributed to luxurious tastes, loose morals, Europeanization of values, and enmeshing all social ranks together. Furthermore, they claimed that the rise in theater paralleled national decay, analogous to the fall of Athens at the end of the Periclean age. Proponents countered that plays were instructive in eloquence and that in the presentations virtue always triumphed over vice; far from being a corrupting influence, they emphasized, the theater provided youth with "rational entertainment" that kept them from taverns and brothels.

English farces, such as those by George Farquhar and Joseph Addison, dominated the American theater much as they had before the war. John Gay's *The Beggar's Opera* retained its drawing power. Two plays, popular in America throughout the century, reminded audiences of public virtue: Nicholas Rowe's *Tamerlane* (in praise of William III and the Glorious Revolution) and Addison's *Cato* (involving an attempt to establish a small republic within Caesar's empire).

American playwrights of the Revolutionary era wrote in imitation of the English farces but with a difference—the major theme being the contrast between American virtue and European corruption. Mercy Otis Warren led the way in this genre with four plays (1772–76), the last being *The Blockheads*, written in reply to General John Burgoyne's *The Blockade of Boston* (1775). *The Blockheads* is so scatological in parts that questions have been raised whether a proper Boston lady could have written it. *Sans Souci. Alias Free and Easy: or an Evening's Peep into a Polite Circle* (1785), possibly also written by Mrs. Otis, shows luxury as a disease of republics.

Robert Munford (c. 1730–84), a southside Virginia planter, who had already satirized colonial elections in *The Candidates* (1771–72), wrote perhaps the most incisive play of the Revolutionary era by an American. *The Patriots* (1777–78), modeled somewhat after the favorite comedy of colonial America—Farquhar's *The Recruiting Officer*—has the bold message that self-appointed Tory-hunters and superpatriots were the least patriotic of all. As far as known, the play was never produced until the 1970s, although it was published by his son William Munford in 1798.

The first play by an American playwright produced in New York (April 6, 1787) and an immediate success was *The Contrast* by Royall Tyler. The hero, Captain Manly, fresh from subduing Shays's Rebellion, contends with a wealthy fop, Billy Dimple, in romance. Manly denounces pretentiousness and says: "I have humbly imitated our illustrous Washington, in having exposed my health and life in the service of my country, without reaping any other reward than the glory of conquering in so arduous a contest."

William Dunlap (1766–1839), who was also an artist and art historian, was so inspired by the success of *The Contrast* that he wrote *The Father, or American Shandyism*, a comedy of manners, first performed in New York on September 7, 1789. Dunlap, regarded as the Father of the American Theater, in all wrote seventy-five plays, thirty of them original and the rest adaptations.

Science

Scientific progress would display the "genius of America." As Brooke Hindle writes (1956): "The cultural nationalism of the Revolution" gave "important dimensions to the demand for attainment in science. Patriotism and pride . . . led men who were sensitive to intellectual values to feel that scientific accomplishment was a necessary measure of national justification" (p. 38).

Americans continued to make progress in cartography, navigation, surveying, and instrument-making, but still showed little interest in pure science. Even though the colleges lagged in the expansion of the study of science, the popularization of science advanced. Almanacs, evening schools, and public lecture–demonstrations brought scientific knowledge to the masses. Americans applied ingenuity to inventions, perhaps the most notable of the period being John Fitch's demonstration of the steamboat in the Delaware River in August 1787 and James Rumsey's similar feat in the Potomac four months later.

In an age of Enlightenment, science became an end unto itself. Yet, Americans perceived no conflict between religion and science, only the belief that knowledge of nature resulted from discovery and not divine revelation. Even deists, who rejected institutional religion, did not disown a Supreme Force. As Herbert M. Morais writes (1934): "Most American deists . . . contented themselves with the innocuous common-sense truths of 'the pure and simple Religion of Nature' with its basic premise of a First Cause, its acceptance of a future state and its emphasis upon virtuous living" (p. 15). Ethan Allen, of Revolutionary War fame and a deist, commented in *Reason the Only Oracle of Man* (1784) that "if mankind would dare to exercise their reason," they would "rid themselves of their blindness and superstition, gain more exalted ideas of God and their obligations to him and one another . . . and acquire many powerful incentives to the practice of morality."

Americans felt that astronomy was the key to understanding the laws of nature. The almanac writers were amateur astronomers. Joseph Pope (1750–1826) succeeded in making an orrery (a device determining the relations of bodies in the solar system), as the self-educated David Rittenhouse (1732–96) had done before the war. Rittenhouse also invented a metallic thermometer, constructed a refractory telescope, and calculated the solar parallax.

Before the Revolution, certain Americans had achieved international recognition in the pursuit of natural history (study of natural objects in the field, especially botany and zoology). Naturalist–collectors frequently sent specimens of fauna and flora to England and wrote about them in the Royal Society's *Transactions*. Natural history had a special appeal to Americans because of the ample latitude for discovery of new species. Americans believed that plants and animals thrived better in the New than in the Old World. Thomas Jefferson, in his *Notes on Virginia* (1782), went to great lengths to disprove the theories of the French naturalist, Georges-Louis Buffon, which argued the degeneracy of fauna and flora and even of the Indians in America.

Although the Revolutionary War interrupted channels of communication between America and England and Europe, which were so vital in the scientific collaborative endeavors, American naturalists still went about their work. America's preeminent naturalist of the Revolutionary and postwar years was William Bartram (1739–1823), son of the famous colonial botanist John Bartram. William Bartram went on a four-year journey (March 20, 1773–January 1, 1777) from Philadelphia through the Carolinas, Georgia, Florida, and the southwestern Indian country, and published his findings in *Travels* . . . (1791). This work became immensely popular in Great Britain and Europe, going through nine foreign editions within a decade. Bartram developed a philosophy of the dignity of animal nature and devoted one-fourth of his book to an idealization of Indian life. His narrative ability and rhapsodic enthusiasm made the *Travels* a literary as well as a scientific masterpiece. The book had enormous influence on English and European writers, not the least being poets William Wordsworth and Samuel Taylor Coleridge. In botany, Humphrey Marshall published a catalog of American trees, *Arbustrum Americanum* (1785), and Thomas Walter issued *Flora Caroliniana* (1788).

The most renowned American-born scientist of the early Republic was Benjamin Thompson (1753–1814), who achieved reputation and fortune in Great Britain and Europe. A Tory and a spy for the British, he left with Howe's army at the evacuation of Boston in 1776. Thompson returned to America only briefly as a British lieutenant-colonel of dragoons. Among his varied activities, he served the elector of Bavaria in implementing social reform and reorganizing the army, and he became a count of the Holy Roman Empire (Count Rumford). His scientific accomplishments included the development of the science of ballistics and the formulation of the theory of caloric heat. Thompson founded the Royal Institution in London. To renew ties with America, he established the Rumford professorship at Harvard. Amazingly, in 1799 President Adams offered the turncoat scientist an appointment as the first superintendent of the United States Military Academy, which Thompson declined.

Learned societies proliferated, many of them giving emphasis to agricultural improvement. Even Kentucky had a Society for Promoting Useful Knowledge in 1787. The American Academy of Arts and Sciences, founded in Boston in 1780, rivaled the older American Philosophical Society in Philadelphia. In the 1780s both societies began publishing *Memoirs;* the Philadelphia organization continued issuing its *Transactions,* first appearing in 1771. The beginnings of a museum movement included Charles Willson Peale's museum of natural history (1787), which offered the viewer "a world in miniature," Robert Leslie's museum of models of machines in Philadelphia, and John Pintard's American Museum of the Tammany Society (1789) in New York. Although such activity further evidenced a growing appreciation of science among the public, the community of science professionals remained quite small. A catalog of all books printed in America before 1804, issued by a Boston bookseller, listed only twenty books (excluding medical treatises) on science. European studies, of course, could be found in American libraries. The average American had little use for anything that was not of utilitarian value and considered the pursuit of happiness as attainment of wealth and prestige. Still, science in American life was becoming more conspicuous and diffusive.

CHAPTER 22

A More Perfect Union

The delegates from the state legislatures who assembled in Philadelphia during the summer of 1787 were men of destiny. They accepted the task of not only saving the American Union but also recasting it on stronger foundations. Their achievement was to be revolutionary by demolishing the government and instituting a new one, and yet also counterrevolutionary by curtailing state sovereignty and providing checks and balances to restrain democracy. From the viewpoint of the framers, however, adoption of the Constitution of 1787 enabled Americans, as stated in the Preamble of the document, "to form a more perfect Union, establish Justice, insure domestic Tranquility, provide for the common defence, promote the general Welfare, and secure the Blessings of Liberty to ourselves and our Posterity."

The formation of the Constitution represented a process that was extralegal and unconstitutional. On February 21, 1787, Congress, endorsing the Annapolis conference proposal, resolved that "it is expedient" that delegates from each state meet in Philadelphia on the second Monday of May (May 14) "for the sole purpose of revising the Articles of Confederation"; the "alterations and provisions" adopted at the Convention would become part of the existing constitution when approved by Congress and the state legislatures. No state authorized its delegates to draft a new constitution. Although radical change had long been advocated by prominent nationalists such as George Washington, Alexander Hamilton, James Madison, James Wilson, and Robert and Gouverneur Morris, there was little anticipation before the delegates arrived in Philadelphia that the Convention would bypass the Confederation entirely and introduce a new frame of government. Richard Henry Lee, who as a member of Congress declined an appointment as a delegate to the Constitutional Convention because he thought serving would constitute a conflict of duty, wrote just after the adjournment of the Convention: "Had the idea of a total change been started, probably no state would have appointed members to the convention." The states were "unsuspecting, and not aware that they were passing the Rubicon . . . and, probably, not one man in ten thousand in the United States . . . had an idea that the old ship was to be destroyed."

By May 17, only the Virginia and Pennsylvania delegations were present. Rain and muddy roads delayed the arrival of others. Certain delegates already intended to establish a new constitution. The Virginians, led by Madison, met for several hours each afternoon, while waiting for the convention to start, for the purpose of forming a plan that would address "the great subject of our mission"—a strong central government. The Pennsylvania delegates also joined in the discussions. Wrote George Mason to his son, on May 20: "The most prevalent idea in the principal States seems to be a total alteration of the present federal system," especially the creation of a national legislature of two branches, based on proportionate representation and "with full legislative powers upon all the subjects of the Union," and an "Executive" and giving the national legislature power to negate state laws "contrary to the interest of the Federal Union."

At last, on Friday, May 25, twenty-nine members from seven states and one delegate each from Massachusetts and Georgia formed a quorum. George Washington was elected president of the Convention and William Jackson, secretary. On May 28 the Convention adopted rules prepared by a committee, consisting of Charles Pinckney, Alexander Hamilton, and George Wythe: each state delegation would have one vote; a quorum of seven states was required; questions already voted on could be reopened; each delegate was limited to two speeches on an issue, unless granted an exemption; and the proceedings were to be secret. From Paris Thomas Jefferson wrote John Adams, in London, on August 30: "I am sorry they began their deliberations by so abominable a precedent as that of tying up the tongues of their members. Nothing can justify this example but the innocence of their intentions, & ignorance of the value of public discussions." Jefferson added that he had "no doubt that all their other measures will be good & wise. It is really an assembly of demigods."

Members scrupulously abided by their pledge of secrecy, although occasionally letters home afforded information on the direction of the proceedings. Two sentries guarded the entrance to the meeting room, and whenever the door opened the delegates ceased talking. The Constitution would long be in effect before the public had any knowledge of the proceedings of the Convention. The official journal, which was entrusted to Washington as president of the Convention, was kept from public view until it was deposited at the Department of State in 1796, and Congress neglected to have it published until 1819. The fullest and most careful notes of the Convention, kept by James Madison, were first printed in 1840, four years after his death. The shorter and fragmentary records of other Convention participants also came slowly to light: notes by Robert Yates, published in 1821, followed by those of William Pierce, 1828; George Mason, 1892; Rufus King, 1894; William Paterson and Alexander Hamilton, 1904; and James McHenry, 1906. All of the records have been reproduced together to form a daily journal of the Convention proceedings (Max Farrand, ed., *The Records of the Federal Convention of 1787*, vols. 1 and 2 [1927]).

On the morning of May 29, Governor Edmund Randolph of the Virginia delegation was recognized and, after bowing to Washington and Benjamin Franklin, "opened the main business" by submitting a plan that would provide a focus for debates as to the extent of change. The next day Washington stepped down from the chair, and the Convention resolved itself into a Committee of the Whole, which allowed informality in debate. Nathaniel Gorham of Massachusetts, chosen chairman of the Committee of the Whole, presided at all the daily sessions.

Two broad questions facing the Convention were how much power should be conferred on the national government, without abridging freedom, and what should be the definite jurisdictions of that government. All delegates expected some substantial change. Many were alarmed by the present state of events, such as Washington, who wrote Jefferson on May 30: "The situation of the general government, if it can be called a government, is shaken to its foundation, and liable to be overturned by every blast. In a word, it is at an end; and, unless a remedy is soon applied, anarchy and confusion will inevitably ensue." Virtually everyone at the Convention favored granting the national government authority to regulate foreign and domestic commerce, levy and collect taxes, and provide for the common defense and general welfare, and prohibiting the states from impairing obligations of contracts and issuing paper money. Three general attitudes were evident among the delegates: the aristocratic one, which distrusted popular participation and favored a strong central government; the moderately conservative, which also had a mistrust of the populace but supported a decentralized or weak central government; and the outright democratic, which emphasized liberty and the right of the common people to self-government.

The Convention progressed through four phases. From May 29 to June 19, the delegates agreed on the principles to be incorporated into the Constitution. The Great Compromise resulted from the debates of June 19–July 16. From the deliberations of July 17–September 7 came a draft Constitution. Lastly, the Constitution was put into final form, with a few additional minor changes, on September 8–17.

The Framers

Of seventy-four delegates to the Convention, fifty-five attended. Eleven who were elected declined to serve, including Patrick Henry. Luther Martin, who was a powerful force on behalf of states' rights until almost the end of the Convention, and his Maryland colleague, John Francis Mercer, withdrew in opposition to the Constitution (leaving September 4 and August 17, respectively), as did Robert Yates and John Lansing of the New York delegation (July 10). Alexander Hamilton left June 29, returned for a day, on August 13, and did not come back until September 6–17. Thus, New York was not represented during much of the Convention. Delegates from New Hampshire did not arrive until July 23. Rhode Island did not send any delegates at all. The average attendance was thirty to forty.

"There are gentlemen of great abilities employed in this Convention," wrote Robert Morris to his sons on June 26. All fifty-five delegates who attended the Convention had held public office. There were three present and four former governors, eight judges, and twenty who had assisted in writing state constitutions; forty-two had served in Congress; and thirty had seen active military service. Eight had signed the Declaration of Independence, and six, the Articles of Confederation. Thirty-four had practiced law, three were physicians, and twenty-six were college graduates. All members were of moderate to wealthy means. None came from the working poor or even from among skilled craftsmen, although several had humble beginnings, such as Benjamin Franklin (printing). But Franklin was now addressed as Doctor, having received an LL.D. from the University of St. Andrews in 1759. There were big landowners, especially the southern planters, including George Mason and George Washington. Sixteen of the plantation owners held productive slaves. Agewise, the members were relatively young, averaging forty-two years of age. Franklin was the oldest at 81, Roger Sherman, the second oldest at 66, and Jonathan Dayton of New Jersey, at 26, was the youngest.

The prime movers of the Convention, the men who carried the weight of the discussions and made brilliant tactical decisions, were James Madison, Gouverneur Morris, and James Wilson, for the nationalists, and Roger Sherman, Luther Martin, and William Paterson, for the local interests. Madison spoke 161 times; Morris 163; Wilson, 168; and Sherman, 138. The other main participants were Charles Pinckney, Oliver Ellsworth, William Samuel Johnson, Elbridge Gerry, Edmund Randolph, George Mason, Pierce Butler, John Dickinson, Nathaniel Gorham, John Rutledge, and Hugh Williamson. Alexander Hamilton and Benjamin Franklin had influence at crucial points.

William Pierce of Georgia left an undated memorandum sizing up the character and ability of each of his fellow delegates in the Convention (Farrand, III, 87–97). Following are a few of his assessments of the main participants:

James Madison, age 36: "In the management of every great question he evidently took the lead in the Convention . . . he always comes forward the best informed Man of any point in debate."

Gouverneur Morris, age 35: "is one of those Genius's in whom every species of talents combine to render him conspicuous and flourishing in public debate:—He winds through all the mazes of rhetoric, and throws around him such a glare that he charms, captivates, and leads away the senses of all who hear him. . . . He has been unfortunate in losing one of his Legs, and getting all the flesh taken off his right arm by a scald, when a youth."

James Wilson, age 35: "ranks among the foremost in legal and political knowledge. . . . All the political institutions of the World he knows in detail. . . . No man is more clear, copious, and comprehensive."

Roger Sherman, age 66: "the oddity of his address, the vulgarisms that accompany his public speaking, and that strange New England cant . . . make everything that is connected with him grotesque and laughable;—and yet he deserves infinite praise,—no Man has a better Heart or a clearer Head. . . . He is an able politician, and extremely artful in accomplishing any particular object;—it is remarked that he seldom fails."

Rufus King, age 32: "His action is natural, swimming, and graceful, but there is a rudeness of manner sometimes accompanying it. But take him *tout en semble,* he may . . . be ranked among the Luminaries of the present Age."

Oliver Ellsworth, age 32: "He is very happy in a reply . . . selecting parts of his adversary's arguments . . . so as to admit the power of his own." *George Mason, age 32:* "one of the best politicians in America." *Edmund Randolph, age 34:* "in whom unite all the accomplishments of the Scholar, and the States-man." *Charles Pinckney, age 30:* "intimately acquainted with every species of polite learning, and has a spirit of application and industry beyond most Men." *Elbridge Gerry, age 43:* "possesses a great degree of confidence and goes extensively into all subjects that he speaks on, without respect to elegance or flower of diction."

The Founding Fathers acted in what they considered the public's best interests. But were their decisions influenced by expectations of personal gain and holding democracy in check? At the beginning of the twentieth century, the time was ripe for inquiry into the motivation of the Founding Fathers. The new social sciences were calling attention to behavioral patterns, and muckrakers were exposing robber barons and corrupt politicians. Historians for over a century had held the Constitution and its framers in awe. But now, in the Progressive era, all government was suspect. Thus, efforts were being made to demythologize both the Constitution and the "demigods" who framed it. *The Spirit of American Government* (1907) by J. Allen Smith, a political scientist, paved the way by expounding on his thesis that the framers sought to "perpetuate the ascendancy of the property-holding class" and to establish "legal and constitutional guarantees which would check the tendency toward democratic legislation" (pp. 298–99).

Charles A. Beard's *An Economic Interpretation of the Constitution of the United States* (1913) stirred the greatest controversy. Beard did not set out to establish a conspiracy theory, so much as to introduce new dimensions of historical inquiry. His theme was that the Constitution "was originated and carried through principally by four groups of personalty [property other than real estate] interests which had been adversely affected under the Articles of Confederation: money, public securities, manufacturing, and trade and shipping." The members of the Constitutional Convention were, "with a few exceptions, immediately, directly, and personally interested in, and derived economic advantages from the establishment of the new system." The Constitution was not created by the people or the states, but by "a consolidated group whose interests knew no state boundaries and were truly national in their scope" (pp. 324–25). Beard also claimed that only one-sixth of adult males approved ratification of the Constitution. Using Treasury records for 1792–1804, Beard showed that five-sixths of the framers stood to gain from the restoration of public credit in regard to ownership of securities, land for speculation, and slaves. He observed that the value of their holdings in public securities appreciated $40 million after the Constitution went into effect.

Robert E. Brown (1956) and others have discredited the "Beard thesis." They have shown that Beard erred in not using Treasury and tax records for the period of 1785–87, thereby including the time when the Constitution was written. Furthermore, Beard often did not distinguish between real and personal property. The framers had far more investment in land than in securities. Only six of them had personal property in excess of realty (George Clymer, Thomas Fitzsimmons, Nicholas Gilman, Elbridge Gerry, Robert Morris, and Hugh Williamson). Gerry, who opposed the final Constitution, had the largest holdings of public securities, while Hamilton, a staunch nationalist, had only $800 in securities.

Jackson T. Main (1960) is representative of those who criticized Beard for the narrowness of his investigations. To Main, "the real question "is not whether a member of the Convention held securities, but the distribution of these in the country at large and the extent to which delegates reflected the desires of security holders" (p. 91). Interestingly, Main finds that at the ratifying stage much of the Beard thesis holds true. Richard Hofstadter (1968) declares that "on two fundamental counts" Beard was "basically right": the elites "took charge of events and framed and established the Constitution," and "the cosmopolitan trading classes of the towns" had an "active and dynamic role" in "making the Constitution." But, to Hofstadter, all this is actually moot because the "central issue" was "whether the American union should become a national state," and, secondarily, whether such a government would preserve and protect liberties and self-government (pp. 226, 231). Inclusive of such goals, the personal motivation of the framers of the Constitution notwithstanding was to safeguard the public credit and property interests.

The Virginia Plan Prevails

Edmund Randolph's speech of May 29 recited the shortcomings of the Confederation and warned of the expansive and unchecked democracy in the states. He referred to the alarm of Shays's Rebellion. "Look at the public countenance from New Hampshire to Georgia. Are we not on the eve of war, which is only prevented by the hopes from this convention?" For "remedy" in the central government Randolph submitted fifteen resolutions (to be known as the Virginia Plan). The first was: "resolved that the articles of Confederation ought to be so corrected and enlarged as to accomplish the objects proposed by their institution, namely, 'common defence, security of liberty, and general welfare.' " The proposed resolutions advocated a bicameral legislature, with proportionate representation in each house according to "quotas of contribution, or to the number of free inhabitants," the lower house to be elected by the people and the upper by the lower house. The national legislature would have power "to negative all laws passed by the several States, contravening in the opinion of the National Legislature the articles of Union." A council of revision, consisting of the executive and part of the national judiciary, would have a veto over national and state legislation. The executive (with one fixed term) and the judiciary (with appellate and limited original jurisdiction) would be chosen by the legislature. The federal government would guarantee each state its territory and a republican form of government. Amendment to the Constitution should be by state conventions, independent of the state legislatures. Also under the Virginia Plan, the national legislature could exercise coercive authority against any state "failing to fulfill its duty under the articles thereof."

Charles Pinckney of South Carolina followed with a plan that "was grounded on the same principles" as the Virginia Plan and remarkably similar to it in details. Pinckney proposed a single executive with a seven-year term and a judiciary appointed by the state legislatures. Andrew C. McLaughlin (1904) has noted that thirty-one or thirty-two of Pinckney's suggestions found their way into the Constitution. The Virginia Plan, however, became the basis for the ensuing discussions.

The Convention immediately began consideration of the Virginia Plan. Randolph, on May 30, himself moved that the first proposed resolution of his plan regarding the strengthening of the Articles of Confederation be replaced with a three-part resolution that acknowledged the inadequacy of the Confederation. He stated that "a national government ought to be established consisting of a supreme legislature, judiciary and executive." This was the most radical proposal of the Convention—to put an end to the government of the Confederation; the use of "national" signified that the new government would not be just a confederation. Although some delegates were offended by "national" and "supreme," the substitute resolution passed by a vote of six to one. The members of the Convention had crossed the "Rubicon."

For the next two weeks, the delegates mostly debated whether population should be the basis for representation in both houses of the legislature. On June 13, a committee reported nineteen resolutions, which confirmed the principles of the Virginia Plan but also noted changes in details. There would now be no council of revision. Section eight of the report mentioned proportionate representation in the Senate as well as the lower house, thereby signifying a total departure from the unit rule in the Confederation Congress. This proposition elicited determined opposition from the small-state men. William Paterson, on June 15, introduced a counterplan in the form of nine resolutions. The New Jersey Plan, as it was called, would give the national government powers to raise revenue through impost, stamp, and postal duties and to regulate commerce. If revenue were insufficient, requisitions could be placed on the states, and means should be provided to enforce collections. Treaties would be the "supreme law," and a plural executive would be elected by Congress. The most controversial feature was a single legislature, with unit representation by state delegations—the same as the Confederation Congress. On Saturday and Monday, June 16 and 18, a heated debate developed over the New Jersey Plan. Paterson argued that state sovereignty must be retained, whereas James Wilson, always a champion of popular representation, emphasized that in the Confederation Congress delegates had been hardly more than diplomats and lacked a will of their own.

On behalf of the nationalist position, Alexander Hamilton, "hitherto silent," tried the patience of the delegates with a speech nearly six hours long on June 18. He examined historical precedents and then offered new proposals. He suggested a permanent Senate, with members serving on good behavior. The Senate as well as the executive would be selected by an electoral college chosen by the people. The Senate would have sole power to declare war and to approve the heads of the Foreign Affairs, Finance, and War departments. The supreme judiciary could declare state laws contrary to the Constitution void. Hamilton shocked his audience when he asked that governors of each state be appointed by the national government and that they have the right to negate state laws; they would serve indefinitely on the basis of good behavior. Hamilton's state executives would essentially be the same as the colonial royal governors. Madison also spoke at length against the New Jersey Plan.

On June 19, the question as to whether the propositions of the Virginia Plan "should be adhered to as preferable to those of Mr. Patterson" passed in the affirmative by a vote of seven to three, with Massachusetts, Connecticut, Pennsylvania, Virginia, North Carolina, South Carolina, and Georgia in favor; New York, New Jersey, and Delaware against; and Maryland, divided. Connecticut, which had been in the small-state column, switched upon assurance of compromise.

The foundations for the Constitution were set, and the Convention now had the task of working out specifics. However, since all votes could be reopened, subsequently the Convention decided against three basic principles of the Virginia Plan: coercion of the states by force (which was not really necessary since the Constitution would operate on the people directly and provided for enforcement of laws thereof); a general grant of legislative powers to Congress (instead, Congress would have specific legislative authority); and a political rather than a judicial guardianship of the Constitution. A "negative" of state laws by Congress, a principle so dearly held by Madison and other ardent nationalists, failed by a vote of seven to three on July 17.

The Great Compromise

Constituting the new bicameral legislature, even more so than determining the range of its authority, proved one of the most difficult tasks of the Convention. Much of the debate for four weeks was devoted to working out agreements in this area. The small-state bloc adamantly insisted on a single state vote in the Senate. On June 30, Oliver Ellsworth made a motion to this effect. In opposition, James Wilson responded that if the resolution were adopted small states would dominate the national legislature. "Can we forget for whom we are forming a Government?" he asked. "Is it for men, or for the imaginary beings called States?" While the debates heated up, Benjamin Franklin injected some advice: "When a broad table is to be made, and the edges of planks do not fit, the artist takes a little from both, and makes a good joint. In like manner here both sides must part with some of their demands, in order that they may join in some accommodating proposition."

On Monday, July 2, a vote on Ellsworth's resolution ended in a deadlock— five–five–one. There was danger that the Convention had reached an impasse and might have to dissolve. Roger Sherman pointed out that "we are now at a full stop"; yet he had faith that a solution could be found. On his motion a committee of eleven, one from each state, was appointed, with Elbridge Gerry as chairman, and the Convention adjourned for three days. On July 5, Gerry, for the committee, reported a compromise. The states would have an equal vote in the upper house, while the lower house would possess the sole authority to originate money bills, which "shall not be altered or amended by the second Branch" (though the Senate could reject money bills). Representation in the lower house would be proportionate to the population of free persons, with slaves to be counted as three-fifths of a free person. Membership in the lower house was fixed at sixty-five members; the actual representation per state would be adjusted in the future on the basis of a census taken every ten years. Interestingly, the compromise resolutions never mentioned slavery, only that representation be "according to the ratio recommended by Congress in their resolution of April 18, 1783." What the Convention did was to take the formula that the Confederation Congress had suggested for levying requisitions and applied it to an entirely different purpose—representation. The Great Compromise, as it became known largely because it saved the Convention, passed on July 16 by a vote of five–four–one. Connecticut, New Jersey, Delaware, Maryland, and North Carolina voted for; Pennsylvania, Virginia, South Carolina, and Georgia voted against; and Massachusetts was divided.

Nationalists were disappointed with the victory of the small-state bloc in winning equal state representation in the Senate. But the overall compromise definitely abridged state sovereignty by having the lower house represent the people, at the exclusion of the states. The Senate, in its final form, would not quite have unit-representation. On July 23, the Convention voted (nine to one) that the two members from each state would vote "per capita" (that is, as individuals).

Even the three-fifths slave clause weakened state sovereignty. It "was instrumental in bringing about a national union in which representation was related to the changing distribution of population," writes Howard A. Ohline (1971). But "the regrettable paradox of American Revolutionary republicanism was that the new nation had to acknowledge the existence of slavery in its legislature in order to be republican" (pp. 567, 584).

A Draft Constitution

Having overcome the legislative hurdle, the Convention gave more attention to the executive and the judiciary. For selection to the federal bench, Benjamin Franklin said that he preferred "a Scotch mode, in which the nomination proceeded from the Lawyers, who always selected the ablest of the profession in order to get rid of him, and share his practice (among themselves)." The Convention agreed on a "single person" executive chosen by the national legislature (this was later to be changed) and invested with powers of veto, execution of the laws, and appointment of officials not otherwise provided for. Besides a Supreme Court, the federal judiciary would also consist of inferior tribunals, and appointment of judges would be made by the executive, with confirmation by the Senate. Areas of original jurisdiction of the judiciary were also determined. Congressional terms were fixed at two years for representatives and six years for senators.

The Convention recessed from July 27 to August 6, while a five-man Committee of Detail, headed by John Rutledge, put all the decisions and resolutions into some format. On August 6 the committee presented a draft constitution of twenty-three articles. It had accomplished more than a compilation, having ventured into making decisions on its own. The draft constitution set forth eighteen enumerated powers of Congress, along with authority for this body to implement these powers, the role of the executive and the judiciary, restraints on the states, and certain prohibitions on Congress (such as no ex post facto laws or suspension of habeas corpus). Only in a few instances did this document not contain provisions to be found in the finalized Constitution.

The draft constitution made three concessions to the South: no export duties; no prohibition or taxation of the slave trade; and a two-thirds vote in Congress for navigation acts. For several weeks, the Convention wrangled over the slave trade and navigation laws, with lengthy debates between northerners and southerners over the feasibility of slavery altogether. During one round of the slave trade debates, Luther Martin of Maryland complained that the three-fifths clause already encouraged slavery, that an increase in the number of slaves created a potential for slave insurrection, "which the other parts were bound to protect," and that slavery "was inconsistent with the principles of the Revolution, and dishonorable to the American character." Charles Pinckney of South Carolina replied that, in the event of slave insurrection, there would be no need for northern aid in suppressing it; "religion and humanity had nothing to do with this question," and northern shipping would benefit by keeping the slave trade open.

George Mason, pointing to the need to diminish slavery, warned: "By an inevitable chain of causes and effects, Providence punishes national sins by national calamities." Pinckney gave assurance that in all probability South Carolina would eventually outlaw the importation of slaves as Maryland and Virginia had already done. Roger Sherman pleaded for a compromise, which would enhance ratification of the Constitution. As to navigation laws, southerners, who had few ships of their own and depended on exports, did not want to make it easy for Congress to levy export duties and to confine trade to American vessels.

On August 25 and 29, the Convention adopted its other famous compromise. First, by a vote of seven to one, Congress would not prohibit the slave trade until 1808, but until then, it could levy a maximum duty of $10 on each slave imported. In addition, by a vote of eight to three, Congress could enact navigation laws by majority vote. The decision on the slave trade gave encouragement to both slavery's defenders and opponents; slavery was acknowledged on one hand, and on the other, Congress had gained entry into the regulation of slavery, even if only in reference to the slave trade.

From August 31 to September 4, another committee of eleven—the Committee on Unfinished Parts of the Constitution, chaired by David Brearley of New Jersey—cleared up a few remaining items, such as providing a four-year term for the president.

Style and Arrangement

A Committee of Style and Arrangement met on September 8–12 to cast the Constitution into proper headings and language. William Samuel Johnson chaired the five-man panel, which included Alexander Hamilton (only two days back in the Convention), Gouverneur Morris, Rufus King, and James Madison. The committee took upon itself the task of inserting several changes. Two-thirds instead of three-fourths of Congress could override a presidential veto. An important change was made in the Preamble: "We, the People of the States of [the individual states are then mentioned]" was replaced by "We the People of the United States." Although this change was made primarily because it was not known how many states would ratify, the substitution left no doubt that the new government rested on the people and not the states.

The final Constitution compressed twenty-three articles into seven. Morris had a major role in putting the Constitution into its final form; in fact, the document is in his handwriting. Commented James Madison to Jared Sparks on April 8, 1831: "the *finish* given to the style and arrangement fairly belongs to the pen of Mr. Morris."

At the last minute, an effort was made to include a Bill of Rights. On April 12, Gerry presented a motion to this effect, seconded by Mason. The Convention previously had given little thought to the subject. Charles Pinckney's proposal in August to guarantee freedom of the press had been voted down on grounds that Congress would be granted only specific powers. Mason argued that without a federal Bill of Rights "the laws of the United States are to be paramount to the State Bills of Rights." But Sherman contended that the state declarations of rights were not repealed by the Constitution. The motion for a Bill of Rights failed unanimously by a vote of ten states to zero.

On Saturday, September 15, the Convention approved the final draft of the Constitution, "by unanimous consent" of eleven state delegations and Alexander Hamilton of New York. On Monday, September 17, an engrossed copy of the Constitution was read, and Washington resumed the chair. He and Franklin gave valedictories. Franklin said that he consented to the Constitution because "I expect no better and because I am not sure that it is not the best." When finished, he moved that the Constitution be signed. Of the forty-one members present, thirty-eight signed, with George Read of Delaware also affixing the name of his absent colleague, John Dickinson.

Three of the members present refused to put their names to the document. George Mason objected because of the lack of a Bill of Rights and a "Constitutional Council" to advise the president. He also had particular complaints about the excessive powers given to the judiciary, president, and Senate. Gerry, fearing "that a Civil War may result from the present crisis of the U.S.," thought that the Constitution should have been "in a more mediatory shape, in order to abate the heat and opposition of parties." Gerry also criticized a weak executive and the absence of a two-thirds majority for passage of navigation acts. Randolph, though saying that he did not oppose the Constitution, wanted "only to keep himself free" for his "future judgment."

As its final action, the Convention resolved that the Constitution be sent to the Confederation Congress and "afterwards" be submitted for ratification by state conventions; it also called for establishing the new government upon approval in nine states. A letter to that effect was addressed to Congress, to be delivered by secretary Jackson.

"The business being thus closed," Washington observed in his diary on September 17, "the Members adjourned to the City Tavern, dined together, and took cordial leave of each other; after which I returned to my lodgings, did some business with and received the papers from the Secretary of the Convention, and retired to meditate on the momentous work which had been executed."

With only one-third of its members present, the Confederation Congress resolved on September 26, 1787, that the Constitution be sent to the states. A clear majority in Congress favored the Constitution and popular ratification, but there was powerful opposition. Therefore, a compromise was made to forward the document to the states without endorsement. Congress, however, paid the costs of the Convention, $1,165, which included the salaries of the secretary and doorkeepers and the expense of engrossing the Constitution.

The delegates of the Constitutional Convention had attended to essential principles but left certain important decisions to the future, such as the debt, suffrage requirements, and judicial review. The Convention had abandoned the doctrine of strict separation of powers and instead settled for a system of interdependent functions. As Saul K. Padover states (1962), the Constitution was a "masterpiece of interlocking compromises." It provided for

> an intricately equilibrated political structure, wherein power was to be balanced by counterpower, and authority checked by countervailing authority. Inside the Federal system, a tripartite mechanism was designed to prevent any one element from dominating the others or from combining to form a potentially tyrannizing unity. The confederated states, equally balanced, were, in their totality, to serve as a counterpoise to the national government. Flexibility, needed for future changes and adjustments, was supplied by a fairly elaborate amendment process. (p. 72)

The Constitution eased rivalry between small and large states, and attempted sectional compromise, which, however, was not fully attainable. It made for a change in the structure of government and granted Congress important new powers. There were possibilities for expanding congressional authority by way of the "general welfare" and "necessary and proper" clauses of Article I, section eight. The Constitution would be the supreme law of the land, although the "judicial power" was limited to "cases" of original jurisdiction and to "controversies" as enumerated in Article III, section two.

Although the Constitution rested on popular sovereignty, the new government would not be a pure democracy. As James Madison wrote in 1830, "the Constitution was created by the people, but by the people as composing distinct States, and acting by a majority in each." Democracy would be tempered by aristocracy (as evidenced by representation in the lower house based on broad constituencies), an unlimited number of terms for the president and congressmen, the selection of the president by an electoral college, the election of senators by state legislatures, and checks and balances affecting the popular will among the three branches of government.

CHAPTER 23

Constitutional Debate
in the Press

 The published commentary of summer 1787 overwhelmingly expressed the high expectations of the Constitutional Convention, despite the secrecy of its proceedings. The *Pennsylvania Herald* on May 19, 1787, had set the tone: the decision at Philadelphia would determine "whether the shattered fabric of the original constitution is to be repaired and enlarged, or a new and stately building erected upon the old foundation." In September, before the Constitution was released to the public, the press still hyped the unknown new government. A correspondent in the *Pennsylvania Packet* on September 6 declared that "the year 1776 is celebrated" for "a revolution in favor of liberty. The year 1787, it is expected, will be celebrated with equal joy, for a revolution in favor of Government."

The lines of battle were being drawn, however, between proponents and opponents of the Constitution. As early as August 7, the *Salem Mercury* observed that there were "many men of illiberal sentiments, base and selfish views, and also of weak intellects," who would seek to scuttle the new government. On the other side, "A Federal Centinel," in the *South Carolina Weekly Chronicle,* October 9, noted: "A swarm of paltry scribblers, possessing posts of high emolument . . . the confirmed tools and pensioners of foreign courts" and "men interested in securing a monopoly of our markets . . . are uniformly conspiring against the majesty of the people and are at this moment fabricating the most traiterous productions which human depravity can devise."

The debate over acceptance of the Constitution was fought in newspapers and pamphlets and ultimately in the proceedings of the state ratifying conventions. The fundamental issue was whether republican government should be established at the national level or remain with the states. The great majority of newspapers endorsed the Constitution. Thus, in shaping public opinion, opponents of the Constitution were at a disadvantage, although most newspapers, at one time or another, opened their columns to letters opposing the Constitution.

One ploy greatly enhanced the cause of the Constitution's proponents. The contest over ratification was essentially one between nationalists and localists. Those who had advocated a strong central government in the past had not objected to being styled nationalists. But realizing that "national" had the connotation of a consolidated government at the expense of state sovereignty, supporters of the Constitution seized on the opportunity to call themselves Federalists. Actually, this name was more fitting for the critics of the Constitution because it derived from the Latin word meaning a league or treaty as opposed to union. In appropriating Federalist for themselves, the nationalists successfully cast the opponents of the Constitution as Antifederalists.

To dissipate fears of too strong a government, the Federalists tried to sell the Constitution as preserving, at least partially, the principle of federalism. James Madison emphasized that it was the people, "as the supreme authority in each state," who passed on ratification. "In this relation, then the new Constitution will, if established, be a *federal,* and not a *national* Constitution." Furthermore, the jurisdiction of the central government "is limited to certain enumerated objects, which concern all the members of the republic." In sum, the Constitution "is neither a national nor a federal Constitution, but a composition of both" (*The Federalist,* numbers 14 and 39).

Although a war of words ensued among most newspapers, the contest over the Constitution received the greater attention in those large states that had significant economic, political, and sectional divisions within their borders—Massachusetts, New York, Pennsylvania, and Virginia. For both the adoption of the Constitution and the creditable establishment of the new government, acceptance by those states was of high importance. In most instances, the published letters and essays were written for the purpose of influencing delegates to the state ratifying conventions. Frequently, the press debates turned into a series of assertions and rebuttals by two individuals, who wrote under pseudonyms. This was the case in the opening round of the debate in New York.

Seven "Cato" letters (attributed to Governor George Clinton of New York), appearing between September 27, 1787 and January 3, 1788, argued Antifederalist views, and two letters of "Caesar" (with Alexander Hamilton purportedly the author), published on October 1 and 17, 1787, defended the Constitution. "Cato" advised against the hasty adoption of the Constitution and predicted that if the new government went into effect, "the science of government will become intricate, and perplexed, and mysterious for you to understand and observe." He objected to the Constitution primarily because of the wide taxing power it gave, because it encouraged a monarchical presidency, and because of aristocratic features in both houses of the national legislature; republicanism was viable only in small nations or states. "Caesar" charged "Cato" with exploiting the passions and prejudices of the common sort of people, and declared: "I am not much attached to the majesty of the multitude."

Two Federalist authors received a wide audience. Oliver Ellsworth published thirteen letters of a "Landholder" in several Connecticut newspapers from November 1787 to March 1788, and these were soon reprinted in other states. "Landholder" argued that the Constitution would greatly benefit farmers. In Number I, he said: "Every foreign prohibition on American trade is aimed against the holders and tillers of the land, and they are the men made poor. Your only remedy is such a national government as will make the country respectable; such a supreme government as can boldly meet the supremacy of proud and self-interested nations." Noah Webster's fifty-five-page pamphlet, *An Examination into the Leading Principles of the Federal Constitution,* appeared in

Philadelphia on October 1787. Webster claimed that the Articles of Confederation had hardly brought the people beyond a state of nature; "the first object of the Constitution is to *unite* the states into one *compact society*, for the purposes of government."

The Federalist Papers

The Federalist brilliantly presented the case for the Constitution by showing how the new government would remedy the defects of the Confederation and provide for energetic and representative government by and for all the people. John Quincy Adams, in a eulogy for James Madison in 1836, said that as "a commentary on the Constitution of the United States," it was "of scarcely less authority than the Constitution itself." Despite its redundancies, *The Federalist* has held its own as America's preeminent political treatise. It combines knowledge of historical experience and political theory. Essentially, it calls for a nationalist solution for the crisis in government.

The Federalist aimed not so much to educate the public as to influence delegates to the New York ratifying convention and, secondarily, similar gatherings in other states. In all, the papers consisted of eighty-five letters from "Publius." The first *Federalist* paper appeared in the New York *Independent Journal* on October 27, 1787, and the last in newspaper print on August 15–16, 1788 (though previously published in a book collection). The first volume edition (numbers 1–36) appeared on March 22, 1788, and the second (37–85) on May 28, 1788, well before the New York convention began meeting in Poughkeepsie on June 17. The pseudonym "Publius" affixed to each *Federalist* essay was derived from the name of Publius Valerius, who had founded the Roman Republic after the fall of the last king, Tarquin. Plutarch (ca A.D. 46–120) said of him that "instead of terrible, he was familiar and pleasant to the people."

Although historians have differed over the authorship of some of *The Federalist* papers, it is now reasonably established that Alexander Hamilton wrote 1, 6–9, 11–13, 15–17, 21–36, 59–61, and 65–85; James Madison, 10, 14, and 37–48; and John Jay, 2–5 and 64. Madison most likely also penned 49–58 and 62–63, and he and Hamilton collaborated on 18–20. While *The Federalist* papers had ample distribution in New York, they reached a very small audience elsewhere. Only twenty-four of eighty newspapers published any of *The Federalist* papers; the four Virginia newspapers carried just 1–6 and 16.

Jay examined the question of America's relationship with foreign countries; Hamilton described the deficiencies of the Articles of Confederation and defended the strong powers to be granted by the Constitution; and Madison, with much reference to ancient, medieval, and modern confederacies, argued the worth of a national republic. Some historians have pointed to the "split personality" of *The Federalist*. Specifically, Hamilton emphasized power concentration, and Madison power balance; Madison wrote as a federalist and an exponent of limited government, and Hamilton, as a nationalist and an advocate of energetic government.

A fundamental premise of *The Federalist* is that people cannot subsist together in a society without the protection of government. Men by nature are given to the destructive force of passion, which embraces vanity, pride, and ambition and emotions such as hatred, joy, grief, and fear. Passion influences opinion and action. Ways need to be found to prevent men from acting upon passion, without reason, and doing harm to one another.

Hamilton wrote (15): "Why has government been instituted at all? Because the passions of men will not conform to the dictates of reason and justice, without constraint." Madison (51): "But what is government itself but the greatest of all reflections on human nature? If men were angels, no government would be necessary." Thus, it follows that "if individuals enter into a state of society, the laws of that society must be the supreme regulator of their conduct" (Hamilton, 33). The "vigor of government is essential to the security of liberty," and government should have "the quantity of power necessary to the accomplishment" of the "objects to be provided by a federal government" (Hamilton, 1)—the means adequate to meet the ends. Under the new Constitution, the central government would operate on the people as a whole and as individuals, and would be supreme in its assigned spheres.

Energetic Union

"The great and radical vice in the construction of the existing Confederation," wrote Hamilton (15), "is in the principle of LEGISLATION for STATES or GOVERNMENTS, in their CORPORATE or COLLECTIVE CAPACITIES, and as contradistinguished from the INDIVIDUALS of whom they consist." The central government should have powers to enforce its laws upon the people. "It is essential to the idea of law that it be attended with a sanction." Powers were needed in order to answer "the principal purposes" of the union: namely, common defense, including "the preservation of the public peace"; the "regulation of commerce with other nations and between the States"; and "the superintendence of our intercourse, political and commercial, with foreign countries." Above all, Hamilton stressed the need to maintain the common defense through full military powers of the central government. "These powers ought to exist without limitation, *because it is impossible to foresee or to define the extent and variety of national exigencies, and the correspondent extent and variety of the means which may be necessary to satisfy them*" (23).

Hamilton carefully argued that there was no need to fear oppression from the national government. The Constitution provided for only a "partial union or consolidation," with the states retaining "all the rights of sovereignty" not "*exclusively* delegated to the United States" (32). Furthermore, "the resources of the Union would not be equal to the maintenance of an army considerable enough to confine the larger States within the limits of their duty" (16).

Madison noted that the Constitutional Convention had faced squarely the problem of "combining the requisite stability and energy in Government, with the inviolable attention due to liberty and to the Republican form" (37). In 41–45 he discussed six areas of powers that were necessary for the new government to exercise:

1. Security against foreign danger; 2. Regulation of the intercourse with foreign nations; 3. Maintenance of harmony and proper intercourse among the States;

4. Certain miscellaneous objects of general utility; 5. Restraint of the States from certain injurious acts; 6. Provisions for giving due efficacy to all these powers.

By "general utility," Madison meant a variety of powers, such as determining the location of the nation's capital, admitting new states, providing for territorial governments, and upholding the validity of the public debt. "Due efficacy" equated with the "necessary and proper" and welfare clauses of the Constitution.

"Energy in the executive is a leading character in the definition of good government," wrote Hamilton (70). A strong executive was needed for protection against "foreign attacks"; "steady administration of the laws"; "the protection of property against those irregular and high-handed combinations which sometimes interrupt the ordinary course of justice"; and "the security of liberty against the enterprises and assaults of ambition, of faction, and of anarchy."

To Hamilton, the new federal judiciary would bring "firmness and independence" in checking the excesses of the legislature and the executive. Although Jay and Madison avoided any definite discussion on this topic, Hamilton, in 65 and 78–83, argued that the federal judiciary would not only serve as a safe counterpoise of power to the legislature and the presidency but would also have a unique role as preserver of the Constitution. It would also put a check on too much democracy. The federal judiciary, however, could not infringe on the republican principle that the legislature was the supreme lawmaking body.

Of the three branches,

> the judiciary from the nature of its functions, will always be the least dangerous to the political rights of the Constitution; because it will be least in a capacity to annoy or injure them. The executive not only dispenses the honors but holds the sword of the community. The legislature not only commands the purse but prescribes the rules by which the duties and rights of every citizen are to be regulated. The judiciary, on the contrary, has no influence over either the sword or the purse; no direction either of the strength or of the wealth of the society, and can take no active resolution whatever. It may truly be said to have neither FORCE nor WILL but merely judgment (78).

Hamilton believed that the Constitution by implication conferred on the federal judiciary the right of judicial review. "The interpretation of the laws is the proper and peculiar province of the courts" (78). The Constitution is fundamental law and superior to statutory law. The Supreme Court, therefore, can decide whether legislation conforms to the Constitution. This did not mean that the judicial authority rated higher than the legislative, but only that the power of the people was superior to both.

The Extended Republic

In *The Federalist*, Madison sought to assure Americans that the Constitution incorporated principles of federalism and republicanism. "The people will be represented in the same proportion and on the same principle as they are in the legislature of a particular state," and the Senate has equal state representation. "The executive power will be derived from a very compound source" (39). The operation of powers is divided between the national and local governments, with separate jurisdictions. But the question that challenged Madison the most was whether the new government could be a republican one. If the Constitution "be found to depart from the republican character, its advocates must abandon it as no longer defensible" (39).

Only a republican government, Madison thought, was "reconcilable" with the "principles of the Revolution." He defined a republic as "a government which derives all its powers directly or indirectly from the great body of the people, and is administered by persons holding their offices during pleasure for a limited period, or during good behavior" (39). Madison emphasized that the people's ability to be heard and the protection of their rights could best be procured by an extended republic, such as to be created by the Constitution.

Madison, in 10 and 51, as proved by historians Douglass Adair and Garry Wills, borrowed heavily (ideas, words, and even sentences) from the writings of Scottish philosopher and historian David Hume in constructing a theory that in a large republic a majority will arise, out of a multiversity of interests while also protecting liberty. The core of Madison's thought on the value of a national republic is found in Hume's essay, "Idea of a Perfect Commonwealth" (*Essays*, I, 492):

> In a large government, which is modelled with masterly skill, there is compass and room enough to refine the democracy, from the lower people . . . to the higher magistrates. . . . At the same time, the parts are so distant and remote, that it is very difficult, either by intrigue, prejudice, or passion, to hurry them into any measures against the public interest.

In Madison's extended republic, a public will is created independent of the majority, while also allowing factions to exist but curing them of baneful effects. To Madison (10) a faction is "a number of citizens . . . who are united and actuated by some common impulse of passion, or of interest, adverse to the rights of other citizens, or to the permanent and aggregate interests of the community." Factions could be removed by destroying liberty or making everyone think and act alike. To preserve liberty, therefore, factions must be allowed: "liberty is to faction what air is to fire." There is nothing to fear from factions, however, in an extended republic because each faction or a given minority has to hone down its edges to be accommodated into a majority will. Under the Constitution, both the majority and minority rights are protected.

The Federalist argued that the Constitution did not incorporate the traditional European conception of mixed government—a balance among monarchical, aristocratic, and democratic elements. Instead, a system of checks and balances was set up among the branches of government without relation to social classes. In 14 Madison said that "America can claim the merit of making the discovery of unmixed and extended republics." He agreed with Montesquieu that "there can be no liberty where the legislature and executive powers are united in the same person, or body of magistrates" and if the judiciary is "not separated from the legislative and executive powers." To Madison, though "each department should have a will of its own" (51), the constitutional system allowed a "partial agency" or control of one department over another, thus preventing any concentration of power (47).

Thus, in the national republic, citizens have a double protection against tyranny. A majority will is refined from multivaried interests, and there is the mutual restraint on power by the branches of government that exercise it.

The Antifederalist Response

Many Antifederalists and Federalists agreed on the basic form of the new government—a bicameral legislature, a strong executive, and a national judiciary. But Antifederalists objected that the Constitution created an overly consolidated government, destroying state sovereignty, and that it had provisions that tended to promote a monarchical and aristocratic government. There was also resentment that there had been no legal mandate to create a new constitution. A major concern was stampeding ratification before the new frame of government could be thoroughly examined and discussed.

Most Antifederalists wanted to hold a second convention to make corrections. It was thought that the Constitution resulted from an inordinate overreaction to the disturbances of 1786–87—the fear of anarchy. Richard Henry Lee believed that most of the old government could have been retained and that the supporters of the Constitution were acting as if "we should kill ourselves for fear of dying."

Compared to the Federalists, the Antifederalists generally wanted a weaker central government and more democratic control. But being disorganized, in possession of disparate views, and pressed for time, the Antifederalists had no definite alternative to offer the public. Essentially loyal to the Articles of Confederation, though willing to accept reforms such as those presented in the New Jersey Plan offered at the Convention, the Antifederalists, rather than the Federalists, found themselves on the defensive.

Only five major newspapers persistently supported the Antifederalist cause: the *Independent Gazetteer*, *Freeman's Journal*, and *Pennsylvania Evening Herald* in Philadelphia; and the *New-York Journal* and *American Herald* in Boston. The *American Herald*, the only Antifederalist newspaper of any importance in New England, suffered loss of subscriptions and moved to Worcester in January 1788.

Certain Antifederalist writers made brilliant and substantial contributions, but, for the most part, their writings found only limited distribution. The sixteen essays of "Brutus" (probably Robert Yates), appearing in the *New-York Journal*, from October 18, 1787 to April 10, 1788, attacked the Constitution chiefly for the reach of congressional and judicial authority, a lack of a Bill of Rights, and the failure to fully separate the branches of government.

The eighteen "Centinel" essays (by Samuel Bryan) ran in the Philadelphia newspapers from October 5, 1787 to April 9, 1788. Bryan contended that the "reluctance to change" was "the greatest security of free governments and the principal bulwark of liberty." In the fourth essay, "Centinel" noted: "The evil genius of darkness presided at its [the Constitution's] birth, it came forth under the veil of mystery, its true

features being carefully concealed, and every deceptive art has been ᵕ
to have this spurious brat received as the genuine offspring of heaven-b
To the "Centinel," the supporters of the Constitution were "false detestable ᵣ
(18), "crafty and aspiring despots" (2), and "avaricious office-seekers" (6). Bes.
making specific objections, "Centinel" observed that the power to suppress insurrection worked against freedom, and he predicted civil war in the future.

"Agrippa" (James Winthrop), in eighteen essays in the *Massachusetts Gazette*
that ran from November 23, 1787 to February 5, 1788, considered the chief pitfalls
of the proposed new government to be excessive powers relating to commerce and
the lack of a homogeneous constituency, necessary for successful republican government. Probably the ablest and most influential of the Antifederalist writings was
Observations . . . in a Number of Letters from the Federal Farmer to the Republican
(possibly by Richard Henry Lee); it was carried in few newspapers but achieved
great popularity as a 40-page pamphlet (1787), going through four editions in a few
months. In January 1788 a sequel, *An Additional Number of Letters from the Federal
Farmer* was published, though it was less successful. The "Farmer" emphasized the
Constitution's too eager ratification, consolidation, and lack of a Bill of Rights.

Observations on the New Constitution and on the Federal and State Conventions
(1788), a 19-page pamphlet by "A Columbian Patriot" (reputedly Mercy Otis
Warren), is valuable for its enumeration of eighteen objections to the Constitution.
The author condemned the "fraudulent usurpation at Philadelphia" and the "parti-
zans of monarchy in the state conventions," and predicted "uncontrouled de-
potism." The "Columbian Patriot" called for "a new general Convention, who may
vest adequate powers in Congress, for all national purposes, without annihilating
the individual governments, and drawing blood from every pore by taxes, impositions and illegal restrictions."

Consolidation

All the Antifederalists had criticisms relating to the latitude of powers conferred on
the central government at the expense of the states. "Agrippa" (6) noted that "the
proposed constitution is an actual consolidation of the separate states into one
extensive commonwealth."

Government over a large territory would lose touch with the people, and even
more so as American empire expanded. "Brutus" (1) observed: "The different parts
of so extensive a country could not possibly be made acquainted with the conduct of
their representatives, nor be informed of the reasons upon which measures were
founded"; the "great officers of government would soon become above the controul
of the people, and abuse their power to the purpose of aggrandizing themselves, and
oppressing them." "A Farmer," writing in two Philadelphia newspapers in April
1788, complained:

> The authority of government in a large republic does not equally pervade all the
> parts; nor are the political advantages equally enjoyed by the citizens remote from

the capital . . . ,combinations consequently prevail among the members of the legislature, and this introduces corruption and is destructive of that confidence in government, without which a free republic cannot be supported; besides, the high influential trusts which must be vested in the great officers of state, would at particular times endanger the government, and are necessarily destructive of that equality among the citizens.

"Sydney," writing in the *New York Journal and Daily Patriotic Register* in June 1788, feared that "the happiness of the people may be totally prostrated," with "the general government arrogating to itself the right of interfering in the most minute objects of internal police, and the most trifling domestic concerns of every state, by possessing a power of passing laws" for the general welfare.

Antifederalists considered a standing army, as did "Brutus" (10), as "dangerous to liberty" and a "means of overturning the best constitutions of government." There was also fear of national control of militia.

The necessary and proper, general welfare, and supreme law of the land clauses in the Constitution would provide for a progressive encroachment on the authority of the states. Powers to coerce obedience from the people and to levy and collect direct taxes would especially enhance the consolidationist tendencies of the new government.

Aristocracy

The Constitution "is a most daring attempt to establish a despotic aristocracy among freemen that the world has ever witnessed," declared "Centinel" (1). The new political system "is devoid of all responsibility or accountability to the great body of the people, and that so far from being a regular balanced government, it would be in practice a *permanent* ARISTOCRACY."

Because of inadequate representation of the people and a large territory to be governed, Antifederalists thought that mostly "natural aristocrats" would be elected to the House of Representatives. The "Federal Farmer" (7 and 9) claimed that normally three categories of persons would stand for the legislature: "men who form the natural aristocracy"; "popular demagogues"; and "the substantial and respectable part of the democracy." Occasionally, the demagogues "are often politically elevated. . . . they often have some abilities, without principle, and rise into notice by their noise and arts." Members of the third category, which includes "the yeomanry, the subordinate officers, civil and military, the fishermen, mechanics and traders, many of the merchants and professional men," would not be well enough known to be elected from large districts.

Most Antifederalists felt that the failure to establish a clearly delineated separation of powers among the branches of government would encourage corruption and rule by a cabal. George Mason's *Objections to the Constitution of Government Formed by the Convention* (1787), published as a broadside, lamented that there was no constitutional council to assist the president. Thus, the president will generally be directed by Minions and Favourites—or He will become a Tool to the Senate—or a Council of State will grow out of the principal Officers of the great Departments; the worst and most dangerous of all Ingredients for such a Council, in a free Country; for they may be induced to join in any dangerous or oppressive Measures, to shelter themselves.

The Senate could become an aristocratic junto. Antifederalists did not object so much to the representation by states in that body, but they disliked its independence from the states. The six-year terms for senators were too long, and, without limitation, senators could serve indefinitely. There was too much fusion of power of the Senate with that of the executive, especially relating to treaty-making, appointments, the vice president as head of the Senate, the trial of impeachment, and rejection (or veto) of money bills.

The absence of term limitations in officeholding would bode ill for the national republic in the future, the Antifederalists said. Once in office, a person would have the resources of incumbency to draw on to aid reelection. Mercy Otis Warren, in her pamphlet attacking the Constitution, stated a common Antifederalist view:

> There is no provision for a rotation, nor any thing to prevent the perpetuity of office in the same hands for life; which by a little well timed bribery, will probably be done to the exclusion of men of the best abilities from their share in the offices of government—By this neglect we lose the advantages of that check to the overbearing insolence of office, which by rendering him ineligible at certain periods, keeps the mind of man in equilibrio, and teaches him the feeling of the governed, and better qualifies him to govern in his turn.

Congress's authority to determine the salaries of its members and to regulate the time, place, and manner of federal elections would also contribute to aristocratic government. "Aristocracy," Mercy Otis Warren cautioned, is "a formidable foe to public virtue, and the prosperity of a nation—that under such a government her patriots become mercenaries—her soldiers, cowards, and the people slaves."

Bill of Rights

The Antifederalists agreed on the necessity for a Bill of Rights. But by placing so much emphasis on such a remedy, they helped obscure other arguments in the public forum.

The Federalists contended that the Constitution, with its enumerated powers conferred on the national government and certain limitations on the states, was in itself a Bill of Rights. They realized, however, the importance of the issue of a declaration of rights—the fulcrum on which the Constitution would be accepted or rejected in the ratifying conventions. Thus, the Federalists themselves made a Bill of Rights sort of "a campaign pledge." They believed that a Bill of Rights would not materially alter the Constitution or the new government to be created. In the Antifederalist view, however, a Bill of Rights would further protect the rights of minorities and individuals against the majority.

The very idea that the American government is derived from the consent of the people meant that the people could contract for expressed guarantees of their liberties. "A bill of rights is essential to the security of the persons and property of the people," said "Agrippa" (18). "It is an idea favourable to the interest of mankind at large, that government is founded in compact." "Brutus" (2) stated that a Bill of Rights was an obligation of a government created by the people:

> When a building is to be erected which is intended to stand for ages, the foundation should be firmly laid. The constitution proposed to your acceptance, is designed not for yourselves alone, but for generations yet unborn. The principles, therefore, upon which the social compact is founded, ought to have been clearly and precisely stated, and the most express and full declaration of rights to have been made.

Power corrupts and therefore should be limited. As "Centinel" (2) commented: "Universal experience demonstrates the necessity of the most express declarations and restrictions, to protect the rights and liberties of mankind, from the silent, powerful and ever active conspiracy of those who govern." A Bill of Rights in itself will inspire a spirit of liberty. Thus, "A Delegate Who Has Catched Cold," in the *Virginia Independent Chronicle,* June 18 and 25, 1788, said that an enumeration of rights, "in [the] head of the new constitution, can inspire and conserve the affection for the native country, they will be the first lesson of the young citizens becoming men, to sustain the dignity of their being."

Neither the states' declarations of rights nor the Constitution itself offered any protection of rights from infringement by the national government. Thus, George Mason, in his *Observations,* stated: "The laws of the general government being paramount to the laws and constitutions of the several States, the Declaration of Rights in the separate States are no security." The Antifederalists thought the necessary and proper clause was similar to Parliament's Declaratory Act of 1766, which had claimed legislative jurisdiction over the colonies "in all cases whatsoever."

The Antifederalists challenged such a Federalist view as held by James Sullivan in his "Cassius" letter (8) in the *Massachusetts Gazette* on December 14, 1787, that if Congress or the federal government in general wanted to establish "an aristocratical or despotick government," a Bill of Rights would not "be any obstacle to their proceedings." "Agrippa" (18), in rebuttal, said that any legislature without checks regarding the rights of individuals constituted a forfeiture of the power of the people as well as denial of protection of minority rights. "It is therefore as necessary to defend an individual against the majority in a republick as against the king in a monarchy."

Antifederalist authors demanded guarantees for three kinds of rights: freedom of the press, freedom of conscience, and due process in legal procedure. The Constitution is silent on the freedom of the press. In prohibiting religious qualifications for office, the Constitution, by implication, left open religious tests in all other areas. Thus, a need existed for a declaration of separation of church and state. As to procedural guarantees, the Antifederalists wanted recognition of due process such as the right to grand jury indictment, trial by jury, and confrontation of witnesses, and prohibition of general search and seizure and cruel and unusual punishment.

In addition, Antifederalists sought to have certain specific powers granted to Congress removed or narrowed, in such areas as determining the election procedure, regulating interstate commerce, and levying direct taxes. Judicial power should be limited to original jurisdiction (thus excluding the trial of cases between a state and citizens of another state). Each state should have sole command over its own militia, and no federal troops should be stationed within a state except to guard public stores. Some Antifederalists wanted a clause in the Constitution stating that document did not deprive persons of the protection of state bills of rights. As an immediate goal, the Antifederalists called for a second convention, which, besides making changes in the Constitution itself, would adopt amendments for the guarantee of rights and also the affirmation of ungranted powers being reserved to the states.

CHAPTER 24

Triumph of the Federalists

 "The Ratification of the Conventions of nine States, shall be sufficient for the Establishment of this Constitution between the States so ratifying the Same." So read the final article of the Constitution. The framers, hoping for a quick acceptance, did not want the document to be mired down in the politics and deliberations of legislative assemblies. Undoubtedly aiding a decision for ratification was the poor voter turnout to select delegates to the state conventions. Because of haste in calling conventions in most states, apathy, inclement weather, and muddy roads, only one-third of qualified citizens participated in the elections for convention delegates.

Most delegates at the state ratifying conventions agreed on a stronger union and a republican form of government. The leading question in most of the state conventions, however, was whether to approve the document as it was or whether to insist on amendments that would place further limits on federal power and also specify guarantees of liberties for individual citizens.

In three states, the Constitution was approved unanimously, and in four others, by substantial majorities; a decidedly partisan battle ensued in the other six states. In the end, seven states coupled ratification with a nonbinding recommendation for amendments, which emphasized rights protection. Although the conventions produced some bitterness, which would be carried over into subsequent political rivalry, few persons sought to overturn the decision once it was made. Write Michael Gillespie and Michael Lienesch (1989): "Ultimately ratification was not a war, which one side won and the other lost; it was more like a plan for peace, preconditioned by shared frustrations and shared hopes, a process in which, in the end, both sides emerged as winners" (p. 18).

Federalist/Antifederalist Profile

Delegates to the state ratifying conventions reflected the views of the majority of their constituents. No single factor explains why persons chose one side or the other. Although the ratification contest may be regarded as "fundamentally an economic conflict," writes Forrest McDonald (1958), there was no "single set of alignments on the issue of ratification that would explain the contest as one in which economic self-interest was the principal motivating force" (pp. 398–99).

360

Geographical location and sections were important determinants as to Federalist or Antifederalist support. Federalists were more likely to be found at ports, market towns, settled and urban areas, and along navigable rivers. Opponents tended to live in scattered, isolated areas. Except for the far frontier, debtors and small property holders in the hinterland did not feel they had anything to gain from the Constitution and hence were either indifferent or hostile to ratification. Farmers, who accounted for 75 percent of the total American population, were split mainly as to whether or not they produced for subsistence only (Antifederalist) or for export or at least had commercial expectations (Federalist).

Historians now discount Charles A. Beard's contention that ownership of personalty (chiefly public securities) played an important role among supporters of the Constitution in the state ratifying conventions as well as among the framers of the document (see Chapter 22). To Beard, the contest involved agrarianism versus fluid capital. Rather, a variety of economic interests, as they relate to specific location, influenced decisions on the Constitution.

McDonald (1958) investigated the personalty holdings of members of the ratifying conventions and found that such ownership was about equal on each side. The fact that no votes were cast against the Constitution in Delaware, New Jersey, and Georgia in itself disproves ownership of personalty as a compelling factor. Very few members of the ratifying conventions of New Hampshire and North Carolina on either side held securities (a combined total of 12.7 percent for New Hampshire, and 3.5 and 5.9 percent for each of the two North Carolina conventions). McDonald found personalty holders among delegates in Rhode Island to be 50 percent for Federalists and 47 percent for Antifederalists; Virginia, 40.5 percent to 34.2 percent; and Maryland, 17.4 percent to 27.3 percent, respectively. In Pennsylvania, South Carolina, and New York, Antifederalists held more personalty than did the Federalists: in Pennsylvania, 50 percent for Federalists and 73.9 percent for Antifederalists; in South Carolina, 43 percent to 71 percent; and in New York, 50 percent to 63 percent, respectively. Only in two states did delegate supporters of the Constitution have substantially more securities than did opponents: Massachusetts, 31 percent for Federalists and 10.1 percent for Antifederalists, and in Connecticut, 36.7 percent to 15 percent. Robert E. Brown (1956) observes that at the New York convention fourteen nonsecurity holders voted with the sixteen security holders to ratify the Constitution.

Wealth in land and slaves among the planter aristocracy also did not serve as an indicator of whether a person was for or against the Constitution. Robert E. Thomas (1953) notes that for delegates to the Virginia convention, twenty-three Antifederalists had 962 slaves for an average of 42 per owner (the slaveholdings of fifty-five Antifederalists were not determined), and twenty-six Federalists possessed 1,019 slaves for an average of 39 per owner (no information was available for the other sixty-three Federalists). Jackson T. Main (1961/1974) found that sixty-seven Virginia delegates (thirty-six Federalists and thirty-one Antifederalists) had 1,000 or more acres of land. Of the largest landholders with 5,000 or more acres, eleven were Federalists and seven Antifederalists.

Alexander Hamilton was not far off the mark as to who would likely support or oppose the Constitution; he made the estimate in his "Conjectures about the

New Government," written September 17–30, 1787. Supporting the Constitution, he said, would be those who were influenced by the framers, such as George Washington; "most men of property" who wished protection "against domestic violence and the depredations which the democratic spirit is apt to make on property"; persons with commercial interests; "Creditors of the United States"; and simply those who were convinced of the inadequacy of the Confederation and the need for change. Opposed to the Constitution would be

> many *inconsiderable* men in possession of considerable offices under the state governments . . . some *considerable* men in office possessed of talents and popularity . . . for their own aggrandizement. . . . add to these causes the disinclination of the people to taxes, and of course to a strong government—the opposition of all men much in debt who will not wish to see a government established one object of which is to restrain the means of cheating Creditors—the democratical jealousy of the people which may be alarmed at the appearance of institutions that may seem calculated to place the power of the community in a few hands and to raise a few individuals to stations of great eminence.

Opponents to the Constitution were likely to be found among debtors, state paper money advocates, and those who wanted to prevent recovery of loyalist property. On the other hand, shippers and manufacturers favored the Constitution. Shipowners wanted to control the carrying trade for themselves and also have entry into the international carrying trade. Manufacturers and urban craftsmen wanted protection for the domestic market. There was also need to protect and expand American fisheries. Large landowners who were heavily involved in the export trade wanted federal trade and navigation laws.

Traditional partisan politics and class antagonism within the states, usually indicative of east-west tensions, affected the views of delegates at the ratifying conventions. To some, Whig ideology became rooted in the context of local and states' rights. A cosmopolitan outlook, rather than a provincial one, certainly inclined a person toward a national government more so than a loose confederation of states. Religion, however, had no significant role in determining support for or against the Constitution, with members of denominations being divided because of other interests. One exception was the Virginia Baptist Association's unanimous opposition to the Constitution because of that document's failure to offer protection to religious liberty.

The Nine "Pillars"

The Constitution sailed through the Delaware, New Jersey, Georgia, Connecticut, and Maryland conventions, but met ardent opposition in the Pennyslvania, Massachusetts, South Carolina, and New Hampshire delegate gatherings. Delaware was the first to ratify, on December 7, by a vote of 30–0. The *Massachusetts Centinel* of December 26 printed the Delaware acceptance resolution, prefacing it with "FEDERAL CONSTITUTION The FIRST PILLAR of a great FEDERAL SUPERSTRUCTURE." The

Delaware ratifiers, mainly small farmers, expected the new government would protect commerce and flour milling and assume the state's indebtedness.

The first real test over the Constitution occurred at the Pennsylvania convention. Division between Federalists and Antifederalists followed the state's traditional party alignment—the Republicans (Federalists) versus the Radicals, or Constitutionalists (Antifederalists). The latter wanted to preserve the state constitution of 1776, with its democratic emphasis, and feared permanent political domination by Philadelphia lawyers and merchants. The Federalists, led by Robert Morris, James Wilson, Thomas McKean, and Noah Webster, had support from the great merchants, creditors, nearby farmers, and urban artisans and tradesmen. John Smilie, William Findley, and Robert Whitehill were the floor managers for the Antifederalist delegates, who came almost entirely from the western section of the state, where the population was mostly Scotch-Irish yeomen. One-half of the convention delegates had seen military service, but among the Antifederalists, only one had held a rank higher than captain. The Antifederalists ran the gamut of objections to the Constitution, not the least being the fear of a standing army and the exclusive authority of the national government to issue money. The convention, meeting November 21–December 15, witnessed heated debates. Finally, the Federalists quashed an Antifederalist effort to declare for amendments and a second Federal convention, and instead called for a vote on the Constitution, which passed 42–23.

No opposition appeared in the New Jersey convention, which, on December 18, became the third state to ratify, by a vote of 38–0. Lacking a good port, New Jersey was dependent on New York and Philadelphia for shipping, and wanted a federal government that would remove the impost duties of New York and Pennsylvania. Besides its diversified agriculture, New Jersey had 1,200 manufacturing establishments, chiefly ironworks, sawmills, and gristmills. The state hoped that the nation's capital would be located on the Delaware River.

Georgia followed in January 2, 1788, with a vote of 26–0. Factors propelling ratification were the immediate danger of a Creek Indian uprising; a disputed border with Spanish Florida and in the western country; and currency depreciation. Otherwise, the state had little motive to ratify, for it was undergoing economic prosperity.

Connecticut ratified on January 9 (128–40). In the doldrums economically, the state, like New Jersey, would gain from the federal government's sole power to levy tariffs. It was expected that a new federal government would assume the state's debts. With a dense population and no new farmland available, Connecticut hoped to promote manufactures. The Antifederalist ranks were made up of men who held state office and represented debtor interests.

When delegates to the Massachusetts convention assembled on January 9, 1788, a majority by twenty were opposed to the Constitution. If the Constitution failed in Massachusetts, the later narrow victories in Virginia and New York might not have occurred, and with the refusal of North Carolina and Rhode Island, there would not have been the requisite nine states. Forty-six Massachusetts towns, of which two-thirds were probably Antifederalist, did not select delegates. The coastal counties were strongly Federalist, and the interior region, Antifederalist.

From the outset of the convention, Federalists had by far the superior leaders, men of distinction: Nathaniel Gorham, Theophilus Parsons, Theodore Sedgwick, Fisher Ames, former governor James Bowdoin, and Generals William Heath and Benjamin Lincoln. Much depended on the stance taken by the revered leaders Samuel Adams and John Hancock, both of whom were noncommittal at the start of the proceedings. Wrote Rufus King, also a Federalist delegate, to James Madison on January 30: "If Mr. Hancock does not disappoint our present Expectations our wishes will be gratified. But his character is not entirely free from a portion of caprice." Leading Antifederalists—men such as Nathan Dane and Elbridge Gerry—did not attend, and the Antifederalist cause was taken up by obscure individuals, namely, William Widgery, Phaneul Bishop, Samuel Thompson, and Samuel Nasson.

The Massachusetts Antifederalists, with Shays's Rebellion fresh on their minds, were afraid of extending government powers at any level. They viewed themselves as championing the "little folks" against privileged merchants, lawyers, and speculators. Amos Singletary, an elderly delegate from Worcester County, declared:

These lawyers, and men of learning, and moneyed men, that talk so finely, and gloss over matters so smoothly, to make us poor illiterate people swallow down the pill, expect to get into Congress themselves; they expect to be the managers of this Constitution, and get all the power and all the money into their own hands, and then they will swallow up all us little folks, like the great *Leviathan*, Mr. President; yes, just as the whale swallowed up *Jonah*. This is what I am afraid of.

The Federalists succeeded in the delaying tactic of having the Constitution considered section by section, thereby postponing a vote for three weeks. Samuel Adams was won over, being influenced by 400 Boston mechanics in a meeting endorsing the Constitution unanimously. John Hancock also declared for the Constitution upon receiving promise of Federalist support for governor and vice president, even possibly for president if Washington should decline the office. The Federalists also took leadership in the pledge to work for amendments in the Congress. On February 6, the Massachusetts convention approved the Constitution, 187–168; the coastal region 131–29 for, and the west, 139–56 against.

The Maryland convention, held on April 21–28, made fast work in adopting the Constitution (63–11), even though the opposition consisted of important leaders such as Luther Martin, three-term governor William Paca, Samuel Chase, and John F. Mercer. It was hoped that the funding of the national debt would cause appreciation of state specie certificates. Merchants and manufacturers of Baltimore and planters raising wheat on exhausted tobacco lands for the export market wanted a stronger federal government.

The main debates over the Constitution in South Carolina occurred in the legislature during the January 1788 session, as it considered whether to call a ratifying convention. Rawlins Lowndes ably led the Antifederalists. Not unexpectedly, division followed an alignment of westerners versus lowcountry "nabobs." Opponents feared subordination of states' rights and curtailment of state powers over currency. They also stressed northern domination, especially interference with commerce and the slave trade. Lowndes declared during the legislative debates: "We are now under a most excellent constitution—a blessing from Heaven, that has stood the test of time, and given us liberty and independence; yet we are impatient to pull down that fabric which we raised at the expense of our blood." The convention met on May 12–23, with Aedanus Burke championing the Antifederalist cause and Charles Pinckney and Edward Rutledge the Federalist. Assumption of state debts and military protection were influential arguments for the Federalists. The vote for the Constitution, 149–73, was divided along sectional lines: 121–16 of the lowcountry for, and 57–28 of the backcountry against.

A majority of delegates to the New Hampshire convention, which met on February 13, 1788, at Exeter, opposed the Constitution. Federalist support came from representatives of those who lived along the coast and the Connecticut, Merrimack, and Piscataqua rivers. It was expected that federal regulation would benefit fishing, shipping, and the export trade in lumber and farm commodities. The Antifederalists had the disadvantage in that most of their delegates were poor farmers and debtors, with unknown leaders such as Abel Parker, Joshua Atherton, and Charles Barrett. Men of public experience and superior ability headed the Federalist cause: John Langdon, Governor John Sullivan, Chief Justice Samuel Livermore, and John Taylor Gilman. The Federalists succeeded in obtaining a recess after a week of debate; the delegates then reconvened at Concord. During the long interruption, Maryland and South Carolina had ratified, and the Federalists assiduously promoted their cause among the public. With recommendations for amendments similar to those of Massachusetts, a vote of 57–47, on June 21, afforded New Hampshire the distinction of being the ninth state to ratify the Constitution.

Virginia

When the 170-member convention met in Richmond on June 2, eight states had ratified the Constitution, and New Hampshire was about to do so. Although Patrick Henry estimated that four-fifths of the delegates opposed the Constitution, actually the number of Federalists and Antifederalists was about equal. William Grayson noted that the decision would be "suspended by a hair." Four of the state's most prominent citizens were absent: George Washington, Thomas Jefferson (in France), Richard Henry Lee, and the dying Thomas Nelson. Washington's well-known preference for the Constitution and the certainty that he would be the first president if Virginia ratified made the former commander in chief present in spirit if not in fact. Men of great ability lined up on both sides: for the Antifederalists, Patrick Henry, George Mason, William Grayson, James Monroe, Benjamin Harrison, and John Tyler; and for the Federalists, James Madison, Edmund Randolph, John Marshall, George Nicholas, Henry Lee, George Wythe, and Edmund Pendleton. The 104 war veterans among the delegates were equally divided. Debates between the shy and soft-spoken Madison and the flamboyant Henry dominated the convention proceedings.

Most issues were national: debts owed British merchants, control of trade (international and interstate), and western concerns—Indian depredations, opening the Mississippi, and internal improvements. The Federalists tried to assuage fears of a stronger central government and pointed out that, although the new system would function directly upon the people, it was still dependent on the states. The Antifederalists objected principally to consolidation, unlimited powers, vastness of territorial jurisdiction, loss of military and taxation authority, exclusion of guarantees of state residual powers, and northern domination. George Mason noted that concurrent powers could not exist—one must destroy the other.

Patrick Henry argued that there was no urgency about establishing a new government. "The first thing I have at heart is American liberty," he said; "the second thing is American Union." A decision to adopt the Constitution "is a resolution as radical as that which separated us from Great Britain," Henry also declared; "our rights and privileges are endangered, and the sovereignty of the states will be relinquished." Virginians would be binding themselves "hand and foot." Henry denounced the scheme for representation: "Virginia is as large as England. Our proportion of representatives is but ten men. In England they have five hundred and fifty-eight." The presidency would be too much like a monarchy: "If your American chief be a man of ambition and abilities, how easy is it for him to render himself absolute! The army is in his hands."

On June 25, Patrick Henry's motion to adopt amendments before a vote on ratification failed, 88–80. Then the delegates gave approval to the Constitution, 89–79. Two days later, the convention, before adjourning, ordered twenty-one amendment recommendations be sent to the new Congress.

The Virginia delegate vote on the Constitution showed distinctions according to seven geographical sections. Delegates from the Tidewater region decided 49–29 against the Constitution. The Antifederalists there had greater attachment to Whig political principles and the state government than did their opponents. The Northern Neck, which was mainly Federalist because of commercial interests, went in the affirmative, 19–5. Southside (south of the James River) and Piedmont (just east of the Blue Ridge) rejected the Constitution by 28–2 and 12–8, respectively. The small farmers of the two regions saw little advantage to a stronger central government, and the Baptists felt that religious liberty would be less secure. The Shenandoah Valley unanimously (14–0) favored ratification. The primary concerns in that region were putting an end to payment of interstate duties to Maryland; improvement of navigation; protection of marketing in grain, whisky, and hemp; more equitable representation and taxation; and opposition to paper money because it drove out specie. The trans-Allegheny area (present-day West Virginia) had interests similar to the Valley, and also wanted protection against Indians as well as expulsion of the British from western posts; the vote went Federalist, 13–1. The small farmers of Kentucky (then part of Virginia) disapproved of the Constitution 11–3 largely because they feared that a central government, dominated by the northern states, would not open navigation of the Mississippi.

New York

In the April election of delegates to the New York ratifying convention, the Antifederalists won forty-six of the sixty-five seats. The convention opened on June 17, with the Antifederalist governor, George Clinton, named as president. Melancton

Smith, John Lansing, and Robert and Abraham Yates led the opposition; prominent Federalist delegates were Alexander Hamilton, Robert R. Livingston, Gouverneur Morris, John Jay, and William Duane. The Antifederalists consisted mostly of yeoman farmers, persons from old families of middle rank, and the newly rich, all of whom wanted greater economic and political opportunity. Upstate isolated farmers especially opposed federal impost duties, which would displace a New York levy and cause higher land taxes. Federalist backing came from commercial landlords and their tenants, creditors, and supporters of loyalist interests and a state bank. New York City merchants and mechanics solidly advocated ratification.

During the debates, the Federalists warned that if New York stayed out of the Union, parts of the state might secede. News of ratification by New Hampshire arrived on June 24 and that of Virginia on July 3. After much debating, the issues narrowed to two: whether ratification should be conditional on acceptance of amendments and whether the state retained a right to withdraw from the Union within a specified time. Hamilton sought the advice of Madison, then in New York City, on the question of conditional acceptance. Madison replied, in a letter of July 20:

> My opinion is that a reservation of a right to withdraw if amendments be not decided on under the form of the Constitution within a certain time, is a *conditional* ratification, that it does not make N. York a member of the New Union. . . . The Constitution requires an adoption *in toto,* and *for ever.*

Hamilton read this opinion to the convention.

A major factor causing some Antifederalists to switch sides was knowledge that other state conventions had forwarded amendments to be considered by the new Congress. On the amendment question, Samuel Jones's motion to substitute "in full confidence" for "upon condition" carried by a vote of 31–29 on July 23. Three days later, the convention approved both the Constitution and a long list of amendments appended to it that were expected to be taken up by Congress (by a vote of 30–27). Strictly considered, New York's ratification was not absolute, but it was sufficient for the state to enter into the Union.

North Carolina and Rhode Island

North Carolina and Rhode Island delayed ratification until after the new government was created. North Carolina's predicament was similar to that of other states. "In all parts of the country," as Jackson T. Main has observed (1961/1974), "the commercial interest with its ramifications, including those who depended primarily and directly upon commerce, were Federal, and the 'non-navigating' folk were Antifederal" (p. 274). Despite sand reefs off the North Carolina coast thwarting deepwater navigation, there was sufficient access to watercraft that the counties around Albemarle and Pamlico sounds were experiencing commercial growth. This area and only three interior and one western (Tennessee) counties were Federalist. Much of the Piedmont region was divided, and other western counties and the southern Tidewater were completely against the Constitution. On the issues, the

Antifederalists denounced federal interference with state paper money and slavery and treaties as law of the land (a major fear was surrender of control of the Mississippi River to Spain).

A convention met at Hillsboro on July 21–28, 1788. James Iredell, William R. Davie, and Governor Samuel Johnston led the Federalists, and Willie Jones, Samuel Spencer, and Griffith Rutherford, the Antifederalists. The convention adopted a declaration of rights but rejected the Constitution (by a vote of 184–93). The ratification of eleven states, however, ended the hope of North Carolina Antifederalists for a second convention. The new government was firmly established, with George Washington as president. North Carolinians held another ratifying convention, at Fayetteville, on November 16–23, 1789, and adopted the Constitution by a vote of 194–77.

Facing the same discrimination from the federal government as North Carolina for being outside the Union, Rhode Island eventually gave up its resistance to the Constitution. Opposition came from a well-organized rural party that had gained power in the spring 1786 elections on a paper money platform. No longer did merchants dominate the legislature. Antifederalists, besides favoring state paper money, advocated direct democracy and opposed increased land taxation. A federal impost duty, instead of a state one, would deprive Rhode Island of a main source of revenue.

The Rhode Island legislature, circumventing the procedure for ratification set forth by the Philadelphia Convention, scheduled a popular referendum on the Constitution in March 1788. The result was a vote of 237 for the Constitution and 2,708 against. The cities of Providence and Newport boycotted the referendum.

For a year, the Rhode Island Assembly managed to forestall authorization of a ratifying convention. But external pressure mounted. In 1789, Congress passed a tariff law, exempting North Carolina and Rhode Island only until January 15, 1790, and a congressional committee recommended that the United States sever "all commercial intercourse" with Rhode Island, beginning on July 1, 1790. By staying out of the Union, Rhode Island would also have to pay its own war debt. There was the possibility that Newport and Providence might secede from the state. At last the legislature reconsidered, and a convention met at South Kingston on March 1–6, only to adjourn until a later time. Henry Merchant, a Newport Federalist, estimated that among the delegates "the Antie's are about ten majority." A few members, however, had a change of mind during the recess. The convention reassembled on May 24, and five days later ratified both the Constitution and twelve amendments proposed by Congress, by the narrowest of any margin in the states, 34–32.

Interregnum

Some diehard Antifederalists did not take their defeat lightly. Riots between Antifederalists and Federalists occurred in Albany on July 4 and in Carlisle, Pennsylvania, on December 26–27, 1788. Otherwise, in the major cities the Constitution was received with exuberance.

On May 1, 1788, Baltimore staged a festival to mark Maryland's ratification. At the firing of seven guns and the shouts of a large crowd, a parade began. The procession included a horse-drawn "Ship Federalist," and each trade marched together under such banners as "May our Trade succeed, and the Union enrich us" and "No Importations, and we shall live." At "Federal-hill" townsmen were treated to dinner and drink at a 3,600-foot circular table. On the Fourth of July, Federalists in ten states celebrated victory. A parade in Philadelphia featured a mobile Corinthian-style temple. Federalists in New York City, not to be outdone, on July 23 conducted a "federal procession" that boasted a 27-foot frigate, *The Hamilton*, pulled by ten horses and manned by sailors and marines who fired the ship's thirty-two guns along the way.

Meanwhile, Congress prepared to turn over the reins of government. Although often lacking a quorum, which had been a long-standing problem, it did amazingly well in clearing up business. Even all thirteen states were in attendance briefly in July and twelve in August. Several laws were passed. On August 28 Congress made its last requisition on the states. Activity in the executive departments greatly dwindled. The secretary at war, Henry Knox, spent the last four months of the year at his home in Maine and in Boston; one of his obligations was to find material for a suit of clothes that George Washington would wear to his inauguration.

Having received notice of ratification of the ninth state, New Hampshire, Congress, on July 2, appointed a committee to report on recommendations "for putting the said constitution into operation in pursuance of the resolution of the late federal Convention." On September 13 Congress voted that the first Wednesday in January "be the day for appointing Electors"; the first Wednesday in February for the electors to "vote for a president"; and the first Wednesday in March "be the time for commencing proceedings under the constitution."

The last time seven states attended Congress was October 8–10. The national legislators had before them a double motion relating to procedures for the commissioners of accounts and to prohibition of the secretary at war from issuing land warrants to former army officers who had not cleared up their paymaster and recruiting records. On October 10, the congressional journal stated, "so the question was lost"—an expression that punctuated the final business of the Confederation Congress.

One or several delegates attended Congress thereafter, although at the end of January 1789 six states and several single delegates from other states presented themselves. From February 19 to March 2 no delegate appeared. On March 2, Secretary Charles Thomson collared Philip Pell on the street and brought him into his office to sign in as an attending delegate. Thomson resigned his secretaryship of Congress on July 23, 1789, and two days later, his former deputy, Roger Alden, on behalf of the new government, became temporarily the custodian of the congressional records and the Great Seal.

At dusk on March 3, in New York City, the nation's capital, thirteen cannon resounded, signaling the end of the Confederation. At dawn the next day, chimes and bells and more cannonade ushered the government under the Constitution into the world.

Signing of the Constitution. **This recent painting by Louis S. Glanzman of the event of Sept. 17, 1787 is the most accurate portrayal of the Constitutional Convention. Standing in the center is George Washington, president of the Convention. On a raised level to his right are (from the viewer's left to right): Thomas Mifflin; Nathaniel Gorham, who chaired the Convention's sessions; and James Wilson. To Washington's left is James Madison. The secretary of the Convention, William Jackson is seated, tucked into the crowd to the left of the picture. Benjamin Franklin is directly in front of Washington. John Dickinson, on bended elbow, lost in concentration over a document, gives appearance of being the odd man in the group. Directly behind Dickinson, with hand on chin, is Roger Sherman.** *Commissioned by the Pennsylvania, Delaware, New Jersey State Societies, Daughters of the American Revolution Independence National Historical Park Collection. Copyright Louis Glanzman, 1987*

Even the new Congress started off with high absenteeism. Not until April 1789 did both houses of Congress jointly have a quorum and thereupon counted the sixty-nine electoral votes from ten states. George Washington was unanimously elected president, and John Adams, with thirty-four votes, vice president.

Independence, Republicanism, Union

The ratification of the Constitution brought to an end the era in which Americans won their independence and created a nation. It remained to build American character committed to the new order, as Michael Lienesch states (1988), "to create a psychology to perpetuate their government" (p. 176).

Out of a growing sense of national identity, Americans had sought national liberty, and consequently nationhood. As J. R. Pole writes (1977):

American unity began as a means rather than an end. The aim in view was liberty in the widest sense, liberty from a form of rule that leading colonials felt to be increasingly out of sympathy with their own interests, oppressive, and humiliating. But they also sought liberty to fulfill their increasingly ambitious aims for the expansion of territorial settlement and commerce, and political unity proved no less valuable as an instrument of these aims than of the original act of national liberation. (p. 143)

In declaring for Independence, Americans embraced certain ideals: all men are created equal and have fundamental rights to life, liberty, property, happiness, and freedom of conscience. Derivative of these ideals are freedom of expression, representative government, free elections, and due process of law. Government arises from the free associating of equal men into a body politic for defined purposes. For the good of the whole society, government is entrusted with control over the exercise of persons' rights, but not their abridgment. To protect rights, government needs to be limited on a constitutional basis, to be an empire of laws and not of men. Since government is derived from the consent of the people, it should be responsive to the general will; if not, the people as a last resort may resist and establish government anew. Ratification of the Constitution by conventions emphasized popular sovereignty and limited the authority of the federal government.

The Founding Fathers expected that virtuous citizens of the future would work to keep the Republic responsive to the will of the people and constrained from arbitrary expansion of its powers. But the new extended Republic ran the hazard of turning into a majoritarian state; although minority dissent would be tolerated, it could not come to full expression. The Constitution, in part, was a document designed to correct excessive democracy and, in so doing, converted an ideology of revolution to one of nationhood.

The government under the Constitution may be considered a failure in public liberty, so notes Hannah Arendt (1963):

> The Revolution, while it had given freedom to the people, had failed to provide a space where this freedom could be exercised. Only the representatives of the people, not the people themselves, had an opportunity to engage in those activities of "expressing, discussing and deciding" [a quote from Ralph Waldo Emerson] which in a positive sense are the activities of freedom. (p. 238)

The Constitution provided "public space only for the representatives of the people, and not for the people themselves" (p. 241). Arendt further contends that "one might even come to the conclusion that there was less opportunity for the exercise of public freedom and the enjoyment of public happiness in the republic of the United States than there had existed in the colonies of British America" (p. 238). "The spirit of revolution" did not "find its appropriate institution" (p. 284).

If some Americans were disappointed that the Revolution had become more conservative than they would have liked and that the new government checked popular democracy, they nevertheless could join with their fellow citizens in the expectation of a new era of freedom and prosperity. Wrote Alexis de Tocqueville a generation later, in an essay on "The Federal Constitution" in his *Democracy in America* (1966 ed.): "How wonderful is the position of the New World, where man has as yet no enemies but himself. To be happy and to be free, it is enough to will it to be so." The American "Union is free and happy like a small nation, glorious and strong like a great one."

The American Revolution indeed had gone full cycle, with the establishment of the new government under the Constitution; but it, too, left the inspirational legacy of the unfinished task of making further reality of full freedom and equality, a beacon at home and abroad. De Tocqueville noted, "the American Revolution ended exactly when ours began."

George Washington, writing to Lafayette on January 29, 1789, expressed contentment in the American achievement:

> While you are quarreling among yourselves in Europe—while one King is running mad—and others acting as if they were already so, by cutting the throats of subjects of their neighbours: I think you need not doubt, My Dear Marquis we shall continue in tranquility here.

The "Spirit of '76" had given birth to a unique experiment in government of the people that would endure if cared for by a virtuous citizenry; then truly the Revolutionaries had bestowed a new order of the ages.

Bibliography

Selected References

Berg, Fred A. *Encyclopedia of Continental Army Units*. Harrisburg, Pa.: Stackpole Books, 1972.

Blanco, Richard. *The American Revolution: An Encyclopedia*. 2 vols. Hamden, Conn.: Garland Publishing, 1993.

Boatner, Mark M. *Encyclopedia of the American Revolution*. New York: David McKay Co., 1966.

Freeman, Douglas S. *George Washington*. Vols. 1–6. New York: Charles Scribner's Sons, 1949–54.

Gephart, Ronald A., comp. *Revolutionary America, 1763–1789: A Bibliography*. 2 vols. Washington, D.C.: Library of Congress, 1984.

Greene, Jack P., and Pole, J. R., eds. *The Blackwell Encyclopedia of the American Revolution*. Cambridge, Mass.: Basil Blackwell, 1991.

Heitman, Francis B. *Historical Register of the Officers of the Continental Army*. Baltimore: Genealogical Publishing Co., 1973, originally published 1914.

Katcher, Philip R. N. *Encyclopedia of English, Provincial and German Army Units, 1775–1783*. Harrisburg, Pa.: Stackpole Books, 1973.

Ward, Christopher. *The War of the Revolution*. 2 vols. New York: Macmillan Co., 1952.

Selected Source Collections
(Other listings in chapter bibliographies)

Boyd, Julian P., ed. *The Papers of Thomas Jefferson*. Vols. 1–14. Princeton, N.J.: Princeton University Press, 1950–58.

Burnett, Edmund C., ed. *Letters of Members of the Continental Congress*. 8 vols. Washington, D.C.: Carnegie Institution, 1921–34.

Butterfield, Lyman H., et al., eds. *The Adams Papers*. Series I, Diaries: *Diary and Autobiography of John Adams*, 4 vols.; Series II, *Adams Family Correspondence, 1761–1782*, 4 vols.; and Series III, the *Papers of John Adams*, 4 vols. to date. Cambridge, Mass.: Belknap Press of Harvard University Press, 1961–79.

Clark, William B., and Morgan, William James, eds. *Naval Documents of the American Revolution*. 9 vols. to date. Washington, D.C.: Naval History Center, 1964–86.

Commager, Henry S., and Morris, Richard B., eds. *The Spirit of 'Seventy Six: The Story of the American Revolution as Told by Participants*. 2 vols. Indianapolis: Bobbs-Merrill Co., 1958.

Davies, Kenneth G., ed. *Documents of the American Revolution*. 21 vols. Shannon, Ireland: Irish University Press, 1972–81.

Elliot, Jonathan, ed. *Debates on the Adoption of the Federal Constitution.* 5 vols. New York: Burt Franklin, 1965, originally published 1888.

Farrand, Max, ed. *The Records of the Federal Convention of 1787.* 4 vols. New Haven, Conn.: Yale University Press, 1911–37.

Ferguson, E. James, et al., eds. *The Papers of Robert Morris, 1781–84.* 7 vols. Pittsburgh: University of Pittsburgh Press, 1973–88.

Force, Peter, ed. *American Archives.* 4th Series, 6 vols. and 5th Series, 3 vols. Washington, D.C.: M. St. Clair, Clarke and Peter Force, 1848–53.

Ford, Worthington C., ed. *Journals of the Continental Congress, 1774–1789.* 34 vols. Washington, D.C.: U.S. Government Printing Office, 1904–37.

Gates, Horatio. Papers. Microfilm edition, New-York Historical Society.

Hutchinson, William T., et al., eds. *The Papers of James Madison.* Vols. 1–11. Chicago and Charlottesville: University of Chicago Press, University Press of Virginia, 1962–77.

Idzerda, Stanley J., ed. *Lafayette in the Age of the American Revolution: Selected Letters and Papers, 1776–1790.* 5 vols. to date. Ithaca, N.Y.: Cornell University Press, 1977–83.

Jensen, Merrill, Kaminski, John P., and Saladino, Gaspare J., eds. *The Documentary History of the Ratification of the Constitution.* Vols. 1–3, 8–10, and 13–16 (projected 20 volumes), Madison, Wis.: Madison House, 1976–93.

Knox, Henry. Papers. Microfilm edition, Massachusetts Historical Society.

Labaree, Leonard W., et al., eds. *The Papers of Benjamin Franklin.* Vols. 1–28. New Haven, Conn.: Yale University Press, 1959–90.

Loyalist Transcripts (Benjamin F. Stevens). Manuscript Books and Papers of the Commission of Enquiry into the Losses and Services of the American Loyalists . . . , 1783–1790. Audit Office Records at the Public Record Office, London. 60 vols. Microfilm edition, New York Public Library.

Moore, Frank, comp. *Diary of the American Revolution, from Newspapers and Original Documents.* 2 vols. New York: Charles Scribner, 1860.

Papers of the Continental Congress. Microfilm edition. National Archives.

Revolutionary War Pension and Bounty-Land Warrant Application Files, Microfilm edition (M804), 2,670 rolls, National Archives (records before 1800 destroyed by fire).

Showman, Richard K., ed. *The Papers of General Nathanael Greene.* 7 vols. to date. Chapel Hill: University of North Carolina Press, 1976–94.

Smith, Paul M., ed. *Letters of Delegates to Congress, 1774–1789.* 19 vols. to date. Washington, D.C.: Library of Congress, 1973–92.

Steuben, Baron von. Papers. Microfilm edition. New-York Historical Society.

Storing, Herbert J., ed. *The Complete Anti-Federalist.* 7 vols. Chicago: University of Chicago Press, 1981.

Syrett, Harold C., ed. *The Papers of Alexander Hamilton.* Vols. 1–5. New York: Columbia University Press, 1961–62.

Washington, George. (1) Papers (complete collection). Microfilm edition, Library of Congress. (2) Fitzpatrick, John C., ed. *The Writings of George Washington.* 39 vols. Washington, D.C.: U.S. Government Printing Office, 1931–44. (3) Abbot, W. W., et al., eds. *The Papers of George Washington.* Revolutionary War Series, 5 vols. to date; Confederation Series, 2 vols. to date. Charlottesville: University Press of Virginia, 1983–93.

Suggested Reading*

CHAPTER 1

Adams, James T. *The American: The Making of a New Man.* New York: Charles Scribner's Sons, 1943.

*A work is cited in the chapter of primary relevance; abbreviated cross-references are included where source is specifically mentioned in the text.

Andrews, Charles M. *The Colonial Background of the American Revolution*. New Haven, Conn.: Yale University Press, 1924.

Axtell, James. *The European and the Indian: Essays in the Ethnohistory of Colonial North America*. New York: Oxford University Press, 1981.

Bailyn, Bernard. *Voyages to the West: A Passage in the Peopling of America on the Eve of the Revolution*. New York: Alfred A. Knopf, 1986.

Berens, John F. *Providence and Patriotism in Early America, 1640–1815*. Charlottesville: University Press of Virginia, 1978.

Bridenbaugh, Carl. *The Spirit of '76: The Growth of American Patriotism Before Independence*. New York: Oxford University Press, 1975.

Brown, Robert E. *Middle-Class Democracy and the Revolution in Massachusetts*. Ithaca, N.Y.: Cornell University Press, 1955.

Buillion, John L. "The Ten Thousand in America": More Light on the Decision on the American Army, 1762–1763." *William and Mary Quarterly*, 3d ser., 43 (1986): 646–57.

Bumsted, J. M. " 'Things in the Womb of Time': Ideas of American Independence, 1633–1763." *William and Mary Quarterly*, 3d ser., 31 (1974): 533–64.

Chichester, Henry M. and Burges-Short, George. *Records and Badges of Every Regiment and Corps of the British Army*. London: Galand Polden, 1902.

Christie, Ian R., and Labaree, Benjamin. *Empire or Independence, 1760–1776. A British-American Dialogue on the Coming of the American Revolution*. Oxford, England: Phaidon Press, 1976.

Colbourn, H. T. *The Lamp of Experience: Whig History and the Intellectual Origins of the American Revolution*. Chapel Hill: University of North Carolina Press, 1965.

———, ed. "A Pennsylvania Farmer at the Court of King George: John Dickinson's London Letters, 1754–56." *Pennsylvania Magazine of History and Biography*, 86 (1962): 241–86, 417–53.

Crevecoeur, J. Hector St. John (Michel-Guillaume St. Jean de). *Letters from an American Farmer*. New York: Fox, Duffield & Co., 1904, originally published in 1782.

Davies, Samuel. *Sermons on Important Subjects*. Vol. 3. New York: J. & J. Harper, 1828.

Dickerson, Oliver M. *The Navigation Acts and the American Revolution*. 2d ed. Philadelphia: University of Pennsylvania Press, 1951.

Dinkin, Robert J. *Voting in Provincial America: A Study of Elections in the Thirteen Colonies, 1689–1776*. Westport, Conn.: Greenwood Press, 1977.

Egnal, Marc. "The Economic Development of the Thirteen Colonies, 1720 to 1775." *William and Mary Quarterly*, 3d ser., 32 (1975): 191–222.

———. "An Economic Interpretation of the American Revolution." *William and Mary Quarterly*, 3d ser., 29 (1972): 3–32.

Evans, Emory G. "Planter Indebtedness and the Coming of the Revolution in Virginia." *William and Mary Quarterly*, 3d ser., 19 (1962): 511–33.

Fischer, David Hackett. *Albion's Seed: Four British Folkways in America*. New York: Oxford University Press, 1989.

Gipson, Lawrence H. "The American Revolution as an Aftermath of the Great War for the Empire, 1754–1763." *Political Science Quarterly*, 65 (1950): 86–104.

———. *The British Empire Before the American Revolution*. Vol. 10. New York: Alfred A. Knopf, 1967.

Greene, Jack P. *Peripheries and Center: Constitutional Development in the Extended Polities of the British Empire and the United States, 1607–1788*. Athens: University of Georgia Press, 1986.

———. *Pursuit of Happiness: The Social Development of Early Modern British Colonies and the Formation of American Culture*. Chapel Hill: University of North Carolina Press, 1988.

———. *The Quest for Power: The Lower Houses of Assembly in the Southern Royal Colonies, 1689–1776*. Chapel Hill: University of North Carolina Press, 1963.

———. "The Seven Years' War and the American Revolution: The Causal Relationship Reconsidered." In *The British Atlantic Empire Before the American Revolution*, ed. Peter Marshall and Glyn Williams. Totowa, N.J.: Frank Cass, 1980, pp. 85–105.

———. "The Social Origins of the American Revolution: An Evaluation and an Interpretation." *Political Science Quarterly*, 88 (1973): 1–22.

Harper, Lawrence A. *The English Navigation Laws: A Seventeenth-Century Experiment in Social Engineering*. New York: Octagon Books, 1964, originally published in 1939.

Higham, John. "Hanging Together: Divergent Unities in American History." *Journal of American History*, 61 (1974): 5–28.

Jones, Alice H. *Wealth of a Nation to Be: The American Colonies on the Eve of the Revolution*. New York: Columbia University Press, 1980.

Kammen, Michael. *Empire and Interests: The American Colonies and the Politics of Mercantilism*. Philadelphia: Lippincott, 1970.

———. *A Rope of Sand: The Colonial Agents, British Politics, and the American Revolution*. Ithaca, N.Y.: Cornell University Press, 1968.

Knollenberg, Bernhard. *Origin of the American Revolution, 1759–1766*. New York: Macmillan Co., 1960.

Kraus, Michael. *Intercolonial Aspects of American Culture on the Eve of the Revolution*. New York: Columbia University Press, 1928.

Labaree, Leonard W. *Royal Government in America: A Study of the British Colonial System Before 1783*. New Haven, Conn.: Yale University Press, 1930.

Leder, Lawrence H. *Liberty and Authority: Early American Political Ideology, 1689–1763*. Chicago: Quadrangle Books, 1968.

McCusker, John J., and Menard, Russell R. *The Economy of British America, 1607–1789*. Chapel Hill: University of North Carolina Press, 1985.

Merritt, Richard L. *Symbols of American Community, 1735–1775*. New Haven, Conn.: Yale University Press, 1966.

Mintz, Steven, and Kellogg, Susan. *Domestic Revolutions: A Social History of American Family Life*. New York: Free Press, 1988.

Morris, Richard B., ed. *The Era of the American Revolution*. New York: Harper & Row, 1965, originally published in 1939.

Nash, Gary B. *Red, White, and Black: The Peoples of Early America*. Englewood Cliffs, N.J.: Prentice-Hall, 1974.

———. *The Urban Crucible: Social Change, Political Consciousness, and the Origins of the American Revolution*. Cambridge, Mass.: Harvard University Press, 1979.

Pargellis, Stanley M. *Lord Loudoun in North America*. New Haven, Conn.: Yale University Press, 1933.

Perkins, Edwin J. *The Economy of Colonial America*. 2d ed. New York: Columbia University Press, 1988.

Pole, J. R. *The Gift of Government: Political Responsibility from the English Restoration to American Independence*. Athens: University of Georgia Press, 1983.

Rogers, Alan. *Empire and Liberty: American Resistance to British Authority, 1755–1763*. Berkeley: University of California Press, 1974.

Sachs, William S., and Hoogenboom, Ari. *The Enterprising Colonials: Society on the Eve of the Revolution*. Chicago: Argonaut, 1965.

Savelle, Max. "The Appearance of an American Attitude Toward External Affairs, 1750–1775." *American Historical Review*, 52 (1947): 655–66.

Simmons, R. C. *The American Colonies: From Settlement to Independence*. New York: W. W. Norton & Co., 1976.

Tucker, Josiah. *Four Tracts Together with Two Sermons on Political and Commercial Subjects*. Gloucester, England: R. Raikes, 1774.

Varg, Paul A. "The Advent of Nationalism, 1758–1776." *American Quarterly*, 16 (1964): 169–81.

Walton, Gary M., and Shepherd, James F. *The Economic Rise of Early America.* London: Cambridge University Press, 1979.

Ward, Harry M. *Colonial America, 1607–1763.* Englewood Cliffs, N.J.: Prentice Hall, 1991.

———. *Unite or Die: Intercolony Relations, 1690–1763.* Port Washington, N.Y.: Kennikat Press, 1971.

Wells, Robert V. *The Population of the British Colonies in America Before 1776.* Princeton, N.J.: Princeton University Press, 1975.

———. *Revolutions in Americans' Lives: A Demographic Perspective on the History of Americans, Their Families and Their Society.* Westport, Conn.: Greenwood Press, 1982.

Wise, John. *A Vindication of the Government of New-England Churches* (1717). Gainesville, Fla.: Scholars' Facsimiles & Reprints, 1958.

Zuckerman, Michael. "The Fabrication of Identity in Early America." *William and Mary Quarterly,* 3d ser., 34 (1977): 183–214.

CHAPTER 2

Alden, John R. *Stephen Sayre: American Revolutionary Adventurer.* Baton Rouge: Louisiana State University Press, 1983.

Andrews, Charles M. *The Colonial Period of American History.* Vol. 4: *England's Commercial and Colonial Policy.* New Haven, Conn.: Yale University Press, 1959, originally published in 1938.

Ayling, Stanley. *The Elder Pitt, Earl of Chatham.* New York: David McKay Co., 1976.

Bailyn, Bernard. *The Ideological Origins of the American Revolution.* Cambridge, Mass.: Harvard University Press, 1967.

Bargar, B. D. *Lord Dartmouth and the American Revolution.* Columbia: University of South Carolina Press, 1965.

Bolingbroke, Henry St. John, viscount. *Letters on the Spirit of Patriotism and on the Idea of a Patriot King.* Oxford, England: Clarendon Press, 1926.

Bonwick, Colin. *English Radicals and the American Revolution.* Chapel Hill: University of North Carolina Press, 1977.

Bradley, James E. *Popular Politics and the American Revolution in England.* Macon, Ga.: Mercer University Press, 1986.

Brewer, John. *Party Ideology and Popular Politics at the Accession of George III.* Cambridge, England: Cambridge University Press, 1976.

Brooke, John. *The Chatham Administration, 1766–1768.* New York: St. Martin's Press, 1956.

———. *King George III.* New York: McGraw-Hill Book Co., 1972.

Chapman, Gerald W. *Edmund Burke: The Practical Imagination.* Cambridge, Mass.: Harvard University Press, 1967.

Clark, Dora M. *British Opinion and the American Revolution.* New York: Russell & Russell, 2d ed., 1966.

Derry, John. *English Politics and the American Revolution.* London: J. M. Dent & Sons, 1976.

Dickinson, H. T. "Whiggism in the Eighteenth Century." In *The Whig Ascendancy: Colloquies on Hanoverian England,* ed. John Cannon. New York: St. Martin's Press, 1981, pp. 28–50.

Donoughue, Bernard. *British Politics and the American Revolution: The Path to War, 1773–75.* New York: St. Martin's Press, 1964.

Feling, Keith G. *The Second Tory Party, 1714–1832.* London: Macmillan & Co., 1938.

Floud, Roderick and McCloskey, Donald, eds. *The Economic History of Britain Since 1700,* vol. 1. (1700–1860). New York: Cambridge University Press, 1981.

Foord, Archibald S. *His Majesty's Opposition, 1714–1820.* Oxford, England: Clarendon Press, 1964.

Guttridge, George H. *English Whiggism and the American Revolution.* Berkeley: University of California Press, 1966, originally published in 1942.

Hay, Carla H. *James Burgh: Spokesman for Reform in Hanoverian England,* Washington, D.C.: University Press of America, 1979.

Hill, B. W. *British Parliamentary Parties, 1742–1832*. London: George Allen & Unwin, 1985.

Hinkhouse, Fred J. *The Preliminaries of the American Revolution as Seen in the English Press, 1763–1775*. New York: Columbia University Press, 1926.

Horn, D. B., ed. *English Historical Documents*. Vol. 10 (1714–1783). New York: Oxford University Press, 1957.

Kemp, Betty. *King and Commons, 1660–1832*. New York: St. Martin's Press, 1965, originally published in 1957.

Knorr, Klaus E. *British Colonial Theories, 1570–1850*. Toronto: University of Toronto Press, 1968, originally published in 1944.

Langford, Paul. *The First Rockingham Administration, 1765–1766*. London: Oxford University Press, 1973.

————. *A Polite and Commercial People: England, 1727–1783*. Oxford, England: Clarendon Press, 1989.

————., ed. *The Writings and Speeches of Edmund Burke*. Vol. 2 (1766–74). Oxford, England: Clarendon Press, 1981.

Lawson, Philip. *George Grenville: A Political Life*. Oxford, England: Clarendon Press, 1984.

Marshall, Dorothy. *Eighteenth Century England*. London: Longmans, Green & Co., 1962.

Mumby, Frank A. *George III and the American Revolution: The Beginnings*. Boston: Houghton Mifflin Co., 1923.

Namier, Lewis. *England in the Age of the American Revolution*. New York: St. Martin's Press, 1966, originally published in 1930.

————. *The Structure of Politics at the Accession of George III*. New York: St. Martin's Press, 1963, originally published in 1929.

O'Gorman, Frank. *The Rise of Party in England: The Rockingham Whigs, 1760–82*. London: George Allen & Unwin, 1975.

————. *Voters, Patrons, and Parties: The Unreformed Electoral System of Hanoverian England, 1734–1832*. Oxford, England: Clarendon Press, 1989.

Osborne, John. *John Cartwright*. Cambridge, England: Cambridge University Press, 1972.

Owen, John B. *The Eighteenth Century, 1714–1815*. London: Thomas Nelson & Sons, 1974.

Pares, Richard. *King George III and the Politicians*. Oxford, England: Clarendon Press, 1953.

Pole, J. R. *Political Representation in England and the Origins of the American Republic*. New York: St. Martin's Press, 1966.

Potts, Louis W. *Arthur Lee: A Virtuous Revolutionary*. Baton Rouge: Louisiana State University Press, 1981.

Rea, Robert R. *The English Press in Politics, 1760–1774*. Lincoln: University of Nebraska Press, 1963.

Ritcheson, Charles R. *British Politics in the American Revolution*. Norman: University of Oklahoma Press, 1954.

Robbins, Caroline. *The Eighteenth-Century Commonwealthmen*. Cambridge, Mass.: Harvard University Press, 1959.

Rudé, George. *Wilkes and Liberty: A Social Study of 1763 to 1774*. Oxford, England: Clarendon Press, 1962.

Sainsbury, John. *Disaffected Patriots: London Supporters of Revolutionary America, 1769–1782*. Kingston, Canada: McGill-Queen's University Press, 1987.

Smith, Paul H., comp. *English Defenders of American Freedoms, 1774–1778*. Washington, D.C.: Library of Congress, 1972.

Sosin, Jack M. *Agents and Merchants: British Colonial Policy and the Origins of the American Revolution, 1763–1775*. Lincoln: University of Nebraska Press, 1965.

Spector, Margaret. *The American Department of the British Government*. New York: Octagon Books, 1976, originally published in 1940.

Sutherland, Lucy S., and Guttridge, George H., eds. *The Correspondence of Edmund Burke*. Vols. 2–3. Chicago: University of Chicago Press, 1960–61.

Thomas, Roland. *Richard Price: Philosopher and Apostle of Liberty.* London: Oxford University Press, 1924.

Toohey, Robert E. *Liberty and Empire: British Radical Solutions to the American Problem, 1774–1776.* Lexington: University Press of Kentucky, 1978.

Tucker, Robert W., and Hendrickson, David C. *The Fall of the First British Empire: Origins of the War of American Independence.* Baltimore: Johns Hopkins University Press, 1982.

Turner, Edward R. *The Cabinet Council of England in the Seventeenth and Eighteenth Centuries, 1622–1784.* 2 vols. New York: Russell & Russell, 1970, originally published in 1932.

Wickwire, Franklin B. *British Subministers and Colonial America, 1763–83.* Princeton, N.J.: Princeton University Press, 1966.

Winstanley, D. A. *Lord Chatham and the Whig Opposition.* Cambridge, England: Cambridge University Press, 1912.

CHAPTER 3

Anderson, George P. "A Note on Ebenezer Mackintosh." *Publications of the Colonial Society of Massachusetts,* 26 (1926): 348–61.

Andrews, Charles M. *The Boston Merchants and the Non-Importation Movement.* New York: Russell & Russell, 1968, originally published in 1916.

Bailyn, Bernard. *The Ordeal of Thomas Hutchinson.* Cambridge, Mass.: Harvard University Press, 1974.

———., ed. *Pamphlets of the American Revolution, 1750–1776.* Vol. 1. Cambridge, Mass: Harvard University Press, 1965.

Brown, Richard D. *Revolutionary Politics in Massachusetts: The Boston Committee of Correspondence and the Towns, 1772–1774.* Cambridge, Mass.: Harvard University Press, 1970.

Bullion, John L. *A Great and Necessary Measure: George Grenville and the Genesis of the Stamp Act, 1763–1765.* Columbia: University of Missouri Press, 1982.

Butterfield, L. H., ed. *Diary and Autobiography of John Adams.* Vol. 4. Cambridge, Mass.: Harvard University Press, 1961.

Chaffin, Robert J. "The Townshend Acts of 1767." *William and Mary Quarterly,* 3d ser., 27 (1976): 90–121.

Champagne, Roger J. "Liberty Boys and Mechanics of New York City, 1764–1774." *Labor History,* 8 (1967): 115–35.

———. "The Military Association of the Sons of Liberty." *New-York Historical Society Quarterly,* 51 (1957): 338–50.

Channing, Edward, and Coolidge, Archibald C., eds. *The Barrington-Bernard Correspondence and Illustrative Matter, 1760–1770.* New York: Da Capo Press, 1970, originally published in 1912.

Christie, Ian, and Labaree, Benjamin W. *Empire or Independence, 1760–1776.* See Chapter 1 references.

Conser, Walter H., Jr., McCarthy, Ronald M., Toscano, David, and Sharp, Gene. *Resistance, Politics, and the American Struggle for Independence, 1765–1775.* Boulder, Colo.: Lynne Rienner Publishers, 1986.

Davidson, Philip. *Propaganda and the American Revolution, 1763–83.* Chapel Hill: University of North Carolina Press, 1941.

Dickerson, Oliver M., comp. *Boston Under Military Rule, 1768–1769, as Revealed in a Journal of the Times.* Westport, Conn.: Greenwood Press, 1971, originally published in 1936.

Ernst, Joseph A. *Money and Politics in America, 1755–1775: A Study in the Currency Act of 1764 and the Political Economy of Revolution.* Chapel Hill: University of North Carolina Press, 1973.

Ford, Paul L., ed. *The Political Writings of John Dickinson, 1764–1774.* New York: Da Capo Press, 1970, originally published in 1895.

Greene, Jack P., ed. *Colonies to Nation, 1763–1789: A Documentary History of the American Revolution.* New York: W. W. Norton, originally published in 1967.

Hutchinson, Thomas. *The History of the Province of Massachusetts-Bay.* Vol. 3 (1749–74). New York: Arno Press, 1972, originally published in 1828.

Jacobson, David L. *John Dickinson and the Revolution in Pennsylvania, 1764–1776.* Berkeley: University of California Press, 1965.

Jensen, Merrill. *The Founding of a Nation: A History of the American Revolution, 1763–1776.* New York: Oxford University Press, 1968.

———, ed. *Tracts of the American Revolution.* Indianapolis, Ind.: Bobbs-Merrill Co., 1967.

Johnson, Allen S. "The Passage of the Sugar Act." *William and Mary Quarterly,* 3d ser., 16 (1959): 507–14.

"Journal of a French Traveller in the Colonies, 1765." *American Historical Review,* 26 (1920–21): 726–47.

Knollenberg, Bernhard. *Growth of the American Revolution, 1766–1775.* New York: Free Press, 1975.

———. *Origin of the American Revolution, 1759–1766.* New York: Macmillan Co., 1960.

Koebner, Richard. *Empire.* Cambridge, England: Cambridge University Press, 1961.

Labaree, Benjamin W. *The Boston Tea Party.* New York: Oxford University Press, 1964.

Leslie, William R. "The Gaspee Affair: A Study of Its Constitutional Significance." *Mississippi Valley Historical Review,* 39 (1952): 233–56.

Longley, R. S. "Mob Activities in Revolutionary Massachusetts." *New England Quarterly,* 6 (1933): 98–130.

Lord, Donald C., and Calhoon, Robert M. "The Removal of the Massachusetts General Court from Boston, 1769–1772." *Journal of American History,* 55 (1969): 735–55.

Lovejoy, David S. "Rights Imply Equality: The Case Against Admiralty Jurisdiction in America, 1764–1776." *William and Mary Quarterly,* 3d ser., 16 (1959): 459–84.

Maier, Pauline. *From Resistance to Revolution: Colonial Radicals and the Development of American Opposition to Britain, 1765–1776.* New York: Alfred A. Knopf, 1972.

———. "Popular Uprisings and Civil Authority in Eighteenth-Century America." *William and Mary Quarterly,* 3d ser., 27 (1970): 3–35.

Miller, John C. "The Massachusetts Convention 1768." *New England Quarterly,* 7 (1934): 445–74.

———. *Origins of the American Revolution.* Boston: Little, Brown, & Co., 1943.

———. *Sam Adams: Pioneer in Propaganda.* Boston: Little, Brown, & Co., 1936.

Morais, Herbert M. "The Sons of Liberty in New York." In Richard B. Morris, ed., *The Era of the American Revolution.* New York: Harper & Row, 1965, originally published in 1939.

Morgan, Edmund S. "Colonial Ideas of Parliamentary Power, 1764–1766." *William & Mary Quarterly,* 3d ser., 5 (1948): 311–41.

———, ed. *Prologue to Revolution: Sources and Documents on the Stamp Act, 1764–1766.* Chapel Hill: University of North Carolina Press, 1959.

Morgan, Edmund S. and Morgan, Helen. *The Stamp Act Crisis: Prologue to Revolution.* Chapel Hill: University of North Carolina Press, 1953.

Reid, John R. *In a Rebellious Spirit: The Argument of Facts, the Liberty Riot, and the Coming of the American Revolution.* University Park: Pennsylvania State University Press, 1979.

Schlesinger, Arthur M. *The Colonial Merchants and the American Revolution, 1763–1776.* New York: Frederick Ungar Publishing Co., 1964, originally published in 1918.

———. *Prelude to Independence: The Newspaper War on Britain, 1764–1776.* Westport, Conn.: Greenwood Press, 1979, originally published in 1958.

Shaw, Peter. *American Patriots and the Ritual of Revolution.* Cambridge, Mass.: Harvard University Press, 1981.

Shy, John. *Toward Lexington: The Role of the British Army in the Coming of the American Revolution.* Princeton, N.J.: Princeton University Press, 1965.

Sutherland, Lucy S. *The East India Company in Eighteenth-Century Politics.* Oxford, England: Clarendon Press, 1962.

Tate, Thaddeus W., Jr. "The Coming of the American Revolution in Virginia, 1763–76." *William and Mary Quarterly*, 3d ser., 19 (1962): 323–43.

Thomas, Peter D. G. *British Politics and the Stamp Act Crisis: The First Phase of the American Revolution, 1763–1767*. Oxford, England: Clarendon Press, 1975.

————. *The Townshend Duties Crisis: The Second Phase of the American Revolution, 1767–1773*. Oxford, England: Clarendon Press, 1987.

Ubbelohde, Carl. *The Vice-Admiralty Courts and the American Revolution*. Chapel Hill: University of North Carolina Press, 1960.

Walsh, Richard. *Charleston's Sons of Liberty: A Study of the Artisans, 1763–1789*. Columbia: University of South Carolina Press, 1959.

Weslager, C. A. *The Stamp Act Congress, with an Exact Copy of the Complete Journal*. Newark: University of Delaware Press, 1976.

Zobel, Hiller B. *The Boston Massacre*. New York: W. W. Norton & Co., 1970.

CHAPTER 4

Alden, John R. *General Gage in America: Being Principally a History of His Role in the American Revolution*. Baton Rouge: Louisiana State University Press, 1948.

Ammerman, David. *In the Common Cause: American Response to the Coercive Acts*. Charlottesville: University Press of Virginia, 1974.

Barker, John. *The British in Boston: Being the Diary of Lieutenant John Barker of the King's Own Regiment from November 15, 1774 to May 31, 1775*. Cambridge, Mass.: Harvard University Press, 1924.

Birnbaum, Louis. *Red Dawn at Lexington*. Boston: Houghton Mifflin Co., 1986.

Bowen, Catherine D. *John Adams and the American Revolution*. Boston: Little, Brown & Co., 1950.

Bowman, Larry G. "Virginia and the Continental Association, 1774–1776." Ph.D. diss., University of New Mexico, 1966.

Boyd, Julian P. *Anglo-American Union: Joseph Galloway's Plans to Preserve the British Empire, 1774–1788*. Philadelphia: University of Pennsylvania Press, 1941.

Brown, Richard D. *Revolutionary Politics in Massachusetts: The Boston Committee of Correspondence and the Towns, 1772–1774*. Cambridge, Mass.: Harvard University Press, 1970.

Butler, Lindley S. *North Carolina and the Coming of the Revolution, 1763–1776*. Raleigh: North Carolina Department of Cultural Resources, 1976.

Butterfield, L. H., ed. *Diary and Autobiography of John Adams*. Vol. 2. Cambridge, Mass.: Harvard University Press, 1961.

Caley, Percy B. "Dunmore: Colonial Governor of New York and Virginia, 1770–1782." Ph.D. diss., University of Pittsburgh, 1939.

Carter, Clarence E., ed. *The Correspondence of General Thomas Gage with the Secretaries of State and with the War Office and the Treasury, 1763–1775*. 2 vols. New Haven, Conn.: Yale University Press, 1931 and 1933.

Champagne, Roger J. *Alexander McDougall and the American Revolution in New York*. Schenectady, N.Y.: Union College Press, 1975.

Conser, Walter M., Jr., McCarthy, Ronald M., Toacano, David J., and Sharp, Gene, eds. *See* Chapter 3 references.

Donoughue, Bernard. *See* Chapter 2 references.

Fortescue, Sir John, ed. *The Correspondence of King George the Third from 1760 to December 1783*. Vol. 3. London: Frank Cass & Co., 1967.

French, Allen. *The Day of Concord and Lexington: The Nineteenth of April, 1775*. Boston: Little, Brown, & Co., 1925.

————. *General Gage's Informers: New Material upon Lexington and Concord*. New York: Greenwood Press, 1968, originally published in 1932.

Frothingham, Richard. *History of the Siege of Boston and the Battles of Lexington, Concord, and Bunker Hill*. New York: Da Capo Press, 1970, originally published in 1903.

———. *Life and Times of Joseph Warren*. Boston: Little, Brown, & Co., 1865.

Galvin, John R. *The Minute Men: A Compact History of the Defenders of the American Colonies, 1645–1775*. New York: Hawthorn Books, 1967.

Gerlach, Larry R. *Prologue to Independence: New Jersey in the Coming of the American Revolution*. New Brunswick, N.J.: Rutgers University Press, 1976.

Gipson, Lawrence H. *The Triumphant Empire: Britain Sails into the Storm, 1770–1776*. Vol. 12 of the *British Empire Before the American Revolution*. New York: Alfred A. Knopf, 1965.

Godbold, E. Stanly, and Woody, Robert H. *Christopher Gadsden and the American Revolution*. Knoxville: University of Tennessee Press, 1982.

Hoffman, Ross J. S. *Edmund Burke, New York Agent, with His Letters to the New York Assembly and Intimate Correspondence with Charles O'Hara*. Philadelphia: American Philosophical Society, 1956.

Jellison, Charles A. *Ethan Allen: Frontier Rebel*. Syracuse, N.Y.: Syracuse University Press, 1969.

Jensen, Merrill, ed. *English Historical Documents: American Colonial Documents to 1776*. Vol. 9. New York: Oxford University Press, 1955.

———. *The Founding of a Nation: A History of the American Revolution, 1763–1776*. London: Oxford University Press, 1968.

Lincoln, Charles H. *The Revolutionary Movement in Pennsylvania, 1760–1776*. Philadelphia: Ginn & Co., 1901.

Lingley, Charles R. *The Transition in Virginia from Colony to Commonwealth*. New York: Columbia University Press, 1910.

McCloskey, Robert G., ed. *The Works of James Wilson*. Vol. 2. Cambridge, Mass.: Harvard University Press, 1967.

Mackenzie, Frederick. *Diary of Frederick Mackenzie . . . An Officer of the Regiment of Royal Welch Fusiliers . . . 1775–1781 . . .* Cambridge, Mass.: Harvard University Press, 1930.

Marston, Jerrilyn G. *King and Congress: The Transfer of Political Legitimacy, 1774–1776*. Princeton, N.J.: Princeton University Press, 1987.

Mason, Bernard. *The Road to Independence: The Revolutionary Movement in New York, 1773–1777*. Lexington: University of Kentucky Press, 1966.

Meade, Robert D. *Patrick Henry: Practical Revolutionary*. Vol. 2. Philadelphia: J. B. Lippincott Co., 1969.

Neuenschwander, John A. *The Middle Colonies and the Coming of the American Revolution*. Port Washington, N.Y.: Kennikat Press, 1973.

Parliamentary History of England from the Earliest Period to the Year 1803. Vols. 17 and 18. New York: AMS Press, 1966, originally published in 1813.

Rakove, Jack N. *The Beginnings of National Politics: An Interpretive History of the Continental Congress*. Baltimore: Johns Hopkins University Press, 1979.

Ryerson, Richard A. *The Revolution is Now Begun: The Radical Committees of Philadelphia, 1765–1776*. Philadelphia: University of Pennsylvania Press, 1978.

Sosin, Jack M. "The Massachusetts Acts of 1774: Coercive or Preventive?" *The Huntington Library Quarterly*, 26 (1962–63): 235–52.

Tourtellot, Arthur B. *Lexington and Concord: The Beginning of the War of the American Revolution*. New York: W. W. Norton & Co., 1963.

Upton, Richard F. *Revolutionary New Hampshire: An Account of the Social and Political Forces Underlying the Transition from Royal Province to American Commonwealth*. Hanover, N.H.: Dartmouth College Publications, 1936.

Walsh, Richard. *Charleston's Sons of Liberty: A Study of the Artisans, 1763–89*. Columbia: University of South Carolina Press, 1959.

CHAPTER 5

Beebe, Lewis. "Journal of a Physician on the Expedition Against Canada, 1776." *Pennsylvania Magazine of History and Biography,* 59 (1935): 321–61.

Bird, Harrison, *Attack on Quebec: The American Invasion of Canada, 1775.* New York: Oxford University Press, 1968.

Boyd, Julian P. "The Disputed Authorship of the Declaration on the Causes and Necessity for Taking up Arms, 1775." *Pennsylvania Magazine of History and Biography,* 74 (1950): 51–73.

Brown, Weldon A. *Empire or Independence: A Study in the Failure of Reconciliation, 1774–1783.* Port Washington, N.Y.: Kennikat Press, 1966, originally published in 1941.

Butler, Lindley S. *North Carolina and the Coming of the Revolution, 1763–1776.* Raleigh: North Carolina Department of Cultural Resources, 1976.

Callahan, North. *Henry Knox: General Washington's General.* New York: Rinehart & Co., 1958.

Cann, Marvin L. "Prelude to War: The First Battle of Ninety-Six, November 19–21, 1775." *South Carolina Historical Magazine,* 76 (1975): 205–14.

Chidsey, Donald B. *The Siege of Boston: An On-the-Scene Account of the Beginning of the American Revolution.* New York: Crown Publishers, 1966.

Elting, John R. *The Battle of Bunker's Hill.* Monmouth Beach, N.J.: Philip Freneau Press, 1975.

Fleming, Thomas. *Now We Are Enemies: The Story of Bunker Hill.* New York: St. Martin's Press, 1960.

———. *1776: Year of Illusions.* New York: W. W. Norton, 1975.

Fortescue, John, ed. *The Correspondence of King George the Third.* See Chapter 4 references.

French, Allen. *The First Year of the American Revolution.* New York: Octagon Books, 1968, originally published in 1934.

Gerlach, Don R. *Proud Patriot: Philip Schuyler and the War of Independence, 1775–1783.* Syracuse, N.Y.: Syracuse University Press, 1987.

Griffith, Samuel B. *In Defense of the Public Liberty: Britain, America, and the Struggle for Independence—From 1760 to the Surrender at Yorktown in 1781.* Garden City, N.Y.: Doubleday & Co., 1976.

Hatch, Robert M. *Thrust for Canada: The American Attempt on Quebec in 1775–1776.* Boston: Houghton Mifflin Co., 1979.

Hume, Ivor Noel. *Another Part of the Field.* New York: Alfred A. Knopf, 1966.

Huston, James A. "The Logistics of Arnold's March to Quebec." In *Military Analysis of the Revolutionary War: An Anthology by the Editors of Military Affairs,* 106–20. Millwood, N.J.: KTO Press, 1977.

Jordan, Winthrop D. "Familial Politics: Thomas Paine and the Killing of the King." *Journal of American History,* 60 (1973): 294–308.

Ketchum, Richard M. *Decisive Day: The Battle for Bunker Hill.* Garden City, N.Y.: Doubleday & Co., 1974.

Lambert, Robert S. *South Carolina in the American Revolution.* Columbia: University of South Carolina Press, 1987.

Lancot, Gustave. *Canada and the American Revolution, 1774–1783.* Cambridge, Mass.: Harvard University Press, 1967.

Landrum, J. B. O. *Colonial and Revolutionary History of Upper South Carolina.* Spartanburg, S.C.: Reprint Co., 1977, originally published in 1897.

Leroy, Perry E. "Sir Guy Carleton as a Military Leader During the American Invasion and Repulse in Canada, 1775–1776." Ph.D. diss., Ohio State University, 1960.

Livingston, William F. *Israel Putnam: Pioneer Ranger and Major-General.* New York: G. P. Putnam's Sons, 1905.

Meyer, Duane G. *The Highland Scots of North Carolina, 1732–1776.* Chapel Hill: University of North Carolina Press, 1961.

Pell, John. *Ethan Allen*. Boston: Houghton Mifflin Co., 1929.

Perry, Clay. "Big Guns for Washington." *American Heritage*, 6 (April 1955), 12–15, 102.

Rankin, Hugh F. "The Moore's Creek Bridge Campaign, 1776." *North Carolina Historical Review*, 30 (1953): 23–60.

Roberts, Kenneth, ed. *March to Quebec: Journals of the Members of Arnold's Expedition*. Garden City, N.Y.: Doubleday, Doran & Co., 1945.

Robson, Eric. "The Expedition to the Southern Colonies, 1775–1776." *English Historical Review*, 66 (1951): 535–60.

Salsig, Doyen. *Parole: Countersign: Ticonderoga: Second New Jersey Regimental Orderly Book, 1776*. Rutherford, N.J.: Fairleigh Dickinson University Press, 1980.

Shy, John, ed. "Confronting Rebellion: Private Correspondence of Lord Barrington with General Gage, 1765–1775." In Howard H. Peckham, ed., *Sources of American Independence: Selected Manuscripts from the Collection of the William L. Clements Library*. Vol. 1, pp. 1–139. Chicago: University of Chicago Press, 1978.

Stanley, George F. G. *Canada Invaded, 1775–1776*. Toronto: A. M. Makkert Ltd., 1973.

Stevens, Benjamin F., ed. *General Sir William Howe's Orderly Book at Charleston, Boston and Halifax, June 17, 1775 to May 26, 1776*. Port Washington, N.Y.: Kennikat Press, 1970, originally published in 1890.

Stewart, Mrs. Catesby W. *The Life of Brigadier General William Woodford of the American Revolution*. 2 vols. Richmond: Whittet and Shepperson, 1973.

Wheeler, Earl M. "The Role of the North Carolina Militia in the Beginning of the American Revolution." Ph.D. diss., Tulane University, 1963.

Wickersham, Cornelius W., and Gilbert, M. Montague, eds. *The Olive Branch: Petition of the American Congress to George III, 1775 and Letters of the American Envoys, August–September 1775*. New York: New York Public Library, 1954.

Willard, Margaret W. *Letters on the American Revolution, 1774–1776*. Boston: Houghton Mifflin Co., 1925.

Willcox, William B., ed. "The Clinton-Parker Controversy over British Failure at Charleston and Rhode Island." In Howard H. Peckham, ed., *Sources of American Independence* . . . Vol. 1, pp. 188–225. Chicago: University of Chicago Press, 1978.

CHAPTER 6

Adler, Mortimer J., and Gorman, William. *The American Testament*. New York: Praeger Publishers, 1975.

Arendt, Hannah. *On Revolution*. New York: Viking Press, 1963.

Arieli, Yehosha. *Individualism and Nationalism in American Ideology*. Cambridge, Mass.: Harvard University Press, 1964.

Barrow, Thomas C. "The American Revolution as a Colonial War for Independence." *William and Mary Quarterly*, 3d ser., 25 (1968): 452–64.

Becker, Carl. *The Declaration of Independence: A Study in the History of Ideas*. New York: Vintage Books, 1960, originally published in 1922.

———. *The History of Political Parties in the Province of New York, 1760–1776*. Madison: University of Wisconsin Press, 1960, originally published in 1909.

Boyd, Julian P. *The Declaration of Independence: The Evolution of the Text as Shown in Facsimiles of Various Drafts by Its Author, Thomas Jefferson*. Princeton, N.J.: Princeton University Press, 1945.

Buel, Richard, Jr. "Democracy and the American Revolution: A Frame of Reference." *William and Mary Quarterly*, 3d ser., 21 (1964): 165–90.

Burnett, Edmund C. *The Continental Congress*. New York: Macmillan Co., 1941.

Burrows, Edwin G., and Wallace, Michael. "The American Revolution: The Ideology and Psychology of National Liberation." *Perspectives in American History*, 6 (1972): 166–306.

Butterfield, L. H., ed. *Diary and Autobiography of John Adams.* Vol. 3. Cambridge, Mass.: Harvard University Press, 1961.

Cappon, Lester J., ed. *The Adams-Jefferson Letters: The Complete Correspondence Between Thomas Jefferson and Abigail and John Adams.* 2 vols. Chapel Hill: University of North Carolina Press, 1959.

Chinard, Gilbert, ed. *The Commonplace Book of Thomas Jefferson: A Repository of His Ideas on Government.* Baltimore: Johns Hopkins University Press, 1928.

Connor, Robert D. W. "North Carolina's Priority in the Demand for Independence." *South Atlantic Quarterly,* 8 (1909): 234–54.

Douglass, Elisha P. *Rebels and Democrats: The Struggle for Equal Political Rights and Majority Rule During the American Revolution.* Chapel Hill: University of North Carolina Press, 1955.

Dumbauld, Edward. *The Declaration of Independence and What It Means Today.* Norman, Okla.: University of Oklahoma Press, 1950.

Egnal, Marc. *A Mighty Empire: The Origins of the American Revolution.* Ithaca, N.Y.: Cornell University Press, 1988.

Fisher, Sidney G. "The Twenty-eight Charges Against the King in the Declaration of Independence." *Pennsylvania Magazine of History and Biography,* 31 (1907): 257–303.

Friedenwald, Herbert. *The Declaration of Independence: An Interpretation and an Analysis.* New York: Macmillan Co., 1904.

Ginsberg, Robert, ed. *A Casebook on the Declaration of Independence.* New York: Thomas Y. Crowell Co., 1967.

Hawke, David. *Honorable Treason: The Declaration of Independence and the Men Who Signed It.* New York: Viking Press, 1976.

———. *A Transaction of Free Men: The Birth and Course of the Declaration of Independence.* New York: Charles Scribner's Sons, 1964.

Hazelton, John. *The Declaration of Independence: Its History.* New York: Dodd, Mead & Co., 1906.

Head, John M. *A Time to Rend: An Essay on the Decision for American Independence.* Madison: State Historical Society of Wisconsin, 1968.

Hellenbrand, Harold. *The Unfinished Revolution: Education and Politics in the Thought of Thomas Jefferson.* Newark: University of Delaware Press, 1990.

Hoffer, Peter C. *Revolution & Regeneration: Life Cycle and the Historical Vision of the Generation of 1776.* Athens: University of Georgia Press, 1983.

Hoyt, William. *The Mecklenburg Declaration of Independence.* New York: G. P. Putnam's Sons, 1907.

Hutchinson, Thomas. *Strictures upon the Declaration of the Congress at Philadelphia in a Letter to a Noble Lord (Earl of Hardwicke).* London: 1776. Virginia State Library.

Hutson, James H. "The Partition Treaty and the Declaration of American Independence." *Journal of American History,* 58 (1972): 877–96.

Jefferson, Thomas. *Notes on the State of Virginia.* Ed. William Peden. Chapel Hill: University of North Carolina Press, 1955.

Koch, Adrienne. *Power, Morals, and the Founding Fathers: Essays in the Interpretation of the American Enlightenment.* Ithaca, N.Y.: Cornell University Press, 1961.

Lind, John. *An Answer to the Declaration of the American Congress.* 4th ed. London: 1776. Virginia State Library.

Malone, Dumas. *Jefferson the Virginian.* Boston: Little, Brown & Co., 1948.

Powell, J. M. "The Day of American Independence, July 1, 1776." Chapter 7 of *General Washington and the Jack Ass and Other American Characters, in Portrait.* Cranbury, N.J.: Thomas Yoseloff, Publisher, 1969.

Rakove, Jack N. "The Decision for American Independence: A Reconstruction." *Perspectives in American History,* 10 (1976): 215–75.

Royster, Charles. "Founding a Nation in Blood: Military Conflict and American Nationality." In *Arms and Independence: The Military Character of the American Revolution,* eds.

Ronald Hoffman and Peter J. Albert. Charlottesville: University Press of Virginia, 1984, pp. 25–49.

Warren, Charles. "Fourth of July Myths." *William and Mary Quarterly*, 3d ser., 2 (1945): 237–72.

Wills, Garry. *Inventing America: Jefferson's Declaration of Independence*. Garden City, N.Y.: Doubleday & Co., 1978.

Wishy, Bernard. "John Locke and the Spirit of '76." *Political Science Quarterly*, 73 (1958): 413–25.

CHAPTER 7

Billias, George A. *General John Glover and His Marblehead Mariners*. New York: Henry Holt & Co., 1960.

Blivens, Bruce, Jr. *Battle for Manhattan*. New York: Henry Holt & Co., 1956.

Bowler, R. Arthur. *Logistics and the Failure of the British Army in America, 1775–1783*. Princeton, N.J.: Princeton University Press, 1975.

Bradford, S. Sydney. "A British Officer's Revolutionary War Journal, 1776–1778." *Maryland Historical Magazine*, 56 (1961): 150–75.

Curtis, Edward E. *The Organization of the British Army in the American Revolution*. New Haven, Conn.: Yale University Press, 1926.

Diament, Lincoln. *Chaining the Hudson: The Fight for the River in the American Revolution*. New York: Carol Publishing Group, 1989.

Dwyer, William M. *The Day Is Ours!: November 1776–January 1777—An Inside View of the Battles of Trenton and Princeton*. New York: Viking Press, 1983.

Fortescue, John W. *A History of the British Army*. Vol. 3. London: Macmillan & Co., Ltd., 1911.

Greene, Francis V. *The Revolutionary War and the Military Policy of the United States*. Port Washington, N.Y.: Kennikat Press, 1967, originally published in 1911.

Gruber, Ira D. *The Howe Brothers and the American Revolution*. New York: W. W. Norton & Co., 1972.

Harcourt, Edward W., ed. *The Harcourt Papers*. Vol. 11. Oxford, England, n.d.

Hibbert, Christopher. *Redcoats and Rebels: The American Revolution Through British Eyes*. New York: W. W. Norton & Co., 1990.

Higginbotham, Don. *The War of American Independence: Military Attitudes, Policies, and Practices, 1763–1789*. New York: Macmillan Co., 1971.

———, ed. *Reconsiderations of the Revolutionary War: Selected Essays*. Westport, Conn.: Greenwood Press, 1978.

Jackson, John W. *With the British Army in Philadelphia, 1777–1778*. San Rafael, Calif.: Presidio Press, 1979.

Johnston, Henry P. *The Campaign of 1776 Around New York and Brooklyn*. New York: Da Capo Press, 1971, originally published in 1878.

Ketchum, Richard M. "England's Vietnam: The American Revolution." *American Heritage*, 22 (June 1971): 7–11 and 81–83.

———. *The Winter Soldiers*. Garden City, N.Y.: Doubleday & Co., 1973.

Lobdell, Jared C. "Two Forgotten Battles in the Revolutionary War." *New Jersey History*, 85 (1967): 225–34.

Lundin, Leonard. *Cockpit of the Revolution: The War for Independence in New Jersey*. New York: Octagon Books, 1972, originally published in 1940.

Mackenzie, Frederick. *See* Chapter 4 references.

Mackesy, Piers. *The War for America, 1775–1783*. Cambridge, Mass.: Harvard University Press, 1964.

Manders, Eric I. *The Battle of Long Island*. Monmouth Beach, N.J.: Philip Freneau Press, 1978.

Mitchell, Joseph B. *Discipline and Bayonets: The Armies and Leaders in the War of the American Revolution*. New York: G. P. Putnam's Sons, 1967.

Palmer, Dave R. *The Way of the Fox: American Strategy in the War for America, 1775–1783.* Westport, Conn.: Greenwood Press, 1975.

Reed, John F. *Campaign to Valley Forge, July 1, 1776–December 19, 1777.* Philadelphia: University of Pennsylvania Press, 1965.

Robson, Eric. *The American Revolution in Its Political and Military Aspects, 1763–1783.* New York: Oxford University Press, 1955.

Rossie, Jonathan G. *The Politics of Command in the American Revolution.* Syracuse, N.Y.: Syracuse University Press, 1975.

Smith, Samuel S. *The Battle of Brandywine.* Monmouth Beach, N.J.: Philip Freneau Press, 1976.

———. *The Battle of Princeton.* Monmouth Beach, N.J.: Philip Freneau Press, 1967.

———. *The Battle of Trenton.* Monmouth Beach, N.J.: Philip Freneau Press, 1965.

———. *Fight for the Delaware, 1777.* Monmouth Beach, N.J.: Philip Freneau Press, 1970.

———., ed. *At General Howe's Side, 1776–1778: The Diary of General William Howe's Aide de Camp, Captain Friedrich von Muenchhausen.* Monmouth Beach, N.J.: Philip Freneau Press, 1974.

Stryker, William S. *The Battles of Trenton and Princeton.* Boston: Houghton, Mifflin & Co., 1898.

Tatum, Edward H., ed. *The American Journal of Ambrose Serle, Secretary to Lord Howe, 1776–1778.* San Marino, Calif.: Huntington Library, 1940.

Thompson, Ray. *Washington at Germantown.* Fort Washington, Pa.: Bicentennial Press, 1971.

Tustin, Joseph P., ed. and trans. *Diary of the American War: A Hessian Journal—Captain Johann Ewald, Field Jager Corps.* New Haven, Conn.: Yale University Press, 1979.

Ward, Harry M. *Duty, Honor or Country: General George Weedon and the American Revolution.* Philadelphia: American Philosophical Society, 1979.

———. *Major General Adam Stephen and the Cause of American Liberty.* Charlottesville: University Press of Virginia, 1989.

Weigley, Russell F. *The American Way of War: A History of United States Military Strategy and Policy.* New York: Macmillan Publishing Co., 1973.

Willcox, William B. "Too Many Cooks: British Planning Before Saratoga." *Journal of British Studies,* 2 (1962): 56–90.

CHAPTER 8

Alden, John R. *General Charles Lee: Traitor or Patriot?* Baton Rouge: Louisiana State University Press, 1951.

Bodle, Wayne K. *The Vortex of Small Fortunes: The Continental Army at Valley Forge, 1777–1778.* Final Report. Vol. 1. The Valley Forge Historical Research Project, 1980.

Chase, Philander D. "Baron von Steuben in the War of Independence." Ph.D. diss., Duke University, 1973.

Clark, Jane. "Responsibility for the Failure of the Burgoyne Campaign." *American Historical Review,* 35 (1930): 542–59.

Clinton, Sir Henry. *The American Rebellion: Sir Henry Clinton's Narrative of His Campaigns, 1775–1782, with an Appendix of Original Documents.* Ed. William B. Willcox. New Haven, Conn.: Yale University Press, 1954.

Deardon, Paul F. *The Rhode Island Campaign of 1778: Inauspicious Dawn of Alliance.* Providence, R.I.: Rhode Island Bicentennial Foundation, 1980.

Dunbar, Louise B. *A Study of "Monarchical" Tendencies in the United States from 1776 to 1801.* New York: Johnson Reprint Corp., 1970, originally published in 1922.

Fleming, Thomas. *The Forgotten Victory: The Battle for New Jersey—1780.* New York: Reader's Digest Press, 1973.

Furneaux, Rupert. *The Battle of Saratoga.* New York: Stein & Day, 1971.

Gerlach, Larry R., ed. *New Jersey in the American Revolution, 1763–1783: A Documentary.* Trenton: N.J. Historical Commission, 1975.

Gottschalk, Louis. *Lafayette Joins the American Army*. Chicago: University of Chicago Press, 1937.

Hargrove, Richard J., Jr. *General John Burgoyne*. Newark: University of Delaware Press, 1983.

Higginbotham, Don. "Military Leadership in the American Revolution." In *Leadership in the American Revolution*, pp. 91–111. Washington, D.C.: Library of Congress Symposium in the American Revolution, 1974.

Howson, Gerald. *Burgoyne of Saratoga: A Biography*. New York: Times Books, 1979.

Hufeland, Otto. *Westchester County During the American Revolution*. White Plains, N.Y.: Westchester County Historical Society, 1926.

Johnston, Henry P. *The Storming of Stony Point on the Hudson Midnight, July 15, 1779*. New York: James T. White & Co., 1900.

Knollenberg, Bernhard. *Washington and the Revolution: A Reappraisal: Gates, Conway, and the Continental Congress*. New York: Macmillan Co., 1940.

Kohn, Richard H. "The Inside History of the Newburgh Conspiracy: America and the Coup d'etat." *William and Mary Quarterly*, 29 (1970): 187–220.

The [Charles] Lee Papers. Vol. 3: 1778–82. *Collections of the New-York Historical Society*, 6 (1874).

Leiby, Adrian C. *The Revolutionary War in the Hackensack Valley: The Jersey Dutch and the Neutral Ground*. New Brunswick, N.J.: Rutgers University Press, 1980, originally published in 1962.

Lowell, Edward J. *The Hessians and the Other German Auxiliaries of Great Britain in the Revolutionary War*. Williamstown, Mass.: Corner House Publishers, 1970, originally published in 1884.

Lydenberg, Harry M., ed. *Archibald Robertson, Lieutenant-General Royal Engineers: His Diaries and Sketches in America, 1762–1780*. New York: New York Public Library, 1930.

Mackesy, Piers. "British Strategy in the War of American Independence." *The Yale Review*, 52 (1962–63): 539–57.

Martin, Joseph P. *Private Yankee Doodle: Being a Narrative of Some of the Adventures, Dangers and Sufferings of a Revolutionary Soldier*. Ed. George F. Scheer. Boston: Little, Brown & Co., 1962.

Mintz, Max M. *The Generals of Saratoga: John Burgoyne and Horatio Gates*. New Haven, Conn.: Yale University Press, 1990.

Moore, Howard P. *A Life of General John Stark of New Hampshire*. Boston: Spaulding-Moss Co., 1949.

Nelson, Paul D. *Anthony Wayne: Soldier of the Early Republic*. Bloomington: Indiana University Press, 1985.

———. *General Horatio Gates*. Baton Rouge: Louisiana State University Press, 1976.

———. "Horatio Gates at Newburgh, 1783: A Misunderstood Role," with a "Rebuttal" by Richard H. Kohn. *William and Mary Quarterly*, 29 (1972): 143–58.

———. *William Alexander, Lord Stirling*. University: University of Alabama Press, 1987.

Nickerson, Hoffman. *The Turning Point of the Revolution, or Burgoyne in America*. 2 vols. Port Washington, N.Y.: Kennikat Press, 1967, originally published in 1928.

Patterson, Samuel W. *Horatio Gates: Defender of American Liberties*. New York: Columbia University Press, 1941.

Reed, John F. *Valley Forge: Crucible of Victory*. Monmouth Beach, N.J.: Philip Freneau Press, 1969.

Ritchie, Carson I., ed. "A New York Diary of the Revolutionary War (Brig. Gen. James Pattison, 1778–79)." In *Narratives of the Revolution in New York . . .* , pp. 206–303. New York: New-York Historical Society, 1975.

Rossman, Kenneth R. *Thomas Mifflin and the Politics of the American Revolution*. Chapel Hill: University of North Carolina Press, 1952.

Skeen, C. Edward. "The Newburgh Conspiracy Reconsidered," with a "Rebuttal" by Richard H. Kohn. *William and Mary Quarterly*, 31 (1974): 273–98.

Smith, Samuel S. *The Battle of Monmouth.* Monmouth Beach, N.J.: Philip Freneau Press, 1964.

Stewart, Frank H. "Foraging for Valley Forge in Salem and Gloucester Counties, N.J., with Associated Happenings." *Proceedings of the New Jersey Historical Society,* new series, 14 (1929): 144–63.

Striker, William S. *The Battle of Monmouth.* Princeton, N.J.: Princeton University Press, 1927.

Thacher, James. *A Military Journal During the American Revolutionary War, from 1775–1783.* 2d ed. Boston: Cottons & Barnard, 1827.

Thayer, Theodore. *The Making of a Scapegoat: Washington and Lee at Monmouth.* Port Washington, N.Y.: Kennikat Press, 1976.

Trussell, John B. B., Jr. *Birthplace of an Army: A Study of the Valley Forge Encampment.* Harrisburg: Pennsylvania Historical and Museum Commission, 1976.

Tustin, Joseph P., ed. *Diary.* 1979. See Chapter 7 references.

Uhlendorf, Bernhard A., ed. *Revolution in America: Confidential Letters and Journals 1776–1784 of Adjutant General Major Baurmeister of the Hessian Forces.* New Brunswick, N.J.: Rutgers University Press, 1957.

Wallace, Willard M. *Appeal to Arms: A Military History of the American Revolution.* New York: Harper & Brothers, 1951.

Ward, Harry M. *Charles Scott and the "Spirit of '76."* Charlottesville: University Press of Virginia, 1988.

Willcox, William B. "British Strategy in America, 1778." *Journal of Modern History,* 19 (1947): 97–121.

———. *Portrait of a General: Sir Henry Clinton in the War of Independence.* New York: Alfred A. Knopf, 1964.

CHAPTER 9

Agniel, Lucien. *The South in the American Revolution, 1780–1781.* Myrtle Beach, S.C.: Artpress International, 1980.

Bennett, Charles E. *Southernmost Battlefields of the Revolution.* Bailey's Crossroads, Va.: Blair, Inc., 1970.

Bennett, Charles E., and Lennon, Donald R. *A Quest for Glory: Major General Robert Howe and the American Revolution.* Chapel Hill: University of North Carolina Press, 1991.

Bulger, William T. "The British Expedition to Charleston, 1779–1780." Ph.D. diss., University of Michigan, 1957.

Cashin, Edward J. *The King's Ranger: Thomas Brown and the American Revolution on the Southern Frontier.* Athens: University of Georgia Press, 1989.

Cavanagh, John C. "American Military Leadership in the Southern Campaign: Benjamin Lincoln." In W. Robert Higgins, ed., *The Revolutionary War in the South: Power, Conflict, and Leadership,* pp. 101–31. Durham, N.C.: Duke University Press, 1979.

Coleman, Kenneth. *The American Revolution in Georgia, 1763–1789.* Athens: University of Georgia Press, 1958.

Davis, Robert S. and Thomas, Kenneth H., Jr. *Kettle Creek: The Battle of the Cane Brakes: Wilkes County, Georgia.* Atlanta: State of Georgia Office of Planning and Research, 1974.

Draper, Lyman C. *King's Mountain and Its Heroes.* Baltimore: Genealogical Publishing Co., 1983.

Ferguson, Clyde R. "Carolina and Georgia Patriot and Loyalist Militia in Action, 1778–1783." In *The Southern Experience in the American Revolution,* eds. Jeffrey J. Crow and Larry E. Tise. Chapel Hill: University of North Carolina Press, 1978, pp. 174–99.

———. "General Andrew Pickens." Ph.D. diss., Duke University, 1960.

Grimké, John F. "Journal of the Campaign to the Southward, May 9th to July 14th, 1778." *South Carolina Historical and Genealogical Magazine,* 12 (1911): 60, 118–134, and 190–206.

Gruber, Ira D. "Britain's Southern Strategy." In *The Revolutionary War in the South: Power, Conflict, and Leadership,* ed. W. Robert Higgins. Durham, N.C.: Duke University Press, 1979, pp. 205–56.

Higginbotham, Don. *Daniel Morgan: Revolutionary Rifleman.* Chapel Hill: University of North Carolina Press, 1961.

Hough, Franklin B., ed. *The Siege of Charleston by the British Fleet and Army.* Spartanburg, S.C.: Reprint Co., 1975, originally published in 1867.

Jackson, Harvey H. *Lachlan McIntosh and the Politics of Revolutionary Georgia.* Athens: University of Georgia Press, 1979.

Johnson, William. *Sketches of the Life and Correspondence of Nathanael Greene.* 2 vols. New York: Da Capo Press, 1973, originally published in 1822.

Lambert, Robert S. *South Carolina Loyalists in the American Revolution.* Columbia: University of South Carolina Press, 1987.

Landers, H. L. *The Battle of Camden, South Carolina, August 16, 1780.* Washington, D.C.: U.S. Government Printing Office, 1929.

Lawrence, Alexander A. "General Robert Howe and the British Capture of Savannah in 1778." *Georgia Historical Quarterly,* 36 (1952): 303–27.

————. *Storm over Savannah: The Story of Count D'Estaing and the Siege of the Town in 1779.* Athens: University of Georgia Press, 1951.

Lennon, Donald R. " 'The Graveyard of American Commanders': The Continental Army's Southern Department, 1776–1783." *North Carolina Historical Review,* 67 (1990): 133–58.

Lumpkin, Henry. *From Savannah to Yorktown: The American Revolution in the South.* New York: Paragon House, 1981.

McCrady, Edward. *The History of South Carolina in the Revolution, 1775–1780.* New York: Russell & Russell, 1969, originally published in 1901.

Mowat, Charles L. *East Florida as a British Province, 1763–1784.* Berkeley: University of California Press, 1943.

Nelson, Paul D. "Major General Horatio Gates as a Military Leader: The Southern Experience." In *The Revolutionary War in the South: Power, Conflict, and Leadership,* ed. W. Robert Higgins. Durham, N.C.: Duke University Press, 1979, pp. 132–58.

Pugh, Robert C. "The Cowpens Campaign and the American Revolution." Ph.D. diss., University of Illinois, 1951.

————. "The Revolutionary Militia in the Southern Campaign, 1780–1781." *William and Mary Quarterly,* 3d ser., 14 (1957): 154–75.

Roberts, John M., ed. *A Revolutionary Soldier [James Collins].* New York: Arno Press, 1979, originally published in 1859.

Robertson, Heard. "The Second British Occupation of Augusta, 1780–1781." *Georgia Historical Quarterly,* 58 (1974): 422–46.

Searcy, Martha C. *The Georgia-Florida Contest in the American Revolution, 1776–1778.* University: University of Alabama Press, 1985.

Schenk, David. *North Carolina, 1780–81: Being a History of the Invasion of the Carolinas by the British Army.* Spartanburg, S.C.: Reprint Co., 1967, originally published in 1889.

Shy, John. "British Strategy for Pacifying the Southern Colonies, 1778–1781." In *The Southern Experience in the American Revolution,* eds. Jeffrey J. Crow and Larry E. Tise. Chapel Hill: University of North Carolina Press, 1978, pp. 155–73.

Uhlendorf, Bernhard A., trans. and ed. *The Siege of Charleston . . . Diaries and Letters of Hessian Officers From the von Jungkenn Papers in the William L. Clements Library.* Ann Arbor: University of Michigan, 1938.

Ward, Christopher. *The Delaware Continentals, 1776–1783.* Wilmington: Historical Society of Delaware, 1941.

Waring, Alice N. *The Fighting Elder: Andrew Pickens (1739–1817).* Columbia: University of South Carolina Press, 1962.

Weller, Jac. "The Irregular War in the South." *Military Affairs*, 24 (1960–61): 124–30.
White, Katherine K. *The King's Mountain Men: The Story of the Battle, with Sketches of the American Soldiers who Took Part*. Dayton, Va.: Joseph P. Ruebush Co., 1924.

CHAPTER 10

Bass, Robert D. *Gamecock: The Life and Campaigns of General Thomas Sumter*. New York: Holt, Rinehart & Winston, 1961.
―――. *The Green Dragoon: The Lives of Banastre Tarleton and Mary Robinson*. New York: Henry Holt & Co., 1957.
―――. *Swamp Fox: The Life and Campaigns of General Francis Marion*. New York: Henry Holt & Co., 1959.
Chadwick, French E., ed. *The Graves Papers and Other Documents Relating to the Naval Operations of the Yorktown Campaign, July to October, 1781*. New York: De Vine Press, 1916.
Chinard, Gilbert, ed. *Lafayette in Virginia: Unpublished Letters*. Baltimore: Johns Hopkins Press, 1928.
Clinton, Sir Henry. *The American Rebellion: Sir Henry Clinton's Narrative of His Campaigns, 1775–1782, with an Appendix of Original Documents*. Ed. William B. Willcox. New Haven, Conn.: Yale University Press, 1954.
Davis, Burke. *The Campaign That Won America: The Story of Yorktown*. New York: Dial Press, 1970.
―――. *The Cowpens-Guilford Courthouse Campaign*. Philadelphia: J. B. Lippincott Co., 1962.
Feltman, William. *The Journal of Lieut. William Feltman of the First Pennsylvania Regiment, 1781–82*. Philadelphia: Historical Society of Pennsylvania, 1853.
Fleming, Thomas J. *Beat the Last Drum: The Siege of Yorktown, 1781*. New York: St. Martin's Press, 1963.
Gottschalk, Louis. *Lafayette and the Close of the American Revolution*. Chicago: University of Chicago Press, 1942.
Gregorie, Anne K. *Thomas Sumter*. Columbia, S.C.: R. L. Bryan Co., 1931.
Johnston, Henry P. *The Yorktown Campaign and the Surrender of Cornwallis, 1781*. New York: Harper & Brothers, 1881.
Landers, H. L. *The Virginia Campaign and the Blockade and Siege of Yorktown*. Washington, D.C.: U.S. Government Printing Office, 1931.
Larrabee, Harold A. *Decision at the Chesapeake*. New York: Clarkson N. Potter, 1964.
Lee, Henry. *The Campaign of 1781 in the Carolinas: with Remarks Historical and Critical of Johnson's Life of Greene*. Spartanburg, S.C.: Reprint Co., 1975, originally published in 1824.
Nolan, J. Bennett, comp. *Lafayette in America Day by Day*. Baltimore: Johns Hopkins University Press, 1934.
Palmer, John M. *General Von Steuben*. New Haven, Conn.: Yale University Press, 1937.
Pancake, John S. *This Destructive War: The British Campaigns in the Carolinas, 1780–1782*. University of Alabama Press, 1985.
Rankin, Hugh F. *Francis Marion: The Swamp Fox*. New York: Thomas Y. Crowell Co., 1973.
―――. *Greene and Cornwallis: The Campaign in the Carolinas*. Raleigh, N.C.: [N.C. State] Division of Archives and History, 1976.
―――. *The North Carolina Continentals*. Chapel Hill: University of North Carolina Press, 1971.
―――. *The War of the Revolution in Virginia*. Williamsburg: Virginia Independence Bicentennial Commission, 1979.
Riley, Edward M., ed. *St. George Tucker's Journal of the Siege of Yorktown, 1781*. Offprint from *William and Mary Quarterly*, 3d ser., 4 (1948).

Sands, John O. *Yorktown's Captive Fleet.* Charlottesville: University Press of Virginia, 1983.

Schenck, David. *North Carolina, 1780–91: Being a History of the Invasion of the Carolinas by the British Army under Lord Cornwallis in 1780–81.* Spartanburg, S.C.: Reprint Co., 1967, originally published in 1889.

Simcoe, Lt. Col. John Graves. *A Journal of the Operations of the Queen's Rangers from the End of the Year 1777 to the Conclusion of the Late American War.* New York: 1844, originally published in 1787.

Tarleton, Lt. Col. Banastre. *A History of the Campaigns of 1780 and 1781 in the Southern Provinces of North America.* Spartanburg, S.C.: Reprint Co., 1967, originally published in 1787.

Thayer, Theodore. *Nathanael Greene: Strategist of the American Revolution.* New York: Twayne Publishers, 1960.

Trabue, Daniel. "The Journal of Colonel Daniel Trabue." In *Colonial Men and Times,* ed. Lillie D. Harper. Philadelphia: Innes Sons, 1916, pp. 3–156.

Treacy, M. F. *Prelude to Yorktown: The Southern Campaign of Nathanael Greene, 1780–1781.* Chapel Hill: University of North Carolina Press, 1963.

Ward, Harry M., and Greer, Harold. *Richmond During the Revolution, 1775–83.* Charlottesville: University Press of Virginia, 1979.

Weelen, Jean-Edmond. *Rochambeau: Father and Son.* New York: Henry Holt and Co., 1936.

Wickwire, Franklin, and Mary. *Cornwallis and the War of Independence.* London: Faber & Faber, 1971.

Wild, Ebenezer. "Journal of Ebenezer Wild." *Proceedings of the Massachusetts Historical Society,* 2d ser., 6 (1890): 78–160.

Willcox, William B. "The British Road to Yorktown: A Study in Divided Command." *American Historical Review,* 70 (1946): 1–35.

CHAPTER 11

Abler, Thomas S., ed. *Chainbreaker: The Revolutionary War Memoirs of Governor Blacksnake* (Seneca chief). Lincoln: University of Nebraska Press, 1989.

Arnow, Hariette S. *Seedtime on the Cumberland.* New York: Macmillan Co., 1960.

Bakeless, John. *Background to Glory: The Life of George Rogers Clark.* Philadelphia: J. B. Lippincott Co., 1957.

———. *Daniel Boone.* New York: William Morrow & Co., 1939.

Barnhart, John D. *Henry Hamilton and George Rogers Clark in the American Revolution, with the Unpublished Journal of Lieut. Gov. Henry Hamilton.* Crawfordsville, Ind.: R. E. Banta, 1951.

———. "A New Evaluation of Henry Hamilton and George Rogers Clark." *Mississippi Valley Historical Review,* 37 (1951): 643–52.

Butterfield, Consul W. *An Historical Account of the Expedition Against Sandusky and Col. William Crawford in 1782.* Cincinnati: Robert Clarke & Co., 1873.

———. *History of George Rogers Clark's Conquest of the Illinois and the Wabash Towns 1778 and 1779.* Columbus, Ohio: F. J. Herr Press, 1904.

Campbell, William W. *Annals of Tryon County, or, The Border Warfare of New York, During the Revolution.* New York: Dodd, Mead & Co., 1924.

Clark, George Rogers. *Col. George Rogers Clark's Sketch of His Campaign in the Illinois in 1778–9.* New York: Arno Press & The New York Times, 1971, originally published in 1869.

Coleman, J. Winston, Jr. *The British Invasion of Kentucky: With an Account of the Capture of Ruddell's and Martin's Stations, June, 1780.* Lexington, Ky.: Winburn Press, 1951.

Cook, Frederick, comp. *Journals of the Military Expedition of Major General John Sullivan against the Six Nations of Indians in 1779.* Hallandale, Fla.: 1972, originally published in 1887.

Corkran, David H. *The Creek Frontier, 1540–1783.* Norman: University of Oklahoma Press, 1967.

Cruishank, Ernest. *The Story of Butler's Rangers and the Settlement of Niagara.* Owen Sound, Ontario: Richardson, Bond & Wright, 1975, originally published in 1893.

Dowd, Gregory E. *A Spirited Resistance: The North American Indian Struggle for Unity, 1745–1815.* Baltimore: Johns Hopkins University Press, 1992.

Downes, Randolph C. *Council Fires on the Upper Ohio: A Narrative of Indian Affairs in the Upper Ohio Valley Until 1795.* Pittsburgh: University of Pittsburgh Press, 1940.

Driver, Carl S. *John Sevier: Pioneer of the Old Southwest.* Chapel Hill: University of North Carolina Press, 1932.

Durrett, Reuben T. *Bryant's [Bryan's] Station and the Memorial Proceedings . . . . Filson Club Publications,* no. 12. Louisville: John P. Morton & Co., 1897.

Eckert, Allan W. *The Frontiersman: A Narrative.* Boston: Little, Brown & Co., 1967.

Evans, E. Raymond. "Notable Persons in Cherokee History: Dragging Canoe." *Journal of Cherokee Studies,* 2 (Winter 1977): 176–89.

Flick, Alexander C. "The Sullivan-Clinton Campaign in 1779." *Proceedings of the New Jersey Historical Society,* new series, 15 (1930): 64–72.

Graymount, Barbara. *The Iroquois in the American Revolution.* Syracuse, N.Y.: Syracuse University Press, 1972.

Harding, Margery H., comp. *George Rogers Clark and His Men: Military Records, 1778–1784.* Frankfort: Kentucky Historical Society, 1981.

Hassler, Edgar W. *Old Westmoreland: A History of Western Pennsylvania During the Revolution.* Pittsburgh: J. R. Welden & Co., 1900.

Jones, Dorothy V. *License for Empire: Colonialism by Treaty in Early America.* Chicago: University of Chicago Press, 1982.

Juday, Richard. *The Battle of Piqua: Revolutionary Encounter in Ohio.* Dayton: Grove-Merritt Publications, 1976.

Kelsay, Isabel T. *Joseph Brant, 1743–1807.* Syracuse, N.Y.: Syracuse University Press, 1984.

Merrell, James H. *The Indians' New World: Catawbas and Their Neighbors from European Contact Through the Era of Removal.* Chapel Hill: University of North Carolina Press, 1989.

Mohr, Walter. *Federal Indian Relations, 1774–1788.* Philadelphia: University of Pennsylvania Press, 1933.

O'Donnell, James H., III. *Southern Indians in the American Revolution.* Knoxville: University of Tennessee Press, 1973.

Parker, Arthur C. "The Indian Interpretation of the Sullivan-Clinton Campaign." *Publication Fund Series of the Rochester Historical Society,* 8 (1929): 45–59.

Pieper, Thomas I., and Gidney, James B. *Fort Laurens, 1778–1779: The Revolutionary War in Ohio.* Kent, Ohio: Kent State University Press, 1976.

Ranck, George W. *Boonesborough: Its Founding, Pioneer Struggles, Transylvania Days, and Revolutionary Annals. Filson Club Publications,* no. 16. Louisville: John P. Morton & Co., 1901.

Redd, John. "Reminiscences of Western Virginia, 1770–1790." *Virginia Magazine of History and Biography,* 6 (1899): 337–46.

Seinke, Katherine W., ed. *The George Rogers Clark Adventure and Selected Documents of the American Revolution at the Frontier Posts.* New Orleans: Polyanthos, 1981.

Shaw, Helen L. *British Administration of the Southern Indians, 1756–1783.* Lancaster, Pa.: Lancaster Press, 1931.

Skaggs, David C., ed. *The Old Northwest in the American Revolution.* Madison: State Historical Society of Wisconsin, 1977.

Sosin, Jack M. *The Revolutionary Frontier, 1763–1783.* New York: Holt, Rinehart & Winston, 1967.

———. "The Use of Indians in the War of the American Revolution: A Re-Assessment of Responsibility." *Canadian Historical Review,* 46 (1965): 101–21.

Swiggett, Howard. *War Out of Niagara: Walter Butler and the Tory Rangers.* Port Washington, N.Y.: Ira J. Friedman, 1963, originally published in 1933.

Talbert, Charles G. *Benjamin Logan: Kentucky Frontiersman.* Lexington: University of Kentucky Press, 1962.

Thwaites, Reuben G., and Kellogg, Louise P., eds. *Frontier Defense on the Upper Ohio, 1777–1778.* Millwood, N.J., 1977, originally published in 1912.

———. *The Revolution on the Upper Ohio, 1775–1777.* Port Washington, N.Y.: Kennikat Press, 1970, originally published in 1908.

Van Every, Dale. *A Company of Heroes: The American Frontier, 1775–1783.* New York: Arno Press, 1977, originally published in 1962.

Whittemore, Charles P. *A General of the Revolution: John Sullivan of New Hampshire.* New York: Columbia University Press, 1961.

Williams, Edward G. *Fort Pitt and the Revolution on the Western Frontier.* Pittsburgh: Historical Society of Western Pennsylvania, 1978.

Williams, Samuel G. *Tennessee During the Revolutionary War.* Knoxville: University of Tennessee Press, 2d. ed., 1974.

Wilson, Samuel M. *Battle of the Blue Licks, August 19, 1782.* Lexington, Ky.: no publ. listed, 1927.

Wright, Albert H., ed. *The Sullivan Expedition of 1779: Contemporary Newspaper Comment and Letters.* Ithaca, N.Y.: A. M. Wright, 1943.

CHAPTER 12

Allen, Gardner W. *A Naval History of the American Revolution.* 2 vols. Williamstown, Mass.: Corner House Publishers, 1970, originally published in 1913.

Augur, Helen. *The Secret War of Independence.* New York: Duell, Sloan, & Pearce, 1955.

Barton, H. A. "Sweden and the War of American Independence." *William and Mary Quarterly,* 3d ser., 23 (1966): 408–30.

Bemis, Samuel F. *The Diplomacy of the American Revolution.* Bloomington: Indiana University Press, 1957, originally published in 1935.

Bendiner, Elmer. *The Virginia Diplomats.* New York: Alfred A. Knopf, 1976.

Bolkhovitinov, Nikolai N. *Russia and the American Revolution.* Tallahassee, Fla.: Diplomatic Press, 1976.

Caughey, John W. *Bernando de Gálvez in Louisiana, 1776–1783.* Berkeley: University of California Press, 1934.

Clowes, William L. *The Royal Navy: A History from the Earliest Times to the Present.* Vol. 3. New York: AMS Press, 1966, originally published in 1898.

Cummins, Light T. *Spanish Observers and the American Revolution, 1775–1783.* Baton Rouge: Louisiana State University Press, 1991.

Dill, Alonzo T. *William Lee: Militia Diplomat.* Williamsburg, Va.: Virginia Independence Bicentennial Commission, 1976.

Dull, Jonathan R. *A Diplomatic History of the American Revolution.* New Haven, Conn.: Yale University Press, 1985.

———. *The French Navy and American Independence: A Study of Arms and Diplomacy, 1774–1787.* Princeton, N.J.: Princeton University Press, 1975.

Dupuy, R. Ernest, Hammerman, Gay, and Hayes, Grace P. *The American Revolution: A Global War.* New York: David McKay Co., 1977.

Feiling, Keith. *Warren Hastings.* New York: St. Martin's Press, 1955.

Fowler, William M. *Rebels Under Sail: The American Navy During the Revolution.* New York: Charles Scribner's Sons, 1976.

Griffith, David M. "American Commercial Diplomacy in Russia, 1780 to 1783." *William and Mary Quarterly,* 3d ser., 27 (1970): 379–410.

Hutson, James H. *John Adams and the Diplomacy of the American Revolution.* Lexington: University of Kentucky Press, 1980.

James, Coy H. *Silas Deane—Patriot or Traitor?* East Lansing: Michigan State University Press, 1975.

James, W. M. *The British Navy in Adversity: A Study of the War of American Independence.* London: Longmans, Green & Co., 1926.

Kaplan, Lawrence S. *Colonies into Nation: American Diplomacy, 1763–1801.* New York: Macmillan Co., 1972.

———., ed. *The American Revolution and "A Candid World."* Kent, Ohio: Kent State University Press, 1977.

Lewis, Charles L. *Admiral De Grasse and American Independence.* Annapolis, Md.: U.S. Naval Institute, 1945.

Lewis, James A. *The Final Campaign of the American Revolution: Rise and Fall of the Spanish Bahamas.* Columbia: University of South Carolina Press, 1991.

Lint, Gregg L. "Preparing for Peace: The Objectives of the United States, France, and Spain in the War of American Independence." In *Peace and the Peacemakers: The Treaty of 1783,* eds. Ronald Hoffman and Peter J. Albert. Charlottesville: University Press of Virginia, 1986, pp. 30–51.

McGuffie, Tom H. *The Siege of Gibraltar, 1779–1783.* Philadelphia: Dufour Editions, 1965.

Macintyre, Donald. *Admiral Rodney.* New York: W. W. Norton & Co., 1962.

Maclay, Edgar S. *A History of American Privateers.* New York: D. Appleton & Co., 1899.

Mahan, Alfred T. *The Major Operations of the Navies in the War of American Independence.* London: Sampson Low, Marston & Co., 1913.

Miller, Nathan. *Sea of Glory: The Continental Navy Fights for Independence, 1775–1783.* New York: David McKay Co., 1974.

Morison, Samuel E. *John Paul Jones: A Sailor's Biography.* Boston: Little, Brown & Co., 1959.

Morris, Richard B. *The Peacemakers: The Great Powers and American Independence.* New York: Harper & Row, 1965.

Neeser, Robert W., ed. *Letters and Papers Relating to the Cruises of Gustavus Conyngham, A Captain of the Continental Navy.* New York: De Vine Press, 1915.

Nordholt, Jan W. S. *The Dutch Republic and American Independence.* Chapel Hill: University of North Carolina Press, 1979.

Patterson, A. Temple. *The Other Armada: The Franco-Spanish Attempt to Invade Britain in 1779.* Manchester, England: Manchester University Press, 1960.

Potts, Louis W. *Arthur Lee.* See Chapter 2 references.

Richmond, Herbert. *The Navy in India, 1763–1783.* London: Ernest Benn Ltd., 1931.

Rush, N. Orwin. *Spain's Final Triumph over Great Britain in the Gulf of Mexico: The Battle of Pensacola, March 9 to May 8, 1781.* Tallahassee: Florida State University Press, 1966.

Schoenbrun, David. *Triumph in Paris: The Exploits of Benjamin Franklin.* New York: Harper & Row, 1976.

Seitz, Don C., comp. *Paul Jones: His Exploits in English Seas During 1778–1780: Contemporary Accounts Collected from English Newspapers with a Complete Bibliography.* New York: E. P. Dutton & Co., 1917.

Smith, Charles R. *Marines in the Revolution: A History of the Continental Marines in the American Revolution, 1775–1783.* Washington, D.C.: History and Museum Division, U.S. Marine Corps, 1975.

Stinchcombe, William C. *The American Revolution and the French Alliance.* Syracuse, N.Y.: Syracuse University Press, 1969.

Stourzh, Gerald. *Benjamin Franklin and American Foreign Policy.* Chicago: University of Chicago Press, 1954.

Tilley, John A. *The British Navy and the American Revolution.* Columbia: University of South Carolina Press, 1987.

Tuchman, Barbara W. *The First Salute*. New York: Alfred A. Knopf, 1988.

Van Alstyne, Richard W. "Great Britain, the War for Independence, and the 'Gathering Storm' in Europe, 1775–1778." *Huntington Library Quarterly*, 27 (1964): 311–46.

Wharton, Francis, ed. *The Revolutionary Diplomatic Correspondence of the United States*. 6 vols. Washington, D.C.: U.S. Government Printing Office, 1889.

CHAPTER 13

Abrahamson, James L. *The American Homefront: Revolutionary War, Civil War, World War I, World War II*. Washington, D.C.: National Defense University Press, 1983.

Adams, James T. *New England in the Republic, 1776–1850*. Gloucester, Mass.: Peter Smith, 1960, originally published in 1926.

Alexander, John K. "The Fort Wilson Incident of 1779: A Case Study of the Revolutionary Crowd." *William and Mary Quarterly*, 3d ser., 31 (1974): 599–612.

Bezanson, Anne. *Prices and Inflation During the American Revolution—Pennsylvania, 1770–1790*. Philadelphia: University of Pennsylvania Press, 1951.

Buel, Richard, Jr. *Dear Liberty: Connecticut's Mobilization for the Revolutionary War*. Middletown, Conn.: Wesleyan University Press, 1980.

Butterfield, L. H. "General Washington's Sewing Circle." *American Heritage* (Summer 1951): 7–10; 68.

———., ed. *Letters of Benjamin Rush*. 2 vols. Princeton, N.J.: Princeton University Press, 1951.

Chastellux, Marquis de. *Travels in North America in the Years 1780, 1781, and 1782*. Ed. Howard C. Rice, Jr. 2 vols. Chapel Hill: University of North Carolina Press, 1963, originally published in 1786.

Clark, Victor S. *History of Manufactures in the United States*. Vol. 1 of 3 vols. New York: McGraw-Hill Book Co., 1929.

Collins, Varnum L., ed. *A Brief Narrative of the Ravages of the British and Hessians at Princeton in 1776–77*. Princeton, N.J.: University Library, 1906.

Cometti, Elizabeth. "The Labor Front During the Revolution." In *The American Revolution: the Homefront*. *West Georgia College Studies in the Social Sciences*, 15 (1976): 79–90.

———. "Women in the American Revolution." *New England Quarterly*, 20 (1947): 329–46.

Crane, Elaine F. *A Dependent People: Newport, Rhode Island in the Revolutionary Era*. New York: Fordham University Press, 1985.

———., ed. *The Diary of Elizabeth Drinker*. Vol. 1 of 3 vols. Boston: Northeastern University Press, 1991.

Davis, Andrew M. "The Limitation of Prices in Massachusetts, 1776–1779." *Publications of the Colonial Society of Massachusetts*, 10 (1904–06): 119–34.

East, Robert A. *Business Enterprise in the American Revolutionary War*. New York: Columbia University Press, 1938.

Evans, Elizabeth. *Weathering the Storm: Women of the American Revolution*. New York: Charles Scribner's Sons, 1975.

Flick, Alexander C., et al. *The American Revolution in New York: Its Political, Social and Economic Significance*. Albany: University of the State of New York Press, 1926.

Foner, Philip S. *Labor and the American Revolution*. Westport, Conn.: Greenwood Press, 1976.

Gross, Robert A. *The Minutemen and Their World*. New York: Hill & Wang, 1976.

Grossman, Jonathan. "Wage and Price Controls During the American Revolution." *Monthly Labor Review*, 96 (September 1973): 3–9.

Handlin, Oscar, and Handlin, Lilian. *A Restless People: Americans in Rebellion, 1770–1787*. Garden City, N.Y.: Anchor Press/Doubleday, 1982.

Handlin, Oscar and Mary F. "Revolutionary Economic Policy in Massachusetts." *William and Mary Quarterly*, 3d ser., 4 (1947): 3–26.

Harlow, Ralph V. "Aspects of Revolutionary Finances, 1775–1783." *American Historical Review,* 35 (1930): 46–48.

Hoerder, Dirk. *Crowd Action in Revolutionary Massachusetts, 1765–1780.* New York: Academic Press, 1977.

Hoffman, Ronald. *A Spirit of Dissension: Economics, Politics, and the Revolution in Maryland.* Baltimore: Johns Hopkins University Press, 1973.

Jackson, John W., ed. *Margaret Morris: Her Journal with Biographical Sketch and Notes.* Philadelphia: George S. MacManns Co., 1949.

Jensen, Merrill. "The American Revolution and American Agriculture." *Agricultural History,* 43 (January 1969): 107–24.

Letters Written by Ebenezer Huntington during the American Revolution. New York: Charles F. Heartman, 1914.

Longley, R. S. "Mob Activities in Revolutionary Massachusetts." *New England Quarterly,* 6 (1933): 98–130.

McClusker, John J., and Menard, Russell R. *The Economy of British America, 1607–1789.* Chapel Hill: University of North Carolina Press, 1985.

Main, Jackson T., 1973b. *See* Chapter 18 references.

Mason, Bernard. "Entrepreneurial Activity in New York During the American Revolution." *Business History Review,* 40 (Summer 1966): 190–212.

Meyer, Edith P. *Petticoat Patriots of the American Revolution.* New York: Vanguard Press, 1976.

Mitchell, Broadus. *The Price of Independence: A Realistic View of the American Revolution.* New York: Oxford University Press.

Morris, Richard B. *Government and Labor in Early America.* New York: Columbia University Press, 1946.

Myers, Albert C., ed. *Sally Wister's Journal . . . 1777–1778.* Philadelphia: Ferris & Lesch Publishers, 1902.

Nevins, Allan. *The American States During and After the Revolution.* New York: Augustus M. Kelley, 1969, originally published in 1924.

Norton, Mary B. *Liberty's Daughters: The Revolutionary Experience of American Women, 1760–1800.* Boston: Little, Brown & Co., 1980.

Post, Lydia M. *Personal Recollections of the American Revolution: A Private Journal.* Ed. Sidney Barclay. Port Washington, N.Y.: Kennikat Press, 1970, originally published in 1859.

Reed, Esther DeBerdt (?). "The Sentiments of an American Woman." *Pennsylvania Magazine of History and Biography,* 18 (1894): 361–66.

Reed, William B. *The Life of Esther deBerdt Afterward Esther Reed of Philadelphia.* Philadelphia: C. Sherman, 1853.

———., ed. *Life and Correspondence of Joseph Reed.* 2 vols. Philadelphia & Blakiston, 1847.

Rosswurm, Steven. *Arms, Country, and Class: The Philadelphia Militia and "Lower Sort" During the American Revolution, 1775–1783.* New Brunswick, N.J.: Rutgers University Press, 1987.

Salay, David L. "Arming for War: The Production of War Material in Pennsylvania for the American Armies during the Revolution." Ph.D. diss., University of Delaware, 1977.

Schulz, Constance B. "Daughters of Liberty: The History of Women in the Revolutionary War Pension Records." *Prologue: Journal of the National Archives,* 16 (fall 1984): 139–53.

Scott, Kenneth. "Counterfeiting in New York During the Revolution." *New-York Historical Society Quarterly,* 42 (1958): 221–59.

Smith, Barbara C. "Food Rioters and the American Revolution." *William and Mary Quarterly,* 3d ser., 51 (1994): 3–38.

Upton, Richard F. *Revolutionary New Hampshire: An Account of the Social and Political Forces Underlying the Transition from Royal Province to American Commonwealth.* Port Washington, N.Y.: Kennikat Press, 1970, originally published in 1936.

York, Neil L. *Mechanical Metamorphosis: Technological Change in Revolutionary America.* Westport, Conn.: Greenwood Press, 1985.

CHAPTER 14

Applegate, Howard L. "Constitutions Like Iron: the Life of the American Revolutionary War Soldiers in the Middle Department, 1775–1783." Ph.D. diss., Syracuse University, 1966.
Aptheker, Herbert. *The Negro in the American Revolution.* New York: International Publishers, 1940.
Berlin, Robert H. "The Administration of Military Justice in the Continental Army during the American Revolution, 1775–1783." Ph.D. diss., University of California, Santa Barbara, 1976.
Bernath, Stuart L. "George Washington and the Genesis of American Military Discipline." *Mid-America,* 49 (1967): 83–100.
Bodle, Wayne K., and Thibaut, Jacqueline. *Valley Forge Historical Research Report.* 3 vols. Valley Forge: Valley Forge Historical Park, 1980.
Bolton, Charles K. *The Private Soldier Under Washington.* Port Washington, N.Y.: Kennikat Press, 1964, originally published in 1900.
Bowman, Allen. *The Morale of the American Revolutionary Army.* Port Washington, N.Y.: Kennikat Press, 1964, originally published in 1943.
Bradford, S. Sydney. "Discipline in the Morristown Winter Encampments." *Proceedings of the New Jersey Historical Society,* 80 (1962): 1–30.
Bray, Robert C., and Bushnell, Paul E., eds. *Diary of a Common Soldier in the American Revolution, 1775–1783: An Annotated Edition of the Military Journal of Jeremiah Greenman.* DeKalb: Northern Illinois University Press, 1978.
Carp, E. Wayne. *To Starve the Army at Pleasure: Continental Army Administration as American Political Culture, 1775–1783.* Chapel Hill: University of North Carolina Press, 1984.
Dann, John C., ed. *The Revolution Remembered: Eyewitness Accounts of the War of Independence.* Chicago: University of Chicago Press, 1977.
Echeverria, Durand, and Murphy, Orville T., eds. "The American Revolutionary Army: A French Estimate in 1777," attributed to Louis de Récicourt de Ganot. In *Military Analysis of the Revolutionary War: An Anthology by the Editors of Military Affairs.* Millwood, N.J.: KTO Press, 1977, pp. 201–17.
Ellis, John. *Armies in Revolution.* New York: Oxford University Press, 1974.
Ferling, John E. *A Wilderness of Miseries: War and Warriors in Early America.* Westport, Conn.: Greenwood Press, 1980.
Foner, Philip S. *Blacks in the American Revolution.* Westport, Conn.: Greenwood Press, 1975.
Ford, Worthington C., ed. *Correspondence and Journals of Samuel Blachley Webb.* 3 vols. Wickersham Press (Lancaster, Pa.), 1893–94.
Frey, Sylvia R. "Between Slavery and Freedom: Virginia Blacks in the American Revolution." *Journal of Southern History,* 49 (1983): 375–98.
———. *The British Soldier in America: A Social History of Military Life in the Revolutionary Period.* Austin: University of Texas Press, 1981.
Glasson, William M. *Federal Military Pensions in the United States.* New York: Oxford University Press, 1918.
Greene, Lorenzo J. "Some Observations on the Black Regiment of Rhode Island in the American Revolution." *Journal of Negro History,* 37 (1952): 142–72.
Hartgrove, W. B. "The Negro Soldier in the American Revolution." *Journal of Negro History,* 1 (1916): 111–31.
Hatch, Louis C. *The Administration of the American Revolutionary Army.* New York: Burt Franklin, 1971, originally published in 1904.
The Heath Papers. Collections of the Massachusetts Historical Society. 7th Series. Vols. 4–5. Boston, 1904–5.

Jackson, Luther P. "Virginia Negro Soldiers and Seamen in the American Revolution." *Journal of Negro History,* 27 (1942): 247–87.

Jordan, John W., ed. "Orderly Book of the Second Pennsylvania Continental Line, Colonel Henry Bicker." *Pennsylvania Magazine of History and Biography,* 35 (1901): 333–42 and 463–86 and 36 (1902): 30–59, 236–53, and 329–45.

Kaplan, Sidney. *The Black Presence in the Era of the American Revolution, 1770–1800.* Washington, D.C.: Smithsonian Institution, 1973.

Lauder, Almon, ed. *Orderly Books of the Fourth New York Regiment, 1778–1780 and the Second New York Regiment, 1780–1783 by Samuel Tallmadge and Others, with Diaries. . . .* Albany, N.Y.: University of the State of New York, 1932.

Lender, Mark E. "The Enlisted Line: The Continental Soldiers of New Jersey." Ph.D. diss., Rutgers University, 1975.

———. "The Social Structure of the New Jersey Brigade: The Continental Line as an American Standing Army." In *The Military in America: From the Colonial Era to Present,* ed. Peter Karsten. New York: Free Press, 1980, pp. 27–44.

Lender, Mark E., and Martin, James K., eds. *Citizen Soldier: The Revolutionary Journal of Joseph Bloomfield.* Newark: New Jersey Historical Society, 1980.

McBride, John D. "The Virginia War Effort, 1775–1983: Manpower Policies and Practices." Ph.D. diss., University of Virginia, 1977.

McMichael, James. "Diary of Lieutenant James McMichael of the Pennsylvania Line, 1776–1778." *Pennsylvania Magazine of History and Biography,* 16 (1892): 129–59.

Martin, James K., and Lender, Mark E. *A Respectable Army: The Military Origins of the Republic, 1763–1789.* Arlington Heights, Ill.: Harlan Davidson, 1982.

Martin, Joseph Plumb, 1962. *See* Chapter 8 references.

Mayo, Robert, and Moulton, Ferdinand, comp. *Army and Navy Pensions Laws, and Bounty Land Laws of the United States . . . from 1776 to 1854.* Baltimore: Lucas Brothers, 1854.

Middlekauf, Robert. "Why Men Fought in the American Revolution." *Huntington Library Quarterly,* 43 (1980): 135–48.

Papenfuse, Edward C., and Stiverson, Gregory A. "General Smallwood's Recruits: The Peacetime Career of the Revolutionary War Private." *William and Mary Quarterly,* 3d ser., 30 (1973): 117–32.

Peterson, Harold L. *The Book of the Continental Soldier.* Harrisburg, Pa.: Stackpole Co., 1968.

Powell, William S. "A Connecticut Soldier Under Washington: Elisha Bostwick's Memoirs of the First Years of the Revolution." *William and Mary Quarterly,* 3d ser., 6 (1949): 94–107.

Quarles, Benjamin. *The Negro in the American Revolution.* Chapel Hill: University of North Carolina Press, 1961.

Rankin, Hugh F. *The North Carolina Continentals.* Chapel Hill: University of North Carolina Press, 1971.

Resch, John P. "The Continentals of Peterborough, New Hampshire: Pension Records as a Source for Local History." *Prologue: Journal of the National Archives,* 16 (Fall 1984): 169–83.

Royster, Charles. *A Revolutionary People at War: The Continental Army and American Character, 1775–1783.* New York: W. W. Norton & Co., 1981.

Scheer, George F., and Rankin, Hugh F. *Rebels and Redcoats.* Cleveland: World Publishing Co., 1957.

Sellers, John R. "The Common Soldier in the American Revolution." In *Military History of the American Revolution,* ed. Stanley J. Underdal. Washington, D.C.: Office of Military History, 1976, pp. 151–61.

———. "The Virginia Continental Line, 1775–1780." Ph.D. diss., Tulane University, 1968.

Shy, John. *A People Numerous and Armed: Reflections on the Military Struggle for American Independence.* New York: Oxford University Press, 1976.

Smith, Jonathan. "How Massachusetts Raised Her Troops in the Revolution." *Proceedings of the Massachusetts Historical Society*, 55 (1922): 345–70.

Smith, Samuel S. *Winter at Morristown, 1779–1780: The Darkest Hour*. Monmouth Beach, N.J.: Philip Freneau Press, 1979.

Stillé, Charles J. *Major-General Anthony Wayne and the Pennsylvania Line in the Continental Army*. Philadelphia: J. B. Lippincott Co., 1893.

Stoudt, John J. *Ordeal at Valley Forge: A Day-to-Day Chronicle from December 17, 1777 to June 18, 1778, Compiled from the Sources*. Philadelphia: University of Pennsylvania Press, 1963.

Thacher, James. *Military Journals of the American Revolution*. New York: Arno Press, 1969, originally published in 1862.

"Valley Forge, 1777–1778: Diary of Surgeon Albigence Waldo, of the Continental Line." *Pennsylvania Magazine of History and Biography*, 21 (1897): 299–323.

Van Doren, Carl. *Mutiny in January*. New York: Viking Press, 1943.

Wright, John W. "Some Notes on the Continental Army." *William and Mary Quarterly*, 2d ser., 11 (1931): 81–105 and 185–209 and 12 (1932): 79–103.

CHAPTER 15

Alexander, Arthur J. "Desertion and Its Punishment in Revolutionary Virginia." *William and Mary Quarterly*, 3d ser., 3 (1946): 383–97.

———. "Exemptions from Military Service in the Old Dominion During the War of the Revolution." *Virginia Magazine of History and Biography*, 53 (1945): 163–71.

———. "A Footnote on Deserters from the Virginia Forces During the American Revolution." *Virginia Magazine of History and Biography*, 55 (1947): 137–46.

———. "How Maryland Tried to Raise Her Continental Quotas." *Maryland Historical Magazine*, 42 (1947): 184–96.

Blackwelder, Ruth. "The Attitude of the North Carolina Moravians Toward the American Revolution." *North Carolina Historical Review*, 9 (1932): 1–21.

Blanco, Richard L. "Continental Army Hospitals and American Society, 1775–81." In *Adapting to Conditions: War Society in the Eighteenth Century*, ed. Maarten Ultee. University: University of Alabama Press, 1986, pp. 150–73.

———. *Physician of the American Revolution: Jonathan Potts*. New York: Garland STPM Press, 1979.

Blumenthal, Walter H. *Women Camp Followers of the American Revolution*. Philadelphia: George S. McManus Co., 1952.

Boothe, Allen S. *The Women of '76*. New York: Hastings House, 1973.

Bowman, Allen. *The Morale of the American Revolutionary Army*. Washington, D.C.: American Council on Public Affairs, 1943.

Brock, Peter. *Pacifism in the United States from the Colonial Era to the First World War*. Princeton, N.J.: Princeton University Press, 1968.

Buel, Richard, Jr. *Dear Liberty: Connecticut's Mobilization for Revolutionary War*. Middletown, Conn.: Wesleyan University Press, 1980.

DePauw, Linda G. "Women in Combat: The Revolutionary War Experience." *Armed Forces and Society*, 7 (1981): 209–26.

Edmonson, James M. "Desertion in the American Army During the Revolutionary War." Ph.D. diss., Louisiana State University, 1971.

Frey, Sylvia. 1981. See Chapter 14 references.

Fridlington, Robert, ed. "A 'Diversion' in Newark: A Letter from the New Jersey Continental Line." *New Jersey History*, 105 (Spring/Summer 1987): 75–78.

Gillett, Mary C. *The Army Medical Department, 1775–1818*. Washington, D.C.: Center for Military History, 1981.

Griffenhagen, George B. *Drug Supplies in the American Revolution*. Washington, D.C.: Smithsonian Institution, 1961.

Hamilton, Kenneth G. "John Ettwein and the Moravian Church During the Revolutionary Period." *Transactions of the Moravian Historical Society,* 12 (1940): 85–429.

Kopperman, Paul E. "The British High Command and Soldiers' Wives in America, 1775–1783." *Journal of the Society for Army Historical Research,* 60 (1982): 14–34.

Lesser, Charles H. *The Sinews of Independence: Monthly Strength Reports of the Continental Army.* Chicago: University of Chicago Press, 1976.

"Letters of Ebenezer Huntington, 1774–1781." *American Historical Review,* 5 (1900): 702–29.

Marietta, Jack D. *The Reformation of American Quakerism, 1748–1783.* Philadelphia: University of Pennsylvania Press, 1984.

Martin, James K. " 'Most Undisciplined Profligate Crew': Protest and Defiance in the Continental Ranks, 1776–1783." In *Arms and Independence: The Military Character of the American Revolution,* eds. Ronald Hoffman and Peter J. Albert. Charlottesville: University Press of Virginia, 1984, pp. 119–40.

Mayer, Molly A. "Belonging to the Army: Camp Followers and the Military Community During the American Revolution." Ph.D. diss., College of William and Mary, 1990.

Mekeel, Arthur J. *The Relation of the Quakers to the American Revolution.* Washington, D.C.: University Press of America, 1979.

Meyer, Edith P. *See* Chapter 13 references.

New Jersey Archives: Documents Relating to the Revolutionary History of New Jersey. Newspaper Abstracts, Vols. 1–5. Trenton: 1901–17.

Risch, Erna. *Supplying Washington's Army.* Washington, D.C.: Center for Military History, 1981.

Rosswurm, Steven. *See* Chapter 13 references.

Schlissel, Lillian, ed. *Conscience in America: A Documentary History of Conscientious Objection in America, 1757–1967.* New York: E. P. Dutton & Co., 1968.

Schulz, Constance B. "Revolutionary War Pension Applications: A Neglected Source for Social and Family History." *Prologue: Journal of the National Archives,* 15 (Summer 1983): 103–14.

Seibert, Russell H. "The Treatment of Conscientious Objectors in War Time, 1775–1920." Ph.D. diss., Ohio State University, 1936.

Tate, Thaddeus W. "Desertion from the American Revolutionary Army." M.A. thesis, University of North Carolina, 1948.

Thayer, Theodore. *Israel Pemberton: King of the Quakers.* Philadelphia: Historical Society of Pennsylvania, 1943.

Treadway, Sandra G. "Anna Maria Lane: An Uncommon Soldier of the American Revolution." *Virginia Cavalcade,* 37 (Winter 1988): 134–43.

Trussell, John B. B., Jr. *See* Chapter 8 references.

Valley Forge Orderly Book of General George Weedon . . . in the Campaign of 1777–8. New York: Arno Press, 1971, originally published in 1902.

White, John T. "The Truth About Molly Pitcher." In *The American Revolution: Whose Revolution?,* eds. James K. Martin, and Karen R. Stubaus. Huntington, N.Y.: Robert E. Krieger Publishing Co., 1977, pp. 99–105.

Wiener, Frederick B. *Civilians Under Military Justice: The British Practice Since 1689 Especially in North America.* Chicago: University of Chicago Press, 1967.

CHAPTER 16

Abell, Francis. *Prisoners of War in Britain, 1756 to 1815: A Record of Their Lives, Their Romance and Their Suffering.* London: Oxford University Press, 1914.

Alexander, John K. "Forton Prison During the American Revolution: A Case Study of British Prisoners of War Policy and the American Prisoner Response to That Policy." *Essex Institute Historical Collections,* 103 (1967): 365–89.

Amerman, Richard H. "Treatment of American Prisoners During the Revolution." *Proceedings of the New Jersey Historical Society*, 78 (1960): 257–75.

Anburey, Thomas. *Travels Through the Interior Parts of America.* 2 vols. New York: New York Times & Arno Press, 1969, originally published in 1789.

Anderson, Olive. "The Treatment of Prisoners of War in Britain During the American War of Independence." *Bulletin of the Institute of Historical Research*, 27 (1955): 63–83.

Bakeless, John. *Turncoats, Traitors and Heroes.* Philadelphia: J. B. Lippincott Co., 1959.

Bowden, David K. *The Execution of Isaac Hayne.* Lexington, S.C.: Sandpiper Store, 1977.

Bowie, Lucy L. "German Prisoners in the American Revolution." *Maryland Historical Magazine*, 40 (1945), 185–200.

Bowman, Larry G. *Captive Americans: Prisoners During the American Revolution.* Athens: Ohio University Press, 1976.

———. "The New Jersey Prisoner Exchange Conferences, 1778–1780." *New Jersey History*, 97 (1979): 149–58.

Boyd, George A. *Elias Boudinot: Patriot and Statesman, 1740–1821.* Princeton, N.J.: Princeton University Press, 1952.

Brown, Marvin L., ed. and trans. *Baroness von Riedesel and the American Revolution: Journal and Correspondence of a Tour of Duty.* Chapel Hill: University of North Carolina Press, 1965.

Bryan, George S. *The Spy in America.* Philadelphia: J. B. Lippincott Co., 1943.

Burnett, Edmund C. "Ciphers of the Revolutionary Period." *American Historical Review*, 22 (1916–17): 329–34.

Chapin, Bradley. *The American Law of Treason: Revolutionary and National Origins.* Seattle: University of Washington Press, 1964.

Crary, Catherine S. "The Tory and the Spy: The Double Life of James Rivington." *William and Mary Quarterly*, 3d ser., 16 (1959): 61–72.

Dabney, William M. *After Saratoga: The Story of the Convention Army.* Albuquerque: University of New Mexico Publications, no. 6, 1954.

Dandridge, Danske. *American Prisoners of the Revolution.* Baltimore: Genealogical Publishing Co., 1967, originally published in 1911.

Flexner, James T. *The Traitor and the Spy: Benedict Arnold and John André.* New York: Harcourt, Brace & Co., 1953.

Ford, Corey. *A Peculiar Service.* Boston: Little, Brown & Co., 1965.

Greene, Albert, ed. *Recollections of the Jersey Prison Ship from the Manuscript of Capt. Thomas Dring.* New York: Corinth Books, 1961.

Hall, Charles S. *Benjamin Tallmadge: Revolutionary Soldier and American Businessman.* New York: Columbia University Press, 1943.

Hatch, Robert M. *Major John André: A Gallant in Spy's Clothing.* Boston: Houghton Mifflin Co., 1986.

Hawkins, Christopher. *The Adventures of Christopher Hawkins, Containing Details of His Captivity.* New York: New York Times & Arno Press, 1968, originally published in 1864.

Herbert, Charles M. *A Relic of the Revolution . . . American Prisoners Captured on the High Seas, and Carried into Plymouth, England, During the Revolution of 1776.* New York: Arno Press, 1968, originally published in 1847.

Intelligence in the War of Independence. Washington, D.C.: Central Intelligence Agency, 1977.

Johnston, Henry P. "The Secret Service of the Revolution." *Magazine of American History*, 8, pt. 1 (1882), 94–105.

Kaplan, Roger. "The Hidden War: British Intelligence Operations During the American Revolution." *William and Mary Quarterly*, 3d ser., 47 (1990): 115–38.

Klein, Milton M., and Howard, Ronald W., eds. *The Twilight of British Rule in Revolutionary America: The New York Letter Book of General James Robertson, 1780–1783.* Coopers-town, N.Y.: New York Historical Association, 1983.

Knepper, George W. "The Convention Army, 1777–1783." Ph.D. diss., University of Michigan, 1954.

Lindsey, William R. *Treatment of American Prisoners of War During the Revolution.* Emporia: Kansas State Teachers College, 1973.

Lowell, Edward J. *The Hessians and the Other German Auxiliaries of Great Britain in the Revolutionary War.* Williamstown, Mass.: Corner House Publishers, 1970, originally published in 1884.

McCowen, George S., Jr. *The British Occupation of Charleston, 1780–82.* Columbia: University of South Carolina Press, 1972.

Metzger, Charles H. *The Prisoners in the American Revolution.* Chicago: Loyola University Press, 1971.

Miller, Nathan. *Spying for America: The Hidden History of U.S. Intelligence.* New York: Paragon House, 1989.

Onderdonk, Henry J. *Revolutionary Incidents of Suffolk and Kings Counties . . . with an Account of . . . the British Prisons and Prison Ships at New-York.* Port Washington, N.Y.: Kennikat Press, 1970, originally published in 1840.

Parritt, B.A.M. *The Intelligencers: The Story of British Military Intelligence up to 1914.* Ashford, England: 1971.

Pennypacker, Morton. *General Washington's Spies on Long Island and in New York.* Brooklyn, N.Y.: Long Island Historical Society, 1939.

———. *The Two Spies: Nathan Hale and Robert Townshend.* Boston: Houghton Mifflin Co., 1930.

Pickering, James H., ed. "Enoch Crosby, Secret Agent of the Neutral Ground: His Own Story." *New York History,* 47 (1966): 61–73.

Prelinger, Catherine M. "Benjamin Franklin and the American Prisoners of War in England During the American Revolution." *William and Mary Quarterly,* 3d ser., 32 (1975): 261–94.

Seymour, George D. *Documentary Life of Nathan Hale.* New Haven, Conn.: Tuttle, Morehouse & Co., 1941.

"The Story of the Convention Army." *Magazine of Albemarle History,* 41 (1983).

Tourtellot, Arthur. "Rebels, Turn out your Dead." *American Heritage,* 2 (August 1970), no. 5, 16–17, 90–93.

Van Doren, Carl. *Secret History of the American Revolution.* New York: Viking Press, 1941.

Volm, M. H. *The Hessian Prisoners in the American War of Independence and Their Life in Captivity.* n. pl.: 1937.

West, Charles E. "Prison Ships in the American Revolution." *Journal of American History,* 5 (1911): 122–28.

CHAPTER 17

Allen, Rolfe L. "The Legislation for the Confiscation of British and Loyalist Property During the Revolutionary War." Ph.D. diss., University of Maryland, 1937.

Barnwell, Robert W., Jr. "Loyalism in South Carolina, 1765–1785." Ph.D. diss., Duke University, 1941.

Benson, Dale E. "Wealth and Power in Virginia, 1774–1776: A Study of the Organization of Revolt." Ph.D. diss., University of Maine, 1970.

Brown, Stuart E., Jr. *Virginia Baron: The Story of Thomas 6th Lord Fairfax.* Berryville, Va.: Chesapeake Book Co., 1965.

Brown, Wallace. *The Good Americans: The Loyalists in the American Revolution.* New York: William Morrow & Co., 1969.

————. *The King's Friends: The Composition and Motives of the American Loyalist Claimants.* Providence, R.I.: Brown University Press, 1965.

Calhoun, Robert M. *The Loyalist Perception and Other Essays.* Columbia: University of South Carolina Press, 1989.

————. *The Loyalists in Revolutionary America, 1760–1781.* New York: Harcourt Brace Jovanovich, 1973, originally published in 1963.

Callahan, North. *Flight from the Republic: The Tories of the American Revolution.* Indianapolis, Ind.: Bobbs-Merrill Co., 1967.

Chapin, Bradley. *See* Chapter 16 references.

Crary, Catherine S., ed. *The Price of Loyalty: Tory Writings from the Revolutionary Era.* New York: McGraw-Hill Book Co., 1973.

DeMond, Robert O. *The Loyalists in North Carolina During the Revolution.* Durham, N.C.: Duke University Press, 1940.

East, Robert A., and Judd, Jacob, eds. *The Loyalist Americans: A Focus on Greater New York.* Tarrytown, N.Y.: Sleepy Hollow Restorations, 1975.

Egerton, Hugh E. *The Royal Commission on the Losses and Services of American Loyalists, 1783–1785. . . .* New York: Burt Franklin, 1971, originally published in 1915.

Einstein, Lewis. *Divided Loyaties: Americans in England During the War of Independence.* London: Cobden-Sanderson, 1933.

Fingerhut, Eugene R. "Uses and Abuses of the American Loyalists' Claims: A Critique of Quantitative Analyses." *William and Mary Quarterly*, 3d ser., 25 (1968): 245–58.

Flick, Alexander C. *Loyalism in New York During the American Revolution.* New York: AMS Press, 1970, originally published in 1901.

Harrell, Isaac S. *Loyalism in Virginia: Chapters in the Economic History of the Revolution.* Durham, N.C.: Duke University Press, 1926.

Hast, Adele. *Loyalism in Revolutionary Virginia: The Norfolk Area and the Eastern Shore.* Ann Arbor, Mich.: UMI Research Press, 1979.

Hull, N. E. H., Hofer, Peter C., and Allen, Steven L. "Choosing Sides: A Quantitative Study of the Personality Determinants of Loyalist and Revolutionary Political Affiliation in New York." *Journal of American History*, 65 (1978): 344–66.

Jones, E. Alfred. *The Loyalists of New Jersey.* Bowie, Md.: Heritage Books, 1988, originally published in 1927.

Klein, Rachel N. *Unification of a Slave State: The Rise of the Planter Class in the South Carolina Backcountry, 1760–1808.* Chapel Hill: University of North Carolina Press, 1990.

Kozy, Charlene J. "Tories Transplanted: The Caribbean Exile and Plantation Settlement of Southern Loyalists." *Georgia Historical Quarterly*, 75 (1991): 18–42.

Lambert, Robert S. "The Confiscation of Loyalist Property in Georgia, 1782–1786." *William and Mary Quarterly*, 3d ser., 20 (1963): 80–94.

————. *South Carolina Loyalists in the American Revolution.* Columbia: University of South Carolina Press, 1987.

Nelson, William H. *The American Tory.* Oxford, England: Clarendon Press, 1961.

Norton, Mary B. *The British-Americans: The Loyalist Exiles in England, 1774–1789.* Boston: Little, Brown & Co., 1972.

————. "The Fate of Some Black Loyalists of the American Revolution." *Journal of American History*, 58 (1973): 402–26.

Oliver, Peter. *Peter Oliver's Origin & Progress of the American Revolution: A Tory View.* Ed. Douglas Adair and John A. Schutz. Stanford, Calif.: Stanford University Press, 1961.

Ousterhout, Anne M. *A State Divided: Opposition in Pennsylvania to the American Revolution.* Westport, Conn.: Greenwood Press, 1987.

Overfield, Richard A. "The Loyalists of Maryland During the American Revolution." Ph.D. diss., University of Maryland, 1968.

Ramsay, David. *History of South Carolina.* 2 vols. Spartanburg, S.C.: Reprint Co., 1968, originally published in 1809.

Ranlet, Philip. *The New York Loyalists.* Knoxville: University of Tennessee Press, 1986.

Sabine, Lorenzo. *Biographical Sketches of Loyalists of the American Revolution.* 2 vols. Baltimore: Genealogical Publishing Co., 1979, originally published in 1864.

Seabury, Samuel. *Letters of a Westchester Farmer (1774–1775).* Ed. Clarence H. Vance. White Plains, N.Y.: Westchester County Historical Society, 1930.

Siebert, Wilbur H. *The Legacy of the American Revolution to the British West Indies and Bahamas: A Chapter out of the History of the American Loyalists.* Columbus: Ohio State University Press, 1913.

Smith, Paul H. "The American Loyalists: Notes on Their Organization and Numerical Strength." *William and Mary Quarterly,* 3d ser., 25 (1968): 259–77.

———. *Loyalists and Redcoats: A Study in British Revolutionary Policy.* Chapel Hill: University of North Carolina Press, 1964.

Stark, James H. *The Loyalists of Massachusetts.* Boston: W. B. Clarke Co., 1907.

Van Tyne, Claude H. *The Loyalists of the American Revolution.* New York: Macmillan Co., 1902.

Walker, James W. St. G. *The Black Loyalists: The Search for a Promised Land in Nova Scotia and Sierra Leone, 1783–1870.* New York: Africana Publishing Co., 1976.

Wilson, Ellen G. *The Loyal Blacks.* New York: G. P. Putnam's Sons, 1976.

Young, Henry J. "Treason and Its Punishment in Revolutionary Virginia." *Pennsylvania Magazine of History and Biography,* 90 (1966): 287–313.

Zeichner, Oscar. "The Rehabilitation of the Loyalists in Connecticut." *New England Quarterly,* 11 (1938): 308–30.

Zimmer, Anne Y. *Jonathan Boucher: Loyalist in Exile.* Detroit: Wayne State University Press, 1978.

CHAPTER 18

Abbot, William W. "The Structure of Politics in Georgia, 1782–89." *William and Mary Quarterly,* 3d ser., 14 (1957): 47–65.

Adams, Willi P. *The First American Constitutions: Republican Ideology and the Making of the State Constitutions in the Revolutionary Era.* Chapel Hill: University of North Carolina Press, 1980.

Brunhouse, Robert L. *The Counter-Revolution in Pennsylvania, 1776–1790.* Harrisburg: Pennsylvania Historical Commission, 1942.

Buel, Richard, Jr. "Democracy and the American Revolution: A Frame of Reference." *William and Mary Quarterly,* 3d ser., 21 (1964): 165–90.

Chambers, William N. *Political Parties in a New Nation: The American Experience, 1776–1809.* New York: Oxford University Press, 1963.

Cochran, Thomas C. *New York in the Confederation: An Economic Study.* Philadelphia: University of Pennsylvania Press, 1932.

Countryman, Edward. *A People in Revolution: The American Revolution and Political Society in New York, 1760–1790.* New York: W. W. Norton & Co., 1989, originally published in 1981.

Corwin, Edward S. "The Progress of Constitutional Theory Between the Declaration of Independence and the Meeting of the Philadelphia Convention." *American Historical Review,* 30 (1925): 511–36.

Daniell, Jere R. *Experiment in Republicanism: New Hampshire and the American Revolution, 1741–1794.* Cambridge, Mass.: Harvard University Press, 1970.

Douglass, Elisha P., 1955. *See* Chapter 6 references.

East, Robert A. "The Massachusetts Conservatives in the Critical Period." In *The Era of the American Revolution,* ed. Richard B. Morris. New York: Harper & Row, 1939, pp. 349–91.

Flick, Hugh M. "The Council of Appointment in New York State: The First Attempt to Regulate Political Patronage, 1777–1822." *New York History,* 15 (1934): 253–80.

Green, Fletcher M. *Constitutional Development in the South Atlantic States, 1776–1860: A Study in the Evolution of Democracy.* New York: W. W. Norton & Co., 1966, originally published in 1930.

Haines, Charles G. *The American Doctrine of Judicial Supremacy.* New York: Russell & Russell, 1959, originally published in 1932.

Hall, Van Beck. *Politics Without Parties: Massachusetts, 1780–1791.* Pittsburgh: University of Pittsburgh Press, 1972.

Jensen, Merrill. *The American Revolution within America.* New York: New York University Press, 1974.

————. "Democracy and the American Revolution." *Huntington Library Quarterly,* 20 (1957): 321–41.

Kenyon, Cecelia M. "Republicanism and Radicalism in the American Revolution: An Old-Fashioned Interpretation." *William and Mary Quarterly,* 3d ser., 19 (1962): 153–82.

Lutz, Donald S. *Popular Consent and Popular Control: Whig Political Theory in the Early State Constitutions.* Baton Rouge: Louisiana State University Press, 1980.

McCormick, Richard P. *Experiment in Independence: New Jersey in the Critical Period, 1781–89.* New Brunswick, N.J.: Rutgers University Press, 1950.

McDonald, Forrest. *The Formation of the American Republic, 1776–1790.* Baltimore: Penguin Books, 1965.

Main, Jackson T. "Government by the People: The American Revolution and the Democratization of the Legislatures." *William and Mary Quarterly,* 3d ser., 23 (1966): 391–407.

————. *Political Parties before the Constitution.* Chapel Hill: University of North Carolina Press, 1973a.

————. *The Sovereign States, 1775–1783.* New York: New Viewpoints, 1973b.

————. *The Upper House in Revolutionary America, 1763–1788.* Madison: University of Wisconsin Press, 1967.

Nadelhaft, Jerome J. *The Disorders of War: The Revolution in South Carolina.* Orono: University of Maine Press, 1981.

Nettels, Curtis P. *The Emergence of a National Economy, 1775–1815.* New York: Holt, Rinehart & Winston, 1962.

Nevins, Allan. 1969/1924. *See* Chapter 13 references.

Pole, J. R. *See* Chapter 2 references.

Rutland, Robert A. *The Birth of the Bill of Rights, 1776–1791.* Chapel Hill: University of North Carolina Press, 1955.

————., ed. *The Papers of George Mason, 1752–1792.* Vol. 2. Chapel Hill: University of North Carolina Press, 1970.

Schecter, Stephen L., ed. *Roots of the Republic: American Founding Documents Interpreted.* Madison, Wis.: Madison House, 1990.

Shalhope, Robert E. "Toward a Republican Synthesis: The Emergence of Republicanism in American Historiography." *William and Mary Quarterly,* 3d ser., 29 (1972): 49–81.

Thorpe, Francis N., ed. *The Federal and State Constitutions, Colonial Charters, and Other Organic Laws of the United States.* 7 vols. Washington, D.C.: U.S. Government Printing Office, 1907.

Wachtell, Harvey M. "The Conflict Between Localism and Nationalism in Connecticut, 1783–1788." Ph.D. diss., University of Missouri, 1971.

Williamson, Chilton. *American Suffrage: From Property to Democracy, 1760–1860.* Princeton, N.J.: Princeton University Press, 1960.

Wood, Gordon S. *The Creation of the American Republic, 1776–1787.* Chapel Hill: University of North Carolina Press, 1969.

Zagarri, Rosemarie. "Representation and the Removal of State Capitals, 1776–1812." *Journal of American History*, 74 (1988): 1239–56.

CHAPTER 19

Baker, LeGrand L. "The Board of Treasury, 1784–89: Responsibility without Power." Ph.D. diss., University of Wisconsin, 1972.

Barnby, H. G. *The Prisoners of Algiers: An Account of the Forgotten American-Algerian War, 1785–1797.* New York: Oxford University Press, 1966.

Bemis, Samuel F., ed. *The American Secretaries of State and Their Diplomacy.* Vol. 1: "Robert L. Livingston," by Milledge L. Bonham and "John Jay," by Samuel F. Bemis. New York: Alfred A. Knopf, 1927.

Berkhofer, Robert F., Jr. "Jefferson, the Ordinance of 1784, and the Origins of the American Territorial System." *William and Mary Quarterly*, 3d ser., 29 (1972): 231–262.

Bourguignon, Henry J. *The First Federal Court: The Federal Appellate Prize Court of the American Revolution, 1775–1787.* Philadelphia: American Philosophical Society, 1977.

Brant, Irving. *James Madison: The Nationalist, 1780–1787.* Indianapolis, Ind.: Bobbs-Merrill Co., 1948.

Burnett, Edmund C. *The Continental Congress.* New York: Macmillan Co., 1941.

Carter, Clarence D., ed. *The Territorial Papers of the United States.* Vols. 2 and 3. Washington, D.C.: U.S. Government Printing Office, 1934.

Cress, Lawrence D. "Republican Liberty and National Security: American Military Policy as an Ideological Problem, 1783 to 1789." *William and Mary Quarterly*, 3d ser., 38 (1981): 73–96.

Crowley, John E. *The Privileges of Independence: Neomercantilism and the American Revolution.* Baltimore: The Johns Hopkins University Press, 1993.

Cutler, William P. and Julia P. *Life, Journals, and Correspondence of Rev. Manasseh Cutler.* Cincinnati: Robert Clarke & Co., 1888.

Feer, Robert A. "Shays's Rebellion and the Constitution: A Study in Causation." *New England Quarterly*, 42 (1969): 388–410.

Ferguson, E. James. *The Power of the Purse: A History of American Public Finance, 1776–1790.* Chapel Hill: University of North Carolina Press, 1961.

Fiske, John. *The Critical Period of American History, 1783–1789.* Boston: Houghton Mifflin Co., 1888.

Henderson, H. James. *Party Politics in the Continental Congress.* New York: McGraw-Hill Book Co., 1974.

Horsman, Reginald. *Expansion and American Indian Policy, 1783–1812.* East Lansing: Michigan State University Press, 1967.

Jacobs, James R. *The Beginnings of the U.S. Army, 1783–1812.* Princeton, N.J.: Princeton University Press, 1947.

Jensen, Merrill. *The New Nation: A History of the United States During the Confederation, 1781–1789.* New York: Vintage Books, 1950.

Marks, Frederick W. *Independence on Trial: Foreign Affairs and the Making of the Constitution.* Baton Rouge: Louisiana State University Press, 1973.

McCormick, Richard P. "The Ordinance of 1784?" *William and Mary Quarterly*, 3d ser., 50 (1993): 112–22.

Morrill, James R. *The Practice of Politics and Fiat Finance: North Carolina in the Confederation, 1783–1789.* Chapel Hill: University of North Carolina Press, 1969.

Morris, Richard B. "The Confederation Period and the American Historian." *William and Mary Quarterly*, 3d ser., 13 (1956): 139–56.

———. *The Forging of the Union, 1781–1789.* New York: Harper & Row, 1987.

Olson, Gary D. "Between Independence and Constitution: The Articles of Confederation, 1783–1787." Ph.D. diss., University of Nebraska, 1969.

Onuf, Peter S. *The Origins of the Federal Republic: Jurisdictional Controversies in the United States, 1775–87.* Philadelphia: University of Pennsylvania Press, 1983.

———. *Statehood and Union: A History of the Northwest Ordinance.* Bloomington: Indiana University Press, 1987.

Pattison, William D. *Beginnings of the American Rectangular Land Survey System, 1784–1800.* Chicago: University of Chicago Press, 1957.

Philbrick, Francis S. *The Rise of the West, 1754–1830.* New York: Harper & Row, 1965.

Phillips, Howard J. "The United States Diplomatic Establishment in the Critical Period, 1783–1789." Ph.D. diss., University of Notre Dame, 1968.

Quincy, Josiah, ed. *The Journals of Major Samuel Shaw, the First American Counsul at Canton.* New York: Paragon Book Gallery, 1968, originally published in 1847.

Rakove, Jack N. 1979. *See* Chapter 4 references.

Ritcheson, Charles R. *Aftermath of Revolution: British Policy Toward the United States, 1783–1795.* Dallas: Southern Methodist University Press, 1969.

Sanders, Jennings B. *Evolution of the Executive Departments of the Continental Congress, 1774–1789.* Chapel Hill: University of North Carolina Press, 1935.

Singer, Charles G. *South Carolina in the Confederation.* Philadelphia: privately printed, 1941.

Starkey, Marion. L. *A Little Rebellion.* New York: Alfred A. Knopf, 1955.

Szatmary, David P. *Shays' Rebellion: The Making of an Agrarian Insurrection.* Amherst: University of Massachusetts Press, 1980.

Taylor, Robert J. "Trial at Trenton." *William and Mary Quarterly*, 3d ser., 26 (1969): 521–47.

U.S. Department of State. *The Diplomatic Correspondence of the United States, from the Signing of the Definitive Treaty of Peace, 10th September, 1783 to the Adoption of the Constitution, March 4, 1789.* 7 vols. Washington, D.C.: F. P. Blair, 1833–34.

Ver Steeg, Clarence L. *Robert Morris: Revolutionary Financeer.* New York: Octagon Books, 1972, originally published in 1954.

Ward, Harry M. *The Department of War, 1781–1795.* Pittsburgh: University of Pittsburgh Press, 1962.

CHAPTER 20

Alexander, John K. *Render Them Submissive: Responses to Poverty in Philadelphia, 1760–1800.* Amherst: University of Massachusetts Press, 1980.

Armes, Ethel, ed. *Nancy Shippen: Her Journal Book.* Philadelphia: J. B. Lippincott Co., 1935.

Berlin, Ira. "The Revolution in Black Life." In *The American Revolution: Explorations in the History of American Radicalism*, ed. Alfred F. Young. DeKalb: Northern Illinois University Press, 1976, pp. 349–82.

Berlin, Ira, and Hoffman, Ronald, eds. *Slavery and Freedom in the Age of the American Revolution.* Charlottesville: University Press of Virginia, 1983.

Bloch, Ruth M. "American Feminine Ideals in Transition: The Rise of the Moral Mother, 1785–1815." *Feminist Studies*, 4 (1978): 101–26.

Brissot de Warville, Jacques R. *New Travels in the United States of America, 1788.* Ed. Duran Echeverria. Cambridge, Mass.: Harvard University Press, 1964.

Brobeck, Stephen. "Images of the Family, Portrait Painting as Indices of American Family Culture, Structure and Behavior, 1730–1860." *Journal of Psychohistory*, 5 (1977): 81–106.

Bruns, Roger, ed. *Am I not a Man and a Brother: The Antislavery Crusade of Revolutionary America, 1688–1788.* New York: Chelsea House Publishers, 1977.

Buchan, William. *Advice to Mothers, on the Subject of Their Own Health; and . . . Their Offspring* (Boston, 1809), in *The Physician and Child-Bearing.* New York: Arno Press, 1972.

Chalou, George C. "Women in the American Revolution: Vignettes or Profiles." In *Clio Was a Woman: Studies in the History of American Women*, eds. Mabel E. Deutrich and Virginia C. Purdy. Washington, D.C.: Howard University Press, 1980, pp. 373–90.

Coleman, Peter J. "The Insolvent Debtor in Rhode Island, 1745–1828." *William and Mary Quarterly*, 3d ser., 22 (1965): 413–34.

————. *Debtors and Creditors in America: Insolvency, Imprisonment for Debt, and Bankruptcy, 1607–1900*. Madison: State Historical Society of Wisconsin, 1974.

Cott, Nancy F. "Divorce and the Changing Status of Women in Eighteenth-Century Massachusetts." *William and Mary Quarterly*, 3d. ser., 33 (1976): 586–614.

Crow, Jeffrey J. "Slave Rebelliousness and Social Conflict in North Carolina, 1775 to 1802." *William and Mary Quarterly*, 3d ser., 37 (1980): 79–102.

Davies, Wallace E. "The Society of the Cincinnati in New England, 1783–1800." *William and Mary Quarterly*, 3d ser., 5 (1948): 3–25.

Davis, David B. "The Movement to Abolish Capital Punishment in America, 1787–1861." *American Historical Review*, 63 (1958): 3–25.

————. *The Problem of Slavery in the Age of Revolution, 1770–1783*. Ithaca, N.Y.: Cornell University Press, 1975.

DePauw, Linda G., and Hunt, Conover. *Remember the Ladies: Women in America, 1750–1815*. New York: Viking Press, 1976.

Egerton, Douglas R. *Gabriel's Rebellion: The Virginia Slave Conspiracies of 1800 & 1802*. Chapel Hill: University of North Carolina Press, 1993.

Essig, James D. *The Bonds of Wickedness: American Evangelicals against Slavery, 1770–1808*. Philadelphia: Temple University Press, 1982.

Feer, Robert A. "Imprisonment for Debt in Massachusetts Before 1800." *Mississippi Valley Historical Review*, 48 (1962): 252–69.

Fliegelman, Jay. *Prodigals and Pilgrims: The American Revolution Against Patriarchal Authority, 1750–1800*. Cambridge, England: Cambridge University Press, 1982.

Frey, Sylvia R. *Water from the Rock: Black Resistance in a Revolutionary Age*. Princeton, N.J.: Princeton University Press, 1991.

The Gentleman and Lady's Town and Country Magazine, May–December 1784 and February 1789–August 1790. American Antiquarian Society, microfilm ed.

George, Carol V. R. *Segregated Sabbaths: Richard Allen and the Emergence of Independent Black Churches, 1760–1840*. New York: Oxford University Press, 1973.

Gough, Robert J. "Towards a Theory of Class and Social Conflict: A Social History of Wealthy Philadelphians, 1775–1800." Ph.D. diss., University of Pennsylvania, 1977.

Greven, Philip. *The Protestant Temperament: Patterns of Child-Rearing, Religious Experience, and the Self in Early America*. New York: Alfred A. Knopf, 1977.

Gunderson, Joan R., and Gampel, Gwen V. "Married Women's Legal Status in Eighteenth-Century New York and Virginia." *William and Mary Quarterly*, 3d ser., 39 (1982): 114–32.

Hawes, Joseph M., and Nybakken, Elizabeth. *American Families: A Research Guide and Historical Handbook*. Westport, Conn.: Greenwood Press, 1991.

Hawke, David F. *Benjamin Rush: Revolutionary Gadfly*. Indianapolis, Ind.: Bobbs-Merrill Co., 1971.

Heale, M. J. "Humanitarianism in the Early Republic: The Moral Reformers of New York." *Journal of American Studies*, 2 (1968): 161–75.

Henretta, James A. *The Evolution of American Society, 1700–1815: An Interdisciplinary Analysis*. Lexington, Mass.: D. C. Heath & Co., 1973.

Hoff, Joan. *Law, Gender, and Injustice: A Legal History of U.S. Women*. New York: New York University Press, 1991.

Hoffman, Ronald, and Albert, Peter J., eds. *Women in the Age of the American Revolution*. Charlottesville: University Press of Virginia, 1989.

Howe, M. A. DeWolfe. *The Humane Society of the Commonwealth of Massachusetts: Historical Review, 1785–1916*. Cambridge: Riverside Press, 1918.

Jameson, J. Franklin. *The American Revolution Considered as a Social Movement*. Princeton, N.J.: Princeton University Press, 1926.

Jordan, Winthrop D. *White over Black: American Attitudes Toward the Negro, 1550–1812.* Chapel Hill: University of North Carolina Press, 1968.

Kerber, Linda K. *Women of the Republic: Intellect and Ideology in Revolutionary America.* Chapel Hill: University of North Carolina Press, 1980.

Kulikoff, Allan. "The Progress of Inequality in Revolutionary Boston." *William and Mary Quarterly,* 3d ser., 28 (1971): 375–412.

Lewis, Jan. "The Republican Wife: Virtue and Seduction in the Early Republic." *William and Mary Quarterly,* 3d ser., 44 (1987): 689–721.

Lockridge, Kenneth A. "Social Change and the Meaning of the American Revolution." *Journal of Social History,* 6 (1973): 403–47.

MacLeod, Duncan J. *Slavery, Race and the American Revolution.* London: Cambridge University Press, 1974.

Main, Jackson T. *The Social Structure of Revolutionary America.* Princeton, N.J.: Princeton University Press, 1965.

Malmsheimer, Lonna M. "New England Sermons and Changing Attitudes Toward Women, 1672–1792." Ph.D. diss., University of Minnesota, 1973.

Miller, William. "The Effects of the American Revolution on Indentured Servitude." *Pennsylvania History,* 7 (1940): 131–41.

Mohl, Raymond A. *Poverty in New York, 1783–1825.* New York: Oxford University Press, 1971.

Morris, Richard B. *The American Revolution Reconsidered.* New York: Harper & Row, 1967.

———. "Class Struggle and the American Revolution." *William and Mary Quarterly,* 3d ser., 19 (1962): 3–29.

Nash, Gary B. *Forging Freedom: The Formation of Philadelphia's Black Community, 1720–1840.* Cambridge, Mass.: Harvard University Press, 1988.

———. *Race and Revolution.* Madison, Wis.: Madison House, 1990.

Nash, Gary B., and Soderlund, Jean R. *Freedom by Degrees: Emancipation in Pennsylvania and Its Aftermath.* New York: Oxford University Press, 1991.

Norton, Mary B. *Liberty's Daughters: The Revolutionary Experience of American Women, 1750–1800.* Boston: Little, Brown & Co., 1980.

O'Brien, William. "Did the Jennison Case Outlaw Slavery in Massachusetts?" *William and Mary Quarterly,* 3d ser., 17 (1960): 219–41.

Quarles, Benjamin. "The Revolutionary War as a Black Declaration of Independence." In *Slavery and Freedom in the Age of the American Revolution,* ed. Ira Berlin and Ronald Hoffman. Charlottesville: University Press of Virginia, 1983, pp. 283–301.

Renier, Jacqueline S. "Rearing the Republican Child: Attitudes and Practices in Post-Revolutionary Philadelphia." *William and Mary Quarterly,* 3d ser., 39 (1982): 150–63.

Rorabaugh, W. J. *The Alcoholic Republic: an American Tradition.* New York: Oxford University Press, 1979.

Rothman, David J. *The Discovery of the Asylum: Social Order and Disorder in the New Republic.* Boston: Little, Brown & Co., 1971.

Runes, Dagobert D., ed. *The Selected Writings of Benjamin Rush.* New York: Philosophical Library, 1947.

Salmon, Marylynn. *Women and the Law of Property in Early America.* Chapel Hill: University of North Carolina Press, 1986.

Scholten, Catherine M. *Childbearing in American Society, 1650–1850.* New York: New York University Press, 1985.

Smith, Billy G. *The "Lower Sort:" Philadelphia's Laboring People, 1750–1800.* Ithaca, N.Y.: Cornell University Press, 1990.

Smith, Merril D. *Breaking the Bonds: Marital Discord in Pennsylvania, 1730–1830.* New York: New York University Press, 1991.

Soderlund, Jean R. *Quakers and Slavery: A Divided Spirit.* Princeton, N.J.: Princeton University Press, 1985.

Taylor, John. *Arator: Being a Series of Agricultural Essays, Practical and Political.* Ed. M. E. Bradford. Indianapolis, Ind.: Liberty Classics, 1977, from the 1814 edition.

Tolles, Frederick B. "The American Revolution Considered as a Social Movement: A Reevaluation." *American Historical Review,* 60 (1954): 1–12.

Ulrich, Laurel J. *A Midwife's Tale: The Life of Martha Ballard Based on Her Diary, 1785–1812.* New York: Alfred A. Knopf, 1990.

Wells, Robert V. "Quaker Marriage Patterns in a Colonial Perspective." *William and Mary Quarterly,* 3d ser., 29 (1972): 415–42.

White, Shane. *Somewhat More Independent: The End of Slavery in New York City, 1770–1810.* Athens: University of Georgia Press, 1990.

Wiecek, William M. *The Sources of Antislavery Constitutionalism in America, 1760–1848.* Ithaca, N.Y.: Cornell University Press, 1977.

Wilson, Joan H. "The Illusion of Change: Women and the American Revolution." In *The American Revolution: Explorations in the History of American Radicalism,* ed. Alfred F. Young. DeKalb: Northern Illinois University Press, 1976, pp. 383–445.

Wood, Gordon S. *The Radicalism of the American Revolution.* New York: Alfred A. Knopf, 1992.

Zilversmit, Arthur. *The First Emancipation: The Abolition of Slavery in the North.* Chicago: University of Chicago Press, 1967.

CHAPTER 21

Albanese, Catherine L. *Sons of the Fathers: The Civil Religion of the American Revolution.* Philadelphia: Temple University Press, 1976.

Andrews, Doris E. "Popular Religion and the Revolution in the Middle Atlantic Ports: The Rise of the Methodists, 1770–1800." Ph.D. diss., University of Pennsylvania, 1986.

Anthony, Katherine. *First Lady of the Revolution: The Life of Mercy Otis Warren.* Port Washington, N.Y.: Kennikat Press, 1972, originally published in 1958.

Baine, Rodney M. *Robert Munford: America's First Comic Dramatist.* Athens: University of Georgia Press, 1967.

Bedini, Silvio A. *Thinkers and Tinkers: Early Men of Science.* New York: Charles Scribner's Sons, 1975.

Bloch, Ruth H. *Visionary Republic: Millennial Themes in American Thought, 1756–1800.* Cambridge, England: Cambridge University Press, 1985.

Boles, John B. *The Great Revival, 1787–1805.* Lexington: University Press of Kentucky, 1972.

Brauer, Jerald, ed. *Religion and the American Revolution.* Philadelphia: Fortress Press, 1976.

Chastellux, marquis de. *See* Chapter 13 references.

Commager, Henry S. "The Search for a Usable Past." *American Heritage,* 16 (February 1965): 4–9 and 90–96.

Cowie, Alexander. *John Trumbull: Connecticut Wit.* Chapel Hill: University of North Carolina Press, 1936.

Cremin, Lawrence A. *American Education: The National Experience, 1783–1876.* New York: Harper & Row, 1980.

Daniels, George H. *Science in American Society: A Social History.* New York: Alfred A. Knopf, 1971.

Davidson, Cathy N. *Revolution and the Word: The Rise of the Novel in America.* New York: Oxford University Press, 1986.

Ellis, Joseph J. *After the Revolution: Profiles of Early American Culture.* New York: W. W. Norton & Co., 1979.

Emerson, Everett, ed. *American Literature, 1764–1789: The Revolutionary Years.* Madison: University of Wisconsin Press, 1977.

Fagin, N. Bryllion. *William Bartram: Interpreter of the American Landscape.* Baltimore: Johns Hopkins University Press, 1933.

Flexner, James T. *The Light of Distant Skies: American Painting, 1760–1835*. New York: Dover Publications, 1954.

Frankenstein, Alfred. *The World of Copley, 1738–1815*. New York: Time-Life Books, 1970.

Golden, James L., and Corbett, Edward P. J., eds. *The Rhetoric of Blair, Campbell, and Whatley*. New York: Holt, Rinehart & Winston, 1968.

Greene, John C. "Science and the Public in the Age of Jefferson." In *Early American Science*, ed. Brooke Hindle. New York: Science History Publications, 1976, pp. 201–13.

Hamlin, Talbot. *Greek Revival Architecture in America*. New York: Oxford University Press, 1944.

Harper, Francis, ed. *The Travels of William Bartram*. New Haven, Conn.: Yale University Press, 1958.

Hatch, Nathan O. *The Democratization of American Christianity*. New Haven, Conn.: Yale University Press, 1989.

———. *The Sacred Cause of Liberty: Republican Thought and the Millennium in Revolutionary New England*. New Haven, Conn.: Yale University Press, 1977.

Hindle, Brooke. *David Rittenhouse*. Princeton, N.J.: Princeton University Press, 1964.

———. *The Pursuit of Science in Revolutionary America, 1735–1789*. Chapel Hill: University of North Carolina Press, 1956.

Howard, Leon. *The Connecticut Wits*. Chicago: University of Chicago Press, 1943.

Humphrey, Edward F. *Nationalism and Religion in America, 1774–1789*. Boston: Chipman Law Publishing Co., 1924.

Jaffe, Irma B. *John Trumbull: Patriot–Artist of the American Revolution*. Boston: New York Graphic Society, 1975.

Jones, Howard M. *O Strange New World: American Culture: The Formative Years*. New York: Viking Press, 1964, originally published in 1952.

Kastner, Joseph. *A Species of Eternity*. New York: Alfred A. Knopf, 1977.

Kimball, Fiske. *Domestic Architecture of the American Colonies and the Early Republic*. New York: Charles Scribner's Sons, 1927.

Loveland, Clara O. *The Critical Years: The Reconstruction of the Anglican Church in the United States of America, 1780–1789*. Greenwich, Conn.: Seabury Press, 1956.

Martin, Edward. *Thomas Jefferson: Scientist*. New York: Henry Schuman, 1952.

Mathews, Donald G. "The Second Great Awakening as an Organizing Process, 1780–1830: An Hypothesis." *American Quarterly*, 2 (1969): 23–43.

May, Henry F. *The Enlightenment in America*. New York: Oxford University Press, 1976.

McLoughlin, William G. "The Role of Religion in the Revolution: Liberty of Conscience and Cultural Cohesion in the New Nation." In *Essays on the American Revolution*, eds. Stephen G. Kurtz and James H. Hutson. Chapel Hill: University of North Carolina Press, 1973, pp. 197–255.

Morais, Herbert M. *Deism in Eighteenth Century America*. New York: Columbia University Press, 1934.

Morrison, Hugh. *Early American Architecture From the First Colonial Settlements to the National Period*. New York: Oxford University Press, 1952.

Nye, Russell B. *The Cultural Life of the New Nation*. New York: Harper & Row, 1960.

Robinson, William H., ed. *Critical Essays on Phillis Wheatley*. Boston: G. K. Hall & Co., 1982.

Robson, David W. "College Founding in the New Republic, 1776–1800." *History of Education Quarterly*, 23 (1983): 323–41.

Rudolph, Frederick, ed. *Essays on Education in the Early Republic*. Cambridge, Mass.: Harvard University Press, 1965.

Seilhamer, George C. *History of the American Theater to 1797*. 3 vols. New York: Benjamin Blom, 1968, originally published in 1888–89.

Sellers, Charles C. *Charles Willson Peale*. 2 vols. Philadelphia: American Philosophical Society, 1947.

Shaffer, Arthur M. *The Politics of History: Writing the History of the American Revolution, 1813–1815.* Chicago: Precedent Publishing, 1975.

———. *To Be an American: David Ramsay and the Making of the American Consciousness.* Columbia: University of South Carolina Press, 1991.

Shalhope, Robert E. *The Roots of Democracy: American Thought and Culture, 1760–1800.* Boston: Twayne Publishers, 1990.

Silverman, Kenneth. *A Cultural History of the American Revolution.* New York: Columbia University Press, 1987, originally published in 1976.

Smith, Wilson, ed. *Theories of Education in Early America, 1655–1819.* Indianapolis, Ind.: Bobbs-Merrill Co., 1973.

Sonneck, O. G. *Early Concert-Life in America, 1731–1800.* New York: Musurgia Publishers, 1949.

———. *Early Opera in America.* New York: B. Blom, 1963, originally published in 1915.

Sparrow, W. J. *Knight of the White Eagle: Sir Benjamin Thompson, Count Rumford of Woburn, Mass.* New York: Thomas Y. Crowell, 1964.

Spencer, Benjamin T. *The Quest for Nationality.* Syracuse, N.Y.: Syracuse University Press, 1957.

Struik, Dirk J. *Yankee Science in the Making.* Boston: Little, Brown & Co., 1948.

Teunissen, John J. "Blockheadism and the Propaganda Plays of the American Revolution." *Early American Literature,* 7 (1972): 148–62.

Tyler, Moses C. *The Literary History of the American Revolution.* 2 vols. New York: G. P. Putnam's Sons, 1905.

Ziff, Larzer. *Writing in the New Nation: Prose, Print, and Politics in the Early United States.* New Haven, Conn.: Yale University Press, 1991.

CHAPTER 22

Beard, Charles A. *An Economic Interpretation of the Constitution of the United States.* New York: Free Press, 1967, originally published in 1913.

Belz, Herman, Hoffman, Ronald, and Albert, Peter J., eds. *To Form a More Perfect Union: The Critical Ideas of the Constitution.* Charlottesville: University Press of Virginia, 1992.

Billias, George A. *Elbridge Gerry: Founding Father and Republican Statesman.* New York: McGraw-Hill Book Co., 1976.

Bowen, Catherine D. *Miracle at Philadelphia: The Story of the Constitutional Convention, May to September 1787.* Boston: Little, Brown & Co., 1966.

Brant, Irving. *James Madison: Father of the Constitution, 1787–1800.* Indianapolis, Ind.: Bobbs-Merrill Co., 1950.

Brogan, D. W. "The Quarrel over Charles Austin Beard and the American Constitution." *Economic History Review,* 18 (1965): 199–223.

Brown, Richard D. "The Founding Fathers of 1776 and 1787: A Collective View." *William and Mary Quarterly,* 3d ser., 33 (1976): 465–73.

Brown, Robert E. *Charles Beard and the Constitution: A Critical Analysis of 'An Economic Interpretation of the Constitution.' "* Princeton, N.J.: Princeton University Press, 1956.

Butzner, Jan, comp. *Constitutional Chaff—Rejected Suggestions of the Constitutional Convention of 1787.* New York: Columbia University Press, 1941.

Carr, William G. *The Oldest Delegate: Franklin in the Constitutional Convention.* Newark: University of Delaware Press, 1990.

Clarkson, Paul, and Jett, R. Samuel. *Luther Martin of Maryland.* Baltimore: Johns Hopkins University Press, 1970.

Collier, Christopher and James L. *Decision in Philadelphia: The Constitutional Convention of 1787.* New York: Reader's Digest Press and Random House, 1986.

Diamond, Martin. "Democracy and *The Federalist:* A Reconsideration of the Framers' Intent." *American Political Science Review,* 53 (1959): 52–68.

Diggins, John P. "Power and Authority in American History: The Case of Charles A. Beard and His Critics." *American Historical Review*, 86 (1981): 701–30.

Dumbauld, Edward. *The Constitution of the United States*. Norman: University of Oklahoma Press, 1964.

Eidelberg, Paul. *The Philosophy of the American Constitution: A Reinterpretation of the Intentions of the Founding Fathers*. New York: Free Press, 1968.

Elkins, Stanley, and McKitrick, Eric. "The Founding Fathers: Young Men of the Revolution." *Political Science Quarterly*, 76 (1961): 181–216.

Hobson, Charles F. "The Negative on State Laws: James Madison, the Constitution, and the Crisis of Republican Government." *William and Mary Quarterly*, 3d ser., 36 (1979): 215–35.

Hofstadter, Richard. *The Progressive Historians: Turner, Beard, Parrington*. New York: Alfred A. Knopf, 1968.

Holcombe, Arthur N. "The Role of Washington in the Framing of the Constitution." *The Huntington Library Quarterly*, 19 (1956): 317–34.

Jillson, Calvin C. *Constitution Making: Conflict and Consensus in the Federal Convention of 1787*. New York: Agathon Press, 1988.

———, and Anderson, Thornton. "Realignments in the Convention of 1787: The Slave Trade Compromise." *Journal of Politics*, 39 (1977): 713–29.

Levy, Leonard W., ed. *Essays on the Making of the Constitution*. 2d ed. New York: Oxford University Press, 1987.

McDonald, Forrest. *Novus Ordo Seclorum*. Lawrence: University Press of Kansas, 1985.

McLaughlin, Andrew C. "Sketch of Pinckney's Plan for a Constitution, 1787." *American Historical Review*, 9 (1904): 735–47.

Main, Jackson T. "Charles A. Beard and the Constitution: A Critical Review of Forrest McDonald's *We the People*." *William and Mary Quarterly*, 3d ser., 17 (1960): 86–110.

Mee, Charles L., Jr. *The Genius of the People*. New York: Harper & Row, 1987.

Meister, Charles W. *The Founding Fathers*. Jefferson, N.C.: McFarland & Co., 1987.

Miller, William L. *The Business of May Next: James Madison and the Founding*. Charlottesville: University Press of Virginia, 1992.

Mitchell, Broadus. *A Biography of the Constitution of the United States: Its Origin, Formation, Adoption, Interpretation*. New York: Oxford University Press, 1964.

Murphy, William P. *The Triumph of Nationalism: State Sovereignty, the Founding Fathers, and the Making of the Constitution*. Chicago: Quadrangle Books, 1967.

O'Conner, John E. *William Paterson: Lawyer and Statesman, 1745–1806*. New Brunswick, N.J.: Rutgers University Press, 1979.

Ohline, Howard A. "Republicanism and Slavery: Origin of the Three-Fifths Clause in the United States Constitution." *William and Mary Quarterly*, 3d ser., 28 (1971): 563–84.

Onuf, Peter S. "Reflections on the Founding: Constitutional Historiography in Bicentennial Perspective." *William and Mary Quarterly*, 3d ser., 46 (1989): 341–75.

Padover, Saul K. *To Secure These Blessings: The Great Debates of the Constitutional Convention of 1787, Arranged According to Topics*. New York: Washington Square Press, 1962.

———. "Unsurpassed and Unrivaled—Our Constitution." *New York Times Magazine* (September 30, 1962): 18, 20, and 70–73.

Peters, William L. *A More Perfect Union*. New York: Crown Publishers, 1987.

Prescott, Arthur T., ed. *Drafting the Federal Constitution*. Baton Rouge: Louisiana State University Press, 1941.

Reardon, John J. *Edmund Randolph: A Biography*. New York: Macmillan Co., 1974.

Roche, John P. "The Founding Fathers: A Reform Caucus in Action." *American Political Science Review*, 55 (1961): 799–816.

Rossiter, Clinton. *1787: The Grand Convention*. New York: Macmillan Co., 1966.

Smith, J. Allen. *The Spirit of American Government*. New York: Macmillan Co., 1907.

Ulmer, S. Sidney. "Charles Pinckney: Father of the Constitution?" *South Carolina Law Quarterly* (Winter 1958): 225–47.

Van Doren, Carl. *The Great Rehearsal: The Story of the Making and Ratifying of the Constitution of the United States.* New York: Viking Press, 1948.

Warren, Charles. *The Making of the Constitution.* Boston: Little, Brown & Co., 1937.

CHAPTER 23

Alexander, John K. *The Selling of the Constitutional Convention: A History of News Coverage.* Madison, Wis.: Madison House, 1990.

Belz, Herman, Hoffman, Ronald, and Albert, Peter J., eds. *To Form a More Perfect Union: The Critical Ideas of the Constitution.* Charlottesville: University Press of Virginia, 1992.

Borden, Morton, ed. *The Antifederalist Papers.* East Lansing: Michigan State University Press, 1965.

Colbourn, Trevor, ed. *Fame and the Founding Fathers: Essays by Douglas Adair.* New York: W. W. Norton, 1974.

Cooke, Jacob E. "Alexander Hamilton's Authorship of the 'Caesar Letters.' " *William and Mary Quarterly,* 3d ser., 17 (1960): 78–85.

———., ed. *The Federalist.* Middletown, Conn.: Wesleyan University Press, 1961.

Crane, Elaine F. "Publius in the Provinces: Where Was *The Federalist* Reprinted Outside New York City?" *William and Mary Quarterly,* 3d ser., 21 (1964): 589–92.

Dahl, Robert A. *Preface to Democratic Theory.* Chicago: University of Chicago Press, 1956.

Diamond, Martin. "Democracy and *The Federalist:* A Reconsideration of the Framers' Intent." *American Political Science Review,* 53 (1959): 52–68.

———. "*The Federalist's* View of Federalism." In *Essays in Federalism,* eds. George C. S. Benson et al. Claremont, Calif.: Institute for Studies in Federalism, 1961, pp. 21–64.

Dietze, Gottfried. *The Federalist: A Classic on Federalism and Free Government.* Baltimore: Johns Hopkins University Press, 1960.

Draper, Theodore. "Hume and Madison." *Encounter,* 58 (February 1982): 34–47.

Epstein, David F. *The Political Theory of The Federalist.* Chicago: University of Chicago Press, 1984.

Finkelman, Paul. "Antifederalists: The Loyal Opposition and the American Constitution (Review of the *Complete Anti-Federalist,* ed. Herbert J. Storing)." *Cornell Law Review,* 70 (1984): 182–207.

Ford, Paul L., ed. *Essays on the Constitution of the United States Published During Its Discussion by the People, 1787–1788.* Brooklyn, N.Y.: Historical Printing Club, 1892.

Furtlanger, Albert. *The Authority of Publius: A Reading of the Federalist Papers.* Ithaca, N.Y.: Cornell University Press, 1984.

Howe, Daniel E. "The Political Psychology of *The Federalist.*" *William and Mary Quarterly,* 3d ser., 44 (1987): 485–509.

Hume, David. *Essays Moral, Political, and Literary.* Vol. 1. London: Longmans, 1875.

Humphrey, Carol S. *"This Popular Engine": New England Newspapers During the American Revolution, 1775–1789.* Newark: University of Delaware Press, 1992.

Hutson, James H. "County, Court, and Constitution: Antifederalism and the Historians." *William and Mary Quarterly,* 3d ser., 38 (1981): 337–68.

Kaminski, John P. *George Clinton: Yeoman Politician of the New Republic.* Madison, Wis.: Madison House, 1993.

Kenyon, Cecelia M. "Men of Little Faith: The Anti-Federalists on the Nature of Representative Government." *William and Mary Quarterly,* 3d ser., 12 (1955): 3–43.

Kesler, Charles R., ed. *Saving the Revolution: The Federalist Papers and the American Founding.* New York: Free Press, 1987.

Kramnick, Isaac. "The Discourse of Politics in 1787: The Constitution and Its Critics on Individualism, Community, and the State." In Herman Belz, Ronald Hoffman, and

Peter J. Albert, eds. *To Form a More Perfect Union: The Critical Ideas of the Constitution.* Charlottesville: University Press of Virginia, 1992, pp. 383–445.

Main, Jackson T. *The Antifederalists: Critics of the Constitution, 1781–1788.* New York: W. W. Norton & Co., 1974, originally published in 1961.

Mason, Alpheus M. "The Federalist—A Split Personality." *American Historical Review,* 57 (1952): 625–43.

Millican, Edward. *One United People: The Federalist Papers and the National Idea.* Lexington: University Press of Kentucky, 1990.

Morgan, Robert J. "Madison's Theory of Representation in the Tenth *Federalist.*" *Journal of Politics,* 36 (no. 4): 852–85.

Mosteller, Frederick, and Wallace, David. *Inference and Disputed Authorship: The Federalist.* Reading, Mass.: Addison-Wesley Publishing Co., 1964.

Rossiter, Clinton. *Alexander Hamilton and the Constitution.* New York: Harcourt, Brace & World, 1964.

———, ed. *The Federalist Papers.* New York: New American Library, 1961.

Smith, Maynard. "Reason, Passion and Political Freedom in *The Federalist.*" *Journal of Politics,* 22 (1960): 523–44.

Smyth, Linda Q. "*The Federalist:* The Authorship of the Disputed Papers." Ph.D. diss., University of Virginia, 1978.

Stourzh, Gerald. *Alexander Hamilton and the Idea of Republican Government.* Stanford, Calif.: Stanford University Press, 1970.

Warren, Charles. "Elbridge Gerry, James Warren, Mercy Warren, and the Ratification of the Federal Constitution in Massachusetts." *Massachusetts Historical Society Proceedings,* 64 (1930–32): 142–64.

Webking, Robert H. "Melancton Smith and *The Letters from the Federal Farmer.*" *William and Mary Quarterly,* 3d ser., 44 (1987): 510–28.

White, Morton. *Philosophy, The Federalist, and the Constitution.* New York: Oxford University Press, 1987.

Wills, Garry. *Explaining America: The Federalist.* Garden City, N.Y.: Doubleday & Co., 1981.

CHAPTER 24

Arendt, Hannah. *See* Chapter 6 references.

Bancroft, George. *History of the Formation of the Constitution of the United States of America.* Vol. 2. New York: D. Appleton and Co., 6th ed., 1903.

Beeman, Richard R. *The Old Dominion and the New Nation, 1788–1801.* Lexington: University Press of Kentucky, 1972.

Benson, Lee. *Turner and Beard: American Historical Writing Reconsidered.* New York: Free Press, 1960.

Boyd, Stephen R. *The Politics of Opposition: Antifederalists and the Acceptance of the Constitution.* Millwood, N.J.: KTO Press, 1979.

Brooks, Robin. "Alexander Hamilton, Melancton Smith, and the Ratification of the Constitution in New York." *William and Mary Quarterly,* 3d ser., 25 (1967): 339–58.

Brown, Robert E. *Charles Beard and the Constitution: A Critical Analysis of "An Economic Interpretation of the Constitution."* Princeton, N.J.: Princeton University Press, 1956.

Carson, Clarence B. *The Rebirth of Liberty: The Founding of the American Republic, 1760–1800.* New Rochelle, N.Y.: Arlington House, 1973.

Conley, Patrick T. "Rhode Island in Disunion, 1787–1790." *Rhode Island History,* 31 (1972): 99–115.

Conley, Patrick T. and Kaminski, John P. *The Constitution and the States: The Role of the Original Thirteen in the Framing and Adoption of the Federal Constitution.* Madison, Wis.: Madison House, 1988.

Cornell, Saul. "Aristocracy Assailed: The Ideology of Backcountry Anti-Federalism." *Journal of American History*, 76 (1990): 1148–72.

Crowl, Philip A. *Maryland During and After the Revolution: A Political and Economic Study.* Baltimore: Johns Hopkins University Press, 1943.

De Pauw, Linda G. *The Eleventh Pillar: New York and the Federal Constitution.* Ithaca, N.Y.: Cornell University Press, 1966.

De Tocqueville, Alexis. *Democracy in America.* Eds. J. P. Mayer and Max Lerner (new trans. by George Lawrence). New York: Harper & Row, 1966.

Elkins, Stanley and McKitrick, Eric. "The Founding Fathers: Young Men of the Revolution." *Political Science Quarterly*, 76 (1961): 181–216.

Gillespie, Michael A., and Lienesch, Michael, eds. *Ratifying the Constitution.* Lawrence: University Press of Kansas, 1989.

Harding, Samuel B. *The Contest over the Ratification of the Federal Constitution in the State of Massachusetts.* New York: Da Capo Press, 1970, originally published in 1896.

Hart, Freeman H. *The Valley of Virginia in the Revolution, 1763–1789.* Chapel Hill: University of North Carolina Press, 1942.

Haws, Robert J., ed. *The South's Role in the Creation of the Bill of Rights.* Jackson: University Press of Mississippi, 1991.

Kaminski, John P. "Controversy and Consensus: The Adoption of the Federal Constitution in Georgia. *Georgia Historical Quarterly*, 58 (1974): 244–61.

Kammen, Michael. *A Machine That Would Go of Itself.* New York: Alfred A. Knopf, 1986.

Kukla, Jon. "A Spectrum of Sentiments: Virginia's Federalists, Antifederalists, and 'Federalists Who Are for Amendments,' 1787–1788." *Virginia Magazine of History and Biography*, 96 (1988): 277–96.

Libby, Orin G. *The Geographical Distribution of the Vote of the Thirteen States on the Federal Constitution, 1787–8.* New York: Burt Franklin, 1969, originally published in 1894.

Lienesch, Michael. *New Order of the Ages: Time, the Constitution, and the Making of Modern American Political Thought.* Princeton, N.J.: Princeton University Press, 1988.

McDonald, Forrest. *We the People: The Economic Origins of the Constitution.* Chicago: University of Chicago Press, 1958.

McMaster, John B., and Stone, Frederick. *Pennsylvania and the Constitution, 1787–1788.* 2 vols. New York: Da Capo Press, 1970, originally published in 1888.

Main, Jackson T. 1974. *See* Chapter 23 references.

Meleney, John C. *The Public Life of Aedanus Burke: Revolutionary Republican in Post-Revolutionary South Carolina.* Columbia: University of South Carolina Press, 1989.

Munroe, John A. *Federalist Delaware, 1775–1815.* New Brunswick, N.J.: Rutgers University Press, 1954.

Nedelsky, Jennifer. *Private Property and the Limits of American Constitutionalism: The Madisonian Framework and Its Legacy.* Chicago: University of Chicago Press, 1990.

Nelson, William. "Reason and Compromise in the Establishment of the Federal Constitution, 1787–1801." *William and Mary Quarterly*, 3d ser., 44 (1987): 458–84.

Pole, J. R. *The Idea of Union.* Alexandria, Va.: Bicentennial Council of the Thirteen Original States Fund, 1977.

Polishook, Irwin H. *Rhode Island and the Union, 1774–1795.* Evanston, Ill.: Northwestern University Press, 1969.

Pool, William C. "An Economic Interpretation of the Ratification of the Federal Constitution in North Carolina." *North Carolina Historical Review*, 27 (1950): 119–41, 289–313, and 437–61.

Risjord, Norman K. *Jefferson's America, 1760–1815.* Madison, Wis.: Madison House, 1991.
———. "Virginians and the Constitution: A Multivariant Analysis." *William and Mary Quarterly*, 3d ser., 31 (1974): 613–32.

Roll, Charles W., Jr. " 'We, Some of the People:' Apportionment in the Thirteen State Conventions Ratifying the Constitution." *Journal of American History*, 56 (1969): 21–40.

Rossiter, Clinton. *Seedtime of the Republic: The Origin of the American Tradition of Political Liberty.* New York: Harcourt, Brace & Co., 1953.

Rutland, Robert A. *The Ordeal of the Constitution: The Antifederalists and the Ratification Struggles of 1787–1788.* Norman: University of Oklahoma Press, 1966.

Schechter, Stephen L. *The Reluctant Pillar: New York and the Adoption of the Federal Constitution.* Troy, N.Y.: Russell Sage College, 1985.

Steiner, Bernard C. "Maryland's Adoption of the Federal Constitution." *American Historical Review,* 5 (1899–1900): 22–44 and 207–24.

Thomas, Robert E. "The Virginia Convention of 1788: A Criticism of Beard's 'An Economic Interpretation of the Constitution.' " *Journal of Southern History,* 19 (1953): 63–71.

Trenholme, Louise I. *The Ratification of the Federal Constitution in North Carolina.* New York: AMS Press, 1967.

Turner, Lynn W. *The Ninth State: New Hampshire's Formative Years.* Chapel Hill: University of North Carolina Press, 1983.

Wren, J. Thomas. "The Ideology of Court and Country in the Virginia Ratifying Convention of 1788." *Virginia Magazine of History and Biography,* 93 (1985): 389–408.

Index

Abercromby, Lt. Col. Robert, 152

Adair, Douglass, 353

Adams, Abigail, 52, 209–10, 304–5

Adams, John,* 12, 28, 38, 42–43, 52–53, 56, 61–62, 80–85, 88, 116–17, 119, 182–83, 191–92, 202, 210, 212, 259, 275, 279, 281, 292–93, 310, 323, 335, 337, 370

Adams, John Quincy, 287, 350

Adams, Samuel,* 36, 39, 41–44, 53, 61, 63, 79, 81, 125, 310, 364

Adams, Willi Paul, 278

Addison, Joseph,* 333

Adkins, Elizabeth, 202

Administration of Justice Act, 48

Admiralty courts, 23, 32–33, 37; jurisdiction (U.S.), 290

Africa, 5, 13, 311

African Americans, 88–89, 127, 311–16, 322; in the armies, 130, 216–17. See also Slaves

African Union Society, 313

Agents (colonial), 12, 46

Alamance, b. of (1771), 70

Albanese, Catherine L., 321

Albany, N.Y., 11, 40, 69, 74, 112, 118, 171, 215, 236

Albany Plan of Union, 11, 288

Albemarle, George Keppel, earl of, 24

Alden, Col. Ichabod, 171

Alden, Roger, 369

Alexander, Robert, 79

Alexandria, Va., 11, 167

Allen, Ethan,* 61, 68, 165, 256, 334

Allen, Richard, 313

Almanacs, 7, 326, 334

Alsop, Mary, 200

Amboy, N.J., 99, 103–4, 257

American Academy of Arts and Sciences, 335

American Board of Customs, 23, 38, 41

American character, 3–4, 370–71

American Convention of Abolitionist Societies, 315

American Museum, 335

American Philosophical Society, 335

Amerman, Richard H., 253

Ames, Fisher, 364

Ames, Nathaniel,* 7

Amherst, Gen. Jeffery, 94

Ammerman, David, 56

Anburey, Lt. Thomas, 252

André, Major John, 242, 244–47

Anglicans, 4, 23–24, 43, 315, 318, 322

Annapolis, Md., 58; conference of 1786, 301, 336

Antifederalists, 349, 354–68

Antigua, 268

Arbuthnot, Adm. Marriot, 124, 131

Arendt, Hannah, 371

Architecture, 330–32

Armstrong, Gen. John, 127

Armstrong, Major John, Jr., 125

Army See British Army; Continental Army; French Army

Arnold, Gen. Benedict, 61, 67–69, 113, 115, 118, 124, 149, 151–55, 245–48, 250

Arnold, Margaret Shippen (Mrs. B. A.), 245

Art, 8, 329–30

Articles of Confederation, 280, 289–90, 292, 299, 301, 338, 354; amendments, 341, 336; evaluation of, 292, 342, 350

Asbury, Rev. Francis, 322

Asgill, Capt. Charles, 256

Ashe, Gen. John, 129

Associated Loyalists of America, 267

"Association" (Cong.), 55–57, 81

Astor, John Jacob, 309

Atherton, Joshua, 365

Attucks, Crispus, 43

Augusta, princess, 24

Augusta, Ga., 129, 146, 148, 160, 256; Siege of, 138

Austria, 81, 182–83

Bach, Carl Phillipp Emanuel, 332

Bache, Sarah Franklin, 201

Backus, Rev. Isaac, 322

Bacon, Anthony, 21

Bacon, Nathaniel, 8

Bahamas, 190, 268

Bailey, Philip, 228

Baillie, Col. William, 191

Baird, Capt. Sir James, 129

Bakeman, Daniel F., 214

Baker, Col. John, 128

Balfour, Lt. Col. Nisbet, 255

Baltimore, 167, 202, 216, 315, 322, 333, 364, 369

Bank of London, 44

Bank of North America, 284, 291

Banneker, Benjamin, 313

Baptists, 313, 322, 362, 366

Barbados, 188, 254

Barbary states, 293

Barbé-Marbois, François, marquis de, 305

Barclay, Thomas, 293

Bardstown, Ky., 322

Barker, Lt. John, 60

Barlow, Joel,* 296, 326–27

Barras, Adm. Jacques-Melchior Saint-Laurent, comte de, 158

Barré, Col. Isaac, 34, 47

Barren Hill, b. of, 116

Barrett, Charles, 365

Barrington, Rear Adm. Samuel, 188

Barrington, William Wildman, viscount, 25, 52, 64

Barron, Lt. William, 172

Barrow, Thomas C., 86

Barton, Lt. William, 234

Bartram, John, 335

Bartram, William,* 335

Bates, Mrs. Ann, 250

Baton Rouge, La., 176, 190

Baum, Col. Friedrich, 113

Bayard v. Singleton (1787), 280

Baylor, Col. George, 122–23, 136, 211, 225

Beard, Charles A.* 287, 340–41, 361

Beatty, Col. John, 251

*Indicates title of a work by this person is cited in the text.